D1566353

The
Anatomy of
Psychotherapy

*To My Mother
and the Memory of My Father*

The Anatomy of Psychotherapy

Lawrence Friedman

THE ANALYTIC PRESS

1988   Hillsdale, NJ   Hove and London

The Analytic Press.

Distributed solely by

Lawrence Erlbaum Associates, Inc., Publishers
365 Broadway
Hillsdale, New Jersey 07642

Set in Goudy type by
Lind Graphics, Woodcliff Lake, NJ

Printed in the United States of America by
Braun-Brumfield, Inc., Ann Arbor, MI

Library of Congress Cataloging-in-Publication Data

Friedman, Lawrence, 1931–
   The Anatomy of psychotherapy.

   Includes bibliographies and index.
   1. Psychotherapy.   I. Title.   [DNLM: 1. Psychotherapy.
WM 420 F9109a]
RC488.F74   1987   616.89′14   87-17125
ISBN 0-88163-053-5

10 9 8 7 6 5 4 3 2

Contents

III
Theory of the Mind:
The Tool of Psychotherapy

IV
Debate About Theory of the Mind: Revisions

V
What is a Psychotherapist?

VI
Implications

Preface

Most psychotherapists sense that their work is vague and its image misleading, and they are occasionally reminded that they have no authentic place in society because society doesn't know what they are up to.

Each profession, of course, has its secret strains and shelters; it would not be a profession if it were transparent to outsiders. But in the case of psychotherapy the outsider's image will be not incomplete but wrong, which shows that the profession is a more private enterprise than most.

Recent efforts to define psychotherapy may help the profession to go public. For the present, however, their effect is to make a very private enterprise even more private as the old consensus vanishes and each therapist shops for himself among a welter of proposals.

Even the shopping tends toward anarchy, theories being accepted or rejected as they are found agreeable or distasteful, their authors often content to leave the unpersuaded to their folly. Although recently more comparisons and cross-translations have been published, the profession has been slow to develop a tradition of detailed, discipline-wide argument.

And that is a shame. New theories for therapists deserve the same careful probing that theories in other fields receive and should have to be defended in sharp colloquy of the sort that engages philosophers and literary critics, economists and political scientists, and, more sedately, physicists and physiologists who offer new ideas. Such was my reason for previously publishing the critiques that appear here mostly in Part IV.

But I also had an ulterior motive for undertaking those studies. I thought that, in observing what therapists need from their articulate theories, I was actually witnessing the silent predicaments that squeeze them at work. I supposed that one way the ghostly essence of therapy manifests itself is by pressing shapes into visible theory – theory of the mind no less than theory of therapy. And that is why I include these theoretical critiques here: Although they are self-contained studies of individual systems, together they are part of an argument about the nature of psychotherapy.

Compared to these theoretical critiques, the argument as contained in other chapters is so much more common and coarse that many will scold me for mixing the sublime with the ridiculous. I have learned that even those who yawn at theory are likely to wince at informal descriptions of treatment. And who can blame them? Nontechnical accounts of therapy, unless they are poetically inflated, are apt to sound superficial and naive, undignified, uninformed, and unedifying. It is natural for therapists to react to an "ordinary life" description of therapy as though it were an attack on the profession and a threat to training. Of course, therapists do talk plainly to each other, especially when they need help. But when they gather in a written or spoken forum to discuss what therapy is, their gut knowledge of their daily work suddenly seems less real to them than the wildest flight of theoretical fancy carried on ingenious wings. I am afraid that, because it must dissect common experience, an anatomy of psychotherapy will often yield a homely portrait. Although one of my arguments is that a refined theory is always at the heart of psychotherapy even when it looks like a wrestling match, another principle is that no description of treatment will be accurate if it remains dignified and respectful. My wish is to explain – not to conform with – the custom of separating chaotic experience from sedate theory. If the reader is annoyed by the clash of hieratic and ordinary styles in these chapters, I ask him to note that his annoyance is respected here as itself a central aspect of the therapist's dilemma.

But an anatomy of psychotherapy cannot free itself from this mixture of tongues. Which is not to say that a confused subject deserves a confused presentation. The simplest account is the best. The reason we appreciate stylistic variety in life is that the simplest account of a vague and various world must include Darwin, Shakespeare, and Bach, as well as the 10 o'clock news and the police blotter. In its untidiness, psychotherapy is a little like life in general. I sometimes fear that it is so much like life in general that there is no special description of it to be had. But if therapy can be described, it certainly won't be in one tone of voice. We have a tone for theorizing. We have a tone for sharing troubles with colleagues. We have a tone for talking to ourselves at work, another for supervision, and yet another for professional meetings. Each reflects a truth. None is comprehensive. We should be suspicious of descriptions that are too homogeneous. They are likely to have been selected for the occasion rather than the subject.

And, of all tones, a homogeneous loftiness is the most suspect. There is no challenge to his honesty so difficult for the therapist as the trick of memory that brightens his work the instant its pressure recedes. Everything else in the therapist's life softens the concentrated tension of his moment with the patient, and nothing does it as artfully as professional reading and writing, which are cultivated partly for that effect.

The larger the view, the more it is tinted. (Skylines tell us little about engineering.) Whatever we might wish it to be, the experience of therapy is so different from tranquil reflection that when we are able to reflect, we will probably be reflecting on a slightly different subject matter than we have at work. To the extent that we do recapture the actual experience we must expect an anatomy of psychotherapy to be often disagreeable.

So I can blame pedantry, plainness, and pain on my subject. But I must take responsibility for some repetition in these chapters. It is the consequence of approaching therapy in a variety of ways, folding in studies that were once freestanding essays. The same basic themes are found in all the sections of the book, so that readers who are interested in theory but not my views on therapy can find those themes in Part IV; and therapists who hate theory but seek validation for the strain of their work can bypass the systematic studies and hear my sermon in the vernacular. Finally, those who patiently read through the whole book may share my belief that few ideas are clear until they are embedded in different contexts.

I owe an apology to authors who are represented only by their early work and relevant authors who are not represented at all. One has to stop somewhere, and I use references more to illustrate problems and options than to assess historical contributions. Human frailty is my excuse for influences unacknowledged by citation. Certainly, cited authors have influenced me in more ways than I indicate.

I particularly wish to emphasize that this is a book about general psychotherapy, not psychoanalysis. If I seem to be writing about psychoanalysis it is because careful theory has been written by and for analysts and I have had to kidnap it for psychotherapy. I hope the reader will forgive the mixed references to "the analyst" and "the therapist."

So that I don't seem the last to notice that everything here is speculative, I apologize in advance for my know-it-all manner of transcribing what are, in fact, experimental thoughts. My excuse is that an unjustified positiveness makes a train of ideas easier to follow than if they were properly hedged.

Credits

Ch. 2 first appeared as: The therapeutic alliance. In *International Journal of Psycho-Analysis*, 50: 139–153, 1969 (Part 2).

Ch. 4 first appeared as: Trends in the psychoanalytic theory of treatment. In *Psychoanalytic Quarterly*, 47:524–567, 1978.

Ch. 5. Portions of this chapter appeared first in *Issues in Ego Psychology*, 4:8–15, 1981.

Ch. 13. An extended version of this chapter appeared as: A view of the background of Freudian theory. In *Psychoanalytic Quarterly*, 46:425–465, 1977.

Ch. 14 first appeared as: Reasons for the Freudian revolution. In *Psychoanalytic Quarterly*, 46:623–649, 1977.

Ch. 15 first appeared as: Conflict and synthesis in Freud's theory of the mind. In *International Review of Psycho-Analysis*, 4:155–170, 1977 (Part 2).

Ch. 16 first appeared as: Cognitive and therapeutic tasks of a theory of the mind. In *International Review of Psycho-Analysis*, 3:259–275, 1976 (Part 3).

Ch. 18 first appeared as: Difficulties of a computer model of the mind. In *International Journal of Psycho-Analysis*, 53:547–554, 1972 (Part 4).

Ch. 19 first appeared as: The barren prospect of a representational world. In *Psychoanalytic Quarterly*, 49:215–233, 1980.

Ch. 20 first appeared as: Problems of an action theory of the mind. In *International Review of Psycho-Analysis*, 3:129–138, 1976 (Part 2).

Ch. 21 is reprinted in slightly altered form with the permission of *Contemporary Psychoanalysis*. It originally appeared in *Contemporary Psychoanalysis*, the journal of the William Alanson White Psychoanalytic Society and the William Alanson White Institute, Volume 10, No. XX, pages 125–142, 1974, with the title: Perspectivism in psychotherapy.

Ch. 22 incorporates material that appeared as: A criticism of Gendlin's theory of therapy. In *Psychotherapy: Theory, Research and Practice*, 8:256–258, 1971, and is reprinted with permission of the Editor.

Ch. 23 is reprinted (with slight changes) from *The Psychoanalytic Review*, 67 (2), 1980, through the courtesy of the Editors and the Publisher, National Psychological Association for Psychoanalysis, New York, NY (Originally part of a Symposium)

Ch. 24 is reprinted from *The Psychoanalytic Review*, Vol. 59, No. 4, 1972, through the courtesy of the Editors and the Publisher, National Psychological Association for Psychoanalysis, New York, NY (Original title: Structure and psychotherapy.)

Ch. 25 first appeared as: Piaget and psychotherapy. In *Journal of the American Academy of Psychoanalysis*, 6 (2), 1978. Portions of this chapter were taken from a discussion of a paper by Anita Tenzer, reprinted with the permission of *Contemporary Psychoanalysis*. It originally appeared in *Contemporary Psychoanalysis*, the journal of the William Alanson White Psychoanalytic Society and the William Alanson White Institute, Vol. 19, No. 2, 1983, pp. 339–348.

Ch. 26 first appeared as: Kohut: A book review essay. *Psychoanalytic Quarterly*, 49:393–422, 1980.

Ch. 27 originally appeared as: The humanistic trend in recent psychoanalytic theory. In *Psychoanalytic Quarterly*, 51: 353–371, 1982.

Ch. 28 contains material originally published as: Potentiality shrouded: How the newer theories work. In *Psychoanalytic Quarterly*, 54:379–414, 1985.

Ch. 32. Much of this chapter appeared as: Reconstruction and the like. In *Psychoanalytic Inquiry*: 3:189–222, 1983. Reprinted with the kind permission of the Editor.

Ch. 33 includes material that appeared as: Pictures of treatment by Gill and Schafer. In *Psychoanalytic Quarterly*, 53:167–207, 1984.

Ch. 34 is a slightly modified version of: Seeing something new in something old. In *The Future of Psychoanalysis*, ed. A. Goldberg, New York: International Universities Press, 1983, pp. 137–163.

Acknowledgments

T his book exists because Dr. Paul Stepansky, Editor-in-Chief of The Analytic Press, first imagined its possibility, caringly saw to all of its needs, and paved a smooth road to its completion. Its incubator was the Section on the History of Psychiatry of the New York Hospital–Cornell Medical Center, where disciplinary boundaries melt in a friendly ferment designed by Dr. Eric T. Carlson and cultivated with him by Dr. Jacques M. Quen. I am indebted to them for that atmosphere, and to them and my other comrades in the Section for access to their wide erudition.

Many of my ideas crystalized in discussions with Dr. Patricia Noel, who brought to our joint study of the rationale of psychotherapy her rare ability to preserve the mysterious, fluctuant life of a therapy session while staining it with conceptual dyes.

Certain chapters have benefited from the comments of Dr. Shelley Orgel, Dr. Dale Boesky, and Dr. Arnold Goldberg. Their empathic fostering seems to me a particularly altruistic form of extramural psychotherapy.

Most of the gifted therapists who have informally shared their perspectives with me already know how important they are to my thinking and will know that I have them in mind as I thank them here. My debt and gratitude are as great, though possibly less evident, to those who have indulged me in that irresponsible gallery-walk known as supervision. And, like all of my colleagues, I am indebted to the brave and skilled therapists who have made samples of their work available for public scrutiny.

I thank my first reader, Carol Lachman, who, though burdened with preparing a complicated manuscript, accepted the role of interlocutor, protected me from stylistic blunders as far as my stubbornness would allow, and offered her lively intelligence for needed dialogue, her cheerful wit for needed morale. To my editor, Eleanor Starke Kobrin, I owe thanks for the many ways she improved the manuscript, for her patience, wisdom, and kindness, and for teaching me that the secret to grace under pressure is a combination of good sense and good humor. I am indebted to my intrepid copy editor, Robin Weisberg, for the fidelity and skill with which she met abundant challenges. I also thank Josephine Shapiro of *The Psychoanalytic Quarterly* for her editorial assistance with some of the essays that appear here.

An author knows, especially if his book is lengthy, that it is just the public part of an invisible campaign. I am deeply grateful to my wife for her characteristic loving support in that campaign.

It is difficult to spell out my debt to Dr. Jules V. Coleman of Yale University. To say that he influenced me would be a shameful understatement. Dr. Coleman arranged a training experience that has been my touchstone for everything tried, every theory weighed, every technique evaluated. Coleman is the most creative teacher I have known and, to my mind, the most sophisticated psychotherapist of our day. For the reader's convenience I have listed some of his publications in my bibliography, but his influence on my thinking came entirely from a nondidactic learning experience that cannot be conveyed in print. It is long after the fact that I note in his writings the same tolerant, psychoanalytically informed realism, the Aristotelian respect for the specific virtues proper to psychoanalysis and psychotherapy (and social work and education), the sensitivity to the troubles encountered by all parties in giving and receiving care, that were implicit years ago in his teaching. Because Coleman's teaching was nondidactic his students took away differing lessons, some of them probably not what he intended. Mine may be such a misconception, so Coleman cannot be held responsible for my sins. But it will always be true that anything I write may be a mere gloss on—perhaps even a memory of—what I learned from him.

Introduction

Three interrelated themes appear repeatedly in these pages: (a) Psychotherapy is a relationship interfered with by theory. (b) The way therapists argue about and modify theory shows their practical needs better than they can tell you outright, and so the history of theory is a dissection of therapy. (c) Theory—especially theory of therapy—cannot be understood apart from the immediate practice problems it is designed to help and these practice problems can only be learned by feeling their bite.

The zig-zag organization of the book follows from these principles. We move back and forth between impressions of practice and the fine points of theory, and between the structure of theory and its evolution.

I begin with what it feels like to do psychotherapy, emphasizing its uncomfortableness. In Part I, I look at the psychoanalytic literature for evidence of this discomfort, and note how theory responds to the therapist's cries for help.

Seeing the practical comfort afforded by theory, I return in Part II to the therapist's raw experience, and describe it in ordinary language as an effort to maintain various kinds of balance. This examination leads to two questions that I believe any account of therapy must answer: (a) How does the therapist select what he will attend to? and (b) What meaning does the patient give to the therapist's selection?

The "naturalistic" description of two people involved in therapy shows that theory—and now I mean especially theory of the mind—is a real, central, and distinctive presence in their midst. Therefore, in Part III, I turn to our most complete theory of the mind, namely Freud's, to find out what a theory of the mind is and how its universal features bear on the action of psychotherapy.

Having examined theory of the mind (in the shape of Freud's theory), and believing that we learn what psychotherapists' needs are by seeing how they push their theory around, I use Part IV to examine a group of modern revisions. From the direction of these revisions, I infer that a therapist cannot afford to recognize everything about himself at once: He must sometimes be able to ignore his eliciting so he can feel himself to be perceiving. And he must allow his wishes to pick up human meaning from patients, even though wishing is forbidden because it limits the relationship. He must be oblivious to his wishes, and yet able to take sight of them when patients do.

In Part V I try to show how the therapist's characteristic behaviors can be explained by this predicament: A therapist is required to conform to contradictory rules. Ambiguity is remorselessly required of him. A therapist is not just more ambiguous than most people. He is required to be so ambigous that to obey the requirement would render him incapable of interaction. It is not surprising, then, that he is always sliding temporarily into various defined roles that make real contact with patients and become his public image: reader, historian, and operator (this last in the form of physician, teacher, coach, etc). None of these by itself is a truly psychotherapeutic role, but because at any given time the therapist is likely to be acting in one of these capacities with huge consequences for the shape of treatment, I examine the way each role does its part to keep therapy flexible, and to meet the patient's needs, for good and ill.

In Part VI, I summarize the anatomy of psychotherapy. Such a diagram is bound to have implications for teaching, and I try to draw those implications as concretely as possible, ending with a glance at the future.

I
Theory and Practice:
The Trouble with Psychotherapy

1

Whatever Happened to the

Therapist's Discomfort?

Doing psychotherapy is stressful. Close-up, it does not look at all like its self-portrait. Its literature shows some patients occasionally upsetting their therapists, and therapists sometimes being too readily upset. We see an occasional hint that these are really most times, most therapists, and most patients. But generally speaking, reports do not disclose the extent to which stress is part of doing therapy.

Patient's stress is more apparent in the literature. At the very least, a shrewd reader of case histories would remark how frequently words of trouble appear. But he might conclude that even patient distress, although frequent, accompanies a process that *need* not be stressful at all.

Considering that the one thing a therapist knows with assurance is that he is constantly managing tensions between himself and his patient while about everything else he is never sure, the evaporation of this large fact in published accounts is impressive: What therapists know best is least apparent in their writings.

That puts psychotherapy into a different class from other treatments. A tense surgeon is essential to surgery no more than a tense driver is to driving, and accordingly, surgical textbooks do not dwell on tension. Viewing his work in a parallel fashion, the beginning psychotherapist may regard it as a technical fault if he is upset during therapy, and looks forward to a time free of strain. Indeed, the more steeped he is in the literature, the more sanguine will be his hopes.

In this sense, surgical texts are honest and psychotherapy texts are not. And this specific dishonesty is as useful a clue to the subject as anything that is written in the texts, because it shows us two important facts of treatment:

5

Therapists function in a sea of trouble and they talk as though they don't. Respect and attention abound, to be sure, but the identifying truth about psychotherapy is that it is an uncivil, threatening, even brutal struggle, instigated by gently reflective intellectuals dedicated to delicate speculations.

On the one hand, what the therapist lives with is the pressure of person on person, with its attendant anxieties, satisfactions, cautions, and effort. On the other hand, what he identifies with is a finicky theory of the mind.

In its collegial preoccupation, psychotherapy seems to be an applied set of scholastic doctrines. Its hallmarks are Freudian theory, one of the most elaborate hypotheses ever devised, and a famous *odium theologicum* that has supplied much fun for critics. Yet anyone can see that the working therapist is not usually a self-conscious theoretician. In daily practice he is less cognizant of his science than, for example, internists are of theirs. Compared with surgery, his practice involves a greater degree of inadvertence and make-shift, and I suspect that even folk-healing has a more predictable method. Patients control therapists to a greater extent than clients control their lawyers. Custom carries farther than theory, until colleagues get together, when theory becomes useful socially. The practicing psychotherapist sits in a broth of interpersonal pressures, and dries himself off in the arid atmosphere of meticulous or at least ambitious, theory: specifiable, cerebral, and debatable.

This contrast provides both a difficulty and an opportunity for the observer. The opportunity is that the difference between the doing and the thinking shows the sinews of treatment. The difficulty is that one of these two parts (the theory part) is the instrument used to dissect the whole thing: It seems impossible to delineate the personal pushings and pullings except by using a theory that is part of the pushings and pullings. For instance, to take a much investigated example, transference is both a description of a field of forces, and it is itself (as a concept) a force used by the therapist to arrange his interaction with the patient.

That would be no problem if treatment simply consisted of unfolding the theory. The theory would then be the treatment. For long stretches of time, many therapists thought of "interpretation" that way. In effect, Kurt Eissler (1953) elaborated the theme that everything that counts in psychoanalysis can be compressed into verbal propositions. If we settled on that, we could say that those truths are both the theory and the treatment.

Unfortunately, we hardly know what a proposition is, let alone a belief, and we are thus ill equipped even to approach the question of how information is communicated and how general information is integrated with individual universes.

But if using psychotherapy theory as the explanation of its own action is fruitless, the prospect of another theory to explain treatment is even more dismal. What point is there in making up a new theory to encompass the one we are describing when what we have is probably the best we can forge? And there is no third choice: we cannot think without theory.

But if there is no theory-free description, there is a common language. And even if a theory, as an interlocking network of terms, does not translate easily, still it is only those ideas that are statable in various ways that are really understood. We are not looking for theory-free descriptions; we are simply looking for multiple expressions.

Critics of psychoanalysis dimly recognize but misunderstand this need. They scold metapsychology for using a model that misleadingly apes natural science or childishly explains things by anthropomorphisms. We are told that analytic theory reifies abstractions, making aspects look as though they are real things. I have more to say about these admonitions in Part IV. But here I want to observe that, although undesirable use can be made of "energies" and "superegos" and the like, the mischief is done not by picturing them as things, but by supposing that mentioning them together in a plausible syntax automatically solves a problem. Real-life problems cannot be solved like crossword puzzles.

I think there is no other way to go about looking at psychotherapy than the way we begin to understand anything else, that is, by relying on the low-level theory of common sense, trying to talk about our subject in ways that are neither confined to, nor incompatible with, whatever sophisticated theories we have. The aim is not to find a better theory, but to find out what is at stake in composing theory. Because no epistemological profundity is claimed, no epistemological circularity is risked. (The risk is rather in not trying to say things in a common-sense fashion, for then we may close ourselves into a parochial jargon, like the savage tribes of Lévi-Strauss.)

And yet, I must admit that this is too slick an escape from the problem of how to prefigure the field without recourse to the theories that play within it. It is all very well to talk about common sense, but any conversation between two psychotherapists reveals that whatever sense they have is not common to both of them. Shall we invite sociologists and ethologists to use their common sense about what we are up to? Of course we should and we do, but the time comes when we have to see things in some light and one perspective will stand out.

The questions psychotherapists want answered are the questions that grow out of their own practice—not those from another discipline. And the experience that answers them must be the experience of doing therapy.

But whose experience? To some extent it may be the shared experience of many therapists. For instance, this book has been influenced by conversations with colleagues at various stages of their careers, as well as by process recorded in print and on tape. But it is all inevitably filtered through what I recognize from my own experience. In the last analysis, then, one begins with one's own experience of practice.

It would not be overly mystical to say that one can only describe his own psychotherapy. The awful converse would be that one reveals only himself when he talks about psychotherapy. (Most therapists are too smart to write all they know about their work.) If someone reads what follows and concludes that I have a penchant for discord or an intolerance of it, an impulsive nature or a too careful one, inability to keep a proper distance or shyness of involvement, excessive concern with technique or failure to master it, obsessive doubting about rationales or theoretical gullibility, I cannot refute him. I might answer that my critic is denying what he daily experiences, but I certainly cannot know that. I may harbor the low suspicion that if his experience is different from mine, it is not psychotherapy.[1] But more realistically, the heterogeneity must be accepted as a continuing problem for the profession because nobody is going to describe psychotherapy to the satisfaction of every therapist. It is not just that practices vary; we need only dub these variations *techniques* or *modalities*, and we have transformed the profession's apparent shapelessness into evidence of its advanced technology. That temporarily solves the public relations problem, although no profession can hope for much of a future if it is defined as a little of this and a little of that (Friedman, 1976).

No, the really serious problem is the difference between the *experience* of one therapist and another. For although therapists act differently according to their personalities and the needs of the patient, if therapy is any one thing, it must operate within a particular field of forces, and one would expect those forces to be felt by all, even if in varying degree and differently by therapist and patient.

Naturally we would discount for the fact that what is easy for one person is harder for another, and we would not expect all therapists to feel the same degree of strain in a given situation. Even such stresses as are felt by all will have different private meanings. (Considering, for instance, that we define our role in conversation partly by what we attend to, we may presume that a profession that permits no role definition will make some practitioners worry about what to attend to, and others worry about the propriety of their attention.) But if a dissection of psychotherapy has any merit, what it describes should be recognized by most therapists at least at moments of difficulty, and if the troubles outlined in these pages do not seem familiar to the reader, I have failed at my task.

A much easier challenge is the one that says that *psychoanalysis*, properly defined, is not well described in what follows. There is no reason it should be;

---

[1]There are times when it seems to me that psychotherapy occurs only when the process is uncomfortable, and I think of the comment attributed to Sullivan, "God protect me from a therapy that is going well," or Levenson's (1983) suggestion that analysis begins only when discomfort is experienced, or Gill's (1982) method for keeping discomfort alive.

that is not my objective. Coherent theory is almost exclusively psychoanalytic, so it may seem as though I am talking about psychoanalytic treatment, and here and there I may be, but it is always with the intention of exploring the experience of general psychotherapy.

Nor am I describing every treatment that is not analysis. I do not have in mind behavior therapy, hypnotherapy, group or family therapy. These are surely psychotherapies; any planned helpfulness at a distance can fairly claim that title. In this book, *psychotherapy* refers to a tradition of individual talking treatment, which flourished in the 1950s and 1960s in the wake of psychoanalysis, copied the duration of the analytic "hour," did not ask patients to recline on a couch out of sight of the therapist, and programmed no more than three sessions per week. It is this tradition that I dissect, as I know it from training, practice, supervision, and gossip, and from sharing its culture during the height of its popularity. I begin with no definition; perhaps one will emerge.

My argument so far is that the experience of psychotherapy is an experience of stress and an experience of theory: that the stress is obscured in the theory; and that the theory is used not just to describe, but to perform the treatment. We must look at psychotherapy from a vantage point outside of theory, so that we can see the role theory plays in practice. We must describe the scene in plain and ordinary ways.

If a reader dislikes theory, he can read a commonsense description in Part II, and skip to Part V for a somewhat less plain, but still non-technical, elaboration of the therapeutic interaction.

But that will yield only a ghost of therapy. Strange as it seems, if we want to talk vividly and specifically about psychotherapy, we cannot just talk plainly. For theory is literally a part of practice; it sits (or hides) in the therapist's mind. Like it or not, theory is half of the doing.

Our task would be simpler if we could just let theory call out "present and accounted for," and go on to describe two people in action. Unfortunately, even when we approach psychotherapy non-ideologically we are not excused from studying theory. One is obliged to study a theory even if he feels it is wrong, because the theory is effective in doing things to therapist and patient, and thus partly reveals what is being done and what the therapist needs in order to do it.

Fortunately it works both ways: We are helped to understand theory by watching how it is used in treatment. We can understand abstract concepts in the light of what we experience as therapists.

That requires some temporary desanctifying of theory—a look at its "cash value," to use William James' ugly term. But before we do that we must be sure what exactly it is that we are cashing in. We cannot translate a theory into a collection of opportunistic maneuvers. In order to see what a theory does, we have to understand it as a system. Thus, even an ordinary, non-ideological, practical, common sense description of psychotherapy must include descriptions of what an intricate belief system does to each party in the therapeutic set-up.

It is harder to understand belief systems than many people think. Even quite sophisticated writers often fail to appreciate the systematic requirements of a theory. The theory's friends frequently regard each of its features as independently mandated by experience, while critics grasp it in the easiest way, which is to consider it copied from a "model," as an automobile chassis is molded by steel dies. (The term *paradigm* is also used to create this impression, using Thomas Kuhn's authority without his subtlety.)

Writers wishing to junk an old theory, or even simply to discourage dogmatism, can forget that a theory often resembles its model because it shares the same inner systematic requirements, rather than because it seeks reflected glory from a passingly popular science.

Theories must be given careful and sometimes excruciatingly boring study, if we are not to have an even more simple-minded vision of therapy than we have of other human phenomena. (Sociologists do not think they have finished describing a society when they have pointed out that it has "a religion" or "some social customs," or has built its institutions "on a Judeo-Christian model." They do not feel they have made an interesting contribution by revealing that societies all have their own way of life. The details are what count.)

In summary, to understand the theory used in psychotherapy, we should give theory many readings (to eliminate mere verbal recognitions); we should let details of theory reveal the problems of treatment that they are designed to help; we should make the heat of treatment bring theoretical concepts to a boil; and we should examine the functioning of theory as an interrelated system.

Only laziness prevents us from explaining theory in other words. And only effort is required to follow out theory's systematic structure. But when we try to integrate troublesome practice with comfortable theories, we pit ourselves against a basic, practical instinct that deserves to be respected, and studied in its own right. It is the instinct responsible for the subdued way that treatment stress is depicted in theory and it is to this problem that I now return.

. . . . .

I do not mean to imply that nobody has noticed how messy and stressful psychotherapy is. Unflinching descriptions of struggle may be found in Freud, Reich, Rank, and Nunberg. Heinrich Racker (1968) is a good representative of a host of writers who depict treatment as a continuous pressure on the analyst. Melanie Klein (1952) shows the analyst being "done to." (Even these writers tend to make the analyst appear to be on top of the situation.) Outside the Freudian tradition, descriptions of the strain tend to be more vivid. Jay Haley's (1963) work is an excellent example. Edgar Levenson (1972) discusses the analyst's helplessness and the patient's distress. Whitaker and Malone (1953) describe normal therapist distress most dramatically, although they make it seem self-inflicted.

Yet, as noted, someone learning about psychotherapy from books and journals would have a distinctly different impression. It would seem to him that psychotherapy was only incidentally a situation of mutual stress, and primarily the perception of configurations.

It is ironic that a psychology of passions has made treatment seem like a cognitive exercise. But it is not surprising. The therapist's most deliberate and conscious effort is the effort to perceive, and it is one of the few efforts he can describe. Psychoanalysis is analysis, and, even aside from the construction of personal history, it attempts to tag ingredients in a problem. There is also the fact that the parties to a therapy have historically seen themselves as explaining things. Something in the nature of an understanding is supposed to emerge from therapy.

As always in psychotherapy, the reality may be quite different. Sometimes "understanding" is a sullen trade-off by the patient—something he has to put up with in exchange for a secret gratification left unchallenged, or payment for a promised gratification. (Few patients leave therapy without feeling betrayed, however slightly, and that is not because they expected more research.) Sometimes understanding goes by the board, and open warfare breaks out. Patients who will not accept bargains tacitly are the ones who teach us about stress and dysharmony. But these patients (often called borderline or narcissistic) are considered exceptional.

If psychoanalysis, having emphasized the importance of frustration in treatment and the dangers of gratification, has not drawn the logical conclusion that treatment is first and foremost conflict and disharmony, one suspects it is because there is more harmony than theory logically implies, and more disharmony than it graphically portrays. (There is both more and less gratification than we are accustomed to thinking.) Tension can be felt moment-to-moment by the therapist. And it can be seen dramatically at the beginning and end of treatment, although with the exception of Rank (1936) and his followers, therapists tend to view beginnings and endings as specialized events, bounding a less agitated process. (Gill's [1982] approach is partly designed to correct that formalism: In his account everything may go on at once.)

All that being said, it is true that people do not let themselves get hurt any more than they have to, and they acquire the knack of getting along, thus obscuring the inner negotiations of therapy. Being listened to and perhaps even being understood is genuinely satisfying in addition to falsely implying a promise of personal attachment. And if seeking and receiving under-standing is what therapy is supposed to look like, both parties have an incentive to see it that way. Thus, the field of tension I have described usually has the guise of an amicable, mostly one-sided conversation, with the therapist in the role of helper.

In addition, therapists also have an orienting reason for emphasizing the cognitive nature of therapy. Stressful and bewildering as the first efforts at psychoanalysis were, they were summarized as an orderly procedure in Freud's (1895) contribution to "Studies on Hysteria." As soon as newer types of stress were encountered, parallel improvements in theory assimilated them to the original, relatively stressless description of psychoanalysis. Of course, Freud did not conceal the difficulties he encountered. And troubles are evident in the descriptions of later theoreticians of Narcissism and Borderline conditions. The therapist can recognize the intensity of those problems by comparing them with his own vivid experiences. But the theory of the mind and the theory of treatment are written in such a way as to drain those troubles of their ache. One might almost say that the effect of theoretical terminology is to make the *Sturm und Drang*, which became increasingly evident in psychoanalysis, seem as much as possible like the clean retrieval of memories that had once been its rationale. Both esthetic and conceptual means are used in this transformation as psychoanalysis acknowledges the analyst's frustration, and the patient's insistence and disappointment.

Phrases such as "working through," and "analyzing a resistance" convey an altogether quieter drama than the scene they describe. For purposes of "real life," (as, for instance, to guide someone who is uncertain whether he wants to become a therapist), it would be more useful to say that Freud, in the 1890s, had to allow himself to be played with and fought with by his patients, and that, in the 1920s, psychoanalysts recognized that they had to let themselves in for opposition. That would describe the therapy vocation better than talking about how the analyst learned to exploit the transference or turned from analysis of id to analysis of defense, and so on. (See Gill's [1982] reminder that Freud's word *tummelplatz*, which is translated as "playground" of the transference, has rather the meaning of a wrestling arena.)

The transformation of practical stress into theoretical tranquility has led to an uneasy feeling that something is being left out. If treatment as written about seems so discursive and intellectual and neat and cool, perhaps treatment as it happens really works on the basis of what every psychother-apist feels daily: personal push and pull; nameless, theory-less, shapeless, swarming interaction. (The account given by Whitaker and Malone [1953] moves in that direction.)

Just a few years ago it was only therapists far from the analytic center (e.g., Fritz Perls, 1966) who declared that accepted theory did not mirror their work, often reacting with a brutal anti-intellectualism. Nowadays, however, one can find distaste near the center of psychoanalysis for the whole theoretical apparatus that analysis has so painstakingly built.

The idea that what actually happens in the consulting room is inaccurately reflected in theory has inspired more and more thinkers to elaborate less and less theory. They are not, on that account, more attentive to stress. (For example, Schafer and even Kohut make therapy seem benign and benignly perceived; compare Kohut with Nunberg!) But they do seek to avoid the apparent mismatch of a highly cerebral theory laid on a field of active striving.

We might take another approach: As against the natural tendency of theory to smooth over the dislocations of practice, if we could find in the literature a concept that stands for the tension between therapist and patient, it might help us to view the tension more searchingly, and we would also see how theory soothes it. Because we begin this book with the therapist's stress, we want to find a marker in theory that points to the therapist's tension. We will have that marker when we spot the theoretical description of what the therapist strains for or against.

Resistance might be thought of, but it is not a good tool for our purpose. It is a concept that is clearest when most blatantly misused. Properly used, the concept of resistance describes the struggle in therapy from the standpoint of the patient's wishes, and only by reading it backward does it describe what the therapist wants. We are looking for a concept that designates the therapist's wishes—what he has at stake that can subject him to stress; what it is that would make him happy or unhappy.

That, I think, is a perfect description of the concept of the therapeutic alliance. It has the air of an ad hoc term, so it is likely to have sprung directly from exigencies of practice. And by its very title it points to an effort that arises from the analyst's desire.

At the time that I wrote the following review, Elizabeth Zetzel (1958, 1966) had brought the concept to recent attention. Having in mind a particular group of patients, she warned about covert threats to the alliance. I should probably have mentioned her famous contribution, although she suffered little because everybody noticed the omission. She is so much identified with the therapeutic alliance that, not having used the concept for her purposes, I was accused of inventing my own definition (See chapter 3). But the therapeutic alliance is an old concept. And I turned to it not because it was currently much talked about but precisely because it ran through most of psychoanalytic history and promised to show, throughout that span, what it is that the analyst wants, what effects his wanting it has, and how he uses its theoretical statement to help himself.

2

Discomfort Reflected in Theory:

The Therapeutic Alliance

T he concept of the therapeutic alliance originates in Freud's "The Dynamics of Transference" (1912a) as the resolution of a paradox encountered in the theory and practice of therapy. Freud had previously (1910b) described the transference as a helpful bond which prevents the patient from again "taking flight" as he had done in building his neurosis. But elsewhere (1910a) he had noted that the transference often constitutes the major resistance to analysis. In "The Dynamics of Transference" he characteristically confronts this paradox head-on. How, he asks, can the transference, which largely motivates a patient to struggle against his neurosis, at the same time be the major weapon that the neurosis uses against those efforts? He answers that the transference is composed of different kinds of attachment, some of which interfere with the patient's cooperation by lending themselves to the resistance, while others induce the patient to persevere. The non-cooperative elements are negative feeling and the unconscious erotic component. The helpful part of the transference is the "conscious" and "unobjectionable" positive feeling of the patient toward his analyst.

This simple answer is not as clear as it seems. First of all, the focus on conscious and unobjectionable positive feelings comes immediately after the statement that "all the emotional relations of sympathy, friendship, trust, and the like, which can be turned to good account in our lives are genetically linked with sexuality and have developed from purely sexual desires" (1912a, p. 105). Second, Freud (1912a) has declared that "*every* single association, every act . . . must reckon with the resistance" (p. 103; italics added). Thus the helpful and unhelpful feelings of the patient toward the analyst may be not separate feelings (in the way that love and hate are separate), but different aspects of the same feeling. Freud seems to be saying that, whatever its origins and overtones which unconsciously may work against analysis, much of the friendly feeling toward the analyst which the patient can accept is what helps the analysis along.

But even with this qualification, the formulation raises disturbing questions. Previously, as we have noted, Freud had observed that the patient "must have formed a sufficient attachment (transference) to the physician for his emotional relationship to him to make a fresh flight impossible" (1910b, p. 226). Can this kind of attachment be described as *conscious* and *unobjectionable*? Moreover, Freud holds that the attachment that makes it possible to progress beyond the routine restrictions of the resistance is a consequence of the identification of the analyst with a figure(s) from whom the patient received love or kindness (1912a, p. 99). The papers on therapy generally make it very clear that overcoming the resistance requires exactly those unconsciously erotic and (to the patient) often objectionable forces that alone are commensurate with the forces of resistance.

If positive, mild, non-erotic aspects of the transference are not only inseparable from unconscious forces, but do not even abstractly represent the physician's prime ally within the transference complex, why did Freud bother to make the distinction? A possible reason might be to account for the phenomenological difference between those feelings that keep a patient talking and those that make him stop. Angry or intense, erotic feelings may inhibit speech, while mild friendliness facilitates conversation. But for Freud, who came to analysis from hypnosis in which mild friendliness is not the facilitating factor, this cannot have been impressive enough to inspire an important part of an important essay on the transference. It is much easier to show that Freud distinguished between pro-analytic and anti-analytic elements in the transference because he wanted to call attention to the existence of negative transference. But though the negative transference may be the main target of the paper, it is not the only one. Another reason for the distinction between pro- and anti-analytic forces may be found in what immediately follows in the text, namely a plan of action for the analyst. The analyst "detaches" the two interfering components of the relationship from the person of the physician, while the conscious and unobjectionable part remains and brings about the successful result. Here Freud is grappling with a technical paradox which corresponds to the previously described theoretical paradox: The analyst uses the transference to persuade the patient in a certain way, but on the other hand the transference as an agent of the resistance must be dissolved. To resolve the paradox, he has divided the transference into helpful and interfering factors and proposes that the analyst utilize one and eliminate the other. Because the two are intimately related, the plan is threatened with the same difficulties we have already explored, only now the difficulties are increased because we are not talking about two elements abstracted from a single attitude, but an actual separation of two kinds of feeling. (The process might be considered a training in sublimation.) But although the apparent difficulties in this practical formulation (detaching interfering transference and leaving the unobjectionable one) are even greater than the difficulties of the theoretical paradox (abstracting transference as resistance from transference as assistance), at least this formulation shows why Freud required a division: Where it would have been easy to say that transference is in some ways a help and in some ways a hindrance, it would not have been so easy to say that what the analyst counts on for his effectiveness is also what he must destroy. The analyst has a practical need for a distinction that will enable him to hold on to one thing while trying to alter another.

The significance of this distinction becomes more apparent when we find in this (1912a) essay two other pairs of alternative ways of regarding resistance generally and transference in particular. The first pair has to do with the stereotypy of transference. On page 100 Freud speaks about an inevitable stereotype of loving that is retained from childhood. On page 102 he speaks about the introversion of libido from external figures to infantile imagos. Finally, he resolves the opposition of these aspects in favor of the latter:

> The *mechanism* of transference is, it is true, dealt with when we have traced it back to the state of readiness of the libido which has remained in possession of infantile imagos; but the part transference plays in the treatment can only be explained if we enter into its relations with resistance. [p. 104]

The second pair of alternatives concerns the aim of transference, and emerges at the end of the paper when Freud says that the storms precipitated by exposing the infantile unconscious complexes cannot be explained by the factors considered up to that point. Up to that point he had discussed aspects of the transference which provide a handy vehicle for resistance, i.e., transference as defence. Now he says that another aspect which must be taken into account is transference as longing, i.e. transference in its appetitive aspect, object-seeking as contrasted with complex-protecting.[1]

---

[1]"In all these reflections, however, we have hitherto dealt only with one side of the phenomenon of transference; we must turn our attention to another aspect of the same subject. Anyone who forms a correct appreciation of the way in which a person in analysis, as soon as he comes under the dominance of any considerable transference-resistance, is flung out of his real relation to the doctor, . . . will feel it necessary to look for an explanation of his impression in other factors besides those that have already been adduced. Nor are such factors far to seek: they arise once again from the psychological situation in which the treatment places the patient. . . . The unconscious impulses do not want to be remembered in the way the treatment desires them

Remembering that Freud has spoken both of a necessary deep attachment to the physician and also of transference as primarily resistance, we may ask: Is this object-seeking helpful because it binds the patient to the analyst or is it a hindrance because of its inflexibility? The double description of the transference as a stereotype of loving and as introversion of libido suggests that when transference is viewed as a reflection of introverted libido attached to infantile imagos the analyst will be in the position of fighting it so as to attach libido to his real self and other contempories (1920b, p. 395), while if transference is viewed as the form of loving (a stereotype) which infantile imagos imprint on the patient's relationship with the analyst, he will at least partly welcome it (1915a, p. 168).

Again we might ask why Freud dignifies these alternatives as separate considerations. It would be easier to say that, while the patient's neurotic wanting is what inspires therapeutic progress, the analyst must try to change the styles and goals of wanting. However, from the practical standpoint, the analyst would like to see plainly that what he is encouraging is what motivates therapy, and he is therefore inclined to separate a way of loving the analyst from a way of withholding love. Alternatively, he can settle for one of these ways of looking at transference. He can rule, as Freud does in this paper, that the chief function of transference is resistance. And he can minimize the ambiguous role of transference by contrasting the whole quest for transference gratification with another, totally different, more disciplined attitude which is favorable to, and favored by, the analyst, i.e. the abandonment of the wish for gratification in favor of recovery of memories. Such a solution has the same disadvantages as the solution offered for the other paradoxes: it does not fit easily with the postulated intensity of the attachment that the patient must feel for the analyst. It does, however, reassure the analyst that what he is fostering is clearly distinguished from what he is countering.

Freud's paper may be considered a first effort to resolve a treatment paradox by the series of distinctions that are summarized at the paper's conclusion (1912, p. 108): Analysis is a struggle of the physician versus the patient; intellect versus instinct; recognition versus discharge. But the paradox is not resolved and Freud will continue to emphasize that the physician must not struggle with the patient until the patient is in some sense firmly attached to the physician; that interest and understanding are of limited usefulness as a motive force compared to persuasion or guidance by the physician; and that with many (non-hypnotic-type) patients the compulsion to repeat is not readily replaced by recollection and is turned into a motive for remembering by "admitting it into the playground of the transference." The physician wants to win the reluctant patient to his recommended pursuit of

---

to be, but *endeavour to reproduce themselves* in accordance with the timelessness of the unconscious and its capacity for hallucination" (1912, p. 107; italics added).

the dominance of intellect and renunciation of discharge; but to reach his goal he must follow the tide of the patient's instinctual press for discharge. Through 1919 the paradox remains in this form. There is the emphasis on the need for a strong emotional tie to the physician to increase his persuasiveness, and there is the emphasis on the use of that persuasiveness to diminish the insistence of the drives. Beyond this there is a need, and a preliminary attempt, to distinguish the patient's influenceability from his regressive acting out, partly to pave the way for actually separating these in the course of the analysis.

II

We have noted that in 1912 Freud had been puzzled by the fact that unconscious complexes are not only disguised and elusive, but that when one attempts to track them down the patient's cooperation, good-will and suggestibility evaporate (1912a, p. 107). Not only is an (unconscious) part of the mind unwilling to come to light, but the patient "himself" does not want to do what he agreed to do. In a sense it was this discovery that the analyst does not really have the patient on his side that led to the structural theory. But in 1919 Freud's reaction to the puzzle was to stress the appetitive aspect of the patient's relation with the physician, as distinguished from the defensive aspect.

In 1937, when "Analysis Terminable and Interminable" was published, the structural theory had been formulated, Sterba had already reworked the problem in its terms, and now Freud described the breakdown of cooperation first mentioned in 1912 in the following way. The analyst makes a pact with the ego against the id, and enables the ego to do its share by building confidence and positive transference, despite which, when he demonstrates ego resistance to exploration of the id, the ego breaks its pact, positive transference turns negative and confidence disappears. The success of the analysis depends on how closely the patient's ego approximates an ideal normal ego and how much it is modified by defence formations.

While structural terms make it more precise, this is substantially the same story as before. In the newer terms, our former paradox appears this way: the agency (the ego) whose aid the analyst enlists in subduing the demands of the impulses, is also more or less the executor of those impulses. Perhaps the earlier notion of "introversion of the libido" is continued in the structural theory as "id resistance" or libido adhesiveness. The "other aspect" mentioned in the earlier paper (the appetitive significance of the transference resistance) is now represented as ego modification. In the new light of the structural theory, therefore, what seemed to be two ways of looking at the same thing (resistance as defence and as striving for fulfilment) now appear more as separate functions (id resistance and ego deformity).

Let us examine the notion of ego modification in the context of "Analysis Terminable and Interminable." In that essay Freud (1937) said:

> The effect brought about in the ego by the defences can rightly be described as an 'alteration of the ego' if by that we understand a deviation from the fiction of a normal ego which would guarantee unshakable loyalty to the work of analysis [p. 239].

Now, in Freud's writing the analytic compact obliges the patient to do more than merely talk, and defaulting on that compact may be shown not just by the patient's silence, but by his loss of confidence, his incredulity, animosity, imperviousness to logic, and loss of interest (1937, p. 239). So ego modification concerns not simply volitional acts (such as speaking, keeping secrets, etc.), but also the kind of relationship to the analyst that the patient is able to sustain.

At this point, I think, one reaches a great crossroads for theories of the therapeutic alliance. We have seen the somewhat ambiguous attempt to resolve the paradox of having to rely on something in the patient which must be dissolved. Generally speaking, unconscious complexes are elusive not only because they are hiding, but also because they are seeking (the analyst), and the elusiveness thus has shifting significance in the analysis. In the structural theory, however, it looks as though it may be possible to resolve the paradox into a distinction as follows. The breaking of the Fundamental Rule, loss of confidence, incredulity, animosity, unreasonableness and loss of interest are the result of a structural enslavement of the ego to the id, but adherence to the Fundamental Rule, confidence, amiability, suggestibility, convincibility, openmindedness and enthusiasm are to be explained as a relative freedom from the id. (In later discussions, this position takes the form of contrasting an ego turned to the id, with an ego turned to "reality.") This distinction can be found in Freud's often ascetic portrayal of the struggle to win the patient away from futile attempts at drive indulgence and to direct him toward intellect and reality. But, on the other hand, Freud never loses sight of what might be called the seductive element in analysis (1912, p. 105; 1919, p. 159; 1920, p. 387), and this modifies the picture. So that with Freud, at least, one is still at the cross-roads and can follow the alternative course which is that confidence, amiability, suggestibility, convincibility and enthusiasm, and not just their absence, are the result of the ego seeking satisfaction on behalf of id impulses. However, although this possibility is open, it leads us back to the paradox of using the impulses to counter the impulses. Until recently, when there has been a reaction in favour of this view, discussions of the therapeutic alliance have tended to follow the first course which, instead of a paradox, provides a simple principle, to wit, the success of the analysis depends on the degree of "disinterestedness" of the ego vis `a vis the id; the analyst uses its sense of reality to counter the impulses.

In summary, the double aspect of unconscious complexes as avoiding disturbance by outside reality (the analyst as interpreter) and also seeking actual fulfilment (in the analyst as transference figure) poses a problem since it is only the analyst as transference figure who can function effectively as interpreter and he thus draws for his power on what he is trying to reduce. An attempt is made to segregate transference feelings into those helping and those hindering treatment (hostile or unconsciously erotic, and unobjectionable friendly feelings), but this does not seem a strong solution. A second (structural) suggestion is then made that the analyst relies on an aspect of the patient's psyche (unmodified ego) which is not defensively committed to id impulses. But while this does segregate pro-analytic and anti-analytic factors, it leaves ambiguous the relationship between unmodified ego and the influencibility which has been repeatedly stressed as the vehicle for therapy. Once again the paradox has reasserted itself.

III

Three years before "Analysis Terminable and Interminable," Sterba (1934) had (as I would construe it) already appreciated how useful the structural theory might be in resolving the paradox by opposing "those elements in the ego which are focused on reality to those which have a cathexis of instinctual energy." With this the therapeutic alliance emerges in its familiar form. In order to mark out a clear platform for the alliance Sterba endorsed segregation of pro- and anti-analytic forces even at the cost of leaving the transference out of the alliance. By now it should be clear that the question that must always arise about such a proposal is: What then drives the analysis? What is the motive force behind it? Even Sterba's language betrays this uncertainty when he compares those elements in the ego which are "*focused* on reality and those which have a *cathexis* of instinctual or defensive energy" (italics added). There is a tendency to play down the role of the transference in developing the alliance. For instance, Sterba says that the dissociation of the contemplative ego is fostered by analysis (and presumably reduction) of the transference, together with identification with the analyst, which Sterba does not relate in a definite way to the transference. It is not clear exactly what relationship identification with the analyst has to the transference. But later in the essay Sterba does describe the role of suggestion and transference in establishing this identification.

> In order that this new standpoint [i.e., a new point of view of intellectual contemplation] may be effectually reached there must be a certain amount of positive transference, on the basis of which a transitory strengthening of the ego takes place through identification with the analyst. This identification is

induced by the analyst. From the outset the patient is called upon to "co-operate" with the analyst against something in himself. Each separate session gives the analyst various opportunities of employing the term, "we," in referring to himself and to the part of the patient's ego which is consonant with reality. The use of the word "we" always means that the analyst is trying to draw that part of the ego over to his side and to place it in opposition to the other part which in the transference is cathected or influenced from the side of the unconscious. We might say that this "we" is the instrument by means of which the therapeutic dissociation of the ego is effected [p. 121].

Sterba makes full use of the structural theory to resolve the paradox when he proposes that autonomous functions are set up within the ego. For then it is not so much what the patient seeks from the physician that keeps him going. Rather the physician strengthens an uncathected, autonomous part of the ego, enabling it to function on its own; the transference no longer serves to attach the patient to the physician so much as it enables the patient to assume independently the attitude of the physician. What motivates the patient to identify with the analyst or accept his partly uncongenial insights becomes less important after identification is completed. Perhaps Sterba's attempt to resolve the paradox works by dividing temporally what motivates a patient from what is helpful in analysis.

There are a number of empirical factors which make this description convincing. In human development personal attachments develop into impersonal guide-lines. (Although when Sterba cites the development of the superego as a model for analytic aims, we may reflect that the superego is powered by drives, and ask if the same is true of the ego ally.) Moreover, in analysis one can see the unfolding of a supervisory, disinterested viewpoint of intellectual contemplation. (Sterba refers to the shift from affective response to intellectual contemplation, and a new point of view of intellectual con-templation.) Furthermore, insofar as it portrays the "focus" on reality of part of the ego as able to counterbalance a "cathexis" of another part of the ego by instinctual energy, this picture of analysis finds a comfortable place in the rationalistic current in psychoanalytic thought that treats instinct as at war with reality.

And finally, citing Herder, Sterba is able to appeal to the undeniably self-reflective and autoscopic nature of human consciousness (although he does not attempt to integrate that with the doctrine that ego division comes from conflict).

On the other hand, one cannot fail to notice how far this view is from the main tendency of Freud's technical papers. With Sterba the emphasis has left "cures of love" and "suggestion," "persuasion of the patient," and so on, and the analyst appears more as one who "strengthens" an autonomous ego, while presumably reality does the rest. For all his love of reason and reality, Freud saw in the analytic process a struggle of such magnitude against such powerful forces that intellectual interest and understanding were negligible allies (1913, p. 143). Therefore Freud's therapeutic alliance was largely a libidinal attachment of patient to physician. Freud joined in referring to "our allying ourselves with the ego of the person under treatment, in order to subdue portions of his id which are uncontrolled—that is to say to include them in the synthesis of the ego" (1937, p. 235), but he continued to say that positive transference "is the strongest motive for the patient's taking a share in the joint work of analysis" (1937, p. 233). He notes that a distortion of the ego makes difficulties and sometimes impossibilities for analysis. But he does not look for an autonomous, uncathected, instinct-free ego factor to make the analysis move (1920, p. 387). Compared to Sterba's alliance, Freud's is much more a colonization. (After all, Freud, like Nunberg, regarded a hypnotic type of response by the analysand as ideal in analytic work [1914, p. 151] and that can hardly be described as an alliance with an autonomous, independent ego!)

At the end of "Analysis Terminable and Interminable" we were left with some uncertainty as to whether the patient's confidence, amiability, suggestibility, and so on are the result of the ego's independence from the id, or are, just like their opposites, the product of the ego's bondage. Sterba attempted to set aside this ambiguity by saying in effect that whatever the nature of those attachment factors, their importance is overshadowed by a factor which certainly is a reflection of the ego's independence of the id. The ego ally thus seems to have a life of its own, apart from instinctual cathexis, and therefore apart from any affective association with the analyst. The ego ally works with the analyst not because of the personal relationship between patient and physician, but because at least as regards that fragment, patient and physician share the same purposes. Having said this, of course, we should immediately be struck by the immense difficulties involved in attributing such purposes to part of the ego. How much independent and painful striving can be ascribed to the synthetic function of the ego? The suspicion arises that we have been able to establish a drive-free ally possessed of great motivating energy only by attributing to it drive properties.

But if we view Sterba's therapeutic alliance as more a motivated than a motivating arrangement, then it may be regarded as the outcome of what Freud described as the attempt to persuade a patient "of the inexpediency of the repressive process established in childhood and of the impossibility of conducting life on the pleasure principle" (1919, p. 159). What in Sterba is briefly alluded to as identification with the analyst and acceptance of information from him is the whole of what Freud was wrestling with in the discussions we have considered. All of the problems that were encountered in Freud's extended discussion are latent in Sterba's incidental reference to how the therapeutic alliance is fostered. Sterba's therapeutic alliance, in this view, is the behavior within the analysis that shows the success of the analysis.

(Therefore analysts should be careful about using these terms to judge suitability for analysis or to explain failures, for fear of tautology.) This is not to deny the alliance an instrumental value in the process of analysis, a function that may be pictured as analogous to—and perhaps an aspect of—working through. But just as working through is capitalizing on an achieved success, so the classical therapeutic alliance should not claim to explain the achievement which it propagates.

But if that is so, why would Sterba's vision have had such a long life and played such an important role in discussions of analytic mechanisms? Suppose that it never pretended to be more than a description of analytic achievement. How has it been found to be so useful in describing the patient–analyst transactions? I suggest that it is because Sterba's view provides the illusion of escaping our paradox: how are we to draw from the patient the interest and energy necessary for analysis while subduing the impulses which seem to provide that interest and energy? If the interest and energy come not from libidinal sources but from a natural "focus" of the mind; if the transference relationship does not define a resultant relationship but merely non-specifically "strengthens" an autonomous ego fragment, while the analyst does not so much use a patient's love to urge him onward, as he provides realistic information which fosters a natural tendency to ego-splitting; if the patient will imitate the analyst's approach without exacting or expecting a *quid pro quo*; if all these things should be as Sterba tells us, then there is no paradox.

IV

As an account of the process of therapy, Sterba's description is not a resolution of the paradox but a minimizing of half of it—the half that says that the main propulsion mechanism in the analysis is the patient's attachment to the physician. It falls to Nunberg to rescue that half of the paradox. Nunberg recognizes a split-off ego fragment as important in analysis, and like Sterba he gives central significance to identification with the analyst. Of course, if Sterba's therapeutic alliance is regarded as the outcome of psychoanalysis, Nunberg's alliance can be thought of as a means to it. But insofar as Sterba regards the therapeutic alliance as a major "tool" of analysis, a radical difference in outlook separates him from Nunberg. For Nunberg sees the basic aims of the analyst as simply opposed to those of the patient (1932, p. 334; 1926, p. 76). The patient at first wants (1) to fascinate by speech and not yield secrets, (2) to gain the analyst's love and attention, (3) to become involved in himself for narcissistic gratification, and (4) to exercise his intellect (1928, p. 111). He wants "complete liberation of impulses," freedom from inhibitions (1932, p. 336). He wants magic protection, absolution from his guilt, privacy for his shame, and a static symbiotic relationship to the analyst (1928, p. 116). Surely much of this will disguise itself as the discovering of a new intellectual point of view, but none of it, according to Nunberg, not even the intellectual interest, promotes treatment. It is possible that not all the clinical phenomena which Sterba would consider steps in the formation of the dissociated ego would be so charitably judged by Nunberg.

But when Nunberg says that the patient's interests and purposes do not promote treatment, he means that they are not part of the analytic work proper and must be replaced by a different kind of work. He does not mean that they play no part in the progress of the analysis. These hopes and activities lead to confession, for instance, and confession leads to transference. Magic expectations lead to a kind of therepeutic alliance which, it should be noted, is illusory (the analyst is not really allied with the patient in the way the patient thinks), but which is nonetheless effective in diminishing anxiety and creating the atmosphere of protection essential to the uncovering of repressions (1928, pp. 112–115). Protected by an illusory endorsement from a strong, magical confessor who is felt to love him as he loves himself, the patient develops an almost hypnotic attitude toward the analyst. Only when the patient raises the analyst to the status of an hypnotic ideal can the analysis succeed (1928, pp. 112–113). The reason for this is that the time must come when the analytic work proper must be done (recovery of memories, etc.), and that can be accomplished only by the threat of the loss of the analyst's love. "When the analysis is threatened; when he sees the analyst lose interest," then the patient first gets to work and is willing to accept insight (1928, p. 116; 1932, p. 354). (Note that this forces him not only to understand but to *accept* insight.)

What Sterba briefly alluded to as giving information and promoting identification here takes on near-tragic proportions. Nowhere else are the implications so boldly spelled out of Freud's requirement that the physician attach the patient to him in such a way that he can no longer take flight. Freud said that "our cures are cures of love" and Nunberg makes it clear that this means that it is the threat of loss of love that persuades the patient along the paths that will be useful to him. Gone is the analyst's alliance with a split-off, uncathected, reality-focused ego fragment. Instead we have an indulgent, magical alliance with a fantasy analyst followed by a desperate appeasement of him as the fantasy mask slips from his countenance. Words like bondage or enslavement, if they were not so melodramatic, would in fact seem to characterize the relationship more exactly than alliance.

Where Sterba is spare, Nunberg is full. Sterba concentrated on the end stage of a persuasion process. What is misty is the factor of motivation. Nunberg, on the other hand, has the motivation problem mainly in view, and since he recognizes that motivation is tightly tied to pathology, he is concerned to discover how it is converted to a force for cure. Somehow work done for the wrong (pathological, fantastic) reasons must result in a change of motives. It will do this if the work encompasses revival of repressed memories and acceptance of the analyst's interpretations. It is as though the patient works and believes as a bribe to induce the analyst to perform his magical protection and facilitation, but after the work is done and the conviction established he finds that he does not require the protection and facilitation for which he labored. The patient may not be working toward the same goal as the analyst, as Sterba suggested, but whatever goal he may have, he can be made to do the right work. But what fundamentally is the work that the analyst insists on? Is it the offering to a magical analyst-figure of gifts, bribes, and sacrifices in the form of credulity and the recovery of memories? Freud says that what the analyst wants is to persuade the patient in favour of the reality principle and against insistence on unbridled gratification. Tarachow (1963, p. 20) points out that, for the patient, accepting an interpretation means abandoning a wish, and it has often been emphasized that recollection means foregoing the attempt to gratify impulses. Perhaps, then, in recollecting and accepting insight at the analyst's behest the patient is in that very act modifying his purposes, altering his motivation, and therefore changing his picture of what the analyst has to offer him. But if this is so, what shall we say about the postulated motivation which is pathological and unrealistic? Is it sensible to say that in order to bribe the analyst the patient must abandon his request? How does an analyst persuade a patient to be more realistic by coercing him with magical threats and blandishments? If Sterba dwells primarily on the end stages and achievement of persuasion, leaving obscure the problem of how it is reached, Nunberg seems to concentrate on the beginning, leaving it uncertain how the particular power of persuasion which he describes can persuade to the goal he wishes. As a choice between a therapeutic alliance without a motor or an energetic alliance without an obvious therapeutic orientation, this is another manifestation of our complex of paradoxes. Contrasted with Sterba's position that the patient has hidden within him, needing only encouragement for its emergence, the same outlook and purposes as the analyst, Nunberg's view that the analyst must use the patient's wrong reason to make him do the right thing raises the question of how commensurate reasons must be with results. The general problem is how a patient who wants only fulfilment of his infantile demands can be made to relinquish them by someone who is not sympathetic with that purpose; how a physician whose importance to a patient lies in his illusory promise of fulfilling infantile demands can derive from them the leverage and authority to undermine them. But however many problems it may raise, Nunberg's is a powerful description of one horn of a very persistent dilemma. It does not seem to have become a popular view, and the popular view may have suffered from its absence. We shall later suggest some reasons why it is not a comfortable position to hold.

V

With the two strong voices on either side of the paradox—Sterba's on the rationalistic, Nunberg's on the libidinal side—Fenichel (1941) seems to place himself as a moderator. In regard to our paradox he is closely aligned with Sterba. He believes that the irrational purposes described by Nunberg represent a "pathological" variant (p. 26), while one can usually rely on a normal wish for recovery, which is associated with a "reasonable ego." Following Sterba, he divides the ego into an observing and experiencing portion. If the reasonable ego is sufficiently fostered, it can pull its own weight, and there is a basic similarity between the patient's wishes for health and the analyst's wishes for him. Ideally no inducement is needed if the realistic ego is confronted with the genesis of its resistance. To be sure, interpretations are accepted not only because of their recognized truth, but also because of identification with the analyst and because the "rational transference" (aim-inhibited positive transference) induces the patient to take a less skeptical view concerning anything expressed by the analyst. But although he acknowledges its usefulness in overcoming certain resistances, Fenichel's appreciation of the transference is tempered by his recognition that, no matter how positive and no matter how aim-inhibited, a transference is a transference: "the impulses belong to infantile objects, and therefore a time must come when these same transference impulses become resistances" (p. 28). With this in mind, Fenichel raises a question which seems to be addressed to Nunberg: if the transference perpetuates infantile longings and expectations, would not its prolongation and intensification be anti-therapeutic? (p. 46). If transference is not interpreted in the beginning, that makes it more difficult later on when it has become interwoven with reality. We might add that failure to interpret transference all along might constitute a tacit encouragement of it, a promise to fulfil its associated fantasies. In that case the reality that transference eventually becomes interwoven with would be the analyst subtly grown into his transference role.[2] Nunberg agreed that transference satisfactions are totally in lieu of therapeutic progress. The difference is that Nunberg felt that they are at least a pre-condition for progress, while Fenichel thought that they hamper it, and should be neutralized as they occur. "The analyst must not offer his patients any *transference satisfactions*. . . . The fulfilment of what the patient longs for most in the analysis serves as a resistance to further analysis and therefore must be refused him" (p. 29). Fulfilment removes the incentive to analytic work. But

---

[2]In theory this problem is usually solved by referring to the patient's ability to reverse a regression in the service of the ego, and the analyst's ability to dissolve an earlier transference distortion by genetic interpretation. These factors, however weighty, should not completely exclude from consideration the fact that experience is cumulative, patients are taught from the outset and learning goes on minute by minute.

what if there is no fulfilment, no transference gratification? Does not that remove the incentive to analytic work? Nunberg thinks so; Fenichel does not. But Fenichel's acknowledgement that positive transference and identification with the analyst facilitate insight and "are very welcome during long periods of analysis" (p. 28) speaks against this view since it would be very difficult to maintain that these aids to acceptance have nothing to do with gratification. (A totally frustrated transference is no transference.) Fenichel makes another comment which constitutes a major qualification to his asceticism despite its casual formulation: "Whoever is blocked in any piece of work to which he is devoted, becomes annoyed: whoever foresees a new advance in knowledge is always glad" (p. 74). It requires no subtle reasoning to discover in this annoyance and gladness a rich area of transference gratification.

If we look at Nunberg and Fenichel together, Nunberg regarding the patient's strivings as totally opposed to what the analyst stands for but indispensable in moving the patient healthward, Fenichel seeing those strivings as not so pernicious and also quite helpful, but their satisfaction as totally detrimental to therapeutic progress, the outline of our old paradox emerges in a slightly altered form: To the extent that a patient is satisfied he has no incentive to change; but to the extent that he is not satisfied he has no willingness to change (to accept interpretations, etc.).

VI

While understandable in its theoretical context, the notion that a patient should ideally get no transference gratification from the analytic hour is an absurdity. To say that someone might engage in a prolonged, highly ab-sorbing and demanding interchange without seeking and getting personal gratification is simply not to talk psychoanalytically, nor is it reasonable to suppose that this personal gratification might be free of transference. In terms of the dilemma we have been discussing, the pendulum of opinion has swung back to an emphasis on the role played by gratification in the progress of therapy. If (to oversimplify) Sterba spotlighted an alliance with a non-striving ego fragment which corresponded to the analyst's purposes, while Nunberg concentrated on the patient's libidinal strivings which were entirely opposed to the analyst's purpose, the quest in this decade has been to find in the patient something in the nature of a striving which is harmonious with what in fact the analyst is doing.

In this project Loewald's germinal paper (1960) has inspired many of the others. Loewald suggested that one sort of childhood need which is not only sought in analysis, but is also fulfilled by analysis, is the need to identify with one's growth potential as seen in the eyes of a parent. Being reacted to like that not only provides hope in general but structures reality in a relevant and promising fashion.

It is this something more, not necessarily more in content but more in organization and significance, that 'external reality', here represented and mediated by the analyst, has to offer the individual and for which the individual is striving [p. 26].

Note the difference between this picture and that of a simple reality presented to an ego fragment focused on reality.

Similarly, Gitelson (1962) writes:

The analyst's empathic imbrication with his patient's emotions provides a sustaining grid of "understanding" [or "resonance"] which leads towards cooperation and identification, to the partial relinquishment of the anaclitic attitude, and in the end to a collaboration which Sterba has called "therapeutic alliance" [p. 199].

In the beginning of this relationship there is a primitive rapport nourished by the patient's optimistic feeling of "hope" or "expectation" that the diatrophic response which he looked for in coming into analysis, can be fulfilled. At first the rapport represents the illusory narcissistic gratification: "the analyst loves me as I love myself." This belief leads to a "new beginning." It should be noted that in this Gitelson is describing what Nunberg had felt to be an antitherapeutic wish, opposed to the real direction of the analyst. Gitelson, however, shares with Loewald the belief that there is some reality in this narcissistic rapport insofar as it reflects the analyst's help in synthesizing the patient's needs and integrating them with reality after the fashion of a good parent. Doing that is a kind of equivalent of loving, of "making everything right." (Perhaps this is embodied in greatly magnified fashion in magical omnipotence fantasies.) With this realistic core satisfaction, there is room for the patient to maintain something of what attaches him to the analyst while relating to him in a more separate (dyadic) way, thus bridging the chasm that Nunberg had left open before us. Greenson (1967) also prefers to speak of a working alliance no longer confined to a reality-attuned ego-fragment and having rational and irrational components. (These include "the non-sexual, non-romantic, mild, mild forms of love" [p. 225], which is similar to Freud's first attempt to isolate the analyst's "agent" in the patient's camp and would not carry us further were it not that, unlike Freud, Greenson explicitly relates these feelings to unconscious motherly and fatherly appearances [p. 240].)

Perhaps Stone's (1961) formula best summarizes recent trends: what is always wanted by a patient is the primal parent, the primary mother, the mother of bodily contact. But the patient also wants the parent who fosters growth, the secondary mother, the mother of separation who provides understanding, control and teaching (p. 72) and in whom, as Loewald observed, the child can see himself being seen in terms of his potential (1967, p. 24). The therapeutic alliance thus includes (1) the mature transference derived from this need for guidance; (2) the tender part of the erotic transference, friendly adult feelings and ego identification (Freud's early suggestion); (3) genuine need for help and rational and intuitive appraisal of the analyst, together with adult appropriate confidence in him; and (4) the primordial transference from the wish for the nurturing, body-contact mother as the driving force.

The theoretical need to combine motivational energy with appropriateness to what the analyst really has to offer may be seen in the following:

> In any case, to most adults, the transference "tag" of the parentallike function is at once a stable, dependable, non-seductive reality, and at the same time, a stimulus through deep, archaic reverberation, of the anaclitic, and still more profound symbiotic, elements in the struggle against separation, which find representation in the various shades of the therapeutic transference [Stone, 1967, p. 30].

VII

A theme that recurs frequently in recent discussions of the therapeutic alliance is the importance of hopefulness. It is implicit in Loewald's picture of the child identifying with the growth potential seen in him by his parents. When Loewald writes that there is something special 'in organization and significance that "external reality", represented and mediated by the analyst, has to offer the individual and for which the individual is striving', he is saying that the analyst is not just a disciplinarian rubbing unsatisfying reality in the ego's face, so to speak, but a guide to the promise that reality potentially affords this particular patient. Gitelson stresses the importance of an optimistic feeling of hope and expectation in the collaboration with the analyst.

Of course, it has always been implicitly recognized that hope was involved somewhere in analysis, if only by logical entailment from the notion of transference. What has not always been clear is what part it played in therapeutic progress. By implication, in Nunberg's outline hope for unrealistic gain is what ties the patient to the analyst and what allows him to overcome repression. In Sterba's paper and in Fenichel its locus is not so explicit. But that is probably because the function of hope is hidden in such notions as the strengthening of the ego by the positive transference (Sterba), and the diminishing of skepticism that comes from identification with the analyst and from the rational transference (Fenichel). 'Strengthening of the ego' is a kind of engineering metaphor (one of the areas where structural concepts tend to invite the substitution of a picture for an explanation), and while it is a commonplace of everyday experience that positive feelings diminish skepticism (Freud, 1920, p. 387), how and why is not part of the commonplace. In both formulations it seems likely that hope has a great deal to do with it.

Where the later writers tend to diverge from the earlier, then, is not in stressing the importance of hope in analysis, but in trying to find something realistic in that hope, or more precisely, some correspondence between the patient's hopes and what the analyst has to offer.

It is curious that in recent discussions of the issue, the work of French is rarely exploited. In his examination of therapeutic process, the role of hope is not only central, but is carefully spelled out and clinically documented (French, 1958). French shows that the ability to re-open poorly resolved questions, to de-repress threatening issues, is related to periodic resurgence of hope for greater fulfilment.[3]

The earlier authors differ from French in portraying hope as favoring the status quo. They tend to regard hope as necessary for building the bond that allows the analyst leverage but in itself a conservative or reactionary force, reflecting false confidence in the achievability of infantile demands. (This is most clearly indicated in Nunberg.) Problems arise in visualizing the use of this backward-pointing energy for forward-pointing movement. French's commentary bridges the gap. According to him the reawakening of hope in the transference calls into question the necessity of neurotic solutions to earlier problems. The work of uncovering repressed material is aided by the transference not just because the transference inclines a patient to please the analyst, but also because it gives the patient himself a reason to review settled matters, the reason being a live hope of a better fulfilment. It should be noted that *this* incentive, unlike the first, is not predicated on a conditional attitude of the analyst; it is not a result of an implied threat.

However hope fits into a theory of therapy, its awakening depends on a perception of some kind of congruence of the outlook and aims of the patient and those of the analyst, whether the congruence is illusory, as Nunberg suggests, or partially realistic as later writers have indicated. With this in mind consider Freud's vivid description of what happens when, in some cases, pointing out ego resistances leads to a break-up of the whole analytic situation: "The patient now regards the analyst as no more than a stranger who is making disagreeable demands upon him, and he behaves toward him exactly like a child who does not like the stranger and does not believe anything he says " (1937, p. 239). This remarkable passage, with its emphasis

---

[3]Seen in this light such factors as the analyst's magical protection may appear as more than a hallucinatory wish for unbridled instinctual gratification. No doubt it is that; but being that, it is also perforce a representation of the confidence that the emotional compromises that have been made can be improved. Nunberg describes this situation as a two-stage process. First, the patient's ego is strengthened by the illusion of magical protection; second, the stronger ego is better able to deal with anxiety-producing material. But that may be an artificial subdivision of a process which is just an awakening of dormant hope *accompanied* by the inevitable fantasies concerning the analyst who stirred it up. This possibility has been extensively explored by Kohut (1977).

on "stranger," has not received the attention it deserves, though the phenomenon is a familiar one. Many theorists would no doubt say that a feeling that
the analyst is alien is simply a sign of lack of suggestibility and convincibility.
But perhaps it works both ways. (For instance, Nunberg says that the patient
finds "in his ego some points of contact with the analyst" (1928, p. 110) and
comments on the importance of the patient's feeling when he comes into
analysis that he is no longer alone (1932, p. 340).)

What are the ways that an analyst becomes *not* a stranger? Specifically, of
course, he takes on certain transference roles. Less specifically, according to
Freud, Loewald, Stone and Gitelson, he performs some actual parental
ministrations. Most generally, then, he becomes other than a stranger by
somehow fitting into the need pattern of the patient. *Insofar as confidence and
suggestibility are related to the analyst's not being a stranger, id impulses help to
produce that state by rendering the figure of the analyst recognizable and familiar.*
The same congruence between analyst and patient that awakens hope also
makes the analyst not a stranger. I have elsewhere speculated that human
drives act as discriminating feelers in perceiving the external world, by
relating what is new and strange to what is old and familiar and thus
facilitating its understanding (Friedman, 1968a). Loewald (1960) says that
"there is neither such a thing as reality nor a real relationship, without a
transference." In saying this he emphasizes the straining of perception
through the grid of drives and feelings which provide its comprehension and
"meaning." (See also Friedman, 1973.)

VIII

We are led, then, to the position that a congruence between patient and
analyst makes the analyst something other than a stranger, naturalizes
otherwise alien interpretations, and awakens hope in the patient. But this
seems to intensify our dilemma, for the purpose of analysis is change, and
familiarity and hope are usually thought of in terms of the old patterns and
old cravings. What makes it less paradoxical is the ancient truth that change
is a synthesis of old and new.[4] This is as true of the change involved in
forming a new idea or perception as it is of change in behaviour. We always
read the present in terms of the past. Something totally alien cannot be
comprehended. Similarly, the direction behaviour takes is determined by our
past and present goals. What is totally unconnected with them cannot move
us (Friedman, 1968b).

It is therefore only to be expected that, as Nunberg emphasizes, what a
patient wants on entering analysis is the fulfilment of the infantile wishes

---

[4]This is empirically investigated in detail in the work of Jean Piaget. See chapter 25.

which underlie his symptoms without their attendant discomfort. What else could he possibly want? If that is what he wanted before analysis, that must certainly be what he wants on entering analysis. It is those wishes which help him to welcome the analyst's insights as 'hitting home', and it is those wishes which, finding hope in the arrival of the analyst on the scene, impel movement, renunciation and the necessary endurance. People move toward their opportunities and opportunities are compounded out of old hopes and new circumstances. That which makes the analyst relevant must lie somewhere among the patient's strivings. The branch of analytic literature that follows Sterba endeavours to isolate it from the illness, but being associated with strivings it probably cannot be isolated from the illness. The only hope a patient can have is a present hope, manifesting itself in the form that hope takes at the present stage in his life. New opportunities will tend to be related to present hopes, and then if all goes well the form of the hope may change.

One must address the patient as he is or one is not addressing the patient; and one must fit into his present need pattern in some way or one is a stranger. In psychoanalysis this addressing and fitting typically takes the form of understanding, articulation, acceptance or tolerance. The analyst may be familiar and gratifying also in a purely fantastic way, as Nunberg points out. But at the stage in analysis when, according to Nunberg, the analyst dispels the illusion of unlimited acceptance, there must be something other than illusion which entices the patient forward.

On the other hand, he who seeks personality change must bring something new to the patient. Being completely familiar, offering to satisfy hopes only in their present expression, gives no vector to the process. Further, meeting the patient on the terms of present personality arrangements alone is not meeting him as he really is, or acting really as a familiar object because the present personality is an inadequate compromise obscuring impulses and aspirations. (Similarly parents would fail if they did not treat their child as a future adult, cf. Loewald. [1960].) In Freud's terms, one must not be a stranger, but one must be a persuader with a new and different vision. The task of allowing oneself to be seen in old, familiar terms, and meeting (by accepting and tolerating) needs expressed in terms of old compromises, while at the same time not settling for them is the source of the paradoxes we have been examining.

We have already referred to Stone's requirement that the physician and analyst must be felt by the patient to be the same person – the analyst's functions of primary mother of bodily contact and secondary mother of separation must seem to inhere in the same figure (1961, p. 110). Here the paradox we have been dealing with is reduced to its primary significance. The psychoanalyst (like all psychotherapists) must convey to the patient not only the direction he wants the patient to move in, but also the confidence that the movement is inherent in the patient, which means that what the uncured patient wants is indeed a representation, however distorted, of what the cured patient will get. To the extent that the analyst fails to convey this promise he will naturally lose significance to the patient. How he succeeds is more difficult to say, but it must have something to do with the acceptance or tolerance referred to from Freud's early papers on. The notion of tolerance deserves far more investigation than it has received. For instance, there would seem to be an opposition between "acceptance" and "persuasion." Also acceptance seems quite different from Nunberg's hard-line ultimatum. Fenichel forthrightly states that whoever is blocked in his work becomes annoyed,without commenting on the problems this raises regarding the analyst's traditional tool of tolerance. The acid test of the analyst's attitude toward the drives and their derivatives, after all, is not his willingness to hear them verbalized, but his reaction to their manifestation in the analytic session where they are bound to block the analyst's work in varying degrees. If, for instance, a patient says that he feels guilty about his pleasure in talking about himself, and the analyst, mindful of Nunberg's warning that this narcissistic indulgence replaces difficult confrontations, directs the patient to concentrate on uncomfortable subjects, the analyst has conveyed to the patient a judgement on his exhibitionistic impulses more decisive than the "acceptance" he shows in allowing the patient to talk *about* his exhibitionistic impulses without criticism.

It follows that the concept of resistance is a tricky one. Resistance may be described as a trade concept, a job term for the analyst, an abstraction designed to be relevant to the analyst's working purposes. Since it is an abstraction, what it points to can obviously be looked at in other ways (for instance, as the implementing of a wish). Since the phenomenon referred to as resistance has these other significances, the analyst's attitude toward resistance will appear to be his attitude toward those other factors. Resistances are a part of a patient's wishing, part of his hope, part of his identity, as well as part of his handicap. It would therefore be impossible for an analyst to show great tolerance of a patient's instinctual drives while manifesting impatience with his resistances. It is the analyst's response to the patient's resistances that teaches the patient which of his wishes and drives are acceptable and which are not. In comparison the mere freedom to talk of taboo subjects is almost inconsequential. Freud says that by moralizing it is possible for the analyst to forfeit the natural advantage of being identified with earlier love objects (1913, p. 140). When Fenichel condones the intervention, 'You are in a state of resistance' (1941, p. 36), should we not consider this a form of moralizing? This is one of the reasons for the truth of Glover's (1955, p. 204) statement that analysing the negative transference without tracing its origin is a reproach. Loewenstein (1963), citing Kris, cautions against the posture of the "angry analyst" toward resistance, even in conceptualizing the analytic process. One must be alert to the low-keyed, apparently technical maneuvers, seemingly devoid of passion, which can embody and convey an angry message (e.g., some disguised way of saying "You are not cooperating with me").

IX

We are now in a position to understand the origin of the paradox that generated the therapeutic alliance concept. Hope is what makes a patient move, and what re-opens sealed (defended) solutions. Hope can only be a present hope, in the shape given it by the patient's present psychological configuration. It may have its illusions, which Nunberg has so clearly outlined, but if it is to withstand the realities of treatment, there must also be a hope that is founded on a real congruence between patient and analyst (Loewald, Gitelson, and Stone have investigated this real congruence). This means that there must be some sense in which the patient perceives the analyst's interest as identical with his own current interest. There are a lot of corollaries to this: the patient must feel that what he takes as himself, the analyst also to some extent takes him to be (Coleman, 1968), that his aspirations, however neurotically distorted, are in some sense endorsed by the analyst. This congruence is the foundation for the non-congruent persuasiveness of the analyst, who in another sense does not settle for what the patient takes as himself, and tries in a way to change the patient's aspirations (Loewald, Gitelson, and Stone). Thus the analyst's attitude must combine a kind of acceptance with a kind of non-acceptance in the sense of not settling for the way things are. Accepting and not settling means depriving a patient of his illusions (cf. Tarachow, 1963) while at the same time valuing them for the possibilities they represent. In other words, the analyst must accept the patient on his own terms, and at the same time not settle for them. If he does not accept the patient on his own terms, it is as though he is asking him to be someone else, the patient will not have cause for hope, and he will not recognize the analyst's vision. If the analyst settles for the patient's terms, he is ignoring the concealed part of the personality and betraying the patient's wish for a greater fulfilment.

This task may be even more difficult to describe than to perform. Acceptance of the patient with his strivings (and the congruence, familiarity and hope this generates) is recognized throughout the literature as fundamental to move the patient. But the persuasion necessary to move the patient is thought to undercut it. Thus arises the initial paradox that the analyst depends for his influence on something he must destroy. It is at this point that the therapeutic alliance is postulated to indicate something (ultimately an ego fragment) which is in the patient, can be accepted and endorsed, and is not inimical to change. Whatever kind of maneuvering may be necessary to strengthen or reinforce it or split it off, it is an institution in the patient which guarantees congruence with the analyst even while the analyst is busy detaching himself from the patient's fantasy grasp.

The therapeutic alliance thus postulates a congruence between patient and analyst on the analyst's terms. We have seen that the account runs into difficulties on the score of patient motivation. As a description of success in analysis, it is not without merit. The patient's observation of id derivatives, the exposing of unconscious fantasies — these activities of the patient constitute a partial renunciation of direct fulfilment, and are in themselves a sublimation. From the beginning Freud described analysis as an attempt to persuade patients to give up their insistence on living by the pleasure principle. The development of realistic sublimations therefore shows that the patient is being persuaded. The appearance of the therapeutic alliance is a sign of the accomplishment of analytic objectives. To say that analysis depends on the therapeutic alliance is a little like saying that analysis depends on sublimation or that analysis depends on maturity.

But it is as a fulcrum of movement, not a sign of achievement, that the alliance was designed. It was intended to permit the analyst an escape from the position which theory originally put him in, namely to fit into the need pattern of a neurotic patient in order to become important enough to him to change that pattern. By virtue of the therapeutic alliance the patient was implicitly endowed with another set of needs (though they were not explicitly called needs), which were happily the same as the analyst's. The patient was in effect thought to share the analyst's professional aims.

When we consider how difficult it is to perform and conceptualize the therapeutic task of simultaneously accepting and persuading, being primary and secondary mother, mother of body contact and of separation, etc., it is not surprising that the analyst should crave a division of the patient into aspects that he might relate univalently to. But I wonder if there is not also another reason for the attractiveness of the concept of the therapeutic alliance. Anesthesiologists sometimes say that the operating surgeon really wants his patient to be a cadaver, albeit temporarily. Bearing in mind Fenichel's frank avowal that whoever is frustrated in his task is annoyed, is it not likely that the analyst archetypically wants as his patient — what? a normal person? — rather, another analyst, i.e. someone who shares his own motives. His theory as well as commonsense tell him, of course, that this is out of the question, but the job itself may create a hunger for cooperation. And the therapeutic alliance with its slight vagueness about the patient's motivation, but its great emphasis on the similarity between analyst and patient, might answer this need.

It would be unrealistic to expect to evade completely the bite of Fenichel's dictum about the analyst's reaction to frustration, and to some extent, I suppose, it must be accepted as a built-in handicap of practice. But one should accept it grudgingly, because it *is* a handicap. To reduce it the analyst should try to envisage his task in such a way as to minimize his frustration. (That, after all, is one of the important services theory renders to practice.) This will be helped by remembering that, while the process of analysis is a part of the analyst's life work, a major portion of his identity, and the chief expression of his creativity, the patient's situation is not the same. If the analyst finds himself impatiently longing for the patient to relax his drive-determined gropings in the analysis, and adopt instead the analyst's more detached viewpoint, he should remind himself that his own activity does not float in the air, that he, the analyst, is not without motivation, and that part of his motivation has to do with the significance of analysis as his life work. He should remind himself further that Freud's self-analysis was motivated not just by the urge to overcome suffering, nor even solely by a wish to understand himself, but had a powerful incentive in the ambition to pioneer a new science and make great discoveries about the human condition. The notion of a bloodless and gutless therapeutic alliance may simplify the analyst's picture of his relationship to his patient. But insofar as the analyst holds up as an ideal a more austere and disinterested mode of activity than he himself pursues, he makes an unreasonable demand on the patient and exposes himself to needless frustration.

From this standpoint Nunberg's apparently more cynical view of the fundamental *discordance* of patient and analyst with its consequences of emotional blackmail by the analyst, is much kinder, more generous and tolerant than the postulation of the therapeutic alliance comradeship. For Nunberg's view allows the patient his own motivation—I might say *a* motivation—which the alliance implicitly does not; and while even Nunberg insists that the patient-analyst congruence must be achieved by the patient coming over to the analyst, it does place more responsibility for accomplishing this on the analyst.

In very general terms, the paradoxes we have examined relate to the obligation of the analyst to find some kind of concordance in the midst of apparent discordance between the patient's direction and his own. I have argued that this search is hindered rather than helped by any approach which does not recognize that the analyst has motives for analysing that the patient *cannot* share. Yet an analyst can hardly be kept from hoping for, and expecting, such a sharing, and being frustrated to the extent that it is missing, and this sharing is desired nowhere so much as in enthusiasm for what is supremely important to the analyst, namely the analytic process. The result is a concept like the therapeutic alliance. Perhaps it would be a useful corrective to regard the patient as having *no* attitude toward analysis as a process, but only an attitude toward his relationship with his analyst, including all that he wants to get from him and all that he suspects the analyst wants from him. In his life the patient wants freedom from the pain of symptoms and realization of his wishes and fantasies. In the consulting room these are adjusted to the person and procedure of the psychoanalyst. Any idea that *apart from these desires* the patient wishes to, or should wish to, engage in a process *per se* is supported by neither analytic theory nor commonsense, but solely by the analyst's natural desire for cooperation, since the analyst *does* wish to engage in a certain process *per se* for which reason he has chosen it as an occupation. A paradigm for this principle would be that it is reasonable to ask a psychoanalyst whether he really wants to analyse, but it makes no sense to ask a patient whether he really wants to be analysed.

According to Freud, as analysis progresses the patient is weaned from his unreasonable demand for direct libidinal gratification. The abandonment of his insistence is heralded in analysis by, among other things, the acceptance of interpretations about these demands and consideration of them in a detached fashion. Since this relinquishment of demands is not only a step toward recovery but also narrows the discordance between himself and the analyst, the analyst will feel this to be a therapeutic alliance. And so it is. But if the analyst begins by looking for it as a fulcrum of treatment, he will be maximizing his chances of frustration and annoyance (in accordance with Fenichel's dictum) and thus unnecessarily interfering with his function of acceptance.

3

Looking to Theory for Help

I n the last chapter we watched theory express a practical dilemma involving cross-purposes between therapist and patient.

Therapists do not write to confess trouble. If they betray strain in their theorizing, it is because they are trying to rid themselves of it. What was the practical problem that the therapeutic alliance was supposed to relieve? Evidently it was not the kind of problem that required experiments in technique. Rather, it was the kind of problem that could be solved by postulating a therapeutic alliance. Such a problem is the need for a rationale to explain an effective procedure. A solution to that kind of problem says "It is reasonable to believe that analysis is possible if one can suppose an alliance of such and such a sort." The concept is designed to make sense out of the pure, austere kernel of analyzing. How to achieve an alliance is a different problem, of secondary interest to early analysts. The implication of their work is that analyzing as such does not build an alliance but presupposes it. The oldest significance of the concept of the therapeutic alliance is to express a professional need of the analyst. The therapeutic alliance is that which the analyst wants. (That is why we can use it to investigate the discomfort of therapy.)

Thus to begin with, most alliance concepts were descriptive rather than prescriptive: The picture of an alliance was mainly a way of reassuring the analyst that he and his patient have a common purpose. Only by implication was the alliance a technical program for increasing the harmony.

Of course, no concept is without technical consequences. From the beginning, an alliance also suggested that the therapist had to win over a

38

patient or educate him before analysis proper could begin. And because, as in all human encounters, analysts are bound to behave differently at first than later on, the therapeutic alliance naturally came to be seen as a preliminary, technical objective. Nevertheless until recently the main function of the concept was to orient the analyst toward his patient during the phase of analysis proper.

Later, with the "widening scope of analysis," the therapeutic alliance became interesting for different reasons, and primarily as a technical challenge. In the last decades, analysts have increasingly sought to match their methods to a variety of patients. Zetzel (1958, 1966) advised special care with some patients to avoid aggravating pre-oedipal sensitivities that might otherwise interfere with analysis by inducing "fruitless regression." She was thinking of patients who had difficulty attaining or maintaining a therapeutic alliance. But this is merely a shift of interest: She, too, considered analysis proper to be that which happens on the basis of an achieved therapeutic alliance. For her, too, the therapeutic alliance is "a secure, basic relationship," which is "a fundamental feature of the analytic relationship" (1958, p. 185). Conceptually, the notion remains the same, although its use is more obviously practical. The alliance becomes a guiding principle for action rather than the explanation of an established fact.

Zetzel's concept of the therapeutic alliance combines many of the positions discussed in chapter 2. For her, as for Sterba whom she cites, the core of the alliance is an ability to recognize reality. But, like Gitelson and Stone whom she also cites, she feels that being realistic involves a personal, trusting attitude, with a traceable personal history. Like Nunberg, she feels that the alliance must eventually be subjected to analysis, but like most of the others, she also feels that some aspect of the alliance must be kept alive at all times. The conceptual difficulties we have seen in this double imperative are not crucial to Zetzel's presentation, because her chief interest lies not in describing the alliance, but in devising practical measures to preserve it.

When it serves as a guide to technique, the concept of the therapeutic alliance arouses different concerns than when it is simply a description of how analysis works. To illustrate the newer worries, I am drawn to Spence's (1982) discussion because he uses my essay as his example.

This is what Spence thinks I have done to the therapeutic alliance concept (as in chapter 2 of this book):

> The reference to the mother–child relationship has been dropped; instead the therapeutic alliance has come to describe the analyst's need to see himself in the patient. He wants to turn the patient into a mirror of his hopes and fears. To strengthen the alliance, therefore, he [the analyst] has projected onto the patient his own needs and tries to behave in such a way that the patient will begin to act like him [pp. 206–207].

With that as his reading of my essay, Spence understandably concludes that I use the term *therapeutic alliance* in a peculiar—he might have said incoherent—way. (How could the therapist expect to actually strengthen an alliance by projecting anything onto his patient, let alone "his hopes and fears?")

Not by itself an intelligible picture, what Spence finds provocative in my sketch (as he sees it) is its utter irrelevance to Zetzel's, which, despite her citations, he judges to be the only authoritative version of the concept. Thus, he writes that from Zetzel to Friedman, "The relationship has moved from the imbalance of the early months of infancy [in Zetzel's formula] to a pairing of equals [in Friedman's]" (p. 207).

This is a truly arresting summary, for it attributes to Zetzel the opposite of what she says.

Zetzel's therapeutic alliance does not represent the imbalance of the early months of infancy. It represents the mastery of that imbalance (as we find in adults). It depends, for instance, on "The capacity to maintain basic trust . . . The capacity to maintain self-object differentiation . . . The potential capacity to accept realistic limitations" (1966, p. 92). Zetzel writes,

> I am neither suggesting that the new patient resembles a newborn infant nor that the analyst's role is explicitly maternal. I am, however, proposing that from the outset, the analytic situation demands from the patient maximal mobilization of ego characteristics which in large part depend on the success achieved at a relatively early stage of psychic development. Such mobilization will be fostered by intuitive adaptive responses on the part of the analyst which may well be compared to those of the successful parent [1966, p. 97].

However innovative her methods, Zetzel's concept of the therapeutic alliance was the established one. In her writings, the alliance continues to be the sharing of a (mature) vision of reality between patient and analyst, and an inclination to pursue shared analytic goals. Zetzel explicitly aligns herself with this tradition. What she adds is the suggestion that the analytic situation itself, especially when newly experienced, may render an otherwise analyzable patient too infantile to form a therapeutic alliance, and in these circumstances the analyst should temporarily normalize her behavior, especially during the initial impact of artificially induced regression. For Zetzel, what resembles mothering is not the therapeutic alliance, but the analyst's concern for the patient who cannot yet achieve it.

When we find a concept persisting through the analytic literature, Spence has advised us to look for "a felt need in our collective clinical experience" that it satisfies (p. 201). This is an extremely important principle, and if there is something compelling about Spence's odd reading of Zetzel, we should ask what collective clinical experience his reading illustrates.

For one thing, Spence's pages suggest that, like many others, he is disturbed by Zetzel's very act of comparing the analyst's functioning with the role of mother. Zetzel's willingness to explore a possible similarity overshadows the details of her argument. Even though Zetzel's main point is that "a relatively mature object relationship should first be achieved and maintained in order to avoid fruitless regression" (1958, p. 196), Spence is transfixed by her willingness to think about tact in terms of parental function.

And second, Zetzel's veiled suggestion that, with some vulnerable patients, especially early in analysis, the analyst should manifest herself more tangibly, dispelling infantile transferences rather than cultivating them for interpretation, makes Spence worry—again for good reason along with much of the profession—that Zetzel is actively participating in the patient's transference drama.

Both of these are perennial and legitimate concerns, prevalent more at some times and places than at others. The first concern can be expressed in this warning: "If you compare your analytic activities to the actions of a mother, you will act like a mother, even if *what* you are talking about is how to avoid being seen as a mother. Therefore, you should be careful about the wording of your analogies, and avoid attributing any fixed genetic meaning to the analyst role (because that will always bring in a parental anlage); we have to watch not just what our theories say, but also what they *do* to us."

The other worry can be stated this way: "If analysts feel that they must fiddle with the therapeutic relationship in order to avoid being misunderstood, they will inevitably be drawn into a neurotically defined role."

Although Spence is ostensibly tracing vagaries in the description of the therapeutic alliance, what really concerns him is the sort of personal approach that a therapist's belief will encourage. It is as though Spence asked himself, "By describing the alliance in this way, what is the author trying to get the analyst to do?" I discuss such nondescriptive uses of theory in chapter 5.

In Zetzel's work and Spence's reaction to it one can see the concept of the therapeutic alliance becoming part of a highly charged debate about how much the analyst should accommodate his technique to a difficult patient. And one can also see a worry that this concept, which was originally supposed to define analysis, could instead be used to change the paradigm.

These days, a wide variety of patient is analyzed. Patients stress the analyst in more ways, demand different types of intervention, invite more glaringly different kinds of thinking. All of that is nothing new for the general psychotherapist. He never was able to escape irregularities in practice style even if he pretended to while writing papers. But now he has access to a greater variety—not to say confusion—of analytic paradigms. In a time of proliferating paradigms, the therapeutic alliance is likely to be invoked as the imaginary vanishing point that binds together otherwise unrelated techniques.

But even if treatments were more similar than they appear, each patient behaves differently at different times. Strain is variable from hour to hour, and theory has been asked to explain what is happening when things are not going well. The therapeutic alliance, considered not as an invisible component of analysis, nor as a preliminary to it, but as an harmonious state that can come and go, is often mentioned in informal conversation. It appears in the literature too, although there we are likely to encounter it in the form of "the good analytic hour."

The bad analytic hour is not featured in the literature (although Langs [1975] has made a study of it). The preferred picture is of slow, steadfast progress, with occasional high points of collaboration. It is a rare writer who refers to frequent bewilderment. (Exceptions are Gardner [1984], who describes it, and Havens [1982, 1986], who recommends it. Lichtenberg [1983] makes difficulty between analyst and patient central to the action of treatment.) Nevertheless, the concept of therapeutic alliance explicitly or implicitly offers the therapist a somewhat tautological knowledgeability about low points in treatment.

To summarize, we have seen that the therapeutic alliance serves the therapist as a comforting image of rapport; it seems to be a common denominator among different treatments; it provides by its absence, a reassuring way of naturalizing a difficulty; it is a bridge between treatments that are and are not going well; it balances the therapist when he is up and down with a single patient.

Most generally, the therapist can use the concept of the therapeutic alliance as a way of telling himself that it is possible to get what he needs in order to do his work; that there is a final resting place; that comfort is not always deceptive, and he is therefore entitled to it. I have suggested that the therapist requires that reassurance because the basic discomfort of treatment makes it often seem doubtful that harmony is attainable or genuine.

Of course, pure theory is not all the therapist uses. There are other writings that help therapists more tangibly. Practical hints for building an alliance may be found especially in case histories (e.g., Zetzel, 1958). But the practical consequences of an occasional effort to build an alliance pale in comparison to the pervasive coloring given a whole therapy by the mere fact of the therapist thinking in terms of a therapeutic alliance.

The next three chapters enlarge our view of the therapist's predicament as it is reflected in the general psychoanalytic theory of therapeutic action. We discover that different aspects of the same theory are emphasized at different times in history. Such variations amount to a natural dissection of the issues involved.

History, it is true, also dissects ideas in ways that have little to do with their cognitive content. Some enthusiasms have economic and social reasons; some reflect fashion. Group pressures mold thinking, and so do opportunities for personal advancement. New professions are conspicuously swayed by these influences, to the delight of debunkers intent on exposing the base motives underlying supposedly reasoned arguments. Debunkers often ignore the fact that ideas generate other ideas. After all, what warrant has an historian of any stripe to take a momentary concept as a natural unit to account for? Theories may be *research programs* (to use Lakatos's [1970] term), and their initial form may be only an outline of what takes time to work out. Even if social forces alone dictated the shape of theory, wouldn't they be likely to shape the tradition as a whole, leaving the elaboration of its details to experience and reflection?

But what concerns us here is that ideas are ideas only in relation to each other, and therefore, latent meaning emerges only in conversation. (Every psychotherapist should recognize that process!) This conversation exists within professional groups at a given moment, but it also takes place over the years. We cannot know what issues underlie a set of terms until we see what arguments it starts. Only historical controversy can unveil the import of a doctrine. We must give dialectic its due: An error hides in a truth until the truth meets its opposition, which may come in the form of a violent factional reaction at the next international congress.

In the following chapter, we recruit history of theory to assist us in ferreting out the immediacies of practice. Because theory of therapy is a way of positioning the therapist in a difficult situation, an opposing theory can expose an overlooked facet of that difficulty by showing how the first solution aggravates it. One theory helps the therapist out of the frying pan, while the contradictory theory screams, "Fire!"

4

Descriptive Help from Theory:

Trends in the Psychoanalytic

Theory of Treatment

F reud introduced the two major presences on the therapeutic scene that have haunted all later discussion. The first is usually called "understanding" and is characteristically represented by intellectual understanding, although it is sometimes given a broader meaning (emotional understanding, deep understanding, understanding that is not just verbal, etc.). The second is described more variously, and I shall give it the rough title of "attachment," meaning some sort of binding emotional reaction to the analyst. Less explicitly, a third factor, integration, was also isolated.

UNDERSTANDING IN FREUD'S THEORY

In 1904 Freud implied that through psychoanalytic treatment, a "better understanding" would modify representations instituted by the "automatic regulation by unpleasure" (p. 266). In 1910 he said that giving "the patient the conscious anticipatory idea [the idea of what he may expect to find] . . . is the intellectual help which makes it easier for him to overcome the resistances between conscious and unconscious" (1910a, p. 142, Strachey's brackets). In the same year, Freud said that "informing the patient of what he does not know" is "one of the necessary preliminaries to the treatment," albeit only a part that should never be thought of as the paradigm of psychoanalysis (1910b, p. 225). In 1912 Freud spoke about the issues of intellect versus instinctual life and understanding versus seeking to act (p. 108).

In 1913, a little more ambiguously, Freud said that "communication of repressed material to the patient's consciousness . . . sets up a process of thought in the course of which the expected influencing of the unconscious recollection eventually takes place" (p. 142). In this essay, he made it clear that instruction is part of the curative factor, but only in a restricted and special way, to which we shall return when discussing other factors.

In 1914 Freud said that the main instrument for curbing the compulsion to repeat and turning it into a motive for remembering consists in the handling of the transference, which renders it "harmless." He thus emphasized that the healing process partly consists of representing a wish rather than implementing it, though in other places he allowed that even remembering is an instinctual, gratifying process.

Freud's 1926 emphasis on ego alteration as an obstacle to treatment (pp. 157, ff.) could be taken to suggest that understanding is a crucial factor in treatment, although the meaning of the term "ego" is too broad to assure that inference. In any case, in *Inhibitions, Symptoms and Anxiety*, Freud continued to stress the importance of making resistances conscious and of opposing them with logical arguments, promising the ego advantages and rewards. This is clearly an established part of psychoanalytic procedure, though Freud went on to say that even when the ego "agrees" with these arguments and decides to go along, the impulses themselves will be found to have a stubborn strength of their own.

In 1937, the analyst was referred to as a teacher, as well as a model (p. 248). In 1938 Freud said, "We serve the patient in various functions, as an authority and a substitute for his parents, as a teacher and educator. . ." (p. 181). Thus "educator" was one of the analyst's accepted roles.

ATTACHMENT IN FREUD'S THEORY

At no time from his first psychoanalytic writings to his last did Freud ever lose sight of or minimize the importance of the affective relationship between patient and analyst. Throughout his work on the process of treatment a kind of running battle may be detected between the respective claims of understanding and attachment, although when one looks more closely one sees that it is not equal combat, but a struggle for survival on the part of understanding. To be sure, Freud was very much the champion of the voice of reason, but while he was cheering it on, he seemed to be advising his friends not to bet on it.

In 1913 Freud said that the analyst must first attach the patient to him by taking a serious interest in him, giving him time, avoiding mistakes, and clearing away certain resistances (p. 139). In the same paper he emphasized that instruction is used only insofar as the transference permits, and described both instruction and transference as ways in which the analyst offers the patient "new sources of strength." Instruction that is useful only in a transference atmosphere could not be considered a mere transmission of information, and indeed it was envisioned more as a training, an exercise, a guidance in the distribution of psychic energy (1913, p. 143). This is the kind of instruction that requires a certain relationship with the instructor. In 1916 Freud said that positive transference, not intellectual insight, is "what turns the scale" (1916-1917, p. 445).

In 1918 Freud wrote, "[We exploit] the patient's transference to the person of the physician, so as to induce him to adopt our conviction of the inexpediency of the repressive process established in childhood and of the impossibility of conducting life on the pleasure principle" (p. 159). The attachment of the patient, Freud asserted, allows the analyst to convert him to a new, different approach, and it is clear that it is the attitude of the physician that accomplishes this and not just information.

In 1937 Freud referred to the analyst not only as a teacher but as a model for the patient (p. 248). In 1938 Freud referred to educational exploitation of the transference (p. 175). He pointed out that there comes a time when it is the unconscious that is on the side of the analyst in opposition to the ego (p. 179). He stated that the analyst serves as a parent substitute, among other roles, and stressed that the positive transference is the most important factor in treatment effect.

Connected with the role of attachment in psychoanalysis was the suggestion that introverted libido of the patient is lured out and drawn onto the analyst. Thus in 1912 Freud depicted the libido as fixated on old objects because of frustration in the outer world and subsequent attraction of the unconscious (p. 102). The course of analysis, he felt, is characterized by the patient's struggle to hold on to the old objects, and the transference serves both as a means of holding on to them and as a possible inducement to give them up.

In 1916 Freud said that we draw introverted libido into the transference and thereby prevent repression from occurring again, with the result that more libido is at the disposal of the ego (1916-1917, p. 454).

INTEGRATION IN FREUD'S THEORY

Besides the two main elements of understanding and attachment, it is possible to find a factor among the Freudian mechanisms that does not precisely fit into either of these categories. It may be called integration.

Thus in 1912 Freud made the familiar comment that unconscious impulses do not want representation in memory but expression in action (p. 108). That passage does not contain all of Freud's thoughts on the matter, because he was aware that there is a sense in which unconscious impulses are gratified by *any kind* of expression of them. It is an open and continuing question for the theory of therapy whether any therapy is possible if unconscious impulses are not at all satisfied by expression in memory. Indeed, the conception of the transference that Freud developed is that unconscious impulses, seeking satisfaction in action rather than reproduction in memory, build a transference by which the impulses are more amenable to mnemic association than they are in their original unconscious state (1914, pp. 153-155). Freud said:

> The main instrument . . . for curbing the patient's compulsion to repeat and for turning it into a motive for remembering lies in the handling of the transference. We render the compulsion [to repeat] harmless, and indeed useful, by giving it the right to assert itself in a definite field. We admit it into the transference as a playground in which it is allowed to expand in almost complete freedom and in which it is expected to display to us everything in the way of pathogenic instincts that is hidden in the patient's mind [1914, p. 154].

If we ask very generally why unconscious impulses do *not* want expression in memory, we are inclined to answer, first, that action is what an impulse primarily seeks. In "The Dynamics of Transference" Freud made it clear that transference does not exist only to serve resistance; it is also a love pattern (1912, pp. 99-100). But it is not just out of preference for action that memory is avoided. Freud referred to the stimulation of transference by a specific disinclination to bring repressed contents into memory (p. 104), and, in the same pages, he referred to transference as being unconcerned with reality (p. 108). To be sure, these are tendencies which make transference useful to resistance, but they do not necessarily come into being for that purpose. We might put this in other terms and say that unconscious impulses seek to preserve themselves unmodified (following the compulsion to repeat), while memory would willy-nilly bring them into modifying contact with cognition and with other impulses.

As a playground, the transference allows impulses relatively unmodified expression, because in a playground the impulse does not have to take much account of other factors. At the same time, the circumscribed setting and the known variables make it possible for the analyst and subsequently for the patient to bring those "actions" into relation with other psychic forces (and with "reality"), just as a memory would have done. The transference is thus a method of slowly bringing into synthesis elements that tend to resist synthesis. Freud wrote:

In actual fact, indeed, the neurotic patient presents us with a torn mind, divided by resistances. As we analyse it and remove the resistances, it grows together; the great unity which we call his ego fits into itself all the instinctual impulses which before had been split off and held apart from it [1919, p. 161].

And in 1915 Freud pointed out that by not responding to the transference, the analyst makes the patient feel that it is safe to allow more of his impulses to be realized (p. 166). We must suppose that safety means that the analyst will respect other, divergent interests of the patient and will not act on the patient's transference presentation of himself. This suggests that what makes the transference a satisfactory middle ground between implementation of an unconscious impulse, on the one hand, and memory, awareness, integration, and compromise of it, on the other, is precisely the guarantee that it will not *remain* unintegrated. A synthesis is promised, so to speak, although deferred.

This rationale is implicit in Freud's definition of instruction as guidance in the distribution of energies (1913, p. 143). And it was explicit in "Analysis Terminable and Interminable" (1937, pp. 220, 225), where Freud referred to a "taming of instinct" which brings instinct into harmony with other trends of the ego, so that it no longer seeks independent satisfaction.

Finally, the integrative action of therapy is implied in passages such as the following: "[We exploit] the patient's transference to the person of the physician so as to induce him to adopt our conviction of the inexpediency of the repressive process established in childhood and of the impossibility of conducting life on the pleasure principle" (1919, p. 159). What is conveyed to the patient is an attitude or approach to the self, and clearly that attitude is one of greater confidence in the possibility of a satisfying integration.

Of these elements in Freud's writings, Nunberg (1926, 1932) concentrated on the attachment factor, and Sterba (1934) on the factor of understanding. It was believed that both aspects were essential to the cure, but Nunberg elaborated the affective motivation and Sterba the organizing and structuring outcome. The integrative factor was not explored with the same attentiveness until later.

THE MARIENBAD SYMPOSIUM

The Symposium at Marienbad in 1936 on The Theory of the Therapeutic Results of Psycho-Analysis utilized many of Freud's basic suggestions on the subject. But what was most conspicuous at Marienbad was a special emphasis on introjection. Glover (1937, p. 126) said explicitly that the discussion of introjective mechanisms in the transference proved technically more helpful than the new ego psychology. Two introjective mechanisms had become important by the time of Marienbad. Both derived from Freud's suggestion that the patient is persuaded to adopt the analyst's attitude. One application was Sterba's formulation that the patient imitates the analyst's disinterested way of observing and alters his own ego to match. The other was Strachey's (1934) idea that the patient incorporates the analyst's greater tolerance, thus altering his own superego.

These two kinds of alteration are by no means theoretically equivalent. The observing ego described by Sterba, which the patient copies from the analyst, can be, and often has been, thought of as a simple receptor of reality. To be sure, it theoretically entails some yielding not just to reality but to the reality principle, which is what Freud said was the aim of the analyst's persuasion. And the reality principle involves a disciplining, channeling, and defining of id drives (see Glover, 1937, pp. 129-130). But in Sterba's formulation, what Freud described almost as a philosophical conversion came to look like simply opening the patient's eyes. The analyst is seen more as a guide than as a reformer; instead of a victory he achieves an "alliance." Since the implicit molding of the patient is more or less hidden in the terminology, attachment factors can be looked upon as mere preliminaries, while understanding is presented as the essence of the analytic process (see chapter 2).

By and large the Marienbad participants did not follow Sterba's path. Nunberg (1937, pp. 168-169) recalled that not the ego alone, but the superego as well, helps to define reality, and, therefore, if perceptions are to be corrected, it will require not only an ego alliance, but also an alliance of the patient's and analyst's superego. Only Fenichel (1937, p. 134) seemed a little uncomfortable with the emphasis on the superego, preferring Sterba's ego terms and complaining that it is not necessary for the patient to introject the analyst in order to admit that he is right; in other words, the analyst's simple rightness gives him access to the patient's ego without a lot of complicated motivation (p. 138). But even Fenichel admitted that the pedagogical influence of the analyst is only occasionally important (p. 138).

Strachey's (1937) contribution to the Symposium is probably the best remembered. Unlike the more intellectually oriented concept of the affect-free ego-alliance, Strachey's ideas about introjection of the analyst's superego referred to an attitudinal, affect-laden conversion. Such an introjection obviously takes something that belongs to the analyst, and the process cannot masquerade as a mutual orientation toward an impersonal reality. Alteration of the superego was a useful concept with which to explain therapeutic influence because the superego is both a rule-bound structure and an affect-determining organ, and, perhaps even more important, it is a structure whose origin is most specifically traceable to the influence of other people.

Strachey's contribution was not just to suggest that analytic effectiveness depends upon introjection of the analyst's superego. He used the notion of introjection to connect the factors of understanding and attachment that otherwise seem to group themselves into separate camps. Anticipating modern perspectivists (e.g., Levenson, 1972), Strachey (1937) recognized that introjection is partly controlled by the patient's affective and motivational situation. It is, therefore, not automatically an agent of change. The patient is inclined to introject the analyst as a whole object (pp. 143-144), which is tantamount to equating him with objects previously introjected. (Strachey said that the patient introjects the physician as part of the id rather than of the superego, which, since the patient is ill, makes the physician into a bad object.)

> Giving non-transference-interpretations is, in fact, like trying to untie a knot in an endless ring of rope. You can untie the knot quite easily in one place, but it will re-tie itself at the very same moment in some other part of the ring. You cannot *really* untie the knot unless you have hold of the ends of the rope, and that is your situation only when you make a transference-interpretation [Strachey, 1937, p. 143].

In order for the patient to experience the analyst as a real person, he must first be able to discriminate the analyst's own principles. Thus, paradoxically, the analyst hopes to be introjected piecemeal rather than swallowed whole. In effect, the analyst must insure that it is his own superego rather than the patient's libidinal structure that defines the introject. He can do this only by a transference interpretation of a pressing urge which shows that the analyst knows how the patient feels about him and yet is neither anxious nor angry. Such a response grips the patient's personal interest while making it difficult for him to reduce the experience to a customary formula.

Thus Strachey implied that the curative factors in analysis would come to light as we acquire understanding of introjection (1937, pp. 143-144). Most of the other Marienbad participants agreed. Glover (1937, p. 129) thought that psychoanalysis brings about a "modification of earlier and more archaic *processes* of introjection" (p. 129, italics added) and that it does so by arranging dosed introjection (probably to be distinguished from global introjection, as with Strachey). Both Glover (1937, p. 130) and Bergler (1937, p. 155) pointed to the alternation of projection (which makes the analyst desirable, for instance, as an ego ideal) with subsequent introjection. Bergler in particular stressed how much the patient's wishes decide what he introjects of the analyst. He pointed out that the analyst's permissiveness is measured by the patient in terms of participation in his sexual wishes rather than by mere tolerance of speech (1937, p. 152). Thus the analyst's superego, as introjected by the patient, is a strict one, and it is partly because of its general severity that its allowances are respected.

Bibring (1937, pp. 181-182), among others, drew attention to the affective component in introjection when he pointed out that gradual frustration within a two-person love relationship is what leads to introjection. In saying this, he recalled classical theory and anticipated the work of Kohut.

THE EDINBURGH SYMPOSIUM

From the heavy emphasis on introjection at Marienbad, one might have concluded that psychoanalysis had found a way to investigate how attachment brings about structural change and how affective elements transmit understanding.

But when we turn to the Symposium twenty-five years later at Edinburgh on The Curative Factors in Psycho-Analysis (1962), we find no such research program confidently underway. The conference even resisted Gitelson's invitation to look again at the problems which introjection was used to explain. Whereas attachment had first been dealt with by Sterba as preliminary to understanding, and then by Strachey as a vehicle for structural change, Gitelson (1962) now implied that attachment can be an integrating or restructuring experience in itself. Correspondingly, instead of an operation on the ego (Sterba), or an operation on the superego (Strachey), analysis was studied as an operation on the entire psychic apparatus. (Of course, all factors had been considered periodically along the way. It had been known that changes in the ego lead to changes in the id, that superego changes alter the ego, and that nothing happens to one apparatus in isolation from the others. I am discussing the shifting focus of interest, not the totality of accepted theory.)

Gitelson portrayed attachment to the analyst as a process that defines and integrates motives. He argued that the primal need for a maternal matrix is not just a libidinal need, but is also a need for support and guidance (1962, pp. 196-197). Every psychic system is served by guidance. The development of the transference itself reflects a maturation of chaotic needs (p. 197). At the beginning, narcissistic libido is attracted to the physician in the readiness for transference.

> . . . even as we see in the course of development of psychic structure the evolution of primary process towards preconscious thinking, and from this the gradual appearance of secondary process function, so do we see in the first phase of analysis the gradual transformation of rather chaotic derivatives of unconscious activity into the structured manifestations which we ultimately identify as the transference neurosis. . . . [Transference] remobilizes the instincts and drives, and redeploys them for a new developmental beginning. In this sense it is really another aspect of Bibring's 'developmental drive'. Thus, from the beginning, the opening phase provides an element of 'structure' to narcissistic and primitive libido [pp. 197, 198].

Freud's theory that the analyst draws out introverted libido was picked up again by Gitelson when he said,

Even as the first external objects receive the primitive narcissistic transference, so does the analyst in the first phase of analysis evoke towards himself the narcissistically regressed libido of the patient and initiate its transformation into 'object cathexis' [p. 197].

Gitelson was saying that what is "taken in" is not just part of the analyst's personality, but also the structure of the relationship. (In a sense, that harks back to the suggestion of Glover [1937, p. 129] at Marienbad that new *processes* of introjection are developed and that there is something in the attitude of the analyst that is intrinsically helpful. Loewald did a great deal more with this idea in his seminal paper of 1960.)

Gitelson left Marienbad still further behind when he found an infantile prototype for the *optimum* use of the therapeutic relationship. One would hardly expect psychoanalysts to be upset by the suggestion that the psychoanalytic situation has an ontogenesis, since psychoanalysts are accustomed to finding an ontogenesis in all human situations. Works of art and theatrical dramas have been analyzed with much less data; why not the psychoanalytic situation? Yet what is noteworthy about the Edinburgh Symposium is the extreme caution and defensiveness with which Gitelson analyzed analysis, and the extreme unhappiness that it nevertheless caused the participants (with the exception of Nacht).

Gitelson pleaded that if this dimension of psychoanalysis was not shown to be already accounted for, nonanalytic techniques would claim to be founded on the oversight. He was anxious to assure his audience that he did not gratify patients more than his colleagues did (1962, p. 202, n.). And he inaugurated the custom of relegating emotionally determined attachment factors to a preliminary stage of treatment, allowing one to reserve the title of psychoanalysis proper for what follows (pp. 194, 196, 201). (This device had been prepared by Sterba.) Much of his paper seemed designed, to use his word, to "detoxicate" unavoidable ingredients of manipulation, suggestion, and seduction, present in psychoanalysis (pp. 200-201). But apparently most of the panelists remained uneasy. They did not want to hear about any curative factor except understanding as conveyed by interpretation.

Segal (1962) said that insight is the curative factor. It reclaims lost parts of the ego and replaces omnipotence with more realistic ways of dealing with feelings and with the world (p. 213). But she also added that the analyst heals by setting an example of someone willing to face hard reality. (She did not, however, discuss how and why the example is internalized, or deal with the more puzzling question of what lesson in courage is to be found in the analyst's facing the patient's hard realities.) Kuiper (1962, p. 218) kept Gitelson's description at arm's length by stating that it is significant only in borderline conditions. (Gitelson [1962, p. 234] replied that we have learned a good deal about neuroses from borderlines, and he warned that just because some factors are less palpable in transference neuroses, it does not mean they are absent.) For Garma (1962, pp. 221-224) the curative factor was the correctness of the interpretation.

The siege atmosphere that hung over this conference distinguished it radically from Freud's writings and from the Marienbad Symposium. Freud, as we noted, took it as a matter of course that love, suggestion, persuasion, and attachment operate powerfully in psychoanalysis. He only moved to rule them out as biases to the *findings* of psychoanalysis. My impression of Freud's approach is that he assigned to the psychoanalytic theory of the mind the task of setting the goals of treatment and left to the theory of therapy the specification of the forces available to bring it about. The psychoanalytic theory of the mind being what it is, there are a great many manipulations that make no sense. But one never gets the feeling that manipulating certain forces has less dignity than manipulating others (except for manipulations requiring dishonesty). The "pure gold" of psychoanalysis refers to the over-all balance of analytic procedure, not to its sometimes base ingredients.

Similarly, the participants at Marienbad gave no sign of struggling to *avoid* a forbidden path; they even felt comfortable referring to unknown influences between patient and therapist. What, then, had happened to make the participants at Edinburgh tread so carefully? Why had interpretation become a battle cry?

Some answers spring instantly to mind. By 1961, as Gitelson's introductory comments acknowledged, psychoanalysis no longer had a monopoly on dynamic treatment. Consequently, as a profession it had a vested interest in advertising what was superior in its approach, namely, exact interpretation. Even aside from consideration of pride, analysts would tend to isolate what is distinctive in their approach and play down what is nonspecific. Although these are powerful incentives for the majority position at Edinburgh, they do not completely explain its militancy because later, while competitors' threats grew noisier, psychoanalytic militancy softened considerably.

Perhaps a clue to the crisis of Edinburgh lies in the remarks of King and of Heimann. King (1962, p. 225) said bluntly that the analytic relationship is different from every other and therefore cannot be described, in Gitelson's fashion, as an outgrowth of an earlier relationship. At first blush this claim appears presumptuous. It seems to deny the fundamental psychoanalytic principle that life meanings are determined by an evolving nexus of psychological prototypes. Why did King put herself in such an untenable position? It is because she felt that any other approach would compromise the patient's freedom. She wrote, "I sometimes think of the analytic relationship as a psychological stage on which I as analyst am committed to take whatever role my patient may unconsciously assign to me" (p. 226). She added, "In these circumstances the communication to the patient of any feelings of either love or hate may make the analyst of less use to the patient as a recipient of *some* of his unconscious, internal imagos" (p. 227). It turns out to be quite reasonable for King to maintain that the analyst preserves an ambiguity unique in human relationships (cf. Friedman, 1975a, 1975b). If the analyst were actually to *maintain* any one attitude toward a patient, he would close to the patient certain possibilities of development. Heimann (1962) pointed out that empathy is not an irreducible given, and should be subjected to careful analytic inspection, presumably to detect the motivations and desires it conceals. She further reminded the audience that in fact the analyst is not a mother and the patient is not an infant. Her point is well taken: patients' freedom to explore themselves can be seriously hampered if analysts vaguely and quite inaccurately identify themselves as mothers and the patients as their infants. (If analysts were encouraged by Gitelson's description to suppose that they are discharging parental duties simply by carrying out the austerely limited service called psychoanalysis, their grandiosity would interfere in all kinds of ways with the conduct of their work [cf. Anna Freud, 1969, p. 148; also Friedman, 1976]). King and Heimann were particularly concerned that if the physician is one thing to the patient, he cannot at the same time be something else.

In our terms we could say that Gitelson disturbed the conference by treating attachment factors as curative. He would not have seriously disturbed anybody if he had simply discussed preoedipal elements of transference. What offended so many sensibilities was his description of *how* those factors were involved in cure. Had he said that they were the subject of study and revision, he would have been applauded; had he said that they inspired the patient to work constructively, he would have been endorsed. Any such statement would have indicated that the patient's affects are structured by the analyst's (and subsequently the patient's) understanding. But Gitelson implied that valid understanding is built into these affective factors. While such a view might seem to accord actual parental power to the analyst, the audience perceived that they were really being portrayed as captives of their patient's emotional structures. And they recoiled from being embroiled in their patient's affective net. They wanted to be above it, looking at it. If they were caught inside it, they felt, both patient and analyst would be thrown together in a position designed by the patient's neurosis. They wanted to say, "I do not need to fit into some ancient, personal pattern for my interpretation to be effective; interpretation gets its healing power from its objective truthfulness alone."

But lest, after our initial surprise that Gitelson's message would offend anyone, we are now tempted to regard opposition as inevitable, we must again remind ourselves that Freud was completely unworried about fixed, affective roles. For instance, in "The Dynamics of Transference" he said, "If the 'father imago' . . . is the decisive factor in bringing this about [i.e., the insertion of the analyst into the psychical series of transference templates], the outcome will tally with the real relations of the subject to his doctor" (1912, p. 100). Something has changed in the analytic scene from the time that was written. By the time of the Edinburgh Symposium psychoanalysts were alarmed over the possibility that the analyst and his communications (and not just his variable transference image) were partly defined by the patient's affective structures. Both King and Heimann were anxious to keep the analyst unattached by such structures. At Edinburgh we saw a profession that studies the universal impact of affect on structure defining itself as a trade in affectless truths.

Freud, no less than Gitelson, felt that the patient's affective structuring could be *consonant* with the analyst's actual behavior rather than restricting and distorting it. Why did not the participants at Edinburgh comfort themselves with that solution? I suggest that it may have been because even consonant or realistic structuring, if it is heavily affective, is hard to conceptualize, and it is therefore hard to be sure that it remains within "proper" bounds. Correctness, reality, and exactness of interpretation seem clear and transparent. The imbrication of mother and child, diatrophic and anaclitic relationships, etc., are much harder to define. Perhaps King wanted the analytic situation to be totally different from any other so that it would not be so difficult to think about and would therefore be more controllable. In fact, the kind of loving relationships discussed by Nacht (1962), Gitelson's only sympathetic commentator, are quite vague. A cognitive focus for Gitelson's, and still more for Nacht's considerations, is not yet optimally developed, and great reliance must be placed on metaphor and analogy to childhood experience, which, far from clear today, was even less clear in 1961.

But we are left with the puzzle that twenty-five years previously the Marienbad Symposium had shown none of these concerns. There the participants were perfectly willing to see the patient introject parts of the analyst as children introject parts of their parents. Evidently at that time the accepted paradigm of introjection made a structuring kind of affective relationship clear enough to allow it to be thought about comfortably. It seems that by 1961 the concept of introjection had lost its reassuring, explanatory promise.

Also, at Marienbad the superego had served as a familiar model of the organizing power of affect. In other words, by looking at the superego, one could see how the patient's affect takes the analyst's attitude and makes it into psychic structure. If this model was no longer so satisfying in 1961, the reason may have been that psychoanalytic cure was found to involve much more than modification of the superego (especially among the wider variety of conditions treated). And there may have been nothing to take its place as a type of "introject."

Without the wrappings of introjection and superego, naked affect is too exposed as a definer of objects. Introjection dresses up attachment and affective processes in structural terms. (For contrast, see Schafer [1968], who stripped it down to volitional terms.) Sterba's ego fragment takes notice of pure structuring activity and discretely hides its affective basis among preliminary maneuvers. But bare of familiar, structured forms, affect cannot be allowed an organizing role without subverting the orderly direction of treatment. Gitelson offered to dress affects in the garb of infantile needs, but the participants at Edinburgh did not feel that they made attachment forces sufficiently precise and recognizable to safely allow them a determining role in treatment. They could be admitted only as a "matter" to which the "form" of analytic understanding would be applied. The participants at Edinburgh had reached an agreement that affect and attachment in the analytic situation represent what is to be changed, not a way of changing it. It was therefore most unpleasant to hear from Gitelson how definitively the analytic situation is drenched in affect and inescapably molded by attachment.

OBJECT-RELATIONS THEORY

Probably one reason that the Edinburgh Symposium took a dim view of Gitelson's project was that in England an attempt to be more specific about the molding effect of attachment had already been tried and found disastrous to Freudian theory.

The object-relations school can be thought of as seeking an entity which, though broader than the superego, would similarly serve to combine an affective and (at least in a vague sense) a structuring force. They called this the "ego" (thus misleading those accustomed to Freudian usage).

Since the object-relations theorists do not distinguish between a structuring ego and an affective id (Fairbairn, 1963), they hold (more consistently than did Melanie Klein) that restructuring must occur through developments in the affective relationship with the therapist. The object-relations school is united in its belief that permanent changes are brought about when the therapist provides a relationship that the patient needs.

At the same time, these writers recognize that the sick person's affective structuring of the situation *prevents* change. Fairbairn (1958) says that psychoanalysis consists of the struggle between a patient who tries to "press-gang" the therapist into his closed system and a therapist who endeavors to resist. Guntrip (1969, p. 285) describes a vicious circle in which fear blocks ego development and the resulting weak ego experiences fear. The difficulty of reconciling the therapeutic and antitherapeutic implications of the patient's "press-ganging" is reflected in the tortured grammar of Guntrip's (1961) restatement of Fairbairn's formulation: "Pathogenic relations are repeated under the influence of transference into a new kind of relationship which is at once satisfying and adapted to the circumstances of outer reality" (p. 414). (Fairbairn [1955, p. 156] had used the verb "developed" rather than "repeated.")

In general, the object-relations school seeks to solve this typical paradox in therapy theory by postulating a saving core of receptiveness to good objects (corresponding to the Freudian "unmodified ego") hidden behind fear-instilled, distorting perceptual grids.

The writings that emanate from this tradition have always been clinically apt. This is because its theory is articulated in terms of particular *attitudes*, a procedure which ensures vivid and concrete application. (Its vividness and immediacy make the theory especially useful to popularizers such as Perls and Janov.) The price paid for this concreteness is that general principles of mental functioning are reduced to the simplest and fewest. No system of needs is elaborated. A need for an object glosses them all. Fundamentally, the basic, undefined, irreducible, unanalyzed terms are "ego" and, by implication, "gratification." By itself the ego is not structured (see, for example, Fairbairn, 1963; Guntrip, 1969, p. 425). Frustration structures it. The distorting emotional grid placed on the analyst is thus the reaction to frustrating internalized objects or aspects of objects. A gratifying relationship with the analyst would ideally impose no private configuration on either party. Thus, if the analyst allows the patient to return to a state of undefended affectivity, the relationship will not be distorted. (Winnicott [1963; 1974, p. 137] is an exception.) The general idea is that "growth" is a non-structured phenomenon that occurs automatically if it is not interfered with (see also, Maslow, 1968, p. 33; 1970, p. 68). In this respect, the object-relations school escapes the therapeutic dilemma by conceiving the good object as permissive but *nonformative* in development, which is why the healthy ego is pictured as unstructured. Compared with instinct theory's view of the normal mind, specific object relations are not important to object-relations theory, and the ego is far more independent of the details of the world. If one can accept this view, then the rest of the solution is easy: once rid of pathological accretions, the patient's ego goes its own healthy way, and the therapist need not worry about the configurations of the attachment. Affects will not distort because they impose no structure whatsoever.

Unfortunately, this leaves us with no meat to hang on the bones of attachment. But the new "ego" concept allows the object-relations school to find at least something in the patient that affectively "entraps" the therapeutic relationship without obstructing therapy. It thus revives Freud's emphasis on love as the mainspring of therapy and blends it with the factors of understanding and integration. Except for Balint (1968) and Winnicott (1963, 1971), writers close to the object relations school still tend to emphasize conventional types of understanding (see, for example, Guntrip, 1969, p. 413). (Guntrip [1969, p. 213] even goes so far as to suggest that interpretation fosters therapeutic regression.) But the message of the movement is over-whelmingly that *relationships* structure, and good relationships integrate.

In trying to identify the site where attachment joins growth, the object-relations school has described psychoanalysis as replacement therapy. But the very idea of re-creating and improving the mother-child relationship of the first years of life underscores the dangerous vagueness of the forces involved, a vagueness represented in object-relations theory by the notion of an unstructured "ego" in communion with the mother. This is unsatisfactory to an analyst who wants to be sure that he is not reinforcing pathological patterns. As Anna Freud (1969, pp. 147-148) points out, it is an illusion to think that one is re-creating an undifferentiated state with the patient. Despite Fairbairn's efforts, the object-relations school does not offer a struc-ture that can be visualized at the level at which therapy is supposed to repair injury. (They offer only structures that interfere with repair.)

From North America, however, Gitelson brought a very different ap-proach to the problem. The dangers that had to be skirted by his compatriots were more practical than theoretical. It is true that they encountered efforts to belittle maturational and structural determinants of illness in favor of environmental influence (Gitelson, 1962, p. 195). But his introductory remarks clearly indicated that the challenge to the mainstream of Freudian thinking in the United States was an activist and sentimental approach to treatment, rather than a critique of theory.[1] And new efforts to relate attachment factors to restructuring in analysis proceeded within the frame-work of Freudian theory. As a result, the main innovators did not emphasize return to the inchoate first year of life and repair of deprivation. Rather, they pointed out what might be called the continuing uses of some maternal functions throughout life. These were describable in terms of Freudian structure and structure-building and were thus more reassuring to the analyst who wants to keep his embroilment with the patient's templates under cognitive control.

LOEWALD AND STONE

Loewald's (1960) influential paper proposes that the patient identifies with the analyst's work. Stated this way, the idea may seem not so different from Sterba's. But for Loewald, the analyst's work is not simply proclaiming reality, nor does he view the patient's identification as affectless. And, like Gitelson, he traces the origin of the identification to earliest relationships and thus relates attachment to understanding. He suggests that the patient's work

---

[1]Gitelson (1962, p. 196) made the extremely important observation that deficiencies in *theory* have caused compensatory aberrations in *practice*.

in translating between his experience and the analyst's more integrated perception is itself internalized and serves as a model to bridge the gap from unconscious to preconscious (p. 25). Attachment is an exercise in integration (p. 31).

In 1961 Stone described a "primal transference" to the omnipotent parent as a useful and appropriate vehicle for analytic work. He regards transference as a quest for the original maternal object who both nurtured the child and fostered independence (p. 72). And Stone feels that it is beneficial to the analysis that these affective structures envelop the analyst, because the patient's structures correspond to what the analyst actually offers as a physician. To this extent the patient's affective structures correspond to the analyst's professional structures. A few years later he compared analytic treatment to Winnicott's "transitional object" (Stone, 1967). Stone and Loewald agree with Gitelson that some of the patient's affective structures are "progressive," not just trivially, as seducing the patient into accepting the analyst's interpretations, but materially, as contributing to their understanding. In the elaboration of these ideas Freud's integrative factor is found useful to bridge the gap between attachment and understanding.

What was it that allowed some analysts to overcome the misgivings of Edinburgh about more complex factors than interpretation and understanding? No doubt the cumulative effect of child research played a role. (Spitz [1956] himself applied his findings to the analytic situation.) The study of infancy makes it easier to think about preoedipal relationships and to use them in the theory of therapy. But these studies, as far as they had been developed, were just as available to his audience as they were to Gitelson. What may have made the difference was that instead of an argument for a brand new, sketchy object-relations theory, Gitelson's use of preoedipal factors grew out of a milieu in which sophisticated refinements of the psychoanalytic theory of the mind were being made. I believe that these refinements of theory allowed analysts to cope with the interplay of affect and structure and permitted them to stray from the few established models, such as the superego, into more general conceptualizations. Perhaps Hartmann's work on the transmutation of affective forces into affect-free structures paved the way. Critiques of the structural theory and the practice of intertranslating the three psychoanalytic models of the mind (as in Arlow and Brenner, 1964; Gill, 1963; Schur, 1966) strengthened command over the elements of the theory and opened up the possibility of dealing anew with common features of the therapy situation.

KOHUT AND KERNBERG: THE EDINBURGH DEBATE RE-ENACTED

When Kohut (1971) takes up the theme of deficiency substitution which previously led proponents of object-relations theory to discard the Freudian theory of the mind, he is able, as they were not, to specify the pathological deficit in structural terms. He draws upon the original Freudian formula that links gratification and frustration together as the generator of structure. Thus Kohut continues the project initiated at Marienbad without jettisoning the Freudian theory of the mind. For Kohut, the affect net which the patient throws over the analyst, provided it is handled properly, has a tendency to build new structure even though it has preformed features. But, one might ask, will not these preformed features of the patient's attachment prevent change from occurring? This alarm, which Gitelson inspired in the Edinburgh participants, Kohut now evokes in Kernberg (1974). A comparison of these two authors will show how much of the Edinburgh conflict is still with us and how much it has been transcended.

Both authors agree that premature and excessive disappointment prevents the development of the psychic structures which provide secure self-esteem. Idealized object images are not optimally integrated into ego ideal and superego (Kernberg, 1975, p. 282; Kohut, 1971, p. 45). Kohut blames this on environmental shortcomings that do not offer children the necessary strong, endorsing figures to incorporate within their own structures. Kernberg acknowledges this possibility but more frequently suggests that, because of an inborn excess of aggression, the infant does not make use of the objects that are available for this purpose. Hate, envy, and fear of any needed object are not only features of the narcissistic disorder, but the cause of it as well. Since children do not use their parents to grow, the structures that they build are pathological from the beginning. The adult narcissistic illness is the developed state of an original pathological organization of experience. So Kernberg emphasizes the defensive nature of narcissism from start to finish.

Kohut, on the other hand, sees the narcissist-to-be as working normally with inadequate parental materials and so describes narcissistic pathology as a frustrated development of normal structure. Kohut emphasizes the deprivation involved in the illness.

But both descriptions of the narcissistic state imply deprivation (either from internal or environmental causes) and both imply defensiveness, at least as a result of the deprivation. Where they differ is in Kernberg's belief that the same excess aggression that started the sickness keeps it going and Kohut's belief that only the defensive action of the abortive narcissistic structure prevents the patient from accepting the needed materials of the environment.[2] Both believe that the pathological structure makes it hard for

---

[2]There are many ironies, paradoxes, and intriguing questions in this debate. In practice Kohut's looks more like an object-relations theory than does Kernberg's. And Kernberg's seems much more of an energy theory than Kohut's. That is, Kohut's patients need an object, but their defensive structures stand in the way; Kernberg's patients need to have their aggression neutralized. For Kernberg, the patient's goal is really a state of satisfaction (with self, object, and the relationship between them). If a person will forfeit an object because his inborn rage makes it unsatisfactory, should we still call that an object-relations psychology? Should we not rather

patients to see the analyst as someone who can serve their needs. But Kohut holds that there are some aspects of the structure that welcome the analyst's reparative task, while Kernberg sees the structure as wholly designed to exclude the analyst (cf. Wangh's 1974 summary of the difference in attitudes). That is the mirror of the Edinburgh debate.

There is, however, a difference from the Edinburgh debate. Like Kohut, Kernberg (1975, p. 315) postulates a new type of stucture as the focus of therapy: a self-representation in relation to object representation, together with an affective disposition. He thus holds out the possibility that the nature of the attachment to the analyst will affect psychic structure. If Kernberg's treatment approach is designed to prevent him from being annihilated or annulled by the patient, that can only help insofar as he thereby presents a dependable, nonretaliating object that can be used even by an orally envious patient to build a less autistic structure of self-esteem. Just like Kohut, Kernberg must disappoint the patient only enough to allow him to gratify the underlying need (see Kernberg, 1975, p. 337; 1976, p. 128). While his theory describes those aspects of the patient that fend off objects, other aspects are implicit in the treatment strategy. Ultimately both Kohut and Kernberg agree that a childhood need is gratified in treatment. That is the difference from the Edinburgh debate.

REFORMULATION BY SCHAFER AND KLEIN

Schafer's (1968) work on internalization takes as its subject something more general than a narcissistic structure. Schafer focuses on motives, systems of motives, and representations. These entities each involve at once understanding, affect, and integration. The use of *motivational* systems for *cognitive* purposes is illustrated by the orienting function of motivationally relevant representations.

> . . . the id motive . . . supports the representations pertinent to it. . . . the motive establishes a contextual organization of representations [pp. 63-64].

> . . . the elaborations and transformations of motives are necessarily influenced by the subject's current supply of information or representations. In turn, this supply depends partly on the subject's previous motivational states [p. 66].

Citing Alice Balint's (1943) eloquent paper (he might also have cited Piaget), Schafer says that identifications help in "comprehending and mastering

---

say that Kernberg is dealing with problems of integrative capacity as related to congenital levels of frustration tolerance? (Kernberg himself considers this possibility [1975, p. 234; 1966, p. 245]). Should we not say that this is a traditional object-formation theory rather than an object-relations theory? And why not consider Kohut's narcissistic cathexis to be the unspoken ego-building or ego-sustaining aspect of the object which is presumed by the object-relations school? Why not consider narcissistic cathexis a name for the relevance to the self of Kernberg's tripartite good-object-good-self-good-relationship representation?

objects in the environment that are new and strange—and therefore experienced as unexpected, unpleasant, reproachful, and threatening . . ." (p. 169). Even primary process "presences," such as introjects, ". . . are ideas that recur or persist under specific intrapsychic and situational conditions. In this respect they are like attained concepts, mastered logical relations, and stable memories, though they differ from these intellectual contents in adhering relatively more to the modes of the primary process . . ." (pp. 130-131).

Motivationally organized representations are grids for understanding. They supply information that in turn influences the elaboration and transformation of motives (p. 66).

Because of this "complementary relation between representations and motives" (p. 67), treatment requires not only new information about current reality and old aims, but also the introduction of new motives, because the old ones cement self-confirming representations into place (p. 67). Thus identification, which serves to master current experience, is brought about through modification of relevant old motives and their corresponding representations (p. 147).

Not only are understanding and motivation intertwined, integration is also connected with both. According to Schafer, one of the paramount early aims of a person is the aim of anticipation, and that aim (traditionally attributed to the ego) *uses* other aims (and their representations) to master future experience. It does so by creating structuralized hierarchies of motivational systems in which some aims serve as means to other aims (p. 56). Even the "interaction [between primary and secondary process] . . . normally . . . imparts that quality of mobility within organization or spontaneity-within-control that conveys aliveness and authenticity of experience" (p. 127).

Psychoanalysis has often been called a closed system that inappropriately studies people who are really open systems. This is a gross oversimplification. Psychoanalysis is definitely a theory of social relations. To be sure, its focus is on the theory of the mind as an entity. The type of structures into which the mind was divided were determined by the need to harmonize parts with a whole (see chapter 15). But it cannot be said that the outcome failed to account for interpersonal effects. All of the factors subsequently used to explain the curative elements in psychoanalysis were present in Freud's writings. The sociological emphasis given by most of the neo-Freudians was just that—an emphasis, designed to conform to the *Zeitgeist*. I am aware of no environmentalist who provided more details of the therapy relationship. On the contrary, their theories tend to be less developed in this respect than the original doctrine; they work with far fewer elements and clues.

Nevertheless, the psychoanalytic account of structure-*building* was naturally rudimentary at the beginning and was concentrated on areas of current interest to the theorist—primarily conflicts related to illness. An evolution of the ego was hypothesized. Treatment considerations then led to the evolution of the superego concept.

We might call this a macroanalysis of the mind. A macroanalysis is bound to look more like a closed system than a microanalysis: the big picture is likely to show us the already developed mind at work (cf. Gendlin's [1964] succinct account of this problem). Psychoanalytic treatment is a subtle, refined, delicate interplay, and its full understanding requires a microanalysis of the very general processes of personal interaction. Compared to a broad description of a person's life course, a highly sophisticated understanding of therapeutic efficacy will tend to look like a different kind of theory—more like an "open system" theory (Gitelson [1962, p. 196] makes the same point).

These considerations may be stated in another way: when we seek to understand therapy, we take a somewhat different entity as the subject of study than when we seek to understand the mind. Our gaze is focused specifically on the conjunction of two systems of meaning, one of them inside and one of them outside the patient's mind. For a long time the model for the intermingling was the giving and receiving of objective truth. The model had the virtue of neatness and simplicity. But it would not do (see Friedman, 1973). That does not oblige us to move into sociology or small group systems for a theory of psychotherapy. Those are different sciences altogether, even though they study the same phenomenon. Ours is still a science of intrapsychic processes. But the units of those processes at a microlevel will be somewhat different from those at a macrolevel. The fear that psychoanalysis would lose its identity in the shuffle was inevitable, but the fear has been worn away by time and practice.

In a sense, the study of the therapy process takes a direction exactly opposite to that of the study of the mind. Freud started from the notion of a unitary mind assaulted from without and gradually recast his terms to suit a mind warring within itself (see chapter 15). The student of psychotherapy must now return and again picture, if not a unitary mind, at least a unitary *state* of mind, attacked from without—that is, by a therapist. And the terms of analysis will shift when going in that direction, opposite to their shift when moving in the original direction. This is the reason for the construction of new entities to handle the interplay of patient and therapist.

This return to the original paradigm of psychoanalysis is dramatically illustrated by the last works of George Klein (1976), who considered the central task of the mind to be the resolution of "incompatibility." He wrote that ". . . motives arise from crises of incompatibility. . . . The 'imbalances' that make for motivational change are not the results of instinctual drives disciplined to the 'exigencies of reality'; they come about from a state of maladaptedness to new requirements" (p. 182). "It is not that conflicts *produce* disturbances in identity; rather, conflict is a 'symptom' of imbalanced identity" (p. 187; see also p. 267).

Klein's formulation harks back to the original Freudian starting point so directly that "incompatibility" is used again as a key term. Klein's "self" is the reincarnation of the original "ego" of psychoanalysis, assaulted either by unassimilable traumatic incidents or by unacceptable parts of the self. The apparent move backward in theorizing is simply a way of gaining a general perspective on the process of structure-building. The generality of Klein's perspective, which is entirely consistent with the philosophy of analytic theory, may be seen in his recognition of the human being as conservative, but with the capacity to change, requiring him to wrestle with the paradox of the responsiveness of a unified self to the sense of change (p. 181).

This overlaps with Schafer's work. But while Schafer shows how representations express and create motivational states and so tie together affect and understanding, Klein was primarily interested in procedures of integration and therefore addressed himself to the concept of the "self." Thus Klein said that "the outcome [of a crisis or trauma] is an internalization of conflict, along with a modification of cognitive structure reflecting the changes in the aims and motivation that constitute the resolution" (p. 197). "Affects thus exemplify different varieties of incompatibility; at the same time they are functional and are linked to the possibilities of purpose and of change. . . . Emotions connoting incompatibility become a way for the self to acquire understanding or sense its position in the world. They are the occasions, as well as the outcome, of the reactive and adjustive motivational structuring" (pp. 192-193). Thus, for both Klein and Schafer, affect-laden structures help a person to adapt—they integrate him as he is with what is new in his experience; they connect the familiar and the unfamiliar. Klein saw in this situation an opportunity to apply Piaget's categories to dissect out of psychoanalysis the operations that build and integrate structures.

According to Piaget (1951), novelty is tamed in the following way: preformed approaches to new stimuli are progressively modified until a master plan (a "reversible schema") is achieved, which allows one to take one's perspective into account and imagine a procedure that would make the apparent novelty familiar.

An example of Klein's use of these ideas is what he called "reversal of voice" from passive to active. If reversible schemata allow the mind to comprehend changing phenomena, perhaps reversible mental actions allow a person to consolidate identity in the face of affliction. Maybe identification with the aggressor is a psychoanalytic counterpart to a Piagetian mechanism. Maybe other representational reversals occur all the time. Then we should draw the Piagetian conclusion, which is that reversal of voice from passive to active not only protects against helplessness, but establishes a sense of self. Active reversals ". . . make the encounter of the conflict self-*syntonic*, rather than dystonic as in repression. The outcome is therefore *accommodative* in respect to self-identity, giving rise to an enlarged region of differentiation of what is 'me' and 'mine,'—and a greater differentiation of motives that will deal with future events without feelings of estrangement and dissonance" (Klein, 1976, p. 201). (Shands [1963] developed a similar theme.)

Unfortunately, most of Piaget's work has dealt with cognition, and it is not easy to see what Piagetian meaning we should give to "reversal of voice" beyond what is involved in any active representation (and all representations are active, according to Piaget). Klein tried to broaden the applicability of Piaget's concepts from the psychology of cognition to personality development. He took his lead from the dis-integration known as repression and was inclined to equate integration with consciousness (again one of the original conceptions of psychoanalysis). Consciousness accommodates to reality, while repression simply assimilates reality to fixed schemata (p. 254). "For Piaget, the conscious implementation of a wish is an important accompaniment, even a requirement, of accommodative behavior" (p. 254).

The trouble with the formula, as we have seen, is that *all* mentation seems to make some contribution to understanding. Klein knew this well: thus he noted with regard to repressed schemata that "preserving an encounter in a schematized form, as a dissociated prototype, makes possible the coding of related encounters in the future—events that may be more easily recognized and dealt with even if not anticipated" (p. 295). And, again, "While its affective aspects are uncomprehended, the schema is still very much an organizing influence in behavior" (p. 296). Again, an unconscious fantasy "gives meaning to an event or an encounter, defining it as useful or harmful . . ." (p. 299). And, again, unconscious fantasy ". . . has properties that Tolman . . . has described as a 'cognitive map,' acting as a guide to scanning and encoding" (p. 256). And, again,

> A defense is a structure in the sense that unrelated cognitive matrices are combined in such a way that a new level is added to the hierarchy of control— by containing previously separate structures in the new configuration of excitation. The defense is, in this sense, a synthesis of two frames of reference. It becomes a basis for organizing experience, a motive or disposition toward action in certain circumstances, and a basis of emotional appraisal. Such internalized representations of conflict and their defensive aspect are features of that created *inner environment* which serves as the person's notions of and disposition toward the 'real world,' providing the means of encoding it and making it meaningful [p. 199].

Thus we *cannot* say that integration is always marked by intentional appropriation into the self-schema, and we cannot say that it is always marked by the emergence of conscious awareness. Unrepressed and repressed are simply examples of more and less integrated, more and less adaptive schemata. And the self to which schemata are integrated, since it cannot be separately characterized by consciousness or intentionality, no longer adds anything to the account. (It approximates Herbart's concept of "apperceptive mass," being the dominant collection of representations from which others are included or excluded. It is in fact here a quantitative concept, a name for the victorious mental majority.)

Klein was a pioneer in refining clinical description, and he was alert to the promise of Piagetian ideas. Holding both themes in his hands, he unfortunately lost the vital link that he had helped to forge between them: the principle that schemata are always to some extent integrative and adaptive. It is no longer necessary to conjure up some separate process, such as understanding or reality testing or even accommodation, to drag affective, assimilative schemata into reluctant contact with the rest of the personality and reality. Affect, the unconscious, fantasy, all have a role to play in understanding. Piaget would never agree that accommodation means conscious comprehension, or that "conscious implementation of a wish is an important accompaniment, even a requirement, of accommodative behavior." Accommodation occurs with the first suckling. No behavior can be purely accommodative or purely assimilative. Piaget's concepts in their strictest sense would never lead one into the quagmire of purely assimilative primary process that seizes aspects of the environment to distort them. (Seizing is selecting, and that entails accommodation.) No purely assimilative schema would be able to relate itself in any way to anything, and would not in fact be a schema. (Perhaps a spinal reflex would satisfy the definition, but it is also accommodative on a neurological level.)

But Klein has pointed the way to a microanalysis of therapeutic interaction. We learn from him that affect-laden schemata are more or less integrated with each other, just as purely cognitive schemata are; they are *more or less* equilibrated with the environment, that is, more or less lop-sidedly assimilative. We learn from him that adaptation amounts to some kind of "reflection" or "acknowledgment" of these schemata by other schemata (p. 194), and a failure of "reflective acknowledgment" causes conflict, pain, and inefficiency.

"Reflective acknowledgment" requires further elucidation. We may suppose that the process and its elements are analogous to the decentering, reflective schemata that Piaget has shown to coordinate schemata of physical orientation. But what place affect and motive will have in the analogy remains to be said.

PIAGET: THE NEXT STEP?

Piaget (1951) offers us a theory of mental processes designed to describe the interaction of individuals with their environment. Such a theory should be useful in describing psychotherapy. According to Piaget, to adapt means to adjust mental structures that are prepared for the world to features in the world for which they are not prepared. It is therefore an interplay between a conservative and an innovative tendency. The goal of adaptation is to obtain an equilibrium between these two tendencies. It has been said that psychoanalytic structures are configurations with a slow rate of change (Rapaport,

1967, p. 701). Piaget provides terms applicable to organizations with both slow and fast rates of change. (He calls them schemata.) In that sense we could say that his is a microtheory of the mind, and Freud's a macrotheory.

Piaget has used his theory mostly to show how objective, logical thought develops. Before it can be used to describe psychotherapy, we have to decide where affect and human attachment enter into it. This question can be put more exactly: with regard to the cognitive aspect of experience, equilibrium between conservative and innovative requirements is achieved by the development of the concept of the physical object. The concept of the physical object is a schema that is fully prepared for the unexpected, because it is basically a procedure for mentally discounting unexpectedness without ignoring it. For instance, when someone makes allowance for his perspective (which Piaget calls "decentering"), he is able to picture an action which would return appearances to their previous state. (Piaget calls that "reversibility.") For the theory of therapy, then, the big questions are: What does decentering do to affect? How does affect influence decentering? What is the affective equivalent of cognitive reversibility? And what role does human attachment play in this process?

Morality has always been the first example of affective structure to be examined because it is the easiest, and Piaget (1967) has applied his theory to it. In the area of morality, Piaget proposes that the "will" does for impulses what the concept of the physical object does for perceptions. He says that the will counterbalances automatic arousal of desires (pp. 59-60). Piaget draws an analogy between this counterbalancing of temptation by the will and the counterbalancing of optical illusion by operational reasoning:

> The system of interests or values, which changes at every moment depending on the activity in progress, thus incessantly commands the system of internal energies by means of a quasi-automatic and continuous regulating process. However, it is only what might be called an intuitive regulator, since it is partly irreversible and subject to frequent displacements of equilibrium. Will, on the other hand, is a regulation that has become reversible, and in this sense it is comparable to an operation. When a duty is momentarily weaker than a specific desire, will re-establishes values according to their pre-established hierarchy and ensures their subsequent conservation. Will gives primacy to the tendency of less strength by reinforcing it. Thus it acts exactly like the logical operation when the deduction (equivalent to the superior but weaker tendency) is at odds with a perceptual appearance (equivalent to the inferior but stronger tendency) and operational reasoning corrects actual [but misleading] appearances by referring to previous states [1967, pp. 59-60, translator's brackets].

The operations of the will are like reasoning about physical objects. Both serve to accept novelty while at the same time reducing it to pre-existing rules.

While knowledge of the world is being structured by logical operations, desirability is being organized by a hierarchy of values.

What, then, is reversibility in moral terms? Reversibility is the conservation of the subject's hierarchy of values in the face of temptations that would tend to rearrange them. The tendency to react "out of character" is not, however, obliterated; there is no will without subordinate desires to be overruled—no morality without temptation. The organism accommodates by recognizing and subordinating the temptation according to a more general affective schema.

In this instance the will corresponds to the superego. But the principles also describe the functioning of any psychic institution. In many respects "will" could be translated (with considerable loss of specificity) into the more popular terms of personal identity or self (as George Klein did), or into "ego" in the loose sense of the object-relations school. The will also corresponds to the synthetic function of the ego in the strict Freudian sense.

Let us then make the following generalization: our action on the world analyzes the world, and the progressive schematization of our actions is a way of understanding the objective world. Accordingly, the interests or affect behind action pick out meaning in the world. Coordination of the affects involved in action does two things: it modifies the significance of our purposes, which means it modifies those purposes, and it creates an affect-relevant reliability or rule-boundness in the object—an understanding of its principles of goodness or badness, so to speak.

In the Piagetian framework, if affective reversibility is not achieved, there should be consequences for both inner and outer worlds. Internally a person would be vulnerable to much greater conflict (whether it shows itself in anxiety, inefficiency, loss of self-esteem, helplessness, or aimlessness). Externally, if affective reversibility is not achieved, the subject would not be able to evaluate the object fully in terms of all the analyzers that his wishes potentially provide. He would be centered on the paramount reaction of the moment.

As the individual progresses to affective equilibrium, a gradual integration—and thus modification—of affective meanings and wishes will occur. In psychoanalytic terms this corresponds to redistribution of energies among psychic structures, sublimation, character formation, etc. At the same time the object becomes increasingly rich and stable in affective values. This shift in the quality of affect and wishes, as well as in the nature of the object, can be illustrated by the development of moral feeling. As moral rules are perfected, the quality of the moral feeling changes. (Witness the difference between the quality of an archaic superego and a more mature one, apart from the difference in standards.) And of course regularity and coherence in solving moral problems is improved.

Optimum affective equilibrium would be that state in which the subject is assured that no matter what the stimulus, his reaction will ignore none of his purposes. A stimulus will be relevant to more than any partial inclination toward it. The subject can react affectively to the total object rather than to a single aspect of it, for example to a particular person in authority rather than simply to an authority figure. This kind of reversibility does not ensure that the subject will not be frustrated. But after all, neither do his conceptual schemata ensure that he will never be surprised. What reversibility does ensure is that he can allow himself to be frustrated without feeling defeated, just as he can allow himself to be surprised without giving up his view of the objective nature of reality.

Complete reversibility is never achieved, either on the cognitive or affective level. I have elsewhere argued that the limits of affective reversibility impose limits on the cognitive (cf. Friedman, 1974). The limits of affective reversibility are illustrated by such principles as Hartmann's (1958, p. 94) dictum that a normal ego must be "able to must." Mourning is the most flagrant demonstration that affective reversibility is incomplete. The work of mourning is an illumination of the *process* of decentering as it occurs in the affective sphere. It shows us how dysfunctional and maladaptive complete decentering would be, such as would make mourning unnecessary. Just as total cognitive decentering would amount to geometrical rather than geographical perception, total affective decentering would be tantamount to an impersonal, "philosophical" kind of independent unreactiveness. A completely decentered person would know laws of psychology but no individual people.

The net effect of both cognitive and affective operations is that no matter what is presented to the subject he can fit it with minimal distortion into a pre-existing framework – a framework of perception and a framework of volition.

But knowledge of affective organization is not all that we need in order to describe the relation of affect to understanding. There is one line of *cognitive* development that Piaget has yet to work out, and unfortunately it is the one psychoanalysts are most interested in: the development of the concept(s) of the human object(s). This is infinitely more complicated than the already extremely complicated development of physical object concepts. We should be able to apply the same principles to it, for instance, the role of integrated action schemata in defining the object. But in the case of the human object, the actions on the object that are relevant are affective appeals, and the shaping responses of the object are other people's affects.[3] (Everyone should

---

[3]Freud's theory shows us the accommodations of intrapsychic schemata to each other. For therapy we must employ concepts of accommodation and assimilation *between* two people's schemata. It is the understandable wish to avoid this departure from theory of the mind that led many orthodox analysts to describe the ultimate "object" in analysis as an "interpretation." That

read Stern's [1977, pp. 98-107] evocative sketch of how this might happen.)

This complexity is hidden by the unique example that Piaget studied—the moral code. Piaget shows how persons learn to conceive of the Good as an object in the same way as they learn to conceive of bodies as objects. But the great variety of human moral systems tells us that what the object is learning is the "object-ness" of parental emotions, that is, the principles behind their reactions.

Unlike the physical object, or even the moral "object," human objects do not indefinitely become more and more understandable as they are embraced in larger and larger schemata. Their individuality is far more important than that of physical objects. Piaget's analysis implies that the more unique the objects dealt with, the less decentering the subject can achieve.[4]

This is what makes therapy so difficult to conceptualize. Those who have emphasized the role of interpretation have been stressing the decentering purpose of therapy. On the other hand, those who have emphasized attachment have been attending to the inherent limitations of decentering when dealing with personal objects. Both theories, however, have been designed to account for the analyst's usefulness in fostering integration of the patient's schemata. The two streams of thought nowadays are converging to an acceptance of the interconnection between understanding and attachment at all stages of therapy.

What we learn from Piaget is that the patient's analysis of himself goes hand-in-hand with his analysis of the physician, following the Piagetian rule that differentiation of the self and of the object are two sides of the same coin. The therapist's services must enhance both analyses because they are aspects of the same process. The traditional role of neutrality facilitates this exploration by providing as simple and general a human object as possible, while holding feedback consistent and minimal. This provides a freedom and clarity that one usually enjoys only when exploring nonhuman objects. It is probably for this reason that all therapies limit involvement with the patient, at least in terms of time. But after all, the analyst is not an inanimate object and could not facilitate the integration of affective schemata if he were one. The patient's growth can only come about through the impact of his desires and provocations on the analyst's meanings and reactivities, since it is through this impact that the analyst's human objectness and the patient's

---

would be relatively rigid "aliment" for the patient to schematize, and the interaction would therefore be easier to describe. But perception of human beings is more complicated than that.

[4]The less decentering by the subject, the vaguer his identity. Consequently the overwhelming importance of individual human beings to each other sets a built-in limit to how individuated a person can be—or stated more philosophically, there is a limit to how much a person can stand apart from his human *Umwelt*, and a degree to which he is simply the nexus of his relationships (cf. George Mead, 1934).

human identity achieve definition. (For elaboration of this point, see chapter 25 and Shands [1976].)

It is only by seeing an impact on the analyst (as one initially sees on one's parents) that the patient can build representations of his own actions (cf., Loewald, 1960, p. 19). He cannot know what he is doing until he has been able to abstract from the response of the other person. When the analyst tells a patient what he is doing, the patient experiences it as a *response* of the object. As such it will contribute to a concept of the object (the analyst) and of the patient's action, and of the patient's nature. But it does not do that by sheer exposition. One must first have a tacit concept of one's action before talking about it can be useful. (A concept of a physical object cannot be provided to a child by labeling the object. Nor can morality be taught by the statement of a code.) Interpretations are simply the most controllable and focused parts of an informative reaction by the analyst, and their impact is mediated by other, subtler reactions of timing and attitude.[5] The significance of an interpretation is always the significance of a reaction from someone perceived as a certain kind of person, though it is to be hoped that it also changes the analyst's image slightly.

Strachey knew that there was something about himself (his superego) that he had to make his patient discover. But he also realized that the patient finds his predominant wishes less threatened and threatening if he refrains from exploring this new object. Strachey (1934) therefore concentrated on ways ("mutative interpretations") which would take advantage of subordinate, less exercised, unintegrated schemata that *would* map the analyst's superego. In this way he presented the patient with an easier task of integrating a somewhat new human object with his predominant schemata, incidentally reshuffling the patient's awareness of himself.

At the opposite pole to the newness of the analyst, Gitelson tried to find the initial affective understanding of the analyst which all patients start out with. In Piaget's terms, we could say that Gitelson found an aspect of the analytic relationship on which the patient could exercise and develop his will. Those who recoiled from this idea were afraid that the patient's will was too poorly established to counterbalance driving, neurotic needs and that those needs would bias the concepts of patient and analyst. But our microanalysis suggests that such is nevertheless the only way that a human (as opposed to a physical) object can be identified.

Balint (1968) most explicitly raises the question of concern to the object-relations school: How can an undeveloped will start *de novo* as it should have

---

[5]This was implied by Gitelson (1962) when he wrote, "I think that so-called 'pedagogy,' 'clarification,' 'suggestion,' and 'manipulation' are 'verbal-nonverbal' *preparatory incomplete interpretations. . .*" (p. 204).

done in infancy? Suppose that affective schemata are not sufficiently organized and, correspondingly, that perception of the object is not sufficiently
objectified to permit Gitelson's level of recognition. Suppose there is relatively no self and no object. How does learning begin to take place? Most
object-relations theoreticians seem more interested in the problem than in
the answer, as though sympathy alone would solve it. Winnicott and Balint
are exceptions. They feel that if the therapist does not require the patient to
grasp the therapist's nature to begin with, he can (by play or unobtrusiveness)
offer an undifferentiated, global opportunity for the patient to integrate his
desires. In this way the analyst, like the mother, will gradually build up the
various partial schemata that must go into larger, coordinated schemata. To
do this he must initially remain as vague as the patient's own identity, since
otherwise the patient's task would be too formidable.

It is in these terms that we must understand the role of gratification in
treatment. All treatment involves attachment and all attachment involves
gratification (see Friedman, 1975b). Gratification does not put something
into the patient temporarily or permanently. It does not drain off something
from him, either helpfully or harmfully. For better or worse it is a structuring,
teaching, more or less defining, more or less integrating response. In an
attachment, gratification says something, albeit something not easily put into
words. In analysis it says something about who the patient is and who the
analyst is. That is why therapists must be so careful about it. *Insofar as it is
therapeutic* it causes a helpful restructuring of the patient's perceptions and
self-feeling, as well as his feeling about—and, therefore, the nature of—his
wishes. *To the extent that it does this* it is not binding but freeing, and leads not
to dependence but to independence. (Maslow [1968, 1970] argues this on
empirical grounds.) Attachment is integrative and is a form of understanding. The full implication of Piaget's approach is that in human relations,
attachment is how learning proceeds.

SUMMARY

Freud catalogued factors of understanding, attachment, and integration in
psychoanalytic cure. Understanding and attachment were explored by
Sterba and Nunberg. At the Marienbad Symposium, introjection seemed to
combine the factors. Later, at the Edinburgh Symposium, when Gitelson
suggested that integration is fostered by an infantile attachment pattern
partially repeated in the analysis, he was met with the vigorous reply that
only understanding (from interpretation) can do that. Among the reasons for
this reluctance to acknowledge what had previously been freely admitted was
the difficulty of imagining how the analyst could be embraced by the patient's
affective structures and still be free to help the patient change.

Object-relations theory was an attempt to resolve this problem, but the destruction it wrought in the theory of the mind discouraged some analysts from pursuing the line of thought. As analysts became more familiar with their theory and were increasingly supplied with models from child observation, they developed terms to deal with this problem, as in the work of Loewald and Stone. The controversy between Kohut and Kernberg illustrates how much of the Edinburgh debate is resolved and how much it is still with us.

Attempts to conceptualize therapeutic efficacy moved theory backwards from the description of gross structures of the mind to common processes of structure formation. This line of march is illustrated by Schafer's work on internalization and Klein's attempt to exploit Piaget's developmental concepts. Piaget's terms do seem to be useful in solving some treatment riddles.

5
Other Uses of Theory

As Kenneth Burke (1954) wrote, we interest someone by dealing with his interests. Nothing can be done with a patient unless we are important to him. But our importance is directly related to how well we fit into his structures. And we do not want to be fitters; we want to be changers. That is the problem.

If we deal with a person the way he wants to be dealt with, we do not allow him to be different; we conspire with him to restrict his freedom. If, however, we don't deal with him the way he wants to be dealt with, we cannot expect him to see any hope—no hope to enjoy any kind of freedom whatever.

The therapist's task seems paradoxical, and therapists use theory to picture it in a less paradoxical way. We have found several ways that therapists are helped by theoretical descriptions. Therapists want theory to make them feel less alone, and so theory describes an alliance. Therapists want to feel that they are not being taken in by their patients, so theory provides a clear description of the transaction. Many other needs are served by theory, but in our account so far, theory seems always to serve by picturing the therapy scene. That is the way the last chapter explained what was at stake at the Edinburgh Symposium.

But the difference between the Marienbad Symposium in 1936 and the Edinburgh Symposium in 1962 is not just a disagreement about which pictures describe treatment accurately. There is disagreement also about what attitude to take toward picture-making.

At Marienbad the participants eagerly discussed all kinds of therapeutic influence and interaction. They canvassed many extreme and moderate positions. The imaginative discussion at Marienbad sharply contrasts with the later one at Edinburgh, where a rigid standoff between the keynote speaker and most of the discussants signals a new concern. Rough ideas are no longer freely circulated as possible images of treatment. Treatment factors are either admitted or dismissed, no longer played with or left hanging. What new priorities have arisen since 1936 to account for this? What makes one generation willing to experiment with descriptions and another shy away? Evidently there are competing, non-descriptive functions of theory that were not important at Marienbad but became important by 1963.

I suggest that when the story of treatment gets so complicated that the therapist cannot be sure what to focus on, theory will stop describing the whole scene and start stabilizing the therapist's position. Its mission then will be to focus the therapist's attention and consolidate his reactions.

First let us look at the 1920s. Ferenczi and Rank (1925) recognized that their colleagues were faced with the question of all beginners: "What on earth am I to make out of all this? What is some thing to hold on to?" Traumatic memories had been something to hang on to. Patient's silences were conspicuous but infrequent somethings to pounce on. If Ferenczi and Rank are to be believed, "complexes" were being seized on as handy somethings, and the spice of psychosexual stages was used to add piquancy. To bring order to this ad hoc variety, Ferenczi and Rank pointed out that theory makes the transference central, and therefore a good way to pick things out of process is to decode the patient's behavior by the way it fits into the treatment relationship. That sort of focus selects items that are both relevant and handy. I want to emphasize that these are two separate functions: to reassure the therapist that there is something to grasp, and to indicate how to spot it. Sometimes theory helps with the first but not the second. For instance, when a trainee first undertakes "long-term, intensive, psychodynamic psychotherapy," he profits from a theory that tells him that there is something to grasp. But the theory as he knows it might not tell him what it is. On the other hand, I have the impression that some current hermeneutic theories give no assurance that there is anything to grasp, but provide a pretty clear idea how to grasp it!

Ferenczi and Rank, Wilhelm Reich, Melanie Klein, and Strachey all offered the analyst a practical focus. But sophisticated analysts shortly began to recognize that their field of study is especially thick, and moreover, no reality can be exhaustively characterized or univocally described. A holistic trend set in early, represented by the object relationists in Great Britain, and in the United States by Waelder, Hartmann, Rapaport, and now Schafer (see chapter 27).

Every theory has its perspectives. A sophisticated theory is aware of its bias and implies that reality has more ambiguity than is described. As theory of the mind becomes more sophisticated, and the winds of complexity dishevel the therapist's purpose, he must lean in the opposite direction in order to keep his balance. He needs to dig himself in. He must feel himself less problematically involved so that he can retain a clear, unambiguous working orientation—a nonspeculative vision on which to base decisive action. A psychoanalyst may philosophize about theory of the mind, but as a therapist he has to act. It may be that the more sophisticated a theory of the mind becomes, the simpler must be the theory of therapy that goes with it.

Here is another example: The original paradigm of psychoanalysis was that, when the patient's infantilisms are exposed he willy-nilly has to give them up (working-through being just a more detailed exposure). By the time of Marienbad (1936), a monumental theory shift had made it apparent that reality itself is not such a simple thing. (For a more recent review see also Friedman, 1973). Reality is not so easily and sharply contrasted with the patient's secret vision. And even if reality could be neatly expressed, experience shows that patients can uncover what the analyst knows to be infantile fantasies and still go on behaving as though they are more realistic than the analyst's reality. It is not sufficient use of the analyst's ingenuity to force infantile attitudes into play, as Ferenczi had tried. It is not sufficient to make experience intense. Experience has to be redefined. That was the problem Strachey tried to solve with his mutative interpretation in the 1930s. His triumph was to find a means of simultaneously controlling both the intensity and the definition of a patient's experience.

Now let us turn to Edinburgh in the 1960s. What were most of these later thinkers doing with the problem of how one can control the meaning that the patient makes out of an interpretation? Essentially nothing. They acted as though that was no longer a problem: Interpretations point out reality. The term *interpretation* stands in lieu of a discussion about how reality is defined and communicated. Why was the later theory of effectiveness less sophisticated than the earlier one? Maybe because at the later time theory had another job to do and it could not afford to be distracted: While preventing the analyst from oversimplifying a complex reality, theory had to let him feel not only that a steady point of view was available, but also that he could selectively get that point of view across to his patient. Theory of therapy is here being used in the first place to discipline and privilege the analyst's listening (by the principle of a balanced attention to all psychic institutions), and secondly, to embolden his teaching (by supposing that a good interpretation is free of interpersonal complications). In these ways the analyst uses theory not as an investigative tool but as a cognitive brace, so that he can undertake more particular investigations of his individual patients.

And that is not all that we see here. Theory is not just used as a cognitive brace. At Edinburgh it is also used as a constraint on behavior. Earlier writers felt that they could separate their analysis of patients from their analysis of analysis. They could treat people in one fashion, and speculate about how they were achieving their results in another. Later analysts were overwhelmingly concerned that such speculations would invariably affect practice. The participants at Edinburgh had foremost in mind that if an analyst thinks that primitive or libidinal or relationship aspects of treatment are instrumental, he may end up dealing with his patients in a more primitive, libidinal, or "related" ("human," that is to say, sentimental) way. Now of course that does often happen. Nevertheless, theorists do not always worry about it. The Marienbaders did not worry much about the immediate effect that speculating about the relationship might have on the conduct of treatment. Glover (1937) was a very proper, reserved analyst, but he could suggest that the analyst as a person is more important than his specific maneuvers. (Indeed, Leo Stone [Langs and Stone, 1980] appreciates Glover's endorsement of this view just because Glover was not a "soft" analyst.) But at Edinburgh theory is no longer a free-wheeling speculation in the evening about the morning's perfectly adequate practice. Theory has become a way for the working analyst to insure his acceptable behavior. (See King's statement, pp. 54–55 of this volume.)

Thus, theory is many things to a therapist. Theory of treatment is sometimes a *post facto description* of a treatment; it is sometimes *a prospective guide to action*. It is sometimes *a way of picking out items* from continuous process (or at least reassuring the analyst that such is possible). Finally, theory is also *a participant in the consulting room* (for example, a chaperone). Theory is not used just to describe: It is fashioned for its effect as a belief.

It is in regard to this last function that the biggest difference between the Marienbad and Edinburgh frame of mind can be found. We should not shrink from identifying it as an ideological function of theory.

Professions try to keep their distance from ideology because it seems to compromise their expertise. When sociologists study the ideology of professions, they often do it with their own ideology, that is to say, they work toward a preferred result, most often to discredit what they regard as a predatory imposture.

It is itself an ideological belief that ideology exists only to line someone's pocket or to let him dominate his fellows. Our age has lost the innocent (some would say smug) assurance that ideology is a narrow interest which sociologists can rise above (as Mannheim [1936] believed). Today we are more inclined to understand ideology as an orienting scheme that facilitates practices of every kind. Ideology is the dramatic background of our living. It is part of everyone's psychology and, because the therapist's psychology is his main tool, his ideology will greatly affect how he carries out his professional task. If we notice something tendentious or impassioned or even venomous in the way therapists argue, we cannot automatically attribute that to tribal or pecuniary interest, or even "the narcissism of small differences." These may be involved. But if the style is characteristic of therapists, we should first of all treat that characteristic as a possible clue to the nature of their trade. We should always ask, what is there about this work that makes people who do it behave like this? One approach to the therapist's ideology is Schafer's (1980a) demonstration of the organizing function of the typical life history learned in psychoanalytic training. This is a study of the role of ideology in practice because Schafer is interested in how, leaving aside its truth claim, the psychoanalytic form of narration keeps the therapist in a position to do therapy. Because Schafer is not challenging the truth of analytic theory (he is, rather, re-defining "truth"), his message is that, even if it is "true," analytic theory also serves as a useful myth.

But there are many more ideological functions of theory than myth-making. And some of these ideological functions become apparent when we see that certain doctrines are felt to be attitudinally incompatible with others. It may be difficult to maintain a non-committal relationship with a patient while imagining that one is functioning as a "mother of distance." When we find that believing one sort of thing to be true, a therapist finds it *anathema* to attend to another, we can sense that theory is sometimes used to position the therapist, and we can understand that such a set-up might be spoiled by another thought. If we first think that we are imparting a neutral comment, and then add that even a neutral comment expresses a personal attitude by virtue of its timing, and so on, we might be in danger of giving up on neutrality altogether. If a therapist only had to heed logical compatibility and empirical evidence, we observers could forget about this aspect of ideology. But if we find practical concerns that forbid mixing one sort of theory with another, in other words, a "postural" use of theories, we can use this as a clue to the therapist's adversities—a signpost pointing to those personal predicaments he faces from moment to moment, predicaments that theory helps not as a map but as an ideology.

I suggest that the shift we have been examining illustrates this postural use of theory: Because neuroses were visualized in different ways over time, early and later analytic theories of treatment were required to position the analyst in different attitudes or stances.

Neurosis was early depicted as an organic whole, a structure that can be transplanted into the treatment as a transference neurosis. This conception goes back to the beginning of psychoanalysis. Freud (1895) represented the neurosis as a system of complex, core and peripheral, affect-laden, interconnected memories, with a velocity that directs them, according to a natural order, through the defile of consciousness, when summoned by the analyst who has removed obstacles at the defile.

For the purpose of our comparison, what is crucial in this conception is the self-definition and self-containedness of the pathogenic wish-structure, its orderliness, impetus, and potential ability to begin again and revise itself.

It is back to this vision that Ferenczi and Rank called their erring colleagues, who had been looking here and there, describing whatever they saw like so many birdwatchers in a disorderly aviary.

According to Ferenczi and Rank (1925) a whole, preformed libidinal structure will emerge in the transference during a properly conducted psychoanalysis. It will unwind from its hidden spool within the patient and onto the visible analyst. Interpretation helps the transference neurosis to develop and resolve itself. But what is crucial in this is the actual development of the transference neurosis.

The theory of Ferenczi and Rank is not as simple as it is sometimes portrayed. But it is safe to say that a paramount theme of the book is that analysis takes a privately conserved and restricted fantastic attachment and socializes it in the transference, thus allowing incompleted beginnings to fulfill themselves and adapt to their new social reality. In this respect, it resembles Balint's and Kohut's and other object relations theories. With only slight exaggeration, one might say that, when treatment begins, a shaped libidinal organization is already present *in statu nascendi*, defined, latent, and liberatable.

If that is the case, it cannot be a life and death matter what conceptual *frame* the analyst uses, or even what *influences* he brings to bear on the patient. Although coiled in the patient's unconscious, the hidden thread is there and given half a chance it will be transferred to the analyst. Ferenczi and Rank even permit themselves to experiment with manipulations that might unwind the thread faster and more completely. The imagination of historians has been drawn to these early experimental techniques. Less dramatic, but perhaps more important, is the conceptual freedom that these experiments testify to. In asking practicing analysts to consider these experiments, Ferenczi and Rank had no trouble supposing that their colleagues could comfortably imagine relationships with their patient that seem to us extraordinarily adventuresome.

Perhaps their reception was hostile, but the mere fact that they would advertise such experiments indicates a climate of unusual intellectual freedom. And I think the reason for that freedom is that the notion of a well-formed infantile libidinal organization, inevitably destined to be transcribed in the transference, left Ferenczi and Rank and their contemporaries free to envision their relationship to the patient in many variable ways. Coiled libido is already defined, and it doesn't matter whether it exactly matches the analyst's perception. It is activation that is important. Definition is secondary.

What happened after Ferenczi and Rank? The illness, which had earlier been thought of as a slightly irritating foreign body composed of traumatic memories, came to be regarded as a systemic disease of the whole psyche. The ego does not just fight off formed id impulses. Instead, the ego is modified by its efforts to abort them.[1] It conspires with the repressed id, and it integrates these split off developments, and the like. In short, the neurosis is no longer visualized as a self-contained organism within a personality. All kinds of interests are served by the illness. There is not even an unequivocal illness to refer to.

This process occurred in the 1930s. Psychoanalysis was then at a cross-roads: At the very moment that analysis was passing beyond easy distinctions, those distinctions that it had perfected were just becoming useful in conceptualizing treatment. The superego is an enduring, internal monitor that had once been directly influenced by real persons. It seemed to be both the organ of resistance and an institution accessible to influence. It was a godsend for explaining how the analyst can move minds.

This focus on the superego carried the enthusiastic theorist back to an earlier, simpler notion of resistance as a force that keeps a hidden organization apart from the rest of the mind. That hidden organization, a set of childish purposes, was given renewed plausibility by the concept of another thing (the superego) that obstructs it. And by good fortune, the notion of "introjection," which initially builds the superego, makes it possible to see how the therapist can overcome resistance.

Thus the Marienbaders were at liberty to explore the nature of influence, confident that the hidden structure of attachment and desire has its own natural form and definition. Strachey stands just one step beyond Ferenczi and Rank. Like the earlier authors, he aims to ease the infantile anxiety that prevents the repressed structure from flourishing. True, he knows better how hard it is to change the perceptions that support that anxiety. But once Strachey's new technique has overcome that problem, the picture of treatment is similar to that of Ferenczi and Rank: what has been repressed is free to start a new beginning. Others at Marienbad (e.g., Bibring) with slightly different conceptualizations share a similar general outlook.

It is a brief moment of unworried experimentation in the history of theory, and it faded quickly. A growing holism destroyed the reassuring belief in an encapsulated neurotic "organism" waiting to be freed, possessing its own form independently of how it is described when it is freed (cf. chapter 27.) Anna Freud (for example, in The Ego and the Mechanisms of Defense [1936]) examined the many other things a person does with intolerable impulses besides repressing them. Defenses are no longer thought to be a lid resting uncomfortably over bubbling longings. The shape of wishes is partly defined

---

[1]There remains considerable equivocation about this (for example, see Eissler, 1953.)

by the defenses. A defense may amount to an inability to imagine useful possibilities. Unlike id-transferences, defenses, when exposed, are not experienced by the patient as a strange, other self that can be contemplated with the analyst in shared wonderment. It is not sufficient to get rid of what holds back stuck wishes, and just let them blossom. The whole layout of the garden is awry. The patient must learn to redefine himself, and the analyst must take care not to mislead him by biased discriminations, descriptions, and conceptualizations. Now it is important for the analyst to know that he has not made a one-sided or arbitrary choice of perspective. For if he felt that he was randomly cognizant of, e.g., impulse, defense, transference, dreams, or any individual item of process, he would fear that he might be endorsing a bad compromise. Ferenczi and Rank, in contrast, could have counted on the emerging libido to take care of itself if the obstacles were cleared away. The earlier and later theories can be translated into each other, but they represent outlooks of different complexity.

The Marienbaders had been enthusiastic about the superego; Anna Freud studied the ego. And there is this difference between them: The ego stands for everything, but everything considered as a problem, rather than as forms looking to be actualized, or as captives struggling for liberation. One can understand a problem best by subjecting oneself to all the pressures that make it up, whence the injunction that the analyst remain equidistant from all psychic institutions. It is essential to be unbiased among the perspectives the mind takes on itself, and that means always being sensitive to the aspect of conflict. There are latent forces to be liberated, but there is no pre-defined libidinal organism to be liberated. Indeed, what the analyst counts on most is a re-defining force (the synthetic power of the ego). The neurosis is a state of the whole person, and its *definition* is crucial to treatment. That definition must do justice to all forces. No driving or unwinding, patterned libido can be relied on to brush aside a sloppy definition by the analyst. What the analyst hopes to revive is something that has not just been masked from view but something that has been actually transformed and distorted in its being. Considering that new descriptions, so to speak, do the liberating, and that simple descriptions are arbitrary and governed by various interests (the product of conflict), the best approach is to take all factors into consideration, and be careful to keep thought and comment confined to what is clearly definable and unqualifiedly helpful. For the analyst, judgment, poise, and balance become overwhelmingly important.

Insofar as it remained for Anna Freud to exploit the subtleties of late psychoanalytic theory, we must say that her father, in his theory of treatment, did not make use of his own developed theory of the mind. Gray (1982) has brought this strange fact to attention, and studied it in detail.

Gray points out that Sigmund Freud's basic attitude toward treatment did not change much over the years. The hypnotic model remained his ideal. Although he occasionally moved toward other positions, he kept coming back to the hypnotic model. His theory might lead to resistance analysis, and defense analysis. But as Strachey (1934, pp. 132-133) adduced in defense of his interpersonal model, even after Freud's late revisions produced an ego psychology, Freud still held that it was through personal influence that resistance is ultimately overcome.

Gray suggests that Freud neglected his daughter's book and adhered to a hypnotic model because of an authoritarian style that made it hard for him to shift into the modern analytic attitude. Rather than reflecting on how a patient handles transference problems, Freud was inclined to persuade him to accept an account of deep, disowned wishes.

Freud continued to emphasize the analyst's personal influence while others began to use terms that minimize it. The new trend undoubtedly led to a less authoritarian practice, but it is not so clear that it produced a less authoritarian theory. It seems to me that one of the most difficult riddles in psychotherapy is whether a theory is more or less authoritarian for dwelling on the therapist's influence. By agreeing with Bernheim that hypnosis involves a universal process of suggestion Freud accepted the authority of the hypnotist *and* the onus that goes with it. By denying that he was influencing his patients, Charcot imposed his suggestions and disavowed his responsibility.

My guess is that in his work, Freud continued to visualize treatment as an effort to liberate a secret organization of wishes that lies inside a protective shell of resistance. Even if his theory of the mind ultimately made this formula untenable, its persisting image left Freud free to speculate on the cracking of shells, so to speak. Therefore he could retain his interest in the *forces* at work in treatment. Perceiving that her father's later theory no longer suggested shells to be cracked, Anna Freud saw that the analyst's influence would be used by patients in complex ways. The nature of influence was no longer so clear, its effects no longer reliable. As a consequence, I suggest, analysts tended not to allow themselves to study the nature of the power they wield, in order that they should not behave like wielders of power.

I do not mean to say that analysts gave up the postulate of an infantile neurosis, the elucidation of which is the ultimate aim of treatment. But I am suggesting that analysts stopped believing in it as a self-contained, self-defined potential experience, and along with it they gave up the trust in a real, natural, pre-definition of wishes, a trust that had allowed earlier analysts to let their theories wander wherever they wished. (Bibring [1937] was a notable wanderer, for example.)

In answer to the question, why analysts are more theoretically open minded at some times than they are at others, the following hypothesis might be explored: How freely theory of therapy is allowed to wander depends on the current belief about whether wishes heal themselves by their own natural direction, or whether they must be newly shaped in partnership with the analyst. The less he believes that the patient has a fixed, hidden, segregated meaning within him the more the analyst will require his theory to reassure him that his perceptions are balanced and impartial, and that he is not influencing his patients.

Compared to Ferenczi and Rank, and compared to Strachey, Anna Freud thought that the ultimate definition of wishes was more influenced by the accuracy of the analyst's perception. And because she recognized accuracy to depend on a balance of perspectives, she used the theory of treatment as a guarantor of cognitive sobriety and of behavioral restraint. (See for example Tausend, 1959.)

Perhaps, then, a certain austerity in describing the analyst's action is the price that must be paid for a theory of treatment that accompanies a more comprehensive theory of the mind.

We can test my hypothesis by asking whether extremely pale theories of influence are found only associated with highly perspectival, complex, and sophisticated theories of the mind. My hypothesis fails the test right from the beginning. If this is a rule, it is surely not the only rule. The same conservatism and stereotypy in theory of treatment can be found in the tradition of Melanie Klein (1952), along with a theory of the mind quite different from Anna Freud's. None of Anna Freud's interpretive moderation, and none of her multiple cognitive grids are used by the Kleinians. The Kleinians prefer to work with the very pre-oedipal images that Anna Freud considered too poorly defined for precise conceptualization. And yet Kleinians, too, restrict the mechanism of treatment to interpretation, reclaiming of areas of the ego, and so on.

But I would suggest that the Kleinians have another, equally strong, reason to keep the theory of the therapeutic interaction simple. The preponderantly primitive significance that their theory gives to all interaction makes it hard to say how the therapeutic interaction exempts itself. It seems to me that Kleinian theory provides the least assurance that the analyst can step out of the role she is cast in by the patient. It would therefore be necessary for this theory to say, if I may exaggerate a little, that in reality the analyst is in *no* way what the patient wants her to be: she is just an analyst (cf. Segal, 1962).

But now the reader may say that I am trying to have it both ways. And perhaps I am. It is only as an illustration that I timidly offer the hypothesis that a complex theory of the mind requires a simple paradigm of the therapeutic relationship, whereas simpler theories of the mind allow more complex images of the relationship. I am only trying to illustrate how one might explore the ways that a theory's cognitive form may be determined by the attitudinal impact the therapist needs from it.

CONCLUSIONS

Here are some of the services we have seen theory pressed into:

1. To describe the mechanism of cure.
2. To assure the therapist that he is not imposing artificial perspectives on the patient.
3. To assure the therapist that he is not being manipulated by his patient (i.e., that he is not being co-opted by the illness), and that he can communicate his own intentions despite the difference of perspective.
4. To assure the therapist that there are objective things to grasp in the process of therapy, whether or not they are currently in view.
5. To actually identify particular configurations one may look for in process.

This last function of theory is the one that practitioners are most conscious of. Even those who see no other use of theory agree that it makes useful patterns out of phenomena.

Therapists need to identify situations and to imagine other situations that represent their translated "meaning." I have already suggested that one reason Ferenczi and Rank wrote their book was to help with this task. The eternal appeal of Melanie Klein's approach is the confidence the Kleinian analyst gains in his own perception. We are beginning to see a major critique of this whole endeavor (see Schafer, 1980a, and Spence, 1982). But I am not sure that the critics fully realize how committed therapists are to a belief in some perception, if nothing else then a perception of the therapeutic situation. The therapist, of course, would like to see everything that is going on here and there, now and then. But at the very least, he must work with some overarching picture of the therapy situation.

Theory of therapy is not just an optional description of treatment. In order for a therapist to work he must have at least a subliminal picture of his role and activity. That picture should not be thought of as a mere battle plan. Having the picture in mind is part of the activity. It is the cannons and gunpowder, if I may be excused the martial metaphor.

At the center of the therapist's approach to his work is a philosophy of potential developments. He may not see it very clearly, and we may not either. But, depending on how the patient's potential is conceived, other features of the treatment theory will take their place accordingly. For example, I have suggested that if the patient's potential is thought of as initially undifferentiated the analyst will require a theory of precise, interpretive definition, whereas a theory that describes the patient's potential as virtually already determined will allow exploration of fuzzier influences between patient and therapist.

It can hardly be controversial to say that psychotherapy is a personal attitude biased by a conception of human potentiality. That is one reason that theory is so important to it. In chapter 28 I discuss the relation between potentiality and theory more specifically. It is a more variable and complicated matter than one would expect.

RECOMMENDATION

We have seen theory work in different ways. We should therefore reflect on theory in different ways; in particular, as pointing to what happens, and as part of what happens.

How can we think best about these two aspects of theory? First, when we use theory to look *at* treatment, we should try to do without technical terms. Jargon makes us feel that we are answering questions when we are really just posing them. Specialized terms are necessary to tie complex theory to complex reality, but we can never be sure we understand the terms unless we can say the same thing in several different ways. So we should find other ways of expressing our ideas than in "acceptable" language. Psychoanalytic theory needs the term *ego*. But when it comes to explaining treatment, talking in terms of the ego answers questions before they are even asked. There is nothing wrong with postulating mental entities. Indeed, in Part III I argue that one cannot think without them. The concept of the ego makes it possible to describe conflict. But it begs all the treatment questions. Once the ego is named, there is nothing more to be said, except that the therapist helps it all he can.

Interpretation is not much better. In any particular case we hardly know the difference between the impact of a silence and that of a question, much less the difference between various species of declarative sentences. Look at our vocabulary: interpretation, clarification, confrontation, and so on. Is that adequate for describing human interaction? Students of speech would laugh at us (see Havens, 1986). Of course, many writers including Strachey (1934) and Gitelson (1962) have referred to *implicit interpretations*, existing in non-interpretive form. But if an interpretation is not a form of statement, then it is just whatever has the effect we are looking for. That will not help us to explain the effect. And if interpretation designates nothing very definite, how much vaguer is the contrasting term, *relationship*! Isn't every relationship in some sense an interpretation of one person by another?

Interpretation and *insight* and words of that sort simply stand for what it is we want to know. They are specialty terms for the mobilizing and synthesizing influences that we are investigating. When they were building a theory of the mind they showed us something new; now that theory of the mind is ingrained in us and we turn to issues of treatment, we must not be satisfied with simply combining and recombining words. That will not tell us anything about treatment forces.

What is the alternative? We cannot feign naiveté as though we had no theory. We must not settle for just any description that feels right and good. A "clinical theory" purified of metapsychology is probably a self-contradiction. And picturable metaphors with little discursive content (such as "the holding environment") can fake an answer as deceptively as theoretical jargon. In the end we have to use our theory; there is no alternative. But we should use it, that is, break it down into its meaning components, and not just reiterate it over and over again in different contexts.

We might follow the lead of the early analysts and look at treatment in a disinterested, almost anthropological way, the way a psychoanalyst would look at any other intimate relationship. That probably must be done first, before it is safe to bring in patented terms reserved for the therapeutic relationship. It would be most unpsychoanalytic to exempt the phenomena of treatment from the laws of psychology.

We cannot learn anything unless we are willing to be surprised. And because psychotherapists have naturally tended to describe their activity the way they wish to see it, any surprise is likely to be unpleasant. I think the early analysts were willing to be unpleasantly surprised, and we should recapture their bold curiosity.

We should actually welcome critical and hostile attacks (e.g., Haley, 1963), and the funhouse mirror images of analysis in faddish therapies, not in order to reform our technique but to revisualize it.

Help can also come from tangling with other studies that deal with change of meaning, such as infant development and literary criticism, historiography and philosophy.

Engaged in all these researches, we can ignore the history of psychoanalytic theory of therapy. But it would be a mistake to stop there. *Another type of scrutiny is also required.*

After we have ruthlessly shunned incantations masquerading as solutions, we must go back to the old formulas and savor them respectfully. We should ask what is the *attitudinal* value of this theory or that concept, soaked as it is in tradition. In this second type of examination we should not try to shake out of a term its bare, cognitive, cash value. Instead we should fully imagine what it is like to work with a given ideology and what it would be like to work without it. And, most important, we should be honest with ourselves about what is likely to take its place if we discard it, for a concept's chief value may sometimes be that it keeps another one out.

If, with Glover and Stone, we believe that the person of the analyst has a fundamental effect, will we inevitably become "saintly" practitioners? Will we overvalue our charm and our gifts and forget the bumbling work of therapy?

Will we tend to just let ourselves go? Will we invite patients to idealize us? Analogous and equally disturbing questions can be addressed to the opposite, purist view of the analyst as an interpretive technician: Will he develop grandiose over-investment in his ideas? It is not a question of whether these practical side effects are compelled by the doctrine, but whether the therapist is likely to behave in a certain way if he believes the doctrine.

If we see our project the way Schafer (1979) does, as a joint work on a series of narratives, will we tend to make an elegy out of what is really an uneasy struggle? Will we deprive our patients of their grounds for complaint? Will we expect more cooperation than is warranted? Will we lose the persistence and curiosity that comes from tracking down objective truth no matter how elusive or illusory? Will we forfeit some of the power that is available to more dogmatic therapists? Whatever it is that we actually do, we are bound to do it differently in the role of hermeneutic critic than as would-be scientists.

If we think of ourselves as interpreters of transference only, will we become too seductive, or will we spoil a necessary seductiveness? Will our biographical curiosity shrivel, our useful voyeurism starve? And will that limit what we discover even within the transference? Will we get used to dealing only with what we find convenient and familiar? (see Schafer, 1985a). Will we become too ideological or too predictable? On the other hand, if we do not adhere to a rule of transference interpretation, will we lose the acuity and discipline necessary to discern it when it is unpleasant? Will we slide into judging the patient's life in general?

"What does it *do* to a therapist to hold an idea like this?" That is one question we must always ask. The answer, in turn, might indicate what internal balance a therapist needs, and shed light on how he accomplishes his mission.

SUMMARY

Attachment, understanding, and integration were always recognized as the powers of treatment. And yet debate abounded. One difficulty is that some of these factors express the therapist's need to be germane to a patient's strivings, whereas others reflect the therapist's need to avoid collusion with his neurosis.

But theory is at various times asked to do many things besides explain. Theory was once used to pick out "real," thinkable forms from a confusing continuum of phenomena. Sophisticated thinking in later years made those earlier forms seem too simple. Theory was then required to give the analyst a mind-set that would do justice to the ambiguity of reality while also guaranteeing a balanced view. Having been assigned that task, the steadying effect of a theory became as important as its descriptive power. When theory is used to discipline perception and attitude, it cannot afford to be as flexible as when it just "calls them as it sees them."

We must therefore look at theory in a number of different lights. We should examine it as a description of happenings, resolutely shaking off jargon that conceals unsolved problems, and stripping off honorific innuendo that makes treatment look like what we want it to look like. But we also have to reckon with other ways that theory helps therapists to think about things, and then we have to examine how each concept molds an effective attitude within the therapist. This kind of study requires respect for the resonances, associations, and the general milieu of time-honored terms, as well as an appreciation of how some concepts serve to keep out other, unwanted attitudes.[2]

Theory of therapy is not a study made by a group of disinterested observors. Describing how treatment works is just one of the things theory can be called on to do. Theory is a tool of the practicing therapist (whether he knows it or not), and as a tool, it may sometimes be used for picking and hacking, sometimes for smoothing and pasting, sometimes for leaning against when tired. It may have to do different things at different times in its history, and it may not be able to do everything at once.

---

[2]Michels (1983) gives a straightforward account of the analyst's many uses of his theory: cognitive, perceptual, heuristic, pragmatic and companionate. Sandler (1983), while focusing mainly on theory's cognitive use, describes how analysts develop tacit, personal bits of theory to make themselves comfortable with their intuitive accommodation to individual patients.

6

Overview

At this point, the reader may reflect with some bitterness that what I have written is just another dreary illustration of how the literature falsely represents practice as an intellectual exercise.

My argument for taking theory seriously is that stress and theory go hand in hand, and define a balance problem that any therapist can discover in his practice—if not at every moment, then at least at those times that feel most special to his profession. The therapist finds a resting place in his theory, but theory also disturbs his rest.

There is a central strain in treatment due to the different intentions of patient and therapist, and when a therapist feels that strain, he cannot doubt that he uses theory to make himself feel better. (Sophisticated patients rely on theory that way too!)

While looking at how theory helps with this strain we noted a few other balance problems for which theory serves as an anchor. For instance, the therapist may have trouble identifying a theme, in which case theory is what he turns to, even if identifying the subject of a conversation does not feel like an exercise in theory. Or a therapist may find himself simultaneously in the position of being misunderstood, being accountable for the misunderstanding, and being responsible for making the misunderstanding profitable without correcting it. In trying to cope with such a deluge of responsibility, a therapist is likely to think theoretically, whether he knows it or not. Or the therapist may react in a way he immediately regrets, and at that moment he will run straight to his theory as his confessor and rescuer. There are many ways that a therapist can be thrown off balance, and every time that happens, some aspect of theory will become important to him.

Psychotherapy is an unnatural relationship, albeit one that includes many conventional, social forms. And the therapist's belief in a theory (however rudimentary or implicit) is both what makes it unnatural and what blends its unnaturalness with what is ordinary in the interaction.

The presence of a theory has effects of its own. If one talks only in the language of the theory one loves, he will not see its impact. His theory will be the invisible photographer of the treatment. Only when the theory itself is posed as a third presence in the room alongside the therapist and patient, will its role be visible. Theory, as I have tediously repeated, is a tool as well as a description: One has to look at it, as it functions in treatment, as well as through it at the treatment.

We must now, therefore, discuss psychotherapy in a nontechnical way, so that we can put theory into it as one item among others.

II
Practice Observed

Whoever is blocked in any piece of work to which he is devoted, becomes annoyed; whoever forsees a new advance in knowledge is always glad.

—Otto Fenichel (1941)

In doing psycho-analysis I aim at:

Keeping alive

Keeping well

Keeping awake

—D.W. Winnicott (1962)

7

Leaving Theory Temporarily

_____

Theory answers to many demands, some empirical (to integrate experience), some schematic (to answer questions raised by the theory itself), and some purely logical (to make its terms consistent). It isn't always easy to know which influence accounts for which theoretical wrinkle. But at least when it comes to picking out of theory those features designed to elaborate the therapist's basic efforts, we can be guided by the therapist's aches and pains. In the realm of psychotherapy, one cannot fully understand elaborate theoretical systems unless one has experienced the universal troubles of practice.

It also works the other way around. Among the ordinary difficulties of practice it isn't easy to know which are mandated by theory and which are due to personal clumsiness. Here it is our conceptual grasp of the implications of theory that enable us to separate difficulties that are part of the project from those that are part of our personalities.

In short, we must consider intellectual theory and mundane practice together to understand this profession.

In some ways, the relationship between theory and practice of psychotherapy is similar to the relationship between rules and practice of language. In both cases, there is a subtle interplay between stable, abstract, textbook principles and the uncertain moment of their actual use when new features are felt out. (In the case of language, Bakhtin [1981] refers to these as centripetal and centifugal movements.)

Consider speech: We have to know the context of an utterance (for example, "fine weather!") in order to know its meaning. The context includes the speaker's state of mind, as evidenced by clues in his behavior and in his environment (for example, the actual state of the weather). The isolated sentence does not explain how it is to be understood.

But the grammatical and lexical meaning of the sentence is itself one of the clues to its own context. If the sentence meant nothing in its own right, we would lack an essential clue to the speaker's state of mind. Of course some context can be detected without language. If it is hot, the speaker is probably uncomfortable, and when he says, "It's hot," he probably isn't being sarcastic. But if it weren't for the fact that "hot" has some invariant lexical tie to temperature, and a declarative sentence has an invariant way of putting meanings together, a thermometer would not suffice to make sense out of his comment. A thermometer would not tell us whether the speaker wasn't perhaps asking for the time of day.

Therefore, what we do is to go back and forth between our linguistic understanding and our other clues to the speaker's intent, which we often explore by engaging him in further conversation. The language core is a tether that the speaker keeps lengthening beyond pre-existing rules (see Ricoeur [1977] on how metaphor expands language and allows continually new reference).

We need to know about language as a unique, formal system. We would get nowhere studying speech as just another physical activity. (It hardly seems necessary to cite Chomsky.) But it is also true, as Austin (1962) and the semiologists and sociologists of language have been telling us, that we will not know how meaning is actually determined unless we see how language is actually used.

To see how language is used we need to know something about the world, about social meanings, and about roles and their implications (cf. Dell Hyams, 1964; Goffman, 1974). These give us a deeper understanding of language use and meaning. But it is just as true that we learn about social meaning by studying the rules of local language use, and how the formal structure of language makes it possible for it to convey social symbolism. (e.g., McGinn, 1985.) In other words, we need to understand language as a unique formal system, and we also have to watch its daily use.

Now I do not suggest an exact parallel between language and speech on the one hand, and theory and practice of psychotherapy on the other. But there is a similarity. The system of a theory of therapy allows new, creative, highly individualized sense to be made out of unforeseen occasions. Just as with rules of language, so also we cannot know how theory of therapy works unless we know its articulation as a system, its coherence as a closed, internally articulated, intellectual structure. And conversely, we cannot really understand the articulation of theory until we see how it is used, both to define roles of patient and therapist and to get new meaning from those roles. Looked at as a system, theory is a set of interrelated propositions. In use, it is a concrete, momentary, personal mediator between the therapist and patient—something more like an ideology.

We suppose that the general enterprise of psychotherapy is carried on under the gun of immediate, personal pressures, much as speech develops from momentary social pressures. Therefore, in order to understand the therapy enterprise, we will look at the momentary pressures in their particular, personal aspect. At the same time we will try not to forget the many threads that tie theory-system to therapy-event. Just as it would be unfruitful to investigate speech simply as behavior without acknowledging the unique, rule-giving system of language that allows it to expand, so also it would be misleading to look on the conduct of patient and therapist as a social ritual devoid of theoretical guidelines (as Frank [1961] and Haley [1963] have both done, each in his own way). I have said that theory functions as ideology, and that might make theory seem to be merely a gloss on practice. But theory isn't *only* an ideology. It is true that when we describe the tiny provocations that decide the therapist's ultimate reactions, our account will seem to trivialize therapy and make it look like a floundering improvisation, loosely held together by an ideology. That is because in the picture we will draw, the theoretical justification of therapy waits off stage. But theory is there waiting, and while we look at the all-too-human reality of the therapist-in-action, we have to remind ourselves that the therapist would not be in this floundering position at all if he were not trying to be consistent with the cognitive content of his theory.

8

What Moves the Therapist?

Te therapist's responses are what make therapy different from other meetings. The aim of this chapter is to determine what causes the therapist to react to one thing rather than another, and in one way rather than another. We do not ask the therapist for his reasons; we want to draw our own conclusions. We observe the scene as though, lacking any idea of what therapy is, we have to figure out what accounts for the behavior of the partner who is called a therapist. Later, in chapters 10 and 11, we look at the same scene again, but there we take into account the special rules of the conversation, and our question is how the partners communicate within those constraints, and what comes of their difficulties and successes. There the subject matter is re-examined from above, so to speak, as the product of certain conventions. But in the present chapter, we are working with the therapist from the ground up.

Our starting point is simply stated: We can look for many different things in conversation. But when we study someone as a partner to a dialogue what we do is to assume that he is not just rising to one occasion after another, but making decisions that gravitate around larger interests. Thus, a therapist imagines his patient to be constantly balancing himself in various kinds of equilibrium, for instance, to sustain a fantasy, or stabilize self-esteem. But if that is how we make the patient an object of study, we must do the same thing to the therapist when we make him the object of our study. We must learn to see the therapist's momentary decisions as efforts to balance himself when challenged by the exigencies of the moment.

Psychotherapists do not usually think of themselves that way. On the contrary, they see themselves as craftsmen, deliberately selecting features of the patient that are germane to their theory of therapy. No doubt the therapist's responses are guided by explicit plans. Yet when we consider how dense the therapy scene is, the myriad possible cues it offers to perception, and the unplanned urgency of its interaction we must suspect that the finer principles of the therapist's selection and response are not a matter of studied decision.

In order to highlight the finer principles that decide what the therapist sees and does, I discuss his efforts to preserve his equilibrium in the same way we would describe a patient — on the grounds that human psychology must bear equally on all heads present.

Until recently, the analytic literature has described the analyst's balancing effort as a minute, controlled, and constricted movement that leaves behind only a residue of information for the analyst to use in his deliberate reactions. Departures from the ideal, although inevitable, require self-analytic scrutiny or re-analysis. Fliess' (1942, 1953) conscientious work in this area may be considered representative. Fliess used metapsychology to draw a useful picture of kinds and degrees of error in analytic reactivity. (He also made brilliant use of Freud's psychodynamics of humor to explain the analyst's emotional deflection of stimuli [Fliess, 1942].) Further than that, and despite his effort to avoid merely terminological answers to problems, his account does not really explain how the analyst can be both emotionally reactive and attitudinally unaffected. Rather, what Fliess did was to say how such an ideal might be described metapsychologically. How does the analyst deal with the emotional pressures put upon him? And what motives operate within him when he is pressed? Fliess (1942) wrote:

> The answer is that the analyst must make possible what rightly seems impossible, because it is actually impossible for the average person, and must do so by becoming a very exceptional person during his work with the patient. To this end he will have to acquire a "work-ego" with the special structure which we are attempting to analyze by means of our metapsychological description . . .
>
> Economically such an ego transformation is feasible for the limited working period of the analytic hour largely because the voluntary submission to these severe deprivations constitutes a proportionately intense superego gratification [pp. 221–222].

Fliess deserves credit for pointing to "intense superego gratification," instead of settling for the reference to a temporary transfer of "powers" from the superego to the ego. He does not (merely) disguise motivation as perception. But on the other hand, he did not pursue the question of the analyst's minute motivation. We know what superego gratifications he had in mind, but although a list of superego motives may begin with discipline and the love of truth, it does not stop there. When we imagine all the meanings of the technical phrase, "intense superego gratification," we might wonder whether a preponderance of such gratification is the optimal inclination of an analyst. Once a motive has been mentioned, all its implications should be scrutinized.

Lacking that scrutiny, what Fliess' picture of an analytic "work ego" amounts to, I think, is the postulation on the analyst's side of a rationale equivalent to the therapeutic alliance on the patient's side. In other words, it reflects a *predicament*, and it does that by projecting a contrasting image of ease that helps to balance the analyst's puzzlement, as though to say, "If a metapsychology like this is possible, an analyst can be motivated without contaminating the field."

The momentary intrapsychic constellations that have been invoked to explain the analyst's paradoxical selfless hypersensitivity often boil down to theoretically biased attention. Fliess (1942) came close to admitting this when he suggested that the transformations of the analyst's work ego which he postulated are analogous to those "obtained by individuals while engaging in other work" (p. 222n). (Again, he was thinking of scientists, but his formula carries farther.)

Structural theory loses its purpose if we postulate a special superego (or a superego-ized ego) for every activity that requires special standards. Every action has its special motives, and we are many "people" in our various capacities, but if these actions and "persons" don't draw on a single motivational complexion, we should give up the mind business altogether. A psychotherapist does not restructure his personality when he engages a patient; he *uses* his personality in a theoretical scene and with a theoretical aim. He may need specialized psychological skills and unusual freedom from anxiety to do that, but we beg the question of what happens between partners in therapy if we begin by attributing a literally wonderful psychic apparatus to one of the participants.

Our job in this chapter is specifically not to consider the therapist "a very exceptional person." The therapist does not stop being ordinarily human when he works. He is not a set of skills fastened like a pacemaker upon a patient. He is one human being locked in an activity with another. We may suppose that he has acquired the psychological fluidity that he needs for his task, but as an initial hypothesis it is safest to assume that the principles of his behavior do not differ radically from those of his patient. What does differ is his position; he is unmistakably not in the same position as his patient. He has problems that come from being a therapist. Some of his perceptions and reactions arise from that role. He cannot just reverberate with his patient, because the patient has different problems that come from being a patient.

The therapeutic dialogue is the most vivid demonstration of the therapist's ordinariness. But process is not usually picked apart this way, especially if it is the process of an experienced therapist. There are exceptions (e.g., Gill, 1982; Hoffman, 1983; Klauber, 1972; Levenson, 1972). But as regards the therapist's action (we are not considering his feelings) ordinary "human" reactions are usually identified as a cause of error, and in this way the therapist's ad hoc balancing efforts are safely quarantined from the principled action of therapy. When the scene is lighted this way, it appears that therapists do what they should because they know it helps, and whatever they do for other reasons is attributable to human weakness.

But it seems to me that such a conceptualization of therapy is "artless, innocent, unaffected; unconsciously and amusingly simple," which is the dictionary definition of *naive*. It presumes that healthy therapists pick up truths that emanate from a patient and then select their responses deductively from a theory of therapy. Neither epistemology nor neurophysiology supports such a simpleminded story. It would be a poor account of what we do when we dial a telephone number; it will certainly not tell us about our behavior with a troubled and highly expectant person to whom we have an obligation. Nobody these days believes that we passively receive factual data and assemble them by fixed rules into perceptions and theories. In every field but psychotherapy we recognize that interest, choice, and individuality shape our perceptions.

How, then, does a therapist make his minute-to-minute decisions about what to attend to?

We are assisted in this inquiry by two detailed treatment accounts. One is Paul Dewald's (1972) *The Psychoanalytic Process: A Case Illustration.* The other is Winnicott's (1972) "Fragment of an Analysis." My brief excerpts out of context are necessarily unfair to these renowned analysts, who have been generous and brave enough to publish the rare kind of process report about which alone one can ask the necessary questions. The apology is especially due because I am deliberately looking for imbalances.

As psychotherapists we are subject to a barrage of cognitive and affective stimuli. Like everyone else, we try to keep a balance, although as professionals we have special kinds of equilibrium to maintain.

The term *balance* should help in comparing inside and outside views of therapy. The equilibrium concept has proven useful in analyzing organic activity of which psychotherapy is one species. And balance and imbalance are also tangible feelings we experience from time to time in doing therapy.

What are the therapist's common decision principles and the balance problems they solve?

TO ACT LIKE A THERAPIST

Most obviously the therapist picks out things that make him intellectually hopeful about movement. He tries to find a vector of impressions pointed by his theory of therapy. In plain language, he chooses to hear whatever fits into a treatment plan.

The balance problem here is banal: A therapist wants to act like a therapist.

I refer here to a balance problem, not a therapy problem. A therapist can comfortably treat people who do not get well. What he cannot gracefully do is feel like he is not a therapist. It is just as vital a balance problem for the therapist to preserve his role as it is for the patient to preserve his self-esteem. And although this is a run-of-the-mill vocational task, it is often a dreadful problem. All kinds of subtle contortions can arise from awkward efforts to maintain this balance. Michael Balint (1968) wrote: "I think nearly the same irresistible urge to 'organize' operates in most analysts. It compels us to make sense of our patient's complaints at all costs in order to stop them complaining" (p. 108).

In the following excerpt, Winnicott is acting like a therapist:

> P: [Begins the hours with:] It's not about myself today; something has happened that confuses the issue. . . . my wife came back early, crying. She had called in on her boy friend, and he had taken ill—had gone blind, and had a fit. He is dying (this was inevitable sometime; he has a heart, mitral stenosis and endocarditis). This complicates matters for me . . .
>
> P. [After many comments by both patient and Winnicott about this and related matters] Once again outside things have come along and have obliterated the underneath things, and it's not helpful; but it can't be avoided, they have to be gone over.
>
> A: There remains the fantasy of the girl with the penis, and it seems likely that your girl friend is felt to have a need for men while your wife is self-contained and has a penis.
>
> P: I see the first part but not the part about my wife.
>
> A: [Winnicott writes] I admitted muddle, and said I was not clear enough to continue with this interpretation [pp. 507–509].

Winnicott believes that genetic explanations are helpful to the patient. So, as a general rule, he will be doing his duty if he can imagine psychogenesis. But he also seems to be constantly reassuring himself as he goes along that he can place every feeling of the patient into a genetic picture. When he is lost or confused he returns to his canvas. He observes himself with paint brush in hand and his balance is restored. Often it seems that Winnicott is keeping up his spirits by interpreting while the patient basks in the security of his consequent good-nature. (There are, of course, other times when Winnicott is directly responsive.)

The first decision principle, then, is an effort to keep professional balance, and it says: "Perceive something relevant to a treatment plan." That is perhaps the only decision principle that applies to all schools of psychotherapy.

TO SATISFY CURIOSITY

Explanatory psychotherapy involves another decision principle: "Look for unsolved puzzles." The therapist's repertoire is aptly caricatured as: "I wonder why you say that," or "How do you feel about it?" Provided these questions are genuine, they seek to intellectually re-balance a puzzled therapist, and that is the second decision principle. But note that if the questions are *pro forma*, then asking questions is just doing what a therapist is supposed to do: It is just a way of feeling like a therapist, and as such it is designed not to assimilate new material, but to follow the first decision principle, and hold on to a role. Most therapists consider their curiosity to be a main healing device and consequently, for them it is always partly programmed, and therefore, in a sense, partly artificial. By artificial I only mean that therapists do not usually wait until they are aroused from torpor by a burning question. They set out to wonder, because they consider that part of their service. If need be, they seek peculiarities in what seems perfectly clear. They conscientiously make sure that they have an exact idea of whatever they focus on. Dewald has an unashamed formula: He keeps asking, "What's the detail?" He repeats it verbatim, like an incantation, so that it will become a formal rule. I believe he wants the patient to know that he is not personally curious, but is performing a duty that she should take over. It is just part of the job.

In the category of programmed curiosity, we should also place the *fixed bases*. Among the few universally valid guesses we can make are those about beginning, interrupting, and ending treatment. I call them fixed bases because, if the patient does not prompt the therapist to ask about them, he will ask anyway.

But there are only so many fixed bases. A therapist may decide to be curious, but then he has to decide what to be curious about. It is sometimes said that psychotherapy asks, "What is the hidden affect?" whereas psychoanalysis asks, "What is the hidden fantasy?" These questions are not really so different. One cannot identify affect exactly without a picture of a situation. And one cannot appreciate a fantasy without the affective tone of its wish structure. These are really the same, and the formula amounts to a decision to be curious about the exact state of the patient's mind. Undoubtedly it has an extraordinary effect on a patient to talk to someone with this sort of curiosity. But does that general interest in the patient's mind decide precisely where the therapist's attention will go? Would it help a beginner to say to him, "Be curious about the patient's internal world?"

Eugene Gendlin (1964) thinks it would, because he regards affect and fantasy as a single, tangible, developing body feeling (see chapter 22). Some people (e.g., Levenson, 1972) believe that any particular productive attention implicitly attends to everything in the patient. Is there one thing happening in the consulting room that a therapist can simply click into? That is a difficult question that I discuss inconclusively in chapter 33. In any event,experience shows that a lot of selection and exclusion are needed to sharpen a sense of the patient's behavior to the point where it can actually answer a therapist's real curiosity.

Therapists usually pare down a patient's experience to manageable proportions by practicing match–mismatch. They form emotionally relevant patterns and try them out on the patient. But there are many patterns they could try on, and many of them would match. In this chapter we are asking "What determines the therapist's selection?"

Is it his theory? But theory cannot do it all.

For example, theory may suggest analyzing defense before impulse, but it does not predict what it is that we call *defense* rather than *impulse*, or for that matter, which pair of impulse and defense we will gravitate to. That will depend on how the therapist is pushed. Because affects and fantasies do not come framed and labeled, the ultimate focus (like all perceptions) is forced on him by a mixture of what comes at him and what he needs. Afterward he invokes a theoretical exegesis to make decent what he has done to keep his balance.

For instance, theory does not tell a therapist whether at a given moment he should be hearing his patient make a plea or seeing him perform an action. Obviously the patient presents both plea and performance all the time. And theory offers some rules to spot and deal with them. But the actual decision about which to react to, plea or performance, will develop from the therapist's momentary cognitive–affective need.

Here is Dewald reacting to something as a display of behavior:

P: I feel as if someone is trying to overpower me. As if they are trying to . . .
A: What is it you're afraid to say?
P: As if you are trying to sit on me and squash me.
A: I think this is one of your fears about starting analysis. It's as if you fantasy that you're going to end up in my power and that you're going to be helpless.

Now here is Dewald's reaction to something that is heard as an appeal.:

A: [Referring to the patient's sense of futility about her feminine feelings – L.F.] What's the detail of feeling that they [the feelings] have been rejected?
P: I don't know, but I feel that there's no reason for them. If I can't . . . I don't know. There's no reason to be a woman or pretty or to attract other men or to be fun or happy or to laugh, there's just no reason. It's natural to me, but I don't want to feel that way.
A: So you still prefer to think of me as *actively* rejecting you rather than to accept the reality of the situation of this as inevitable and not an active rejection.

Nothing in his theory prevented Dewald from hearing the same kind of plea in the first as in the second example. If he had reacted in the first excerpt according to the principle he used in the second (i.e., responded to a plea), he might have said something like this:

> You prefer to think that I am deliberately getting you into my power, rather than that this is an inevitable part of being cured.

Conversely, in the second excerpt, if Dewald had been destabilized in a different way, he might have felt like a disinterested observer and said something like this:

> You have tried so hard here, and you feel you are leaving defeated, and I don't appreciate you and you wonder whether it is worth it.

But am I right to look for other balance problems than those that theory sets? Doesn't a psychological theory create its own balance problems and thus determine minute decisions? According to a common cynical view of psychotherapy, the therapist's perceptions and actions are all designed to validate his descriptive theory: he is alleged to be constantly demonstrating his general hypothesis.

Obviously some of the therapist's perceptions and reactive decisions are made that way. If the patient illustrates a theory so blatantly that he seems to be offering a testimonial for it, that fact will probably seize the therapist's attention and make him feel negligent if he does not follow the rule laid down for such an event. But I do not believe this happens as often as the stereotype predicts. Process does not usually scream out a familiar theoretical slogan. At any particular moment, the therapist's attention is not usually arrested by an astonishingly precise overlap of a patient's comments with a theoretical formula. The therapist's balance problem does not consist of swinging from one dazzling confirmation to another.

Well then, does theory cause the therapist to look more anxiously for more subtle confirmations of theory? Does it challenge him to try to find theoretical truths, and follow the implicated directions, despite the unpredictable and essentially unclear events of the moment? But if we are talking about subtle demonstrations of theory, that is not usually much of a challenge, since almost any material can be seen to subtly fit any theory and everything always seems to call for just the rules of treatment that are desired. (Only extraordinarily provocative patients block that path.) So this principle cannot pinpoint the therapist's reactions, let alone offer an inspiring challenge.

Is the therapist under pressure to validate his theory in the face of new data? But psychological theories are never in danger of being disconfirmed in a moment. Because no one item shakes his theory, it cannot orient the therapist anxiously toward proof. In other words, it cannot be said that he perceives certain things in order to *save* his theory, because it is never in real danger.

But as therapists we do perceive some things in order to *use* our theory. If we enjoy our theory, we use it a lot. Theory creates balance problems just to the extent that we enjoy theorizing. In that case we do not want to stop, and we try to find ways to continue.

Sometimes theory points to an issue that yields really selfish dividends. A therapist's curiosity may entrain itself onto a subject of his forthcoming publication. A less dramatic, but more frequent kind of theoretical lure is playing up hunches derived from past practice.

Freud, of course, warned against trapping curiosity in theoretical structures. But free-floating attention can never float free of all prefabricated forms (Spence, 1982). We have to use our own focus of curiosity. Here is an excerpt at random from the analysis by Winnicott: The patient has been talking mildly about being passive and dominated in the analysis, a main theme throughout.

P: It's funny that being good-natured as I am supposed to be is linked with a willingness to be dominated.

A: Somewhere in all this is a relation to one or both of your sisters, with a reluctance on your part to be the one with the penis.

P: Two things come to my mind here. One, how do you come into this: Are you to dominate me, or what? I sometimes fear that I dominate the session.

A: Here I am the girl, who has or has not a penis. You wonder what I will feel like being the girl with no penis, when you have one [p. 504].

Later in the analysis the patient explains that he tries to block out the knowledge of other patients in the waiting room. Winnicott replies:

A: When you can admit three people, you get the relief that the third can have the rival penis, so you do not need the idea of a woman with a penis.

To be sure, there are issues here of the philosophy of interpretation. But apart from those issues, Winnicott clearly is *interested* in the theory he uses. Winnicott acts like someone listening to a shortwave broadcast, entranced by the indistinct sound of his mother tongue, and constantly adjusting the dial to bring it in. The fingers on the radio knob make decisions based on imbalances in the ears.

Winnicott's empathic involvement in an imaginary childhood of his patient is close to the excitement of a playwright. It reflects a genuine curiosity about what can be done with his own creative powers, and that is a personal problem—a balance problem if you will—which selects its own solutions. (We further discuss the therapist's role as a reader of texts in chapter 31.)

But now we run into difficulty. It seems that curiosity acts as a specific decision principle only when it is genuine. But genuine curiosity is not as common as we like to think. One reason that genuine curiosity is so scarce is that it may conflict with the first decision-principle, which is to act like a therapist. To some therapists, being a therapist means knowing and not being bewildered (cf. Havens, 1982). A sense of workmanship may conflict with being open to unclassified feelings and tugs. Winnicott is good at wonderings but not at unclassified wondering. Anyone who has supervised a beginning therapist can testify that maintaining a role always takes precedence over curiosity. Some trainees cannot experience curiosity unless it is justified by a clear role. In contrast, they all feel justified in being curious about what they should do.

How can we tell genuine curiosity when we see it? One sign of a curious person is that he can hardly restrain himself from trying out hunches and throwing up possibilities. Certainly the genuinely curious therapist experiments, at least privately. He plays a game with himself: "Have I got it right?" Wondering is even more productive when spoken aloud. We are sometimes inhibited by a grandiose worry that our guesses will prejudice the patient. An inordinate concern about misleading patients with our guesses is a self-fulfilling anxiety. Seeing how reluctant we are to be wrong, a patient will infer that we have an enormous investment in what we finally come out with. "Interpretation" can be a word for a pompous guess. In contrast, undisguised guessing is a powerful stimulus for searching out the lineaments of feeling. It is often more effective to ask, "Is it more like this or more like that?" than to ask, "What comes to mind?" But I digress. What works best is not my topic here. My point is that if we are curious, we will naturally try out possibilities. In fact, I am inclined to think that when we cannot even venture a hunch, curiosity evaporates. (That is a clue to how theory nourishes curiosity.)

Now, if someone who craves an answer is inclined to follow it up with, "Is it this? Is it that?" then there are certainly many therapists who ask for, but do not particularly crave, an answer.

And despite that fact, I still wish to argue that without genuine curiosity of some sort, no final decisions could be made in therapy. I suggest that what seems to be an incurious therapist is simply a therapist who does not ask himself questions about his patients. But asking questions is only one form of curiosity, and by no means the most common one between people. What other forms of curiosity are there?

Let us look again at our two sets of process. Both Winnicott and Dewald obviously seek to balance their professional identity and their intellectual bearings by finding in the patient illustrations of a hypothetical story. They are curious about psychogenesis.

But that is not their only curiosity. It is only so much of their curiosity as can easily be put into words. If we look at their actual experimenting we can find another, less expressible curiosity. Dewald works on the principle that if he acts as though there is something more to be said, the patient will respond. She will do something more—she will say something different. She has a capacity to expand in a way that is congenial to him and he continually hunts for and taps that capacity.

Winnicott's underlying, non-verbal curiosity is harder to pin down. In a sense he does not want to be seen engaging any particular facet of his patient. He gives the patient complete freedom by contenting himself with his own ruminations. But I venture to say that Winnicott is experimenting in this fashion: He says to himself, in effect, "If I act toward this man as though he is continually posing problems for me which I humbly, readily, and steadfastly accept; and if I make no demands at all in return, out of his dull, listless shell will creep a lively creature actively involved with a caretaker; and that is a creature I am most curious to meet." (I am describing the so-called holding environment as an experimental provocation.) I know that is not what Winnicott said to himself. But we may see it as an active principle within him, side by side with his empathy.

Experimentation is exciting. The therapist's mental or practical experiments tell us something important about his balance problem: He is not simply looking for professional or intellectual security. *In general we are curious not just because we do not recognize something. We are curious because we have ways of recognizing that we want to put into action.* And we have more ways of recognizing things than we have theories or words. The therapist enjoys, for instance, discovering anew the power of his theory over people's novelty. Match–mismatch often provides all the excitement a therapist needs. Many an otherwise self-defeating patient has benefitted from his therapist's capacity to entertain himself with his own theoretical games. (Klauber [1972] has shown the many ways interpretation serves the analyst.)

TO ELICIT SOMETHING DESIRABLE

The two guiding principles I have listed—to act like a therapist and to exercise curiosity—therefore have something in common: They are both attempts to enjoy exercising interesting patterns. But genuine curiosity about individual people differs in important ways from the simple pleasure of using learned patterns. Genuine individual curiosity is less explicit, and yet far more pointed and specific than theoretical puzzles. And furthermore, genuine curiosity about an individual is a social excitement. It is not without a tinge of personal attachment. For instance, when it is individualized and personalized, intellectual mastery can mean power and control—a fact of which patients are often exquisitely aware. Any kind of understanding can be aggressively erotic ("I have something in my mind which can be made adequate to yours; I have something which can fit you"). It can be a sexual surrender ("I am at your disposal"). Understanding can have a simple bonding connotation ("I can always find something in common between us"). Understanding is not love, as some therapists have smugly assumed (Levenson [1972] punctures that balloon; see also Friedman [1976]), but it can act as a loving gesture.

All of these types of curiosity help to define the relationship between therapist and patient. At its most objective, even a diagnostic sort of curiosity still defines a personal relationship. The relationship becomes more intimate as the therapist's curiosity becomes more individualized. And if the therapist attempts vague, nonclassifying recognition and discovery, curiosity becomes flagrantly social (Some uneasiness within the analytic community about the recent emphasis on empathy may have to do with the more social quality of the curiosity it involves.)

The converse holds as well: *Any seeking of an interaction is a kind of curiosity.* When we seek interaction we are asking which of the responses that we like are available in the other person. Obviously that is not the kind of curiosity that searches for propositional knowledge or classification. It can yield propositional knowledge afterward, when we ask questions about our interactive appetites and what satisfied them. When the therapist focuses on the countertransference and its consequences, he is surveying the appetites that have been stirred in him. This secondary, deliberate reflection is a theoretical curiosity about his first undeliberate personal curiosity. It is a later, classifying curiosity about his primary, unplanned explorations into the patient's reactivity: He studies both what he was led to look for and what he found.

The therapist's undeliberate search for interactive response plays a special role in psychotherapy. It is one curiosity that is perfectly embodied in the tests it uses. To highlight the contrast with intellectual curiosity one might exaggerate a little and say that personal search does not stumble around trying to find how to ask the right question. It isn't a general question to begin with: It is a personal inclination. It knows where it's going; it knows how to find out what it wants to find out; it knows when it has found it. Theoretical curiosity does not work that way. However apt a theoretical formula may be, it still requires a chain of inference from the data, to rouse it as a possibility and satisfy it as a likelihood. There is no way for the clinical material by itself to gravitate obligingly into a theory and precisely fill its verbalizable, critical pigeonholes. In comparison, a nonverbal, unintentional hope, or expectation, or preference, or wish that canvasses the patient—although it can certainly lead to misunderstanding—need only register its own satisfaction, and that *constitutes* its understanding.

Another reason that undeliberate, personal exploration is important to the psychotherapist is this: Intellectual curiosity squeezes the therapist's impressions into abstract concepts, and even when they fit wonderfully well, we do not know what other good matches might have fit just as well. In contrast, when the therapist's interpersonal questing is satisfied, it is likely to happen at a moment, and with an aspect, that has peculiar value to the patient. Not that a satisfaction of the therapist's inclination is the only possible "take" on the situation, but there is a soft guarantee that it is related to the patient's own "take" on the situation at the moment.

Thus the therapist's unintentional effort to elicit personal reaction helps the therapist select some area for attention out of all that he could experience, and helps him feel his way toward something like a common meaning with his patient. In later chapters I discuss these two services—focus and common reference—in more detail. But here I want to alert the reader to consequences of looking at therapy this way, and warn him that they will become increasingly obtrusive and perhaps annoying as the discussion proceeds, blossoming at last into an unwelcome discussion of the therapist's wishes in chapter 29.

I have suggested in this chapter that the therapist's decisions about what to attend to are influenced by a number of problems, among them the need to act like a therapist, the need to use learned, theoretical forms, and the urge to ignite a satisfying interaction with the patient. It is perfectly possible to trivialize and then ignore the first two of these motives. After all, don't they just say that a therapist tries to help the patient according to his lights and with his learned concepts? These principles are just that banal if we are not using them to pinpoint the therapist's urges at a given moment.

What about the third principle? Can we assimilate it to a comparable banality? In calling attention to the therapist's quest for interactive response are we just saying that he not only uses previously acquired knowledge, but also his empathic sense of the individual patient? The answer is that we cannot sum it up that way. We are trying to identify primarily what moves the therapist, and only secondarily what he is moved toward. We are not concerned here with how or what the therapist knows, but what impels him, activates him, or satisfies him. We are not studying his capacities but his incentives. Suppose that empathy is a faculty and suppose that it picks out not just *a* meaning of the patient's experience, but *the* meaning of that experience. We would then be interested in what the therapist looks for as an end point to his search, since empathy must often be strained for, and does not always fall like the gentle rain from heaven. That which confirms empathic grasp will act as a need on the therapist's part; having the confirmation or not having it will affect his equilibrium. And, of course, if empathic grasp does not close precisely on a central, or main, or real meaning, we would want to know what causes the therapist to empathize with one thing rather than another.

The strongest claims for empathy within the psychoanalytic tradition were made by Heinz Kohut and he allowed that conceptual match goes into it (1984). He routinely used the relative terms, *experience-near* and *experience-distant*, refusing to separate them as radically disparate data. If we think along Kohut's lines, then acting like a therapist and trying to identify theoretical constructs are both parts of empathizing, and we could not say that empathy is propelled by a completely different motive.

If empathy actually designates another *motive* of the therapist, it is a rather different beast than commonly supposed. That is, in fact, what I suggest in chapter 28. Meanwhile, I consider that the third force that is propelling the therapist is his undeliberate reach for a certain desired range of reactions from the patient.

Sometimes it seems to me that the therapist's ultimate decisions about what to do and see are all touched by this quest. I begin to imagine that, although the therapist's gross attention and movements are guided by the wish to exercise intellectual schemas, it is the lure of exercising a special, desired interaction that, microscopically and outside of his awareness, finally decides what he will be curious about.

But then I realize that I am erring equally in a direction opposite to those who exaggerate the therapist's objective curiosity. I am ignoring the many cool, distant sorts of curiosity that pervade the scene. After all, a therapist may react to a patient as he does to a book, and it would be a strange reader who sought a reaction from his book. (I discuss the therapist as reader in chapter 31). Or a therapist may prick up his ears when the patient discloses biographical information that the therapist needs for an hypothesis he is building. (I discuss the therapist as historian in chapter 32.) Indeed, a therapist may follow an entirely pre-programmed timetable of his own making (but here I am inclined to draw the line and declare such a treatment outside my definition of psychotherapy). In short, I must remind myself that therapists are not off balance in all spheres equally at all times, and their "righting responses" are not activated by all their needs at once. Sometimes therapists are indeed objective naturalists, readers, and historians.

But even if it is not the final guide at every moment, the need to elicit personal interaction must be at the heart of psychotherapy, if for no other reason than that it alone can keep the therapist's actions responsive to reality rather than to his own fancy. In chapter 10, I suggest that the inclination to evoke something in the patient serves as a non-arbitrary discriminator of material, and as a bridge between the patient's universe and the therapist's. This seeking must be undeliberate. A rule (e.g., a rule for testing an hypothesis) would not serve the same purpose as an undeliberate seeking. A therapist who employed a deliberate rule for judging reactions would still have to be primed for the responses that add up to a signal that his criteria have been met. (The notion of "the good analytic hour" illustrates this: what is accomplished can be plainly stated in theoretical terms, and in that sense it provides a discriminating rule, but its defining qualities are not neatly specifiable, and its occurrence is partly determined by "feel.")

How should we characterize an undeliberate seeking, a seeking from another person, a search for a reaction of a sort that we want? It seems to me that this is what we ordinarily call a *wish* when it feels pressing, or an *appetite* if it is quieter. And it seems to me that a wish or an appetite is precisely the kind of state that can pick up data without inference. In other words, it can act as a final homing device. (I elaborate this in Part V.)

Along with his theory, the therapist's wishes will figure again and again in what follows. And I write about them with misgivings. The misgivings, too, will be part of the account because I believe they are part of the therapy.

Perhaps it would have been better to use blander words that do less violence to our usual view of the work. Considering that a therapist is supposed to be especially sensitive to certain qualities of his patient's experience, we could talk about "sensitivities" instead of appetites. In our usual picture the therapist is appreciative of what the patient has been through and is now wrestling with, so we could talk about the therapist's ability to value coping efforts. Therapists are presumed to have a keen eye for movement, which allows them to spot small signs of change without tedious inference, so we might talk about "a feeling for the work," or "an intuition of therapeutic engagement."

All of these descriptions capture something of the therapist's set. But they do not capture—indeed, will regularly be used to disguise—the familiar quality and consequences of the therapist's wishing and satisfaction. And so great is the effect on the patient of his therapist's wishing, being frustrated, being satisfied, or being able to savor something of him, and so influential are these states in the course of therapy, that it seems better to risk overdramatizing and vulgarizing the therapist's psychology than to use neutral terms that hide his motivational wellspring (which is, after all, what the patient is focused on.)

Although therapists are likely to be put off by reference to their wishes, I believe that the term *wish* comes closest to what they will see in themselves when they work, and perhaps even more clearly when they watch other patient/therapist pairs at work. Watching others, therapy sometimes looks like the gradual accommodation of two sets of divergent wishes seeking to accommodate each other.

However persuasive these considerations are, they always clash with the professional image of the therapist. When we think of the therapist as a professional, we naturally think of his wishes as professional wishes, and therefore instrumental and non-substantive.

A lawyer wishes his client to be cooperative, but we do not think it useful to describe the practice of law in terms of the lawyer's wishes. Closely viewed, therapy is a scene of two people's wishes tangling. But when we consider therapy from a distance, we tend to think of it as we do the law. And then it seems perverse to dwell on the expert's "wishes." (Fenichel, 1941, must have felt that way when he wrote so offhandedly about the therapist being annoyed by blocked work. See p. 91, this volume.)

But the parallel does not hold. A lawyer wants cooperation from his client, but his objective is what the cooperation will achieve, for example, in a court of law. His wish for cooperation is purely instrumental. (We might have a closer parallel to psychotherapy if the legal client's cooperation all by itself decided the outcome of his case.)

Even that sort of instrumental wish will inevitably grow into what we ordinarily call a personal wish if it operates continuously between two people without external distraction. (The interrupted intervals of therapy help to maintain the professional quality of the therapist's wishes. And if a lawyer saw as much of his client as a therapist does, his wishes might become less lawyerly.)

But there are other forces at work besides "cohabitation" that stretch the therapist's wishes into something more than instrumental, if–then requirements for cooperation, and transform them into personalized wishes.

One such personalizing force we found while examining the notion of the therapeutic alliance (chapter 2): What the therapist needs in order to perform his function is not compliance in this or that act, but an entire attitude from his patient. In referring to a therapeutic alliance, the analyst acknowledges the pervasive attitude that he seeks, but tries to make it seem to be only an instrumental performance (like cooperation) designed for another objective (an improved viewpoint). The therapeutic alliance concept is an effort to portray the therapist's wish as very much like any professional person's demand on his client.

In chapter 2, we saw another way that the therapist's wish is more personal than professional. Discovering aspects of the patient and validating significant movement depends on something like a match between the therapist's enthusiasm and the patient's. And seeking that sort of match is closer to what we ordinarily call wishing than it is to the professional helper's need for compliance by his client.

We should therefore recognize that a psychotherapist operates with a whole spectrum of desires, ranging from the trivial desires that resemble a lawyer's to the more passionate ones unique to psychotherapy.

After all, each balance problem determining the working therapist's response can also be viewed as the outcome of a wish that he brings to the encounter. The problem of acting like a therapist can be said to arise from a wish to perform a professional task. That is evident, for example, when a therapist wishes that the patient would produce some "material" that is workable. Such a wish does not necessarily feel like a wish: it feels like just getting on with the job. At the other end of the spectrum are the more personal and therefore less definable wishes for "connection," "engagement," "movement," "affective discovery," and so on, and these are much more likely to feel to both parties like wishing, wanting, desiring, and the like.

If the reader judges subsequent reference to therapists' wishes to be overly poetic, romantic, anti-intellectual, suited, perhaps to the Big Sur, but not to the sharp contours of Manhattan, he should ask himself whether he isn't selecting the most instrumental of his wishes to represent them all.

But the reader may well ask, If the therapist has appetites that are satisfied by the patient, doesn't that mean that the patient seduces him into a certain relationship? The answer is: It certainly does; the therapist is rewarded and responds accordingly. The reader may also ask whether, by having his wishes satisfied, the therapist isn't seducing the patient into a certain relationship. And the answer is: Yes indeed; for it is obvious that the therapist enjoys the patient in one way more than another. Whereupon the reader must ask: Doesn't that interfere with therapy? And, of course, the answer is that it surely does interfere with therapy, because the patient's future freedom is hampered by the therapist's failure to be neutral. The pivotal question is whether therapy could happen without such "errors" (at least on a subliminal scale), and to that question I think the answer is: No.

Is there any place for seduction in therapy? We are taught a rule of abstinence: A patient should get only fantasy gratifications. A therapist should get only intellectual gratifications. It seems to me that if these were the only gratifications around, a therapist simply would not know what to do. There are too many possibilities to choose from, too many things to hear, too many ways to hear them, too many ways to respond.

What the therapist needs beyond these intellectual gratifications is an impression that reality lies here or there, that the patient is really doing this or that, that the feelings are really of one kind or another. No principle will make that decision for him except the sense of personal effect—the feeling of being operated on by the other person in a way that is recognizably related to the way one is operating on him. That is the ground of the sense of reality about persons. It is a process of mutual induction. It has more or less marked indicators that, unfortunately, tempt us into what *The New Yorker* used to call "vivid writing"—in this case, poetic rhapsodies that dangerously idealize psychotherapy: We recognize engagement by an upsurge of energy and enthusiasm, in a form that is incompletely defined and uncertain of outcome.

Psychodynamically I suppose it is a rapid mobilization of a pack of dormant strivings – a sudden cascade of opportunities seen lighting up the partner.

However you describe it, one gets to engagement by experimenting, and experimenting involves offering a variety of enthusiasms for the patient to seduce and be seduced by. I need hardly add that since nobody is one person only, the caveat is that the variety should be maintained. The only two dangers in psychotherapy are that no seduction occurs or that only one sort of seduction happens.

Experimenting is sometimes called playing. Winnicott (1977, pp. 63 *ff.*) in particular has characterized psychoanalysis as play. For him: No play, no analysis. A sample of his work shows how broadly that word may be construed. With at least one adult, Winnicott's (1972) transcribed technique seems leaden, although it must have come across quite differently to his patients. His own playing is confined to mental experiments, and playfulness shows up as tentativeness and lack of self-importance. The playing this encourages in his patient must be something like shadow play, the patient moving his fingers to see what figure Winnicott's light casts on the wall. In contrast, Dewald's patient – the kind all analysts look for – ran to the playground all by herself. In order to satisfy his appetite for affect, all Dewald had to do was cheer her on.

At work most of the time, most of us therapists are not in a noticeably playful mood, and only real difficulty, or the irresistible appeal of an especially congenial patient, makes us aware that we are trying out one or another capacity to be pleased or entertained or moved or engaged, merely for the experience of the moment.

It is easiest to see this kind of interplay in the beginning of treatment. (Why that is so deserves more reflection than it has received.)

And yet I believe that below the surface, we are always using the patient for a host of satisfactions, fitting him in to as many imaginary forms of companionship as we own, forming minute relationships of every kind, and thereby testing the facets of his reality. At the level of those final choices that count most, we are guided by our sense of the patient's reality; our sense of his reality comes from the way he fits our enthusiasms and vital interests; and our balance depends on finding that fit through experimentation. We are impelled to make these choices by the nonintellectual curiosity that generally leads people to sound out their companions, and if we are unable to follow that curiosity, we will be off balance in everything that transpires (although different therapists accomplish the same thing with different recognizing and responsive templates).

In passing, we should note that even if all of the ultimate therapy choices are efforts to make a person again out of someone whom theory has turned into a patient, these efforts are not always successful. If, for example, because of his theory or his personality, or because of the patient's personality, the therapist cannot exercise those activities that would allow him to minimally enjoy his patient, he will do something else that he can enjoy. A therapist who is unable to experiment (or play) with his patient as he needs to, may, for instance, put all his money on the therapist role. Mr. Harris, who treated Dewald's patient before him could not seem to find a great deal to engage in her, and so was sadly reduced to just doing what he was paid for, namely, giving her "help"—bare help—which took the form of pseudo-sexual solace. When a therapist cannot even enjoy that role, he may discharge the patient. Mr. Harris did just that, and I suspect that it was this ultimate confession of not being able to enjoy her rather than his clumsy attempt to enjoy her through role playing, that left the indelible hurt she exhibited in her follow up interview with Anthony. Dewald, on the other hand, was able to play endlessly with her in many colorful and mutually fascinating ways. (If he had found even more ways to enjoy her would she finally have made peace with her failure to fascinate her first therapist? Which of us can resist such obnoxious second-guessing of another therapist's work?)

This is not a license for impropriety. Although it is likely that therapists exploit patients mostly out of helplessness and unresourcefulness, selfish hedonism in a therapist unquestionably occurs and does harm. The therapist's mission is not to enjoy himself, and not even to enjoy his patient (although that comes closer to the mark). The therapist's job is to balance (a) his role assignment, (b) thought problems, and (c) experimental engagements. Creativity does not need to be conspicuous. The minutiae of therapy usually conceal enough experimental engagements to keep a therapist as happy as he needs to be without recourse to flamboyance. Winnicott was a great believer in play, but there is scarcely enough hanky-panky between him and his patient to keep his patient awake.

Nevertheless, I do not want to burden experimental engagement with too heavy a yoke of traditional sobriety for this reason: I have mentioned that a therapist can completely avoid a patient with whom he is unable to get satisfaction, by entertaining himself with his own professional cerebrations or by acting out the role of therapist. There is an even more common and insidious danger that is usually detected only by the next therapist. An intensely interested therapist, without personal or countertransference problems, can still turn a deaf ear to *sectors* of his patient, even while explicitly talking about them. I have suggested that the fine points of the therapist's perception are governed by what feels lively to him. And I have suggested that what feels lively to him is partly determined by his enthusiasms. It would follow that the limits of the therapist's own liveliness (or enthusiasm) set limits to what he can perceive. Thus one of the reasons for the insistence on touching the "known bases" each time—termination and other standard resentments—is to keep the therapist in practice, to stir him up, so that he will be able to perceive. He acts as though there are hidden troubles between himself and his patient so that he will not begin to go blind to them. It may be that we perceive only what we participate in, and only according to the way we participate. What we deal with one way may register with us quite differently than if we dealt with it another way. If that should turn out to be true, it would be an argument for maintaining a variety of styles as well as a fund of concepts.

Toward the end of his analysis, Winnicott's patient is complaining of increasing inability to feel enthusiasm or excitement, a complaint that brought him to treatment. He has forgotten his daughter's first birthday, is ashamed of his incapacity to match her excitement, and feels generally lonely.

Winnicott points out that the patient feels isolated from the analyst:

A: A mother may be able to be in touch with you when you are remote.

P: If that is so, it is rather difficult. Outside here there is no one to know what I need. In here when I hint that I want you to say something, you never will. You seem pledged not to. It is a hopeless position to know that you have decided not to do the one thing needed.

A: How am I to know what is needed? You are making a search for the experience of not being met because no one was there to be in touch with you.

P: How does this get anywhere?

A: I think you are near feeling anger, which is all the time implied if you are reaching moments at which there was a failure. (Patient asleep) You had a need then to be held with someone else in charge while you slept [p. 661].

One must always comment with caution on a transcript, but it is hard to avoid thinking that if Winnicott had allowed himself more of the playfulness he desired in his patients, he would have reacted differently to "How does this get anywhere?", And, having reacted differently to it, he would have seen a different patient, a patient that the reader sees who is much stronger and more forcefully competitive than Winnicott recognizes. But because Winnicott's enthusiasm is aroused mainly by the affect of deprivation, he conducts himself as someone who has *almost* been attacked, and therefore perceives a patient who is *almost* angry. Anger has not been ignored. It is talked about throughout the session. But Winnicott has not provisionally reacted to the anger, so he cannot savor it; he cannot enjoy it. He is an expert analyst, so he knows it is there, but he does not perceive it. He can infer it; he can name it; he can incorporate it abstractly into a construct from which he can draw further abstract implications. But that anger is not personal: It is not somebody's specific anger. And so it cannot introduce the patient in a new way to Winnicott. Because it does not introduce the patient in a new way, it also does not pick out anything special in the relationship, as witness Winnicott's translating the patient's predicament entirely into a memory of the distant past. Winnicott cannot learn how the patient feels about being shadowed with transference interpretations. He has no way to particularize the current failure. So when the patient falls asleep from the same disappointment, Winnicott can only repeat what he already knows about the holding environment. For Winnicott (at this point) the sleep is real (what therapist can avoid being intrigued by that?); the patient's yearning is real; the anger is not.

Much could be said about the effect on the patient of this interaction. Winnicott would probably have said that the patient was not yet ready to experience his own anger with the attendant risk of hurting his analyst. Others would say that the patient was being instructed not to be angry, because Winnicott was helpless. Or that Winnicott preferred a sleeping baby to a hungry one. None of this is my concern. My point is that with all the data and all the theory, the therapist's final decision about what was real hinged on his active curiosity as revealed by what kind of thing excited him. It seems to have been loneliness that excited him and not anger. So he named the anger, but he *saw* the loneliness. Nobody can say he was wrong. But it seems to me that he would have been better off with a wider appetite for excitements.

This chapter is about what happens in therapy, not why it helps. But it might as well be said that the balance problems we have discussed seem to be helpful, and that is not surprising if we think of therapy very generally as a patient trying to do one thing while his therapist wants him to do something else—not a particular something else, but anything else that he would like to do. The therapist gets his way by not allowing a fixed relationship to congeal, so that the patient's hidden temptations will carry him into the something else. If that is so, then the therapist's attempt to match as many of his own enthusiasms to as many of his patient's not only orients him to the patient's reality, but also prevents the patient from establishing one safe relationship with which to inhibit his conflicted wishes. In other words, it would seem to be a good idea for therapists to act the way we see them inclined to act.

I fear the reader may think, "Well, here is another boring reminder that countertransference is always present and useful." That misses my point. The therapist's governing appetites are closer to transference than to countertransference. They might also be described as transference hoping to be transformed into countertransference; readiness hoping to discover a use. The psychoanalytic ideal (which none of us should ever pretend to have reached) is to leave the patient free of fixed, overpowering, blanket demands from our past. But we know that reality is not something left over when all attitudes have been purged (Friedman, 1973). Transference in its broadest sense is the reality that we give our perceptions, especially our perceptions of people. Transference is recognition (Loewald, 1978a; Gill, 1982; Brenner, 1985). It goes without saying that we should survey countertransference to find material to interpret. And it goes without saying that we must observe what the patient does to us if we want to know what he is looking for. It is obvious that our special vulnerabilities are our antennae. My point is that we will know what a patient does to us only to the extent that we actively seek an assault on our vulnerabilities.

SUMMARY

The question dealt with in this chapter is: What are the therapist's concerns that impel his actions and alert his attention? The answer proposed is that the therapist (a) does what makes him feel like a therapist, (b) looks for a chance to use his anticipations about human behavior, and (c) is compelled to elicit reactions that he can appreciate, which satisfy a more individualized curiosity.

The therapist's actions are efforts to balance these purposes against the swarming topics and forces of the moment. The therapist is busy keeping his role, conducting thought experiments, and trying to engage valued responses in his patient.

That is a rough list of guiding stimuli that determine time, focus and manner of the therapist's response. The next chapter comes up with a similar list, but it emerges from a different question, namely, "What, in general, does therapy require in order to do its job?" Having seen how the therapist's psychology effects therapy, we now look at how the therapy task affects his psychology and that of the patient.

9

Therapy Tasks That Theory
Must Explain

The picture of a therapist using his theory to keep his balance accounts for many details of therapy. For instance, it is useful in studying recorded process. But general psychotherapists find it an offensive picture. They recognize their individual troubles, but their ideal is likely to be a formal psychoanalysis, and they do not picture analysts worrying about their balance. According to a familiar image, the only psychoanalytic balance problem is cognitive ("How can I figure out what this means?"), and even that is popularly imagined to be resolved by unconscious recognition, so there is no fumbling, stumbling and failing. (This view is critiqued by Gardner, 1984; Havens, 1982; Klauber, 1972; Lichtenberg, 1983; Spence, 1982.)

The irony is that the psychoanalyst's balance problems are subtle and can be owned without embarassment (Fliess, 1942; Racker, 1968), whereas the general psychotherapist, a denizen of no-man's-land, whose patients have not agreed to an analytic approach, who has no theoretically grounded response for most of what he encounters, who is possessed of a vague professional identity that is openly and often challenged—this precarious professional who may have trouble even keeping his composure will resist thinking about his career as a struggle for balance. He will confess any inadequacy before accepting such a job description. Rather than surrender the dignity of his office, a therapist will happily let the profession demand a serene *gravitas* far beyond his personal capacity. He can reassure himself that, after all, nobody is perfect. He can get supervision. He can restrict his practice. He is determined to be at least an aspirant to a dignified profession.

To escape the appearance of improvising, some therapists see themselves as consistently sheltered by one stable attitude–for example, curiosity, or sympathy–which they think guarantees professional security. They do not realize that, apart from the impossibility of even briefly adhering to one attitude in the vortex of interaction, these postures are themselves commitments to a theory of therapy (and probably a theory of mind) that they will have to defend under siege. Furthermore, in identifying themselves with a single attitude, they are unknowingly asking for special treatment by their patient because all fixed attitudes solicit reciprocal attitudes. (That is recognized to be one of the dangers of the therapist's character pathology. See Schafer [1959] regarding empathy based on defensive altruistic surrender.)

Therefore, to say that the therapist is anxious to assure himself that he is performing as a therapist, although it may seem to ridicule therapy and may be used as a reproach by patients, nevertheless identifies a frequent and honorable motivation in the practice of general psychotherapy. There is no one, proper mood for a therapist, and yet, in the ebb and flow of process, he cannot always, or even usually, design each act according to deduced principles. Therefore, he must often scramble for what feels like a "right," although difficult, position. That is why the previous chapter was devoted to a blunt description of the therapist's obvious and overt balance problems.

Many therapists use their memory of gratifying moments as exemplary images of their craft. Obviously there is no place for the hard times in a picture chosen for its sublimity. In such a sketch, the hard times appear as exceptions, as blockages caused by "resistance" and "error." We are always tempted to read the essence of therapy out of moments when we and our patient affirm each other. But there is no warrant for that reading. Insofar as our enterprise is characterized by both difficulty and satisfaction, we must regard both as faces of the same coin. (The principle is elaborated by Lichtenberg [1983] and Gardner [1984]; it is the key to understanding resistance [see Schafer, 1973b]). One test of a description is how well it integrates the nice and the not so nice aspects of therapy.

The same admonition, *mutatis mutandi*, applies to me. The preceding chapters have been full of troubles and discomforts. But therapy also has a serene side. One frequently finds a friendly, warm, enjoyable, creative, mutually helpful atmosphere. Therapy is often deeply gratifying. If it has built-in problems, these must be tied to happy opportunities. In the next chapter, we return to what the last chapters considered as problems and think of them now as opportunities. In order to do that, we talk about the objective tasks of patient and therapist rather than their needy, personal struggles. The emphasis now falls on the challenges of mutual interpretation and influence, which treatment, by making them especially difficult, renders especially profitable. We had wanted to keep our feet on the ground, so we began with the therapist's problems, as they are felt, as they are reflected in theory, and as they appear to a therapy watcher. In the next chapter, we consider why the therapist puts himself in the way of these troubles. We will see that these problems are solutions to other problems. For obviously if there were no experience of achievement, nobody would accept such difficulties.

Consider the bare outline of psychotherapy: Two people react to each other in a way that is supposed to help one of them. Even from this minimal description we can see three demands on a theory of therapy. No theory is complete unless it answers these demands: (a) A complete description of therapy must show how the therapist can offer something qualitatively unique — something that other people cannot provide. (b) It must show how the therapist singles out the proper items from the encounter. (c) It must show how the patient chooses items from what the therapist singles out, and why that is useful. We might say that a complete theory of therapy will include an account of the therapist's influence, a theory of the therapist's epistemology, and a theory of the patient's epistemology.

All three questions are interrelated. But if we deal with them all jumbled together, we may settle on some inadvertent answers. Answering one question explicitly, we may decide others tacitly. We may be unaware of a major hypothesis embedded in our favorite paradigm.

For instance, the therapist's epistemological problem may seem to him the only real question. He may think that all of therapy is wrapped up in his knowing. A tolerantly curious therapist may find comfort in comparing a difficult patient to a deprived child, and believe he has thereby settled his professional uncertainties. But we must ask why his visualization is helpful, since it is no more obvious what one should do with a very big, angry child than what to do with an angry patient. If the therapist comes to rest with this "knowing," he shows that he implicitly believes that good things will happen if he can take a parental attitude, or if he can find "naturalness" in somebody who bothers him, or if he can identify a patient's fantasy, or if he can locate an unmastered life crisis, or if he can imagine an imperfectly matured psychic structure. The therapist in question has taken some theory of therapy and some theory of mind; he has assumed the posture that thinking this way puts him in; and he has squeezed theory of the mind, theory of therapy, and style of behavior — all of them — into his sheer *picturing* of the patient. He may suppose that up to this point his theory of therapy specifies only curiosity and understanding. But that is far from the case. There is a hidden doing to the patient and a hidden reading by the patient, assumed and glossed over in this account. (Writers have tended to bleach the awkwardness and complexity out of treatment by being brief about therapy and loquacious about pathology, which makes it seem that knowing accomplishes everything.)

It is an axiom that the therapist cures by hearing rightly. But if the events that this formula summarizes are not understood in their complexity, it becomes a grandiose, smug and complacent mystery. Why does the therapist hear what he hears instead of something else that is also true? How does he get the chance to hear something that everybody else hasn't already heard? What does his hearing have to do with what the patient takes away with him? And why does it make a significant difference?

Answers to these questions can be found within the theories of Freud or Kohut, for example. But many a therapist simply supposes that he hears properly and that does the trick.

And yet, one *can* abstract a separate cognitive problem from among the interpersonal buffetings. One does need to know something in order to do something. The therapist does hear rightly, in some important sense. (And one of the reasons for the therapist's balance problems is that the treatment situation makes it especially difficult to know anything.) Indeed we should be able to study the task of knowing, even if knowing does smuggle in other decisions.

Therefore, even though the problem of influence and the epistemological problems of patient and therapist are all related, we should make sure that we have addressed them each explicitly.

In the first part of this book we examined some ways that therapists picture (and worry about) their influence, and Part V deals with that in more detail. We now have to consider how the therapist's attention finds items to focus on (chapter 10) and how the patient extracts from that a meaning that is important to himself (chapter 11).

Ideally, if we could answer these questions, we would be able to reconstruct the balance problems of the therapist, as seen in chapter 8. Moreover we would acquire standards by which to compare theories. In our present state of knowledge, comparing theories is often a matter of taste, if not blind prejudice. Perhaps someday we will compare theories according to which aspects of the treatment task they are principally concerned with, and what happens to the others as a consequence.

10

Therapy Tasks:

How the Therapist Makes Sense

of the Patient

N o general pattern, however dramatic, signals where it is instanced in experience. Or, to put it the other way around, nothing in nature comes labeled, not even a self-referring creature like man.

How do we pick out things to match our forms? Freud (1912b) warned against hunting for forms. His argument against focused attention is clear and useful. It is much less clear what happens when attention is freely floating: What does the focusing then? (Spence [1982] studies this question.) Gray (1982) has pointed out that analysts abandoned hypnosis because they grew less interested in pasting their own standard id labels on appetitive roots of behavior, and became more interested in how the patient reacts to his own experience. One could say that analysts became more interested in the patient's self-perception, self-definition, and self-manipulation. Today's analyst wants to discover the articulation of experience, and how it grows. He does not wish merely to see through manifest content. Therefore he has to exercise various kinds of attention, and not just resonate with id-ish starting points. Complex meaning requires complex attention. For this advice, Gray salutes Anna Freud, who was more faithful than her father to the practical implications of his late discoveries.

But right from the beginning, at a basic, artisan level, analysts have always had to deliberately structure their field, because otherwise they could not operate in it. An analyst could imagine that he was learning by unconscious communication, but then what he heard on the unconscious telephone had to be categorized before it could cue an action. The analyst has to do something or nothing, now or some other time. What should he look for as a signal? Only the wild analyst would let his unconscious directly decide his *actions*.

At various times, the analyst was told to intervene when the patient stopped talking, or to point out resistances as they arise, or to facilitate the idea closest to consciousness, or to reconstruct the origins of the illness, or to examine dreams as they are reported. These are all attempts to divide up the analytic field.

But none of these rules of thumb selects one part of the patient's private meaning about which the analyst can say, "This is oedipal conflict," or "This is a feeling about me," or "This is a memory." And the reason is not just that these labels are uncertain or incomplete, but because the "this" that they refer to is something very personal and private, and loaded with its own secret order of explicit and implicit connotation, and it cannot easily be identified publicly as a "this" for both analyst and his patient. (Again, see Spence [1982], who makes this very clear.)

How can we know that we have seen the real parts into which the patient divides his experience, or is ready to divide it, so that we can talk about them?

The therapist shares a physical and cultural world with his patient, a language, and life experience. He may teach his patient to share a code of significant life events and a useful narrative pattern. He demonstrates a useful perspective to his patient by looking at the patient's mind as an object of inquiry.

But still that is not enough. None of it can be counted on to draw the eyes of the patient and therapist to the same thing at any given moment.

A wordless glance may suffice to orient someone to a physical thing. But what we are glancing at inside a patient will be different to him than it is to us, because it is part of a different life. When I point to a physical thing, I ask you to lift out from your private context the public fact that is available to both of us. How can I gesture toward internal experience, which is *defined* by this private context? (Spence [1982] has beautifully portrayed the errors this may lead to.)

Ostensive (pointing) definition of material things seems easier than ostension in psychology. But ostensive reference to physical things is not free from problems either. Much of the difficulty is common to thought in general.

According to Quine (1981), no matter how many questions we ask someone, we cannot find out how he carves up his universe, mental or physical, and he cannot know how we do it. In our attempts to find out, neither of us knows exactly what part of the universe the other is asking us to identify. Many modern logicians and philosophers of science have agreed that what usually passes for ostensive definition is really a kind of pointed bulge in a smooth balloon of theory. No non-theoretical pieces of the world are simply pinned to the theory as samples to use in applying the theory to the world. We have to know the interrelation of terms before the terms can guide us to the world. That means we must first be made to see the world a certain way before that way can orient us to the world.

The debate that Kohut stirred up about empathy is to some extent an argument about whether we are at least as able to refer ostensively to items in the mental realm as we are in the physical realm. So one does not dispose of Kohut's challenge by simply showing that there are no theory-free descriptions. There is theory in physical perception, too, but I can see where you are pointing.

There is one feature of the mental world, however, that should make ostensive definition actually easier than it is with physical things. Unlike rocks and trees, people try to make you see them in certain ways.

The therapist is not an eavesdropper. Patients work on their therapist's attitudes. In fact, that is what we all do when we communicate, in order to focus another person's gaze on a shared meaning. Kenneth Burke (1954) showed that even for the simplest instrumental purpose, we propagandize the other to make him see something in a certain light. If I am trying to get you to register a certain meaning, I must maneuver your feelings to converge on it. In conversation we manipulate the other's mind. The meaning of every word and action is uncertain until it is hemmed in by its context. So the speaker must manipulate the context, including his role and relationship to his partner, if he wishes to be understood.

One can count on the patient to manipulate the therapist that much just for the sake of elementary communication. But when, as in therapy, a person is vitally concerned about the meanings he intends, the way he wants to be seen, and how he hopes his wishes will be read, his communicative propaganda will be much more intense than what is needed merely to recruit in the hearer semantic properties that make sentences intelligible. That is why the main feature of therapy is the provision of somebody who listens attentively, that is, somebody for the patient to affect.

Therefore, if a therapist wants to see the most important divisions that the patient makes of his own experience, he should encourage the greatest play of propaganda from him. And, in fact, therapists do bathe themselves in manipulative influence from the patient as much as possible.

Now let us ask how the therapist induces the patient to mobilize this effort. Is it by being inactive, or impersonal, or non-judgmental? All of these attitudes contribute. But I think the most general way that the therapist forces his patient to maximum effort is by holding to a theory. Despite the therapist's attention and the patient's work, the therapist's theory interferes with communication. Because the therapist's participation is encumbered by his theory, the patient cannot establish the dialogue he starts. He cannot guide his therapist's gaze by using their involvement with each other and their place in the world, as we ordinarily do in conversation (cf. Rommetveit,

1983). The patient cannot use familiar social skills to continually coordinate their common vision. Theory not only fails to provide ostensive definition; it does a lovely job of interfering with it. The patient cannot get across what he wants to.

Thus, we have a patient who is invited to affect a therapist who is attentive to him but who is also attentive to a theory of the mind and a customary stance. The therapist is trying harder than anybody else would to make sense out of what is going on, but the patient does not have his undivided attention.

Now it may be objected that this is flagrantly untrue; that the therapist hears the patient's *real* meaning, and his interventions simply reflect it back to the patient. But that is exactly my point. This "real" meaning that the therapist responds to is connected, however distantly, with his theory. Surely something from the patient works directly on the therapist, and I return to that later. But the very fact that the therapist has a notion of real meaning, of superfices and interiors, of appearances and reality, of mental things and their manifestations, makes him not a partner in an ordinary dialogue.

Gesture and speech need a context to give them meaning. For instance, if you change the scene, put something different before or after, accompany it with another expression, you have changed the meaning. Context determines meaning. But the therapist's theory interferes with ordinary contexts in many obvious ways. Although the patient can only address someone within a context, the therapist has detached himself from contexts. The patient has to place the therapist in some role; he has to assume some relationship with him and take for granted a common view of the world, just in order to talk to him. (That is part of what is called transference.) However, because the therapist is loyal to his theory, he will take up no role, relationship, or fixed view of the world.

The listener's context that gives the patient's voice its meaning is thus continually undermined. Trying to shape the therapist's attitudes, the patient works with materials that dissolve in his hands. His message inserts itself in a shifting context that brings out other meanings, and optimally, ultimately, the most private and undeveloped ones.

The famous rule of abstinence begins here. Long before we reach the issue of denying physical gratifications, or even verbal gratifications, the patient has to put up with an inability to communicate in the ordinary way to make his meaning. Of course we know that being listened to satisfies a deep craving. But every practitioner also knows that his *way* of listening is in itself frustrating. It is the base-line outrage. It gives the patient no traction.

It gets worse from there, because any more personal way that the patient wants to affect his therapist—to make himself lovable or detestable and, always, to make himself special, continually comes to grief.

But as a result of this frustration, and assuming that he experiences some taste of success, the patient's scattered, public talk becomes more like a private, structured "work," a work designed by conflicting motives. About this work, Schafer (1970b) is right: It should be looked at in as many ways as possible, as we look at a work of art. Students of hermeneutics and literary criticism have much to tell us about this kind of understanding.

But we must not let this esthetic appreciation of the show distract us from the grim facts of its production. The whole thing emerges because the therapist's attention evades the patient's aim. That is what is involved in looking at an orienting effort rather than allowing oneself to be oriented by it. Refusing to be sensibly cued by the patient, the therapist leaves himself open to some other orienting effort.

It follows that the therapist must have a less passionate interest than the patient wants him to have. Surely that is the basic tension for both parties. Historically, psychoanalysis originated in that mutual stress. "Dialogue" is too tame a word for the psychoanalytic interchange. (cf. Rangell's [1982] review of Leavy [1982].) In their writings, analysts show their continuous need for theoretical support in this difficult position (cf. chapter 1).

Naturally the hurt of conflicting desires is most poignant. But we should not forget the cognitive burden of conversing without the mutual manipulation that conversation depends on. Therapists hope that they will inspire new, more occult speech acts. Meanwhile it is a severe cognitive strain for both parties (cf. again Spence, 1982).

How far does this advance our understanding of the psychotherapist's perception? We see in the next chapter that the strain between patient and therapist induces the patient to manifest himself more clearly. But how does their mutual past-pointing help the therapist to select the particulars that the patient is trying harder to get him to see? How indeed can the therapist pick out anything about the subject, when he does not allow himself to be guided in the way people are normally guided, that is, by ordinary conversation? Theory does not step in and do for therapy what ordinary dialogue does for ordinary conversation: theory does not annotate process as it happens. Even laid on a platter of theory, a protracted interaction does not just fall apart into segments for us to think about.

Of course, theory offers some help by prejudicing experience. Like it or not, the analyst tries to see if he can make a case for story lines that he is familiar with. Nobody can escape this. Like any other thinker, the analyst looks for opportunities to use his chunked knowledge, his ready forms and narratives. (Schafer [1980b] shows this appreciatively, and Spence [1982] critically.)

But what draws Dr. Jones's attention to a fleeting reality about Mr. Smith's mind at 3:45 p.m. on a Thursday, and makes his task different from the historian's or the literary critic's, is a wish to see something move, or to catch sight of something that is just about to move (see Havens, 1984). That is also why psychoanalysis is a natural science, and not simply a hermeneutics.

A familiar story may be useful to tie movements together into an intelligible narrative. But I do not see how a therapist will sensitize himself to the subtle signs of a potential shift of meaning and affect simply by having a story ready in his head.

Before we can make sense out of what appears to us, it has to appear to us. Our eyes must have angle and color receptors before we can discuss the artistic values of a painting. Infants have built-in sensory preferences. The data that we deliberately scrutinize must first be picked out by involuntary scanning. One might say that features have to appeal to us in order to appear to us. I cannot see any way that the therapist can track nodal points where meaning shifts except by the continuous and automatic operation of a rooting appetite, that is, an inclination toward certain turns of affect, or forms of feeling, or liveliness of behavior. An appetite or inclination finds its own satisfaction without much need for explicit theory. One of the reasons a book cannot teach how to do psychotherapy is that one needs to have these appetites cultivated. Training and supervised analyses are designed to do that.

In contrast to, let us say, census taking, this scanning is like meeting someone. A patient introduces himself in a session. The therapist cannot meet him as he would in a social situation. His theory modifies his personal and sensory reactions. For instance, the therapist may know better than he would in a social situation that the patient is afraid of his hostile impulses or of his wish to be loved. But that is the sort of understanding one could obtain through a one-way mirror. While informing the therapist about the patient, his theory makes a cipher out of the patient's personal "come-on" (his invitation to an encounter). And the therapist is therefore more bewildered and less satisfied by this meeting than he would be in a social situation. (Klauber [1972] believed that analysts use interpretations almost obsessively in order to keep their distance.) The urge to refind the obscure person, to bring his dimness to light, to have a reunion, to reanimate what theory has killed—such a surveying urge might be the beacon that tracks the patient's corresponding effort to make contact. That would be the sort of automatic recognizing device needed to pick out the particulars of a momentary event, which is a service that no general concept or theory can provide. An inclination, for example toward liveliness, could bring the therapist's focus to the same place as the patient's, regardless of differences in perspective. And because an inclination is a way of being affected by what is fresh and new, it may be that which keeps the therapist from being an idealogue (cf. Schafer, 1959, p. 349).

When you come right down to it, motives like those I have described are simply the forms that curiosity takes when it bears on people we are engaged with. And nobody has suggested that a therapist could function without curiosity.

Psychoanalysis is sometimes described as a chronic mild bewilderment punctuated by achieved comprehension; and sometimes as a state of passive understanding, punctuated by sudden incomprehension. (Arlow [1979] seems to paint the first picture; Leavy [1980] the second.) Probably both are accurate pictures of psychotherapy.

Both involve comparing experience with images or models (a vital process, classically described by Gombrich [1960]). That comparison is what we are likely to think of when we use the word, "curiosity." It is the judgment that checks "yes" or "no," finding that we do or do not recognize this as an example of that.

But I am concerned with the more minute discriminations that provide the data that can then be greeted with recognition and surprise. The kind of curiosity that *brings in* data will naturally be more personal, not to say libidinal, than intellectual curiosity. (Racker [1968] and Tower [1956] have discussed this issue). Intellectual curiosity is like trying to understand a character in a play. Before you can interpret a character you must perceive the character and not just the actor: You must react to the virtual character projected by the actor. The undeliberate, subliminal curiosity that looks for the character that the actor is portraying—that is the curiosity I am interested in (cf. Ricoeur [1981], who discusses the detachment of the action from the actor; cf. also Gadamer [1975]).

One can see the yearning to refind the patient in the therapist's hunger for recognizable situations. By a situation I mean a dramatic social reality, as opposed to a theoretical outline, a view of an aspiring person in a world of opportunities and limits. A situation, for instance, is somebody competing or being rejected; somebody mothering somebody else, two people fighting, or one person acting as though he were in a fight. Obviously any such situation implies a judgment by the observor. We know that it could be seen in other ways. Studying history, for example, we read many different situations into a single happening.

In psychotherapy, many such situations have proved valuable: the holding environment, symbiosis in its vulgar sense, the therapeutic alliance. The oedipus complex and the primal scene serve as recognizable situations. Conscious integration of a patient's impact on us requires some sense of a situation, as a grossly recognizable, not too theoretical image.

Must we, then, admit that high-level theory cannot introduce us to persons, and that low-level theory decides what we will see? Must we admit, in other words that we are entirely prejudiced by our favorite story lines?

It is true that abstract theory of the mind—metapsychology—will not produce personal recognition. High-level theory tells us that there are continuities and regularities to be found. But before these categories can be applied to anything there has to be something for them to apply to. And it is a person in a situation that they apply to. One has to appreciate a drama, even a very small drama, at least in some vague sense, before one can analyze it. A therapist does not analyze phonemes, or a series of postural shifts. He analyzes a dramatic reality. The therapist has to recover some dramatic reality from the person he is treating (Schafer, 1970b). One of the reasons dreams appeal to analysts is that they seem to be already given *as* situations, and it only remains to analyze them (although Spence, 1982, has challenged this illusion effectively). Elsewhere we are grasping for situations to analyze.

These days, one of theory's hardest jobs is to say what the relationship is between the therapist's preformed images and his open sense of available change. In earlier work, Schafer (1959) pointed out that the analyst's professional estrangement stimulates efforts toward merger and understanding. Lately, though, Schafer dwells on storytelling. Schafer's action language has had the unfortunate effect of separating his work into two parts: an early motivational inquiry, and a more recent cognitive one. That not only makes for a fractured theory of treatment, it even prevents him from giving a full account of cognition. He can no longer refer to deciding principles that tack a narrative here and there to what is going on in the office. Those tacks have appetitive aspects that he no longer cares to elaborate. Schafer may think that he is becoming more practical as he moves from metapsychology to narrative style, but he will not be able to illuminate actual practice until he can account for the interactive stimulus that commands the particular use of a narrative style at a particular moment and in a particular way. For that he will need the old motivations that he has previously discussed so fruitfully.

After all, patients have an empirical response to their therapist's behavior even if we can never agree on what it is, and the therapist's thought is directed toward the patient's movement. As a result of what a therapist does, something actually happens in the world, which does not happen, for instance, when I say that Raphael's *Holy Family* in the Metropolitan Museum is a bore. (The picture doesn't care.)

I understand Gray (1973, 1982) to say that if we want our gaze to alight where the patient's own meanings can shift, that is, on the natural features and segments of his mind, then the situation we should be primarily attuned to is the problem that the patient experiences in presenting himself to the analyst. Gray and his patient find a common situation in the difficulty the patient has with himself in the presence of his analyst. The needed drama that makes the scene alive and compelling is the barest, agonistic drama— almost formal internal conflict. In order to point to the common ground, therefore, Gray has the least need to impose his own definition, and the patient is freest to develop his own private meanings.

I think that is the most accurate knowledge one can have of these matters.

A reliable feature detector for this sort of scanning might include the therapist's enthusiasm for predicament as a point of potential meaning shift, and his taste for the sense of being used by a patient to solve a problem. One reason Kohut is popular is that he has induced a new appetite for a way of being used by a patient. That appetite roots out particular meanings in particular patients, something that no abstract theory by itself could do. It is a powerful operator (see chapters 28 and 33).

Still and all, the patient's experience is the patient's experience. How can we know that the appetite satisfied by students of Kohut really finds what they think it has found? The answer is that we cannot know.

But it is not necessary for the therapist to know exactly what he is encouraging. It is sufficient that he treats the patient as though he were roughly the person he is indeed about to become. (See chapter 34; also Loewald's [1960] classic elaboration of this theme.) The patient will explore being treated that way: He will fill in the personal details himself. The exact meaning to the patient of the therapist's response, the exact nuance of his new self or new view, is something only he can experience, because part of its meaning comes from how it fits with all the rest of his life, which only he has lived. I should think it is now a commonplace that all interpretations are inexact. Only the patient knows what he has learned in treatment. What the therapist can hope to know exactly as the patient does is the place where meaning shifts in the flow of process. I discuss this further in chapter 11.

The therapist's accuracy will be measured by how close he comes to the natural point of change. And that is a matter of when and where he gestures. But it is also a matter of how he gestures because his manner partly defines the direction of the gesture. And his manner, in turn, is partly defined by all the attitudes previously accumulated in the treatment. How well all these attitudes blend with each other will reflect how solid his theory is. His theory will determine how integrated his images are. And his theory will also inspire certain temporary roles and relationships, and train him to feel usable by the patient in certain ways. All of these factors will determine the therapist's special kind of curiosity. A profession so complex cannot be described simply as the cultivation of a point of view. And it will find its test in the actual influence it is able to exert. (On this issue the reader is referred to chapter 33 on Gill and Schafer.) The therapist is accurate if he is responding to natural points of change.

"Natural points of change" refers us to the most difficult question in the psychotherapy enterprise. It is the question that theories of the mind are designed to answer in detail. I use it here simply as a bridge enabling us to conclude our description of the therapist's epistemological problem.

To that end, I recall the principle that a statement has no single meaning and that its meaning depends on its context. If a patient is angry with me while I talk gently about his wish for closeness, he may fairly construe me to be telling him that I would like him better if he were milder, no matter what I thought I was saying or showing. If he is being seductive and I refer to his competitiveness, he may learn that his charm is a dishonorable manipulation. The therapist's response is always heard as a commentary on the patient's efforts to mold him. It is perceived by the patient as a reaction. The school of Lacan has done a good job of hammering this point home. A "natural point of change" must be some ready feeling of promise that the therapist's attitude gives to the patient's intent. A promising attitude by the therapist is one that models a hesitant refinement of meaning that the patient is on the verge of accomplishing. It treats the patient as though he is what he would almost be.

And the patient changes because, situated within that model, he feels the benefit of its greater refinement and harmony. He is in it, so to speak, before he knows it, and it is all right. (In chapter 34, I refer to this as a *performable model* or *metaphor*.) And please note that it depends on there being a new meaning that the patient was truly about to try. People will not be lured into just any old vision of themselves. Whenever a patient really elaborates a wish or a meaning, it is because it is what he really wanted. If the therapist is wrong in his own ideas, and yet the patient genuinely moves, it simply means that the therapist does not realize what he is saying (which must be most of the time).

I should add that treating a person as though something were true is only partly a matter of telling him things. An interpretation is but the tip of an iceberg; underneath the words an attitude spreads out and sets the tone. An interpretation is the most deliberate part of a therapist's attitude—the part whose meaning can be best governed. That is its good side. Its bad side is that it deceives the therapist about his power. Because the therapist governs his speech, he thinks that he governs his message. Actually, an interpretation is not the same thing for him as it is for the patient. To the therapist it is more like an isolated proposition. Eissler's (1953) vision of a pure, non-parametric intervention, although idealized, does truly reflect something about the therapist's experience, but it is that which is different from the patient's experience. Although the honest therapist is often bewildered about what the patient is conveying to him, he usually enjoys an ill-founded certainty about what he has conveyed to his patient. That is the subject of the next chapter.

11

Therapy Tasks:

How the Patient Makes Sense of

the Therapist

H owever deep our understanding of dynamics and pathology, we cannot know what is happening in treatment unless we know what the therapist picks up from the patient and what the patient picks up from the therapist.

The previous chapter discussed the therapist's choices. What happens on the patient's side of the dialogue? That is a more pressing question for, unlike therapists, patients are not licensed and may do as they wish. What they will make out of what goes on is not something we can take for granted. We have to be especially careful not to assume that they give it the meaning we would like them to.

The incredible austerity of psychoanalysis, together with its unsentimental acceptance of human stubbornness, sometimes makes us forget that the analyst's comments have always been offered as new opportunities for satisfaction, real or illusory.

The analyst may count on a sensible ego. But in that context, *ego* means a psychic structure, not a disinterested apparatus. In declaring that effective analysis requires an undeformed ego, Freud (1937) was not thinking of 20/20 vision or perfect pitch. He was referring to plasticity of feeling, the degree to which a patient can ultimately imagine more flexible satisfaction. Maximum satisfaction is what the ego is there for. It is not a receptacle for miscellaneous information. An ego is deformed if it cannot be tempted to greater satisfaction.

According to analytic theory, the patient reacts to the flow of analysis as he does to his whole life, that is, in pursuit of purposes. The real or imaginary opportunities that the analyst presents constitute opportunities to the extent that they answer to the patient's momentary purposes. When an analyst judges the truth of an interpretation by the associations it inspires, he is watching the patient find opportunities in the interpretation. He is measuring its "correctness' by the opportunities it opens up.

The ultimate opportunity the analyst offers is the integrated satisfaction of the patient's wishes. It has therefore been the paradigm of psychoanalysis, unlike other talking treatments, that what comes across to the patient from the analyst is basically the patient's own voice. Analysis distinguishes itself from "educational" treatments on that basis.

At the beginning, when analysis was the recovery of traumatic memories, the figure of the analyst represented the hope for symptom relief. Soon Freud realized that patients see more opportunities than that in their analyst. Some of the particular (interpersonal) aims temporarily overshadow the larger (treatment) aims. But the vividness of their wishes involving the analyst (in the transference) helps patients to see how they limit their general opportunities.

The whole process gives the patient opportunities of his own choosing, defined first by transference, and then by his capacities. At each stage these are distinctly self-defined opportunities. (Nobody has done a better job of showing this stepwise progression of hopes in treatment than the unfairly neglected Thomas French [1958]. See also French and Fromm, 1964.)

Despite that program, Ferenczi and Rank (1925) found many of their colleagues just telling things to their patient, things one supposes such as: "You have a castration complex," "Here is evidence of your father complex," "This is a derivative of an anal fixation." It was the analyst's voice that came across. When the analyst formed an opinion, he simply told it to the patient.

According to Ferenczi and Rank, that is not psychoanalysis. The analyst should comment only to assist the patient's current purposes, allowing repressed intentions to complete themselves. The stunted life plan will then flourish and the patient will ultimately discard it in favor of better plans.

By describing the analyst's goal as the release of a pent up experience rather than the forging of a verbal formula, Ferenczi and Rank made it clear that what the patient gets from the analyst is a chance to develop his own meanings. In their famous metaphor, libido unwinds like a thread from the secret spool within the patient and onto the analyst. I have little doubt that this faith in the patient's preordained, growing self-definition is what allowed Ferenczi and Rank to experiment boldly with provocative techniques (see chapter 5).

A decade later, James Strachey (1934, 1937) pointed out how much easier it is to talk about freeing experience than it is to actually free it. What unwinds onto the analyst isn't just libido – it is also resistance. Strachey wrote with the bitter knowledge of the structural theory. Every kind of resistance represents a vested interest. If you consider a man's purpose as a net product, then overcoming resistance to what he "really" wants is to get him to want something different. (Strachey didn't put it that way, but that is what his attention to the superego amounts to.)

Would we therefore say that patients get opinions from their analyst and find themselves converted? ("You should be tolerant of your infantile wishes.") What else could Strachey mean by offering his superego for introjection? Yet none of us would like to say that, and Strachey did not settle for it either.

Strachey's concept of the mutative interpretation is one of the most beautiful in the history of analysis. In a mutative interpretation the patient introjects the analyst's benign superego. But is the analyst's superego especially tolerant? I think, on the contrary, that Strachey's forebearance in the face of the patient's challenge, shows self-denial, ideological discipline, and aloofness. If the patient introjected *that* superego, he would abandon analysis altogether.

But if Strachey wasn't recommending his superego to the patient, what was he doing?

Strachey had another, more plausible explanation of his effectiveness: He was pinpointing something within the patient. Ordinarily the patient will hear the analyst according to his neurotic pattern, with attendant moral judgments. There is no way the analyst can point out what he wants to, as long as the patient hears him in his transference role. All the patient will hear is some overall attitude, for instance, an implied criticism or threat.

Strachey's famous metaphor of the analyst trying to untie a knot in an endless loop illustrates how difficult it is for the analyst to get across just what he wants. One can imagine Strachey thinking: "I must find a way to make the patient attend to just what I am looking at, rather than what he thinks my overall attitude is."[1]

His answer was to catch a moment when the patient is pressed to deal dangerously with him and then to make the opportunity unmistakably clear.

---

[1] Strachey also had other reasons for his famous formula. When the superego was considered the chief sources of resistance, it was logical to prescribe changing the superego as a preliminary for all other change. But I think Strachey was motivated more by his practical experience, which showed him that, no matter what he intended or said, it was hard to break free of attitudes imputed to him by his patient.

The patient is enabled to experience the desired and feared attitude toward the analyst *as* desired (and even desirable).

What came across from Strachey was a personal reaction to the patient's immediate act, but a special kind of personal reaction that gave a hopeful meaning to the act. Only such a personal response forces the patient to see separate aspects of himself that would ordinarily have been blended in a judgmental attitude projected onto Strachey. In response to his feelers, the patient got back a peculiar variety of attitude, leaving him with more opportunities than he had bargained for.

Ferenczi and Rank and James Strachey were alike intent on liberating sealed opportunities. Strachey went beyond the earlier authors by showing that the patient's opportunities become opportunities only in the light of certain peculiar attitudes from the analyst.

This is a disturbing wrinkle in psychoanalytic theory. If the analyst's attitudes shape meaning, how can we say that the patient discovers his own voice? On the other hand, if the analyst does not plant attitudes, how does he keep his words from being twisted by the patient's attitudes?

We don't often encounter this problem in theory, because we just assume that the patient understands the analyst's words the way the analyst does.

Freud (1913) suggested giving the patient a preliminary idea of what he will discover. Fenichel (1937) argued that truth is its own salesman. If it is truth we are talking about rather than meaning, the patient doesn't need to introject a piece of the analyst, he simply repossesses a lost piece of himself. The truth that has been repressed or disguised could as well drop from Mars, except that a great deal of interpersonal spadework is necessary to make it welcome.

That is the original image of psychoanalytic treatment, and it remains its most succinct and summarizing high-order abstraction. Its classic statement is Kurt Eissler's (1953) meticulous essay that made parameters famous. There we find the ultimate elaboration of the rule that the analyst's attitude should not contaminate the patient's voice. I am going to argue that even Eissler's uninflected truths need therapist attitudes as their vehicles. In particular, they need Strachey's sort of attitude, which regularly emerges from the distorted conversation called psychotherapy.

II

An utterance can only be understood in context. Irony is a simple example: Without knowing if the tone is ironic, we cannot tell whether "A" means "A" or "Not A."

Other examples are more complicated.

A woman says to her lover, "You are angry with me for not seeing you last week." Maybe this is a reproach; maybe she is warning him not to demand too much. If that is her meaning, it will not escape him.

If a therapist says, "You are angry with me for not seeing you last week," he probably does not mean it as a reproach. But only the context, past and present, can make that apparent. If the implication is that the patient's anger is irrational, the therapist's meaning will be the same as the message of the inattentive lover. Context is crucial to meaning.

What is context made of? Here are some components: Patients understand what a therapist says in terms of what they are inwardly concerned with (not necessarily what the therapist wants to address, or even knows about [Michels, 1983a]).

Then again, a patient can only make sense out of his therapist's reaction if he knows what situation the therapist is in. The therapist's situation is strange and hard to read. But part of it is designed by the patient (cf. Hoffman, 1983).[2]

The base line for understanding a reaction to oneself is one's own action on the other person. Even if a therapist wanted to be a blank screen, the patient would know something about the inner reaction he (the patient) calls forth. People are people, and everyone knows it. The therapist's overt response can therefore be read as a commentary on his inevitably covert response.

Hoffman (1983) makes this point in his important essay on "The Patient as Interpreter of the Analyst's Experience": " . . . every patient knows that he is influencing the analyst's experience and that the freedom the analyst has to resist this influence is limited" (p. 411).

I think therapists sometimes exaggerate their ability to react only with empathic associations. They do not like to think that the patient succeeds in stimulating reciprocal feelings. (Lucia Tower [1956] is a great exception. See also Racker [1968] and Brenner [1985]). Some therapists seem to think that, in principle, they can preserve a stable disposition. For them, countertransference is a slip-up, an event that is especially informative because it interrupts a normal therapeutic situation. I agree with those who believe, on the contrary, that without countertransference there would be no significant communication about affect.

But Hoffman's point must be qualified. The therapist does not react just to his patient. Most of the therapist's situation is set up by his theory, beyond the control of the patient, and patients know that.

After all, if someone behaved like a therapist outside of the office, he would rightly be considered mentally ill. Since patients do not usually draw that conclusion, the therapist's behavior must get much of its meaning from the therapy situation.

---

[2]Hearing a transference interpretation, the patient probably knows what he has done to the therapist a little more clearly than when other things are discussed. And that may be part of the special value of transference interpretations. (This, however, is true only when transference interpretations are applied with the specificity that Paul Gray [1973] describes.)

But what is the therapy situation? How well does any practitioner know? And what sense of the therapeutic situation has the patient, who must use it to identify the therapist's meaning? Obviously his own sense, and therefore his beliefs about therapy will partly define the literal meaning of everything that is said.

As received, the therapist's meaning is shaped by the way his actions have been progressively and privately defined by the patient over the whole of the treatment. Something said early in treatment is heard differently than the same thing later. Should we ascribe that only to peeling away defenses? Or should we also say that the same words, early and late, are actually different messages because they are embedded in different contexts—and that they emerge from different speakers, because the therapist later is a person who shares a past with his patient?

To summarize so far, what the patient hears is determined by (a) immediate context, (b) the patient's secret concerns, (c) the position he puts the therapist in, and (d) his changing image of what the therapy is all about. That is a lot of context per word! And on top of this, the therapist interferes with being understood by deliberately confusing the social context. (He cultivates the most thorough ambiguity known to man.)

It would appear that no psychotherapeutic communication is ever a transparent proposition. It is always an historical event with a vague, unique, complex background, and plurivocal meaning.

That does not mean that no abstract truth can be extracted from it. It just means that the chances of one abstraction being made instead of another, will depend on what has happened between the two people involved.

III

What I have considered so far is how the patient catches the therapist's thought: He compares the comment with the context. That would be true even if the therapist did not intend to tell the patient anything. For example, if the patient surreptitiously observed a note the therapist had made about him, he would have to go through all these interpretive efforts to grasp the meaning of the secret notation.

Ordinarily, of course, what comes across to the patient is the result of the therapist's utterance. And so the patient has to grasp not just the therapist's private thought, but also what it means that the therapist decided to tell it to him.

This is an area that therapists have wanted to avoid. Therapists have admitted that some of their speech is manipulative. They catalogue those acts as confrontation, clarification, questioning, and so on. But one reason for labeling these actions was to clear the way for another form of speech—

interpretation—that could be considered a pure description, devoid of personal attitudes that influence people. Eissler called speech that acts a *parameter*: He considered it psychoanalytic only if it can finally be pruned down to speech that only provides information for the patient and does not act on him.

Eissler sums up the Socratic objective of acquainting the patient with himself, which is the central inspiration of psychoanalysis. But more analysts are now allowing that this abstract summary of the purpose of analysis, does not characterize its minute inner workings.

For example, it is not uncommon these days to find psychoanalysts citing the work of the philosopher, John Austin. Austin (1962) recognized that talking always *does* something to someone.

Austin argued that speech is designed to evoke in the hearer other responses than bare, grammatical meaning. He called that extra freight the *illocutionary force* of the utterance. (Think, for instance, of the statement, "I need more light!") Austin suggested that we also consider what he called the *perlocutionary force* of the utterance, which is what the speaker hopes to accomplish by the illocutionary force of his words. (When I say, "I need more light," I hope it will be heard as a request; and I hope that by saying it I will get more light. For a discussion of the role of speech in psychoanalysis, see Shapiro, 1979.)

Roughly speaking, illocutionary force is the manipulative aspect of speech, and the perlocutionary aspect is the speaker's ulterior motive. A therapist's utterance does not float in the air, to be abstracted and absorbed by the patient at leisure. It reaches over to the patient and does something to him. (Indeed, many of the therapist's simplest, descriptive interpretations may have an illocutionary force similar to that of, "I need more light." And the perlocutionary point might be to fit things into a theory.)

You might say that a therapist "does" an interpretation on his patient to make him react some way, in order to accomplish what the therapist has in mind. Like an interlocutor, the patient knows this. If he did not know it, he would not know the simple meaning of the utterance. (To show that grammatical understanding must be supplemented by a grasp of illocutionary and perlocutionary force, it is customary to point to the pseudo-question, "Can you pass me the salt?")

Perhaps Austin's most popular example of words as action is what he called the *performative*: "I now pronounce you man and wife." Said in the right situation by the right person, this does not describe—it accomplishes something. Havens (1986) discusses performative effects that are deliberately used in some therapies, but subtly find their way into all—even analytic—psychotherapies.

A frequent speech act, especially in general psychotherapy, is what Austin called the *verdictive*. When it is said by a psychiatrist, the statement, "You are suicidal" may have physical consequences. Indeed, whenever a therapist puts a different cast on something from the way it sits in the patient's consciousness, he may be ruling on it with a defining authority already bestowed on him by the patient. Any comment by the therapist that resonates with superego transference, or indeed with any parental function, will probably have some performative force because, as far as the child is concerned, parents christen everything in the world.

A therapist may try to avoid performatives by declining to rule on matters. But he cannot avoid the milder, overall performative aspect of psychotherapy speech in general, which implicitly says, "By this token, our action is commissioned a psychotherapy." His words themselves may be quite modest and tentative. But saying them makes what is happening a therapy, according to the convention and roles of the participants.

Anything in the therapist's comment that suggests that the patient is not doing what he should is a performative and not just a description because as far as a patient is concerned therapy is whatever the therapist conducts. Fortunately, therapists are not as inclined as they once were to say, in effect, "I hereby pronounce you a resistant patient. (But you have the keys to the jail in your pocket.)"

(Frustration in work is not easily avoided, as Fenichel [1941], noted with alarming nonchalance. But Davison et al. [1986] demonstrate a way to eliminate the pernicious performative aspect of resistance interpretations.)

But subtle performatives can probably never be entirely eliminated from treatment talk. For instance, any time the therapist even faintly repeats a previous instruction, he is reprimanding the patient.

Whenever a therapist says something, he intends to alter the patient's sensorium. The patient, like any conversationalist, has to grasp the *intent* in order to make sense of the statement. (See Goffman, 1974.) He must get the gist of the therapist's purpose.

Examples of perceived therapist purposes might be: "He want's me to follow his curiosity," "He finds it convenient to his way of thinking if I present myself this way," "He wants me to select this aspect of my thought for further elaboration," "He wants me to stop presenting myself in the same, old fashion," "He wants me not to feel guilty," "He wants me to be brave," "He wants me to trust him," "He wants me to love him," "He wants me to believe that his feelings can't be hurt," "He wants me to know he is with me in my struggle," "He wants me to think he's harmless," "He wants me not to blame him," "He thinks I am not telling the truth," "He wants me to respect his acuity," and so on.

There is always an invitation, demand, requirement, entreaty, a claim, when we talk to someone.

Everything I have written up to this point is true of all discourse. But psychotherapy is a peculiar discourse. Illocutionary elements are both more and less conspicuous than in ordinary conversation.

For instance, the therapist's performatives are usually vague. He will not accept the role he seems to act from, and the patient is never confirmed in a safe status. The therapist reacts variably (by social standards), and thus the manipulative tendency of his statements, their illocutionary force, is somewhat unplaceable.

Therefore, patients say "What is that supposed to mean?" "What are you driving at?" "Does that mean I should change it?" "Why do you always harp on how I feel about you?" "I notice that you only comment when I say something like this, and not when I say something like that." "You often talk but you never *tell* me anything." (which translates roughly into: "I don't know how you feel about me." which means "I can't tell whether you like me, or what you want from me.")

But on the other hand, although vague, the illocutionary force of the therapist's comments—his personal intent, pressure, and expectation—is accentuated, because there is no other business at hand for the meanings to be about: There is nothing else to manipulate. Sailors pulling together on a line are not only clearer about what they want from each other, they are also less demanding because a great deal of their attention goes to the rope. Between patient and therapist there is no rope to agree on, and the whole thing consists of one's imprint on the other. No reflection on the patient is merely incidental to a comment about something else.

In ordinary life, people draw the outside world into their conversation partly to prevent focusing such intense purposes on each other. Compared to ordinary speech, the patient is bathed in personal attitudes from the therapist, but he cannot tell what they are.

IV

I do not suggest that the therapist's words have no public meaning. I am saying quite the opposite: There are many public meanings of a word or sentence, especially about things of the mind. That leaves a lot of uncertainty for the private context to clear up, and the clearing up is impeded by the therapist's ambiguity. Private contexts are thus more important and require greater effort to establish than ordinarily.

This creates a vicious circle. It is hard to know what the therapist's attitude is, so it is possible for the patient to hope for a lot. And the hope makes it doubly important to find out "what he thinks of me."

As a treatment progresses, these private contexts accumulate and form a backdrop of expectations that colors the meaning of everything the therapist says. Every exchange is understood as shedding light on an array of opportunities and expectations that have been conjured between therapist and patient.

The patient learns the therapist's interests, vulnerabilities, and favorite procedures; he learns what words the therapist likes to attach to which phenomena; he has hunches about what the therapist is after, and how he will react. What is more important, the patient has a sense of the therapist's expectations. He imagines his actions plotted onto the therapist's hidden progress chart. He sees everything his therapist does as a sign of an expectation about him—an expectation of a momentary reaction and a future development. All of this is read as a sign of what the therapist thinks is "in" the patient—what his potential is, what is the best part of him.

We are now in the area of transference, and to that extent you may reproach me for belaboring the obvious. But, if the term is used narrowly, we are not *just* in the area of transference, because we are looking at the inevitable construing of any dialogue.[3]

Looking at matters this way, one can see why reason and feeling, so seemingly separate but annoyingly equal in treatment, are really one and the same. Abstract categories, such as anger or jealousy, can be located in oneself only as part of a personal physiognomy. It is different from knowing physical objects. We can locate trees within space because all spatial perspectives on a tree are summarized in a geometrical awareness. But within ourselves personally, there is no objective summary of all possible perspectives—there are no neutral ordinates to locate one thing and another. We locate things not by topography but by setting off familiar views of ourself, a view of our whole self with a particular something in the foreground. (For an elaboration of the foreground/background distinction in the analysand's presentation of himself, see Lichtenberg, 1983.)

We get a few ordinates from our culture (and culture here means mainly parents [cf. Stern, 1985].) These common ordinates are bound up with moral attitudes to our whole person.

And it is those attitudes that focus psychological vision. Attitudes are not just feelings. They are the ways we point to something inside someone or ourself.

But how can somebody's own voice be found by applying attitudes to him?

---

[3]From the standpoint of the patient's phenomenology, the reason that defenses have to be dealt with in an orderly fashion is to allow the patient to *place* the analyst's comments, and avoid an unpleasant surprise about what the analyst's expectations are. See Freud's (1937, p. 239) image of the analyst turning into a stranger.

Can we say that the therapist's attitudes acquaint the patient with free-standing facts that he continues to recognize after the therapist's attitudes have evaporated? Is therapy a one time flash of light that picks out features of the patient's personality, so that he can find his way around even in the dark?

That is close to Eissler's formula. And I am sure that it is true, as far as it goes.

The problem is that if it takes so much attitude and affect to isolate features of a person, it is hard to imagine what those features are all by themselves without the therapist's attitudes, especially since we know that *some* attitudes will always contaminate them.

We cannot be indifferent to ourselves. Reflection is always part of a commentary, hopeful and fearful, and psychoanalysis says that we think the next thought because we are drawn to it. Self-knowledge is always a commentary that has a "therefore" relevant to hopes and fears. A very abstract truth about our personal selves that doesn't make us feel one way or another really isn't anything but words. Attitudes are part of all self-knowledge. If attitudes are acquired in therapy, will they ever be free of the therapist's slant?

V

Let me anticipate the objection that we do not just feel about ourselves, but also think about ourselves. We have empirical knowledge that is more or less accurate by hard, predictive standards. Even without psychotherapy we have a theory of the mind. We know of memories, wishes, fears, habits. Can't the therapist simply refer to those things empathically, without exposing the patient to any attitude of his own?

We now enter the third and most difficult domain of our investigation. First I asked how the patient grasps the therapist's thought in its context. Then I asked how the patient picks up the reason for the therapist's actions. We have now to consider what is going on within the patient when the therapist speaks. What do the therapist's meanings impinge upon? What kind of a home within the patient is waiting for those meanings?

Our question, fundamentally, is this: What is there in the nature of inner experience that allows it to progress? And what happens to that progression when a patient speaks to the therapist and hears from him?

It is not enough to say that removing repression is what allows experience to progress, because we would still have to say what progress amounts to in the absence of repression; in other words, we have to spell out the process that is freed in therapy. And again, we cannot simply say that what the therapist does is to remove defenses, because we have to explain how the therapist can move anything before we can explain how he can move defenses.

At any one moment we are not statically contemplating a map of our mind. In fact, there is no way we could sum up what we are. Any one experience is a version of ourself in relation to what is going on. When I reflect on myself, I am *commenting* on what I see, and responding. I engage in inner conversation.

The therapist's comments intrude on a continuous commentary going on within the patient. Now, if internal speech were an orderly speaker-to-hearer speech, we could think of treatment just as empathic amplification. But internal dialogue is not just between one speaker and one listener. The patient has more than one voice—more than two. The therapist might have to hush one voice to let another speak. Because the patient does not simply speak to himself and listen, the therapist cannot simply echo him.

Moreover, whether we are speaking aloud or to ourselves, speech is not an enactment of a prepared text. Gadamer (1975) writes, "In the act of speaking one word brings another with it and so our thought is eventually set forth" (p. 497). The late Russian linguist and critic, Mikhail Bakhtin (quoted in Todorov, 1984) denied that simple semantic rules describe conversation. He wrote,

> Nor is there a ready-made message X. It takes form in the process of communication between [interlocutors] A and B. Nor is it transmitted from the first to the second, but constructed between them, like an ideological bridge; it is constructed in the process of their interaction [p. 55].

If what Bakhtin wrote is true, then it is not a question of the patient imposing his definitions on the therapist, or the therapist intruding with alien meanings on the patient's reverie. It is the nature of speech (language *in use*) to be open-ended, a device for creating, rather than simply expressing, meaning.

This view had been formulated earlier by the great Russian psychologist, Vygotsky. His disciple, A. R. Luria (1981) wrote of Vygotsky:

> He argued against the notion that a thought is a completely developed formation and that speech serves simply to embody it. Instead, he argued that thought is *completed* in the word, i.e., he argued that the *thought itself is formed with the help of the word or speech* [pp. 151-152].

I cite Bakhtin (1981) again on how talk grows ideas:

> [The speaker's] . . . orientation toward the listener is an orientation toward a specific conceptual horizon, toward the specific world of the listener . . . The speaker strives to get a reading on his own word, and on his own conceptual system that determines this word, within the alien conceptual system of the understanding receiver; he enters into dialogic relationships with certain

aspects of this system. The speaker breaks through the alien conceptual horizon of the listener, constructs his own utterance on alien territory, against his, the listener's apperceptive background [p. 282].

The word in living conversation is directly, blatantly, oriented toward a future answer-word: It provokes an answer, anticipates it and structures itself in the answer's direction. [p. 280].

We can see how even a solitary, inner conversation among several voices might produce a continually expanding vision. We can see how an interlocuter would make expansion more likely. And we can see why Freud's treatment, based on a dialogue of conflict, proved more helpful than Pierre Janet's treatment based on a cacaphony of several monologues.

The sociologist Erving Goffman (1969) describes expression in a similar fashion:

The subject turns on himself and from the point of view of the observer perceives his own activity in order to exert control over it . . . The subject . . . tends to make use of the observer's use of his behavior before the observer has a chance to do so. He engages in impression management [pp. 12–13].

Impression management is a preconscious and conscious process. But we might say that psychoanalysis describes a similar impression management in the unconscious censorship. We might say that a person checks out his awareness of himself to make sure that he knows what attitude he will elicit in himself.

Because self-descriptions are not only ambiguous but feel themselves toward many possible responses, every thought and exchange gives us a chance to find ourselves in a different landscape. Talking gives us a chance to do more justice to our underlying nature. We come closer to feeling our resources, and that makes us hopeful and courageous. That must be the reason that even unfavorable discoveries are often envigorating. Knowledge is power, not because knowing something about ourselves gives us the power to manipulate it, but because, in the act of knowing it, we can feel the capacities it grows from.

But linguists and literary critics can take us just so far in our inquiry. Patients have wishes and needs. They don't just try to get meanings across. They want something from their analysts, and act accordingly.

The ideal patient, such as Sterba (1934) had in mind, is concerned enough about the analyst to engage in impression management, but feels safe enough to tip his hand while doing it, thus disclosing his concerns. He is then in a better position to catch his *internal* impression management. Gray (1973) describes how patients can be trained to do that. But although the patient's openness is important, it is his concern that is the meat of the treatment, and there is nothing to inspect without it.

Psychotherapy is focused on the patient's effort. We explore ourselves in everything we do. But in ordinary conversation, we elicit an attitude that can be used for a purpose and we then move on to exploit it. If I convince you that my harmlessness is lovable, I will then explore what my lovableness can get me. The survey of myself never stops, but in the ordinary course of things it keeps sweeping the terrain from much the same spot. There is nothing to make me see my harmlessness differently. (I am, of course, oversimplifying to make the comparison clear.)

In contrast, psychotherapy provides no satisfactory dialogue. The therapist distorts efforts toward him by straining them through his theory. The theory dislocates the smooth exercise of the patient's habits—it trains individual muscles. (The therapist sees himself as undoing solutions and examining their components.)

To the therapist, his theory is an abstract statement of possibilities. But to the patient, the therapist's theory comes across as a kind of insatiable expectancy. Because the patient continues to want from the therapist, he is arrested in his next step by the sluggish therapist who is always peering behind the patient's efforts, mindful of his other possibilities.

Strachey understood that patients keep looking for personal attitudes. He wanted to distinguish the specific focus of his attention from the broad personal attitude the patient tried to read out of him. The therapist will try in vain to be attitudinally non-committal; the patient cannot *recognize* anything except a personal attitude.

What dissected the patient's interrelated aspects was Strachey's analytic reactivity. He called it his superego. But, as I have argued, it couldn't be his superego. (I am sure that Strachey did not allow himself to be treated uncivilly except when he was analyzing.) Obviously it was his theory and not his superego that modified his reaction. And in some odd sense, it had to be his theory and not his superego that the patient introjected, not of course as theory but in terms of attitudes.

A theory is possibility in abstract terms. I suppose the patient senses it in personal terms. He sees himself suddenly illuminated by a more hopeful attitude (maybe unintended in this shape by the therapist). He mobilizes a more hopeful voice in his internal conversation to match what he hears from the therapist. And it will be undermined in the next moment by a shift in the therapist's attitude, because the therapist does not have one attitude to the patient. With each possibility goes a different interpersonal relationship. As long as the therapist is faithful to his theory, he will be reliably faithless to his human relationship with the patient.

The patient's effort to understand the therapist will successively build full panoramas out of innumerable, shifting contexts. And, in their totality, these will map his mind more finely.

(In his important study of analytic process, Myerson [1981] shows how the patient, searching for the analyst's response, encounters different contexts for his affective experience, and these new contexts make it less risky for him to put his experience into specific, verbalizable form.)

The therapist's words in context spell out attitudes that are inconstant, always focused beyond what is happening, designed to fragment the patient's conversational survey of himself and push him closer to his latent options.

CONCLUSIONS

We will never decide controversies in technique by arguing about generalities such as what needs to be interpreted or what must be analysed. Technique cannot be realistically debated without considering the context and the nature of the momentary speech acts that carry the interpretations. Because context and form are so important, abbreviated case histories have limited value in these controversies, and nothing can be understood except by studying process.

We cannot afford to treat contexts as incidental. It is unrealistic to say, "Of course the therapist has to be tactful, and his timing right." *Where* the therapist's action fits into the sweep of the whole treatment is substantive, not procedural, just like a note in a symphony. Any technical decision always rests on the answer to the question: "What will the patient *make* of this?"

A given therapy is defined by the machinery that it sets up for the therapist's reaction and the patient's uptake. Conversely, unless we can say how in our practice a patient is likely to interpret what we are likely to do, we don't know what treatment we are administering.

III
Theory of the Mind:
The Tool of Psychotherapy

12

Why Bother with Theory of the Mind?

I n chapters 10 and 11 we noted that the therapist's view is spotted with theoretical preconceptions. Theory interferes with his sociable finding-power and intensifies his search for a personally responsive partner.

It is a familiar irony. We saw the therapist ease a strain with theory; then we saw that theory is what put strain there in the first place. Patient and therapist share a problem: They both have to interact with a person and a theory. If it were not for the theory, the two would have just ordinary balance problems that they would handle as in other relationships. It is the obstructive presence of theory that makes the difference. Theory is busy all over the place in therapy.

Up to this point, I have made no effort to separate theory of the mind from theory of therapy. What we have been looking at so far is mostly theory of therapy.

Although never a popular study, theory of therapy is always tolerated. Theory of the mind is not so lucky; it has fallen on bad times. Many regard it as a parasitic hobby. Although theory of therapy maintains its original, stumbling stride, theory of the mind, which led the whole psychoanalytic parade into history, is now regarded as a professional dinosaur—awesome, ungainly, and useless. It no longer seems evident that our effort to help someone depends on how we think he "works."

The thesis of this book is that theory is not a pasttime but a practical instrument. In the previous chapters I have tried to show that the therapist's determination to see his patient as a certain kind of something chisels out the treatment relationship and decides what does and does not get noticed.

Theory of the mind is an expectation of untapped potential. It colors the therapist's attitudes, and his attitudes determine what happens. In a talking treatment there is nothing else but attitudes to entice a patient into new freedom. Considering that fact, how can we not accord theory of the mind a decisive role? A theory of the mind presents the patient as a functioning entity with hidden possibilities; it allows the therapist to hope for new developments because an entity is never exhausted by any set of its manifestations.

Theories have characteristic effects on the therapist's expectations. A theory that describes potentiality in terms of conflict helps the therapist to see well-defined new directions and well-defined triggers for their development. A theory that describes potential in terms of a whole, maturing organism helps the therapist to sense the inevitable next movement, and encourages him to clarify it. Theories that are full of abstraction leave the therapist free to imagine what is specifically happening between himself and his patient, whereas theories that are more lively and experience-near (to use Kohut's term) carry a fixed picture of the therapy interaction, but as a trade-off, they leave the therapist free to imagine innumerable nuances of the patient's inner state.

Theories generally act by suggesting where to anticipate a ready development, telling the therapist: "Here the patient will find an opportunity." We have seen that one way a theory does that is negatively, by immunizing some of the therapist's vulnerabilities, preventing him from being moved by the patient and forcing the patient to his new opportunity (cf. Havens [1986] on "clearing the field" of social forces.) Theories also illuminate opportunities positively by sensitizing the therapist to specific types of change, as when the therapist wonders what a reaction formation is reacting to, when he anticipates that courage will follow secure attachment, or when he assumes that feelings of helpless disintegration will be transformed into manageable feelings of disappointment, or the affect of depression will develop into anger. Theories also work supportively by giving the therapist familiar constraints, so that the patient's novel details can be filled in without disrupting the therapist's orientation, as when variations of oedipal conflict are studied. Theories create opportunity by raising questions in the therapist's mind. Theories help the therapist imagine what he looks like to the patient (e.g., as an object of transference, a container of rage, a calm sustainer, a dry breast), and his theoretical outlines give him a standpoint for criticizing or sympathizing with that construal. Theories create opportunities by identifying certain attitudes or forces as "enemies" of therapy, against which patient and therapist can struggle in comradely fashion. Theories of the mind help the therapist to use the patient while easing his guilt about using him. We have illustrated a few of these uses in chapters 4 and 5, and others occupy us in the remainder of the book.

Over and above all special functions, theory of the mind always serves one general purpose in practice: To have a theory means knowing that there is more to the patient than he shows, and perhaps more than he wants to see.

Theorizing about the mind is not fun. Examining and comparing theories of the mind is a fussy business. It seems a far cry from the near-physical impact of a patient on his therapist that was our starting point. But we should not be deceived. However wearisome the study of theory, it is an investigation of something that hammers hard on the practicing therapist even when he does not know it. No matter what sects they belong to, therapists are always exploring some form of unused freedom, and their exploratory orientation amounts to at least an implicit theory of the mind. One must expect that the style and excellence of a therapist's theory of the mind will determine what kind of potential freedom he can find in his patient.

Theory of the mind is the instrument of psychotherapy. Therapists bring their own talents to the profession and these are discussed later. But individual talents are encouraged and restrained by theory. In the first part of this book we found illustrations showing how the instrument of theory is used. The following two parts study the theory of the mind itself, and alterations that have been suggested for it. That done, we will have looked at the therapist's practical need for an instrument, examined the way the instrument is built and how practice bends it, and we will be in a position to return to the immediacies of practice and say in more detail what therapy is.

To begin with, we want to find out what a theory of the mind is. We take Freud's system as an exemplar. We want it to show us how, in general, a theory of the mind works. Because that is what we are interested in, we do not look on Freud's theory as a philosophy of life, suited to his temperment. We do not regard it as a work of art influenced by popular fashions. We do not view it as a way of joining other, elite sciences. We study it as a system.

The way to examine a theory as a system is to find out what special tasks it has to perform. Tasks are the things a theory has to do to accomplish its objectives. It is sad that so many psychoanalysts are content to understand Freud's system as shaped after scientific "models" of the time. Exposition of a theory in terms of a model barely scratches the surface unless it takes account of the common tasks that the theory and the model accept responsibility for.[1] Comparing Freud's theory with other sciences of his day can help us understand what his system is about, but chiefly by showing us what the special tasks were which had to be faced by all the sciences of the time. From this we learn what demands *required* the features we find in Freud's system (chapter 13).

In chapter 14 we use Freud's early procedure and his schedule of priorities as clues to his mission. In chapter 15 we survey the overall movement of the

---

[1]Exclusive preoccupation with paradigms shows a disrespect for the *problems* that they are designed to deal with. Thomas Kuhn (1970a) cannot be blamed for that because even a cursory reading of Kuhn alerts one to the scientist's concern with problems.

developing theory, noting the specific, persisting demands that the theory answers to. And we conclude, in chapter 16, with a discussion of the kinds of knowing that such a theory facilitates, and the way such a system serves psychotherapy.

13

The Historical Context

My purpose in this chapter is to describe the problems and opportunities out of which Freudian theory grew, so that its objectives can be seen more clearly. The intellectual history of this period is the subject of many specialized accounts, and my broad sketch is only a suggestion of a perspective relevant to the genesis of psychoanalytic theory.

I believe that the basic psychoanalytic hypothesis, already present in "Studies on Hysteria" (Breuer and Freud, 1893-1895), is that within the mind there exist elements that can be traced through many changes and that can be referred to sometimes in physical, sometimes in ideational, and sometimes in affective terms without being completely encompassed by any of them. These parts of the mind can be thought of as "things," which, like ordinary objects, show themselves in various ways. Thus one may be observing the same thing in a hysterical symptom as one observes in an abreaction. The "thing" may be called an idea, a fantasy, or a wish. What is important is that it is not just an aspect of mind, but a real entity having multiform effects of its own.[1]

---

[1]Although it used to be a cliché that psychoanalysis began with the discovery of the unconscious, commentators have long realized that the unconscious per se was by no means a new idea. Ellenberger (1970) summarized the evidence for the fact that the unconscious is not specifically a psychoanalytic discovery. I am certainly not the first to regard variably expressive entities as the real psychoanalytic discovery. Rapaport (1944, pp. 187 *ff.*) considered the hallmark of Freud's theory to be the quest for intrapsychic continuities. Ricoeur's (1970)

Of course, no single formula can sum up the significance of a theory. For instance, in postulating an entity within the mind Freud was defining a part of a whole, and so his theory had to alternate between seeing the part as a separate thing and seeing it as an aspect of the whole mind. The development of psychoanalysis can thus be characterized as guided by a mixed allegiance to part formulas and whole formulas. In addition, part-entities within a single whole may be in conflict. When Freud recognized that the thing he was studying was not just a piece of the instrusive, traumatic, outside world, but part of the mind itself, he was drawn to a theory of conflict of parts of the mind.[2] But if there is indeed one mind, conflicts must be capable of resolution. Freud therefore had to complement his conflict theory with a theory of synthesis of the whole mind. One can describe Freud's genius as an alertness to conflict within a theory that accounts as well for synthesis.

There is also another aspect of Freud's approach. A thing that constitutes a part of the mind is "treated" or "handled" in varying ways by the mind. Therefore, psychoanalytic theory has to refer to things and also to process. Moreover, since the thing is a part of a whole mind and not just an intrusion upon it, it is itself a part of a process, as shown by its origins, development and fate, and it must be described at times in terms of process rather than in terms of things. Conversely, in describing the mental state that causes a certain clinical event, the process involving the whole mind must be broken down into static units. The theory thus has to be a fluctuating mixture of a thing theory (static, phasic, like a snapshot, structural, institutional, etc.) and a process theory (cathectic processes, discharge processes, energic transformations, and over-all directions of mental movement).

Freud's initial step was to identify entities in the mind, the fate of which could be correlated with symptoms and behavior. In doing that he explained how we can look at the mind as a whole and as a collection of parts, as a synthesis of wishes which are also in conflict, and as a flowing process in which we can discern discrete configurations.

I believe that these terms—part and whole, entity and process, conflict and synthesis—can be useful in examining the intellectual history, the relationship to scientific innovations, and perhaps the future of psychoanalysis.

---

profound study of the Freudian system reveals it to be built upon the postulation of an unknowable instinct representative straddling biological and mental worlds. Such an unknowable referent I regard as the sign of any real entity or thing under investigation (see chapter 16). Wyss (1966) holds that the point of departure for Freudian theory was the postulation of an idea with displaceable, quantitative affect. Stewart (1967) suggests that the basic idea of psychoanalysis which was present from the beginning was the "repression of an idea and the displacement of its energy onto a substitute."

[2]Hartmann (1956, p. 277) regarded conflict (and defense) as the key to understanding Freud's theory. Ritvo (1974) holds that conflict dominated Freud's theory from the beginning.

GENERAL BACKGROUND

In one form or another, these terms refer to logical or philosophical problems inherent in any system of thought. They have been of concern at least from the time of the pre-Socratics and possibly from the time of the first "primitive" intellectual systems. At any rate, there seems to have been some special form of crisis involving these problems during the nineteenth century, a crisis manifested by a troubled effort to specify natural entities.

According to Lester King (1975, pp. 290–291), seventeenth century medicine was a field divided between retreating Galenists, iatrochemists, and corpuscularians. From his account it would appear that the theoretical issue was how much abstract conceptualization is needed to understand phenomena. It seems that the Galenists took a realist or rationalist stand in favor of essential abstractions, the chemists a nominalist or empiricist position in favor of particular descriptions, and the atomists occupied intermediate ground.

Evidently, the victor was an empiricism even more radical than that of the chemists. Discussing the lethal tendency of eighteenth century physicians to group diseases into irrelevant classifications, Paul Bernard (1975) says:

> Part of the trouble was that eighteenth-century medicine, like the other sciences, was largely dominated by the taxonomic spirit that characterized the age. Medical theorists concentrated their efforts on arranging diseases in categories and, having done so, did not trouble to reflect that the basis of classification had been external symptoms and not the *causa* or the *sedes morbi*. Thus common colds, dysentery, diabetes, a tendency to miscarry chronically, and gonorrhea were all held to be different manifestations of the same disease [p. 200n].

It seems to me that the pendulum of favor swung so far from reason to observation that by the nineteenth century the very *idea* of a natural category became problematic. Instead of debating rival categories, thinkers argued the skeptical question: What is one looking *for* when seeking the essence of an illness or the subject of a science? That is a challenge that can be addressed alike to Galenists, chemists, corpuscularians, taxonomists, and, later, to physicists and psychologists.

Commentators on Freud have customarily placed him in either a mechanistic age (when examining his theory) or a humanistic setting (when examining his method) (e.g., Peterfreund [1971] and Gedo and Wolf [1976] respectively). Nineteenth century Materialism (in the form of Mechanism) may have been a reaction to Romanticism (in the form of Vitalism). But both currents shared a common concern about what a natural entity was and a new uncertainty about what entities could be studied. The successes of post-Newtonian physics had encouraged scientists to think in terms of forces (see Amacher [1965] on the Helmholtz school). Forces could be represented by laws or rules. But forces act on things, and force itself was sometimes thought of as an entity subject to laws and rules. (Popper, 1974, p. 1120, states that forces and dispositions refer to unobservable entities, of which they are manifestations.) Therefore forces do not dispose of the problem of natural entities.

Underlying the science of mechanics is the implicit assumption that simple bodies of matter are the ultimate entities. But it is also assumed that certain aggregates of bodies are natural entities and that the naturalness of those compound entities is assured by the forces inherent in their supposedly simple components. From the time of Newton, it became necessary to attribute to the ultimate atoms of matter occult powers which natural laws were supposed to make unnecessary. De Santillana (1941, p. 21) states that "against Newton's better judgment, and with much hesitation on his part, atomism was drifting back toward explanations through inherence" – a reversion to the despised Aristotelian notion of entelechies. De Santillana points out that by the beginning of the nineteenth century, a mechanicist physicist, Poinsot, had already realized that mechanics is not fundamental, that its principles have to be founded upon another science, which must rest upon another in an infinite regressive series.

Since even the successfully formalized science of mechanics could not finally encompass entities in its own terms, some nineteenth century empiricists abandoned mechanism, materialism, and atomism, and began a long philosophical march, continuing to our day, in quest of a proper subject of science that would *not* be an entity. The project was to explain the unification of knowledge brought about by scientific laws without attributing it to common underlying natural entities. Reacting to the nineteenth century perplexity about entities, this school would henceforth deride entities as "metaphysical."

The first and traditional empiricist proposal was to say that what the laws correlate is sense data. This seems to designate sense data as primary things.[3] And if laws represent forces, such a formula comes perilously close to the tenet that the world is made out of mind. That is not a congenial statement for those who wish to confine themselves to empirical laws. To avoid this impasse, the empiricists renounced not only entities, but forces as well. A conventionalist interpretation of laws crept into empiricism. Mach suggested that scientific theories are just simple or useful or economical arrangements of "experience" and portray neither natural entities nor a natural order. For Mach, the knowing mind is not to be thought of as a receptor, but rather as

---

[3] Avenarius opted in favor of substantializing sensation, with considerable effect upon later academic psychology (see Titchener, 1929, pp. 115–118).

a biological strategy. It adjusts its contents in a pragmatic fashion that is continually modified by experience (see Joergensen, 1951, p. 7).

As for what seemed to be natural entities, these "things . . . appear to be merely relatively constant complexes of so-called 'qualities' which Mach identified with our sensations and called 'elements' " (Joergensen, 1951, p. 8). Joergensen states that for Mach, "every scientific statement is a statement about complexes of sensations, and beyond or behind these there are no realities to be looked for" (p. 9). Clearly, Mach had not succeeded in disposing of natural entities. He had unwittingly made sensations again into natural entities (see Cassirer, 1957, pp. 25–30). Moreover, without natural entities, he was left with the mystery of what in the objective world makes certain arrangements of experience simple and economical. By abandoning objective reference and regarding natural laws as merely convenient, he seemed to have doomed science to arbitrariness, even though that arbitrariness had a rule (an arbitrary one) of its own. This tendency broke the promise implicit in the very name of empiricism, to promote statements determined by objective fact. According to Mandelbaum (1971, pp. 19–20), late empiricism ironically made other, less rigorous intellectual currents seem more serious and scientific by comparison.

For empiricism and mechanism had no monopoly on thought. The nineteenth century was far from being a purely mechanistic age. Mandelbaum (1971) has described a dominant concern with organicity, that is, the shaping of elements by their collectivity, the whole of which is more than the sum of its parts. Obviously, the whole which is more than the sum of its parts, is a proper entity and not an artificial or arbitrary collection we chance to make on observation. The parts of such a bona fide individual are entities whose fate is influenced by the inherent direction of the whole, a notion that must have been reinforced by Darwin's theory. It follows that if you find the proper whole, you will understand why the parts behave the way they do. And if you correctly observe the functioning of real parts of an organism, you will witness the principles of the organism's development. The nineteenth century interest in evolution and history is well known. What I wish to stress is that a concern with evolution and history is also a concern with the identification of natural entities. (Mandelbaum [1971, pp. 45–46] points out that an emphasis on progress or development presupposes a substance or entity which is developing.)

BIOLOGY

It is sometimes said that mechanism and materialism flourished in the nineteenth century. Such a view ignores what we have seen to be a great dissatisfaction with the attempt to reduce physical phenomena to natural forces and material entities. It ignores even more blatantly the fact that the successes of Newtonian physics did *not* include a Newtonian explanation of biological phenomena. Galaty's (1974) important study shows that members of the so-called Helmholtz school gave up in despair their efforts to find entities common to nonorganic and organic worlds and settled instead for a Kantian common *principle* of explanation, according to which the mind could conceive of change only in terms of the motion of matter and the motion of matter could be explained only in terms of forces of attraction and repulsion.

Current critics of psychoanalysis who hold these "mechanists" responsible for what they regard as Freud's philosophical naïveté would be amazed to find Gilbert Ryle's modern critique of mind explicitly formulated by the very "mechanists" themselves:

> The definition of force as the cause of motion . . . is a comfortable figure of speech which we cannot easily part with and which is still of service to us. . . . As soon as one probes to the basis of events . . . one recognizes that neither force nor matter exists. Both are, from different points of view, adopted abstractions of things as they are [Du Bois-Reymond, as quoted by Galaty, 1974, p. 305].

Where the Helmholtz school differs from the current revisionists is in the former's Kantian recognition that however one regards entities, they are what "understanding" is about.

Thus, as they transposed the problem of the unity of knowledge from the physical to the biological realm, the members of the Helmholtz school offered an alternative solution to Mach's problem. It was neither a materialist nor a conventionalist solution, and, insofar as it influenced Freud, it was extraordinarily fruitful because it permitted natural entities to be located on several levels (see Quinton, 1972, p. 72). But it was not easy to find genuinely fundamental biological entities.

Natural entities in biology were more difficult to come by than in physics and chemistry, where, despite philosophical difficulties, atomic mechanism had been highly successful. Zilsel (1941) states: "Whereas in physics . . . most classifications are elementary and, therefore, can be followed rather soon by causal research, the vaster variety of objects in the fields of zoology and botany is much harder to survey" (p. 74). Nevertheless, by the time of the nineteenth century a great deal of work had already been done on the question of what the lawful entity is that underlies the variety of living forms.

Some eighteenth century workers, such as Bonnet, maintained that the female germ contains in preformed miniature all the offspring that would follow its line (see Nordenskiöld, 1928, p. 245). This supposes an original multiplicity of beings rather than a common identity. In the debate about origins that followed it is possible to see a deliberation about what entities should be considered real.

Viewed this way, one current of thought (exemplified by Erasmus Darwin, Geoffroy, and Lamarck) seems to suggest a single essence of all organisms. Another (represented by Cuvier, Owen, and Lyell) seems to propose several fixed entities underlying different groups of organisms. These probably represent the alternatives that remain when one can no longer believe that individual organisms are specified by a Divine Plan. Formerly the Divine Plan would have been the fundamental entity. It would have been the fundamental entity because order, understanding, regularity, and lawfulness could be derived from that plan, and all particulars could be unified by reference to it (cf. Eiseley [1958, ppl 6ff.] on the "Scale of Being").

To the extent that the Enlightenment had made a Divine entity an unsatisfying explanation of the whole variety of life, another entity had to be found.

In the eighteenth century, several natural entities underlying the various animal forms were gradually defined by the science of comparative anatomy, and ultimately Darwin replaced the overall entity of the Divine Plan with an overall entity of Life, characterized by the property of adaptation. Life is an over-all entity because the defining property of adaptation attaches to Life and not to individuals. (In assessing the influence of Darwin on Freud, Ritvo [1974] referred to Haeckel's dictum that Goethe guessed the unity of nature, but Darwin proved it. Darwin's influence on Freud is the subject of Sulloway's [1979] study.)

The species are not the atoms of Darwin's system, because they are not *programmed* as entities. They are produced by the evolutionary entity, rather than adding up to it. But although not entities in their own right, the species and varieties are not merely concocted groupings; they are part-entities with objective boundaries. To see that this is so, it is only necessary to compare Darwin with Lamarck, for whom species were not even part-entities (cf. Fothergill, 1953, p. 69). Lamarck regarded species and varieties as transitional moments of a sliding passage moving toward inevitable and uniform perfection. Differences among creatures, if not simply the result of unequal evolutionary maturity, reflect a uniform effort to adapt to disparate surroundings, and these differences no more mark off one form from another than the color of a chameleon on a leaf distinguishes its type from that of its brother on a twig. In Darwin's system, on the other hand, biological groupings are entitled to be treated as natural part-entities, because they reflect not only what is common to life processes, but also the real differences *not* arising out of a common direction, which are selected as advantageous by different habitats and are thus transformed from accidental variations into defining essences.[4] Although we tend to think of Lamarck as an environmentalist because he believed in the inheritance of acquired characteristics, the environment for him was simply the clay out of which life's uniform purpose works its will. For Darwin, on the other hand, the environment was not a challenge to be answered in a preordained fashion, but a variable, independent standard that surviving organisms have chanced to incorporate as their own. It was Darwin, not Lamarck, who funneled the environment into the very essence of life's subtypes, thereby separating them from each other in reality and not just for purposes of classification. In this way he produced a proper whole with proper parts.

THE HUMAN SCIENCES

The problem of what laws were laws *of* was never a life-and-death matter for most sciences—certainly not for physics and not really for biology—because the entities with which these sciences work—the items and instruments they deal with in their laboratories and researches—have always had an unquestioned authority at the primary level, and have never needed credentials. That there is some sense in which an animal or a plant or a microscope or a steel ball is a thing has never been in dispute.

Such was not the case with the social sciences as the nineteenth century approached. There, common sense and expertise did not provide clearly demarcated entities to study and relate. Once the "City of God" lost its justification, the nature of man's collective life was harder to understand.[5] The variety and development of collective life no longer illustrated any obvious underlying truth. The eighteenth century had replaced the bustling variety of God's truth by the relatively ethereal, static and, in principle, uniform entity of man's intellect.

That will not do for History. History demands an entity that will allow a focus on differences as well as uniformities.

Ranke clearly described the new historical approach: " . . . our task is to present the characteristic, the essential in the individual, and the coherence,

---

[4]Foucault (1971) tells this story as though it amounted to an arbitrary shift of principles of explanation, in the course of which categories defined by visible characteristics were replaced by categories justified by the specialness of internal structure. I think it is possible, however, to read all of his evidence as arguing for an uninterrupted hunt for unity in diversity, which in my terms amounts to a search for natural entities underlying phenomenal variety.

[5]As with the Freudian revolution, the inspiration for the new social science is sometimes described by commentators as ethical or esthetic. Nisbet (1966, p. 19) has shown that sociology arose as a disgruntled critique of the atomized society that the Enlightenment had substituted for medieval *communitas*. However, social discomfort was not the only pain of transition: Intellectual problems arose as well, and I am suggesting that these can be seen as incentives by themselves.

the connection in the whole" (see Krieger, 1975, p. 13). For historians like Meinecke, who emphasized the individualizing part of Ranke's program, any alleged overall historical processes were artificial constructs; the true entities of history were what was novel and creative. Others, like Marx, who emphasized the reverse side of Ranke's task, tended to see overall human history as the entity under study, with novel part-entities related organically to that whole. For Treitschke, only the state was a true individual to be profitably studied in a social science (see Mauss, 1962, p. 32). According to him, other data were not inherently interconnected, and their relationships were fortuitous and unedifying. Herbert Spencer, on the other hand, managed to combine a belief in society as an organic individual with a respect for the individual person as another such (Mauss, pp. 18–19). Comte did not believe that the state was an entity, but neither did he regard the individual person as one. *Society* was the scientific entity, he argued, and it was precisely because previous generations had failed to see society as an entity that they had not been able to derive the laws of man's development (see Mandelbaum, 1971, p. 65). According to Comte, the individual person was only a recent abstraction from Humanity. *Humanity*, not the person, was the unit that exhibits regular behavior capable of study. "Society," he wrote, "is not more decomposable into individuals than a geometric surface is into lines, or a line into points" (see Nisbet, 1966, p. 59).

But even the new sociologists who regarded the basic scientific human entity as larger than the individual person and broader than the state remained uncertain as to what kind of unit it was. Ward's *social unconscious* resembles Freud's; it is the result of conservative and reproductive forces pitted against each other and against institutionalized moral and esthetic forces. The "creative synthesis" of opposing forces to which he attributed social structure (Mauss, 1962, p. 66) was taken from Wundt and parallels Herbart's dynamics and Freud's ego. (It is worth noting that when culture is objectified a theory of an unconscious results.)

Emile Durkheim thought he perceived a *social fact* that was supra-individual. This kind of entity, which would be studied by statistical analysis of large groups, was distinguishable from its mere manifestations within an individual. Within the individual a sociopsychology might find a distorted reproduction of the pure social fact which influenced the individual because it existed outside of him. Mass emotions were not simply a common denominator of individual sentiments (Durkheim, 1895, pp. 7–13). Religion, for example, was a creative synthesis from the meeting of many minds in the community and stood apart from individual creations (see Mitchell, 1968, p. 182). The social fact was "independent of the individual forms it assumes in its diffusion [among the members of society]" (Durkheim, 1895, p. 10). It was "found in each part because it exists in the whole, rather than in the whole because it exists in the parts" (Durkheim, p. 9). As Mitchell (1968, pp. 79–80) says, the "conscience collective . . . is a determinate system having a life of its own." According to Mauss (1962, p. 79), Durkheim regarded history and the state as too abstract for study: only social groups were concrete. In other words, Durkheim regarded the social fact as an actual object of study, and Julien Freund (1968, p. 11), representing the viewpoint of Max Weber, takes him to task for treating a hypothesis as a fact, much as later critics will complain that Freud reified such concepts as the superego.

Georg Simmel, on the other hand, according to Mitchell (1968, p. 110), "saw no unity that may be called *society* . . . he regards only the individual as real. . . . To describe society is merely to describe the social interactions of individuals; society only *seems* real." It would be a mistake, however, to say that Simmel regarded the individual as an entity. For, as Mauss (1962, pp. 76–77) points out, he took as his subject the abstract form of human relations as found in institutions such as the state, church, and economic system, and it seems to me that the entity he chose as the subject of scientific study is the *pattern of group interaction*, the behavior of dyads, triads, etc. (cf. Mitchell, 1968, p. 110). From our contemporary viewpoint, he would seem to have approached his subject as a transactionalist, in a fashion similar to some current schools of family therapy, with which he shares a preference for a patterned structure as the studied entity and a tendency to regard both the individual and the larger society as distracting factors.

Max Weber took a far more sophisticated, but also more equivocal, position on the entity under study. He did not believe in free-standing social facts or in a collective unconscious. And because he was not swayed by the hegemony that History exercised over prevailing German thought (Mitchell, 1968, p. 86), he did not visualize society as a developing organism in its own right (Freund, 1968, p. 76). This distinguished him from many other important social thinkers of the time, such as Spencer and Marx, who proposed an evolving entity underlying human society. Unlike them, Weber is said by Freund (1968, pp. 111 *ff.*) to have taken the individual person as the underlying entity to be studied. The specific subject of Weber's studies was *goal-oriented action* (Mitchell, 1968, p. 88). All the human sciences were perspectives on this conceptually neutral entity, each perspective selecting its way of categorizing the unit of study according to its own value-orientation. Out of the fluctuating and continuous web of social phenomena, Weber said, a specific social science picks out its proper entity by abstracting various "ideal types," which are clear pictures that exaggerate some regularity in social relations—for example, the ideal type of the modern capitalist or the bureaucrat.[6]

---

[6]An argument could be made that Charcot's "typical case" was a Weberian "ideal type." Certainly, Charcot's medical values helped select the subject that would eventually become the concern of psychoanalysis. Freud's enemies among academic psychologists resembled Weber's sociologist antagonists in their insistence that only a perspective-free, natural entity was truly

Although Weber wished to avoid postulating any natural entity other than the individual's action and accordingly developed a philosophy in which sciences did not have proper, natural entities as their subject, in the last analysis it seems to me that he actually worked with an entity similar to Durkheim's, namely, a social fact (for instance, the Protestant ethic) that gave meaning to the individual's actions. Indeed, it is this entitization of spirit that embroiled him in posthumous controversy over whether the Protestant ethic was an entity or an epiphenomenon (see Tawney, 1926). Weber was aware of the ambiguity of his analysis and explicitly warned against interpreting his use of spirit as a causal entity. But he may not have been able to carry off his relativistic philosophy in practice as well as he thought. Mauss (1962) says that "Karl Löwith has shown that through all these ideal types runs the theory of the over-all social process."

Despite the disagreement among sociologists about the sociological entity and the unhappiness that many, like Max Weber, would have felt about such a formula, I think Durkheim (1895) summed up the quest most bluntly:

> . . . social phenomena are things and ought to be treated as things. To demonstrate this proposition, it is unnecessary to philosophize on their nature and to discuss the analogies they present with the phenomena of lower realms of existence. It is sufficient to note that they are the unique data of the sociologists. All that is given, all that is subject to observation, has thereby the character of a thing. To treat phenomena as things is to treat them as data, and these constitute the point of departure of science [p. 27].

I shall argue that psychoanalysis was the culmination of a similar point of view in psychology.

PSYCHOLOGY

If students of mankind were agitated by a lack of clearly demarcated entities in an age when substances were no longer defined by tradition, students of the mind were even more desperate. It is characteristic of the times that a

---

scientific, although that requires it to be both nonconceptual and well defined! Because of his therapeutic value-orientation, Freud looked to them like a "rough-and-ready" technician (cf. Heilbreder, 1973; Titchener, 1929).

I think there is another important similarity between Weber and Freud. Weber recognized that all science fluctuates between the intuited individual and the general regularity of laws (see Freund, 1968, p. 39). Freud and Weber kept both regularized structure and single-event process in their systems. Those who could not accept this uneasy combination of arbitrary and nonarbitrary, static and dynamic definitions—such as Kierkegaard and Nietzsche (see Mandelbaum, 1971, p. 346), and the contemporary existentialists and experientialists—could never stomach that equivocation. The difference between Freud and Weber in this regard is, I believe, that Freud claimed a special dignity for the psychoanalytic perspective as being one in which the value-orientation was selected by the subject rather than by the observer (cf. Friedman, 1975c)..

Wundt or a Meynert begins his labors by lamenting that psychology has been altogether too subjective a discipline and some way has to be found to fasten it to an objective referent.

Of course psychology did not have to start from scratch. There was aphilosophic tradition to draw on. For instance, Locke's discrete ideas seemed to be reliable entities for psychology to deal with. But ideas were not the only entities in Locke's psychology. There was also the individual mind, characterized by the activities of association and imagination, which linked, distorted, and rearranged ideas. Locke's psychology portrayed mind as both a collection of ideas *and* a system of operations. Since Locke wanted to show how much of thought depended on experience, he called especial attention to the *collection* of ideas (which he felt could be traced to sensation). Hume and Kant, who were interested in the ways that thought did *not* depend on experience, preferred to discuss what the unitary mind *brought to* the accidents of sensation. Although this debate bore more on the philosophy of science than on any particular science, it served to remind fledgling psychology that the mind was not composed simply of Lockean ideas and that inasmuch as Locke's ideas were the *result* of a unitary mind working on outside stimuli, such ideas could not be considered the *elements* of the mind.

Those who, like Kantor (1969, pp. 120, 238), see in this development a naturalistic, individualistic British atomism suffocated by a theologically conditioned German unitary-mind theory, overlook the fact that, at least as regards the development of psychology, both trends were already present in Locke and any simple atomism was permanently ruled out by Hume. Perhaps the elaboration of these trends was influenced by the German fondness for abstruse theorizing. But it is clear that Locke had already postulated a unitary mind and that ideas, as he defined them, did not begin to account for its behavior. In effect, Locke's ideas were the burden of the mind: they were carried and rearranged by its current. For ideas to be explanatory units that would account for the functioning of the mind they would, unlike Locke's ideas, have to possess some kind of permanence and effectiveness.

That is precisely how Herbart's *Vorstellungen* differed from Locke's ideas. Unlike Locke's ideas, Herbart's composed the mind, at least partially. The whole mind was a result, or at least a *resultant*, of those parts and was not just their editor. They had continuity, a life history of their own, and a tendency toward self-conservancy, as one might expect of a regular entity (see Ribot, 1886, pp. 25, 38, 42). They were not food for the mind to digest, nor data for a unitary mind to process, but parts of the mind itself, involved in the digesting or processing. (Brett [1953, p. 532] says that Herbart made the elements do their own work.)

Squeezing a multiplicity into a unity generates paradoxes (see Boring, 1950, p. 254; Kantor 1969, p. 238). As Kantor disapprovingly notes (p. 141), all theories that recognize a unified mind underlying its diverse elements must have recourse to a mysterious unifier in the shape of apperception or else a pure ego as a common stage for all events (see also Andersson, 1962, p. 150); or , in later psychologies, a supremely governing function of attention. (Or, we might add, a metapsychological energetics). After we have described entities underlying a process, we are still always left both with entities and with process.

Nevertheless, Herbart indicated what kinds of entities might be the subject of a science of the mind. Andersson (1962) and others have shown that Freud was exposed to Herbart's ideas throughout his education. Perhaps Herbart's anatomy of mind helped Freud to construct his own. Herbart's (1891, p. 90) dynamic entities appeared to be striving and fighting, very much as Freud's ego, id, and superego often appear to behave. Herbart's influence might account for the fact, noted by Hartmann (1956, p. 278), that Freud replaced the "ideas" of traditional psychology with "purposive ideas." Hartmann (1956, p. 273), however, minimized Herbart's influence on Freud. Perhaps he underestimated the usefulness of an abstract, non-clinical perspective. On the other hand, Hartmann may be right: it is possible that many of the striking parallels between Herbart and Freud are more a matter of convergence than influence. It may be that any picture of a unified mind with real parts will necessarily look something like Herbart's. For example, it may be that such a theory will necessarily be a theory of conflict. Herbart himself seemed to think so, when he wrote that "without . . . antagonism, all the representations would constitute only a single soul" (see Ribot, 1886, p. 31). And, as I have suggested elsewhere (see chapter 16), any theory that treats parts of the mind as entities will perforce ascribe to them the self-conservancy that characterized Herbart's *Vorstellungen*.

Whatever influence on or anticipation of later psychology we can find in Herbart, he himself remained within the area of speculative philosophy because there is really no way to empirically identify the parts into which he divided the mind. Parts that cannot be identified independently, but whose sum equals the mind as we experience it, amount to a giant tautology. Toward the specific task of discriminating an objective psychological unit, Herbart contributed only the aspect of bare, unmeasurable magnitude (see Ribot, 1886, p. 27). But he did show what a theory that includes real parts in a whole mind might look like.

After Herbart had sketched his prospectus of how mental parts might function, what was still needed was to find some actual parts that actually did function within an actual, unitary mind. Objective entities still had to be discovered—items that were not arbitrary designations.

Fechner found one by comparing stimulus intensity with sensation. His discovery was naturally very welcome to Wundt, who, like others we have discussed, was troubled by the arbitrariness of psychological terms (Wundt,1873, p. 249). Fechner's entities—sensations, as they appear to introspection—could be real entities for study and not arbitrary perspectives on an amorphous matter of mind. But if the data of experience are already entities rather than manifestations of an entity, they should be sortable in and of themselves in a closed, defined system, without the aid of intellectual discriminations. Wundt (1894, p. 128) was perceptive enough to realize that this approach was not to be found in any other science. Psychology was the only science that would not study an underlying something by means of its appearances. For psychology, the appearance would constitute the something studied.

This gave Wundt his entities, but with them came a number of difficulties.[7] Many aspects of mind are not directly intuitable with that immediate definition and delimitation that make subjective sensations appear to be objective. Feelings, in particular, seem to form an amorphous and inexhaustible continuum (Wundt, 1897, p. 126). What is worse, feeling and volition seem to blend without objective borders into the whole of experience (see Brett, 1953, pp. 483–484; Wundt, p. 126), which suggests that all apparently separate entities of experience, including sensation, are merely arbitrary abstractions from a unified, unduplicable, constantly shifting panorama. This contradicts the notion that sensations are given in an immediate and nonconceptual fashion.

Moreover, Wundt realized that the study of the mind required *something* underlying appearances that would be illuminated by psychological studies (see Ribot, 1886, p. 191). If everything was blended together and in constant flux, the underlying something had to be a process. Accordingly, Wundt offered a process theory, which made use of apperception and creative synthesis as unifiers (see Brett, 1953, p. 485; Wundt, 1894, p. 128). As a result of Wundt's fidelity to the incompatible demands on his system, a confused picture emerged of a small aspect of mind composed of entities (sensations), which could be studied experimentally, and a large, overarching aspect of mind, which was not composed of entities and could not be studied experimentally.

Clearly, the entities that Fechner had discovered and Wundt had elaborated were in jeopardy as soon as one made an attempt to correlate them with the mind as a whole. Thus when members of the Würzburg school picked up the process aspect of Wundt's psychology, they were able to show that attitudes and set could alter perception, that judgments were arrived at without introspectively available sensory evidence, and that the examination of sensation did not enjoy any particular advantage over the cumbersome examination of any other aspect of mentation.

In the light of renewed attention to the whole mind process, mind "parts" again began to look artificial. Once more it was hard to find a respectable mental entity to study. For example, Titchener (1929) attacked the

---

[7]Behind all the difficulties was the logical problem of nonconceptual definitions. Titchener (1929, p. 100) later pointed out that it is insoluble and tried to make Wundt into a perspectivist instead.

intentionalists and act psychologists on the grounds that their discriminations were arbitrary, which was, in effect, Wundt's complaint about the
Würzburg school. The problem is that the man who sees the mind as a set of
frozen sections can always be shown to have aribitrarily carved them out of
a flowing process. He, in turn, can always retaliate by pointing out that the
words and categories of his rival, the process theoretician, are just as
arbitrarily imposed upon a fluid subject.

To save the "thing-ness" of sensations, Külpe sacrificed their supposed
immediacy and proposed as the subject of inquiry an underlying something
that had outside physical and internal mental determinants (see Titchener,
1929, pp. 127–128). After all, that *was* what Fechner had been dealing with.
The logical implication of Külpe's view was that psychophysics *uses* sensations as an appearance or outward sign of an underlying mental entity, which
today we might call a sensation-processing disposition. The challenge then
was to integrate that entity with other mental entities. But other mental
entities, as Wundt had realized, were a lot harder to define and would have
required something more than psychophysics to discover. Wundt (1873,
p. 250) hoped that these undefinable aspects could be studied by their
reflection in social forms, as in anthropology, presumably because, unlike
mind itself, *products* of mind are objectively definable in terms of entities and
can be studied like the data of any other science. To us, that hope appears
misplaced, in view of the very similar difficulties we have already seen to
afflict the more objective social sciences in their own field when they have to
justify *their* proper units, i.e., their objective entities.

But the fact that even physicists were hoping that sensations could be
made into objective entities for all sciences probably encouraged psychologists to keep looking to psychophysics for entities. Not only was Fechner's
discovery an unrivaled success, but, because of the influence of positivism, it
seemed peculiarly scientific. Psychologists thus suffered from a prejudice
about where entities could be discovered (see Titchener, 1929, p. 138).
Medical men suffered much less from this prejudice. Their freedom was
viewed with a kind of envious condescension by those who lacked it.
Titchener (pp. 250–259), for instance, regarded practical psychologies as
popular, technological contaminants of the proper science of psychology.
Heilbreder (1973, p. 250), while acknowledging the fruitfulness of Freud's
theory, attributes its successes to a lack of concern for scientific protocol. In
fact, what Heilbreder is referring to in this passage is simply the freedom
medical people have enjoyed to look for mental entities wherever they could
be found. Ultimately, Freud left Fechner's entities to Wundt and the acade-
micians, borrowed only Fechner's process theory, and proceeded to look for
entities of his own.

Before him, others, such as Meynert (1885, p. vi), tried to use brain
anatomy as a basis for nonarbitrary discriminations about the mind.
Meynert thought that the unified mental experience which had defied a

consistent analysis in Wundt's scheme could be differentiated in terms of spatial location of brain site and passage of nerve-excitation (p. 153). The entities that Meynert proposed consisted of subcortical patterns of connectedness among cortical sites. Those patterns represent what is constant in the mind, which he called individuality (pp. 16–18).

Except for a few oversimplified examples, Meynert (1885) did not empirically correlate these entities with known mental events. In fact, he did not believe it possible to establish them as empirical entities, since "one cannot estimate how closely an image is tied into the others" (p. 172), as would be necessary if one were to predict the empirical (behavioral) consequences of the patterns. Thus, he called individuality an artificial concept (p. 172). It is true that Meynert's terms and examples, as well as derivative theories of aphasia which Freud criticized, often make him sound like an atomic associationist. In fact, however, Meynert despaired of finding entities within the mind and ended up instead elaborating upon the whole-mind entity. In other words, what he offered was a process theory. According to Meynert, the brain functions along the path of least resistance to discharge (p. 194). In terms of emotion, mental events proceed in such a way as to avoid pain (p. 176). (Equating these two principles, he was forced to the strange conclusion that winning a lottery causes pleasure because it increases association pathways [p. 194].) But ease of discharge alone does not ensure pleasure. In fact, it can cause pain if the discharge is not along patterned channels (p. 190). We must regard Meynert's formula for the direction of mental process as the building of more and better discharge patterns.

By correlating psychological with physical events, Wundt had made one part of the mind (sensation-processing) observable (though he left the overall mental process a mystery.) Meynert made no such correlation: his "associations" were purely speculative and thus were not marked off in any precise, nonarbitrary fashion. He himself called them "artificial." His only real correlation was between brain functioning as a whole and mind as a whole. The only entity he focused on for study was the *process* of mind, fundamentally represented by a selective, self-regulating process of brain nutrition guiding association pathways and manifesting itself in the resulting structured discharge of nervous impulses.

Like so many subsequent process theories, including Janet's (and Piaget's), this theory says that mind is a process of differentiation and integration. For Meynert (1885, pp. 144, 159), as for Wundt, a wish was a successively modified reflex. In this respect, Meynert anticipated Freud's primary and secondary processes (Amacher, 1965, pp. 38–39), which incidentally shows that Freud's originality did not lie, as Jones (1953) believed, in the formulation of these processes. Andersson's (1962, p. 81) theory that Freud repudiated Meynert's system because it reflected an enthusiasm for brain anatomy while Freud was under the sway of more modern physiological concepts ignores the fact that, for all his anatomical diagrams, what Meynert had presented was a physiological theory. If Freud had stuck with Meynert, he would not have developed a brain mythology, but a Janetian psychology. As it was, Meynert provided a formal model of mind process, just as Herbart had provided a formal model of mind structure. What remained to be found was a part entity which could make investigation of the whole mind as empirical as Fechner's discovery had made investigation of sensation processing.

Freud's criticism of Meynertian aphasiology was as much a logical critique of his units as it was an empirical refutation of his physiology, and, in fact, the criticism had been anticipated by Herder (cf. Cassirer, 1957, pp. 32–33), who had noted that associations were not intrinsically separable from what they associated. Indeed, it seems to me fairest to say that Freud did not repudiate Meynert's theory at all, but recognized that a process theory without delim-ited part entities did not offer a foothold for empirical investigation. Meynert's theory was refined to describe the needed process aspects of the mind. But some empirically identifiable elements had to be added for the process to work on.

HYPNOSIS

The quest for these elements was vastly aided by a new understanding of hypnosis.

Mesmer grew up under the sway of Newton (see Walmsley, 1967). He wrote his dissertation on the influence of the heavenly bodies (sun and moon) upon animals. It early seemed to him that just as the moon affects the tides by gravitation, a similar influence must work on animate bodies. He pictured that influence partly along the lines of mineral magnetism, but mainly in the fashion of gravitation. He proposed a physical medium through which the force worked and gave it the same characteristics as Newton's fluid, since, like Newton, he could not accept the notion of action at a distance. Both Newton and Mesmer sought a mechanical causality, and neither was satisfied by a bare Law, although Newton was finally content to enunciate a bare law and became a god of science, while Mesmer could not hide his causal imagery and is today an object of ridicule.

Mesmer's theory preceded his practice: his theoretical interest was primary, utility secondary. Human cyclic phenomena gave early support for his theory (see Walmsley, 1967, p. 52), and he later cited episodic aspects of disease to demonstrate an ebb and flow within people. Only after witnessing a demon-stration of "magnetic healing" did he embark upon a practical career as a therapeutic magnetist. What he always hoped to attain was recognition as the Newton of biology.

But though the motion of the moon can explain a tide, whole-mind motion is not the sort of thing that can explain a change from sickness to health. While Mesmer's principle model had been gravitation and gravitational fluid, his theory of effects on human beings, especially on the nervous system, came to be based on mineral magnetism (Mesmer, 1779, p. 32). He had to develop a rudimentary part-theory of the mind, drifting away from Newton, who did not need to dissect gravitational bodies. Mesmer's picture of the uniform alignment of magnetized parts was an early model of adaptation. (It is a forerunner of the synthetic function of the ego. Mesmer also postulated two forces—a responsive and suppressive principle—which can be compared to Freud's two instincts.) As I understand it, animal magnetism is primarily something within the animal that orients his parts, but it can be secondarily charged, depleted, and communicated to other animals. Mesmer (p. 31) maintained that animal magnetism is that property of an animal that renders it *liable* to the action of heavenly bodies. Sensitivity of the parts of the body to the synthesizing influence of the heavenly bodies is provided, according to Mesmer, so that the harmonious functioning of the animal is not left to chance (p. 32).

Although a vague image of tidal flow within the nerves accompanied the gravitational model, Mesmer did not ask what the elements are that can be harmoniously or discordantly oriented by animal magnetism. Therefore, his explicit theory was a whole-mind theory, or a process theory, in which synthesis depended on outside stimuli plus responsiveness to those stimuli. Implicitly, when the organism was not tuned to its governors, there were unspecified parts which could become disorganized.

Benjamin Franklin headed a French Royal Commission of eminent scientists that investigated Mesmerism. The Commisison has often been criticized for stubbornly refusing to recognize the theoretical challenge and promise of what it observed. A study by Quen (1976) is useful in this regard, since it focuses on the problem of the inertia of scientific theory when confronted with palpable opportunities for advancement.

That this blindness was no simple prejudice is shown by an examination of the report of the Franklin (1785) Commission. The Commission decided that it would be impossible to evaluate Mesmerism by studying claimed cures. It has often been faulted for this crucial exclusion without sympathy for the fact that at the time, etiologies were poorly established and accurate diagnostic criteria were minimal. One can only admire the Commission for recognizing that the natural course of illness was largely unpredictable, especially among the as yet undefined "nervous" diseases for which Mesmerism was chiefly used. Indeed, the Commission was able to call in support Mesmer himself, who fully recognized the weakness of proof by cure and claimed to have much better evidence for his discovery.

The Commission did examine therapeutic effects if they were immediately evident. What they begged off from was evaluating long-term benefit. But the Commissioners readily acknowledged as well known that the mind can influence the body, and they cited in evidence what we would now call autonomic effects as well as healing of illness. They then set about reproducing Mesmeric effects by simple suggestion, which acquits them of the charge of ignoring the phenomena after discrediting the theory. Their final criticism was not that Mesmerism was ineffective, but that, besides being based on an invalid theory, it used the powers of the mind in an unhelpful and potentially dangerous fashion. That conclusion, of course, was presumptuous in view of the fact that long-term outcomes had been excluded from the study. The Commission judged a priori that violent treatments such as Mesmeric convulsions should be used only sparingly, and in this respect they sound like some recent ethical critics of electroshock. Furthermore, one can raise an eyebrow at a society that countenanced extensive bleeding and purging but shrank from a convulsion that leaves the body intact. Nevertheless, one can scarcely consider as a scientific blunder a well-reasoned report establishing Mesmerism as a manipulation of imagination and of the nervous centers that can affect somatic processes and the course of illness through specified psychosomatic mechanisms, and warning that it could be dangerous if used without caution.

The Commission worked with the limited concepts available. Its members could speculate about the influence of concentrated "attention" on bodily processes and sensations and could even imagine how that influence, acting on the diaphragm, could produce a convulsion. But they had no appropriate disease entities in view, no definition of states of consciousness regularly related to each other, no notion of mental constants whose variables could be manipulated by experimentation. Their field of observation was a commonsense continuum of thoughts, feelings, and actions.

The members of the Royal Commission were in need of entities to examine. On witnessing the chaos of group Mesmerism (accompanied by piano music!), they wisely observed that "too many things are seen at once for any of them to be seen well." When they came to experiment upon themselves, they tried to separate at least autosuggestion from Mesmeric influence, and for this critics have chided them, saying that it destroyed the suggestibility required by the technique, as though it would have been possible to investigate, or even to think about, something so ill-defined that it is at once an imposed influence and a spontaneous activity, a perception and an illusion. People had always known that the mind influenced behavior and had long known that it influenced the body. What the Commission showed was that the Mesmerists had offered nothing new to work on. The only new units to think about or to correlate with one another were the operator and the subject, considered as fluid-communicating bodies. Those were the allegedly real entities presented to the commission; and since they were fictions, it is hard to see what its members could have done with them except to dismiss them.

The profitable study of hypnosis began with a shift of focus from the act of hypnotism to the hypnotic subject, for the purpose of dissecting his mind. Puységur adhered to the fluid theory, but he specified that it acted specifically on the mind and more specifically on thought and will (cf. Walmsley, 1967, p. 146). He further isolated a state of mind in which thought and will were altered, which he designated as "artificial somnambulism" (see Ellenberger, 1970, p. 71). Puységur had more confidence than his predecessors in a mental theory because his experiments dealt with a multitude of phenomena that could all be seen as manifestations of a familiar state of mind resembling sleep.

The Abbé Faria shifted the focus even further toward the hypnotic subject. He did not accept the fluid theory, chiefly because he wanted to pay attention exclusively to the subject's attitude, his receptivity (see Goldsmith, 1934, p. 181). The shift was from a two-person theory to a one-person theory, a shift some recent theoreticians have deplored (e.g., Wolstein, 1976). But it was a necessary step toward the localization of a psychological entity (as opposed to the sociological entity of a hypnotist–subject pair). The receptive and non-receptive attitudes postulated by the Abbé paralleled Mesmer's responsive and suppressive forces. But the Abbé was looking for an explanation of them within the organism, a shift that corresponds to Freud's shift from the traumatic memory to a repressed wish.

The work of Bertrand, on the other hand, gives us an idea of how Mesmer's own theory would have evolved after the inevitable obsolescence of the theory of fluid transmission (see Janet, 1925). Bertrand placed the emphasis on the magnetizer's will. He retained Mesmer's two-body theory in the form of an interpersonal psychology. He also carried Mesmer's inquiry further into the anatomy of the subject by implying that in the normal person variables finer than just total synthesis (health) and disorganization (disease) could be studied.[8] But in general the price paid for dispensing with Mesmer's pseudophysics was the postulation of an influence—the will—which is even vaguer than a fluid. (Schopenhauer [1847] liked it precisely because it was such a general concept.)

Elliotson, a clinically minded physician still believing in the fluid medium of transmission, defined the target organ as the brain (see Goldsmith, 1934, p. 205): The patient's will was affected by the influence of the fluid on the subject's brain. The usefulness of this belief was that it served to conceptually dissect the hypnotized subject, explicitly isolating the brain as significant and implicitly implicating whatever in the brain was responsible for will.

---

[8]Mesmer's student, d'Eslon, had told the Royal Commission that "there is but one nature, one distemper and one remedy" (Franklin et al., 1785).

James Braid tried to specify which *parts* of the mind were involved. He allowed that the power of suggestion was the external force, but he readily abandoned theories of mechanical transmission (to the horror of Elliotson for whom that was tantamount to abandoning science). Unlike the Royal Commission, Braid did not have to turn away from Mesmerism as soon as its physical force was discredited, because he was able to construct a hypothetical explanatory system within the subject. He simply set aside the two-person system as no longer of interest. Hypnotic phenomena revealed not "a physical influence from without but a mental delusion from within" (Braid, 1846, p. 191). (Again, this parallels Freud's shift from the seduction theory to the fantasy theory of hysteria.) Braid characterized hypnosis as essentially a state of concentration of nervous energy on an idea, and that continued as the paradigm for hypnosis right through to Janet and Breuer.[9] Braid's contribution, then, was more than a careful and critical examination of the effects of hypnotism and a demonstration of its dramatic use for anesthesia. He also elaborated a rough theory of the mind, emphasizing ideas as parts and a flux of energy that could be more or less invested in those ideas.

This theory was then expanded by Durand de Gros (see Bernheim, 1884, p. 114). Durand's prophetic theory was that afferent nerves require not only tonic central innervation, but also specific attentional impulses. He suggested that hypnosis removes those attentional impulses, after which a simple, homogeneous hypnotic stimulus will concentrate most of the brain's nervous energy in one area. Impressions entering through the half-open door of hypnotism release so much pent-up energy that they awaken a dormant part of the brain and lead to an exaggerated physical response. Durand argued that the suggested idea concentrates available energy wherever the hypnotist desires.

Ambroise Liébeault continued this inquiry into the processes of the mind. He emphasized the desynthesizing effect of hypnosis. He suggested that what happens in hypnosis happens because associations are in the hands of the hypnotist (see Bernheim, 1884, p. 117).

Durand's theory, boldly, and Liébeault's, more subtly, were theories of parts of the mind interrelated by energic distributions. The emphasis, however, was not on the parts but on the energetic *processes*.

It is instructive to reflect upon these beginning stages of dynamic psychol-

---

[9]Braid (1846, p. 191) also noticed that in hypnosis body and mind interact. It is interesting that this skeptical medical man could respect hypnosis only if it fit into a chain of causation between mind and body. He did not care much about the nature of the external force involved (it was just something that concentrated attention), but he cared very much that there be a chain of causation within the body translating the idea into a physical outcome, so that, for instance, hypnosis could be thought of as applied to phrenological capacities, and he liked to picture suggestion as specifically designed to alter a known physical function which can then take proximal credit for the cure (see Bernheim, 1884, p. 112).

ogy. It is so much easier, when confronted with a complete, complex "machine" like the Freudian system, to picture it as a simple copy of mechanical or electrical models than to trace its evolution out of a specific problem. The early medical hypnotists had to find some way of describing a situation in which acuity could be deliberately enchanced or suppressed—in which people could be deliberately made to use the whole of what they potentially know, think, and will, or alternatively, only a portion of it. That the whole-mind process can be concentrated or dispersed is a very modest, low-level theoretical transcription of the observed events. And yet the formulation is already a metapsychology; it is already an account of the fate of a limited fund of energy. It all seems to follow from the assumption that the brain, or at least the nervous system, or perhaps simply a mind, underlies hypnotic phenomena.

Process, however, is only half the lesson of hypnosis. Despine paid attention not just to the predominance of a suggested idea, but also the peculiar kind of activity that it manifests. He held that *all* nervous centers possess, in accordance with the laws that govern their activity, an intelligent power without ego and without consciousness. He proposed that in pathological states such as hypnotism, these centers might be responsible for acts similar to those ordinarily initiated by the ego, whereas in normal states automatic and conscious centers are bound together and act conjointly (Bernheim, 1884, p. 122).

Instead of this group of executives, Bernheim proposed a hierarchy of impulses: lower levels of the mind, he said, tend to react to evidence automatically with belief and evoked sensation, and hypnotism frees such automatisms from the review and control of higher, more skeptical centers (Bernheim, 1884, p. 137). (This is the theoretical line that Janet followed.) Bernheim also allowed that in the ordinary course of their lives some people, whom we would now call suggestible, are less governed by higher processes of mental review than others.

Up to the time of Bernheim's work, the evolution of thought about hypnotism was something like this: the variables were gradually accepted as psychological rather than physical (at least by those who did not regard them as mystical). The items involved came to be seen as the hypnotizer's will and the subject's trust or credulity. The focus of theory then shifted from the interpersonal to the intrapersonal, and the phenomenon of hypnosis became usable as a tool for conceptually analyzing the mind. The mind was seen as working in two ways, not necessarily sharply distinguished from one another (Bernheim, p. 149).

The analysis of the two ways the mind worked varied somewhat. Primarily, a distinction was made between a completely synthesized mind and a fragmented one, i.e., one in which not all of the mind's powers or stores of information were applied at once. (This was the tradition of Braid, Durand, Liébeault, and Janet.) This distinction implied the existence of real parts of the mind, which could be summoned up or ignored. At first, the main debate was whether the distinction was vertical or horizontal. Either the whole mind was vertically split by hypnosis, with higher functions concentrated like a movable spotlight on only a few items of mentation (Braid, Durand), or else automatic levels of the mind were freed by hypnosis from higher ones (Despine, Bernheim, Janet). In either case, the nature of the entities that were encompassed (automatisms or exaggerated, conscious emphases) was only vaguely described, and the main explanation was in terms of types of mental processes or functions.

The major empirical problem that these theories faced was the phenomenon of amnestic suggestion for delayed, organized response and the hypnotic teaching of segregated, complex abilities. Braid had remarked that a second language could be buried in a hypnotic level. Clearly, such a thing as language was neither primitively organized nor restricted in focus. A structure as complicated as normal thinking was separated here from ordinary use.

Prosper Despine, especially, realized that there were theoretical implications of the fact that organized activity of the sort we associate with purpose and intention could be elicited by hypnotic suggestion without a whole mind (conscious) purpose or intention (Bernheim, 1884, p. 122). Therefore, in Despine we find not just a new kind of mind process, but two new kinds of entity in the mind, namely, a segregated, effective, variably expressive purpose and active and intelligent part-mind "centers." Despine thought of these centers as lower forms that normally fuse with a higher, conscious one. Bernheim, on the other hand, pointed out that automatic activity could be just as sophisticated and, indeed, as temporarily conscious as any other form.

An important issue was at stake. Bernheim could have allowed for different modes of processing, but he was not comfortable with a division of the mind into actual entities, that is, into parts which had their own semi-independent, effective activity. A memory could be latent, but it could be effective only when it became actual, i.e., only when it joined the whole mind, however narrowed the whole-mind process might be at the time. Therefore, even when suggestion blunted critical faculties, the whole mind, including consciousness, was seen as functioning when it was functioning at all.

But then Bernheim was confronted with another major empirical puzzle— posthypnotic suggestion. Here an intention seemed to be active on its own and without reference to the intention of the whole mind. To get around this, Bernheim was forced to adopt a strained hypothesis, namely, that a person carrying out a posthypnotic suggestion keeps dipping into his somnambulistic, automatized state in order to consciously sample the buried instruction, and emerging quickly out of it again so as to give the appearance of being unaware of the suggestion. Beaunis quite rightly dismissed this as begging the question (see Bernheim, 1884, p. 157).

Bernheim's quandry was not unique. Even today an analyst such as Roy Schafer (1973a, 1973b) finds it difficult to allow for the existence of part-mind entities, probably for the same reason as Bernheim: entities seem too anthropomorphic. In the spirit of Bernheim, Schafer will not allow for what in Freud parallels Despine's unconscious but intelligent centers. He wants the whole mind to be responsible for its actions, and he echoes Bernheim in describing deeds as actions taken by the whole person.

Charcot's great service, albeit an inadvertent one, was to pick up the emphasis Durand and Despine had placed on the *action* of a split-off piece of mind (which the Nancy school had neglected in favor of the process that accounts for splitting). Durand had tried to account for suggested ideas in terms of pent-up nervous energies. Despine had postulated intelligent centers that were uncovered by hypnosis. Charcot, precisely because of his exclusive and rather dogmatic identification of hypnosis with pathology, elaborated on the *effects* (both physical and mental) of a hypnotic type of idea. He thought he had circumscribed a configuration of effects in terms of a disease, which put him in a position to study this new kind of idea as an agent having its own special kind of effect. Thus we can see that Bernheim's appreciation of the normality of suggestion was not the only reason for his disagreement with Charcot. Bernheim was also prejudiced by his process orientation, which was so far from being empirically based that he had to strain the data in order to uphold it. Charcot's blindness to the universality of suggestion, on the other hand, although it may have distorted both his theory of hysteria and his understanding of mental processes, allowed him to recognize a *part* of the mind as a thing to be studied and to begin to trace its natural history.

As soon as observers began to think in terms of part-entities and whole-entities of mind, hypnosis became an experiment that could fasten psychological terms to objective fact (cf. Freud, 1924, p. 192, who said that hypnosis made the unconscious for the first time subject to experiment).

As regards the whole mind, exemplified in its process, hypnosis (like Fechner's psychophysics) offered a quantitative discrimination: the degree of "dissociation." The mind could be more or less unified. "Attention" was an extremely controllable and, therefore, objectively variable function in hypnosis, unlike Herbart's and Meynert's predominant mental aggregates, which were merely pseudonyms for the mind's unity or net outcome. Herbart's apperceptive unity was a way of imagining parts of the mind being held together. Meynert's pleasure-pain principle was a definition of an invariant mind process. But in hypnosis, the mind, on the one hand in a state of attending to something in itself and, on the other hand not attending to it, diagrammed radical differences in mentation, each with a rich empirical outcome. These states were visible variations of some underlying, constant process. The phenomenon of dissociation, which uncovered a graduated process of synthesis, was the discovery that inspired Janet.

By the same token, if one had empirical evidence that the mind is more or less holding something together, one perforce had empirical evidence of what is or is not being held together. Now the opportunity at last arose to find real parts of the mind, that is, parts that were not arbitrarily defined.

While the Nancy school used hypnotism and suggestion to demonstrate varying degrees of mental synthesis and a bundle of mental entities that were dealt with by that synthesis, Charcot's study of hysteria characterized the synthetic process more sharply and the mental entities more subtly. In the first place, Charcot added another dimension to mind process by distinguishing between pathological and normal processes of synthesis and by establishing regularities in their consequences. Freud (1888a, p. 42) acknowledged this contribution when he said that Charcot had picked hysteria out of the chaos of nervous diseases. Adding to Bernheim's universal personal categories of sleeping and waking and the interpersonal categories of the power of suggestion which had been anticipated by Braid and Bertrand, Charcot supplied the personal variables of hysterical and nonhysterical minds as a device for studying the synthetic process.

This particular category brought medical respectability to the study of hysteria.[10] What is more important, Charcot's work suggested that it might be possible to *describe* the synthesizing process, i.e., the *medium* through which ideas were handled, an opportunity that Freud (1888b, p. 80) was quick to grasp.[11] Furthermore, by correlating them in a medical fashion with variables in the patient's life, Charcot was able to give the mind-parts—the ideas—a more definite and elaborate history than was available to those who simply engaged in suggestion.[12] This further served to establish the parts as real entities.

Charcot's most important contribution, however, was to demonstrate the variety of expressions an idea could display when handled in various ways by the mind process. Specifically, ideas could be manifested in obviously goal-directed behaviors, general somatic status, and ideational awareness.

---

[10]Jones (1953, p. 227) said that Charcot made hysteria a medical matter. Boring (1950, p. 698) noted that Charcot obtained medical acceptance of hypnosis by "mislabeling" hypnotizability as a hysterical symptom.

[11]The Nancy school's skepticism of Charcot's findings repeated the general attitude of the Royal Commission toward hypnosis (cf. Ritvo, 1970, p. 203; Stewart, 1967, pp. 25–26). The Royal Commission reduced mesmerism to "contact, imitation and imagination." Although both Bernheim and the Commission had grounds for skepticism, they allowed their interest in interpersonal factors to distract them from the opportunity to explore the intrapersonal.

[12]Andersson (1962, p. 58) points out that Freud and Charcot both saw that suggestion uses the *patient's* meanings, while Bernheim saw only the meanings imposed by the hypnotist.

Charcot thus laid the groundwork for an entity that was not just a conscious idea, a latent conscious idea (an unconscious idea), or a force determining a resulting idea, but something that could take the form of an ordinary idea *or* some other form altogether. In other words, he pointed to an entity underlying "ideas." Another way of putting this is that Charcot provided a least-arbitrary discrimination of the data based on a relationship between physical and ideational phenomena, just as Fechner had done for sensation.

This initial separation of physical from conscious aspects of an "idea," triangulating an underlying entity, was the starting point of psychoanalysis.[13] Even the Breuer and Freud depiction of an idea as a foreign body in the mind—a parasite—was anticipated by Charcot [see Andersson, 1962, p. 54].) To integrate those part-entities into the whole-mind entity and to amalgamate structure with process was to be the path of development of psychoanalysis (see chapter 15). Freud's theory is distinguished from others by abandoning neither process nor structure aspects.

SUMMARY

Nineteenth century thinkers were concerned about the problem of natural entities. They had difficulty describing the achievements of physics in terms of real objects and difficulty describing that science without reference to entities. Biology pursued the quest for natural entities and was rewarded with Darwin's theory, which made life a kind of organism, with species its part-entities. Sociologists had far more difficulty, but made numerous attempts to confirm the objectivity of some particular unit.

Psychologists experienced the greatest difficulty in establishing empirical entities. Locke's ideas were not sufficiently substantial; Herbart's representations were not sufficiently empirical; Wundt's sensations were not sufficiently representative of mental processes; Meynert's mental process was not sufficiently dissectable. But Herbart did offer a model of mind parts, Wundt, a

---

[13]See, Freud (1924, p. 193), Jones (1953, p. 397), Stewart (1967, pp. 25–26), Wyss (1966, pp. 49, 450). Despite this agreement about its importance, commentators sometimes miss the significance of the detachment of an idea from its physical expression in hysteria. Wyss (pp. 61, 83, 102) believes that Freud simply borrowed from physics the theory of a body with a quantitative charge and transposed it to the realm of ideas. Stewart (pp. 25–26) regards the physical-mental correlation in hysteria as a first problem for Freud to resolve, rather than as a technique for isolating a natural entity. Although Jones (p. 397) regarded the notion of a quantity separable from an idea as an original contribution that psychopathology had made to psychology, he believed that the cornerstone of Freud's theory was the distinction between primary and secondary process, thus identifying Freud's hypothesis more with its account of process than with its structural elements.

model of empirical parts, and Meynert, a model of the processing of mind parts.

What these models needed was an empirical device that would analyze the whole mind into parts. It was only gradually realized that hypnosis was just such a device. By the time of Charcot, students were no longer preoccupied with the relationship of hypnotist to subject and used the phenomenon to make various kinds of distinctions about the contents and process of the mind. It remained for Charcot to find, through hypnosis, parts of the mind that were entitled to be treated as genuine entities because they had ideational, volitional, and physical manifestations and a life history of their own. The stage was set for Freud to relate them one to another, trace their life history, and systematize the process which handled them.

14
Freud's Foothold

THE ISOLATION OF A PSYCHOLOGICAL ENTITY

STUDIES ON HYSTERIA (Breuer and Freud, 1893-1895) investigated an entity consisting of the memory of a trauma. That entity is enmeshed in a larger, whole-mind process of synthesis or discharge. The entity within the mind was later portrayed as a repressed wish. But even before thus refining it, the theory emphasized its distinctness an an entity. Repression, i.e., separation from the rest of the process, was hypothesized even before wishes came on the scene. Breuer proposed, and Freud (hesitantly) accepted, that the separation could be explained in terms of weakness of the synthesizing process. That was the basis of Janet's complaint of plagiarism. But Janet was more one-sided in emphasizing process rather than the segregated entity.[1]

It is illuminating to consider the brief moment in the development of

---

[1] Janet (1919, pp. 235-239) conceived of the "idea" as primarily a command, propelled by instincts. Higher grade, deliberative functioning requires more energy than lower grade functioning. If enough energy is supplied, ideas are synthesized with each other; if energy is deficient, they are more multiform. Janet's accusation that the Freudian catharsis is simply a rewording of his own conception of reversing dissociation (Jones, 1915, p. 381) ignored the difference between a phasic theory, in which an idea, conceived of as a thing, may in a sense be eliminated, and a process theory, in which the idea is adjusted or melded into the whole. Freud's theory ultimately combined both aspects.

Freud's theory between the time he postulated a noxious entity and the time he replaced it with a conflict of wishes (1892–1895). During this time, a conflict of wishes was implicit in Freud's account. But he did not spell it out. As Jones (1953, p. 285) says, the "idea of a volitional repression dawned gradually." In "Studies on Hysteria," Freud was content to describe the relationship of noxious ideas and ego as one of incompatibility, even though his understanding of it as an instance of "moral cowardice" showed that he *could* have defined it more precisely. With regard to "Studies on Hysteria," what is important is the incompatibility – the unassimilability – the separateness of the idea, rather than the reasons for the barrier. Whether the traumatic idea is inadmissible to consciousness because it is simply frightening, because it is embarrassing, or because it is self-defeating, does not seem to matter. What matters is that it is kept separate from other mental processes. Indeed it is a very formal treatment of the problem and not at all the poetic *Sturm und Drang* search for conative conflict that is sometimes imagined to have been Freud's point of departure.

Freud's (1892–1893) order of priorities can further be seen in the casual way he used the notion of the "distressing antithetic idea," which he had borrowed from Charcot, who had borrowed it from Reynolds (see Andersson, 1962, p. 54). (It is also to be found in Herbart [see Ribot, 1886, p. 41].) In his very early writings, this term marked the place that would later be occupied by the whole history of intrapsychic conflict. According to Freud's use of the concept, assumptions that future events and one's own efficacy will be satisfactory are always surrounded by thoughts that, instead, unfortunate events will occur (antithetic ideas aroused by expectations), and one will perform incompetently and shamefully (antithetic ideas aroused by intention). These dismal ideas are normally balanced by the predominant, healthy ones, but in neuroses they may be intensified for a number of reasons, including an unexplained lowering of self-esteem.

As regards antithetic ideas aroused by expectations, the consequences of intensification are just what we would expect, namely, "a generally pessimistic frame of mind" (Freud, 1892–1893, p. 122). Obviously, the concept of antithetic ideas would never have been introduced solely to reach this conclusion, which explains pessimistic thinking by a propensity to think pessimistically. What Freud found useful is the notion of an intensified antithetic idea aroused by *intention*. With regard to such ideas, Freud saw two possible neurotic effects. If intentions were combined with intensified antithetic ideas, the result would be a "distrust of the subject's own capacity," manifested in a *folie du doute*, though Freud added, as though he were simply elucidating the distrust, that the antithetic idea subtracted from the volitional idea and caused "weakness of the will" (1892–1893, p. 122).

But the whole discussion was really designed to introduce those intensified, antithetic ideas produced by intention, *which were dissociated from consciousness*. Such an idea "can put itself into effect." It "establishes itself as a *counter-will*" (Freud, 1892–1893, p. 122; see also Breuer and Freud, 1893–1895, p. 92). It was for this explanation of the apparently counterpurposive activity of his patients (Breuer and Freud, p. 95) that Freud welcomed antithetic ideas.

Whereas the formula concerning antithetic ideas produced by expectation is a simple tautology, the formula for antithetic ideas produced by intention is almost sleight-of-hand. On a common-sense level it is mildly persuasive until we ask what precisely the antithetic idea *is*, and what, in fact, it is antithetic *to*. In the formula for self-doubt, the antithetic idea is a pessimistic expectation, and what it is antithetic to must be another expectation. I suppose one can continue to picture the antithetic idea as a pessimistic expectation, even while it "weakens" the will, on the grounds that hopelessness diminishes striving. But what kind of idea is it that, being put into effect, produces an opposite *striving*? Surely that is not just an expectation. When an expectation is fully in effect, it is simply a fully believed expectation. If, on the other hand, an idea is such that its realization is a purposeful deed or will, then it must have been a volitional idea to begin with, antithetic not to an expectation about one's ability, but *antithetic to a volition*.

That would do well enough for Janet, who assumed that an idea of any kind is primitively an imperative. According to his account, therefore, a dissociated idea would naturally function as a command. However, once Freud had distinguished between volitional and nonvolitional ideas, this path was not open to him. Therefore, to call a dissociated idea an autohypnotic suggestion would not explain whether and why it suggested an action or instead a hallucination. I apologize to the reader for belaboring what has been obvious, even from the vantage point of psychoanalytic theory a bare few years later. I dwell on this equivocation between expectations and wishes—this unconcerned ambiguity about expectant ideas and volitional ideas—because if we can see an area where Freud was lax, this may teach us which matters he was more attentive to. For at least three years Freud entertained the hypothesis that a *doubt* about one's ability, if unchecked by other thoughts, naturally turns into a *decision* to fall. This, I submit, is not the kind of formula that an investigator would propose who was currently focusing on the nature of intrapsychic conflict, and in the next chapter I argue that it was a stage of theory making in which the wholeness of the mind was just about to give way to its division into parts. During this period, Freud's theory included ideas that arose from mere logical possibilities; and it included a will that really sprang from nowhere. Such evidence suggests that his initial interest was to outline a system that handled separate, interfering ideas and purposes, whose origin was at that time of secondary importance[2].

It was only after the separateness of the noxious idea was firmly established

---

[2]This probably also explains why Freud as a therapist continued practicing suggestion, despite his allegiance to Breuer's cathartic technique, a fact which has puzzled historians (e.g.,

that the logic of the situation demanded that the antithetic idea be treated as seriously as the main idea. At this subsequent point, the theory finally concerned itself with the origin of the "counter-will."

I certainly do not mean to deny that empirical findings affected the theory's development. Freud's first experiences, beginning with the story of Anna O, told him about memories, and he only gradually came to hear about wishes. The volitional history of antithetic ideas took a while to reach his ear. But when it did, there was a slot in his theory waiting for it, and conflict and censorship were already in place to serve their purpose. Hartmann (1956, p. 277) accepted Freud's assertion that he disowned the hypnoid hypothesis because he was thinking motivationally. I believe that we have reason to add that he was able to think motivationally because he already had spent some profitable time thinking structurally.

Despite a superficial similarity between Freud's first formulation of antithetic ideas and Janet's hypothesis, there is an important difference which reveals Freud's characteristic approach. Janet was concerned that wherever the ideas came from, there was more or less synthesis, because there was more or less synthesizing power. Freud was concerned that wherever the ideas came from, they maintained a certain separateness, despite their involvement in a common process, and that meant that the process itself could be seen as arising out of certain entitized systems.[3]

On the other hand, where information about the history of pathogenic

---

Andersson, 1962, p. 90). The theory was not ready for the practice. Breuer's discovery was first used to *isolate* the entity. The nature of the entity was of secondary importance. Therefore, treatment was first directed toward exorcising the entity. The theoretical implications of abreaction per se were only gradually worked out and only then did Freud rediscover it for his practice. These theoretical implications have to do with visualizing the traumatic entity as acting from within—rather than against—the mind process, i.e., making it a part of the mind rather than a foreign body. Only after that was established theoretically, could one reasonably use suggestion to make the patient do a piece of psychical work rather than to relieve symptoms directly (Freud, 1925a, pp. 42–43). This is the reverse of Jones's rule (1953, p. 51) that new techniques lead to new theory. No doubt that happens, but the situation is not always as neatly empiricist as that.

It is true that Freud said that he abandoned hypnosis and suggestion because of therapeutic failures (1925b, p. 27). General experience suggests, however, that therapeutic failures do not necessarily by themselves discredit methods of treatment that are attractive for other reasons. Freud himself adds other reasons for having abandoned the techniques, e.g., his feeling of inaptitude for hypnosis and discomfort with the deliberate dishonesty of suggestion.

[3]Pollock (1976, p. 137) holds that Breuer indulged in more psychological speculation than the modest and empirical Freud, partly because Breuer was more removed from the practice of psychotherapy. If that were so, one would have expected Freud to immediately center his thinking upon abreaction, which had been Breuer's main clinical discovery. As we have noted, he did not, and I have tried to show that he did not do so precisely because he was not an "empiric," but a speculator—a theory builder. Breuer wrote the theoretical chapter of "Studies on Hysteria," but my contention is that Freud was, if anything, more theoretical than Breuer, more systematically following the theoretical needs of the moment and temporarily ignoring other empirical problems (e.g., the difference between expectations and desires among antithetic

ideas was lacking, as in phobias and some neurasthenias, Freud, like Janet, discussed those disorders in terms of process theory—synthesis and working-over of libido in the psychic process (Freud, 1895b, p. 193). (The discussion anticipated current process theories, such as that of Gendlin [1964a].) Further empirical evidence was necessary before a comprehensive theory of symptom-formation could be propounded. Freud used this temporary mystery about the psychogenesis of phobias and neurasthenias to flesh out the process aspects of his theory, and for that reason he was probably less impatient than he otherwise would have been to find a psychogenesis for those neuroses. Later, having analyzed process into developmental phases, Freud was in a position to look for the ways in which his memory entities could be transformed into various syndromes. Those entities—now perceived as persistent wishes and fantasies—could at last be correlated with at least some of what he had for a while considered to be nonideational neuroses.[4]

We have noted that the original entity—trauma, idea, wish, wishful fantasy—was chiefly marked by its polymorphous manifestations in both physical and mental areas. (It is not accidental that "vicissitudes" has become the shibboleth of psychoanalysis.) As variations on a given entity were worked out, the forces that affect it were also spelled out, beginning with an ego that at first resembled an institutionalized *amour propre*, but became progressively more specialized. It was a story of a dischargeable entity versus obstructive forces, and as this story was elaborated, it became an account of wishes that were more or less modified by institutions, or by other wishes, and by internal representations of reality. Thus all psychic phenomena could be described as the expression of the wish-entity undergoing modification from its environment (cf. Wyss, 1966, pp. 104–105; Ricoeur, 1970).[5]

The notion of compromise formation, which was finally set down as a

---

ideas). When he later picked up the question of where oppositional ideas come from, it was as much a theoretical next step as it was a result of experience. Freud took this step not just because he listened to his patients, as Stewart (1967, p. 33) makes it seem. The origin of antithetic ideas was something that had to be looked for. According to the way the concept of the antithetic idea was originally formulated (imprecisely), the memories that Freud had already heard from his patients were irrelevant. Even the drift away from the hereditary theory of dissociation, which we can see in the discussion of antithetic ideas, was not just a result of the empirical evidence that some very able people were subject to hysteria, but resulted also from the new availability of an alternative to the hereditary theory, namely, the foreign-body depiction of trauma, which gave dumb clinical experience its tongue and allowed it to speak to Freud. Janet also listened to his patients. But his theory made him less interested in how normal ambivalence and the strength of distinct wishes affected the hypnoid state.

[4]In saying this, I am declining to accept at face value Freud's own statement (1925a, p. 26) that a psychotherapeutic impasse is what led him to attribute a physical rather than a mental causation to neurasthenia and phobias. After all, he had allowed paranoia a mental causation, despite what must have been very limited therapeutic success.

[5]E. B. Holt (1915) was probably the first to recognize the central significance of the wish in Freud's system; he compared it to atomic theory (p. 47). But precisely because Holt treated the wish as a process and not as an entity, his beautiful essay misinterpreted Freud along the lines of

paradigm, was implicit in the theory from the beginning. Freud viewed mental phenomena as expressions of a wish-entity interacting with something else. The ultimate definition of the wish is left to the patient as he free-associates in the course of a psychoanalysis. That is why Ricoeur calls psychoanalysis a *semantics* of desire. In this respect psychoanalysis ends up examining an entity which, in a sense, defines itself. The theory states how it functions in the system, but its precise description is (ideally) the patient's[6] (see Friedman, 1975c).

This, then, was Freud's answer to the nineteenth century problem of how we can make a nonarbitrary definition of elements. One can readily see how it differs from other attempts, such as Marxism, positivism, and historicism, although it approaches most closely to the last.

THE EMPIRICAL FUNCTIONING OF EARLY PSYCHOANALYTIC THEORY

In Freudian theory the mind is regarded as an entity that can be divided into other entities. The whole mind is a divided entity that is characterized by principles of conflict and synthesis (see chapter 15). That much was anticipated by prepsychoanalytic philosophy, which, in Germany, had often referred to the synthesis as apperception, and which, as in the voice of Herbart, had said that if the parts are real, their sharing of the same stage must be represented by conflict. A theory that ignores conflict will emphasize unity at the expense of examinable parts—it will be a process theory, and its variables will tend to be restricted to the categories of more and less, as in Janet or Meynert. Such a theory may satisfy a philosopher, but it will provide little empirical foothold.

In order to say something particular about process, one must be able to trace the impact of external events through the mind process. In order to do that, one must find the parts of the mind that carry that influence and trace the history of those parts; and that requires an identification of parts or entities.

Right from the beginning, Freud's theory generated those parts. The first such entity was a memory of a specific kind. There are an infinite number of memories one might single out. What makes Freud's "memory" a *thing* is the fact that it shows itself in various ways, physical and mental, and is demarcated from the flow of experience by conflict—a demarcation that announces itself in the resistance of the memory to consciousness.

---

functional psychology; that is, he interpreted only the process aspect (anticipating Pribram, 1976). See also, Ritvo (1970, p. 202), who says that all mental process amounted to wish-fulfillment in the "Project for a Scientific Psychology."

[6]Note, in this regard, Andersson's (1962, p. 58) point that Freud and Charcot differed from Bernheim in relying on the patient's meanings, rather than defining the mental happening entirely in terms of the hypnotizer's meanings.

Corresponding to the memory are specific events in a person's life, which can be looked for empirically. Thus Freud's entities enabled him to make specific discoveries about important events in the lives of his patients. His theory spotlighted traumas, pointing to events which could be studied for lawful correlation with psychological states. One example is the correlation of childhood seduction with hysteria, which was shortly after disproved—an empirical fate that could never overtake such purely philosophical theories as Herbart's. The hunt for the trauma was an empirical investigation inspired by a theoretical construct (which had been suggested by an empirical phenomenon). It is not simply because Freud "listened to his patient" that he knew that there was something to hunt for.[7] Others had listened, too, but with no entity in mind to give reality to an underlying regularity which could be studied; they had been at a disadvantage.

Next Freud examined the array of clinical symptoms in traditional functional syndromes and tried to organize them as manifestations of a memory entity undergoing different processes. The result was the theory of defenses. But he was unable to locate the memory entity in several illnesses—neurasthenia and the phobias—so he turned his attention to the process that *deals* with the entity. He postulated a prepsychological phase of the entity that could be expressed either in representation or in anxiety, depending on whether it was taken up and worked over by the mental process or not. Worked over entities, he postulated, could be represented psychologically and then gratified or frustrated, or they could be worked over less and segregated by dissociation (Freud, 1894b).

This energic description of the process in turn implied a redefinition of the psychological entity as a wish. It was the wish that had many embodiments and constituted an empirical entity, whose "vicissitudes" could then form the basis of an empirical study (cf., Stewart, 1967, p. 136). After Freud had established the wish as an entity, he was able to use dreams to examine the process that deals with wishes.[8] This in turn led him to an empirical correlation between dream phenomena and conscious associations.

Freud had already realized the possibility that age variations could account for different processing of similar entities. Traumas at different times in life were handled in different ways. Now that the entity was a wish, he could look for the way age affects desires. This set the stage for the discovery of regularities in psychological (sexual) development, which in turn inspired him to hunt for the disguised wishes that had eluded him earlier (fantasies, etc.).

---

[7]Freud (1925a, p. 21) said that "Studies on Hysteria" "hardly went beyond the direct description of the observations," but this was the modesty of a man whose higher level theory was so elaborate as to obscure the novelty of its elements.

[8]Amacher says that only when Freud saw that wishes were involved did he become interested in dreams (cited by Ritvo, 1970, p. 202).

LESSONS FOR THE PHILOSOPHY OF SCIENCE

Philosophers of science search for the criterion of better and worse among theories and for the reasons why theories are changed. Empiricists demand of a truly scientific theory that it be possible to invalidate it or its component parts (Popper, 1974). But they cannot agree on what the validation and invalidation procedure consists of (Lakatos and Musgrave, 1970).

Thomas Kuhn (1970a, 1970b) wrote that confirming and disconfirming are procedures that relate particular descriptions to general theories, rather than relating either to reality per se. During intervals of what he calls normal science, a theory is assumed, and what is confirmed or disconfirmed are ways of making the theory square with the data: he calls this "puzzle-solving." At certain periods in history, anomalies arise that create dissatisfaction with the theory. Kuhn's special point is that it is extremely difficult to say what differentiates an as yet unsolved normal puzzle from an anomaly. Whatever it is, Kuhn claims that it is not a signal that forces the abandonment of the old theory. What dislodges a theory is something in the evolution of thought that allows the data to be seen (at least by some observers) in such a different way that the discrepancy does not appear to be satisfactorily solvable by the old theory, but makes it look like a normal puzzle for a new theory.

According to Kuhn, the new theory requires a new Gestalt. It cannot be simply described in terms of the old theory, and ultimately it cannot actually be proved. It is conveyed to those who are receptive as a new way of solving puzzles, and when it becomes the standard and accepted theory of its science, that science will continue to be taught by example and practice of solving puzzles in the fashion prescribed by the prevailing theory.

Psychology, according to Kuhn, has not matured to the point at which evolving paradigms are generally accepted by the scientific community. Accordingly, schools of thought multiply, the scientific community never shares a consensus on a paradigm, and there is no unilinear development of theory. This observation seems distressingly apt. But Kuhn may have drawn too sharp a line between preparadigmatic and paradigmatic thought.[9] In general, the *genesis* of a paradigm is what is least clear in Kuhn's account.

Psychoanalytic investigation, whatever one may feel about its "scientific-ness," has certainly been more empirical than, for example, Herbart's specu-lations, and even its critics often take a good many of its terms as simple facts of the mental world that present puzzles which the critics feel better able to solve. If we could show that Freud's theory is an example of scientific paradigm formation, we might have a better idea of what a paradigm is.

We have seen how Freud was able to pose for himself problems in the

---

[9]At the end of his career, Popper (1974, p. 981) has come to believe that the demarcation between "metaphysics" and science must be roughly rather than sharply drawn.

genesis and interrelationship of symptoms by postulating an underlying entity with variable modifications. That postulation allowed him to divide the continuum of psychological phenomena into supposedly natural categories. There is little point in thinking about an arbitrary collection of adjectives, but one can profitably think hard about real things. One can hunt for influences on them and discuss regularities in their interrelationship. Therefore, Freud (1900) very explicitly set out to deal with the mind as though it were an ordinary *thing* in the world: "The unconscious is the true psychical reality; *in its innermost nature it is as much unknown to us as the reality of the external world, and it is as incompletely presented by the data of consciousness as is the external world by the communications of our sense organs*" (p. 613). Just five years earlier, Durkheim (1895), trying to lay a foundation for sociology, had written that "social phenomena are things and ought to be treated as things" (p. 27).

This must be an early phase of every science. We would never have advanced to quantum physics without it. If a photographic plate had no more claim to "thing-ness" than the shadows in the laboratory, nothing significant would have happened in that laboratory. Of course, the underlying reality of these "things" is what the science progressively defines. Their ultimate nature cannot be shown at the start of the investigation. But the assumption that they have an underlying reality is the *basis* for observation.[10]

This is also true in psychoanalysis (see Freud, 1925a, p. 57; 1900, p. 613). The underlying entity, whether it is instinct representative or raw, primitive wish, is known only by its manifestations, as are all objects or entities. But it is by viewing the mind as composed of such entities (and as itself being such an entity) that Freud was able to pose puzzles and propose solutions. As with all paradigms, one shows the entity by the way one specifies important puzzles and goes about solving them. With this in mind the psychoanalyst seems much less arrogant when he says that the truths of analysis can be perceived only by those who submit to it. That is how paradigms are taught and shown.

The Freudian revolution was the discovery of psychological entities that could be seen in multiple guises. Investigation of those entities constituted what Lakatos (1970) called a research program, which culls data and regularities out of emotional life.[11] Perhaps we can generalize and say that scientific

---

[10]When Freud does what all scientists do, i.e., attributes "thing-ness" to what he is studying, Wyss (1966, p. 450) mocks him as reviving Aristotle's entelechies.

[11]Lakatos's description of scientific theories as research programs ought to attract the interest of psychoanalysts, who are continually attacked for the supposedly unscientific suspiciousness with which they view doctrinal modifications. Their parochialism can be defended on the grounds that psychoanalytic theory is a special way of looking for empirical data, and its essence (about which, of course, there might be disagreement) has to remain identifiable in order to carry out that project. Those who feel that the notion of orthodoxy is totally inappropriate implicitly regard scientific theories as patch-works gathered from empirical data. This difference from

revolutions and paradigm formation consist in the discovery of new types of entities or objects. That would be consistent with Cassirer's (1957) view that thinking advances by finding conceptual intermediaries between ourselves and experience, concepts being the epistemological counterparts of objects or entities.

Since a concept supposes an entity that underlies an infinite array of phenomena, no formal definition can be given it without tacitly including the notion of "thing." One cannot make a list of the properties of an actual thing because they are infinite. There are, for instance, innumerable tests that will never be run on it and potential reactions to circumstances that will never occur. To describe it, one can only mention a few of its properties and indicate that they belong to a thing. Accordingly, one illustrates the wish by its "vicissitudes" (or, as Freud said, the unconscious by the data of consciousness). One cannot set out a formula for it, and as Freud pointed out, it is in this respect exactly like any other natural thing.[12] Speaking poetically, we could say that every natural thing has a hidden aspect just as the mind has an unconscious. But in the first place, "hidden" should not be taken as literally as it was before Kant. And in the second place, the unconscious (insofar as it can be "made" conscious) is itself the manifestation of something still more "hidden" (for instance, an instinct representative).

THE TIMING OF THE PSYCHOANALYTIC REVOLUTION

Why did the Freudian revolution occur when it did? In chapter 13, I suggested that thinkers of the nineteenth century were generally in quest of natural entities. But entity-hunting is the universal procedure of science (see chapter 16). What was special about the nineteenth century?

---

conservative attitudes may be analogous to the difference between a road map and the game known to children as a treasure hunt. A road map is put together piece by piece from assembled bits of isolated information. A treasure hunt is a sequence of puzzles, the solution of one leading to the discovery of the next and, ultimately, to a sought treasure. Errors in a road map can be corrected on the spot by a mere erasure and substitution. Tampering with the clues of a treasure hunt before it is completed will destroy it. The most intolerant critics of orthodoxy may be viewing as a road map something that is more akin to a treasure hunt.

[12]Freud wrote that in the light of what was learned from hypnosis, the unconscious no longer remained a philosophical conception, but became something actual, tangible, and subject to experiment. Elsewhere (1925b, p. 217), he wrote, "Analysts, too refuse to say what the unconscious is, but they can indicate the domain of phenomena whose observation has obliged them to assume its existence." He explained (1925a, p. 57–58) that the natural sciences do not begin with clear-cut definitions. Terms are explained to begin with by reference to the realm of phenomena from which they are derived, and are made clear and constant by progressive analysis.

1. Possibly, we must give some credit to the sheer accumulation of philosophical sophistication. Issues of mental atomism and holism, although debated from very early in Western thought, had been worked on more and more specifically, and the experience of coping with more and more difficulties may have rendered models increasingly adequate.

The picture of philosophy as *advancing* may bring a smile to the reader's face. The alternative view is that styles of thought are not strictly comparable with each other and thus cannot be viewed as more or less advanced. The virtue of the relativistic approach is that it highlights the central, organizing principles prevalent at a particular time, rather than viewing earlier beliefs as rudimentary attempts to do what later thought finally accomplishes.

Foucault (1971) has presented a very compelling picture of a shift between the sixteenth and the twentieth century in the sort of thing the intellect sought—the kind of thing that was felt to constitute knowledge—that is, the form it was felt an explanation should take. Foucault argues that the various sciences are born out of their contemporary premises, rather than being inspired by the lure of their "objective" subject matter. In his view, the subject matter itself is a creation of history. Thus he sees nineteenth century organicism as a decision to seek hidden, invisible realities that structure appearances and provide the individual with identity.

Foucault presents his own rather difficult theory of the significance of psychoanalysis and the human sciences. But if we were to take just so much of his general attitude as bears on our approach, it would suggest that psychoanalysis arose in the nineteenth century because the nineteenth century was *sui generis* an age of entity-hunting. If I can be forgiven a crass and oversimplified way of putting it, the mind had to become an entity on its own, not because there was no longer a Divinity for it to mirror, but because mirroring or representing something was no longer of interest—it was no longer felt to be explanatory.

The idea that thinking unaccountably reaches toward totally different goals in different historical periods is a difficult one to accept. In its favor are the evident profusion of man's creative works and the open-endedness of history. But we will certainly not accept it until we have tried every way to demonstrate continuities. Thus, Foucault has been attacked by Piaget (1970) for ignoring the transformational relations between one system of thought and another. Hayden White (1973a, 1973b) tried to reduce Foucault's creative, new epistemes to the sequence of changes determined by the forms of human grammar, thus unifying the history of ideas, in effect, as ringing the changes on possibilities of predication. What is particularly interesting to observe is that Foucault's earlier epistemes bear a striking resemblance both to Piaget's (1951) prelogical stage of infantile thought and to Lévi-Strauss's (1966) "savage thought." Although Lévi-Strauss strongly sides with Foucault against the discrimination of thought as more or less advanced, *his* defense of "savage thought" includes the finding of *similar* styles in our current sciences. All of this strongly suggests that however different their styles of approach, the various epistemes have been trying to attain at least something of the same goal. To me, Cassirer's (1957) picture of the progressive objectivization of knowledge most satisfactorily describes what all of these writers have brought forward as evidence. That is why I think that we cannot do without the factor of increasing sophistication over time, in the sense that men do gradually realize, for instance, that arbitrary classifications will never take on a natural endorsement no matter how long pursued.

2. An argument could be made that eighteenth century secularization diluted the explanatory dynamism previously supplied by theology and thereby created a need for a new way to understand the direction of natural processes. The disintegration of the unified, medieval world-view that distressed the 19th century sociologists (see chapter 13) might have inspired a search for new natural units or objective entities (as it clearly did in sociology)—entities which would contain their own principles of development. That would set the stage for the elaboration of psychoanalytic theory which, I have tried to show, is a combination of process and entity conceptualizations.

3. Since psychoanalysis is a theory concerned with individual persons, one would have to consider what in the times favored a focus on the individual. The mind-body problem, for instance, seems to become an issue in history when the individual is the center of the intellectual and artistic stage, as, for example, in Classical Greece. We have seen that the nineteenth century was preoccupied with the organic. To some extent organicism or historicism *is* just such a focus on the individual. The organicist bias also favors theories that balance static and process elements.[13] In this way, sociopolitical developments may have helped to pave the way for psychoanalysis.

4. Nineteenth century successes in the physical and biological sciences probably made the human sciences seem more likely to pay off. Pribram (1976) has cited the sudden advance in brain anatomy and neurophysiology which, in turn, may have been influenced by improvements in microscopy, etc. I believe that the so-called Helmholtz school offered less a formulation of a structure or model than a declaration of confidence that organic events could be explained.[14]

5. Functional illnesses had to be isolated before constants could be found

---

[13]Gedo and Wolf (1976, p. 43) give credit to the German philosophers—Kant, the Romantics, Schopenhauer—for making the humanist perspective scientifically respectable.

[14]Galaty (1974) has shown that the members of the Helmholtz school were not trying to reduce organic phenomena to physical categories, but were inspired by the belief that organic and specifically neurologic phenomena were subject to the *a priori* Kantian categories of explanation. Cranefield (1966) adds further evidence that these thinkers were not simply reductionists.

within them. That separation itself required the accumulation of knowledge about organic illnesses to set them off from functional.

6. All of the foregoing influences probably converged upon a specific, intrapersonal understanding of hypnosis and hysteria, which is generally recognized to have been the launching pad for psychoanalytic theory. Given that understanding, certain problems were set for the investigators: What determines the outcome of a suggestion? Is it a predisposition? What is a predisposition? How can one conceptualize a mind with divisions that are customarily thought of as mind-like? In other words, how can a unitary mind be decomposed into parts?[15] Furthermore, Breuer's experiment raised questions about the special effects of a certain kind of ideo-affective expression (catharsis) on subsequent behavior. The paradigms then current did not suffice to elucidate his observations.

7. The most popular account is the one about which we should be most cautious. If my argument is correct, it is a mistake to say that psychoanalysis imitated models of mechanical success in physics or economics.[16] In the first place, as Mandelbaum (1971) has shown, the nineteenth century was not exclusively a mechanistic age. Second, mechanism itself can be viewed as a paradigm for a deterministic system rather than as a model in its own right (cf. Galaty, 1974).[17] I have suggested that Freud did not start with a picture of a machine, but with the notion of entity, and in pursuing it he built a system which in some respects, but only some, could be viewed as machine-like. He himself contrasted his outlook with mechanical views (1924b, p. 216). The ways in which current biology influenced Freud should not be oversimplified. Of course, terms and concepts in one branch of biology are likely to resemble those prevailing in others, as, for example, in Darwin's and Jackson's theories that increased nerve energies require discharge (Andersson, 1962, p. 152). It is not with this trivial currency of terms that we are concerned, but with the empirical functioning of the theoretical system. Meynert's psychology was also set in similar terms and produced little of empirical value.

PERSONAL DETERMINANTS OF THE REVOLUTION

Why was Freud the one to develop the new paradigm? There are, first, some obvious and general reasons. Besides boundless ambition, which Freud

---

[15]Ellenberger (1970) has pointed out that there was a burgeoning of poly-mind theories at the time.

[16]See, for example, Arlow (1975, p. 520). Amacher (1965, pp. 73, 81) also feels that, except for repression, Freud's basic picture of mental functioning up through 1895 was borrowed from his teachers. I believe that the "exception" marks a radical revision. If I am correct, Bernfeld (1944, p. 349) exaggerated the theoretical source provided by the school of Helmholtz.

[17]The Helmholtz school presented more of an epistemological than a mechanistic program. On the relationship of mechanism to the general project of explanation, see Meyerson (1930).

possessed, the particular first step in the new science required far more theoretical elaboration than would any subsequent observations. And Freud was a towering figure as a theorist. Very few men have shown such a combination of specific creativity and attention to theoretical demands (cf., Jones, 1953, p. 384). Still fewer have combined that theoretical competence with the kind of empirical interest that Freud had; rather they would have become speculative philosophers. Gedo and Wolf (1976, p. 13) say that Freud considered getting professional training in philosophy. Jones (1953, p. 384) even suggested that Freud used the "Project for a Scientific Psychology" to work off excess philosophizing zeal that would otherwise have undermined his clinical investigation. Surely, one of the reasons for Freud's discoveries was that he lived in an age that respected science more than philosophy and that tended to direct him toward empirical investigation.

Besides the matter of intellectual prestige—that is, aside from where it seemed that the great problems would be solved—Freud probably had his personal reasons for restraining his speculative bent. Jones (1953, p. 384) believed that Freud held a tight rein on his speculative urges until he had found an empirical fulcrum. Freud may have felt that without the iron discipline of observation, his ambition and his speculative powers might run away with him (see Wittels, 1931, p. 80).

But what is more specifically involved in his discovery is that Freud had a structural turn of mind and a structural focus of interest.[18] The author of On Aphasia (1891) is clearly the man to find new entities, and thereby a new paradigm. The kind of mentality required for the discovery of psychoanalysis is the same kind that would perceive that " 'Perception' and 'Association' are terms by which we describe different aspects of the same process. But we know that phenomena to which these terms refer are abstractions from a unitary and indivisible process. We cannot have a perception without immediately associating it" (Freud, 1891, p. 57). Freud recognized that there was an *entity*, of which perception and association were facets or aspects.

Freud concerned himself with systems or structures as the ultimate objects of study. (This, I think, is the explanation of the Freudian trait that Jones [1953, p. 97] described as going directly from particulars to general concepts, or universals, without passing through the realm of the statistical.) Early in his career Freud recognized that perception was no entity and could not be studied unless one found an entity that was reflected in perception. Until that was done, perception was an arbitrary abstraction.[19] Later, he turned the

---

[18]It seems to me unlikely that such a strong bent was a mere second choice stemming from a feeling of inadequacy in physiology, as Bernfeld (1949, p. 42) has suggested. Another suggestion by Bernfeld (1949, p. 41) is that Freud's direction was inspired by his technical inventions (see also, Trosman, 1976, p. 230). But the inventions could as well be used as evidence of his structural point of view.

[19]Andersson (1962, p. 69) believes that Freud's initial attacks on Charcot's and Meynert's

same insight to account in building psychoanalysis: an affect or an idea is not an entity and cannot be studied unless we can find an entity of which both are reflections. Only then can their relationship (and others) be studied.[20] When Freud encountered in his seduction hypothesis the same disappointment that the Royal Commission (see chapter 13) found in hypnosis (both were the result of "imagination"), Freud, unlike the Commission, was ready with an underlying entity—fantasy—to carry the investigation further.

THE FUTURE

The question of origins is doubly significant for psychoanalysis. In the first place, to the extent that we understand the currents upon which psychoanalysis floated into history, we can have some idea about the direction in which today's tides are carrying it.

In the second place, an understanding of the origins of psychoanalysis can itself influence our next theoretical moves. If, as George Klein believed (1969, p. 48), Freud's drive theory was primarily developed to unify mind and body, rather than to put entities into process, we may seek to replace it with a supposedly purely psychological theory. If, like Gill (1976, pp. 95–96), we hold the constancy principle to be really a neurological principle, rather than an aspect of "thing-hood," we may invite neurophysiology to revise it. If we believe, as does Holt (1976, p. 162–163), that Freud borrowed a mechanical preconception from Helmholtz and Brücke, we will not let the same preconception impose itself on our new theories, although if we saw those scientists as deliberately conforming to logical criteria of explanations as both Galaty (1974) and Cranefield (1966) do, we might not be in such a hurry to restructure.

The critiques of Peterfreund (1971) and Schafer (1973a, 1973b) both hinge upon the attribution of a mechanistic genesis to psychoanalysis and an unscientific anthropomorphism to the machinery. If one viewed the matter differently and, for instance, regarded a degree of anthropomorphism as inevitable in a partializing theory of a whole mind, one would be more cautious and self-critical in presuming to be able to dispense with such blemishes (see chapter 20).

---

brain localization theories were merely examples of the way the older anatomical enthusiasm was being modified by the newer physiological way of thinking. Although such an influence may have been at work, the nature of Freud's criticism was at least as logical as it was physiological, and, as it applied to Meynert, it merely recapitulated an older argument of Herder's (see Cassirer, 1957).

[20]Bernfeld (1951, p. 30) points out that the phylogenetic principles which Freud utilized in his Petromyzon study he later applied to the ontogenesis of mind, which I take to show that Freud realized that structure can be perceived in process.

Of course, as with all historical perspectives, if there is a bias in our current view of the origins of psychoanalysis, that bias itself reflects the spirit of the new age. The reason for the endless animadversions against "the mechanical model" to which we are treated by many theoreticians is that mental entities are in disfavor. Entities are thought to be natural only if they are neurophysiological. Among therapists there is a turning away from structural components of theory of the mind and a noticeable comfort and feeling of virtue when dealing with process.

Perhaps this is a reaction to a previous overemphasis upon structure, or maybe it is a simple continuation of the battle between vitalistic and static modes of thought. In any case, the signs point to an abandonment of the quest for entities within the mind (see, for example, Schafer, 1973a, 1973b). If my suggestion about paradigms is correct, this means that few new paradigms for a theory of the mind are likely to emerge in the near future. There are exceptions: Holt (1976), Klein (1969), and Bowlby (1969) have offered possible candidates. A major contender is the Piagetian "schema." Piaget (1951), like Fechner and Freud, has found an entity with multiple expressions and has traced it through a process of development. What is particularly exciting is the way he has interdigitated process with entities in the very definition of a "schema." In chapters 24 and 25 we will see if paramount needs and affects can be included in the picture. We will examine Kohut's mixture of entities and process in chapter 26.

In the meantime, it is likely that some psychoanalysts will go on with the puzzle-solving problems of Freud's old system, while others look for entities of a largely psychosomatic nature. (Rubinstein [1976, pp. 261–262] insists that new models of psychoanalysis must be compatible with physiology, by which he means that mental entities must be potentially physical entities.) Such entities surely can be discovered. A new kind of affect entity might gradually be elaborated as the workings of the limbic system are explored. A new kind of idea entity may emerge from the relationship between action systems and receptive systems, such as Pribram (1971) is developing. The development of new consciousness entities via cerebral disconnection experiments can be witnessed in the debate about how to describe the association of right and left brain functioning (Margolis, 1975; Puccetti, 1975). In each case, we should be cautious about equating these entities with Freud's concepts of affect, idea, and consciousness. We might consider the possibility that these discoveries represent the founding of a new science, or the picking up again of an old neurophysiology, with observable entities slightly different from those dealt with by psychoanalysis.

We should study that possibility attentively. The furniture of the mind, which Freud's theory delineated, has become such an accustomed part of our intellectual scenery that we are likely to think of it as a perceptual given, which it certainly is not. We are unduly disposed to treat clinical data as theory-free observation. There is a powerful tendency to believe that what Freud was doing with his theoretical speculations was enriching and embroidering his clinical discoveries. To balance this optical illusion, which is the likely fate of any theory that successfully establishes useful entities, the background and history of Freud's theory provides a necessary counterweight. It shows us the theory as a *way of perceiving* the separate items in mental life that we can make discoveries *about*.

SUMMARY

An empirical psychology requires not only a description of the processes of mind but the isolation of mental entities that are real. Real entities are not arbitrary collections of adjectives, but instead correspond to regularities in the behavior of several types of phenomena, which can be conceptualized as the manifestations of the entity. Freud built his theory on such entities, concentrating at first on keeping them distinct, in contrast to Janet, who concentrated primarily on the over-all synthesis within the mind. By building a psychology upon objective entities within the mind and proposing a synthesizing process that deals with them, Freud was able to satisfy the nineteenth century demand for legitimate, natural entities.

With such entities and a process to deal with them at his disposal, Freud was able to organize functional, mental illnesses in a nonarbitrary fashion and divide the continuum of mental life in a way that selected certain aspects of a person's life as especially and specifiably consequential. Empirical regularities suggested hypotheses, and the hypotheses suggested the existence of further empirical regularities. This procedure might be the usual format for scientific revolutions. Finding new entities may correspond to Kuhn's emergence of new paradigms.

Of the many aspects of the nineteenth century that would be likely to promote the psychoanalytic revolution as thus conceived, the popularity of mechanistic scientific models is not the most relevant. Of the several aspects of Freud's mind that would be likely to promote such a revolution, a gift for structural thinking seems the most relevant.

Mental entities are not currently fashionable. Those who do not dispense with entities altogether tend nowadays to look for physical ones. In applying the findings of physiological researchers, we should be wary about substituting their very similar terms for the terms of psychoanalytic clinical observations, since analytic data are not simply percepts, but are arrangements of entities selected by Freudian theory.

15

Construction of Freud's

Paradigmatic Theory

F reud was a theoretician. He did not leave us merely a collection of observations, or a poetic image, or some ways to understand sick people. He left us a theory of the mind. Of course his ideas can be viewed as reflexions of the paradigms and prejudices of his times, or as perceptions of clinical problems confronting him. But to understand his work as a theory of the mind, we must identify the theoretical tasks that he accepted, as manifested in the way the theory grew. Only when we have understood the theoretical requirements that the system responds to, can we compare Freud's terms with those of other theoreticians (such as psychologists of meaning and intention) because only then is there a common language in which to compare them, namely the language of problems.

I hope to show that one such important problem that Freud grappled with was how to treat the mind as an entity without ignoring its internal diversity and conflict. One can view his theory as a series of efforts to come to grips first with conflict and then with unity, and after establishing unity, to place conflict in it again, and subsequently to re-establish a unity. It is a dialectical process in that the final outcome gets its meaning from, and does not replace, the dialectical switch-back that constituted its growth, so that the final terms cannot be completely understood by themselves.

FIRST MOVE

"Studies on Hysteria" (Breuer and Freud, 1893–95) is so rich in hypotheses that it is hard to name a psychoanalytic concept not foreshadowed in it.

Nevertheless, there is one overriding paradigm that pervades the enterprise. The authors find a conflict at work in the production of hysterical symptoms. And that conflict is described as a conflict between the person and his environment.[1] That kind of conflict is the easist to imagine. The mind is thought of as an organism and the environment as a noxious impingement from outside it (a trauma). It is a conflict between two whole entities, the mind and the world. But although, or because, that kind of conflict is so easily imagined, it does not explain hysteria. The results of their therapy show the authors that the trauma continues to exert its influence throughout the life of an hysteric, by being carried *within* the mind in the form of a memory. But the conflict is still generally thought of as between a whole mind and its environment. The memory is, so to speak, an offending piece of the outside world, imbedded in the organism. The authors are explicit on this point:

> But the causal relation between the determining psychical trauma and the hysterical phenomenon is not of a kind implying that the trauma merely acts like an *agent provocateur* in releasing the symptom, which thereafter leads an independent existence. We must presume rather that the psychical trauma—or more precisely the memory of the trauma—acts like a foreign body which long after its entry must continue to be regarded as an agent that is still at work . . . [p. 6].

It is an analogy that will later be just as explictly modified by Freud. But it is important to recognize that, although almost all the evidence that would require its modification is available to the authors even at this stage, the first effort to describe a conflict emphasizes the trauma to a whole organism from outside evils.

The terminology reflects that vision. Hysteria is supposed to result from the "incompatibility" of certain "ideas" with the "ego." In its broadest sense, "ideas" means what has been planted in the mind by the outside world. The "ego" means the person, and "incompatibility" stands for the trauma inflicted by the outside world on the person.

RECOIL FROM THE FIRST MOVE

But as the explanation is worked out in detail, these terms take on other significance. "Affect" is added to "ideas," the "ego" comes to represent

---

[1] A brief outline by Rapaport (1960a, pp. 18–19) characterizes the development of Freud's theory in terms very similar to mine. Rapaport's purpose differs, however, in that he wishes to trace the role played by external reality in the theory, whereas I am interested in tracing the form of conflict generally.

something more like a person's moral standards, and "incompatibility" becomes an increasingly complicated and mysterious affair. The outside source of ideas becomes less obvious, as Freud notices that their sexual significance seems unusually prominent. He tries to hold to the original formulation, appealing to the common wisdom that, for whatever reason, sexual matters are often sensitive, and so ideas (experiences) in that area can easily be traumatic. And he essays a few other explanations, such as the effect of sexual ignorance at the time of exposure. But it is easy to see that the motivational aspect of sexuality diminishes the aspect of outsideness or implantedness of ideas that made their conflict with the person easy to grasp.

Then there is the curious concept of the "antithetic idea" (p. 89). Here is an idea that is *born* within the mind. Even while proposing it, Freud tries to hold on to the outside-inside description of conflict. An external danger is represented in the mind by an idea antithetic to a person's wish. And "it is this idea which puts itself into effect" (p. 92). It puts itself into effect in the form of a "counter-will." But although this rather desperate strategem of having the idea put itself into effect obviates the necessity of placing conflict among parts of the person, rather than between him and circumstances, it anyway allows a "counter-*will*" into the theory, and not just an antithetic idea. By referring to an antithetic idea, Freud was able to keep a conflict between the wishes that define a person and the impressions that are foisted on him. But having arrived at a counter-*will*, the unity of the person comes into question, and the ego that represents him is now less self-explanatory.

Finally, the "incompatibility" between the ego and the idea, which has been in jeopardy from the first acknowledgement that part of the mind retains the external trauma, must ultimately come to mean something less decisive than simply "damaging to the mind." After all, any noxious stimulus, by definition, is in some sense incompatible with the organism. This incompatibility is supposedly eliminated by connecting the idea and its affect in consciousness. What further incompatibility tends to prevent this ordinary resolution of an ordinary incompatibility? (Painful memories do not always lead to hysteria.)

There can be only one answer: if the incompatibility between organism and environment is not resolved, it must be because of incompatibility *within* the organism. But that is a difficult notion to grasp. In order to keep the situation as similar as possible to the easily imagined picture of an environment traumatizing an organism, Breuer proposed a variable part of the mind which functions *as though it were part of the outside world:* the hypnoid state carries the impingements of the environment. Even after being forced to divide the mind this way, it is still possible to view the hypnoid state as a kind of Fifth Column representing the outside world, the way it might appear in parlour hypnosis. As a concept, the hypnoid state can be seen alternately as, on the one hand, a representative of the outside world lying inside the person and, on the other hand, a second mind within the person. It thus serves as a bridge between an outside-inside conflict and an inside-inside conflict.

But precisely because of its double service, the hypnoid state can be challenged from both ends. As a carrier of external trauma, it must explain why the trauma is not dealt with normally. And as one of two minds, it must explain how they both represent a single person (as in the production of symptoms). The answer to the first question is that associative pathways are not available to drain off the noxious energy represented by the idea with its affect. But in answer to the second question, it is proposed that both the segregated idea and its affect maintain all kinds of connexions with other pathways.

How can these views be harmonized? The results of therapy suggest that it is *consciousness* of the idea and its connexion with the affect that is required for elimination of the internal carrier of the trauma. But that does not explain *how* the hypnoid state can be both connected and dissociated from the rest of the mind; it merely shows that it is. The traumatic "foreign body" carried in a second state of the mind affects the rest of the mind, but not in a way (becoming conscious) that would eliminate it. The relation of the two states remains obscure, and will remain obscure as long as the second (hypnoid) state is treated as an agent of the world rather than as a part of the mind.

Freud recognized that. Though he still allowed Breuer his hypnoid state for a certain group of hysterical phenomena, he writes: "The incompatible idea, which, together with its concomitants, is later excluded and forms a separate psychical group, must originally have been in communication with the main stream of thought. Otherwise the conflict which led to their exclusion could not have taken place" (p. 167). In other words, an internal conflict is an internal conflict and cannot be treated as equivalent to a conflict with the environment.

The task is to describe the forces on each side of the conflict while still describing the organism as a functioning unit. That is a lot harder than describing a conflict between organism and environment. Its achievement is a goal of Freud's later work. But a beginning is already made in "Studies on Hysteria" for instance in the general outline of a conflict between sexuality and morality, a conflict that one may say was forced on Freud's attention by his patients.

There is, however, an even more general kind of internal conflict, hinted at by Freud, that seems to herald the direction that his *theory* was taking him. One can see it in the following comment:

The situation which has thus been brought about [by the hysterical mechanism of defence]is now not susceptible to further change; for the incompatibility which would have called for a removal of the affect no longer exists, thanks to the repression and conversion. Thus the mechanism which produces hysteria represents on the one hand an act of moral cowardice and on the other a defensive measure which is at the disposal of the ego [1893–95, p. 123].

What does Freud have in mind when he describes repression as an instance of moral cowardice? Does he mean that hysterics are afraid to look danger in the face? Undoubtedly he had some feeling at that time that repression was an ostrich-like strategy. (He uses the analogy in later work.) But we must bear in mind that in the original paradigm of "Studies on Hysteria" what repression avoids is the *elimination* of a trauma. It makes little theoretical sense to hail the elimination of a trauma as an instance of bravery, or condemn its retention as cowardice. When Freud speaks this way, he is obviously visualizing parts of the mind with divergent interests. It may be normal cowardice for the mind as a whole to get rid of a trauma, but it requires bravery on the part of the ego. (That suggests, by the way, that there are different kinds of pain: pain that the organism would avoid by abreacting and pain that would be suffered thereby. And these must be different *kinds* of pain or there would be no opportunity for cowardice.)

Still, that does not entirely account for the phrase. Why *moral* cowardice instead of just plain cowardice? Perhaps the notions of acceptance and repudiation hold the answer:

> The actual traumatic moment, then, is the one at which the incompatibility [of the traumatic idea] forces itself upon the ego and at which the latter decides on the repudiation of the incompatible idea. That idea is not annihilated by a repudiation of this kind, but merely repressed into the unconscious. When this process occurs for the first time there comes into being a nucleus and centre of crystallization for the formation of a psychical group divorced from the ego – a group around which everything which would imply acceptance of the incompatible idea subsequently collects [p. 123].

Probably if we knew the meaning in this context of "acceptance of the incompatible idea," we would know what 'moral cowardice' means. The passage is ambiguous. Freud could mean simply that the connexion of the incompatible idea with the rest of the mind constitutes its acceptance and therefore *any* associated idea must be repressed with it. Or he could mean that some associated ideas are not only connected, but reveal an acceptance, in which case we would have to look further for what "acceptance" means. The case history in which this discussion appears suggests to me that the latter is the case – that what the ego repudiates is some of the person's own purposes which the trauma reveals: "Here the traumatic memory was playing a part: she did not behave as though she had got rid of everything connected with her devotion to her employer" (p. 124). Moral cowardice would be a strange epithet for retaining rather than discharging an external trauma, but it exactly fits refusing to acknowledge one's own purposes.

It may well be, however, that at this stage Freud is deliberately ambiguous, preferring to maintain the theoretical language of "ideas" as representatives of external traumata, while making it clear that for practical purposes, it is *themselves* that hysterical people are offended by. After all, even in 1892 Freud (1892-93) had called hysteria a perversion of the will, and stated that an inhibited impulsion to action is the basis for a theory of the counter-will (Freud, 1892). In 1894 he was content to write, rather informally:

> For these patients whom I analysed had enjoyed good mental health up to the moment at which *an occurrence of incompatibility took place in their ideational life* – that is to say, until their ego was faced with an experience, an idea or a feeling which aroused such a distressing affect that the subject decided to forget about it because he had no confidence in his power to resolve the contradiction between that incompatible idea and his ego by means of thought-activity [Freud, 1894a, p. 47].

"An experience, an idea or a feeling . . ." – this is a much broader specification than simply "an idea." In 1896 Freud (1950, p. 239) declares that an hysterical attack is not a discharge but an action designed to reproduce pleasure. In 1897 he writes (Freud, 1950, p. 256): "Remembering is never a motive but only a way, a method. The first motive for the construction of symptoms is, chronologically, libido. Thus symptoms, like dreams, are *the fulfillment of a wish.*" In 1898, the delayed traumatic effect of early sexual experiences, that is, the trauma that is usually described as an idea, is *equated* with libidinal impulses: "during the interval between the experiences of those [childhood] impressions and their reproduction (or rather, the reinforcement of the libidinal impulses which proceed from them) . . ." (p. 281). In other words, the role played by reproduction of received impressions is reassigned to the arousal of libidinal impulses.

These are just a few examples to show that the first general theoretical solution of the problem of conflict is strained to the bursting point almost as soon as it is formulated.

SECOND MOVE

It would have been convenient if the conflict lay between the environment and the mind. A whole mind is easier to understand than a divided one. But the mind is divided and conflicted, and some way has to be found to describe its conflict within the framework of its unity.

That is the task of "The Interpretation of Dreams" (Freud, 1900). Now the wish replaces the idea. Certainly, memories continue to be important, but what is most important about them is the psychic impulse which *seeks* to revive them (cf. pp. 565–6). Active conation is as central to "The Interpretation of Dreams" as passive response was to "Studies on Hysteria." The clash of wishes has shattered the unity of the responding organism earlier depicted.

Is this theoretical development the accidental result of empirical research? It could well be. Even beyond the details of dreams and associations, the very nature of the dream as a normal and continuing process could be expected to strain a theory designed to account for accidental, pathological and intermittent hysterical phenomena. In particular, dreams will not be as plausibly explained as hysterical phenomena in terms of the disturbance of a unified organism by a fortuitous external event.

But granting that the new subject matter invites a more conflict-laden picture of the mind, it is also true, as we have seen, that the old theory was under strain from the beginning. It was difficult to say, on that theory, why anything should go wrong with the normal way of handling noxious happenings. The postulation of two states of mentation did not really make it any easier. Repression had to spring from a common battleground on which two armies could make contact. And Freud was already trying to find a way to relate trauma to sexuality. There was thus adequate dialectical pressure to open up the unified organism and display its contradictions, and we can consider the subject of dreams a fortunate opportunity for a theoretical necessity.

"The Interpretation of Dreams" thus offers what "Studies on Hysteria" did not, namely a bold, theoretical acceptance of a conflict of wishes within the mind–conflict between the wish to sleep and active urges, between the wish for sexual experiences and the wish not to have them, etc. That done, Freud had to make sure that he did not lose in the process what "Studies on Hysteria" did offer, namely, a unified picture of the mind.

It was only natural to try to preserve this advantage of the earlier theory by devices similar to those the earlier theory employed. Everybody knows what conflict between an organism and its environment is like. We can easily imagine a gazelle trying to escape a lion. Some sort of flight from danger seems to make sense out of conflict even when it is internal conflict. The danger is simply shifted from outside the organism, to outside the mind (but within the organism), that is, to biological stimuli.

> This effortless and regular avoidance by the psychical process of the memory of anything that had once been distressing affords us the prototype and first example of *psychical repression*. It is a familiar fact that much of this avoidance of what is distressing–this ostrich policy–is still to be seen in the normal mental life of adults [Freud, 1900, p. 600].

That tends to make the mind whole again, in the form of the ego or consciousness. But there is really no turning back. After the recognition of a conflict of wishes, the analogy loses its clarity. Something in the mind may be fleeing but something assuredly is not.

Some other kind of coherence within the mind had to be found. It was found in what I will call a "maturational series." I use the word "maturational" not in a necessarily genetic or age-determined sense, but in the sense of one thing developing into another. It refers to ideas like the following:

> The fulfillment of these wishes [derived from infancy] would no longer generate an affect of pleasure but of unpleasure; and *it is precisely this transformation of affect which constitutes the essence of what we term "repression."* The problem of repression lies in the question of how it is and owing to what motive forces that this transformation occurs; but it is a problem that we need only touch upon here. It is enough for us to be clear that a transformation of this kind does occur in the course of development – we have only to recall the way in which disgust emerges in childhood after having been absent to begin with – and that it is related to the activity of the secondary system [Freud, 1900, p. 604].

Thus the progression of unconscious processes into conscious thought, or the dream-work itself, is a mental process identifying the mind as a whole. It is a process which embraces divergent directions within it, the divergent directions being identified generally as the pleasure principle and the reality principle. These principles, though antagonistic in a way, are also at the same time a maturational series.

The difficulty with this refinding of a unity in a conflicted organism is that the divergent principles, pleasure and reality, are only roughly divergent. The maturational series does not as yet really seem to encompass the kind of internal conflict-of-equals – the self-contradiction – that needs to be resolved. The mind is given too much unity under the formula that it strives to avoid pain. The unity was also overstated in "Studies on Hysteria," but its exaggeration becomes much more obvious in Freud's (1900) book on dreams, where responsibility is thrust more completely on the individual, and the avoidance of pain cannot be so neatly contrasted with impingements from the environment. When the conflict is seen as between inside and outside, pain seems to be a transparent concept. It does not demand definition. "Studies on Hysteria" took pain as a given. But when the conflict is within the individual, pain takes on the role of a signifier of relative weights and balances among the interests of the organism. Freud recognized that even in 1898, when he toyed with the idea that pain arises *because* of the repressed state of ideas, rather than simply as a reason for repression (Freud, 1898). This comes close to saying that pain is an epiphenomenon of regulation among divergent interests of the mind. To the extent that it is a sign of regulation, pain loses its explanatory advantage, and the principles of regulation demand elucidation. Another way of stating this is that after conflict of wishes is taken as the focus of inquiry, pain ceases to refer to the violation of the organism's overall purposes, and comes to represent the frustration of various wishes.

"The Interpretation of Dreams" (1900) seeks to unify the mind in a maturational series in which the various competing conative interests of the mind are regulated by fluctuating redefinitions of pleasure and pain. Something that is not painful is experienced as painful because a prudential view has been incorporated in the organism, or rather because the organism has scrutinized a kind of test-run on impulses (see p. 582).

The theory has now reached the stage where various "meaning" and existential psychologies stop (cf. Gendlin, 1964a). If Freud had stopped there, these two schools of thought (and therapy) would be easily assimilable to each other. But Freud did not stop there because he recognized that the progressive development of 'realistic' meaning, governing the assignment of pain and the direction of the organism, does not in fact govern absolutely. There is an internal dissension—some factor of recalcitrance that the theory does not account for. He knows that the mind does not just fight the world, but fights itself. He has found a way of unifying the conflicted forces by arranging them on a single scale and distinguishing them as more or less mature, more or less regulated, more or less detailed and defined. But he recognizes that the theory is now more unified than the mind really is, and he must return attention to the real antagonism among its parts.

RECOIL FROM THE SECOND MOVE

In "Beyond the Pleasure Principle" Freud (1920a) begins a major revision of his theory with an emphasis on the resistance and uncooperativeness that patients manifest in treatment. We can very well suppose that the new developments in theory were brought about by difficulties discovered in clinical practice. The regular march to therapeutic abreaction that "Studies on Hysteria" led us to expect was not generally to be found. The usually successful resolution of intrapsychic conflict in dreams was not the outcome of intrapsychic conflict in neuroses. Inevitably, a practitioner with Freud's years of experience would be at least as much aware of parallel conflict as of the maturational series of ideation and wish formation. I believe that the conflict between therapist and patient is indeed what keeps the hard facts of internal conflict before our eyes, despite the temptations both of theoretical intelligibility and professional comfort to draw a harmonious picture.

Yet we must be struck by the fact that resistance in therapy could have been well accounted for without much more theoretical elaboration than was achieved by 1900. In fact, the dictum (Breuer and Freud, 1893–95, p. 268) that the forces that oppose treatment are the aetiological forces of illness had already guaranteed an explanation of any stubbornness encountered in clinical work. (Indeed, a challenge to "Studies on Hysteria" is that therapeutic *success* could not be predicted from the explanation of the illness, a problem that continues to haunt psychoanalytic theory, and indeed any theory of treatment related to a comprehensive theory of the mind.)

Whatever impetus practical problems gave to the final elaboration of psychoanalytic theory, the need for such elaboration was anyhow present in the state of affairs as of 1900. In effect, explanation of how the mind resolves conflict had outweighed explanation of how conflict can exist. In 1910 Freud made it a point to describe psychoanalysis as a study in conflict, in contrast to theories that rely on dissociation and hypnoid states that conjure conflict away (p. 213). Yet the theoretical current emerging from "The Interpretation of Dreams" kept drifting toward a hierarchical, maturational series of compatible and transmutable levels. "The Interpretation of Dreams" had given a general description of how secondary process takes hegemony over primary process. In 1911 Freud had described the emergence of consciousness as a progression in differentiation:

> It is probable that thinking was originally unconscious, in so far as it went beyond mere ideational presentations and was directed to the relations between impressions of objects, and that it did not acquire further qualities, perceptible to consciousness, until it became connected with verbal residues [p. 221].

In 1915 he envisions a transmutation of pleasure into pain, and wonders how that can come about: "We should have to assume certain peculiar circumstances, some sort of process by which the pleasure of satisfaction is changed into unpleasure" (Freud, 1915b, p. 146). Even the quality of an affect can be experienced in a less and then more precise fashion (Freud, 1915c, pp. 177-8), and the affect itself can develop and change as instinctual impulses find attachment to new conscious ideas: "Often, however, the instinctual impulse has to wait until it has found a substitutive idea in the system Cs. The development of affect can then proceed from this conscious substitute, and the nature of that substitute determines the qualitative character of the affect" (Freud, 1915c, p. 179).

Finally Freud advances the notion that ideas in the system Ucs are of things alone, while in the system Cs, the hypercathexes involved in language, "bring about a higher psychical organization and make it possible for the primary process to be succeeded by the secondary process which is dominant in the Pcs" (Freud, 1915c, p. 202). We can fully appreciate this maturational series if we recall that Freud (1915c, p. 202) portrays language as a sophistication of relational thinking. The unconscious idea of a mere thing, then, is the idea of a thing relatively lacking in relational attributes, which means relatively lacking in attributes. It would be a very rudimentary idea indeed.

So we see that in the years following "The Interpretation of Dreams," the parties to conflict are actually on different levels, in a hierarchy characterized by definedness of ideas, and precision, recognizability and even quality of affect. The contrasts are very much on the order of more or less development, original versus transmuted states. Thus, if conflict is going to be explained at all, it will be necessary to muster all the clues that the theory contains that portray incompatibility, antagonism, and conflict-of-equals. And that is what is done from "Beyond the Pleasure Principle" (Freud, 1920a) onwards.

On the surface, of course, it appears that it is the unconsciousness of defense that necessitated the structural theory. But the original image of flight could have accounted for the unconsciousness of defense. We do not ask whether the fleeing of the gazelle from the lion is in the gazelle or in the lion. And this metaphor could have been stretched to account for the details of repression, as in the possibility suggested in 1900 that repression occurs *between* the system *Cs* and the system *Ucs* (cf. Gill, 1963, p. 100). What does require the structural theory is the need to exemplify conflict, that is, the need to allow the systems a common arena where wishes may battle, rather than a mere ladder on which wishes can ascend from primitiveness to refinement.

Psychic energy provides the common arena. It is, of course, one of the oldest concepts in the history of the theory. When the conflict was viewed along the lines of organism versus environment, the input of energy (in the form of unwanted stimulation) provided the medium of contact between the contestants, and discharge of energy constituted the breaking of contact. When conflict was internalized, but the flight model retained, energy of instinctual drives was appropriately pitted against energy of ego instincts, and countercathexis could be seen as fighting fire with fire. But the very fact that the combatants had so much in common led to a pacification in theory. The pleasure principle, which actually defines psychic energy, is seen to govern both parties. The reality principle that distinguishes one camp is but a refinement of the pleasure principle of its rival. One combatant is simply trying to help the other accomplish what he is unable to do unaided. The theory must find a new *casus belli*.

I hope I have made it clear that this problem is no fortuitous muddle which the theory is saddled with because of some premature biologism. Much has been made of the conspicuous reflex-model of Freud's thinking. But models are not paper patterns; they are persuasive visualizations of relationships. Most often Freud's application of the reflex model is nothing else than a search for causal chains.

Thus when we say that some distinction must be made in the common energy that unites conflicting interests, in order to account for their conflict, we are not indulging in esoteric speculations about a mythical physics. Those are simply the chosen terms for describing a conflict within a unified mind.

If cause and effect in mental life is described in terms of cathexis and discharge, we must say what prevents discharge (Freud, 1920a, p. 9). Throughout the development of the theory, from the beginning to end, undischarged primary processes were alleged to find an especially large number of outlets, in every "system" and almost every fashion. In what sense, then, could they be said to be undischarged? What kind of effect would terminate their action? What was it about secondary processes that allowed discharge, and in what sense could primary processes be said to be active but undischarged?

The earliest answer had to do with association. "Studies on Hysteria" referred to associative disconnexion of the undischarged idea. In 1914 Freud (1914b) referred to a "working over" of an idea that prevents disease (although it can also produce symptoms). As stated earlier (Freud, 1900), primary process proves inadequate because it represents a wish as the insistence on a global repetition of a satisfying experience, rather than as a defined goal coupled to a practical means. Secondary process defines a wish and relates it to other requirements in a way that enables it to find satisfaction. The definition involved in secondary process becomes part of the satisfaction of the wish (Freud, 1920a, p. 25; also Ricoeur, 1970, p. 371). The energy of the wish, i.e. the wish as causal, has extended to include a number of functions which make it fulfilable (though it is now no longer referred to entirely as a wish).

Having established that a wish expressed in primary process finds discharge in secondary process, the problem arises, why it does not always do so. Why should some wishes fail to be educated? Why should education ever be unwelcome? (Freud, 1920a, p. 10, poses a question of this kind.) Some wishes will not undergo secondary process modification. Repressed unconscious contents cannot be made compatible with the rest of the preconscious system by the ordinary process of what Gill (1963, p. 10) calls normal inhibition. The best synthesis that can be made of them is an incomplete one. It is a compromise formation in the form of an anti-cathexis (cf. Gill, 1963, p. 104). The synthetic activity of normal inhibition therefore does not completely characterize the tendency of energic processes. Some contradictory stubbornness is involved.

Our problem is well formulated in Rapaport's (1951) terms. He distinguishes peremptory motives which find expression without secondary process elaboration and delay (or would if they were not repressed) from those which are tamed to tolerate secondary process delay. The distinction between amenable and unamenable motives is usually sought in the difference between bound and unbound cathexes. But the concept of binding is more a marker of the difficulty than a solution to it. Thus Holt (1962) finds three distinct meanings of binding: (1) inhibition of discharge, (2) attachment of cathexes to mental objects, and (3) structure-building. The last two move the process forward in a maturational series, even though the first would seem to block it in an expression of conflict. The concept of bound and unbound cathexis, therefore, does not provide an unequivocal rivalry within the mind statable in terms of energy.

Clearly some other distinction about energies must be found to represent the difference between amenable aims and unamenable aims (a distinction that was anticipated in the contrast between sex and ego instincts).

THIRD MOVE

The pleasure principle and its modification, the reality principle, represent a graduated series of refinements, reforming crude wishes into wishes that incorporate and integrate new varied interests. Some of those new interests may be considered structures. (Structures represent permanent interests which become part of all other motives; cf. Apfelbaum, 1966; Rapaport, 1951.) In contrast, unamenable motives must be, to use Freud's original term, incompatible with that maturation. Unamenable motives, then, are wishes which will not bend to others. The distinction that must be brought into the theory, therefore, is one that will differentiate between what is plastic and what is rigid in wishes. As Holt (1962, p. 520) says, binding is a synthetic process which brings about new organizations. A term must be found to stand for the relatively unbindable or unamenable. (It cannot be "the unbound," because that is merely a potential for integration. It has to be the unbindable.)

But the pleasure principle has been used to *define* energy: it is the general direction that energy takes; it is a statement of the kind of causality embodied in the concept of energy. If it also implies a specifically synthesizing direction, it will be hard to distinguish in energetic terms between the bindable and unbindable.

What in effect must be done is to redefine energy in such a way as to allow for incompatible directions *within it*. If the pleasure principle seems not to allow for contradictory directions, then its significance must be changed. It must become more abstract. It must come to stand for one *aspect* of psychic causality. The predominant theme in Freud (1920a) is that the pleasure principle is only one aspect of psychic movement; it has become a partial definition of psychic causality. To complement the pleasure principle as one aspect of psychic causality, Freud (1920a) nominates another—Eros.

Against this formulation, it must be admitted that Freud did not want to be left with only one energy, no matter how many aspects it was allowed. He granted to each of the two instincts its own energy (Freud, 1920, pp. 53-4; 1923, pp. 44-5). This adds innumerable difficulties to the theory. Apart from the deep obscurity of the notion of a fusion of energies in mental functioning, and apart from the observation that neutral Eros (perhaps even merely sublimated Eros) can serve the death instinct *without* fusion (Freud, 1923, p. 44), the fact that the two instincts are *never* found without each other (Freud, 1920a, p. 57) raises the question of whether they are distinct enough to command separate energies. Indeed it forcefully suggests that while love and hate may be separable and therefore fusable, Eros and the death instinct cannot be fused because they are fused to begin with. One might be tempted to suppose that Freud took a chemical model too literally in proposing mixtures of separate death instinct and life instinct energies. But we will later see some theoretical reasons for his reluctance to rest with his own observation that life as a whole has double aims (Freud, 1923, pp. 40–41), and to draw the implication that no *part* of life, e.g. an energy, can have only one of them.

Two energies have not been found. Energy is, as we said, the common battle ground on which conflict must be located. It is only in an abstract analysis of two *aspects* of energy that the battle can be located. And the aspects have to do with plasticity and rigidity. From this point on, the parallel with Piaget (1951) becomes so striking that it is unnecessary for me to call attention to it at every turn.

As a corollary to this abstract distinction, other distinctions must necessarily be made. Plasticity and rigidity are relative terms. They refer to the possibility of a blending, and blending requires entities to be blended. A single entity alone in the universe could not be considered either plastic or rigid. The abstract contrast between plasticity and rigidity suggests a more concrete contrast between things to be blended, in this case wishes or motives. Thus the contrast of death instinct and Eros carries with it the postulation of organized aims, and must be accompanied by a well-defined theory of multiple structures within the mind. Even if, as Gill (1963) says, structure was present in the theory from the beginning, it must, at this point in the analysis, be set forth explicitly. For this description of a unitary mental functioning in terms of contrasting directions is designed precisely to account for concrete schism and rivalry within it. The death instinct and the structural theory go hand in hand. Without the two-instinct theory, the structures would represent only points of view rather than conflicting aims. (I shall refer to this again when commenting on perspectivism.)

As formulated by Freud, Eros and the death instinct are general organic principles. If we ask what represents the death instinct in mental life, we can easily identify a constancy principle—the perseverative tendency that led Freud to the concept. As for Eros, it is a force that brings things together (Freud, 1920, p. 50; 1923, p. 45). With respect to the mind as a whole, as well as its components, Eros introduces novelty, which is then preserved by the death instinct (which thus serves a purpose similar to Piaget's [1951] assimilative tendency). If we say that the perseverative tendency is the mental embodiment of the death instinct, what is the embodiment of the opposite tendency—the tendency to yield and blend? It is what we are accustomed to calling the synthetic function of the ego (Freud, 1923a, p. 45). The term is unfortunate. Many authors have pointed out that synthesis is a function of the mind as a whole, not a part of it (Loewald, 1960; Rapaport, 1960a, p. 42; Apfelbaum, 1966). And all kinds of synthesis are clearly present in any identifiable aspect of the mind. (Recognizing this fact, Gill [1963] and Schur [1966] have relativized the notion of the ego, and Arlow and Brenner [1964] have done the same thing by referring to variable states of the ego.)

Unless we wanted to make the ego stand for the whole psychic structure, we would have to leave it a factional role and not allow it to be umpire (as Freud wanted it to be). Thus, if the ego represented reality perception and incorporation of novelty from outside the organism, synthesis would stand above it, and draw it into the nexus of other wishes, etc. At any rate, the synthesis of aspects of the mind cannot be an aspect on the same level as what is synthesized. It is, instead, as abstract as the death instinct. The death instinct and the synthetic function of the mind represent the unity of the mind in contrary aspects or tendencies. It is a unity that allows for conflict. The nature of the conflict is statable in terms of organizations of motives named in the structural theory (cf. Schafer, 1968).

RETROSPECTIVE

Let us see how this specific antithesis of death instinct and Eros was fore-shadowed by the dialectic between unity and conflict in the growth of the theory.

In the beginning, the as yet unnamed constancy principle was tacitly applied to the overall identity of the organism, as it sought to protect itself from outside attack. In the ideal model of the flight of the organism, a synthetic function was not necessary (except as one might say that the direction of flight represented an accommodation to the nature of the threat). After internal conflict was memorialized, the same paradigm was tried on it. Consciousness flees from internal trauma. The ego, in the form of consciousness, has the function of the constancy principle, and the ego instincts were thought to flee the sex instincts (Freud, 1920a, pp. 51–52). In order to recognize internal conflict, however, a constancy principle had to be joined by a synthetic principle, for that is what makes the conflict part of a single person. The synthetic function now requires that the trauma has to cooperate with the fleeing. There has to be a meeting, not just a fleeing. If the ego embodies synthesis, and consciousness is what is fleeing, then the synthesizing ego can no longer be identified with consciousness. The synthetic function is now illustrated by the interaction of the system Ucs with the system Pcs-Cs. And the constancy principle is now represented by the sum of the laws of the apparatus. That is tantamount to treating the pleasure principle as the Law of the Mind, and the energy – libido – as the causal chain that it governs.

But a difficulty now arises. The theory set out to explain conflict. But the interaction of the opposed systems is an example of synthesis. It therefore becomes necessary to find a place in the theory for an antisynthetic principle:

> strictly speaking it is incorrect to talk of the dominance of the pleasure principle over the course of mental processes. If such a dominance existed, the immense majority of our mental processes would have to be accompanied by pleasure or to lead to pleasure, whereas universal experience completely contradicts any such conclusion. The most that can be said, therefore, is that there exists in the mind a strong *tendency* towards the pleasure principle, but that that tendency is opposed by certain other forces or circumstances, so that the final outcome cannot always be in harmony with the tendency towards pleasure [Freud, 1920a, pp. 9–10].

The *limits* of synthesis are generalized as the constancy principle, or death instinct, and particularized as the recalcitrance of specific interests, organizations or parts of the mind:

> There can be no doubt, however, that the replacement of the pleasure principle by the reality principle can only be made responsible for a small number, and by no means the most intense, of unpleasurable experiences. Another occasion of the release of unpleasure, which occurs with no less regularity, is to be found in the conflicts and dissensions that take place in the mental apparatus while the ego is passing through its development into more highly composite organizations. Almost all the energy with which the apparatus is filled arises from its innate instinctual impulses. But these are not all allowed to reach the same phases of development. In the course of things it happens again and again that individual instincts or parts of instincts turn out to be incompatible in their aims or demands with the remaining ones, which are able to combine into the inclusive unity of the ego [Freud, 1920a, pp. 10–11].

The constancy principle and the synthetic function overlap to define the concrete identity of the organism.

> For in our hypothesis the ego-instincts arise from the coming to life of inanimate matter and seek to restore the inanimate state . . . [Freud, 1920a, p. 44].

> The emergence of life would thus be the cause of the continuance of life and also at the same time of the striving towards death; and life itself would be a conflict and compromise between these two trends. The problem of the origin of life

would remain a cosmological one; and the problem of the goal and purpose of life would be answered dualistically [Freud, 1923, pp. 40–41].

But once the mind's concrete identity is thought of as variegated or conflicted, the constancy principle and the synthetic function must be raised to a higher level of abstraction where they can refer to two *aspects* of mind: its divisions and its coherence respectively. Logic requires these aspects to be on a higher level than the structures that they separate and connect. But the theory could not quickly accept constancy and synthesis as governing principles of the whole mind because they were originally functions of the ego and the id, which were the original actors in a drama modeled on a person organizing himself to preserve his integrity from assault. Because the ego began as a synonym for the whole organism, it clings forever to the office of synthesizer even after it has also become a contesting interest within the mind.

We cannot imagine the ego except as a synthesizer. That leaves the constancy principle apparently homeless, since it was also embodied in the ego. It will not rest easily with the id, despite that structure's famous obstinacy, because the id is also a notorious provocateur and agitator: "It would be possible to picture the id as under the domination of the mute but powerful death instincts, which desire to be at peace and (prompted by the pleasure principle) to put Eros, the mischief-maker, to rest; but perhaps that might be to undervalue the part played by Eros" (Freud, 1923, p. 59).

So now Freud correctly feels it necessary to make the constancy principle an overriding principle of the mind, impartially applicable to all contesting interests. Or, more accurately, Freud treats the constancy principle as a universal aspect *of* all contesting interests. By so doing, he implicitly elevates its antagonist, Eros, to the same superordinate status.

But in his writing Freud (1923, pp. 45, 56) continues to associate Eros with the synthetic function of the ego. He never quite gets around to removing synthesis from the ego and installing it in its higher seat beside the death instinct. Why was he reluctant to do that? After all, these conflicting aspects of mental process—death instinct and Eros—need to be separated from a substrate that they can pull in opposite directions. For two abstract principles to rule, there must be some common activity for them to rule, and if it is energy we are talking about, then these polar abstractions must be aspects of a common energy.

Indeed, Freud recognizes that and provides such an energy (1923). But it is not, as one would expect, a primary, indifferent energy showing aspects of Eros and the death instinct. Though it is ruled alike by Eros and the death instinct, it comes from Eros and becomes available to the death instinct only be being desexualized. Just as synthesis stays with the ego even while it applies to the whole mind, so energy stays with Eros even while it is also serviceable for every purpose.

> We have reckoned as though there existed in the mind—whether in the ego or in the id—a displaceable energy, which, neutral in itself, can be added to a qualitatively differentiated erotic or destructive impulse, and augment its total cathexis. Without assuming the existence of a displaceable energy of this kind we can make no headway [p. 44].

> It seems a plausible view that this displaceable and neutral energy, which is no doubt active both in the ego and in the id, proceeds from the narcissistic store of libido—that it is desexualized Eros [p. 44].

> If this displaceable energy is desexualized libido, it may be described as *sublimated* energy; for it would still retain the main purpose of Eros—that of uniting and binding—in so far as it helps towards establishing the unity, or tendency to unity, which is particularly characteristic of the ego [p. 45].

Why does Freud require neutral energy to be desexualized energy rather than unsexual energy? Partly because he has identified Eros with love, and the death instinct with sadism and hate. But, then, why that identification? Why does he so vehemently throughout his theory reject the possibility of a neutral energy? (1923, p. 46; 1940, pp. 149–150). And why continue to reject it even when it turns out that he needs it and must desexualize Eros in order to have it? Surely Freud did not mean to suggest that desexualized Eros is secondary *in time*, and that the death instinct has at first no energy to work with! But if desexualized Eros was not previous sexual Eros, and if this energy is not currently dedicated to Eros, than it would be hard to see in what sense it is Eros at all. At this abstract level, "energy" just means a tendency toward a certain outcome. Its outcome defines it.

The theory requires two forces acting on one energy. By the logic of the theory's development, constancy and Eros are two aspects of the same thing, and Freud labors in vain to find some particular mental thing that, for instance, does not show the operation of Eros (Freud, 1923, p. 46).

I suggest that the reason for this loyalty to dualism is as follows. The theory requires conflict within a unity. One needs to find original opposite poles, or there will be no differentiation of developed opposites. The temptation is to describe those poles on the earlier analogy of the fight between the organism and its environment. And that makes it plausible to portray the mind as a living organism attacked by something antiorganic.

The momentum of the theory prepares for another turn of the circle. That would be again an effort to bring the organism together by identifying the death instinct with nonlife and the ego with the living, which flees its enemy as the theory first described the mind fleeing from a trauma. If only we could say that the ego represents the mind, and its vitality is Eros, synthesizing what outside energies would destroy. But that cannot be done anymore. We are beyond that now. The 'enemy' has been situated in the mind for a long time; the ego has as much need as its enemies for conservation and sluggishness, its enemies as much need for synthesis, and everything as much need of the same energy as everything else (Freud, 1923, p. 59; 1940, p. 149). We have reached a plane of abstraction where the final antinomies lie, the kind of opposition that needs no further unification because it will tolerate no concrete incarnation as energies. We are left with an opposition of two aspects of a single process. But that seems finally to abolish the division that the system had sought to account for. So Freud drew a line at a theory of energies and decided to stop the dialectic spiral there. Henceforth two energies would be named to commemorate conflict, even though the system itself was finally using only one energy.

In summary, Freud found conflict in the mind. He tried to patch it over as any theoretician must do. The patching over occurs in successively elevated abstractions. First, conflicting wishes are analysed in terms of potential for development, on the one hand, and developed definition, on the other. But since that makes things seem more harmonious than they are, it is pointed out that each potential for development already has its own definition which will resist further development of "its" potential. There is a sense in which wishes are fulfilled by their synthesis with reality and the rest of the mind. And there is a sense in which wishes are betrayed by that synthesis. (It is a typically Freudian tragic paradox.) Using an anthropomorphic figure of speech, one can say that the strivings of a wish (or an interest, an impulse or motive) are simultaneously conservative and progressive, schismatic and synthetic. The conflict of wishes has been brought under a general theory of a unified mind by finding a more highly abstract conflict between aspects of fulfilment.

Theoreticians commonly perceive the anthropomorphic, willful strivings of psychic institutions as incompatible with the overall synthesis of a whole mind. They do not always realize that this is a phase in a theoretical analysis balanced by other phases. Many theoreticians attempt to find a simple description within or outside of Freud's theory to sew the mind back together. Such a simple description always leaves conflict unaccounted for.

One such description is Rapaport's (1960a) concept of threshold. It is designed to serve both as a definer of impulses and their modifier, cleverly blending the act of conserving the impulses in their own form with the act of synthesizing them together. To begin with, he recognizes that "drive energies can be conceived of only within well-defined systems which have definite thresholds of discharge" (p. 52). Then, when he imagines a clash of impulses, he looks for another threshold to synthesize them. Thus he writes about Freud's earlier hypotheses:

> A conception of psychological life as a continuous clash of drive forces arose, and the abiding character of the interfering factors was lost sight of. Not even the link established between the concepts of censorship and the secondary process . . . conceptualized the abiding character of these two drive-controlling factors [p. 53].

Since, from the beginning, practically all of Freud's conceptualizations are conceptualizations of the abiding character of the interfering factors, in the shape of regular patterns of reaction and symptom formation, Rapaport's criticism is quite mysterious until we realize that he is looking not just for abiding *patterns* of drive interaction, but for an abiding synthetic force to impose those patterns. (Perhaps he felt that the only thing that would make a pattern abiding is a continuously operating force.) The force of impulses, each with its own threshold, can provide conflict. But where, Rapaport seems to ask, is the force that unifies them? The problem is that if another force is postulated as governor, we are back to a conflict of forces and we have lost our synthesis again.

Rapaport seeks a way out of this dilemma by an ambiguity. The original *thresholds to be modified* are portrayed as thresholds *of a drive*. But the *modifying structures* are usually referred to *simply as thresholds*. Because he wants to make structure appear as the agent of synthesis, rather than as a conflicting competitor, he must, on the one side, play down the structure already present in competing impulses and, on the other side, he must soft-pedal what it is that structures proper are structures *of*. He does this chiefly by making drive structure look a little bit like the drives they characterize. Impulses are supposed to have a faster rate of change than the structures proper that modify them, though in fact Rapaport gives us no reason to believe that the *thresholds* of impulses vary so much in constancy. The rate-of-change distinction is designed to covertly suggest an opposition between raw impulse and what gives it form, though Rapaport is forbidden by his own premise from explicitly talking about formless impulses. Having given a structure to impulses as part of their definition, he can only try to make that structure *seem* rather unstructured. He makes drive structure look a little bit less like a pattern and more like a drive, by contaminating it with the sporadicness of drive *occurrences*.

Having done that he is in a position to show structures modifying drives without actually competing with them, since structures give drives what they are explicitly said to need, and what, by implication, they do not already have, that is, well-defined (more permanent) structure. Of course, this tendency to describe resolution of conflict as the imposition of relative form on what is relatively formless is not in fact explanatory. Structure has simply been abstracted from an event and then rejoined to it. An abstraction is not a force that can impose synthesis on something else. But the metaphor of a threshold can make the abstraction look like a concrete force: a raised threshold holds back an impulse. It combats the lower-threshold impulse. But at the same time it is *not* a separate, conflicting, competitive drive, for, in effect, it is part of the new definition of the impulse. Thus the new threshold seems to bring conflict and synthesis together. Conservativeness is depicted both in the building up of drive energies behind a barrier, and then again in the existence of the barrier. And yet the barrier also represents *another* structure and thus serves synthesis. (Actually there would be an infinity of such thresholds, and Rapaport's model would be a stop-motion picture of transmutation of meaning.) But this picture can serve both synthesis and conflict only if we allow it two different interpretations at once.

On one hand, we can consider the raising of a threshold as a simple formula for the changing definition of an impulse. It is as though Rapaport declared that conflict is synthesized by the advent of greater definition. We can therefore read the threshold model as a metaphor for synthesis, whereby the conservatism of many high-rate-of-change structures is sacrificed in favor of a larger synthesis with a lower rate of change, no account of conflict being offered. That would be what I have called a maturational series.

Or we can emphasize the *imposition* of higher thresholds on impulses that tend to maintain their lower thresholds, in other words, the imposition of greater definition on what tends to be less defined. But we have already noted that an abstraction such as "greater definition" is not a force that can impose anything on anything else, even when it is described as a threshold. One has either to confess that the whole project of synthesizing conflict is a mystery (which I think Rapaport does when he admits, p. 107, to being in need of a learning theory, since I cannot see what the threshold model provides if it does not provide a theory of learning), or else one must come right out and postulate a conflicting force, on a level with the impulses, that imposes the greater definition. But as we have already seen, a force that imposes synthesis simply adds another conflict, and does not incorporate synthesis in the system. (If the ego really did impose synthesis on a recalcitrant id, we would still need to find some "abiding character of the interfering factors" between ego and id that regularized this struggle—yet another structure in an infinite regress.) When Rapaport chooses this alternative, he is left with a structure of something that can enforce but is not a force. That is what Apfelbaum (1966) so tellingly mocked as the invention of an "organ with a purpose."

Rapaport's effort to make the very definition of the conflicting forces serve also as a concrete synthesizer in the form of a slightly disembodied structure cannot work out smoothly. (Note the awkwardness of his attempt, 1960, pp. 28-9, to show how the psychological blindness to the object of a drive once its threshold is raised, leads to a more refined search for that object.)

In many respects, Gill's (1963) work exposes the futility of Rapaport's struggle. His emphasis on "the functional inseparability of motive and discharge structure as well as of motive and inhibiting structure" (p. 146) takes the ambiguity out of thresholds and settles for what I have called a maturational series. A synthesizing continuum of increasing structuralization replaces the effort to polarize impulse and structure. But what is sacrificed, as always in a maturational series, is a picture of conflict.

For that reason, Arlow and Brenner (1964), while not denying the presence of a synthetic continuum of structure, insist on superimposing on it patterns of conflicting organization (id, ego and superego) each of which has its own continuum of synthesis. But then they, too, need to identify an overall synthesizer. They find it in the traditional synthetic function of the ego. But this synthetic function is no longer equated simply with increased structuring. Increased structuring may be represented by the growth of the ego, and with regard to that kind of synthesis Arlow and Brenner are in agreement with Gill. But they also describe another kind of synthesis, represented by a balancing of still-conflicted factors, in which there may be *decreased* structuring, for example, in "regression in the service of the ego" or in defensive ego regression. In fact, a measure of this large kind of tolerant synthesis is the ability to make the best of a decrease in the ego-structuring type of synthesis.

By implication, this large kind of synthesis pays homage to the conservatism or recalcitrance of elements in the mind. It suggests a "best possible" and a "less best" synthesis of those elements, and thus points to factors limiting synthesis. But as we have seen in discussing the intermediate stage of Freud's theory, it is only by sleight of hand that this broad kind of synthesis is identified with one of the competing elements of the mind. Only by supplementing the institutional definition of the ego as a structurizer, with the vague notion of it as a purveyor of adequacy or satisfactoriness (or adaptation) of the mind, do we seem to have located this general synthesis in one part of the mind (allowing us to describe conflict), rather than distributing it throughout the mind as Gill had done (which leaves conflict somewhat obscure).

The belief that pictures of conflict fail to portray the continuing synthesis of a unitary mind has made theoreticians less and less structurally oriented. Since it seems so futile to try to localize synthesis as an item, step, event or organ in the mind, there is a tendency to make synthesis an ultimate function of the mind, thus allowing us to take it for granted. That is easy to do, for undoubtedly synthesis *is* a function of the whole mind. But the more one treats synthesis as simply equivalent to mental behavior, the harder it is to define anything other than whole mind, and hence the more difficult to discuss conflict.

Therefore theoreticians act as though they have to choose between paying attention to the individual impulse or to the whole-mind system. The first choice is illustrated by Peterfreund's (1971) computer model. Impulses can be roughly paired with programs which at least superficially can be given good definition and thus allow for conflict. Their synthesis is left to superprograms which reprogram the subprograms in accordance with some major homeostatic identity of the organism. Conflict does not present a problem because it simply is not discussed on the level where the master program does its synthesizing. But enough is said to show that defined elements of the system offer no resistance to synthesis and in that sense are not capable of generating conflict. (That represents Peterfreund's extreme effort to get rid of partial conservatisms in the mind because of their anthropomorphic potential: only the whole mind seeks to conserve itself, and therefore only it is describable in anthropomorphic terms [see chapter 18]).

The second path is taken by Apfelbaum (1966). Having clearly described Rapaport's inability to make a structurizing *force* out of a mere particular structure, Apfelbaum chooses the option of putting synthesis back into the whole mind. The mind is described abstractly in terms of organizations of interests: superego interests, ego interests, interests of defense and interests of impulse. These are all abstract aspects of a concrete "psychic unit" that can display them simultaneously or in succession. That psychic unit is where we will find synthesis. We can still talk about conflict because, for Apfelbaum, the abstract, persisting organizations of interests in the mind are just as real as its "psychic units." But the nature of a psychic unit that can be alternately ego, superego, instinct, and defense is hard to pin down. It is difficult to define it—hard to say what makes it separate, how one points to it, etc. All of the differentiae that we are accustomed to using as designata can be put on and taken off by the same psychic unit. The truth is that, far from being parts of the mind, Apfelbaum's psychic units are the whole mind at work in indivisible and concrete fashion, and the organization of motives are abstractions from them, however regularized and patterned. The nature of conflict will not be easily fitted into such a picture.

Schafer (1973b) goes a step further along Apfelbaum's path, and arrives at a concrete image of an already synthesized mind exemplified in its actions. Abstractions which were allowed a ghostly presence in Apfelbaum's work are exorcised by Schafer. For such a mind it would no longer be true, as Apfelbaum would have it, that "aims are no less innate or invariant for being aims" (1966, p. 469). Schafer's is a type of analysis that forbids innate abstractions and therefore never needs to worry about synthesizing conflicting motives. If one adheres to a wholistic, concrete image of the mind in action, one has undoubtedly rescued synthesis, but only by giving up particulars, and by abandoning the attempt to give a systematic account of conflict. In fact, when looked at sharply one can see that this approach makes it difficult even to talk *about* the mind. Of course, Schafer does talk about the mind, but he is able to talk about particular acts (which are inevitably abstract because they are defined) only because he refuses to be tied down by the requirements of his theory. The mind has been equated to acts, and when those acts are discussed as though they were defined, the mind loses the concrete 'thing-ness' which the theory sought to preserve (see chapter 20).

The most consistent and radical travellers along the road to exclusive synthesis are the existentialists and their friends. One of the most precise and least obscurantist of them, Eugene Gendlin (1964), has explicitly presented a whole-mind theory, in which what I call synthesis is examined in detail. It is, as it must be, a process theory. Psychoanalytic theoreticians should read such work to see what implications lie in wait for them in their understandable rebellion against too much structure. I discuss Gendlin's theory in chapter 22. What is significant here is that when his discussion turns to therapy and therefore to dysharmony—that is, when the exposition reaches the point where conflict would have to make its appearance, Gendlin is forced to incorporate in his whole-mind process a broken, piece-of-mind, static fragment which is not consistent with his general endeavor. (I am referring to the anomaly of a "frozen structure" in a process theory that eschews structure.)

In summary, if we do not approach theory of the mind the way Freud did, with his dialectic of conflict and synthesis, the problem becomes one of finding items in the mind which do no arranging, but are arranged by other items in the mind. Since it proves impossible to make such a distinction consistently, the tendency is to give up the whole project and put synthesis and conservation back into the mind-as-a-whole, and refuse to make any abstractions at all—the point where the theory began—with the result that it becomes difficult to talk *about* the mind and therefore about conflict.

If, on the other hand, we respect the conflict-unity dialectic of development of Freud's theory, we will view psychic institutions as organizations of motives that we have selected on the basis of clinical interests and other human experiences, to focus on the ways that conflict is synthesized in the mind. Conflict and synthesis are dispersed throughout the unitary mind. That is why the two-instinct theory is formulated in such enormously abstract terms in Freud's theory. But to be able to talk about conflict, we must abstract from the unitary mind, and abstraction requires a vantage point. What we have abstracted, besides aspects of synthesis and conflict, are structures or institutions: we have delineated entities which must be synthesized and which tend to hold on to their definition. Having *named* them, of course, the conservative aspect of life takes prominence in our eyes. We seem to have given each of them the unity that properly belongs to the mind, whence the anthropomorphic locutions that are unavoidable. It is the designation of general conservative tendencies in terms of particular conflicts that makes psychic institutions seem to have a will of their own. We have, in effect, temporarily let go of the overall synthetic aspect of the mind (though we may paste it on top, provisionally, by referring to the synthetic function "of the ego").

Of course we must grant the perspectivists that there may be different ways of describing conflict-in-unity (see Levenson, 1972). But if conflict itself is seen as relative, i.e. if abstraction of elements that seek to conserve themselves within the pull of total synthesis is not thought to represent a real disunity within the mind, then no conflict is described—and incidentally, no illness and no treatment.

CONCLUSION

The development of Freud's theory shows an alternating response to aspects of conflict and unity in the mind. It is difficult to respond to both aspects in a simpler fashion. If the alternating respect for both conflict and unity that is already present in Freud's theory is lost, new theories may caricature the old as a machine in which death instinct and Eros fuel the cogwheels of id, ego, and superego. Then these new theories may develop a model of an existential, seamless mind, manifesting no distinctions and therefore no conflicts. In chapter 27 we see that therapists are tempted by such models for reasons of practical advantage as well as theoretical simplicity. But if therapists allowed theory of the mind to evaporate this way, they would be out of a job.

16

Conclusion: The Nature and

Function of a Theory of the

Mind

ADVERTISEMENT

The line of thought that I want to develop in this chapter starts from the premise that psychotherapy must be concerned not only with a theory of the mind, but also with the nature of theories of the mind. Here are three arguments for this: (1) Psychotherapy does not just operate within a theoretical framework; it employs theory *per se* as an instrument of treatment. Of course, a therapist does not discuss theory with his patient. But he does attempt to transmit an organizing principle from his theory to his patient and he presumes that the transmission has something to do with the therapeutic outcome. This fact is reflected in analysts' concern about the nature and exactness of interpretations, and the kind of truth that can be attributed to reconstructions. (2) Psychoanalytic theory grows in a field thick with competing systems. New concepts sprout daily. In order for the analytic therapist to stake out his place in that field, he must know what in general theories of the mind are. Uncertainty about that has led to a protective isolation of analytic theory from other speculation, and random efforts to integrate the latest idiom with analytic understanding. (3) Since theory is used as an instrument in treatment, we cannot finally say how our results are related to the effect of other symbolic healing techniques until we reach an over-all understanding of what a theory of the mind is. Until then we will be saddled with miscellaneous *ad hoc* classifications of therapies according to devices used or outcomes hoped for.

PROSPECTUS

Philosophers of science have found it of limited value to speculate about the nature of theory formation in the abstract. The most fruitful approach is to look at a well worked-out theory and see what it does.

For this purpose, Ricoeur's (1970) monumental study of Freud's theory is immensely valuable. Ricoeur is an "outsider"—a professional philosopher, who has undertaken a detailed examination of Freud's theory as a philosopher would examine any complex argument. His primary objective is not to challenge or support the theory, as those in the profession are almost bound to do, but to *place* it, that is, to grasp its objective and describe its strategy. And that is exactly what is necessary in order to evolve a notion of what a theory of the mind is.

Reflected in Ricoeur's study, Freud's system is a way of dealing with mental phenomena as aspects of a mind which is considered as an object.

I want to place this side by side with Cassirer's (1957) argument that the process of objectivizing is the kernel of experience and that science progresses by postulating less and less imaginable and more and more inferential objects, in accordance with which I suggest that Freud's procedure of postulating a mental object is what a theory of the mind must do.

Inasmuch as a theory of the mind is used as a tool in treatment and seems to involve consideration of phenomena as aspects of an object, I speculate that the therapeutic process involves some shift in the nature of the object that the patient focuses on.

A shift of that sort is similar to the shift of paradigms that Kuhn (1970c) discusses. So, still using the notion of objects as my primary focus, but with an eye to the phenomena of paradigm revolution and paradigm discovery, I suggest that treatment involves the cognitive and affective apprehension by the patient of a more unified object and the emergence of a more comprehensive theory of his mind. I suggest that it is the *procedure* of finding such an object, rather than the descriptive theory itself, that is the effective factor in treatment,[1] and that a relatively new paradigm can be relatively agreed upon, because patient and therapist share a common problem.

This way of looking at the situation reveals a family of treatments, each with its own specialness undiminished by the family relationship.

The drift of the argument is against the stream of thought that regards the

---

[1] In this regard, see Roustang (1982).

term "the mind" as a linguistic sophism and considers "objects" as unscientific short-hand for phenomena. It also involves some strange wording, such as describing the therapeutic relationship as a thing. But my impression is that many conceptual difficulties have arisen from a false sophistication which abhors the indispensable notion of "things."

RICOEUR ON FREUD

One cannot read Ricoeur's study without appreciating how misleading it is to examine isolated pieces of a theory apart from their function in the theory as a whole. Even sympathetic critics have been too quick to suppose that concepts such as psychic energy are deposited by the *Zeitgeist* or arbitrarily dragged in to satisfy a whim of the author. Ricoeur shows that the energetics of metapsychology is an expression of the focus of the psychoanalytic project. Psychic energy emerges from Ricoeur's study as the very substance from which the Freudian picture of the mind is forged; it is the mediator between the meanings the mind entertains and the changes it undergoes. Remove from the term "energy" all of its associations to physics, and a term of that sort must still be found to serve its function in the theory.

An even more startling example is the significance Ricoeur discovers in what many of us have come to regard as Freud's philosophical holidays – the theory of the death instinct, the grand cosmic speculations about the direction of life, the pessimistic pedal-point and occasional heroic *obbligatos*. Ricoeur shows that these are not simply temperamental embroideries but constitute the working out of theoretical problems implicit in Freud's initial conceptualizations.

This coherence of Freud's theory enables Ricoeur to demonstrate its philosophical skeleton. That skeleton, I believe, can be used to instruct us about the tasks of a theory of the mind. The underlying project, which Ricoeur portrays as an advance on Cartesian meditation, is the attempt to objectify our self-knowledge by distancing ourselves from it before returning to introspection. Consciousness must first be separated from its intuitive, unstructured experience and set into a framework of objective relationships. Freud did that by reading consciousness as a translation of a more systematic nexus of relationships. Ricoeur describes psychoanalysis, as a hermeneutics, thus comparing it with the interpretation of cryptic texts. This approach presupposes that conscious phenomena are intelligible in terms of an under-lying pattern.

If we leave Ricoeur for a moment and consider this presupposition, we note that if psychoanalytic hermeneutics were simply a translation from one language to another (one called conscious and the other unconscious), it would be a senseless exercise. A translation from German into English establishes nothing except that both are languages. And a translation from English into a wholly postulated language would prove still less, namely that one can invent another language than English.

Only if the relationship between the two languages points to some fact of the world besides translatability has anything been *discovered*. What makes hermeneutics a process of discovery rather than a formal exercise is its claim that it uncovers a *hidden* meaning. Psychoanalysis translates one language into another, but it treats that translatability as a manifestation of something else, namely an intention to disguise. It finds in its text a principle of organization which cannot be described simply by another language, since it refers also to an intent to conceal or transform. The meaning of the text includes its disguise. Therefore the translation is not arbitrary. The unconscious is not simply another description for conscious processes. It contains within itself the principles that generate conscious processes. That is what gives psychoanalysis the hermeneutic privilege of treating conscious processes as a *manifestation* of the unconscious and not merely an alternate expression of the unconscious.

Now if we return to Ricoeur we find him posing a difficult and, I think, crucial question: for translation from consciousness to be possible, the hidden meanings must be comparable to the conscious text. But a disguising *activity* is part of the translated meaning. How are we to imagine something that is both a language and a force? How can that be the outcome of a *translation*? There is nothing tricky or sophistical about this question. It is echoed in the ambiguity of the concept of the id. Is the id a seething cauldron of desire? If so, what possible relation can it have to formed, integrated thoughts and defined wishes? If not—if the id is formed and integrated, and its wishes discrete, in what sense does it underlie those processes of disguise responsible for conscious wishes? (Cf. Gill, 1963.)

Ricoeur's answer to this question provides what I think is a main tool for understanding the function of theories of the mind, and I will use it as my chief instrument of analysis in this paper. He says that Freud inserted a *construct* in his theory and deputized it to stand for the intersection of meaning and force. That construct is the instinct representative. Neither a formed idea, nor a biological drive, it is that which represents the biological drive to the mind. As such, we can see that, in principle though not in practice, it can be the outcome of a translation while at the same time carrying the intention of concealment. In practice it cannot be the end-point of interpretation because it cannot be given a defined content. It serves as a kind of ideal limit authenticating the direction of interpretation.

From the fact that this mysterious entity is indescribable, it seems to follow that all we can know about it is its effects, namely, all of the psychological phenomena, conscious, preconscious, unconscious, etc., that we are interpreting, or into which we are translating what we are interpreting.

This translation into a category whose content is not independently known allows Ricoeur to suggest that one might translate as well in the opposite direction, i.e. *from* instinctual or biological substrate *into* cultural or idealistic human constructs. Since we can know the instinct representative only by its developments, he asks, why not say that the concept of God, for example, is one of its ultimate aspects? Or, since the interaction of an individual's instinct representative with society results in a moral feeling, why not say that moral feeling is an aspect of this instinct representative, for the deployment of which it need only find a suitable social inductor?

But quite apart from this Jungian implication, what shall we think of this strange conclusion? *The ultimate end-point of interpretation of all phenomena in psychoanalysis is an unrepresentable instinct representative.* Is that a *reductio ad absurdum* of psychoanalysis? Should a theory that leans on such a vacuous metaphysical construct be replaced as quickly as possible? Even Ricoeur, who is anything but hostile, feels that force and meaning (blended in the instinct representative) do not sit perfectly well with each other in Freud's system. Indeed Ricoeur's doubts about the harmony of force and meaning have led to serious misunderstanding of his argument. He has been seen to offer science an excuse for not talking with psychoanalysis, and an opportunity for psychoanalysis to trade scientific discipline for humanistic maunderings.

It must be admitted that those who are inclined to separate psychoanalysis from natural science can find support in Ricoeur. At the outset he restricts hermeneutics to the search for extra meaning in signs that already have a fixed meaning, as when we discover symbolic meaning in written texts that can also be read literally. In so far as Ricoeur's restriction to language-like systems is merely his way of selecting a topic, no issue is involved. We could go on to see if, and to what extent, hermeneutic techniques are also employed in the wider area of representations generally. But Ricoeur implies that we cannot generalize to all of science in this fashion. He rejects Cassirer's suggestion (which I shall discuss below) that we view all knowledge as constituted through symbols. Ricoeur argues that only what we ordinarily call symbols, as contrasted to other, explicit signs, have the properties that call for a hermeneutics. Only when dealing with them,

> ... I am carried by the first meaning, directed by it, toward the second meaning; the symbolic meaning is constituted in and through the literal meaning which achieves the analogy by giving the analogue. In contrast to a likeness that we could look at from the outside, a symbol is the very movement of the primary meaning intentionally assimilating us to the symbolized, without our being able to intellectually dominate the likeness [Ricoeur, 1970, p. 17].

But according to Cassirer that situation is what all representations—all knowledge—builds on. If we did not intuit a meaning in phenomena which led irresistibly to other meaning, we could not construct any formal significating system such as language which we *can* intellectually dominate. Indeed without an involuntary symbolizing, the notion of meaning would never have arisen. Cassirer argues that the the symbol comes first, and from it come explicit signs like language. This argument is largely ignored by Ricoeur, who therefore implies that hermeneutics is a far more unique sort of thinking than his description requires it to be.

From the implication that hermeneutics is radically different than other kinds of understanding, the path leads directly to the segregation of psychoanalysis from natural science. However, a close look at Ricoeur's definition of a symbol may nip that implication in the bud:

> A symbol exists, I shall say, where linguistic expression lends itself by its double or multiple meanings to a work of interpretation. What gives rise to this work is an intentional structure which consists not in the relation of meaning to thing but in an architecture of meaning, in a relation of meaning to meaning, of second meaning to first meaning . . . [p. 18].

The question is whether at bottom, *every* signifying system rests on the relation of meaning to thing. Or alternatively formulated, the question is whether a thing is not itself a meaning, in which case Ricoeur's contrast of hermeneutics with other interpretation is a distinction without a difference. Cassirer holds that the concept of a thing requires abstraction, i.e., it requires us to regard a particular item as representative of a class, an appearance as representative of an underlying reality, phenomena as representatives of laws. Therefore a verbal term that refers to an object also refers to a meaning and satisfies Ricoeur's definition of a symbol. And as for multiple meanings, even that aspect of symbolic meaning is reflected in the natural sciences (see Lakatos and Musgrave, 1970). There is much to be said (and Einstein would have said it) for the view that science generally approaches nature generally as though it were a book with an obvious text and a hidden meaning to be deciphered by a hermeneutics. Even in its primitive beginnings, thinking begins with the assumption that there is an underlying order that is mirrored in obvious natural differences (Lévi-Strauss, 1966). Thus what Ricoeur has discovered in Freud's theory may well be true of science generally, including the tension between force and meaning. And if that is the case, then we would have to let Freud's mysterious, unrepresentable instinct representative teach us something about the theory of the mind, rather than dismissing it as an implausibility or tolerating it as an emblem of a quasi-science.

CASSIRER ON OBJECTS

What Ricoeur says for hermeneutics, Cassirer says for all thought. Starting with the most primitive, vague meaningfulness of a face or a natural event,

Cassirer finds thought progressively distancing itself from the brute immediacy of personal experience. Step by step, rationalized, principled frameworks are interposed, whose elements are intelligible in the sense of being
specifiably interrelated. This culminates in contemporary science where
ordinary language (with its brute and chaotic associations) is replaced by a
completely intelligible mathematical language. Cassirer's account of the
history of thought parallels Piaget's studies of individual development. Piaget
(1962) finds a progressive development of de-centring schemata which classify
singular phenomena according to reversible (and therefore intelligible) operations.

Following Kant, Cassirer points out that for ordinary thought this distancing and rationalizing works by attributing phenomena to *objects*. An
object is the postulated representation of the orderliness and comprehensi-
bility of phenomena. Continuing the tendency of all cognition, modern
science has had to transcend ordinary thought in order to do away with the
remaining incomprehensibility of the world of objects—the inexplicable "it's
just there" quality of space and time and the left-over aspects of objects that
are just "matters of fact" instead of theoretically deducible necessities. Our
familiar space, time and objects are no longer to be found in physics. But
these familiar things are eliminated for the same reason that they were
developed, namely to represent what is just there in sensation by something
that is purely intelligible, and necessarily internally interrelated—finally by
mathematics. Although objects are now considered insufficiently objective,
so to speak, the regularity of phenomena that they represent still finds
representation in science, by a formula, if not by a picture. Physics still
portrays an objective world, albeit one without objects.

But we need not follow Cassirer that far. A science of mental life has got to
deal with mentation. It is not a cosmology and it cannot progress along the
lines of physics without deserting its subject. It must stop at the level of
things. But by the same token, it may not stop till it gets there. One
understands mental life only by representing the mind and its facets as one
represents objects. And objects are curious items. They have more in them
than anything we can say about them. We understand phenomena by
attributing them to objects, that is, by regarding them as attributes of an
object. But what an object is beside its attributes is very hard to say. In fact,
little more can be said than that, over and above its attributes, an object is a
factor X, which stands for a pertinent constancy and interconnectedness
among its known attributes and between them and an infinity of other
potential attributes. But if an object represents the intelligibility of phenomena, it is not itself thoroughly intelligible. Besides fostering understanding, it
also represents the brute fact-ness of its attributes. In a sense, it *causes* those
attributes; it is responsible for what happens. The connexion between its
attributes that cannot be derived from the attributes alone, is there *just*

because they adhere to the same object. That *just because* corresponds to what Ricoeur calls force. And that force coexists in the object with the *meaning* that the object gives to phenomena, the meaning being the interrelatedness it provides among otherwise disparate and shifting events.

The "X factor," which makes an object out of phenomena, is the message imbedded in that which otherwise has no message. It is the ground of intelligibility, the guide to translation, the unity in diversity, the connectedness of the apparently separate, the configuration of reality which gives interpretation a place to fit. Every such X factor, no matter where it is found in science, must claim, on one hand, to be a part of brute, given reality and, on the other hand, to be readable by the proper translation; it must be both the idea behind things and the actuality of the thing. Ricoeur has summarized psychoanalysis beautifully as the semantics of desire. But even a formalized physics is a semantics of a kind of cosmic desire wherein the disparity between force and meaning can be seen in the difference between the abstract physical formula and the concrete workings of the world.

Ricoeur shows that Freud's theory is an attempt to take mental life as an ordered, coherent subject. Ricoeur has shown that in the course of that attempt Freud had to postulate an underlying X factor which is in some ways similar to the data (it has meaning), and in some ways different (it has impetus and cannot be represented). In the light of Cassirer's work, I think we can now say that his X factor—this instinct representative—is nothing else than the X factor that designates the object-ness of what is being studied and which, in turn, corresponds to the conceptualness of our studies. Its amalgam of force and meaning is exactly what we would expect of any natural science object. The mind is understood by treating conscious phenomena as attributes of an object, and the instinct representative constitutes that object. I believe Ricoeur's message is that a semantics of desire presupposes something like an instinct representative. Or more precisely, the lesson is that to look for a semantics of desire is to treat mind as though it contained something like an instinct representative.

APOLOGY FOR MY TERM

By the end of this discussion, if not sooner, the reader will be weary of the term "object." I will have worked it into the ground. To be sure, there is some usefulness in seeing how much can be squeezed out of a given concept. One stretches a concept to see what it can and cannot do. But I am fully aware of the danger of conjuring with words. When it comes to terms, one man's profundity is another man's banality. Little is accomplished by showing that one can talk about a lot of things in his favourite language. Some further justification must be offered.

Certainly terms other than "object" could have been used in this discussion. Many prefer to consider these matters in terms of "models." There is a particular hazard lurking in that approach. Bewitched by the dazzling vividness, detail and up-to-dateness of a system borrowed from some other field, we may forget to ask: What abstract principle are we actually borrowing in making this analogy? The effective principle taken from the model can be very meager, whereas its elaboration in the model may make it seem revolutionary. For example, a theory of the mind based on information-processing theory may borrow from the model merely the principle that the mind is a concatenation of many small causes and effects (see chapter 18). Or the effective principle of comparison to the model may be extremely potent and yet not be spelled out for critical examination of its limits. That is how I feel about Pribram's (1971) discussion of the neurological hologram. To my way of thinking, the hologram offers a physical object that can correspond to a mental object in a way that other neurological objects do not. I think that it may be the object-ness of the hologram (in contrast to the mere connectedness portrayed by other neurological models) that makes it so suggestive and useful as a model for the theory of the mind. After all, what is special about holograms is the way they resemble objects rather than aspects.

In straightforwardly abstract discussions, the most familiar term that has been used for our subject is "lawfulness." It seems more scientific and down to earth, vastly simpler and clearer than the concept of an object. Then why bother with objects at all? My answer is that "lawfulness" is simple and appealing precisely because it slurs over the implications that make it useful. It implies something compelling which it deliberately refuses to describe or even point to. Nobody has yet succeeded in formulating it without recourse to something like objects. I will discuss this further when criticizing Ryle's theory below.

Without doubt, the term that is currently favored in discussion of our subject is "structure." And this term, which seems much more specific and formalizable, could indeed be substituted for "object" in most of the contexts used here (see also Allport, 1955). I believe that those who employ it are working on the same problem and in much the same fashion as those who have tried to understand the concept of an object (see chapter 24). "Structure" has the grammatical advantage of a more natural usage when extended to non-material things (see Piaget, 1970). It would therefore be a better term if it conveyed all that "object" does. But, like "lawfulness," it seems to me to beg those issues which concern us here. It is precisely because "structure" skips over the difficulty of uniting what Ricoeur calls force and meaning, and assimilates it all to meaning, that it suits so many systems with so little strain. After all, the schema in a child's mind is a different kind of potentiality for action than the schema of a mathematical structure. Piaget shows us how the concept of an object arises, but in portraying that development we must suppose an object that is learning. There is some vector at work beside formal logic, else we would have logic without logicians. Perhaps not the theory, but the terminology of structuralism almost persuades us that base matters of fact have been transmuted into the pure gold of reason; logic comes to look like the force of development. Instead of this recent Hegelianism, I choose the Kantian term "object," to call attention again to the matter-of-fact-ness that underlies structure.

In the old days, terms such as "essence" and "substance" would have been used to discuss these issues. They are no longer common. But I offer as a merit of the term "object" that, though common and, I think, indispensable, it is ancient, *un*fashionable, and carries no glamour from the latest development in this or that field. In that respect its usefulness and limitations are transparent. It cannot be pictured; it has no charm. It simply stands for some theoretical necessities and it may be translated by the reader into any term that does the same for him.

For the rest of this chapter, then, I will discuss theory and therapy in terms of objects. I hope this term will not be confused with the psychoanalytic term "object," which is an emotionally invested representation of a person. The "object" that I am referring to is closer to the "object" of everyday speech. The main difference is that I do not confine it to something one can touch or see. I am referring to a concrete entity in contrast to an aspect of something or a manifestation or appearance of something. As I use the term, an object is something that persists over a period of time; it has an infinite number of aspects and can therefore be described in an infinite number of ways; and consequently when we attribute aspects to it we are not only stating a necessary connexion between those aspects but we are stating that those aspects are necessarily connected with another, infinite set of attributes which we cannot specify. Thus in regarding something as an object, we are claiming that our descriptions of it are not an arbitrary collection but a real grouping, not an elective classification but a compelled description; not a definition but a discovery.

Paraphrasing Ricoeur in my terms, I believe he has shown that one theory of the mind—Freud's—is the finding that conscious meanings are the properties of an object.

That does not mean that if he had failed, we would be left without objects. Meanings and feelings by themselves refer to objects of their own. They have the same kind of amorphous, mysterious centre that is not exhausted by their descriptions. When we try to express them, we know that we are inadequately fumbling for an "it." Meanings have their own system of uncountable internal relations, of inexhaustible necessary interconnexions. That is what makes perspectivism plausible (cf. Levenson, 1972). It is why our mental life is not a mathematical reverie. It is what Langer (1953) means when she says that there is no way of following psychic integration. I think it is possible that a feeling is the way the object-ness of our fragments of awareness is signalled to us (Friedman, 1968a; Gendlin, 1962). The simplest perception is surely already cast into object form (see Cassirer's discussion of color perception, 1957, p. 136). In like manner, we would still have the objects of our everyday world even if we did not have a science of physics.

But if we wish to take all of these objects, the various perceptions, feelings, Gestalten and what have you, and find the object of which they are just properties, then we will formulate a theory like Freud's. That is the task of a theory of the mind. A theory of the mind treats conscious mental objects as though they were properties. And although that is the general direction of scientific thought, as I have argued above, it is bound to be disconcerting to anyone who is preoccupied with the initial objects as objects, just as relativity physics is disturbing to the layman. Before reaching any emotional defensiveness, the concept of the unconscious is likely to cause discomfort for this reason alone. In a paradoxical way, behaviorism can be viewed as an attempt to save the ordinary objects of experience from becoming mere properties of another object (mind), by leaving them alone and taking other objects (behaviors) as the properties of the object (the nervous system) that *it* is looking for.

A similar struggle seems to be under way in linguistics. A psychoanalyst could find comfort in the fury and mutual misunderstandings of a conference on psycholinguistics (Aaronson and Rieber, 1975). Chomsky (1972) has noted that there is an infinity of possible sentences, in any language which cannot be specified by ordinary grammatical rules, nor learned by enumeration. That is a very objectlike situation. I think Chomsky has proposed what I would call a language object. His theory of deep structure can be compared to the theory of the unconscious. It is not part of the unconscious, but it serves the same function in the theory of language that the unconscious does in the over-all theory of the mind. (Chomsky, 1980, has tended to confirm this view of his work by proposing to treat language as an organ.)

Understandably, this effort has been greeted by many as a metaphysical nuisance. Behaviorists and others have asked where the deep structure is supposed to live. Foes of Chomsky have tried to preserve the ordinary objects of language as objects – the speech patterns of various peoples, the errors that are made, the influence of context on comprehension, and the like. Some linguists have tried to straddle the fence by placing Chomsky's deep structure in the position of an ideal to which speakers approximate. But what Chomsky calls language "competence" is not an ideal. Competence is the language of a speaker considered as an object, of which his performances are the properties.

A science that takes mental life or language as its object does not evict other sciences which take the *properties* of mental life or language as objects. Chomsky's transformational grammar does not put comparative linguists or developmental psychologists out of business. And Freud's psychoanalysis does not displace phenomenologists, or art critics or sociologists. In some ways the creative artist himself is engaged in finding the object of a delimited area of mental life (Friedman, 1965b). The arts and sciences generated by those endeavours can be thought of as partial theories of the mind. But it must be remembered that the objects of all of these sciences are selected by their investigators. In that respect, a theory like Freud's stands apart. For there is a sense in which the object of psychoanalysis is selected by the subject. It is a curious anomaly that this is an option only for a science of the mind. Only a "semantics of desire" can be said to be literally called for by the subject in the sense that the differentiation of desire is part of its fulfilment. (Sublimation is itself a kind of satisfaction as well as a transformation.)

Needless to say, that does not mean that the descriptions and elements of Freud's system are eternal verities, or formulatable only in his way, much less that the system is a mirror image of mental life. Nowhere in science do we find demonstrable mirroring of theory in fact (cf. Lakatos and Musgrave, 1970): the very consideration of phenomena as attributes of an object guarantees that the resulting theory will not exactly fit. The only thing a theory will exactly fit is an abstract, formal system. An object, on the other hand, is not univocally describable. Thus the tension between force and meaning that bothered Ricoeur in Freud, is found in all scientific theories.

Ricoeur's account does not confirm the details of Freud's theory. After all, Ricoeur is a philosopher, not a psychologist. What emerges from Ricoeur's account is the impression that the *structure* of the theory shows the nature of any theory of the mind. It is that structure which can claim to be not only the project the investigator chooses, but one that the subject himself pursues.

I have already said, following Kant and Cassirer, that all experience is experience of objects. Every person, and therefore every patient, has his own theories, and to the extent that they are integrated, he has his own implicit theory of the mind. Any kind of purposeful or expressive or intentional behavior requires that some *thing* within a person is employed in a certain way, and I mean the word "thing" literally. I mean it literally because any way that the person experiences his psychological act is colored by the fortunes of the moment and could be otherwise experienced. Its expressiveness or intentionality or purposefulness means that there is an underlying "it" (a meaning, intention or purpose) from which the momentary, accidental expression is felt to be derived. (Piaget [1962] has shown that action and perception deploy a previously existing schema.)

The words "object" and "thing" have a cognitive ring. But just as force and meaning are intertwined in the theory of the mind, so also are affect and thought in experience. A feeling has more or less definition, and if feeling could be separated from definition by some qualitative analysis, there would be no theory of the mind, much less a psychoanalysis. That is evident from

Ricoeur's analysis, if it was not already obvious. The whole of psychoanalysis is a description of the vicissitudes of feeling under the influence of definition. (The more recent enthusiasm for the notion of "labeling" is really a step backward, as it depicts an otherwise specifiable feeling, decorated with an affectively laden description, like an iced cake.)

I am saying that we experience our emotions and purposes no less than the world around us in the form of objects. That is not a popular doctrine these days. We are often given to understand that it is the cause of all of our theoretical troubles. The philosopher Gilbert Ryle is frequently credited with this revelation (cf. Schafer, 1973a, 1973b).

DIGRESSION ON RYLE

Since my language is specifically the language that Ryle set himself to discredit, and since many authors seem to take Ryle as "the bottom line" of the history of philosophy, I must say a few words about his book *The Concept of Mind* (1949). I believe that Ryle's scorn for mentalism is the result of his taking Zeno's paradoxes too seriously and induction too casually.

1. Ryle is very impressed by the mystery of the infinite regress. For example, from the fact that an intention to do something would have to be preceded by an intention to have an intention, and so on, he concludes that mental causation is absurd. This is not a difficulty alone for a theory of the mind, nor even a difficulty peculiar to causation. It is ultimately a difficulty in using both discrete and continuous language as we do when we speak about happenings in time. There is much controversy over what Zeno hoped to prove by his paradoxes, but whatever it was, nobody has doubted that an arrow flies from bow to target, or that Achilles catches the tortoise.

2. Moreover, we do not need to resolve Zeno's paradoxes in order to use the kind of causality that allows us to say that an action is a reflexion of a more general intention, etc. That does not involve us in problems of temporal causality, and it is most often what we are getting at when we say that somebody did something because he wanted to, or because of his plans. With regard to this kind of causality, Ryle's general approach is to show that statements that attribute events to a mind can be rephrased as propositions about dispositions of a person. ("To find that most people have minds . . . is simply to find that they are able and prone to do certain sorts of things, and this we do by witnessing the sorts of things they do," p. 61.) But of course this substitution does not take us anywhere unless we have at least a clearer idea of what a disposition is than we have of what minds are. Ryle thinks he has. Dispositions, he says, are statements that refer to laws. Perhaps we can dispense with the concept of mind if we know what laws are. But if laws describe facts, then we have merely substituted statements about mind with statements about the laws of the mind. So Ryle is in the position of saying

that law-statements are a different kind of statement than "singular categorical statements" (p. 122). They do not refer to a realm of existence in the way that statements about minds pretend to. What, then, do they refer to? They do not, according to Ryle, actually refer to anything in the same way that existential statements do. Ryle is fond of saying that they are "used": "A law is used as, so to speak, an inference-ticket (a season ticket) which licenses its possessors to move from asserting factual statements to asserting other factual statements" (p. 121).

What we are to make of this "so to speak" is never quite clear. An "inference-ticket" and a "license" are all that is left of 2,000 years of debate about the justification of induction. But clearly the concept of the mind has not been rendered superfluous by this argument until we are told what matter of fact grants the licence or issues the ticket. Ryle himself notes that dispositions come and go, and that makes them look suspiciously like matters of fact (p. 125). Yet he maintains that "Dispositional statements are neither reports of observed or observable states of affairs, nor yet reports of unobserved or unobservable states of affairs. They narrate no incidents" (p. 125). Even though dispositions come and go, and even though we are accustomed to think that incidents are things that come and go, dispositional statements narrate no incidents and describe no state of affairs, according to Ryle.

It is important to recognize that the apparent force of Ryle's argument against the concept of mind as an object rests squarely on this device. He shows that the concept of mind can be largely reduced to dispositions. And he then asserts that disposition statements do not describe any existences, occurrences, events or state of affairs. In effect, he divides propositions into those that describe events and those that do not describe anything, but are *used* in some way to allow us to predict. (Schafer [1973a, b] has tried to build a psychoanalytic theory using only the first type of proposition.)

Ryle calls it a superstition to believe that these two types of proposition have the same sort of meaning.

Naturally, the addicts of the superstition that all true indicative sentences either describe existents or report occurrences will demand that sentences such as "This wire conducts electricity," or "John Doe knows French," shall be construed as conveying factual information of the same type as that conveyed by "This wire is conducting electricity" and "John Doe is speaking French" [p. 124].

But it requires little philosophical sophistication to see that propositions that clearly refer to events are also disposition statements. "This wire is conducting electricity" means that if it is connected to a lightbulb, the bulb will light up, and if connected with an ammeter, the meter will register a value. (In chapter 20 I prove that attempts to confine psychological descriptions to nondispositional propositions are likewise futile.)

Why this reluctance to accept the matter-of-fact-ness of disposition statements which are so obviously indispensable to any empirical assertion? Because a disposition would be a "hidden" state of affairs that Ryle feels we do not need to describe in order to make our predictions. And that is true to some extent. We cannot describe a disposition completely. But we do need to refer to it *as a state of affairs* in order to make predictions (or any empirical statement). A proposition alone cannot be a licence to anything. Only a state of affairs can licence an empirical prediction. We cannot "use" a proposition if it is just a formula we have cooked up. We cannot write our own "inference tickets." We must be able to refer to something which entitles us to make the predictions that we make. Ryle is really saying that, since we all believe in the factualness of dispositions (as shown by our empirical statements), we do not need to talk about them.

The limits of Ryle's usefulness can be seen in his style of argument:

> . . . the theoretical utility of discovering these hidden goings on [facts designated by disposition statements and the justification of laws] would consist only in its entitling us to do just that predicting, explaining, and modifying which we already do and often know that we are entitled to do [p. 124].

The "only" in that statement is truly dumbfounding. By that one word, Ryle announces that he has not yet accepted the task of the philosopher, which is, of course, to show us *how* we are entitled to think and describe the world the way we do. A philosopher who quits work after showing that one can live without philosophizing is not the man to ask about the implications of our thinking.

To my mind, the modern school of English philosophy is not so much the latest outcome of philosophical inquiry as it is an effort to wipe the slate clean and start thinking again in hopes that it will not be necessary to encounter any of the problems that have possessed thinkers for hundreds of years. We should not be surprised to find the ancient difficulties poking their heads through the simplistic examples and naive formulations that occur when one starts to think *de novo*.

Thus the concept of the object is just the kind of concept that has been developed to authorize the "license" that Ryle uses in inference. A tariff must be paid for inference-tickets and that tariff is respect for objects. We will look in vain to Ryle for any other authorization—another tariff. Actually, there *is* one point where Ryle pushes his inquiry almost to the beginning of philosophy. He writes: "If we wished to unpack all that is conveyed in describing an animal as gregarious, we should similarly have to produce an infinite series of different hypothetical propositions" (p. 44).

Here we have an inference-ticket to an infinity of destinations, a remarkable offering from a man who is so amused by infinite regresses. Such a ticket is no longer a ticket. It is, minus the name, the concept of an object.

PSYCHOANALYTIC THERAPY AS OBJECT-MAKING

I hope my quarrel with Ryle shows that my conception is not so far from ordinary, unsophisticated (what Ryle would consider muddled and misleading) speech. We have a mind. When we think about it, we are inclined to divide it into parts. Most of the time we do not think about it, but, if we reflect at all, we are inclined to think that we *have* feelings or wishes and that they can be expressed or concealed in various ways. Our map of these entities can be roughly construed as a tacit theory of the mind. Our theory can be more or less complete. It can be more or less concerned with the mind as a whole, more or less focused on some subordinate object, such as a wish. Thus we can have more or less of a theory of the mind, and more or less of theories of other objects which a theory of the mind would regard as properties of the mind.

Roughly the same thing, I believe, is what is meant by saying that behavior, including mental behavior, always has some degree of integration and differentiation. At first glance, integration might be thought of as a simple meshing of behaviors, and differentiation as gradual alteration along fixed lines. But there is more to these terms than that. They are terms that designate the combination of constancy and change in the course of time. (Piaget's terms, assimilation and accommodation, make that aspect more explicit.) "Integration" does not just commemorate behaviors that get along with each other. (Anything that coexists with something else gets along with it in some fashion.) It refers to a potential unity concealed by that apparent diversity in behavior. And "differentiation" clearly suggests the flowering of an early potentiality, lurking in what is later differentiated. I suggest that integration and differentiation both assume an object. Integration is the finding of an underlying object of which the integrated behaviours are properties. Differentiation suggests the finding of previously untested properties of an object.

Thus, insofar as therapy is considered to work by increasing differentiation and integration, it can also be said to do something about the objects that comprise the patient's theory of the mind. (Note that these terms are refracted in a highly confusing fashion into the notion of a synthetic function of the ego. Abstract categories like these are best not identified with organizations of motives or styles of functioning, since they are at work in any and every aspect of the mind. To say that they are functions of an agency of the mind is like saying that the object-ness of an object resides in part of the object.)

Other common, general impressions about the direction of therapy also suggest that it operates on the objects of a theory of the mind. Flexibility, for example, implies alternate expressions of a common theme or striving. A patient's recognition of his activity where he felt passive, and responsibility where he felt victimized, suppose that elements of his experience come to be seen as properties of an internal object – an object being something which has innumerable aspects or properties and is not exhausted by any set of them.

Suppose that the patient's tacit theory of the mind is incomplete: he has not taken his entire mind as a principle object. Suppose that he is distracted by other objects and other theories that vitally concern him. For example, he may be concerned with the object that constitutes a particular type of relationship between himself and important figures, past or present. Or he may be possessed of a "consciousness raising" interest that focuses on a social status relationship and is felt to be incompatible with a theory of one's own mind as object. The patient, then, would be dealing with a different object than the analyst. He might feel that the analyst's orientation interferes with his own theory. (People usually resent having even their slips of the tongue pointed out, even when what they reveal is trivial.) Related to this might be the elementary resentment that can arise from not being taken at face value in psychotherapy. What the patient is primarily dealing with is treated by the analyst as a mere attribute of another object. And since we are speaking about wanting and not just about abstract cognition, that means that the analyst is proposing a shift in desiderative aim. If we consider the nature of free-floating attention or free association, it becomes evident that these are processes of treating what one has previously considered objects as mere attributes of a something else.

At best the analyst's theory and the patient's will never exactly coincide, no matter what conversational agreement they have. What the patient hears and learns is never the exact correlate of what the analyst thinks and says. And vice versa. Such disparity is built into human individuality and the cumulative nature of feeling, and it cannot be the essential measure of congruence and incongruence between analyst's and patient's theories. It is a common problem for all human discourse and finds a common solution that is not peculiar to treatment.

But if, on the other hand, the disparity comes from a patient and analyst taking different things as object, the question arises, How can they ever get together?

HOW PATIENT AND THERAPIST CAN AGREE ON A MORE COMPLETE OBJECT

I find Kuhn's (1970c) conception of paradigms relevant to this disparity. A paradigm, according to Kuhn, structures inquiry: it generates relevant questions and procedures for solution. But it is not boldly formulatable. One either recognizes it or one does not: one cannot be forced to see it. If one is inclined to recognize it, he can be assisted by exercises in problem-solving, and that is the customary way of learning a paradigm. For example, at times when paradigms are not changing (Kuhn's "normal science"), physics is taught by making students use theoretical formulas to work out practical problems. They learn the paradigm by using their abstract theory to pose problems and propose solutions.

The psychotherapist will be struck by the similarity of this activity to what happens in treatment. It is useless to instruct a patient in a theory of the mind. No one has been much helped with his personal problems by reading a book on the psychoanalytic theory of the mind. Nor can a person be persuaded to understand himself psychoanalytically by an argument based on that theory. But when, because of personal involvement with his psychoanalyst, a patient is inclined to accept the analyst's view of his mind, then he begins to look for problems relevant to analysis, starts to see questions and answers of an analytic sort, and practices them in many examples (called working through). And at that point he may be said to have grasped the analytic paradigm. That could be one way of defining the therapeutic alliance.

I am suggesting that Kuhn's paradigm corresponds to a particular world of objects. As emphasized above, an object is more than any known set of its properties. It cannot therefore be demonstrated or fully described. But if one is disposed to treat certain known events as properties of an object, then one can observe how those properties can be related as though they were manifestations of an object. One can catch on, so to speak, to the kinds of questions and answers about those events that illuminate them as properties of an object, rather than, for example, as objects in their own right, or as properties of another object, e.g. a sociological object.

Cassirer (1957) has argued that the understanding of an event as a representation of something else is originally a basic intuition, without which no science, knowledge or indeed objective experience could ever be built up. Understanding is an intuition that what is immediately presented expresses something else, and through most of human thought, the something else that is expressed is an object. The epistemological equivalent of objects is concepts. Cassirer makes it clear that concepts could not be derived by a formula (as Locke, for instance, tried to do). To have concepts, we must first treat data as though they were related to an object. Formulas are ways of systematizing that relationship between data and objects. Thus Kuhn's observation that the scientist grasps a paradigm by applying his abstract theories to concrete problems, is what Cassirer's view would lead us to expect. In my terms, the scientist would be hunting for an object with his theory, while scientists working in a different paradigm who were not concerned about the object, would find nothing in the theory to make them be concerned. As Kuhn (1970c) says, "Languages cut up the world in different ways, and we have no access to a neutral sublinguistic means of reporting" (p. 268).

I superimpose Cassirer's views on Kuhn's in order to justify the following speculation: Psychoanalysis trains a willing patient to look for an object within himself, and to treat his array of conscious experience as a property of that object. The analyst does not so much convey information, as introduce an object to somebody who wants to find it, by the practice of applying certain exercises in establishing relationships. The training is akin to Kuhn's training in the use of a paradigm, and requires that the patient already accept that all of his awareness is a property of an object.

The most elementary aspect of psychotherapy, which has great force in itself, and has been described by Gendlin (1964a) as focusing, involves perfecting the object-making of a simple feeling. It is the first step in working again on a theory of the mind. It means taking one's feeling as an object—a thing with many facets, and a unity underlying them.

But how the analyst helps a patient work on his own paramount paradigm is the least interesting challenge of all theoretical and practical questions. It is equivalent to therapy with an established ideal therapeutic alliance. The crucial question is how analyst and patient can get together on a paradigm where they differ to begin with. (It is the difference between Kuhn's normal science and science at a time of paradigm crisis.) If the patient does not accept the analytic paradigm or vice versa, then what must happen to him before he can learn the analyst's paradigm is roughly what happens to a scientist at a time of shift in paradigm—something that Kuhn likens to a conversion experience, and for which, in fact, he has yet to develop an adequate explanation.

Now, according to analytic theory, the object that becomes the main concern for a patient is the relationship between himself and his analyst. And the primary focus and effectiveness of analysis lies in the development of a theory about that relationship. The patient treats the relationship as an object. But the analyst treats the relationship as an attribute of another object. It is not simply a matter of two parties seeking to define the relationship differently, or fighting for the authority to make it one thing or another, as Haley (1963) has described it. That may be part of what happens between patient and therapist, just as it happens between the patient and others in his life. But there is a subtle sense which is special to psychotherapy in which the therapist is not seeking any relationship at all, indeed is not attending to the relationship as important in its own right, but is concerned instead with what the relationship reveals. The therapist's abstinence is not merely self- restraint. It is a way of experiencing the phenomenon of the encounter, just as someone who ignores the dramatic impact of a painting in order to appreciate its painterly or design values is not necessarily resisting a temptation. (I am very much impressed with the recent finding that musically sophisticated people process music in the opposite cerebral hemisphere from that used by the unsophisticated.) And to a large extent it is the therapist's different theory of the mind that orients him differently from the patient.

Concentrating on the object of his own interest, the patient tends to assimilate the analyst's approach into his own primary paradigm. He may perceive the analyst's stance as a familiar rejection, or seduction, a deliberate frustration, disapproval, indulgence, etc. Levenson (1972) has studied that phenomenon in detail. This attitude of the patient is not intrinsically unrealistic. Human relationships cannot be dscribed univocally. Reality in general is not a simple perception (see Friedman, 1973). What has been called realism on the part of the ego has to do with the flexibility that would allow the patient to shift the object of his intellectual and emotional focus – to trade one paradigm for another.

If the patient can shift in that way, that very step will offer possibilities that were not previously felt, because the new object will have alternative properties to the one he has been regarding as his sole object. One could say that his adaptability will increase, his hopefulness will expand (cf. French, 1958). One cold also describe this as increasing his power of sublimation.

Remember that we are not describing a logical exercise, but perception of one's mental life. The shift in paradigm that goes along with a shift in object, is a change in the ways of wanting. If one perceives one's wishes to be aspects of other wishes, they are phenomenologically no longer the same wishes (Gendlin, 1964).

I am describing a process similar to Loewald's (1960) vision of psychoanalysis. He supposes that the patient responds to the reflexion of his growth potential in the eye of the analyst. That would be exactly treating the patient as an object. Just as Loewald says, it is this reorientation, rather than specific information, that allows the patient greater scope. It is also why the content of therapy may be lost while its effectiveness continues. It is why different formulations can lead to the same result.

Such is the benefit of shifting paradigms. But how is that accomplished? How do people who start out with different paradigms, different objects of concern, arrive at a common paradigm? It is this bedrock question that has compelled the uncomfortable conclusion that the analyst must somehow *force* the patient to change his outlook (Friedman, 1975a), a position so contrary to the educative and tolerant spirit of analysis that theory has tended to play hide-and-seek with it. (Surely it is the only aspect of analytic theory that an analyst would rather not disclose to his patient, and that must be significant.)

And yet, viewed as a problem of paradigm clash, the analyst really *cannot* force the issue. Ordinary forcing will simply be assimilated to the patient's paradigm (Levenson, 1972). The threat of the loss of the therapist's love can only be effective if the patient can imagine a kind of love that he can get by making some sort of change. And unfortunately love is defined by his own paradigm.

I think that the force-theory of change represents an awareness that the patient must be set a problem, and a problem that is close to the one that the therapist is working on. (The latter requirement is sometimes overlooked, for example, by Nunberg, 1928.) A problem must be set before the paradigm is accepted. Patient and therapist must be able to identify an object before it is defined, in order to be able to work toward its definition. From their separate perspectives, they must be able to feel a common problem before they can evolve a common goal. Only if they share a common problem to begin with can the conflict in paradigms even be perceived by the patient.

It seems to me that the common problem has to do with the patient's ambivalence toward the therapist . The patient has conflicting wishes toward the therapist . To that extent, his paramount paradigm of the relationship is already in crisis. There is already a beginning fissure in his theory of his mind. The abstinence rule is a wedge in that fissure; it is not just a provocation intended to elicit information for the therapist's theory to work on. The patient finds he has to work on a new paradigm, not because the old one is unacceptable to the therapist but because it is not serviceable in the treatment situation. The patient has not necessarily given up his interest in the relationship as an object. But his old paradigm no longer describes it.

Meanwhile the therapist has, as I have suggested, a quite different object in mind, namely the patient's mind as a whole. But the nature of the relationship is also problematic to him. It is problematic in the sense that it requires his theory of the mind to make sense out of it. He has found that if he takes the relationship as the property of an object consisting of the patient's mind he can respond to the relationship in a coherent fashion. (Hence the dictum that the analyst must put himself in the place of, and give equal respect to, ego, superego, and id.)

The therapist's demonstration of this approach makes it available to the patient for use in evolving a new paradigm for the relationship. Experientially his use of it may vary from the therapist's. But its direction will be the same. That is, it will lead toward taking his own mind rather than the relationship as an object, even though it is the relationship that he started with. Agreement on paradigms comes about because the X factor that makes a person's mind an object is the same one that makes a conflicted therapeutic relationship into an object. That factor—the underlying objectness in the mind, or of the relationship—can be identified by a common problem before any definition is given to it. Indeed, as I have said, analyst and patient may never quite agree on the definition of their common interest, since objects may be described in an infinite number of ways. They certainly begin by defining their common problems differently. There is initially no common explicit paradigm. But the analyst shows a *route* from their shared problem to a common object. (I am reminded of Parmenides' approach to the object in terms of a route, cf. Mourelatos, 1970, p. 192.) And by practicing solutions to the problem, patient and therapist work out, with various differences in formulation, a paradigm for it.

One could state formally that the therapist wants the patient to treat his objects not as objects but as properties. In particular, he wants the patient to treat the therapeutic relationship as a property of something more fundamental. The patient's conflicts make him treat *some* of his own objects—some objects of his interest, and some objects of his mind—as mere properties of other, "realer" objects of his interest and of his mind. Therefore, both therapist and patient are trying to find an underlying object in the therapeutic relationship and in its participants.

THE RELATIONSHIP OF PSYCHOTHERAPIES

If psychoanalysis is viewed as the most ambitious training in perceiving oneself as an object, or perfecting an implicit theory of the mind, its relationship to other formal helping modalities may become clearer.

Generally speaking, two methods have been used to place analysis in the array of treatments. One distinguishes analysis in terms of its techniques, such as the use of free association or the analysis of the transference. The other defines it in terms of its results, such as alteration in character structure. The first method is too modest and the second is too presumptuous. Clearly analysis is distinguished by its aims as well as its tools. But if those aims are described in terms of results, they cannot safely be appropriated by psychoanalysis. The science of the mind is nowhere near precise enough to predict apodictically what consequences will or will not follow a given stimulus. Intrapsychic echoes and reverberations are not so easily mapped. We may be skeptical about the power of a voodoo healer, but we cannot know for sure how a visit to him will affect an individual's psychic economy.

But even if analysis is described in terms of its aim, and its aim is described as a project rather than an outcome, the likelihood is that it will still overlap with other psychotherapies. It is intrinsically implausible that we can tailor our helpfulness to different patients by targeting unrelated impingements on assorted pieces of the mental apparatus, and it is still implausible if one adds that juggling one part of the apparatus causes less improvement than tinkering with another or adjusting the whole machine. Most likely some aspect of the project and some of the benefit are shared by all psychotherapy. (That likelihood leads Frank [1961] to reduce the whole business to what is considered the lowest common denominator—suggestion or persuasion. But suggestion is such a vague and global term as to beg the issue.)

Can we not say, then, that all psychotherapies, including traditional and ritual healing, aim at some sort of restructuring? If so, then we can employ our terminology to make the following distinctions: just as in theory, so in practice, psychoanalysis is the most complete effort to take the mind as an object, undistracted by other objects, such as sociological groupings, aesthetic formations, etc. There is no other psychological theory that could have been investigated as a complete system in the way that Ricoeur has studied Freud. The differences that have distinguished analytic theory from other theories of the mind have always followed from the greater ambitiousness and theoretical meticulousness of analytic theory. Similarly in practice, the objects that the patient begins with, especially the object that he makes out of his relationship with his analyst, are most consistently treated as properties of another, single object (the mind) in analytic practice. Psychoanalysis is a technique for promoting the most persistent and unrelenting regard of the mind as an object.

What is usually called supportive therapy can be described as the pursuit of the objects that the patient is initially concerned with. In formal psychotherapy that would lead to clarification of feelings and situations. In folk healing, the objects would be not feelings or specific personal relationships, but relationship to the community.

This classification might seem superfluous as merely reflecting the degree to which a therapy challenges defences. But in psychoanalytic theory "defense" is really the actualization of a potentiality. Like a sublimation, it makes a differentiated something out of what would otherwise be a little rawer, more "instinctual" (cf. Gill, 1963; Friedman, 1982). A defense is both a reaction to and a derivative of the multipotential instinct representative. In other words, defenses are properties of an object. Thus, while challenging defenses would necessarily set in motion the most thorough quest for the mind as an object, supporting defenses would also lead towards objectifying of an object, though not necessarily the mind as a whole. Supporting someone's defenses therefore may not be as static and conservative an activity as it sounds. And its possible consequences cannot be foreclosed on theoretical grounds alone. Its range of consequences would depend on how far the patient's object-making tendency carried him. If that were not the case, the still-thriving school of Rogerian counseling would probably not have survived.

In the classification I am proposing, the entire spectrum of psychotherapies would share this project: to enhance people's proclivity to experience as aspects of an object what was not previously thought to have such significance.

SUMMARY

1. From Ricoeur's study of Freud, one can draw the conclusion that a theory of the mind amounts to regarding the mind as an object, with conscious phenomena as its properties.

2. Cassirer's theory of experience suggests that this object-making underlies all experience and is the essence of science generally.

3. The practical use of theory of the mind in psychoanalytic therapy suggests that the patient is helped to take his mind as an object, rather than the partial experiences, such as the relationship with his therapist, which are the objects he is initially concerned with.

4. Kuhn's discussion of paradigm clash suggests that it is not easy to shift from experiencing something as an object to experiencing it as the property of another object.

5. In psychotherapy this shift may begin with an agreement between patient and therapist on a problem, felt in common by both parties although described differently by them. The therapist takes the therapeutic relationship to be a property of the patient's mind. Because of his ambivalence, the patient gradually takes his dominant paradigm of the relationship to be the property of some other object, so as to accommodate it to conflicting wishes. The tendency to look for an underlying object is what the therapist communicates, and a common paradigm is more or less arrived at.

6. All psychotherapies may share this object-making enterprise. How far the consequent restructuring goes is an empirical and perhaps individual matter. Psychoanalysis is distinctive among psychotherapies in most diligently pursuing the mind as an object.

IV
Debate About Theory of the Mind:
Revisions

17

Introduction

In the first part of this book we watched an interplay between the therapist's practical dilemmas and his theories. Naturally the part of theory that first came into view was theory of therapy.

But we then noticed that the diffracting lens that filters everything between patient and therapist is theory of the mind. And so, in Part III we set out to see what theory of the mind is. We selected Freud's theory as the most complete one available; we looked for the schematic criteria that guided it; and we tried to understand how those abstract criteria satisfy practical, treatment needs.

In Part I we found that disputes show what is at stake in theory of therapy. In the same fashion, disputes can help us to see what is at stake in theory of the mind. Although few theories rival Freud's in scale, there is no dearth of passionate criticism and partial revisions. We want to see what vital treatment issues hinge on these disputes. It will help make those treatment issues visible to us.

Revisions can be approached in so many different ways, that we could easily lose our path. Schisms are caused by many forces. Theory of the mind is subject to the same diverse influences we chose to ignore when looking at theory of therapy, including socioeconomic forces and institutional politics. But theory of the mind is subject to other vectors as well. Intellectual pride is not a negligible force. The last century saw breathtaking advances in the physical and biological sciences. Psychotherapists, like other "soft" scientists, are likely to feel that their theory is stagnant and out-of-date, and may hunt for where it went wrong.

If we add to this a shift in philosophical fashions we have the recipe for many recent critiques, as stated boldly in almost all of their introductions. But we should beware these philosophical declarations of intent. They may not do justice to the contributions that they introduce. After all, the philosophy of science is a camp follower, and a clumsy, inexperienced one at that. Few problems have been solved either by trying to "think scientifically" or by deliberately thinking unscientifically. Constructive theory probably arises from natural difficulties, even if its maker thinks it comes from a more grown-up world view.

I do not wish to oversimplify the path that leads from practical difficulties to theoretical innovations. Theory has its own momentum, which directs it even while it is interacting with practical problems. My point is that insofar as psychoanalytic revisions resemble current trends in philosophy, they may simply be going through the same periodic resifting of their subject matter that all theories engage in. Rather than building on new philosophical idioms, psychoanalysts may be reacting to their own last theory the way philosophers happen to be reacting to theirs. Both in psychoanalytic theory and in philosophy, there seem to be alternating cycles in which problems are first elaborated and then dismissed. One generation entangles itself with increasingly difficult answers to a riddle, and then the next generation announces that the tangle is unnecessary because there is really no riddle. Then the riddle gradually makes itself felt again, first here and then there, and before long, the process begins anew.

It seems to me that philosophy has traced three or four such cycles in matters of induction, substance, and abstraction. Psychoanalytic theories of the mind seem to be going through a few similar cycles. The best workers in the field once put enormous effort into Freudian exegesis, trying to smooth out Freud's theory and piece it together seamlessly on the drawing board. There followed a tendency to dismiss the whole project as not, after all, just difficult, but fortunately unnecessary. We were told that theory of the mind is confusing only because it is the product of a confusion; something simpler is called for; we should start anew. We watch these new theories develop, and we see that the simpler picture needs a few finishing touches. A few questions are raised, and then a few more, and, creeping in again with different names, we spy elements that led to the Freudian complexity.

Not that we necessarily get back to the earlier stage. The Dialectic insists that we are wiser when we return. But we are probably wearier as well. Who will labor to erect a theory of the mind on the scale of Freud's? Even if another such theoretical genius should come along, the hopefulness of the pioneer can never be recovered.

There is another, less dismal reason for this diminishing spiral of theoretical ambition. We have seen that Freud's theory is comprehensive just because it is a mixed theory. It is mixed in all ways: It is a part/whole theory and a maturation theory. It is a dramatic theory and a causal theory. It is an abstract theory and a humanistic theory. It is not coherent on a single plane. It works by answering questions as they are raised. It cannot be set forth in a homogeneous fashion.

After every effort has been made to recast it in a linear fashion, the inevitable reaction to such a theory is to select one favorite phase to hold on to, and demolish the discordant others. But when theorists see that room has to be made for all of these ill-assorted schemas, will the prospect of building another, equally rambling edifice appeal to anyone's architectonic instincts? Would Freud have gone so far so fast if he knew ahead of time that every answer he developed would be misleading except in the context of its development from his first guess to its final formulation?

But although we will probably never again see a full theory of the mind, there is considerable value in new beginnings and critical revisions. For one thing, a theory that is only elaborated and never shrewdly challenged will become a purely syntactic structure devoid of semantic content. (Nothing could have brought Freudian resistance theory to life again nearly as well as Schafer's reformulation.) And for our investigation, we have special reason to thank the revisionists: The pendular swing of their allegience dissects for us the demands that the practice of psychotherapy makes on theory of the mind.

For even though psychoanalytic theorists are intellectuals, and hold themselves to high speculative standards, they are never disinterested theoreticians. The intensity, patience, and concern behind these revisions of Freudian theory could not come solely from a wish to make theory look better or sound more sophisticated, although the authors frequently ask us to believe that is their motive. Only a felt need, a professional disturbance, a mission that comes out of practice, could sustain these projects. It is clear that even the more "traditional" of these revisions makes a difference in practice—a difference that should be respectfully charted.

With that conviction, we must wrestle with these innovative theories until we can feel some of the fissiparous pulls of practice that had been cinched together in Freud's theory of the mind and now claim special attention.

Of course, if these theories are simply better theories, they might not show us anything about the practice of therapy. They might only show us that therapists now think better than they used to. And because that is what these revisions claim, we must examine them first as rivals for the throne. Having done that, and concluded that they are not, we can use them more interestingly as mirrors of the therapist's dilemma.

II

Some reforms struggle to make psychoanalysis more scientific. Others, disappointed in its truth claims, cut bait and abandon scientific pretensions. But whether promising more or less "science," what the revisions all have in common is a suggestion that theory of the mind has been living in its own world, and some way must be found to reconnect it with reality.

It is impossible not to sympathize with the effort to catch freely flying theory and hold its nose firmly to the real, definite and demonstrable ground. For this laudable purpose, theoreticians use a wide variety of styles. They may insist that we talk about persons and action, or they may insist that we talk precisely about introspectively evident representations, or they may talk demonstrably about body feeling, or they may talk plainly about the self, or humbly about perspectives. These are very different things, but they are all vivid and ordinary. We are invited to compare them with the unreal, esoteric "things" of psychoanalytic theory, and see how far psychoanalytic theory had strayed from the stuff it wanted to explain.

A rebellion against abstraction is in progress, and a longing for concrete items. By and large, what the revisionists do is to palm the discarded abstractions that are necessary for understanding, and use them (without credit) in isolating their concrete items and in talking about those items. Although the revisions start out from many different positions, they all move toward presenting the mind as an organic whole, which is easily identified with concrete reality, and compared with which any generalization or abstraction is artificial and arbitrary, all theory a distortion. That is the trend we will see in the following chapters.

The reader will observe this convergence of dissimilar revisions when he compares Peterfreund's theory with Gendlin's. When we first see it, Peterfreund's theory looks concrete and specific, and by comparison, Gendlin's looks almost mystical and Bergsonian. Peterfreund uses a computer model. (One can visualize discrete circuitry while reading him.) Gendlin hates all "chop–chop" talk of parts and pieces. But we find that Peterfreund's information processing is simply a code for the largest abstraction we can think of. The larger the abstractions denoted by a theory, the farther we get from arbitrary divisions, and the closer to the bare existence of the organism. Accordingly, Peterfreund ends up with a theory that is, no less than Gendlin's, the portrait of a whole undivided organism. Levenson, like Gendlin, does little to hide his distaste for abstractions, and he challenges all particular understandings. Schafer tries to eliminate abstractions, but when faced with the consequences he will not part with the clinical understandings they bring. George Klein sought to straddle the fence, but the terminologic trick of explaining things by "equilibrium" does not save him from falling to the concrete-whole-organism side. Kohut tried the same procedure, and of these theorists, Kohut alone emerges with a statable theory. But that is because he retains the essential lumpiness of a theory of the mind, as found in Freud's theory.

Klein and Kohut tried to make equilibrium the pivot of theory because the concept of equilibrium, unlike other contenders, is one abstraction that seems to keep its hold on reality. Because Jean Piaget's work is the most exhaustive exploration of the equilibrium concept in science, I comment on his work at the end of this section. One test of whether psychoanalysis can be transformed into a more organismic theory is how much use psychoanalysis can make of Piaget. (Loewald's [1980] project is the other promising test of an organismic theory of psychoanalysis.)

I have another reason for discussing Piaget, who, after all, is not a psychoanalytic revisionist. In chapter 8, I portrayed the actions of the therapist and the patient as efforts to establish an equilibrium, and I have claimed that what a therapist does is largely determined by how he seeks to balance himself when upset. So, for his bearing on my own account of therapy, no less than to evaluate revisions of theory of the mind, Piaget must be looked into carefully.

18

Peterfreund's Information-

Processing Theory

THE CHALLENGE

E manuel Peterfreund's book *Information, Systems, and Psychoanalysis* (1971) is an effort to reform psychoanalytic theory by substituting such concepts of computer technology as information, programs and processing.

The book carries a particularly useful appreciation by Benjamin Rubinstein, who argues for Peterfreund's revision in a spirit so different from Peterfreund's as to set up an independent standard for judging the text.

Peterfreund tends to view psychoanalytic concepts as *ad hoc* constructs, shaped by models of a dated physics and influenced by primitive modes of thought such as anthropomorphism. Scientific hypotheses should relate phenomena to progressively more general laws of nature. But, argues Peterfreund, physics has left psychoanalysis behind; analytic concepts once thought to be analogous to concepts of physics are now known to be unrelated. Peterfreund asks that psychoanalytic theory be replaced by concepts compatible with modern brain physiology, and thus put in touch with chemistry, physics and the whole corpus of scientific law.

Rubinstein, on the other hand, recognizes that psychoanalytic concepts are not just images, but express relationships of data. The "core meaning" of a psychoanalytic concept is the empirical hypothesis that it expresses. In other words, after stripping away their pictorial and associational trappings, Rubinstein allows that psychoanalytic concepts have yet a significance in organizing clinical observations.

This recognition does not make Rubinstein less methodologically exacting.

According to Rubinstein, psychoanalytic concepts are not necessarily arbitrary or illogical, as Peterfreund makes them appear, but they get no support from other sciences. Nor can psychoanalysis claim that clinical hypotheses – its core meanings – are credentials enough. For the same core meanings can be expressed in other ways. And since psychoanalytic core meanings are ultimately hypotheses about brain function they should be expressed in terms compatible with brain physiology.

> . . . we can interpret the core model in terms that, by contrast to its energic interpretation, are compatible with what is currently known about neurophysiology. That is precisely what Dr. Peterfreund is trying to do, not only with the psychic energy model, but with the theoretical psychoanalytic model as a whole. I am not suggesting that he first constructed an explicit core model which he then proceeded to interpret in accordance with modern biology. I do believe, however, that this step is generally implicit in the development of theoretical formulations from clinical data and hypotheses [p. 5].

Satisfied that Peterfreund has implicitly taken this step, and observing the large number of psychoanalytic interests that Peterfreund casts into terms of information systems, Rubinstein concludes that the study is "not simply an introduction but a new departure involving a radical reorientation of our thinking" (p. 7).

The claim that Peterfreund's work is a new departure thus rests on the conviction that he has implicitly reinterpreted psychoanalytic core models. After all, the call is not simply to talk more scientifically but to talk more scientifically about what psychoanalysis has been talking about.

Has Peterfreund's work fulfilled the claims of its preface? Certainly the book demonstrates that it is easy to discuss many phenomena in terms of information, feedback and processing. Nor can we demand that such an ambitious undertaking be complete and detailed on first venture. Therefore Rubinstein is not disturbed that Peterfreund approaches the reinterpretation of psychoanalytic core meanings "only in a somewhat general way." He regards it as a deficiency of completeness, not of conception. If Peterfreund is rather general in proposing alternative expressions for psychoanalytic hypotheses, "This is not a criticism but a reminder to ourselves of the fact, freely acknowledged by Dr. Peterfreund, that in spite of his pioneering efforts much work remains to be done." But if Peterfreund's reinterpretation of psychoanalytic core models has indeed made a new departure involving a radical reorientation of our thinking, it must already have dealt in depth with those issues, such as conflict and development, which stimulated the development of psychoanalytic concepts. No matter how effectively he criticizes the ego concept, his new departure can radically reorient us only after it gives us an adequate account of the kind of conflict that prompted Freud to frame his structural theory. A promise will not do for a radical reorientation. According to Rubinstein, psychoanalytic theory has its reasons. If those reasons are not dealt with by another theory we would be inclined to say that an alternative has not been offered. New theories are hardly developed overnight, it is true, but patience cannot deny that there are some nodal aspects of a theory which tell us immediately whether psychoanalytic core models are in fact being reinterpreted.

THEORY OF TREATMENT

A good sample to take for this examination is the theory of psychoanalytic treatment, because there conflict and development are conspicuous issues. To understand a theory of therapy we must first grasp the theory of pathogenesis. Here is Peterfreund's:

> Defective or inadequate programming may lead to pathological activity, behaviour, or subjective psychological experience, and these are often accompanied by stress, pain, and anxiety. In all cases, defective or inadequate programming must be evaluated with reference to a standard or norm. Programs which contain instructions that are logically incompatible with the attainment of a desired goal are important examples of defective programming. Clinically, these programs result in conflict.
>
> Defensive activity, behavior, or subjective psychological experience can be viewed as the clinical manifestations of substitute programming. The organism tends to defend itself by automatically deactivating those programs which result in stress, pain, anxiety, and conflict. Substitute programs are activated; as a result, stress, pain, anxiety, and conflict are lessened. Any information-processing programs, and therefore any activity, behavior, or subjective psychological experience, can serve defensive purposes [p. 170].

No great distinction is made here between defence and ordinary learning. Strictly speaking, any program may be thought of as a "substitute program," which has been activated to replace one that led to "stress, pain, anxiety and conflict," for that is how programs are supposed to be selected. A defense is simply a program that does not maximize the processing of information. Thus Peterfreund's position is that people suffer when they are not flexible or open enough in their programming to respond to as many facets of experience as an average person. They are not open because openness would require programs that conflict with other of their purposes.

Since emotional problems are states of inadequate information, treatment means providing information. The analyst commands information derived from the patient, from his own life, and from his training and experience. The patient is allowed to absorb this information at a gentle pace and to reprogram himself with it. So far the formulation is vaguely reminiscent of the earliest psychoanalytic theory of treatment before the advent of the structural theory, when treatment seemed to be a welcomed enlightenment. But many psychoanalytic concepts (and even the anthropomorphic style of writing that Peterfreund condemns) were inspired by the discovery that patients do not want the new information. Resistance is therefore one of the nodal points for a reinterpretation of psychoanalytic theory. Peterfreund does not actually translate the concept of resistance into his own terms. But we get an idea of what resistance is in his theory by observing his view of transference, since transference is, among other things, one form of resistance.[1] This is how Peterfreund conceptualizes transference: Transference is an error that the patient makes because he is processing the input from the analyst in a narrow range of old programs. It is an error that can be corrected by encouraging the patient to receive input about the error itself.

But how can the patient's unsuitable, primitive and deficient programming be made to correctly program the information about the error in his programs? The possibilities appear to be limited. The analyst might try a new mode of information delivery; he might hope that the patient will use new programs to process his information; and he might seek to convey a new kind of information. All three possibilities are found in Peterfreund's discussion.

1. The analyst can deliver information in a new fashion. Peterfreund leans heavily on the factor of pacing. In analysis, information that might be stressful is percolated at a rate that the patient can tolerate. This might seem to imply that the patient has some adequate programs that have gone unused because they can handle only small items of information, whereas all the information in his world has come in large packages. That, however, is not a sensible sentence in Peterfreund's language. Alternatively we can take comfortable pacing to mean more appropriate pacing, that is, better discrimination. But then, instead of a simple quantitative explanation, we see the question begged.

2. The patient can process the analyst's information with better programs than he ordinarily uses. Useful "switched off" programs are latent in the patient, and the analyst has a way of switching them on again. For instance, Peterfreund says that patients "must abandon attempts to censor or to maintain their familiar self-representations as they permit alien mental

---

[1] In the original version of this chapter (Friedman, 1972), I simply took Peterfreund's explanation of transference to be his theory of resistance. Peterfreund (1973) justifiably objected that resistance is not the same as transference, but, significantly, he did not take the opportunity to offer a different theory of resistance (see Friedman, 1975d). I think he was hard pressed to find one.

contents to emerge" (p. 318). And again, "Other programs must simultaneously be activated. . . ." (p. 319). It is not clear what the analyst provides in
terms of information theory that makes the patient do these things.[2] Since we
are not told how programs are switched off and on we cannot consider this an
answer.

3. The analyst provides a new *kind* of information. Peterfreund refers to a
corrective emotional experience in analysis. I take this to mean that the
patient gets a kind of feedback from the analyst that he does not get from
everyday life. Of course, we know to begin with that the analyst contributes
something special, but how are we to imagine specialness in informational
terms? We must remember that Peterfreund is using the term "information" in
an objective sense (not the newspaper sense), as a pattern of physical events,
or a relationship between such patterns, and there must always be all kinds of
such patterns everywhere. All the analyst could do with information defined
in this way is to produce more of it. More information might fill information
gaps, but it cannot by itself overcome resistance, which processes the analyst's
new input in a narrow range of old programs.

The problem is that Peterfreund defines information as a transmitted
pattern of physical events. Consequently, information is already supplied in
our environment. Thus, while treatment can be said to be the provision of
increased information, it is more accurate to say that treatment is the
modification of programs so as to increase information input. But the theory
of therapy does not tell us how programs are modified. To judge whether
Peterfreund has reinterpreted psychoanalytic core concepts involved in
resistance and response to analysis we must therefore turn to his learning
theory.

LEARNING THEORY

Peterfreund's formula is this: Information is input. It is modified by the
organism's programs. The aim is to reduce stress.

> The essential point is this: In order to reduce stress, in order to attain the
> ultimate goal of homeostasis and survival, or any subsidiary goal, the organism
> must activate the appropriate adapted organismic program—the product of
> past learning and of phylogenetically evolved programming. But if the appro-
> priate program is not present, the organism must proceed to learn; it must
> reprogram itself to reduce stress. . . .

---

[2]A vindictive defender of the ego will here counterattack Peterfreund for the latent anthropomorphism of expecting his patient to switch this on and that off for him.

Thus we can say that because the organism is constantly responding to some potential stressor and constantly attempting to reduce the resulting stress and to restore or maintain homeostatic conditions, the organism is either constantly activating and hence reinforcing the appropriate existing learned programs, or else is attempting to learn; it is attempting to evolve new structures or new programs of information processing which allow stress to be reduced and biological order to be restored [pp. 188-9].

How are new programs developed? For one thing, the organism is programmed to scan its collection of old programs to see if it can find one to fit (p. 189). "Old learning and a wide variety of information-processing levels are activated" (p. 190). Moreover, "New arrangements and combinations are formed" (p. 190). These are then tried out, and feedback establishes the successful ones. The theory of learning is that the organism tries out old and new ways of reacting and preserves the ways that avoid stress. To learn is to select programs fit for a new challenge. Fitness is determined by the elimination of stress. The stressless state is the referee. But what is stress? Stress is the condition of "biological variables moving beyond their normal range" (p. 190, 200n.). The implication is that the normal range of biological variables is a range which the organism can find programs to handle. (This is perhaps a way of saying that the organism is defined by its complement of programs, and I think that is consistent with a computer analogy.) So when Peterfreund says that the organism tries out various programs in its search for stressless feedback, he is saying no more than this: that the organism tries out some programs to see if they work. Stress is what happens when programming is unsuccessful. Unsuccessful programming is programming that leads to stress. Learning is finding successful programs. Peterfreund says, "Indeed, learning, adaptation, and biological order are, in a sense, synonymous" (p. 189).

As a definition this is unobjectionable. As a learning theory it leaves an important question unanswered. Peterfreund believes that in one sense motives are programs. His definition of learning makes lower order motives instrumental to higher order motives. Lower order motives are tried out to see if they satisfy higher order motives.[3] But at the highest level, motives are still instrumental, though they are instrumental for a very abstract supermotive, namely equilibrium or homeostasis. Now the unanswered question is this: With regard to the psychological apparatus as a whole, what is it that is to be equilibrated? I cannot see any other answer than that what is adapted, or is made to survive, or is equilibrated, is a set of programs. But how are the *predominant* programs to be modified for the relief of stress, when

---

[3]Peterfreund believes that primitive programs can also be controlling and peremptory because of their strategic location in the circuit. But he does not seem to want to place them in a separate category, so I assume that they too exist at the pleasure of the larger programs and are simply more difficult to manipulate.

stress is the failure of *those* programs to be realized? I do not mean this as a logical paradox but as a question that a learning theory must answer.

Here is another way of presenting the difficulty: As a learning theory, Peterfreund discusses the choice of subordinate motives that are consistent with larger or more dominant motives. In other words, he shows us how strategies can be learned (or rather he asserts that strategies are selected). What he does not show is how motives per se are learned. We could say that he segregates instrumentalities and motives. He leaves motives to the most abstract areas of the psyche—so abstract that they also define the psyche. His learning theory is clear and simple because it neglects the learning of non-instrumental motives.

Of course, distinctions between instrumental and noninstrumental programs and between strategies and motives are foreign to Peterfreund's discussion. It is part of his general approach (and probably an element in his campaign against anthropomorphism) that all programs are instrumental—all are strategies. The program of the organism as a whole, it seems, is as instrumental as the smallest subprogram. The small program, for example, knee flexion, may be instrumental to a larger one, such as walking. But it seems that the very largest program is still instrumental to adaptation or stresslessness. That is an illusion. Stresslessness is not a motive which can be served. Nor is equilibrium. They are incomplete descriptions, like "success." Equilibrium is a different thing in each of its instances. It signifies that an organism's psyche is functioning, and it cannot be used to explain the configuration of that psyche except in the trivial sense that functionability explains functioning. Peterfreund says that programs are switched on and off depending on how well they serve more general programs. But one cannot say the same about the total organism, or its overall psychological equipment. Adaptation of the organism does not mean manipulation for some higher goal. The organism serves itself, not "equilibrium." Its configuration is determined by how well it can preserve itself as it is. That is what equilibrium means.

But if a total configuration of programs can seek to maintain itself, then why not the subprograms that comprise it? I guess Peterfreund shuns the idea because it leads directly back to the sort of theory he hoped to replace. For instance, a kind of anthropomorphism makes its appearance. Anthropomorphism regards the individual mechanisms of the mind as though each acted like a whole mind. Programs do not seem anthropomorphic because they are simply there or not there, switched on or off. Unlike the superego or id of Peterfreund's critique, programs do not strive to survive or plot to fulfil themselves. Their fate is an indifferent outcome of the objective equilibration of the organism. But if the whole mind which is to be equilibrated is also a program, and each subprogram follows the same laws as the mind—if the same kind of striving which we see in the whole man can be attributed in some degree to his subprograms, why not an anthropomorphic view? How *now* to conjure away "the ego tries . . ." with "programs process"?

Moreover, if we find that subprograms imitate the mind as a whole, the much ridiculed energy theory may hobble back into respectability. For the energy theory is a way of ordering the balance of emphasis and priority in a mind thought of as a federation. As long as Peterfreund's system looks like an imperium serving a common cause—homeostasis—it seems to need no such principle. But if homeostasis simply refers to the effort of a program to preserve itself, and if each of that program's subprograms has its individual *raison d"etre*, then the net product of the mind is not a function of a simple goal; the parts of the mind serve their own interests as well as that of the whole. That may not exactly rehabilitate the energy concept, but it would rescue it from unemployment.

All of this is what Peterfreund wanted to avoid. For that reason he has preferred to abstract the organizing criteria of the mind from the mind that is organized. He has abstracted the organizing criteria into the term "homeostasis." By this notion he has so strained out of the organism its purposes that his learning theory comes close to saying that learning is a successful organism, which in turn scarcely allows a more revealing description of therapy than the assertion that the patient becomes more successful at his life task (information processing).

Even in details Peterfreund prefers to bury fractional organizing purposes as far from the scene as possible. For instance, as regards learning, though he allows that we try out first what worked before (an old part of the mind struggling for survival), he reserves his enthusiasm for the idea of random trials (where only the final purpose is active). Or consider the analytic situation. Peterfreund likes to think that patient and therapist naturally serve the same homeostatic master. Indeed Peterfreund's concept of homeostasis is so abstract that we *can* easily deceive ourselves that it means the same thing to both patient and therapist, with the consequence that resistance can be mistaken for an "error."[4] Peterfreund keeps pushing the problem of learning or criteria for change to the outermost limits of his theory where, as homeostasis, it becomes so rarefied that it is almost empty. What is the alternative? What would happen if the theory were not so preoccupied with

---

[4]It might be argued that the goal of both patient and therapist is to maximize the utilization of information. One might suppose that goal to be the same for both of them. But is that really what the participants are after? Are there not really two goals, each person seeking to maximize the information his already given program can handle? If by some miraculous tinkering with the mental "computer," an enormous increment of information could be programmed, transforming the mind into an indiscriminate consumer of every kind of pattern, who would request such an operation? What each creature wants is not that goals be realized, but that *it* realize goals, which is to say, in terms of Peterfreund's theory, that a person values his programs as well as his information.

automation? We may catch a glimpse of the alternative in Piaget with whom Peterfreund invites comparison.

COMPARISON WITH PIAGET

Superficially Piaget's terms "schema" and "assimilation" seem analogous to Peterfreund's "program" and "processing." But although Peterfreund's "program" operates on increasingly complex information, and is liable to being switched off or replaced, it is nevertheless essentially a fixed conduit. In that respect it is quite different from Piaget's "schema," which is altered by its very use. And therefore Piaget's term "assimilation" does not really correspond to Peterfreund's "processing." *Processing* is the exercising of a program on the information that it is *designed* to handle. But a *schema* can assimilate only to the extent that it accommodates slightly to something it was *not* designed to handle. For Peterfreund, novelty increases the information available to fixed (though replaceable) programmes. (Programs process memory-information in addition to information from outside the organism.) But for Piaget, novelty continually shapes and reshapes the schemata themselves. For Piaget there is no sharp distinction between memory and the organism's schemata. Memory is itself a schema.[5] In short, Piagetian schemata are in constant revision; to use them is to revise them. Change and development need to be studied and described but are not a separate problem for the theory. "Recompute mode" is always operating, or rather, there is no need for such a separate mode. But Peterfreund's programs are preset. Peterfreund agrees that there is constant change, but change and development must be accounted for by more remote operations of the theory.

Piaget's theory is intrinsically developmental because a kind of striving or conation is distributed throughout the theory. Instead of "take it or leave it" programs functioning under the aegis of an abstract criterion of survival, each of the organism's schemata is an attempt to come to terms with an environment. By each reaction the organism seeks to maintain itself amid changing circumstances and therefore the organism must ceaselessly change each type of reaction. But it does not change reactions simply by substituting one element for another, as in Peterfreund's account. Like the whole organism, every schema tries to hang on to the environment—one might say it tries to impose itself on the environment—and modifies itself to that end. In contrast, Peterfreund tries to describe development in a stepwise fashion: Information is provided as input. And then a program processes it. And then the program

---

[5]Why indeed does Peterfreund consider memory to be information rather than a program? Perhaps if memory consisted of programs, there would be less justification for the distinction between information and programs and less clarity in the static, phasic computer model.

is scored by the feedback from its output. And then, perhaps, another program is tried, etc. This stepwise theory, although it looks more concrete than Piaget's, is infinitely more abstract. How abstract it is becomes apparent if we scrutinize Peterfreund's fundamental concept of information.

WHAT IS "INFORMATION" IN THIS THEORY?

Peterfreund defines information as "a pattern of physical events" transmitted by a number of causally related sequences of physical events. "This information is processed, arranged, and rearranged in complex ways from input to output" (pp. 115–17). "Innumerable operations are performed on the input information, operations whose complexity increases as experiences and learning accumulate. The term 'information processing' refers to these operations; the term 'program' refers to the instruction for these operations." This model of the mind seems specific, visualizable and concrete: we picture items of information being put into the mechanism, there to be analysed, abstracted and filtered by programmed processes.

But the concreteness of the model is an illusion that results from thinking that "information" means what it usually means, namely, a relevant selection of data. On the contrary, for Peterfreund it is a technical term meaning "a pattern of physical events." What we ordinarily consider information is the *outcome* of processing. What "goes into" the system is nothing less than the order of the universe – or as much of it as the system can absorb. Peterfreund's definition makes information equivalent to any or all of the patterns that can be found in reality, all of the abstractions that could be made, or, in philosophical terms, simply reality itself. According to his definition, programs are dispositions to react in a certain way, and information is what there is to react to. If we were to adhere strictly to such a physical definition of information its use in psychology would be abstract and trivial. It would enable us to say that what impinges on the organism makes a difference to it; that the organism has dispositions to react; that these dispositions pattern what impinges on the organism; and that what happens within an organism is the result of its dispositions and its environment.

In contrast, Piaget discusses psychological information. He shows how it is developed, not just how it is disposed of. In Piaget's theory, "aliment" takes the place of "information." Aliment is that aspect of reality which more or less fits a schema. Aliment is obviously a relative term, whereas information is only covertly or equivocally a relative term the way Peterfreund uses it. Were we to present Piaget's message in Peterfreund's language, we would always speak of information *for a program*, or information *to a program*. Indeed we would say that information is information *because* it is processed, and *insofar* as it is processed. We would say that processing is not just something that is done to information, or just a way of reacting to information; we would say that processing is what makes information.

How abstract Peterfreund's deceptively electronic terms are may be seen if we identify what in his theory really corresponds to Piaget's concepts. I have said that superficially Peterfreund's "program" resembles Piaget's "schema." Actually programs correspond not to schemata but to Piaget's *abstract tendency of assimilation*, the tendency of an organism to embrace that which it is prepared to meet. But if Piaget is right, this is an *aspect* of a reaction, not a reaction itself. It is balanced by the aspect of accommodation which is the way the organism is affected or changed by what it assimilates.

CONCLUSION

Both Rubinstein in his preface and Peterfreund in his text try to console those who are offended by a computer model of mental life. Peterfreund assumes that what might give offence is the reduction of man to the level of his general biological nature. I think he is mistaken. There are many theories, including Piaget's theory and Freud's philosophical setting for psychoanalytic theory, which put man in his place as a natural creature. What Peterfreund's theory does that these do not is to make conation, purpose or striving seem to be illusory. I think that is why the computer analogy is distasteful. The theory is an effort to eliminate intentionality. (It does so only spuriously, by making organismic purpose vague.)

None of this means that an information-systems theory of the mind is untenable. But Peterfreund's theory does not reinterpret the core models of psychoanalysis. Peterfreund has only shown that one can easily talk about the mind in computer terms, and thus in terms of other sciences. But the universality of this *lingua franca* is hardly cause for rejoicing. Its terms are so broadly applicable just because they are very abstract, and at a certain point abstraction becomes triviality. Peterfreund's information-systems theory is really a meticulous restatement of the principle of causality, insofar as causality refers to general rules or patterns. "Information" is available causal pattern, in other words potential cause. "Programs" are dispositions to react in certain ways to causes, in other words, "programs" are potential effects. "Processing" is the actualizing of some potential effects by actual causes. "Feedback" is the effect of those effects on the organism. "Homeostatic equilibrium" is a nonspecific name for the organism's specific existence. No wonder that these terms bring us on to a common ground with the rest of science! (Some simplified, generalized behaviorism, amounting to very much the same thing, has always beckoned seductively to the simplifying theoretician.) That is how the concept of information "allows one to theorize about aspects of the central nervous system despite the current lack of knowledge concerning many chemical or electrical events" (p. 117).

No doubt such a formal recasting of the principles of causality has its uses. Perhaps it facilitates the mathematical discussion of small, known, finite, well-understood, delimited causes, acting on systems with denumerable and relatively constant alternative reactions. For the same reason, the more that is known in detail about a system, and the less plastic its parameters, the more it can be sorted into a formal, stepwise causal chain. Peterfreund's book gives no indication that the science of the mind is anywhere near that stage.[6] What the book does convey is faith—faith that a formal causal analysis alone can bridge the gap from physics to mind, if only it is worked out diligently enough. ("The 'mobility' of any program results from increasingly elaborate communication networks, elaborate and more precise program selection, and so on" p. 372.)

One has to be very enthusiastic to hope for so much from a *formal* theory.

SUMMARY

Peterfreund has suggested that psychoanalytic theory be replaced by an information-systems theory using the computer as a model, in order to connect psychology with the other sciences.

To account for resistance and therapeutic change in his new terms, Peterfreund uses a new learning theory which represents the mind's reactions as servants of homeostasis.

But I object that homeostasis is not a complete description of a goal. The goal must be adaptation of a specific organism or a specific psyche. And if the mind as a whole tries to maintain its own configuration, there is no reason why the dispositions that compose it should not be thought to do the same. Component reactions would not then be dispensable means to a general goal of homeostasis, but would seek also their own homeostasis and thus constitute motives of their own. But Peterfreund's learning theory explains only the learning of means and not motives. (He simply says that means may be considered as motives.)

Piaget offers the contrast of a theory in which each of the organism's component patterns seeks its own equilibrium. Whereas Peterfreund pictures the organism as trying out one rigid means after another to reach its general purpose, Piaget sees each means as a flexible attempt to attain a subordinate goal. Consequently every "means" is altered by its use and is not just accepted

---

[6]To rush us into psychocomputerology when we hardly even know how to describe behavior seems to me a little like peddling typewriters before an alphabet is invented: It is a very forward-looking enterprise, but it does not help much in communication.

or rejected by the organism's over-all goal management. Piaget, in other words, provides a theory of goal learning.

In Piaget's theory every organismic activity has both an aspect of adapting itself to the environment, and an aspect of selecting out of the environment something that already fits its pattern. Peterfreund artificially separates these aspects of organismic reaction. On the one hand, adaptation to the environment becomes a very abstract goal attributed to the organism as a whole, which, in turn, is extremely flexible in striving for it. On the other hand, the organism's various programs react rigidly and only to those elements of the environment that they are already prepared for.

The distinction between receptive, fixed programs and active, flexible adaptation is an abstraction in the theorist's mind. It comes to look like a distinction between separate phases of an actual system only because of the ambiguity of the concept of information. Information sounds like something relevant enough to fit into a passive, preformed program, and at the same time objective enough to be grounds for revision by the organism's adaptive centers. Because information is already relevant, the right program does not need to seek homeostasis. And because information is independent of programs, the organism's homeostatic centers can, so to speak, use information as a basis to hire and fire programs. But information cannot really have both qualities. One must finally decide whether information is a personally relevant organization of data or simply the way things are in the environment. Peterfreund chooses the latter definition. But that makes information practically the same as reality. And it therefore makes the programs that process information equivalent to potential effects of reality. Equilibrium becomes a mere abstract reference to the organism's identity.

On its face, the information-systems alternative to psychoanalytic theory seems almost industrially concrete, but it turns out to be really a high abstraction of potential causes and potential effects. It is doubtful that so abstract and formal a theory can make a bridge between physics and behavior.

19

Phenomenological Theory:

Mind as a World of

Representations

Serious students of mind quickly discover that they are dealing with a motley variety of abstractions. That is hardly surprising: we could no more describe the mind fully in terms of elementary units and processes than we could describe the physical world with only quantum physics and none of the common things of life and laboratory. For psychologists, the common things of life and laboratory include not only dispositions and feelings, but also hypothetical groupings and systems. Such a scattered assortment of perceptual and conceptual universes presents a problem to the clinician, who struggles to comprehend a lively patient in terms that alternate between widely different levels of generality and many types of theory. Therapists would like to find a single thread that runs from the drama of the office, through loops and tangles of mature structures, and on back to earliest learning.

Object representations have been welcomed as such a thread. To the extent that psychic structure is built out of object representations, therapists see a clear path from theory to practice. Representational theory diagrams component parts of the mind that are available for change.

The trouble with "representation" is that it means so many different things (see Fraiberg, 1969), and almost all its meanings are vague. Since mental life is practically equivalent to signifying activity, the term "representation" is almost synonymous with "mental." In that broadest sense, the language of representation is merely an atomized way of speaking about meanings (cf. Modell, 1968).

But it is not the simple category of meaningfulness—scarcely a dazzling innovation—that has attracted theorists and therapists. It is rather the trend to *confine* psychoanalytic theory to descriptions of meaning. Critics within psychoanalysis have declared that it should concern itself exclusively with reasons and meanings, not causes and entities (Basch, 1973; Gill, 1976; Klein, 1976c; Schafer, 1973b). I do not believe that anyone has succeeded in constructing a clinical psychology on such stringent terms.[1] But the wish to purify theory of anything that does not refer to a meaning has given a new allure to that item of analytic theory that was called a representation. This analytic kind of representation is not just any signifier; it is supposed to signify a coherent object of desire. As such, it subtly combines force and meaning.[2] If one wants to talk about the mind by referring only to meaning, this psychoanalytic sort of representation is a tempting term, because it is a meaning that conveniently carries with it its own principle of selection (desire). Since its implicit conative definition validates its borders, such a representation can be used to map the mind's constitution, whereas simple "meanings" appear to be merely the mind's flickering productions.

It is this theoretical goal of mapping the mind with representations that I wish to criticize. And so I will first try to develop the particular definition of representation that it uses.

Representations that map the mind are prototypically the full mental representatives of whole, loved people in the environment. The term is also used, however, to stand for any significance or aspect such persons might have for the subject. The most frequent aspect that passes for a representation is an image. Are images representations? Answers vary. However, if representation is but another word for image, it samples too small a sector of mental activity to be of much use. Images do not have the mind-mapping power of the traditional psychoanalytic representation. Psychoanalytic theoreticians therefore agree that representation must have a broader definition than image (see Meissner, 1973; Schafer, 1973c). In this respect, their language does not always follow their definition. Thus Sandler and Rosenblatt (1962) say that representations are not images, but "schemata constructed out of a multitude of impressions" (p. 133). But representations are then compared to a radar or television screen (p. 136), which suggests that they are, after all, more like images or a multitude of impressions than like schemata constructed out of them. Unless one holds the term "representation" fast to the high-level abstraction it labels, it travels to a more concrete world and sets itself up as a visual image. One reason for this slipperiness is

---

[1]The purest attempt that I know of is Gendlin's (1962). My reasons for excluding Schafer's theory are given in chapter 20.

[2]For the original function of the term *representation*, see Beres and Joseph (1970), who give a succinct, up-dated account of how representation serves Freudian theory as a necessary complement to concepts of cathexis, binding and neutralization of energy, and as a help in defining conflict. See, also, Ricoeur (1970) on the interplay of force and meaning.

that whatever object representations are, they must come from memory, and whenever we think about memories, we thing about images. We cannot remind ourselves too often that memory is not confined to images. Structuralization, conceptualization, abstraction, symbolization, focalization—all occur on many dimensions of meaning, and it is their interaction that constitutes object representations as the term is used clinically.

But after we decide that object representations are more than images, it becomes difficult to exclude from their nature anything whatsoever. Everything about us—knowledge, mood, valuation—colors our awareness. Everything about us may be reflected in our representations. Representations would seem to be reports on overall mental functioning as it bears on whatever the observer's special interest is. A representation would embody, for instance, id pressures, ego modifications, and superego significances. (Schafer, 1973b, makes essentially this point.) That is to say, if one could fully comprehend any particular representation, one would be sampling the entire psychic apparatus. Taken altogether, the representational world would signify everything that one could experience about oneself and one's environment, as one is presently constituted.

To the extent that representations are synoptic examples of total mind functioning, Stolorow (1978) is right to offer the representational world as an alternative rather than a supplement to Freudian theory. It should be noted, however, that the representational world swallows up Freudian theory only in the sense that what we want explained already contains the grounds of its explanation, just as pointing to something substitutes for its definition. What can we do with the experienced world other than experience it? The moment we do something other than suffer it or enjoy it, it is no longer just the experienced world. It is gone as soon as we focus on some part of it; distinctions destroy it.

What separates one representation from another? Stolorow (1978) appeals to Piaget's theory as a parallel account that successfully maps the physical world by means of representations. But it can be argued (as I do in chapter 25) that Piaget was successful only because his independent knowledge of the physical world gave him a ready conceptual grid of separable, defined concepts (mathematics, geometry, and physics) with which to seive the responses of his little subjects. He could delineate their representations in terms of (and in contrast with) his own scientific representations.

But Stolorow is dealing with a felt, not a physical, world. And when he lists in the plural as "components" of a representational world "distinctive *configurations* of self and object representations" (p. 315; italics added), he supposes a separateness that he has not justified. Of course, what therapists wanted when they welcomed representational theory was indeed just such a set of stable abstractions—something like the concepts of physical objects, but including persons and relationships. Yet even Kernberg (1976), who used to talk about object representations as though they were units that combined themselves into meaningful compounds (p. 29), now seems to talk more about object repesentations as abstractions from a generalized, meaningful state (p. 87).

In short, if representation as image is too trivial to be theoretically useful, representation as the world-for-the-person—the experienceable world—is too encompassing. We must abstract certain features from this "everything" in order to have items to talk about.

Theorists of the representational world (such as Stolorow) assume that they do not need to impose structure on the data, because the representational world has already been carved up for them by the subject into individual representations. They do not take responsibility for making their own abstractions. They think they are obediently recording the lumpings and groupings of experience, abstracted by the person they are studying. They are using the term "representation" to refer to something like intellectual understandings, only affectively tinged, which the subject himself has perfected. The subject's own experience is supposed to tell us where one understanding leaves off and another begins. Schafer (1968) makes this point by using the word "idea," freed of its purely cognitive connotations, but retaining its claim to being a unit. Just as the people we study have more and less abstract ideas in their heads, so also representations exist on many levels of abstraction. We are asked to regard these as the subject's subjectively experienced and lived-with abstractions, rather than categories imposed by the theorist.

Suppose, then, that representations, although they are not images, do somewhat resemble conceptual understandings. Would a warm-blooded understanding stand out as a separate item, independent of the observer's bias? If intellectual understandings are the model, the answer is: No. Intellectual understandings are not self-contained items. They involve each other. Mathematical understandings are related to an entire number system. In geometry, the concept of a triangle cannot be defined apart from the whole world of geometrical figures. Still less when it comes to concepts of physical objects are we dealing with discrete items that can be objectively defined apart from the purpose of the inquiry. We can give a dictionary definition of a flower, and we can point to a flower, but our concept of a flower cannot be simply set out, because it leads into many other concepts. There are some philosophers (Leibnitz, Whitehead) who maintain that every concept is related to every other. Understandings do not come in parcels: they are more like infinite networks.

Here is another way of looking at the situation: if you think, for a moment, about a nearby object, you will realize that you could not possibly describe it completely in however long a list of attributes. So your representation of it would have to be somewhat open-ended. In other words, if a representation is a kind of understanding of an object, it will share some of the real object's undefinableness. A representation that was neatly delimited would not be the representation of an object; it would be the representation of a formal relationship. Thus, if we mean by representation a kind of understanding of an object, then it is not the sort of thing we could flash before our mind, as we could an image, a dictionary definition, or the formula, $E = mc^2$. A representation of an object is too vague, too involved, too ragged, and altogether too much, to be instanced at some particular time. After all, the intellectual understanding of a physical object is not a singular experience. It is something that an observer infers that a person has, based on his mental and physical operations on the world. If the representations of psychoanalytic theory are like understandings, then they are inferences made by the psychoanalytic observer on the basis of people's fantasies and relationships.[3]

What, then, should we say about those actual *experiences* which we are inclined to call representations? What about a primary process presence? What about a voice of conscience? What about a spontaneous image of a commending or condemning parent? What about a hallucinated voice? Shall we say that these, too, are representations which, however, have condensed an understanding (which is a network) into a solid and singular phenomenon? But *every* signifier congeals some understanding. And everything in the mind is significant. Once we have acknowledged that it will get us nowhere to substitute the word, "representation," for the word, "mental," we are obliged to reserve it for a capacity and distinguish it from experience. Accordingly, we should not call a primary process presence or a hallucination a representation of an object. These are, so to speak, glimpses of an object; but they are not *the* understanding or capacity to appreciate the real object. Speaking

---

[3]In this chapter I am mainly concerned to establish that representations are not units set out in unmediated experience, but are abstracted from data by theory. It need hardly be added that, because of the reflexiveness of the human mind, people can theorize about themselves. Indeed, they routinely do so when they undergo psychoanalysis (see Chapter 16). Nor is it only as patients that they do it. Artists probably theorize about themselves; certainly many novelists do. And there are various styles of introspection that amount to fragmentary theorizing. If people abstract representations from their own experience, their representations then become a part of their experience. Thus individuals may have within their own experiences their own representations that they have defined for themselves. What I wish to say is that these are *not* their ways of apprehending objects in the world, but guesses about patterns of apperception. In no way do I belittle these subjective estimates. I think they are of great consequence, and I confine my appreciation of them to this footnote only because they offer no exception to my rule, inasmuch as they are abstracted by principles of theory, however fragmentary; they can be re-formed along different perspectives (for example, psychoanalytic or artistic) according to the interest of the introspector; and they may be quite different from the representations found by a treating psychoanalyst, which does not in the least invalidate them. As part of people's experience of themselves and their relation to the world, their own self-understanding must be taken into account in abstracting their patterns of awareness, but only as one of many aspects of experience that reflect their representations.

psychoanalytically, we would not call the sight of one's mother a representation; no more should we call the hallucination of her a representation. Such experiences of sensation or reverie reflect something *about* a person's representations. But it would be a logical absurdity to maintain both that a representation is a capacity to recognize and that it can be transformed into an experience. For once a representation is transformed and no longer a capacity, how could the hallucinator recognize the real object when it is before him?

Limiting the meaning of "representation" to a capacity is admittedly more single-minded than the usual practice. But I suggest that this is the meaning that is essential to psychoanalytic description, and it is incompatible with other usages.

Modell's (1968) position is in direct opposition to my argument. Using the term, "identification," where others would say "representation," he explicitly requires it to stand both for an ability to recognize an object and an experience of an object (within the self). A common process may indeed underlie both events. But even Modell concedes that such an underlying common process would be neurophysiological, and so it is impossible to give a psychological name to that one thing which is used sometimes as an ability and sometimes as an internal experience. (In other words, it is impossible to say what such a diversely describable "identification" is, unless we are satisfied to leave it as "an affection of the mind.") A capacity to recognize is of a different logical type than a feeling of the self.[4]

So I suggest that most psychoanalytic theorizing implies that when we speak about someone's "representations," we are estimating the kinds of experience that person can have. Representations are not themselves experiences, but potentialities for experiences, and organizations into which experiences may fit, just as physical concepts are not experiences but understandings by which perception can be integrated and differentiated. With increasing understanding, experience becomes increasingly complex and abstract, but it always remains experience. A fantasy has richer organization than an imaged contour, but it is no more a psychoanalytic representation than the image of a contour is an understanding of shape. Fantasy and contour both reflect the kind of sense that can be made of the world. They are, respectively, symptoms of complex and simple representations.

---

[4]Modell rightly scorns the view that the mind consists of a collection of atomic representations, a view he compares to Locke's atomism. But he accepts the separation of ideas from their organized use, which is what critical philosophers identified as Locke's error. The atomism that Modell, despite himself, shares with Locke is the belief that the mind builds a world of objects by connecting disconnected items (ideas of perception for Locke; identifications for Modell). The disconnection of one identification from another in Modell's system is revealed by the fact that the subject can treat an identification as an aspect of himself rather than as an aspect of the world, just as Locke's subject could regard an idea of sensation as a self-contained event.

Those who hope somehow to make immediate experience explain itself welcome representations as pretheoretical, but nevertheless delineated, items. That assumption makes it seem possible to discuss the real, unmediated structure of the mind, rather than what are thought to be the arbitrarily designated, "reified" structures of Freudian theory. But in fact it is only if we consider the whole mind as a Parmenidean unit that we have a naturally given structure (and even then, the social scientist will object that it is a mere abstraction from a social event). To discuss representations in the plural, and persisting trends and motives, the observer must make his own abstractions, according to his purpose and perspective.

In Stolorow's outline (1978), for example, this perspective is probably given in the systems of what he calls "tasks" and "functions." In effect, Stolorow has chosen to *abstract* tasks and functions from the naturally occurring, experienced world; the taskless and functionless *representations* that tasks and functions operate on are manufactured by the *same* abstracting perspectives. They are *all* theoretical constructs. Observe, for example, how Stolorow subtly segregates representations from an otherwise unspecified mental apparatus when he refers to "the various conscious and unconscious functions . . . that may be served by the representational configurations that are established in the course of a person's life cycle" (p. 315). True, we can speak about the way individuals use their environment. But aren't their patterns of use already incorporated in their representations? If a pattern of use is already in a representation, then we cannot speak about the *representation* being used. And if the pattern of use is *not* a part of the representation, then that representation is not a simple fact of experience, but an abstraction we have made as theoreticians, separating it from other interlocking aspects, such as affective coloring and expectancies, so as to create the illusion of a concrete (naturally separate) structure.

Like all psychoanalytic phenomenologists, Stolorow has it both ways: representations have myriad meanings already in them, but there are certain specific sorts of meanings, here designated as functions and tasks, that are set aside as preferred dimensions for discriminating and relating those meanings. And that, I think, is roughly what Freudian theory had already accomplished much more openly and elaborately.[5]

---

[5]Stolorow (1978) claims that, unlike Freudian theory, his makes no "assumptions . . . about the existence of impersonal psychic agencies or motivational prime movers in order to 'explain' the representational world" (p. 315). Yet the ingredients of his theory include not only separable configurations of self- and object representations, but also "developmental tasks" and "various conscious and unconscious functions (for example, wish-fulfilling, self-guiding and self-punishing, adaptive, restitutive-reparative and defensive functions)" (p. 315). We are asked to agree that an "unconscious function" is not a motivational prime mover, that developmental tasks are "assigned" without "moving" the organism, and that a self-guidance function is not the same as an impersonal agency. On that premise, he "aims to elucidate the nature, developmental

In his earlier work, Schafer (1968), too, frequently treated representations as though they can be described independently of the motives to which they are relevant, like a door that can be used to go into or out of. He did that because he wanted to avoid peopling the mind with all kinds of powers determining their own directions. He held that only motives determine directions. (Nowadays even motives seem to him too abstract to command the authority that is properly assigned only to a whole person.)

But Schafer also recognized that motivations partly determine representations, and representations help shape motives. Furthermore, one might argue that Schafer's definition of "regulation" as "higher order forms of restraint, guidance and mastery" (p. 11) would allow us to call representations regulatory agencies since they serve as "guides" and "models" (p. 196). He wrote, in fact, that "positive representations are also among the conditions of the person's capacity to modify drive aims and subordinate them to the regulatory motives" (p. 195). Nor did Schafer shrink from the consequence that representations alter motivation (pp. 66–67). Finally, by referring to them in one sentence as "guides to adaptive change, the models of this endeavor, and the barometers of its success" (p. 196), Schafer effectively summed up the status of representations as a rather inclusive term of mental functioning from which we can abstract such things as motives.

Thus, representations cannot be divided and sorted in the same way as primary process presences, subjectively experienced introjects, hallucinated voices, etc. How, then, are we to identify and arrange them? How do we distinguish one "understanding" from another?

The answer can only be: In all kinds of ways. We have noted that representations share the property of inexhaustibility with the objects they represent. Just like objects, representations can be seen in many different lights, and aspects of them can be selected according to many perspectives.

Psychoanalysis has delineated representations according to their drive or motivational significance. Put more exactly, it has divided the representational world according to drive or motivational meaning. Or still more exactly stated, it has described the transformation of representations in terms

---

origins and functional significance . . . of the representational configurations that permeate a person's subjective world" (p. 316) and find "a methodological system of interpretive principles to guide the study of meaning in human experience and conduct" which "does not postulate a theory of the nature of personality as an 'objective entity.'"

Yet Stolorow's "various conscious and unconscious functions . . . that may be served by the representational configurations" (p. 315) also have their own configurations, invariant ordering and organizing principles (p. 316). The only clear change wrought in Freudian theory seems to be to speak less vividly about forces at work and more vividly about what happens as a result of them. It seems that Stolorow prefers the language of tasks and functions to systems of ego, superego, and id, because he feels that the first set of terms accurately reflects their abstractness, while the names of psychic institutions do not. He fails to recognize that the fallacy of misplaced concreteness (if one regards it indeed as a fallacy) merely shifts to the "representations" that one has carved out of the multilayered, interlocking web of meaning and association.

of motives or wishes and especially in terms of wishes that themselves can be defined because they are conflicted.

I do not say that this summarizes the mission of analytic theory. Psychoanalysis was also designed to describe the transformation of *wishes*. (Looked at that way, the transformation of wishes is described in terms of representations, especially as manifested in fantasy [cf. Loewald, 1971; Ricoeur, 1970].)

My point is that institutions and relations of institutions within the Freudian theory of the mind serve as analyzers or as a descriptive and relating grid for representations. For it is my contention that representations, as such, are as seamless as objects of the world – just as inexhaustible in dimension and character and just as stickily connected with each other as are features of the world. They do not fall apart into meaningful personae all by themselves, but only in regard to some particular perspective (belonging either to the subject or the theorist) of which the Freudian concern with motive, wish, and drive is one.

While it is true that a great deal of psychodynamic description can be carried on in representational language, that can happen only to the extent that the language hides in its margins the aggregation of wish structures that are made visible in Freudian theory. Thus, as soon as an emotionally charged "representation" is referred to, it has already been carved out by an invisible structural theory.

Mapping the mind with representations requires that representations be something like understandings. But even as a kind of understanding, a representation is not sufficiently definable to support a theory of the mind. The reason is not far to seek. There is no way to speak *only* of meaning and still say something significant. For example, to speak of someone's representations is to say what the world means to that person. Hence the proposition that individuals' representations are transformed into psychic structure amounts to proclaiming that what the world has meant to them now influences their way of experiencing it. And that is merely to say that learning occurs. Surely we wanted to say more than that.

What had we wanted to say? Despite the current lively debate about what psychoanalysis properly and improperly is, few would deny that its power has something to do with a way of tracking meanings on their path of change. If we wish to preserve and expand psychoanalytic knowledge, we must try to preserve that *way*. And by a way of tracking meanings on their path of change, I do not mean the treatment situation. *No* situation by itself is a way of analyzing anything (unless we include in "the situation" a lot of conceptual structure).

The psychoanalytic way of thinking brought us long ago to a certain vista of meanings, and we can now make a start from that point. No great harm is done by ignoring how we got there. But we cannot expect to blaze the trail further if we lose sight of where it is we had wanted to go – in other words, the viewpoint from which we had related and defined meanings, a viewpoint revealed in the terms of our theory.

This is not to say that there are no other ways of analyzing meaning, no other paths that can be blazed, no other interesting descriptions of mentallife. Artists, poets, rhetoricians, physiologists, sociologists, ethologists, behavioral scientists of all sorts, have always and will always follow many different paths and divide the universe of mind in a multitude of ways. They are all useful to the psychoanalyst. Complementary perspectives are no threat to the psychoanalytic project. But psychoanalysis *is* threatened by a general impatience with all theoretical perspectives—by the belief that we can go where psychoanalysis was leading without a compass and get there faster if we unload our conceptual baggage. Any psychology would be endangered by a na\"ive belief that if we rid ourselves of a consistent way of abstracting from experience, we will be free to understand experience *tout court*. A good way to get lost is to go everywhere. An example of "everywhere" is the representational world.

In its constructs psychoanalysis hoards abstractions that have been painfully culled from experience by a particular approach to meaning transformation. Representational theory randomly scatters these abstractions back onto undifferentiated experience in order to grow discrete representations out of the representational world. In its impatience to close in on the naked, palpitating reality of mental life, representational theory brushes aside as mere make-believe the abstractions attendant on our perspectives. Representational theory claims to strip terminological camouflage from reality, but it ends up using twigs of raw phenomena to hide the abstract framework that is always present when meanings are being isolated and related.

Unfortunately, although a hidden framework can support data already arranged on it, it is not available for new data. After long use, theories become a part of a world view and can be used without citation. We can use already developed Freudian theory by tacit agreement while talking in terms of representation. What we cannot do, if we are confined to this previous product of the theory, is to find out *more* about how meanings change. We can, for instance, understand, as Stolorow (1978, p. 316) says, that the psychoanalytic situation permits "the structure of a patient's representational world to maximally unfold and find illumination . . .," but we cannot find out more about the relationship of unfolded representations to folded ones, or how a representation ultimately changes.[6]

The work of Margaret Mahler (Mahler et al., 1975) shows how new insight can be gained by analyzing movement of meaning in terms of strivings, and how that opportunity could be lost if we were to see only ˄ cinematic

---

[6]Stolorow et al. (1978) believe they can answer many of these questions on their own terms. It seems to me that they do so simply by asserting that the patient adapts to the analyst.

progression of representations evolving organically, to use Stolorow's (1978, p. 315) terms.

Mahler's studies are distinguished from a host of other infant observations by her interest in the interlocking of striving and perception. Consider what she labels the rapprochement subphase of the separation-individuation process. In the preceding practicing subphase, children acquire the ability to walk, enormous confidence in themselves, and an independent manner. This state of mind is consequent to a maturational action spurt. It is followed by a period of separation anxiety and ambivalence (the rapprochement subphase).

What do we see here? In an optimum environment, a maturational striving puts a particular cast on the world (the "love affair with the world") which we would ordinarily associate with representations of an invulnerable self. And this is followed in the rapproachement subphase by a resurgence of a conflicting wish for attachment, which we associate with representations of a helpless self. Overall, it is not a simple story of progressive consolidation of representations. In the transition from symbiosis through practicing, to rapproachement and resolution, we see the successive substitution of new representations for previous ones (see Kaplan, 1972) partly under the influence of alternating and then conflicting strivings. We can see this influence more clearly than usual in Mahler's account because she points to maturational strivings that are standard and phasic, and thus isolatable. These maturational strivings serve as a natural experiment for studying the effect of strivings on awareness.

Of course, it is not only strivings that enrich awareness. All sorts of cognitive processes occur throughout development, many studied in detail by nonpsychoanalytic observers, for example, students of memory development (e.g., Flavell and Wellman, 1977) and Piagetian observers of structural recombinations and syntheses.

But Mahler's special lesson would be lost if we read hers as an account of how children react to a changing world of representations. Children's representations are partly a product of the actions they are biologically impelled to take. They analyze the world by means of their impetus. Certain kinds of push for independence reanalyze previous meanings. (They modify existing representations.) The representation of the mother that is achieved after rapprochement is the outcome of a progressive mixture and conflict of wishes for independence and nurturance. The final "representation" embodies that history.

Let us note also Mahler's impression that the expansion of children's sensed environment (the nature of their representations, if you please) is limited by the number of activities they can safely exercise and the ambitions they can pursue. If they are forced by maternal indifference to attend too constantly to self-protection (Mahler et al., 1975, p. 58), they will not be free to push for that independence which would have modified their perceptions, and so they will differentiate late. A motivation is blunted and a meaning is unrevised.

Thus, if we ascribe to a patient an immature, "split" or inconstant object representation and react to it as though some strength had not been transferred from the environment to the interior, we have missed Mahler's moral just as surely as we misuse the term "representation." The defective representation testifies to an interpersonal *conflict* (for example, the rapprochement crisis) that was not optimally facilitated and thus did not create new meaning (enriched representations of the self and object). Mahler's study of the interlacing of drive and meaning offers a clue to the machinery of psychotherapy which would be lost in an invidious grading of representations.

Kohut (1971) makes a similar point. If drives do not find tolerable exercise, they cannot progressively redefine and deepen awareness. Kohut's analogs for representations are aspects of the world marked off by their relationship to strivings (e.g., strivings for self-esteem, ideals, etc.). Representations are modified by the exercise and gradual differentiation of strivings. In fact, Kout's impact on therapy probably has much to do with the pragmatic usefulness of reading developmental strivings out of transference representations, along with the attendant hope that elaboration of strivings will change object representations (see also Goldberg, 1978).

The innovation that both Mahler and Kohut offer to psychoanalytic theory is not a new type of mental entity called representation, nor even a new function for such entities as grid-work of the mind, but the possibility that some *organizations of motive* previously subsumed in the tripartite model of the mind may be profitably sorted out and given a standing of their own.

The proper question for theory at the present moment, I think, is not whether the structures referred to by the term, representations can do better what structures such as ego, id, and superego claimed to do, but whether the groups of motives identified as id, ego, and superego are sufficiently coherent and refined to accomplish the kind of analysis of representations that we wish.

Empiricist philosophers like Locke once looked for building blocks of experience that come to the senses predefined. Some psychoanalysts are now looking for components of the mind that come to the theoretician with already separated meanings. The rebellion against abstract structure in theory of the mind has given new appeal to Melanie Klein's prepackaging of meanings in concrete images. It has inspired information-systems theoreticians to rely on data that are meaningful before all processing ("information" ambiguously combining its technical and its ordinary meanings). The same trend accounts for the existentialist effort to make meaning a surd atom of explanation in the form of action.

We cannot study meaning transformation if we take meaning for granted—

if it fills the conceptual universe. Thinking proceeds by contrast. Heterogeneous conceptual instruments will do meaning no dishonor.

SUMMARY

Some theoreticians have grown impatient with terms that do not refer directly to human meaning. Some have thought to use "the representational world" as a way of describing the mind phenomenologically with a minimum of theory. But when we try to make the term "representation" refer to something more specific than just any meaning or mental act, and yet to something more general than an image, it turns out to stand for something close to an understanding. And understandings are really high abstractions. To abstract them, we need a perspective. When "the representational world" is used to describe the mind without explicitly stating the theoretical perspective by which the representations are specified, the method of analyzing phenomena is hidden, giving the illusion of apprehending the mind directly without intervening concepts.

The price paid is that the principles of analysis do not remain conspicuously available to be carried forward consistently in research. For example, without the psychoanalytic principle of studying representations in terms of wish, the contributions of Mahler and Kohut may be trivialized as a mere elaboration of the phenomenology of experience when, in fact, they show how desire and action lead to the transformation of meaning, thus helping to answer interesting etiologic and therapeutic questions which mere description cannot reach.

20
Schafer's Action Language

R oy Schafer (1973a, b) has proposed a reformulation of psychoanalytic theory that is both rich in therapeutic wisdom and troubled with philosophical problems.

SCHAFER'S APPROACH

Appealing to our common understanding that human events are the doings of persons and not of components of persons, Schafer challenges the Freudian picture of the mind as a collection of forces and agencies. Schafer's thesis is that the theme of human action is not compatible with a mechanistic model of the mind. The incompatibility results in anthropomorphisms, which are the "archaic representation of the theme of human action [in mechanistic models]" (1973a, p. 169).

Schafer argues that the theme of human action is indispensable for psychology. Freud's thinking cannot be understood without it. It is ingredient in our view of a person as a person. Without it, the scheme of things leaves no room for the therapist to operate. The theme of human action is what allows us to attribute responsibility to a person and allows a person to assume responsibility for himself. These needs have stretched the neat outline of the mechanistic model into hybrid notions of identity, therapeutic alliance, the "self" and, of course, the explicit structural anthropomorphisms which are so familiar.

Schafer is not as clear about the needs that the older, mechanistic model fills. He is less disdainful of mechanism than other critics, recognizing it as the natural science model of the mind, rather than dismissing it as a toy of the nineteenth century. But he believes that the mechanical model is incompatible with the view that it is a person who acts. And he argues that, since the theme of human action is what allows us to understand man psychologically and deal with him therapeutically, classical, mechanistic, psychoanalytic theory must be dropped and the action theme, detached from its anthropomorphic manifestations, freed to spell out psychoanalytic principles of its own.

As Schafer uses the term, action is not confined to physical or observable behavior. A thought, a wish, an inhibition are all actions. An action can be described in an infinite number of ways. This specification is very important because it tells us that for Schafer an action is something that is concrete rather than abstract.[1]

Schafer's term "action," as I understand it, is designed to refer to *a concrete thing* (it can be looked at in many ways), which reflects the *whole being* of a unitary person (it is a person that acts, not a part of a person), who effected it for a *purpose* having to do with a certain perceived situation (an act is intentional and has a meaning related to its setting).

Though Schafer is sympathetic to the existentialists, it is not his purpose to call attention to man-in-the-world in a romantic or dramatic fashion. He does not mean his account to be read primarily as a summary of human nature (though it cannot help implying one) but as a statement of the logical unit that is most appropriate for a psychoanalytic psychology.

THE CENTRAL DIFFICULTY

Although Schafer's formulation is deceptively like our common-sense way of thinking about people, I believe that it relies on an ambiguity about concreteness and abstraction that makes it uncompetitive with Freudian theory.

Stated in the most general fashion, the ambiguity is as follows: an action and a person cannot both be treated as concrete, individual things at the same time that the action is regarded as an expression of the person. A concrete person and a concrete action would be as separate as two rocks on a hill. Insofar as we consider a branch to be an expression of the tree, or a

---

[1] I apologize for the monstrous term "concrete action," and for the term I shall use later, "concrete person," which I am afraid will put the reader in mind of the Commendatore in *Don Giovanni*. Unfortunately, "concrete" is the most economical antonym of "abstract." Ordinarily it refers to a whole, individual existing thing—thus a whole, individual person, as opposed to an aspect of him. But I cannot simply substitute "individual" for "concrete" because "individual" can also be used for something like a number and for something like a person's spirit, and both of these are abstract. What I call a concrete thing is what people usually call just a thing. A concrete action is an actual, one-time-only, naturally circumscribed happening.

painting to be an expression of the artist, or an utterance to be an expression of the speaker, we are thinking about some *property* of the branch, painting or utterance—some particular *aspect* of its organization, not its concrete entirety. Something about the branch (for example, its material connection or its origin in growth) is a property of the tree; some arrangement of form and color is an aspect of the painter's intention; some meaning in the utterance is an idea of the speaker.

Correspondingly, if the person is treated as a concrete thing, then his action, insofar as it is *his* action, will be an *aspect* of his living; that is, it will be an *abstraction* from him. (Either an observer or the person himself will make that abstraction.) But if action is an abstraction, then it cannot be said—as Schafer does—that it supports a multitude of interpretations. It is, so to speak, one interpretation of the observed person. ("John threw the ball to Jim" would be considered one action, and "John threw the ball at Jim" would be another action.) If we are using "action" in this way as an abstractive description, then saying that a person acted in such and such a way attributes general motives to him. Schafer wanted his theory to deal with a unitary subject who performs diverse actions, but we now discover that he is talking about a subject who is divisible into many aspects, like a man with many motives or a psyche with many interests. (Thus, if it is true both that John threw the ball to Jim and that John threw the ball at Jim, then John is both friendly and hostile.) That is more or less the position of existing Freudian theory, and it brings with it the problems Schafer wanted to avoid, for instance how to describe the interaction of a person's aspects without anthropomorphizing, on the one hand, or losing meaning and intentionality, on the other.

But if it does not suit Schafer's purpose to regard action terms as describing people (and thus making up abstractions about them), the alternative relation between action and person is no more satisfactory. If we regard *action* as concrete and treat the person as an abstraction that is made up out of all of his actions, what we would have on our hands is a radical behaviorism. In that case, the action would have no intention or meaning, since it is not the servant of an intending person or the product of an integrating sensibility. Furthermore, the only sort of explanation such a theory could offer is a statistical correlation, since, underlying the various actions, there is no concrete something in which connections can be supposed to exist. That will not yield the sort of theory Schafer (and every practicing psychotherapist) wants.

There is a way of avoiding this dilemma by regarding both person and action as concrete but abandoning the idea that action reflects the person. Action is not thought of as an abstraction from the person (that is, it is not a view of him), nor is personhood an abstraction from action (the person is not the common trend in a series of actions). Rather, action is considered *equivalent* to the person; both terms are used to refer to the same concrete thing. A person is his action. His actions are the person. This is the path of radical existentialism. This sort of action would not tell us *about* the person, nor would the "nature" of the person shed light on the meaning of his actions. Indeed it is difficult to imagine what, on this view, would shed light on meaning, since we would be forbidden to picture meaning or intention as a relationship of factors the way we usually do, for example when we talk about the meaning *of* a sign, or when we talk about someone intending to do *something* to someone. This pure existentialism is clearly unsatisfactory for organizing any descriptive data such as psychoanalytic observations and Schafer cannot go all the way in that direction.

Schafer's is one of a number of efforts to find a resolution to this problem which will allow us to keep our thinking concrete. In this category belong existentialist psychology (which is not the same as radical existentialism), for example, May (1958), the structuralism of Piaget (1970), process theories of personality, like that of Gendlin (1964a) and the philosophy of Langer (1967, 1972). All these theories are opposed to static formulations of the structural sort. They all use some kinetic concept as their fundamental building block — being-in-the-world, process, transformations, or the act. But they all make their compromises. In practice, existentialist psychology has absorbed a notion of a common human nature and a common life challenge which a person weaves into his unique tapestry. Gendlin describes the living process abstractly, comparing it to digestion. He makes it consist of an interplay of separable and abstract functions, namely abstract signification and body feelings. Langer's "acts" are more akin to abstract tendencies, directions of growth, aims, motives etc. than they are to concrete, momentary happenings. And Piaget's transformations are guided by regular abstract principles of accommodation and assimilation.

But Schafer, bedevilled by the spectre of anthropomorphism, appears not to have made up his mind about how much abstraction to let into his system. He seems to want to retain the brute, concrete, thing-ness of action, as the behaviorists and existentialists do, without giving up the definable-ness that makes it so informative to psychoanalysts. The unwillingness to give up either of these contradictory advantages strains a system in two characteristic ways:

(1) When action and person are both considered concrete, the theoretician finds himself struggling with some concept of *potential* action which he needs but cannot find a place for. He needs it because a concrete person, like anything that is concrete, will have unrealized potentiality. But he can't accommodate it because potential action implies a person who does the acting while being describable in terms other than action. And that makes action a property or attribute or abstraction from the person and violates the premise that action is concrete.

(2) When action is discussed as though it reflected something *about* a concrete person, while at the same time it is employed as the ultimate subject of study, the theoretician will have to equivocate between defining an action *by* its meaning and defining action as something *to which* meaning can be given. That is because the subject of an investigation acquires more and more meaning, but a *reflection* of a concrete person *is* already a meaning.

An examination of Schafer's theory will make these considerations clearer.

THE ANOMALY OF POTENTIAL ACTION

This is how Schafer tackles the problem of potentiality:

> There is a second major referent of the dynamic unconscious, in addition to unacknowledged actions in which the person is engaged. It is the class of actions in which one *would* be engaged were one not avoiding them by engaging in counteractions. These are the so-called impulses one is repressing or other-wise defending against, i.e., *in mechanistic language, they are impulses while, in action language, they are would-be actions.* This means that one's thinking of them ("experiencing" them) as impulses is a matter of obeying a convention of language, for one could just as well follow the action convention and say that, more or less effortlessly, one is restraining one's initiating certain actions; one may be conscious of these would-be actions or may conclude, on the basis of one's apprehensive expenditure of effort, that one is about to engage in them. Through so-called free association in analysis, one frequently discovers that one is acting just this way.
>
> Of course, the person could be mistaken in thinking that he would do something were it not for his specific counter-actions. Actually a would-be action is a prediction in one of its aspects, and as such it might be right or wrong [1973b, p. 274].

Schafer has also made the following translation between the "mechanistic" and action language: ". . . the so-called impulses or drives are actions, too. In the action model, an anal impulse is an anal action that is not being carried out" (1973a, p. 187).

Here, then, are some of the terms that Schafer is forced to integrate into his system: the class of actions in which one would be engaged were one not avoiding them; would-be actions; actions that one is restraining initiating; actions one is about to engage in; an action that is not being carried out; action as a prediction.

At first glance these may seem like perfectly ordinary expressions. But their peculiarity appears when we recall that action is the unit of description in this theory. These potential actions must themselves be actions. We will have to say that one is acting to the extent that one would be acting; that some actions are would-be actions; that one can have acted even without initiating the action, or engaging in it, or carrying it out; that one can have acted even if the action has not yet happened.

Orthodox terms like "motive" represent continuing potential or abstract tendencies. The action language speaks of actualities. Does action language merely *disguise* potentialities by describing them in terms borrowed from the world of concrete actuality? The test of Schafer's project is whether he can explain how potential actions are actions. His explanation follows the pattern set by the positivist philosophers who had a similar objective. The positivists wanted to eliminate reference to mysterious potentialities and confine science to events. Wherever potentiality was referred to in previous metaphysics (generally in the concepts of substance and natural law), they sought to replace it with a predictive statement, thinking in that way to define it in terms of events. In the same spirit, Schafer says, "actually a would-be action is a prediction in one of its aspects, and as such it might be right or wrong" (1973b, p. 274). The grammar alone shows that the concept is in trouble. What kind of action can be right or wrong (in the sense of true or false)? Not, one would think, the sort of action Schafer describes in other contexts. This new kind of action is a proposition, specifically, a conditional proposition. People do not do propositions. Of course people do formulate propositions, and formulating is an action in Schafer's ordinary sense. But as an *action* predicting is neither would-be, nor right or wrong. It is a simple fact. Now, what about the other fact—the content of the prediction? Can that be right or wrong? In Schafer's system, it is unclear what it is that people believe when they formulate a proposition about what they would do if they let themselves. What, in fact, would make the proposition true?

In orthodox theory, we could say that the proposition refers to a tendency or motive strong enough potentially to cause an action were it not counteracted. In Schafer's system, we cannot say that. He offers instead the positivist suggestion that the belief is a prediction of what would happen if a certain (counter) action were not taken.

Let us suppose that prediction here means a simple guess—the kind we make when we call heads-or-tails on the flip of a coin. In that case, it would not be a belief in the strict sense of the word. This sort of action describes nothing else in the mind but a gamble by somebody thinking *about* the mind. The mind can act this way, but certainly no theory of the mind can be constructed on the basis of this sort of action.

Most likely, then, when Schafer calls a would-be action a prediction, he is defining it as an estimate of probability. That kind of prediction refers not only to an action by the observer (i.e. estimating) but also to an action in the subject (whatever makes an outcome more likely). Such a prediction can therefore be a part of a theory of the mind—but only in so far as it spells out what kind of situation in the mind *warrants* a probability judgement. Orthodox theory says that predictions are estimates of relative strengths of motives. Schafer eschews this. He is thus left with the problem of justifying inductive reasoning without recourse to present potentialities, cause-and-effect, and other "mechanized" parephenalia. Whether this can be done has been hotly debated. The burden of proof is on the theoretician who seeks to replace potentiality with probability. Until he can show otherwise, rules determining probability must be presumed to be based on properties of the mind, and thus again on potentialities, previously referred to as motives.

By calling a would-be action a prediction rather than a probability, Schafer appears to keep his account on an action level. One could say that the field consists of actions completed and actions predicted. If he referred to the probability of an action, he would have to speak of other things beside action. The field would then consist of actions and whatever makes actions likely.

But Schafer does not really have a choice. He cannot confine the discussion to prediction as opposed to probability. The would-be action that a person believes he would carry out if he were not currently defending against it, is an action in the present that is not happening; it is not a *pre*diction of a possible future outcome. If such a current, would-be action is not a prediction, then it must be a description. It is, in fact, quite simply the description of a potentiality for an action. In other words, Schafer has replaced a language that speaks of motives and actions with one that speaks of potential action and action. Unless he can say how a potential action is different from a motive, he is laboring to no purpose. The one definition he offers of potential action, namely that it is a prediction, turns out to be another use of a concept of potential action rather than a clarification of it. There is therefore no reason to think that he can manage without the orthodox concepts.

EQUIVOCATION BETWEEN CONCRETE AND ABSTRACT ACTION

Unactualized action is not the only anomalous result of a rebellion against abstraction. It is merely one manifestation of a general need to smuggle abstractions back into the theory. For instance the "mode" in which an action is taken becomes a major variable in Schafer's reconstructed psychoanalytic theory. We can perform an action deliberately, inconspicuously, reflectively, resolutely, affectively, incompletely, unrecognizably, even faultily. A single action that can be found in modes so variable can only be a very high abstraction—it is action as a Platonic Form.

We have only to contrast this with Schafer's description of action as concrete to become aware that the term is being used in two senses: ". . . . there is no limit to the number of vantage points from which an action may be regarded, and therefore no limit to the number of ways in which it may be defined or described" (1973a, p. 178).

As a pattern executed in various modes, action is a generalized purpose or meaning. We use this sense when we say, "That sonata does interesting things with its theme." In contrast, an action that can be seen from unlimited vantage points is a sum total actuality, and from many vantage points it would be quite senseless to separate the action from a mode (e.g., to characterize defensive self-observation as faulty). We use this sense of action when we say about a piece of performed music, "That was a particularly spirited performance," and also that the performer's mannerisms were distracting. Action in the one sense refers to the essence of what a person does; in the other sense, simply to what a person does, including all the ways and means he uses.

If we consider what is left to action when we strip away all of its modes, we come upon the exact equivalent of a tendency or a motive. To call that underlying abstraction an action, just as we call the finished product an action, is to pretend to describe the mind in terms of concrete momentary events while continuing to employ abstract concepts.

The double meaning of action appears again in one of Schafer's most interesting theses:

> The seeking of psychological explanations presupposes an orderly universe, or an orderly approach to it, and to say this is to say that *there cannot be more than one reaction to one situation* and that *there cannot be more than a relatively narrow range of similar reactions to a group of relatively similar situations.* Clearly different actions must imply clearly different situations. The concept of situation is the same as the concept of psychic reality, and so expresses an important aspect of psychoanalytic interpretation [1973b, p. 269].

This profound formulation implies that an action is not fundamentally a re-action to causal circumstances, as mechanistic formulas hold, but a kind of representation of the perceived environment. One reads the nuances of a person's situation from his actions (including his mental actions). (The response defines the stimulus.)

Furthermore, Schafer argues, the reasons for an action are not its *cause*, in a mechanistic sense. The reasons for an action are its meaning. And since action is defined as meaningful, the reasons for an action are not clearly separable from the action; they are included in the action, so to speak, as a cause would not be.

All of this very thoughtful analysis seems to group distinct abstractions that mechanism had separated (cause and effect, stimulus and response, fact and meaning, subject and environment) into a kind of dialectical unity of immediate experience. And Schafer almost accepts this implication: "Thus the four terms—meaning, action, reason and situation—are aspects of the psychological mode of considering human activity, and they co-define or co-constitute each other" (1973b, p. 269). But Schafer does not completely accept the merger. Co-definition and co-constitution suggest something less than equivalence. If meaning were synonymous with action and situation, then there could not be many interpretations of action or situation. The meaning would be already given to it. And Schafer requires that the same action and situation be capable of *various* meanings (1973a, pp. 178–179). But if situation and action are *variously* describable and at the same time synonymous with meaning, then meaning itself would be capable of various meanings and we would have to invent something else (a meaning of meaning) to stand for a univocal meaning, which would then not be equivalent to situation and action. As the reader may expect by now, the "meaning of meaning" would turn out to be the hidden abstraction in the lot.

If co-definition is not plain definition, and co-constitution is not synonymity, then what is the relationship between the terms "meaning," "action," "reason," and "situation"? It is, I suggest, equivocation—a necessary equivocation between, on one hand, abstract, "mechanistic" concepts of cause-and-effect, stimulus and response, and so on, and on the other hand, a more "holistic" view in which concrete realities alone are tolerated. If they are thought of as identical, "meaning," "action," "reason," and "situation" define a final, concrete occurrence. But as separate terms they subtly invoke the necessary discriminatory power of the abstract "mechanistic" view. Since these views cannot actually be blended, what happens is a kind of figure-ground shift, in which the aspect that is desired at the moment is emphasized. At one moment the substance under consideration is a total experience. At that moment in the argument, "holism" prevails, and Schafer acknowledges his debt to existentialism. But the matter cannot be left that way, for there is really nothing that can be said about this whole, though I suppose it can be *expressed* in various ways. It is, so to speak, fully interpreted. Its interpretation is part of what it is. It is thought of as including all the abstractions ("meaning") that can be drawn from it, and any further abstractions, descriptions, distinctions etc. distort it, rather than approximate to it. (Distinctions such as reason, situation etc., are allowable, because they are not real distinction: things that define each other are not really separate.)

So at another moment, in order to have something to talk about, the subject of inquiry becomes an uninterpreted, productlike action, of which there can still be an infinite number of descriptions. In the first moment, we are considering the object with all its predicates together. In the second moment we are considering a subject to which predicates can apply, i.e. a subject (or substance) per se.[2]

---

[2]The term "information" in Peterfreund's information-processing theory of the mind (1971)

How would the problem stand without equivocation? If we feel that separating the subject from its attributes is an artificial operation, we would have to accept the inconvenience of a subject to which we are not free to add attributes. The alternative to the "mechanistic" view is a seamless vitalism, which clearly cannot generate any considerable body of hypotheses and interrelationships, much less the psychoanalytic corpus.[3]

The anomaly of unactualized action and the equivocation between action as concrete and as abstract grow out of the same frustration: The wish to deal always with something concrete—a thing, an ultimate logical subject, a substance (as people feel themselves to be and as they are dealt with by their psychotherapists)—runs up against the recognition that one must abstract from it to think about it.

THE UNDERLYING PROBLEM: PREDICATION

It is commonplace nowadays to regard "mechanistic" models as a holdover from a bygone physics (cf. Peterfreund, 1971). As for anthropomorphism, it is often regarded as a holdover from prehistoric physics. Even Grossman & Simon (1969), who recognize the practical usefulness of anthropomorphism in the growth of psychological theory, dwell more on its phenomenology than on its logic. They grant it a mission at a stage of theorizing, in bridging introspective and systematic levels of consideration. Schafer, who commends them, allows anthropomorphism an even higher station: it reflects psychology's claim to the status of a natural science.

Regarding natural science, Schafer's criticism is very precise: its model lacks a concept of personal responsibility or agency, and so therefore does current psychoanalytic theory which is built on it.

I do not think we can appreciate what is at stake until we set the problem in its broadest perspective. Responsibility and agency are not solely psychological terms. Whenever we try to think about an actual thing, as opposed to a part of a system, and whenever we seek to attribute to that thing its own consequences or properties, we are assigning responsibility and agency. The hunt for agency is the hunt for an ultimate subject which is responsible for its predicates, or, in old-fashioned terms, the hunt for a substance.

The problem is that the ultimate concrete subject eludes us. Predicates are

---

allows a similar equivocation. At some moments we can think of information in its modern, technical sense, as uninterpreted subject or substance, and at another moment, in its older, connotative sense as an interpreted outcome or resultant. (See chapter 18.)

[3]In this respect, Schafer's project risks the same irrationalism that threatens all process theories, from Bergson to Gendlin. It is interesting to compare Schafer's approach with Gendlin's. Schafer's terms are atomistic, while Gendlin's tend to describe a continuum. But for both, movement characterizes the person (see chapter 22).

general, inexhaustible and apply indifferently to many subjects. Moreover, predicates are ultimately comparative and therefore relative to the describer's perspective. Yet it seems to be impossible to think without supposing a concrete, individual subject. (That was Kant's message.) We may suppose the subject to lie in various realms—tangible, mental, energic or what have you. But we must find or suppose such a subject. We ought not to be ridiculed as unsophisticated when we "substantialize" abstractions. It is not because of a shameful immaturity that we do it. It is from cognitive necessity. ("Tough-minded" positivists are apt to substantialize space-time points.) We think about concrete things and we think about them in terms of abstract properties that never quite cover the subject.

Among the first to worry about this state of affairs were the pre-Socratic philosophers. They explored the possibilities of connecting concrete things and abstract properties. Parmenides observed that it is artificial to make abstract divisions of a single, concrete thing. And he so respected that fact, that he was willing to accept its discouraging implication that there is only one thing, namely the whole of reality. It could be said that Parmenides emphasized responsibility or agency, except that with only an agent, nothing was left to be responsible for. Strange as that outcome is, it could also be the logical fate of Schafer's approach: if a person's action is indistinguishable from his situation, he has in a sense, *produced* nothing to be responsible for.

Heraclitus, on the other hand, at least according to his popular reputation, pointed out how impossible it is to make the contradictory and fluctuating descriptions that constitute our knowledge coincide with any persistent, actual thing we know about. Whatever we think or know about anything is relative to a moment and characterizes it in ways that we will contradict at another time. No consistent and enduring thing is adequately bounded by our descriptions. All is in flux. There is plenty to be responsible for, but nothing to be responsible for it. Schafer's theory moves in that direction too. For if a given action always corresponds to a given situation rather than to a person's latent potential, what responsibility can the person have? A series of actions would be very like a Heraclitean flux with no designated core. As Heraclitus banished enduring things, so Schafer banishes motives.

Mourelatos (1973) speculates that the early Greeks regarded all knowledge as knowledge by acquaintance. Nowadays we consider light and dark to be abstract properties (qualities), and philosophers have a hard time affixing them to the underlying concrete thing. But Anaximander regarded qualities as concrete things in their own right, which one could meet, as one meets people. His across-the-board anthropomorphism provided a perfect locus for agency and responsibility, but ignored the abstractness of the qualities. According to Mourelatos, Heraclitus discovered the abstractness of qualities when he realized that such terms as light and dark are logically interrelated (one is the negation of the other). If Mourelatos is right, we would be inclined to say that Heraclitus showed that qualities are different from people and cannot be anthropomorphized. Unlike qualities, people are not logically interrelated; they are not defined in terms of each other; they are just themselves. But in fact, even when we describe people, we find that our descriptions are abstract. And Heraclitus concluded that, far from everything's being like a person, as Anaximander believed, nothing is.

Mourelatos contrasts this attitude with that of Parmenides, who refused to stop "substantializing" qualities and thus ended up with one spatial but indivisible, unchanging and basically uncharacterizable entity, which could simply be pointed to. It could be said that Parmenides depicted the whole world as having a unique personhood.

The implication is that if we look for something in our subject other than comparisons and biased abstractions, we find only "wholeness," or rather, since that too is a comparative term, we are simply forced to take a nonanalytic attitude toward the subject.

THE COGNITIVE PURPOSE OF MECHANISM AND ANTHROPOMORPHISM

I believe that theorizing must straddle the fence between the Parmenidean and the Heraclitean perspectives, or else fall off into the absurdity of individuality without features or features without individuality—agency that swallows up all consequences or consequences that replace any agency.

And what is that old bogey "mechanism" but the archetype of fence-straddling theory? Is not a "machine" the Parmenidean "thing" spread out in space with the contradictory Heraclitean adjectives somehow attached to it? After all, a thing is that which moves and changes and yet stays the same; it is a functioning unit and yet it is composed of parts (cf. Meyerson, 1908).

As a procedure, mechanism sets out to explore an individual thing. In psychology the thing is someone who can actually be met. But mechanism is not satisfied to introduce him. It presumes to describe him, and therefore portrays him as divisible: it catalogues his "parts." These divisions are the result of abstraction. And since the abstractions are drawn from a nonabstract individual, they are arbitrary, for other abstractions could be made instead. Seeing this, some critics castigate a mechanical model of the mind for its reifications of abstract relationships. Yet, while it may be arbitary to characterize an individual by certain abstractions, it is not arbitrary to suppose that he is characterized by abstractions. If we refused to think of an individual as constituted in some way by his abstractions, we could not even think about his unrealized potential or his past qualities that were never tested. We would be dealing not with a person or a thing, but with a

Heraclitean flux or a Parmenidean homogeneity (depending on whether we threw out the person or the abstractions).

By treating the abstract "parts" of the mind as substantive, rather than as capricious inventions, mechanism indicates that something or other does characterize the individual apart from momentary effects that he has on himself and others. In so doing, it lays the groundwork for tying together various behaviors.

To the extent that these "parts" are regarded as real parts and not inventions, they become things in their own right. One can then take *them* as subjects of investigation. One can study a superego as well as studying a person. Mechanism thus has a tendency to move its focus of inquiry and, with it, the seat of "thinghood" from larger and more singular units, such as a person, to smaller and more general ones, such as an ego. It becomes at once microscopic and cosmic as it moves away from the individual it began with.

What it means for the focus of inquiry and the seat of "thinghood" to move away from the individual it began with is that agency and responsibility are attributed to the abstract parts of what was considered the concrete thing. Mechanism attributes to the abstraction some of the concreteness of the whole individual. It distributes the individual's responsibility among his generalities, which then become individuals in their own right. But what kind of individuals do the abstractions become? The answer depends on how the theoretician feels about losing his original subject. Therapists tend to be unhappy about losing their original subject, which is the person. As the inquiry becomes more and more depersonalized, they dig in their heels and try to halt the shift. Being mechanists, they have divided up their subject in order to think about it and have thus created other subjects of inquiry, such as psychic structures, which then claim agency and responsibility. All that they can do to prevent further evaporation of the person is to limit the inquiry to the *type* of agency or responsibility that pertains to personhood; they will have the ego striving and the superego punishing. That is the source of anthropomorphism, and Schafer understands that.

Anthropomorphism is easily ridiculed. It seems to explain an individual by peopling him with other individuals. But the alternatives are funnier still. They are, to repeat, explaining something by pointing to it, explaining something by showing that there is nothing to explain, and explaining something by forgetting about it per se and turning to more general principles. (The first alternative was chosen by Parmenides, the second by Heraclitus and the last is the path of natural science.)

Anthropomorphism can certainly be misleading. It is important to dispel anthropomorphic *myth*. There is no point in stopping halfway between the individual person and whatever destination the further breakdown of the logical subject would lead to, unless we do in some way preserve the individual person as the focus of our thinking. Better a neurological description or a universal, transactional, interpersonal field theory than disembodied egos and superegos floating around.

But we can prevent the illusion that anthropomorphic imagery is a special kind of understanding if we recognize that anthropomorphism is just a half-way house on a journey away from the personal subject. It is a simplified reference to the potentialities that make up an actual, individual person.

A REINTERPRETATION OF SCHAFER'S REINTERPRETATION OF PSYCHOANALYSIS

I think that Schafer's mission is to remind us that we anthropomorphize because we do not want to lose the individual person as our subject of investigation. If, as I have suggested, anthropomorphism is a movement away from that subject stopped *in medias res*, then every once in a while we will need to be reminded of our starting point and encouraged to resist the mechanistic pull away from it. It is that valuable, conservative service that Schafer renders, not a revision of theory.

Schafer's *Aspects of Internalization* (1968) tells us that, in whatever way we have described our psychoanalytic subject, we have always *meant* to describe a something that wants and wishes. Our theories have always dealt, explicitly or implicitly, with conation. In his chapter on "Action" (1973a) he shows that the psychologist is concerned with *personal responsibility*. And in his paper on resistance (1973b) he has, in effect, stressed the *individuality* of the thing psychoanalysis studies, i.e. the concreteness—the non-abstractness—of a person and the consequent relativity of our view of him.

These principles hold psychoanalysis to what it had set out to examine. Schafer's work helps us to keep in mind the nature of the psychoanalytic subject despite the dialectical tensions involved in sticking with it. But he does not eliminate the tensions. Yes, the person is an individual thing, and he or his actions can therefore be described in innumerable ways, as indeed any concrete thing can be. But by the same token, responsibility entails handling something, and requires a nomenclature which distinguishes between a person and his situation, as well as among motives that are separable from their implementation. Yes, we should always remember that metapsychology is just a scheme for interrelating wishes. But at the same time biological factors enter the equation, for instance when we sleep or go into a depression. There is an *it*, otherwise describable, that does the wishing.

These are the representatives of "mechanism" that cannot be exorcised. In contrast to the philosophers he respects, Schafer lets his solutions draw in these paradoxes because at heart, in my opinion, he still believes in the notion of a substance to be investigated, an entity to be described. Since he will not let the subject dissolve into an assortment of sense data, nor allow it to congeal into a total mystery, he is in a good position to clarify psychoanalytic theory. His further work may show how we can steer a course between the unthinkable theories of process and uniqueness and the irrelevant expansion of abstractions. I hope that he will further distinguish himself from the extremists by ceasing to make "mechanism" a scapegoat for the recalcitrance of difficult philosophical problems.

SUMMARY

Schafer's desire to preserve psychology's focus on personal responsibility persuades him to favour a concrete model of the mind and to shun abstraction.

Because abstractions are necessary in our thinking, Schafer's action language cannot substitute for orthodox psychoanalytic descriptions. It does not adequately describe latent responses and it is not consistent. In order to serve Schafer's purpose, the term "action" must be used equivocally as meaning on the one hand a concrete doing and, on the other, the form or nature of a doing.

What makes Schafer's project so difficult is the ancient problem of relating abstract predicates to concrete subjects. The alternative, extreme solutions have been known from the beginning of Western philosophy. They are: regarding things as ceaseless activity—a flux of phenomena—and regarding everything as an organic, unanalyzable whole. Conceptual analysis always compromises between these views.

Mechanism is just such a compromise. Mechanism leads to a progressive substantializing of abstractions, in the course of which the original focus of its inquiry is replaced by others (the study of the person is replaced by the study of the ego, the id, etc., or it is replaced by organizations of motives or energy and so on).

I suggest that anthropomorphism represents an arrest in this shift, allowing one to refer to the original subject's special kind of action, even though that subject has been broken down into abstract components. The action appropriate to the whole is attached to the abstract components, in an effort to stay close to the original inquiry.

On this understanding of anthropomorphism, Schafer's contribution should be welcomed not as a replacement for orthodox psychoanalytic theory, but as a reminder that psychoanalytic psychology was and remains the study of personal responsibility.

21

Levenson's Perspectivism

E dgar Levenson's *The Fallacy of Understanding* (1972) is rare, brilliant, and true. The only comparable work is Frank's *Persuasion and Healing* (1961). But Levenson's is more important to therapists because the anthropological facts that impressed Frank have been roughly common knowledge, whereas the highly abstract background of Levenson's thinking is not. Which is not to say that Levenson has written an abstract treatise. On the contrary, it is replete with particular aphorisms and dicta that are each of immense practical value to therapists. ("Telling someone else what he thinks is always demeaning, even when accurate"; "Successful therapy may not be so much a consequence of what the therapist does as it is of what he does not permit to happen . . ."; "[When a patient disagrees with me] I cannot be sure that I did not say what *he* thinks I said, rather than what I think I said"; ". . . telling the therapist to analyze his countertransference is telling him to stop feeling that way about [his patient]. Actually she permits no alternative.") But these particular insights are a testimonial to a general approach that is so convincing that its power and limitations need to be appreciated.

I will summarize Levenson's argument in six theses.

STRUCTURALIST PSYCHIATRY

First, our conceptions organize the world with much arbitrariness. What we feature or name, what we take to be entities, which relationships we choose to notice and which we don't, ultimately involve a kind of choice—a choice

295

that is made by individuals and by societies, in the context of historical periods. Second, such choices are not discrete decisions, but mutually affect one another. If we (subliminally) analyze one part of the world according to a certain principle, we will have perforce analyzed the other parts according to the same principle. When I cut out a figure, I have also labeled its ground. We do not make a lot of separate choices; we choose an overall pattern. Third, what makes the resulting structure more than a happenstance of unrelated accidents is the organizing principle behind it, which, being a principle, will manifest itself in many—no, every—situation and will have many different appearances. The "structure" of structuralism refers to the real unity among diverse items.

Fourth, we never perceive this structure. After all, it is merely a *principle* of organization, and not an organized *thing*. If our master plan for dividing up the welter of experience were itself a piece of experience to be sliced up by us, we would naturally have to have a super-master-plan to direct its carving. We can never see our seeing. Our world-view is evidence of our basic orientation, but our basic orientations are never a part of our world view, since if they were seen, the way we saw them would be another *instance* of our orientation, another symptom of our set rather than the set itself. This, of course, makes for a certain epistemological relativism or perspectivism: We are led to admit that the only method available to us for examining how someone else or another culture organizes things is by organizing the others and their organizations in our own way.

This has an important application to therapy. While we share more of an outlook with our patients than we do with other cultures, each of us has his own unique view of the world. Levenson rightly calls structuralism a science of the individual. The organizing principle of a patient's world is the sense or the rationale or the harmony in his choice of perceptions. It follows that the patient's structures will overlap and assimilate his therapist. No matter what his therapist does, the patient (like anyone else) will perceive it in terms of his own world view. *This "transformation" of the therapist is a perception, not a distortion.* I do not think that Levenson has evolved a new definition of truth or reality, as would be necessary to cope with the differences we are accustomed to distinguishing on a continuum between "appropriate" perception and hallucination, but he has made the extraordinarily important observation that for the most part, the relationship between patient and therapist can be as well described by the patient's scenario as by the therapist's. Do you think that having cleared yourself of specific, isolated, and therefore removable "counter-transferences," you are exactly what you want to be to your patient? Then learn from Levenson the first lesson of psychotherapy: It is not within the therapist's power to determine his relationship to his patient. That could be done only if there were an objective structure to experience, a built-in univalent meaning which is not a construct. Only our trade-school solidarity could have sustained such an illusion in dealing with people.

Levenson's *fifth* premise is that things really do change as time passes. They do not just get older; something new is added. Just as societies change and habits disappear, just as art produces new visions, so do ways of perceiving the world change definitively. The range of human views of the world, individual and collective, present and evolving, is a continuous creative enterprise, and an individual personality is an esthetic creation.

Sixth, Levenson believes that change is not smoothly continuous. He associates changing vistas with Kuhn's shifting paradigms. According to Levenson, Kuhn holds that an epoch's science is built around a current paradigm, that is, a general picture of how things work, which makes theories comprehensible but also limits their scope until a new paradigm replaces it.[1]

According to Levenson, three paradigms are connected with the evolution of technology: the mechanical, the communications, and the organic (or structural). These paradigms have organized all the structures of their milieu, influencing not only science and technology but personal relations, theories of mind, norms of psychopathology, and methods of treatment.

Our society is different from Freud's. Patients are different. Problems are different. What patients want from treatment is different. Even while retaining the old language, the therapist views his patient's problems and his own function differently. The difference does not reduce these serious matters to whims of fashion. Fashion is a partial epiphenomenon while structure is the common framework of an age. Levenson is not scornful of old paradigms. His principles guard him from fancying his own position to be the top of the hill. He reminds us that time affects everything. There is no paradigm or structure outside time, no immutable vantage point from which to survey what it is that is being looked at differently in different times. But by the same token we can no longer pretend to think the way our teachers thought.

ANOTHER ASSAULT ON MECHANISTIC MODELS

It seems to me that we have become too accustomed to patronizing Freud's "mechanical model." We are overdue for a discussion of what a model is and whether it is indeed merely a selection from an endless array of plausible visualizations. Levenson has opened the discussion by identifying "model" with "structure." But after he has made that translation, it is not clear

---

[1]Kuhn's belief is now less easily summarized than it used to be. One of his first refinements was to locate paradigms within a discipline—even an un-named discipline—rather than using paradigms to characterize all the sciences of an age. (See Kuhn, 1976a.)

whether or not he thinks that scientific structures are progressively out-
moded. Levenson himself glories in the antiquity and universality of his
"new" structuralism. And as for the "old" mechanism, it is hard to imagine
that science stood still from the time of Democritus until after Freud's death,
which is what it would mean to dismiss mechanism as one passing moment in
the progression of paradigms.

I think humanity has used very few models. It looks like these few have
chased each other throughout history without any of them retiring. We are
told, in effect, that Freud was naturally drawn to mechanical models because
steam engines were so conspicuous in his day. Maybe so, but "mechanism" is
also the way we attend to the fact that things are not in a complete flux, that
somehow, something more or less remains the same while other things are
changing (Meyerson, 1908), that there is some kind of continuity over time as
well as the discontinuity Levenson stresses.

AN ASSAULT ON UNDERSTANDING?

In other words, a model may be a period piece and yet also share some
timeless ingredient of the requirements for understanding. Perhaps Levenson
means to challenge this ingredient, even if, as Kant argued, it is inseparable
from knowledge. He has dared to call his book "The Fallacy of Understanding," rather than "New Ways of Understanding." He asks to be read "mythically." And he concludes that religion, myth, and mysticism may share the
future with the human sciences. It seems that Levenson is telling us that
understanding itself is the old, outdated model.

Is understanding a fallacy? Will we say about the old paradigms, "Oh, those
were the days when we thought there *was* such a thing as understanding"? (I
think such a dismissal would swell rather than diminish the ranks of
antiquarians.) Is there no sense in asking whether patient-types have
changed, inasmuch as our thinking about them has changed at the same
time? If the thermometer markings shift with the fever, we cannot take a
temperature. Is our thinking about our patients simply a way of interacting
with them? Shall we say that when our patients were waltzing our thoughts
about them were waltzing, but now we are both dancing differently? These
implications of his argument are fully acknowledged by Levenson, and my
impression is that, with some slight hedging, he is willing to accept them. It
seems to me that he leaves us with the possibility that when it comes to
knowing, there is only resonance or mirroring or a time-specific reacting, but
no such thing as understanding, no valid distinction between subject and
object, and little in common between the Victorian and Aquarian Ages. He
has made an effort to write in the new paradigm, to mirror facets and echo
themes from different aspects of life.

And yet, granted that he has invited us to read him mythically, he has nevertheless chosen to present an *argument* about therapy rather than painting a picture or writing a poem.

HOW, THEN, ARE WE TO UNDERSTAND TREATMENT?

The conceptual argument seems to me to run this way: Since we cannot stand outside of time, our theories about patients are influenced by the same *Zeitgeist* that influences their troubles. We fall in with them generally in their approach to the universe since we share their epoch. If there were nothing more to be said we could close the book on professionalism. A therapist would be an accoutrement to his patient in the same fashion as his symptom (every patient getting the therapist he deserves). But Levenson allows that there is some unevenness in the hold that the age has on its denizens. Psychotherapists do stand a *little* outside time (just as do artists and some others). They are *somewhat* in a position to see what others simply show. They can swim a little bit against the current. Besides that, individuals have some uniqueness, which means that everyone is to some extent out of phase with others, so there is at least a possiblity of a contrast of paradigms within the large, cultural uniformity, even in Levenson's view. The contrast of individual paradigms is not always manifest because people fit into each other's style. Indeed, it is to make individual differences manifest that the therapist tries to resist being fitted into the patient's world view. As Levenson portrays it, that job is exceedingly difficult but apparently not impossible.

But, now, if some people (therapists) are less immersed than the multitude in the spirit of the times, can we go further and say that they are more detached in some ways than they are in others? And if they are relatively independent of the cultural paradigm in some sectors of their life, might not the same be true for the multitude (including patients)? Such a possibility, which Levenson's approach seems to allow, begins to break up the endless hall of mirrors of a dominant paradigm.

In a magnificent rush of therapeutic hints at the conclusion of his truncated theory of therapy, Levenson leaves many questions unanswered, most conspicuously what rationale justifies his practical suggestions for therapy. I believe that he is right about what the therapist does, but in terms of Levenson's own beliefs it is hard to see why anybody should work that way. The therapist is encouraged to resist incorporation in the patient's world-view. But to what purpose? What difference would it make? Has the patient been waiting for someone to force change by noncooperation? What can we say was *wrong* with his disturbing world-view or presenting structure, now that we can no longer say that it is "inappropriate"?

Levenson says that therapy induces structure, which produces first a wider range of feeling and then a greater patterning, better able to include new data. This seems to imply that the patient's structuring is not only unhappy but inadequate, imperfect, imprecise, unequilibrized, ineffectual, too narrow, unusually rigid, etc. None of these faults is easily expressed in Levenson's terms, and I think all of them carry miniatures of a mechanical model within them, because it is the separating of something (a mechanical structure) from something else (e.g., its articulation) that allows one to talk about trouble. In contrast to the mechanical model, organic structure is supposed to be indivisible. All organic structures would seem to be adequate to their situation by definition.

Furthermore, if structures transform everything, is not a therapist who resists structuring at least figuratively and perhaps literally nothing to his patient? (A machine, on the other hand, not only runs its course but can use readjustment.)

And how *can* the therapist resist the patient's structure? Simply by pointing out the master plan the patient uses? But Levenson explains that this activity, like any other, is very easily incorporated in the patient's preexisting structure. In a perspectivist world how can the therapist do or refuse to do anything without the patient's cooperation? Is even the therapist's resistance possible without seduction?

Can these questions ever be answered without a theory of conflict? If the universe of the patient is an esthetic whole, there is nothing to do about it and no reason to do it. If something inside the patient clashed with something else inside him, then we *could* answer the questions: One of the patient's paradigms is at odds with another (whatever that would mean). We might then say that if the therapist resists incorporation by either part, the other can flourish, presumably making for a more satisfying esthetic picture of the world. It would be tough theoretical sledding, but a path would be visible.

However, if we were to talk about conflict, we would be describing separable interests. We could no longer describe the mind as one, cohesive perspective. It would be a multitude of incompatible meanings and values triangulating an outer universe. We would picture a patient as having delimited needs and wishes while living in a world that resists their simultaneous satisfaction. We would be very, very close to a mechanical model.

Similarly if the therapist allows himself to be structured by the patient (so as to be included within the patient's purview), while trying not to be completely overwhelmed by the structure (so as to bring about change), then he is reacting to *parts* of the patient, so to speak, and again we are on the road to a mechanical model.

Over and over again the old paradigms find entree when we are forced to apply standardized categories (conflict, parts, wishes) to the seamless web of creativity. It is hard to use both languages. Yet it is difficult to separate them. After all, speaking clinically, what considerations of Levenson's would not have claimed Freud's respect? A change of paradigm is not supposed to be a mere enrichment of observation, but a new way of perceiving the world. Yet there is nothing in Freud's "mechanical" model that would have prevented him from acknowledging the oversight in his treatment of Dora which Levenson points out. I am sure we would all expect him to concede both the criticism and its importance. What paradigmatic shift can have occurred if the new view is an oversight within the old one? Could Newton thank Einstein for helping him to be a better Newtonian? In his own system, Freud ran into *problems* with Dora which Levenson could have helped solve. So the *systems* do not compete.

WHAT ARE STRUCTURALISTS CONCERNED ABOUT?

If Levenson has retired mechanism prematurely, I think it is because he expects too much from structuralism. And he expects too much, I suggest, because structuralism is not what he thinks it is. He thinks that structuralism is a continuation of man's "search for order and system in the universe" (p. 30). He holds that in a structuralist perspective, ". . . time becomes again the matrix of life . . . all events are related by their immersion in its flow . . ." (p. 24). In other words, Levenson believes that structuralism will show how things are connected spatially and temporally. In that case it could replace earlier ways of explaining the therapeutic interplay and outcome. But I think structuralism (at least his variety of structuralism) is not so much concerned with relationships as with entities. (That is why he can call it the science of the unique.) It is not as respectful of time as it is of timelessness. Structuralism does not search for order and system in the universe; it surveys mankind's search for order and system to discover the root urge behind the search. Myth seeks order and system. Levenson writes as though myth were itself a kind of structuralism. But myth is no more structuralist than science.[2] Both seek order and system. And to the structuralist each is an artifical imposition of arbitrary or culture-bound categories, revealing the action but not the nature of an organizing principle within man.

Fundamentally, structuralism is the modern counterpart of the old philosophy of substance and essence. Its task is to find the real foundation of things in contrast to artificial or abstract or arbitrary entities. Its search is for something that has a natural boundary or border which is not a product of analysis or an ad hoc set-up. Such a thing can somehow remain itself over time, and it is independent of the way it is perceived. In other words, it is separate and it is enduring. But it is also concrete and actual and thus has a

---

[2]Lévi-Strauss explains that he dwells on primitive thought rather than Western science only because he can do so from a greater intellectual distance (1970).

history even though it maintains its identity. It has been identified with the whole culture. Levenson finds it in the whole individual.

The modern revival of the philosophy of substance and essence has brought us existentialism, phenomenology, process philosophy, and now it inspires structuralism. It is not surprising that psychotherapy is frequently the focus of this revival since there we confront essence in the form that is most vivid to us, namely, human individuality. Confronting human individuality, we recoil from generalized categories and standardized descriptions. No wonder the mechanical model has become so hateful! (See Friedman, 1984).

WHAT ELSE SHOULD STRUCTURALISTS WORRY ABOUT?

But Levenson does not seem to realize that this focus on the unique, concrete object makes it hard to connect objects with each other or to show how time affects them. He feels that his system for once does justice to the passage of time, unlike, for instance, Freudian theory where the past is drained of its pastness by being recapturable. However, Freud never said that the past could be relived; according to him, the difference between past and present is what makes memories therapeutic. Freud did believe that the past was in some way woven into the present. Whereas, Levenson, thinking to celebrate time by stressing the newness of the present, places events in time but renders them not of time, since something that does not arise out of the past may have a temporal location but it is not affected by time.

As to who honors time and who does not, I think Levenson has it completely backward. He believes that the ancient interrelatedness of organic cosmologies and the dream-time of primitive thought are examples of taking time seriously. "Time," he writes, referring to the former, "was the matrix of reality" (p. 23). And he believes that the evolutionary picture according to which ape advanced to man is essentially a spatial metaphor. But Lévi-Strauss (1970) has shown that the difference between archaic or mythical thought and Western scientific thought is precisely that the dimension of time, history, previous causes and later effects is of no concern to the former, but is vital to the latter, mentality. The older, or primitive, organization stresses the unity, not the passage, of time. No, I would say that Levenson's view of disjoined paradigms is the ultimate in the spatialization of time that he so much deplores; it is events without ancestors, though—and this is important—he reached that position through an effort to do justice to creativity and newness. But, in fact, only he respects time who recognizes *both* continuity and creativity.

An even subtler confusion is involved in Levenson's view of the relationship between entities. Just as Levenson wrongly assumes that respect for inventiveness can all by itself do justice to the reality of time, so he seems to think that structural "transformations" explain relationships. Indeed the word "structuralism" does have a very relational ring. It seems to promise something much more relational than mere comparative descriptions like "x is bigger than y" or "A is healthier than B." "Bigger" and "healthier" are merely externals; in another perspective x might be smaller than y, health might be meaningless in regard to A and B. But transformations make up a structure; they don't just characterize it. Transformations are not just the way someone chooses to describe the system. They *are* the system. (In philosophy they are known as internal rather than external relations, since they define the entities concerned at the same time as they relate them to each other; the relationship could not be changed without changing the entities.) With some justification Levenson regards himself as the prophet of complete relatedness.

But that complete interrelatedness is of something considered as a self-contained unity. For instance, if we regard society as an entity, its essence is the transformational rules that are reflected everywhere in it, including the relationship between therapist and patient. That is the sense in which "we are trapped in the melody of change."[3] The genius of the times is reflected in our psychotherapy as in our art and sexuality. But this is not a relationship between therapist and patient, it is a relationship that therapist and patient have to society, or to the cosmos, or to whatever is being taken as an entity. At this level, patient and therapist are not considered as entities but as reflections or aspects of a concrete universe.

Now we can, and Levenson does, consider the *patient* as an entity. When we do that, the therapist becomes a part of the patient's preordained world, as a reflection of his essential structural formula. In that case the genius of the *patient* pervades the office, but there is still no relationship between the patient and the therapist. The patient is considered as an entity but the therapist is not. There is no room for the old-fashioned "representation of the therapist." The entity that is being considered—here the patient—is always an irreducible, concrete thing, and what seem to be interrelated parts are in fact aspects of his surd essence.

Very simply, if relationships are accidental abstractions which the observor merely superimposes on the patient's specific, concrete wholeness, then the patient himself can have no relationship with anything, except in the observer's imagination.

The interrelatedness that Levenson propounds is the indivisibility of self-enclosed oneness. But we do justice to relationships only when we recognize the reality of common abstractions as well as unique concreteness.

Neither the proposed solution nor its difficulties are new. Leibnitz, in

---

[3] I overlook the exceptional role Levenson grants the therapist, because, as suggested above, this exception may require a major revision of his theory.

effect, also postulated that the final "it" of a being was its particular synthesis—its perspective—on the world, but he recognized that paradoxically such an identity could have no real interaction with others; it is immune to forced change. He, therefore, had recourse to a divine coordinator of the locked monads whose very mirroring of the world isolates them from each other.

People who are totally defined by their way of synthesizing experience, are ipso facto not really *affected* by experience. Theirs is a Leibnitzian perfect harmony, but without a coordinating God. All things are mirrored in a perspective without a mechanical causing. A disastrous consequence of this is that there are no unrealized possibilities. Consider the Freudian synthetic function of the ego which works at the behest of (mechanical) fragments of the mind, on the one hand, and mechanically "outside" stimuli on the other. It makes a difference to that machine whether or not it meets a therapist. With tongue in cheek we might say that Levenson also describes a synthetic function of the ego, but his synthetic function is a unique esthetic creation flung like a pot of paint upon the universe, therapist and all. The Freudian synthetic function of the ego, like a mechanical filter, waits for its input to make use of it. All kinds of potentialities are inherent in it, depending on the accidents of fortune, because it is really an abstraction. The esthetic projection described by Levenson, on the other hand—an irreducible, novel, unique, concrete creation—is what it is and nothing more; a system which can digest whatever is given it with no room for tension or missed possibilities. In other words, in this system we cannot talk of unrealized potentiality, nor, therefore, I am afraid, of treatment. Each being (or society or group) is a universe unto itself; each is a work of art. A science of uniqueness pushed to its extremes is a science of lonely, timeless harmony.

THERAPY NEEDS STRUCTURALISM AND THE "WHAT ELSE"

But Levenson cannot afford the extravagances that philosophers indulge. Psychotherapy is a field where influence, change and conflict and unrealized potentiality are the order of the day. His account is full of people clashing with their society and with their therapist. He is the bravest chronicler of the therapist's struggle to engage and disengage himself from his patient.

Only the theory lags behind: one suspects that he knows it and, therefore, ends his book in a hurry, before he has spelled out the justification for the therapist to impose a difficulty on the patient.

Levenson's view of alienation is particularly puzzling in this regard. He writes that organic mutuality is the hallmark of our age, and yet alienation is one of its expressions. He holds that the old question "How can I function?" has been replaced by the question "Why should I function?" and he regards this as evidence of a new spirit of interrelatedness, but yet he argues that the lock-step life of past times was a reflection of the old mechanical model. Perhaps this is where Levenson is to be read mythically. In any case I am left with the feeling that he has conjured conflict into his account by using alienation as (and I hope he will pardon the expression) a *deus ex machina*. Somehow he manages to make his perspectivism look like a natural support for rebelliousness, rather than for the Hindu apathy or Hegelian acceptance which is where its logic would take it. The rebelliousness Levenson saw around him when he wrote his book he portrayed as a self-definition on one hand and a pretense of detachment on the other. If that description is accurate, then rebelliousness is either a fashion or a fraud or both. Levenson recognizes both nuances but his sympathies for the rebel prevail.

Yet what agony can there be in a complainer who, as Levenson reveals him, not only is architect of his own prison, but cannot in the nature of things *expect* anything else than a choice of isomorphic surroundings? Levenson shows that we will always be embedded in some way in our culture and that we will in some way endorse this embeddedness. Does this not make an absurdity of our noisy militancies, our bitter protests against oppression and co-optation, sexism, exploitation, consumerism? Maybe these evils are only names for structural embeddedness. Are people now seeking to break out from structure generally, or at least from human structure? Perhaps what is characteristic of our decade is not a recognition of organic wholeness, but a dim view of structure itself. Such a view would also regard structuring activities such as traditional psychoanalysis as oppressive "adjustment" techniques, a view that Levenson unhappily shares. In point of fact, organic societies are not noted for challenging the "why" of functioning.

Levenson does not want to trivialize modern rebelliousness as a mere mood. However, if he wants to portray alienation and "dropping out" as a conflict between older and newer paradigms, rather than simply a lifestyle of its own, he will have to forgo the smooth, separated wholeness of a series of discontinuous structures and give us a theory of conflict.

Levenson is aware that structuralism is not of a piece. But he underplays the selectiveness of his perspective. Piaget, for instance, is far more impressed than other structuralists by the real action of time, undoubtedly because he is a developmental psychologist. His structuralism has in it less of what Levenson calls discontinuity. He sees structures growing out of each other rather than replacing each other. At the root of human structure Piaget finds specifiable problems, such as the problem for an individual of maintaining his individuality while experiencing the buffets of novelty (Piaget 1951). For Piaget, such a problem is not a mere perspective; it is basic to all organisms however it may be conceptualized. By the same token, perhaps, we could say that there is more mechanism in Piaget, insofar as his schemas, although inventive, are not *just* esthetic structures (though they are surely that to an extent) but are also means to an end, levers, tools, which can function for better or worse. They have a task. They are delimited; minds hold many schemas at once. In a manner of speaking, Piaget has built a growing-machine. The machine's principle of growth is an objective task of assimilation and accommodation. Piaget does not feel that a myth is as good as a scientific hypothesis (Piaget 1970).

What I am saying is that structuralism and mechanism are ways of responding to different aspects of experience that are hard to describe together. Like process-ism or vitalism, structuralism tries to do justice to uniqueness and creativity. Mechanism tries to do justice to interaction and potentiality. Both try to grasp continuity during change and in this respect both are inadequate. There will be questions answerable in the one framework which the other can only beg. But neither, in my view, is an accident of the times, and I strongly suspect that "new" conceptualizations will fall into the one family or the other, because the problems that compel them are not artificial, invented, creative, or expressive, but just plain problems.

Levenson's (1983) later work bears out this prediction, for there he swings over to the idea that a preformed semiotic process inside the patient awaits training by exercises with the therapist. Levenson still eschews conflict and thus tends to construct a process theory, but the process is founded on a static structure—an inborn ability, ultimately analogous to a psychic institution or an organ, in the Chomskian sense (Chomsky, 1980).

That is all very well, Levenson might say, if you are talking about "understanding," but understanding itself may be merely a passing fancy. What about the escape hatches: mysticism, religion, new forms of consciousness, etc.? We could answer `a la Kant (and Chomsky?): If you go beyond understanding you go beyond experience. But we might also say that those alternatives are not new, and not escapes. They are the attitudes appropriate to the old, limited conceptual options. When one approaches the perspectivist, unique, process aspect of experience, one attends intuitively, appreciatively, feelingly, and with abandon; when one approaches the interrelated aspect of experience, with a view to what might be that isn't, one will categorize, verbalize, and impose abstractions. No doubt we will attend to these different aspects in different ways at different times. No doubt also there is nothing new under the sun. Making due allowance for the sloppiness of "dialectic," reflection always seems to end with "yes *and* no."

ESTHETIC APPRECIATION VS. PROBLEM IDENTIFICATION

Years ago, when academic philosophy still acknowledged a heritage, there was a school of thought at the University of Chicago that held that every major philosophy was a completely unified creation, and that each was correct "on its own terms." The appearance of internal contradictions or conflicting tendencies was held to be evidence only that the philosopher was being misread. The Chicago tradition brought into American scholarship (temporarily, alas) a new humility and therefore a more acute attention to the details of philosophies that had previously been arrogantly dealt with as patchwork quilts of debates with fellow philosophers.

Levenson's approach reminds me of the Chicago discipline. Unfortunately I am also reminded of some sad consequences of the Chicago style. A new polyscholasticism developed; the architecture of the philosopher's work was reverently traced; the intrinsic necessity of everything from the first word to the last period was dutifully discovered; the text was revealed as a perfect esthetic creation, standing, if not alone, at most side-by-side with similar ones, far from those of a different style. But nowhere was there a care for why the perfect whole of a philosophy was produced; nowhere an admission that it had relevance to another philosophy and might conflict with it; nowhere an allowance that, as a human work, it might uncomfortably embrace divergent aims. Nobody cared about the itch the philosopher was scratching, or observed that another philosopher might be suffering from a similar itch. And certainly none of the scholars felt any corresponding itch themselves.

It is clear that Levenson is far ahead of his colleagues in appreciating the itches his individual patients are scratching, and in discovering what corresponds within himself. But his esthetic attitude and personal world-view strip discomfort of its significance and in theory (though obviously not in practice) deprive his exchange of the bite of dialogue.

The Chicago school performed a much needed service when it insisted that a philosophical system is a functioning structure and not a heap of artifices to be pillaged at will. What the movement lacked was a way of transcending systems so that the scholar could not only resonate with the system but also — and I use the word advisedly — understand it. To understand a philosophical system one must feel a problem *underlying* the author's work. One must share the philosopher's motivating pain which, though colored by the student's perspective, ties him by a real, shared discomfort to the different perspective of the philosopher and thence to the still different perspectives of other philosophers (Gadamer, 1975).

If Piaget is right, wherever we are in history, wherever on the globe, we start our lives with a stretch and become what we are by struggle. In a sea of relativism there must be something at the core of a *problem* which can be a compass to us if we feel it even in our own, idiosyncratic way.

We have needed Levenson's book for a long time. The other side has had more than its day. And yet, lest he make too much of a good thing, it would be wise for him to come half-way back and paint some collective, connecting problems onto his own canvas, some parts inside his patients and some conflict among the parts, some suggestion (seductiveness) in his therapist, some linear causality among objects, some developments of old theory, some brotherhood between ages, some veracity in abstract concepts.

We may never get it all together, but we can try not to let any of it get away.

22

Gendlin's Vitalism

. . . you may say anything you really and truly feel. Anything at all, no matter what it is. I am not afraid, so long as it is your real self that speaks, and not a mere attitude—a gallant attitude, or a wicked attitude, or even a poetic attitude. I put you on your honor and truth. Now say whatever you want to. —Candida, Act III, George Bernard Shaw

In these lines, Candida speaks like a seasoned psychotherapist. She has captured the essence of therapy in one short instruction. Yet there is something devilish in those last two sentences that makes us uneasy about claiming her as a colleague. The young poet wants to win her love, and she says, "I put you on your honor and truth. Now say whatever you want." Here is his response:

MARCHBANKS (the eager expression vanishing utterly from his lips and nostrils as his eyes light up with pathetic spirituality): Oh, now I can't say anything: all the words I know belong to some attitude or other—all except one.

That one, of course, is her name, and that is all her instructions allow him to say. Her invitation to a genuine encounter is actually a ruse to keep him mute. Candida, we learn, is loyal to her husband; she allows *him* to be as hypocritical as he pleases. Indeed Shaw's characteristic twist is that Candida devotes her life to supporting her husband's facade of open-hearted understanding.

If Candida's instruction is such psychiatric wisdom, what about its mocking purpose? When Candida takes care of someone, she lets him strike a pose; she demands authenticity in order to reject someone (who does not need her!). Therapists are supposed to be both responsible and demanding toward patients. They are supposed to permit themselves to be needed, to accept the patient's vocabulary, and at the same time they are hired changers, who ask the "real self" to speak and not a "mere attitude."

How can we fit into a patient's patterns and yet expect to change them? How are we to appreciate someone while struggling with his customs? How can there be both fit and strain between us? It is the puzzle we began with and, in chapter 2, we saw how theorists dealt with it by putting a fragment of the ego on its "honor and truth" while allowing defenses to speak their "mere attitudes."

Mindful of the difference between what people want to say and can truly say, we are bound to be attracted to a theory that holds that the patient's presentation is authentic even while it is designed for persuasion. In Gendlin's (1964, 1967, 1968) process theory, patient and therapist work together with no element of struggle in sight. The therapist can be purely appreciative and never doubtful. Momentary abrasions are depicted, but the basic interaction is cooperation—all fit and no strain between patient and therapist; no divergence of directions; no covert threats or bargains; no insincerity, hidden reservations or bribery. Gendlin seems to have found a way to take from Marchbanks his mere attitudes and still leave him words. I know of no other system that so persuasively describes the concordance a therapist longs for, the personal appreciation the patient demands, the freedom from make-believe the theoretician despairs of. Those who are accustomed to thinking of therapy as a muffled and civilized reenactment of an older, titanic, often life-and-death struggle, sweaty, messy and, tragic, will find Gendlin's vision a welcome change. We will naturally wonder whether he can carry it off theoretically. The examination that follows explains why I believe he cannot quite do so, although his technical suggestions are helpful. His method is not a miraculous tonic, but it is good medicine. And Gendlin's technical device does have significant theoretical import.

In chapter 14, I argued that Freud acquired his initial theoretical leverage by discovering an entity within the mind that can be followed in its transformation. Transformation is so obviously important to a treatment theory that anyone unacquainted with psychoanalysis would imagine it to be replete with accounts of how change happens. And so it is, with regard to growth and development, but theorists are not absorbed with the process of change in general, and certainly not in treatment. Most of the revisions we look at in this part of the book reexamine the standard static picture of the mature mind. (Feffer's, 1982, study of the issue is both unusual and thoughtful.) Many focus on change but few describe transformations of continuing elements, and that is the reef on which revisions tend to founder. Gendlin's special interest is the temporal aspect of the mind. He feels that psychoanalysis set out to explain change but used up all its resources in describing a momentary state of personality. Ignoring the process aspect of Freud's theory (see chapter 5), Gendlin sets out to formulate one of his own. Unlike many Freudian revisionists, what interests him in mental process is not the unity of the mind, but its fluidity. Like other revisionists he recoils from the concept of mental structure, but his concern is not so much that structures are figments of the theorist's imagination, as that such concepts impede the therapist's efforts to facilitate change.

MENTAL PROCESS INSTEAD OF MENTAL CONTENTS

According to Gendlin, psychoanalysis regards ignorance of one's motives as the cause of resistance to change, and it holds the same motives to be the cause of the ignorance. Insofar as ignorance has its motives (as in repression), enlightenment does not seem to explain why change occurs. Gendlin (1964) writes:

> Once we have shown how anything will be distorted which tends to bring these experiences to awareness, we cannot then consider it an explanation to simply assert that personality change is (by definition supposedly impossible) a becoming aware [pp. 105–106].

Actually, Freud (1910b) was the first to point this out. It was his argument against wild analysis. It was also his substantive argument against hypnosis (but with some equivocation; see Gray, 1982).

Continuing with Gendlin's argument, if one wants to explain personality change one must postulate something that can change. Experiencing is such a thing because it is a process. Our feeling states do not come with labels. But as we push on our environment and are pushed by it, the feelings within us take on one meaning after another, some that can be put into words and some that cannot. Gendlin (1964) calls that process *experiencing*. "When felt meanings occur in interaction with verbal symbols and we feel what the symbols mean, we term such meanings 'explicit' or 'explicitly known' " (p. 112). If the interaction is not with verbal symbols, the meaning of the body state is implicit. As we watch the continuously developing interaction, we see that a "felt meaning can contain very many meanings and can be further and further elaborated" (1964, p. 113). In particular, there are always new possibilities of interaction with verbal symbols, so there is always much more implicit (momentarily non-verbalizable) than explicit (currently sayable) meaning to a body state, and the meaning of a body state is never exhausted by any description.

Experiencing stops when the patient and his environment cease to interact with body feelings and therefore do not generate meaning. Neither the audience inside his own head nor feedback from other people picks out any particular significance of his unlabeled body state. In place of meaning, the patient develops stereotyped, prejudged pictures and attitudes that Gendlin calls *frozen wholes*. Like the "bleep" that replaces a forbidden word on television, frozen wholes take the place of actual experiences. For example, a fixed attitude toward authority replaces an encounter with a particular ranking person. Frozen wholes may be described but they are not experienced in their details because they do not allow the particulars of the environment to help the owner find shapes and significance in his body feeling.

A psychoanalyst would say that the patient is actively avoiding a feared experience. But Gendlin does not want to stack the cards against change. If the patient has something in him that *makes* his experiencing stop, experience (in the treatment) is not going to start it up again. Gendlin's more hopeful formula is that a frozen whole signals the *absence* of symbolizing interaction, and the consequent abandonment of the search for the significance of one's body feeling: "experiencing remains structure bound, the structures themselves are not *modifiable* by present occurrences" (Gendlin, 1964, p. 129). "Instead of the many, many implicit meanings of experiencing which must interact with present detail to interpret and react, the individual has a structured feeling pattern" (p. 129).

The job of psychotherapy is to "reconstitute" the stopped process of experiencing. But you cannot reconstitute living experience by pointing to rigidities. No one, Gendlin observes, is much helped by talking to him about how he does not function. One can only respond to that much of experience which is still in process. Therefore, it is a waste of time or worse to nag a patient about his faulty patterns. Those patterns are, so to speak, what is dead about him. You might as well argue with a corpse. The therapist must respond to what is living, "*to the functioning experience, not to the structure*" (p. 132). That is what a therapist does when he reacts to the normal, human, seeking aspect of sick behavior. The therapist's response and the patient's response to that encouragement are events that interact with the patient's body feeling. They therefore develop the meaning implicit in that feeling. And that is the answer to the riddle of personality change: When new meaning is developed the feeling has been to that extent transformed. The old body feeling without a shaped meaning is not the same as the state after interaction has given it meaning. When a patient has felt his purpose, so to speak, he has not just discovered something about himself, he has changed himself; he has shaped something in him that was not shaped before. It must be noted that not every impact has this effect. Looking back over the path that has led to new meaning, one notices that there is a chain of priorities by which one new meaning leads to the next. Some meanings must be discovered before certain others can be felt. This exploration of meaning, which changes what it investigates, indirectly picks up strands of previously ignored feeling and allows the stopped flow to be reconstituted.

The technique of responding to functioning experience rather than to structure is called *focusing*. The therapist trains the patient to listen to his actual body feeling, and helps him to discover the implicit meaning in it. The therapist does not use conceptualizations to "explain" the patient's feeling. Conceptualizations are used to *point* to the momentary body feeling, which is accordingly called *the felt referent*. The therapist's formulation helps the patient to find an appropriate meaning in his feeling, but the formulation is not the meaning. Like all reactions from the environment, the therapist's utterance makes a difference to the targeted feeling. Instead of a formless limbo of potentialities it is now just that kind of a feeling that has evoked that particular pronouncement from a therapist. But what meaning this interaction leads to can only be found by the patient attending to his feeling state — that must be his reference point: a felt referent not a conceptual referent. Good therapists have always known that patients should be looking at their feelings and not at formulas.

The therapist may further reveal some of his own reactions to the patient as clues to the implicit meaning of the patient's body state. When he does that, he emphasizes the "positive" meaning of troublesome or unpleasant expressions — what is succeeding in the patient, not what has failed and ceased to strive. It is not the therapist's job to say what the patient is "really" thinking. His job is to be a special kind of environmental foil for a person who needs reactions to discover the significance of his unstructured feelings. Therapists who pretend to know the meaning of body feeling ahead of their patient are fundamentally misleading him because felt meaning is not knowable that way; it is a concrete linkage of feeling with environmental events. One might almost say that meaning "happens," and the patient is the first to know when it does. When meaning is achieved the feeling state changes and the process continues with a somewhat new body feeling. If the interaction with a therapist has elicited a fresh unfolding of meaning to a previously stopped experience, the patient will feel a peculiar relief of a sort known to all therapists. It is peculiar because the patient is relieved even if the meaning he has found is ugly. This relief is the feeling of a frozen, non-experiencing structure moving again into process and going forward in its development of meaning. It is the specific relief afforded by psychotherapy and the proof of progress.

It is startling to realize how closely Gendlin paralleled, and to some extent anticipated, Heinz Kohut's work, but within a different discipline and tradition. Gendlin writes for psychologists, and there is a lesson here about noncommunication between therapy professions (although Kohut evenhandedly omitted citations from all disciplines alike). But the differences between Gendlin and Kohut are even more illuminating than their similarities. Kohut's patients are paralyzed by fear as well as driven by aspirations, and they create particular relationships to their therapist in order to conserve their functioning. In other words, Kohut wants to have both experiencing *and* structure in his theory. Kohut's mixed theory allows for recurrent unhappiness between patient and therapist, and it puts a value on impasse, even though Kohut resembles Gendlin in the generally "nice" picture he paints of the treatment process. On the other hand, as a more consistent process theorist, Gendlin might say that Kohut's type of empathy exercises a presumptuous authority over another person's world. Gendlin started with the sort of empathy that Kohut (1984) was moving toward at the end of his life (i.e., the act of responding rather than a state of achieved knowledge). Kohut showed us a human relationship in this process, whereas Gendlin shows the intrapsychic event that empathy inaugurates within the patient.

Observe that Gendlin attacks the problem of personality change by picturing the whole of experience as a process rather than as the Freudian mixture of psychic institutions and process. He discards the notion that experience is a flux that is filtered through a fixed personality composed of defined things like wishes, thoughts, attitudes, and structures. Instead, he says that the whole of a person's state is capable of many different meanings or definitions, depending on its interaction with its environment (bearing in mind that one's own soliloquy makes one a part of his own environment). And moreover, he declares that a new meaning induces a new body state that is susceptible to still other kinds of meaning in an unending progression. Therefore, to be an experiencing creature is to be in continual process of definition of body feeling. Thus changing a patient's personality is no longer the impossible task of dissolving a structure that is defined by its unchangeableness, and becomes instead the more hopeful task of restoring mobility to an experiencing process that is defined by its movement. And the therapeutic gift that restores motion is not the ability to see attitudes that are by definition invisible (repressed), but rather the discovery of new opportunities to define body feeling, and give it the ever-changing meaning that makes it experience.

HAS GENDLIN REALLY OFFERED AN ALTERNATIVE?

This looks promising, but the difficulties that beset other theories are not easily dispelled. One notes first that Gendlin says little about why free experiencing stops, why experience becomes structure bound, why patients react by developing frozen wholes. Little is said about why a patient does not respond to his body feeling, or why responses are not elicited from family and friends. Second, the theory deals rather vaguely with the pain that treatment is designed to ease. Because trouble is arrested experience, it must be felt as a sense of lack. Gendlin describes it as a "stuck feeling," but he also compares it to the interruption of a life process. The clinician who sees a vivid spectrum of miseries may feel cramped by having to describe them either as a stuck feeling or a (partial) death. Third, it is not clear from Gendlin's formulation what service the therapist renders that is not rendered by everyone else in the patient's environment. The therapist is supposed to respond to what is "positive" in the patient, and maybe that means he is more appreciative. But because Gendlin wants no libido in his theory, he cannot say why the patient makes it possible for the therapist to respond to parts of him that he does not let others respond to. Finally, it is hard to see how the theory can account for patients who refuse to be diverted from their preferred drama by the therapist's interest in their felt referent.

One could answer these questions with psychoanalytic theory. For instance, a patient may not get what he needs from others because of a self-defeating conflict. The quality of the pain might reflect the drive that is frustrated. The therapist might be useful because he is not put off by defensive aspects of behavior. Patients who do not take advantage of what Gendlin hails as universal nutriment might be said to feed on fantasy.

Alternatively, disliking these terms, Gendlin could use his own: He could say that experience is blocked because childhood discouragement taught the patient to avoid taking risks. (That is part of Kohut's answer.) The painful quality of stopped experience might be a generalized frustration, because all fulfilments require the common process of experiencing. (Cf. Kohut's view of drives as breakdown products of an overall maturational thrust.) Perhaps the therapist's unique effectiveness would be found to hinge precisely on his ignoring, rather than pointing to, the patient's limitations (defenses). And patients who try hard not to focus on their felt referent may simply be said to lack a required aptitude.[1] But until Gendlin commits himself to some answers, he has not resolved the paradox of personality content versus personality change, and of repression versus insight. And if these dilemmas are not really resolved without recourse to the old language, then the enticing impression that this is a non-struggle theory of therapy may be an illusion. For the theory's special amiability, just like its freedom from the content and repression paradoxes, comes from avoiding concepts of struggle, such as drive and defense, repression and conflict, and so on.

To put it briefly, Gendlin makes therapy appear much less a struggle than do psychoanalytic descriptions because on the therapist's workbench, instead of a something—intrapsychic conflict—Gendlin puts a nothing—the absence

---

[1] Gendlin (1969) has offered this as an explanation. It seems to me more like a shrug of the shoulders. But all theorists who try especially hard to avoid any pejorative terminology tend to shrug this question.

of experiencing, and a nothing is naturally less recalcitrant than a something. Therefore, we will not know whether we are better off with this theory than, for instance, with analytic models until we are convinced that the unanswered questions about etiology, varieties of psychological discomfort, the special nature of the therapist's leverage and apparent instances of patient "uncooperativeness" do not point to holes left in the theory by the avoidance of more conventional terms. We must feel sure that Gendlin has not avoided concepts like drive and defense, conflict and repression, by simply refusing to name them. If he is secretly depending on these concepts he will fall by his own sword.

THE PERSONALITY CHANGE PUZZLE IS THE GENERAL PUZZLE OF CHANGE

After seeing Gendlin's theory, we may wonder whether it is any easier to discuss change in a process theory than in the traditional terms of mental contents. It is true that structural theories (such as psychoanalysis) have trouble explaining therapeutic action. The analyst effects change by allowing himself to be molded in fantasy by the patient's current wish-state (as the transference develops). Analysts may bypass this difficulty by looking for a therapeutic alliance with the patient, but rather than solving the problem of change the concept presupposes its resolution. One might say that when the patient is allied (when free associations are free) then the struggle is already won. How the struggle can occur and be successful remains the most difficult theoretical problem of treatment (see chapter 2).

Gendlin's process solution suffers from a similar handicap. Saying that "we cannot explain *change* in the nature of the *content* when our theory specifically defines personality only as content" (1964, p. 106), Gendlin touches not upon a special flaw in content theories, but rather on the general difficulty of imagining how something can change while continuing to be the same thing. It is a difficulty as old as philosophy itself.[2] We have seen how it makes trouble for psychoanalytic theory of mental contents. How does it make trouble for

---

[2]Zeno's Paradoxes show that no set of static descriptions adds up to a description of movement. Another way to feel the problem of change is to wonder why, if something is unstable, it has not already changed. The problem simply expands outward as one adduces changed circumstances. There is something about the date of events that defies explanation. At the beginning of this century, the philosopher–chemist, Émile Meyerson (1908) suggested that time and change constitute an irrational area which it is the purpose of reasonable explanation to erase by substituting real, underlying, unchanging identities. Obviously such an effort can never be finally successful. Friends of change like Gendlin will always be able to exhibit weakness in static descriptions.

Gendlin when he defines personality as process rather than contents? Why, of course, in explaining change in the nature of the process. Substituting the term *self-process* for personality *structure* does not make it easier for the therapist to understand why whatever it is should change for him.

To escape this trap, Gendlin has carefully avoided saying that therapy changes one sort of process into another. Therapy, he shrewdly maintains, is simply an effort to get a process going where as yet there is none. Thus, stereotyped experiencing and maladaptive fantasies are not considered sick process but the absence of experiencing. If the therapist adopts this point of view he may personally feel relieved of the dilemmas of change, but only by a dodge. The old problem is still there: If the therapist can get process going again, why wasn't it going before? And once process has stopped, why should it ever start again?

What Gendlin needs is something that will make a bridge from the state of a patient at one time to his (improved) state at a later time. The concept of experiencing by itself will not do that because there are no grades of lesser and greater, no invidious distinction between sick and well experiencing, and the only distinction left is between experiencing and not experiencing, which is the widest gap possible, posing the greatest challenge (nothing comes from nothing). Gendlin needs a bridge and the bridge consists of equivocating concepts such as (a) the frozen whole, a patient's stereotypical experiencing, which functions (as a prejudicial whole) and yet does not function (in the articulation of its parts); (b) an intrinsic order of precedence in which some elements of experience cannot become functional until others do (and are thus latent in the latter while not actually present); (c) even stranger terms, such as implicit functioning, which is something that "ought to be there" but isn't.[3]

All of these concepts are attempts to bring back into the picture of therapy something like the distinction between sick and well, or repressed and discovered, for movement to happen between, without at the same time making those two conditions look so disparate that movement between them cannot be imagined. But the price of such a concept as a partly functioning frozen whole is the acknowledgment that, even while in process, the mind is structured. And Gendlin cannot come right out and say that, because he began by blaming structure (in the form of mental contents) for making personality change incomprehensible. In effect, we are asked to suppose that the structure of the mind is not the same as the structures described in our theories. Gendlin will keep theoretical "contents" as fictions. And he is right in a way. Any particular thing in this world is infinitely divisible into

---

[3]Gendlin's concept of "implicit functioning" should be compared with Schafer's "would-be actions." They are both efforts to put concepts of content into a language of process.

qualities, dispositions, and attributes. No description of an individual can be definitive or exhaustive, because descriptions are abstract and things are concrete. The mind is the archetypical individual thing because to ourselves we are more individualized than anything else. So vivid is the concreteness and individuality of our experiencing that philosophers such as Bergson contend that the only thing that can be real is something like our human experience, everything else being an artificial construct or an abstraction. Psychotherapists occasionally need to be reminded that "loves his own dirt," "feels guilty about hostility," "has an archaic superego," and so on, are not pieces of the mind, but somewhat arbitrary abstractions—ways of looking at someone for a particular purpose (cf. Waelder, 1936). But although it is good for a therapist to remember that the structure we build into theories is not God's classification, that does not help the theorist explain therapeutic change. We get into difficulty just as quickly when we try to describe how change occurs in a mind of *unknown* structure. It is the structure and not our picture of it that seems incompatible with change.

Philosophically we are left with the paradox of time: Things remain themselves but change as the minutes tick by. Clinically we are left with the paradox of growth: We must allow patients to deal with us in their characteristic ways while doing something to facilitate innovation. We need abstractions about the "contents" of the mind to point to what persists in the mind's flowing river. If we are smart and heed Gendlin's warning we will not let these abstractions seem too real, too concrete, too much like actual entities; we will not let them become theoretical hallucinations to distract us from our patient and our patient from himself. But we cannot afford to let the flow of time hypnotize us so that we see nothing but creativity, development and novelty and only the uniqueness of the individual. If we no longer recognize persisting identities, within people and shared among mankind generally, we are on our way to mysticism, irrationality, and the subordination of thought to intuition.

I conclude that Gendlin has seized one horn of the dilemma of change, opposite to the one chosen by structural theories. Structural theories dwell mostly on the factors preventing change (except for ad hoc concepts like the treatment alliance), whereas process theories like Gendlin's mostly describe the desired change (flexibility in restructuring feeling). The difficulty of explaining change is felt equally by both theories.[4] Freudian theory combines both type of theory (see chapter 15).

---

[4]It is currently fashionable to regard mechanistic psychological models as useless fossils from a dated stage in the history of physics without considering whether such models may be required by the very nature of explanation (cf. Meyerson, 1908). There will be a lot of wasted theory-making and needless hard feeling if the Heracliteans and Parmenideans do not at last learn that they can do nothing without each other (cf. Friedman, 1965a, and chapter 16).

WHAT THERAPEUTIC TECHNIQUE FACILITATES CHANGE?

Even if Gendlin's process theory does not especially explain change, his technique may be useful.

The task is to get the patient to structure his body feeling in a fluid fashion. What kind of therapeutic response would help that? What are the structure-loosening and structure-building aspects of a therapeutic response? Consider Gendlin's idea that experience stops when someone fails to see "a way of interpreting or activity that feels life-maintaining," and begins again when such a way is rediscovered. A helpful response would seem to be one that discloses new structures for body feelings that are in line with the patient's directions. This seems to me a definition of hope. Perhaps frozen wholes are dissolved by stirring up hope.

A further clue that hope may be the therapist's medicine is Gendlin's idea that experience is always with and toward a real other (even when it seems to be self-exploratory). Gendlin maintains that "feeling" is basically a tendency to act and affect our environment. We may infer that reconstituting a patient's experience has something to do with resuscitating his tendency to act and affect the environment—and in therapy the environment is the therapist. That is, again, a definition—now a more particular definition—of hope. So I suggest that what makes Gendlin's response therapeutic is the hope it stirs in his patients.[5]

If therapeutic efficacy has to do with stimulating hope and not just offering a response, then much will depend on how the patient sees the therapist. According to Gendlin the therapist's reaction helps the patient to find the meaning of his body feeling. This implies that the patient has a much clearer picture of the therapist's activity than of his own body feeling. But meaning, in Gendlin's theory, is an interaction between body state and environmental reaction; it does not lie in the one or the other alone. How can we assume that the patient finds the therapist's reaction plainer than his own body feeling? Can we not equally say that the patient's body feeling is a guide to the therapist's significance? (Elsewhere, I have speculated that body feeling in the form of persistent drives may help to give meaning to all perceptions and may provide a structure for the otherwise chaotic flux of novelty [Friedman, 1968a; cf. also Noy, 1969].)

A therapist cannot be thought of as a simple, silhouetted lighthouse by which a patient can orient his internal feeling. Before the therapist can be

---

[5]This hope is framed by past patterns but holds an aspiration for change. It therefore lies somewhere between a frozen structure and freely modifiable experience and consequently somewhere between an aim the therapist cannot endorse and one that he can. Kohut's theory elaborates this, and it was Kohut's mission to work out a way for the therapist to endorse something in the patient provisionally without feeling dishonest or condescending.

used to give meaning to the patient's feeling, the patient must interpret the *therapist's* behavior (see Hoffman, 1983). As therapists, we may tell ourselves that we are focusing on the patient's immediate feeling, or offering him an imaginative guess about what he is feeling, or showing him our reaction to his behavior. But in general what we are up to is by no means so easily described, and the patient knows it. And it is what we are up to that determines the real meaning of our response. For example, the patient will wonder about every reaction of the therapist, "Does this show that he is working to get me what I want, or that he is aiming to take it away?"

In this respect therapy is different from some kinds of learning where the conversation certifies its own usefulness. A man struggling with a conceptual problem finds it helpful to bounce his ideas off any interlocuter who is willing to participate. Gendlin usefully transposes this model to the arena of psychotherapy. But psychotherapy is different from an intellectual conversation. A person struggling with a conceptual problem has a simple and obvious purpose, and so he can tell whether his partner is helpful by simply observing the trend of the talk. The partner's internal aims are of little consequence. In contrast, the purposes of a patient in therapy are not simple or obvious, and they have to do directly with his therapist's own internal aims. (For instance, the patient will always wonder "What does he want from me?".) The patient cannot be sure that his therapist has good intentions merely because he invites him to dwell on his body state. From the patient's standpoint what it means for the therapist to be a helper is that the therapist is for him, i.e., wants for him what he wants for himself, and that is not only always open to doubt—it is, in fact, never entirely true. Gendlin might answer that everyone wants to experience freely and can easily tell when the therapist endorses this basic wish. Maybe that is true with many patients. But even if free experiencing is a basic wish, it must have its individual and momentary coloring, not necessarily the same for the patient as for the therapist. If, for example, the patient sees focusing as a test of talent, it may not be very helpful. One would suppose that focusing on the patient's immediate feeling is helpful only if the patient recognizes the helpful attitude of the therapist who recommends it.

Most of his readers will agree that Gendlin's attitude is not only helpful but conspicuously helpful. How does he make his helpfulness apparent? What is always conspicuous in his treatment is his flexibility in his role and infinite confidence in his patient. He does not claim authority over the patient, not even the customary privilege of defining the patient's experiences. Viewing himself as a foil for the patient's never-ending self-definition, he imposes nothing, and puts up with everything except closure. Under these circumstances a patient's hopes are optimally encouraged without being satiated or mutually cancelled out. The patient has free reign to experiment in building

structures and finding meanings (which entails experimenting with relationships to the therapist). In contrast, a therapist who sets himself up as an
interpreter, validator and touchstone of ultimate truth may suppress the
patient's hopes for autonomy, encourage futile hopes of succor, and teach the
patient how not to listen to himself.

As a process theorist, Gendlin would deny that hopes exist before they are
aroused. He would say that hope is a name for increased activity or freedom.
His point is well taken. Patients get the courage to entertain hopes by seeing
them realized. In that sense hopes follow deeds, but the encouraging deeds
need not be visible and accomplished; they may be planned or imagined.
(After all, hope is usually stirred up even before the first visit to the therapist.)
What must be actually experienced by the patient is the leeway and the safety
to envision himself daring to pursue his wishes. An authoritative interpretation is confining in many ways. It tells how the therapist wants the patient to
regard himself and his wishes. It may "show up" a wish as impossible or
childish (cf. Tarachow, 1963). It may even express the therapist's disapproval.
(How often do therapists interpret a patient's cooperativeness?) To accept an
insight as a final description is also confining. It tells the patient that he is
playing "for keeps" and puts him on guard. It makes him choose and choosing
means excluding something else. Gendlin refuses to insist on a "correct"
interpretation and refuses to accept a given awareness as final, and he thereby
gives his patient a real taste of safe freedom.

SUMMARY

Gendlin thinks of experiencing as a seamless goal of life and therapy,
unbroken by categories (lust, guilt), distinctions (good and bad adaptation),
and levels (conscious and unconscious). He then ignores the problem of how
to change experiencing and speaks only about how to start it. But inevitably
he must concede that experience is not necessarily either fully flexible or at a
dead halt. Otherwise it would be impossible to explain therapeutic difficulty
or the therapist's leverage. It seems instead that whatever is "structure bound"
has yet some interaction, just as free experiencing has some rigidity. With this
qualification, we must agree that satisfactory living requires continual restructuring of experience, and that the therapist's task is to make relatively
rigid structures more flexible (although according to common sense as well as
psychoanalytic theory one cannot dissolve all fixed structure). As noted in
chapter 1, the patient's current strivings are necessarily expressed within the
bounds of his current structure.

Viewed from outside his system, Gendlin's approach relies on the fact that
flexibility springs out of hope of achieving partly structured wishes (while

rigidity is caused by hopelessness). His technique suggests that the therapist encourages hope by being available for all of the patient's feelings and by insisting on an unfixed relationship in the therapy setting.

Practically, then, Gendlin's theory is a valuable reminder that if we want the patient to have maximum flexibility we must create a therapy situation that is not itself frozen. But even therapists find comfort in structures, and our allegiance to openness is often betrayed by imposing or accepting fixed roles in the therapy situation. I remember hearing an experienced psychoanalyst say that he felt obliged to tell many of his patients that masturbation is normal. Most of us have sometime given advice and without doubt it is occasionally helpful. But it is a *freezing* sort of comment (if I may borrow the term from Gendlin's "frozen whole"), freezing the therapist's authority over the patient and freezing an evaluative framework of normality–abnormality. Perhaps one inhibiting structure is broken up: the patient may feel less ashamed of masturbating. But a dozen other structures may have been needlessly installed. Gendlin, it seems to me, is recommending a procedure and rationale for the therapeutic *demonstration* of the flexibility we wish for our patient.

All therapies probably work by creating hope, which breaks down frozen structures. Where therapies differ is in how much further flexibility they create after breaking down initial rigidities; that may depend on how many rigidities are built into the therapy program itself, rigidities ranging from the deliberate plans of behavior therapy and didactic therapies, to the inadvertentcies of counter-transference.

Focusing is a useful tool but it is hard to agree with Gendlin that it is the essence of psychotherapy because the *incentives* for focusing are important in their own right and psychotherapy has a great deal to do with what lures and reassures the patient. Psychotherapy per se may turn out to be the difficult work of inducing patients to focus rather than the act of focusing. And it may be that the inducing is sufficient even if deliberate focusing never occurs. Experience with nondiscursive techniques (such as paradigmatic therapy [see Friedman, 1979]) strongly suggests that focusing is far from essential. Because Gendlin indicates that words are only one of the many kinds of events that give feeling meaning, his own theory would suggest that focusing is just one technique rather than a definition of psychotherapy. Nevertheless if instruction has a place in psychotherapy I am persuaded that training in the art of focusing is one of its clearest and most profitable forms, and Gendlin's theory is one of the best orientations for patients.

Although we have found some difficulties in the doctrine that any experience that is functioning is good and sickness amounts to the absence of functioning, Gendlin's belief dramatizes a cardinal principle usually extolled in therapy and ignored in practice: whatever we may think of what the patient is doing, his present state is the only emissary of his potentialities and must be properly honored.

In the last analysis Gendlin is a therapist's therapist. His writings furnish a demonstration of how not to let our patterned, professional thinking befog the unique and emergent soul we should be thinking about.

23

George Klein's Equilibrium
Theory

O
ne hesitates to evaluate a post-
humously edited book like George Klein's *Psychoanalytic Theory* (1976a). We
can never know what aspect is the result of tragic interruption. It might be
more fitting to use it as a collection of suggestions.

Yet this book has the appearance of system. Half of it was finished before
the author's death. Themes reappear often enough to show what is elaborated and what is not. The editors—friends and colleagues of the author—
assure us that it was intended as a reformation which starts by challenging old
theory and ends by suggesting new. So we have both textual and biographical
reason to read the book as a systematic critique and renovation of psychoanalytic theory.

Klein covered a vast area: philosophy of science; the nature of psychoanalytic explanation; Freud's thinking; Hartmann's ego psychology; the nature
of sexuality; motivation, defense, adaptation, and esthetics. Even if he set out
as a systematic surveyor and builder, we suspect that work on such a broad
front may turn out to be organized around some particular mission that the
author himself regarded as a mere offshoot or secondary consequence of his
plan of operation.

Several aspects of Klein's work warn us that what is most important may lie
below the level of explicit argument:

A good writer, where they are rare, Klein is almost always persuasive. Yet
crucial concepts tend to remain perpetually elusive.

A second peculiarity of the text is its ambivalence. Klein was a sophisticated theoretician, sensitive to the nuances of the beliefs he opposed. He
scorned models but he understood their usefulness (p. 31). He scolded Freud

for his physicalism but acknowledged his constant concern with meaning (p. 117). He wanted psychoanalysis to make a break with other sciences but granted it the same sort of activity as the others (p. 57). He urged a radical departure but sensed that he might be merely explicating conventional concepts (p. 10). No massacre here!

But Klein also wrote as though models were perfectly dispensable (p. 54), proposed new principles of explanation to conform with new data, and tried to convince us that drive theory has failed. On one page Klein shows his broad-minded fairness; on another, his zeal, making it difficult to discern the project's center of gravity.

Last, we do not find in Klein's criticism of psychoanalysis that enormous attentiveness to its over-all workings that we would have expected from such an able thinker, had he been preoccupied with theory. Rather, he deliberately tested bits of theory by holding them up to the clinical mirror.

For all these reasons, I will not assume that the fundamental significance of Klein's work is what it appears to be, namely, a perception of theoretical and philosophical inadequacies in psychoanalysis, which logically dictates remedial reconstruction. Instead, I will consider the possibility, and eventually conclude, that Klein's generative vision had less to do with theory than with fact, and that he was forced by the temper of the times to don the uniform of a theoretical revolutionary.

But first I must evaluate his theoretical innovation as presented.

For Klein, the basic human motivation is movement toward compatibility of meanings, and the basic human threat is incompatibility of meanings, which is tantamount to self-disintegration (p. 191). Vital pleasures that contribute to "well-being" (p. 213) take their meaning from their relation to the environment and the self. If the meaning of an experience or an aim is incompatible with the meaning of the self (one's identity, integrity, self-perception), a person can protect himself in one of two ways: He can segregate the meaning, as in repression. Or he can identify with the external circumstances that rendered the meaning incompatible. Klein described the latter maneuver as change of voice from passive to active, and he regarded it as the major engine of personality development.

THE PIAGETIAN MODEL

This approach borrows initial plausibility from Piaget's (1951) psychology. Piaget showed that cognitive schemas adapt themselves to the world and to each other by slight modifications that preserve as much as possible of their original form. Klein proposed that the mind in general holds its identity the same way. The same process of accommodation that adjusts thought and action to the environment also supports personal identity in the face of challenge.

More specifically, according to Piaget we make the unfamiliar recognizable by imaginarily shifting our perspective. Piaget calls this reversibility. To Klein, Piaget's reversibility seemed very like identification with the aggressor; psychoanalysts use similar words to describe re-working of passively endured trauma. It occurred to Klein that not just a few schemas but a whole person can resolve not just sensory but all sorts of incompatibilities by reversing them in his mind.

In chapter 4, I argued that this analogy is faulty. Piaget's cognitive reversals are not equivalent to the transformation of passively endured events into imaginarily active ones. The objective experience of a passive event is as active a mental process as the experience of an active event. Indeed, the capacity to have both experiences already presumes Piagetian reversibility. A bias in favor of imagining oneself the agent would be a sign of incomplete decentering. In Piaget's theory, appropriating "incompatible" experience amounts to placing that experience in a more general or abstract framework. It is not the *value* of the experience, but its peculiarity, that is tamed by assimilating it. One can take an aggressive role more effectively after that peculiarity has been mastered. But that is a consequence, not a cause, of the other kind of active role which makes the situation *familiar*. Piaget's general point is that *all* psychological functioning is a blend of active and passive.[1]

THE REPRESSION QUANDARY

Piaget's term "accommodation" tempted Klein to make a still more disastrous comparison. He asked himself: Can't we describe "the repressed" as a meaning schema that has been dissociated? And isn't a dissociated schema one that assimilates everything to its stubborn self rather than accommodating to reality? As I point out in chapter 25, Piaget's schemas are always *both* assimilative and accommodating. The combination of assimilation and accommodation defines a schema in action. Admittedly, Piaget hedges on this, and it is possible to find phrases like "purely assimilative" in his writings. It is also true that the *balance* of accommodation and assimilation may vary. But the difficulties of relying on elementary Piagetian terms to re-define repression, as Klein did, are simply insurmountable, as Klein's own text reveals.

---

[1]Klein takes from Piaget the general formula that the organism establishes equilibrium by appropriating what is foreign in the environment one way or another. Klein is not alone in failing to realize that what scientists are interested in is how one way is different from another. What all ways have in common—adaptation or equilibrium—is just being an entity in an environment (see chapter 24).

In his text we find that even repressed schemas have "representation" (p. 251), produce activity (pp. 251, 296), and have "complex affective properties" (p. 245); they cause an "output: a communication, an approach, an aversive action" (p. 244). In the form of introjects, a repressed schema "actively finds replicas in interpersonal encounters" (p. 295). Klein even said that unconscious fixation may serve to "recognize" and anticipate similar situations following trauma (p. 295).

And yet, despite this trafficking with the world, a repressed schema, according to Klein, does not accommodate to reality. Klein wants to say that a repressed schema is not modified by the feedback from the activities it produces, or the situation it recognizes, or the message it communicates. As I have indicated, Piaget does not everywhere bar this kind of locution. But the thrust of his work, and the consistent implication of his principles, is that *nothing* (not even the genome) is sealed off from its surround. A schema that recognizes a situation is to some extent modified by the unique particulars of the occurrence of the situation. For instance, if the schema produces an action, it is modified by the individual exigencies of the action. If it engages in communication, approach, or aversive action, it takes cognizance of, and is modified by, the pathways open to it. *The schema always receives feedback as a concommitant of its action.* At the very least, an active schema abstracts an old figure from a new ground, and having done that it now has more content— it has at least become more general.

A nonaccommodating, purely assimilative schema is a chimera: It has the head of a Platonic Idea and the tail of a Piagetian structure—a Piagetian structure being a structure only by virtue of its structuring something. Actually, a repressed schema must be integrated in some way with the rest of the mind (and therefore with reality) or it would not be part of the self.

Schemas are not cytoarchitecture of mind. The term "schema" is more like the term "adaptation." Its relevance depends on what it equilibrates with what else (see chapter 24). Klein did not clearly specify his schemas this way, but he did hint at what he had in mind.

WHAT KIND OF SCHEMA?

This is what Klein had to say on the subject: A repressed schema acts but its "affective aspects are uncomprehended" (p. 296). There is a missing factor of "intentionality" (p. 253): ". . . the expression of *responsibility* for . . . affects and actions [provoked by the activity of a repressed schema] is disowned" (p. 245); ". . . the cognitive schema which these activities [produced by an activated repressed idea] represent remains unresponsive. . ." (p. 244). (Note that a repressed idea is not just active but is *activated by* something.) "While its [the repressed schema's] affective aspects are uncomprehended, the schema is still very much an organizing influence in behavior" (p. 296). Feedback from actions inspired by repressed schemas does not affect choice (p. 245), though it seems to affect behavior (pp. 243–244). An unconscious motivational schema is "subjected to an inhibition of the functions associated with intentional thinking" (p. 247). "The comprehension of the leading element of the schema is lacking." Self-relatedness and ownership are missing (p. 251). A repressed wish becomes active in a way that prevents "reflective acknowledgment" of its aim (p. 194).

In short, Klein's *schema* is not a simple thing: it is the kind of schema that can be repressed; it has a leading element, which may be secret; but it also includes more engaging elements of action; and each part deals separately with the rest of the mind.

Some of its aspects may be integrated without thereby integrating the others. Some aspects can be accommodated to the world, while others stay locked away. There are schemas within schemas. A single schema maps different kinds of meaning, cognitive and noncognitive (as we learn from Klein's distinction between feedback relevant to cognitive aspects and feedback relevant to other aspects).[2]

WHAT IS INTEGRATION AND WHY IS IT VARIABLE?

Involved so multifariously in schemas of such complexity, meaning cannot masquerade as a simple quality of experience. For example, Klein suggested that repressed meanings are partly integrated and partly separate from the self. They are "segregated from understanding" (p. 251), or from "comprehension," but are otherwise active. This distinction implies that understanding and comprehension are not the only ways that meanings can be integrated. That is a foregone conclusion for all theorists who accept the repression paradigm. It was not, however, a foregone conclusion for Klein, because he wanted to keep "meanings" out front in plain view, where they couldn't turn into metapsychological werewolves. So he came up with a definition of consciousness as "an experienced integration of a meaning" (p. 253).

Nothing could better sum up the several worlds that Klein was trying to have the best of. Since consciousness is the *experienced* integration of a meaning, it would seem that an *unexperienced* integration of meaning could

---

[2]The unsorted out components and aspects of schemas and their respective fates is no trivial oversight in this theory. Klein refused the specific challenge that led Freud to his theory. It is the decision not to spell out and take seriously the various things involved *in* a schema and follow *them* through the operations of mental processes that separates Klein from Freud, much more than disagreements about philosophical, methodological, or scientific issues. It also accounts for Klein's resemblance to Janet.

exist in a state of repression. But read differently, the formula says that in terms of experience, consciousness *is* integration of meanings, as one might say, for instance: "The semantic integration of meaning is metaphor; the experienced integration of meaning is consciousness."

Put bluntly, the question is whether experience is to be considered an epiphenomenon of an underlying system, or whether experience, just as it is, is all there is. Klein thought the latter view was far cleaner, but found, like many another de-mystifier, that it is very hard to talk psychoanalytically in that manner. (See chapters 16, 20.)

Klein hoped that Piaget would help him out of this difficulty with terms that would bridge organism and existential subjectivity. A schema could be a meaning and also an organic potential. He managed to persuade himself that Piaget shared his conviction that integration requires consciousness (p. 254). No doubt he felt he was operating within Piaget's framework when he declared that identity is a peculiarly human problem (p. 177). Nothing could be further from the truth. Piaget (1971b) scorned existential subjectivity (see his comments on "the lived"). In the world of Piaget, every organism (and each of its parts) has a problem with identity. Schemas *need* not have anything whatever to do with consciousness. The meaning mapped by a schema can be any objective importance that any aspect of the environment has for any aspect of mental functioning.

Although Klein's term "meaning" is much more specialized than Piaget's "schema," Klein seems to have felt that Piaget spoke for him and spared him the need to define "meaning" rigorously. Confident that Piaget's "schema" made "meaning" a substantial term, Klein tended to work at establishing meaning as the *only* term. He held that meanings do not *come* from drives, and do not *produce* disturbances in identity (p. 187). There is nothing above them and nothing below them. There are just meanings. But if "meaning schema" is a perfect fusion of structure, feeling, and motive, there are no variables left to ask or answer any question. Meanings are either more or less integrated or they are not. That may be a straightforward description, but it is not a theory. And to make it a theory, the "self" is introduced, so that at least one question can be asked and, it is hoped, answered, namely, *Why* are meanings integrated or not integrated?

Janet (1925) postulated a synthesizing force that holds the parts of mind together. Freud abandoned that solution after "Studies on Hysteria" (Breuer and Freud, 1893–95) (along with Klein's favorite terms, "compatibility" and "incompatibility"). Freud described competing factors within the mind, structural and instinctual. (This conscientiousness spawned the anthropomorphisms that people make fun of.) But Freud's theory of competing parts alternated with a theory of *integration*, which gave the competing factors a common ground for competition to take place on. Insofar as everything is a modification of a single energy, integration has not been forgotten. Insofar as opposing institutions are refinements of a single drive, integration has been respected (see chapter 15). And it has been respected without adding an "integrator." (The synthetic function of the ego was a later embarrassment.)

Klein did not want to go Janet's way. He did not want to say that integration depends on the strength of the glue that holds the parts together. But, on the other hand, neither did he want to account for the integrity of the mind by appealing to something the competing parts have in common, for instance, a common energy or a common lineage. Integration of aspects of mind had to be accounted for in some other way than by cohesive force or common ancestry. And so he opted for a *self* that acts as a blender.

Two equivocations permit this answer: (1) The self is neither a part of the mind, nor a name for the whole mind. According to Klein's own argument against the synthetic function of the ego, if the self were a part of the mind, another agency would be required to adjudicate between it and other parts. On the other hand, if the self were a name for the whole mind, it would not adjudicate among the competing parts; it would merely describe the outcome of the competition. Nothing would have been said about what makes for integration.

This equivocation can be seen abstractly in Klein's definition of the self as a receptive and responsive structure to which instrumental structures are responsive (p. 182). The self as receptive and responsive is the whole mind contrasted with its parts: it *includes* the parts. There would be no way of describing such a structure devoid of its parts, since in fact, it simply designates the organization of the parts. Therefore, to say that the self brings about integration is simply to say that the whole comprises the parts. But because the sentence "The self integrates the parts" carries "self" and "parts" at opposite ends, it seems as though we have connected two items.

(2) The second equivocation is as follows: The term "schema" is said to refer to a cognitive structure (p. 83). And the meanings that the self makes compatible or incompatible are sometimes treated as cognitive abstractions that can be changed to fit the self's needs as it pleases. (For instance, one imagines meanings like "good" or "bad," "his rule" or "my rule," which the judicious self might compromise. Judge that you are being bullied and you might decide to rebel.) In that sense it seems natural to say that motives arise only *from* incompatibility of meanings (p. 182). But at other times, Klein treats meanings as though they *include* motivation (p. 8), in which case incompatibility is a primary fact. Here is an example of both uses together: Klein begins a statement with the first thesis: "The structured residues of incompatibilities are dynamisms, which organize the aims of behavior." In other words, meanings are there first and then their incompatibility generates a force that acts on behavior. But he immediately adds the second thesis: "Structurally, they [the incompatibilities] are meaning schemata" (p. 193). In

other words, those forces *are* the meanings themselves. Though he sometimes treated schemas as cognitive, he did not conceal their impelling nature.

> The peremptoriness of sensual cravings has much to do with the persistent activation of this cognitive structure. It can activate . . . tendencies . . . which promise pleasure. . . . According to the motivational context to which it is itself responsive, the schema is also capable of inducing . . . responses. It is through the schema that memories and accumulated conceptions of sensuality become capable of invoking sensuality or inhibiting it [p. 115].

We can find an even more direct acknowledgment of the motivational nature of schemas on page 110, where Klein refers to "incompatible meanings which simultaneously prescribe and proscribe." And if that isn't clear enough, he goes on to say: "These meanings . . . tell us that the valuations attached to sensual experience, including internalized parental convictions *which act as a demand structure*, become extremely important in arousal itself. . . ." (italics added).

Strictly speaking, all this would imply that the self may be stressed by opposite pulls. But Klein did not want to give such activity to parts of the mind. Indeed, he could not afford to, since the "parts" he works with (meaningful schemas) have no common substance to pull on, as Freud's do, and their independent activity would fragment the hypothesized mind. Therefore Klein found it useful to say, in effect: There is nothing pulling against anything else; the single, unified (active) self has pasted contradictory (but inert) meanings on experience. The use of the word "meaning" to imply, on one hand, valuational appraisal which risks only semantic inconsistency and on the other hand, directional tendencies which risk frustration, is a principle equivocation on which this self theory rests. Schemas are cognitive meanings assigned compatibility or incompatibility by the self. Schemas are directional tendencies that, in the form of wishes, can be frustrated or "aborted" (p. 52).

In the passage from page 115 partially quoted earlier, what Klein deceptively called a "cognitive schema" is clearly a disposition to react to certain stimuli by movement; it is equivalent to aspiration and avoidance. Here is how the system works: To begin with, there is an external "motivational context." That activates an internal "cognitive structure," which is basically "a potential for experiencing sensual need" (p. 116). And that structure activates tendencies of search, etc. According to this passage, an incompatibility of meanings is directly translatable into *conflicting dispositions*. Klein said explicitly: "A conflict involves simultaneously active but contradictory tendencies. . ." (p. 110). But by interposing the term "cognitive schema" he makes it possible to slide from appetitive to descriptive meaning, and from there to supreme governance by a self-conception. At the same time, beginning with conflicting dispositions, the theory presumes to emancipate itself from crude struggling parts. Cognitive schemas sound like viewpoints (p. 187). If a person senses several meanings in an experience, we would not ordinarily say these sensings are parts of the person. Klein would have us say that it is one person who *gives* several meanings to an experience.

This voluntarism of the self is particularly central. After making due allowance for Klein's refusal to cater to causal demands, it is still striking how little this clinical theory says about what *makes* for integration or non-integration. Klein's is a process theory emphasizing unity, and in such theories it is always easier to see how the mind is integrated than why it should ever not be.

Suppose that Klein was right. Suppose that it is inaccurate to say that we develop psychological trouble by being driven in contradictory directions. Suppose that it is more accurate to say that we experience distress when we cannot decide what we want to be or we cannot be what we want to be. Suppose even that these formulations are not only more accurate but also closer to raw experience (though it does not seem to me that experience speaks *any* one language). What would we have gained if we cannot say why we sometimes have more and sometimes less difficulty "deciding" what to be?

Much of the "overconceptualization" (p. 13) Klein finds in psychoanalysis is the inevitable outcome of theoretical responsibility: After theoreticians identified pathogenic traumas, and described how the mind could deal with them more adaptively, they felt obliged to say exactly *why* the trauma was dealt with badly. Klein did not realize it, but what annoyed him was the analytic custom of giving motivational answers as long as possible to a string of questions about mental functioning. It is not difficult to construct a simpler theory. A simpler theory has a briefer string of motivational answers. A simpler theory cuts the inquiry short; it reaches bedrock fast with a quasi-physical explanation in terms of "strength." Of course, Klein did not use that term. But a self that is the final arbiter of conflict can do well or badly only by virtue of its relative strength. It cannot blame an intrinsically difficult assignment because it does the assigning. It is not compelled to serve two masters because it is the master. It does not have to satisfy too many demands because demands are mere off-shoots of the meanings it selects. The mind is divided only if the self has not been doing its job. And *that* is not a matter of motive or meaning. The adequacy of a theory is measured by how quickly it resorts to mere strength as an explanation and how prominent a role strength plays in the theory.

If that seems unfair, consider Klein's brief confrontation with this challenge:

The question arises: When does one resort to reversal of voice, and when to repression? In general, repression is resorted to when experienced dissonance is of traumatic proportions, i.e., when the experience cannot be "re-enacted" by reversal of voice because of overwhelming fear and anxiety. Of course, what is traumatic in the experience is its *meaning* . . . [p. 294].

Quantitative differences in the "stimulus load" and probably constitutional differences of tolerance determine whether the person will resort to repression [p. 295].

Granted that this is a supremely difficult question for any theory of the mind, we may nevertheless feel cheated by such an answer: Trouble arises when meanings are too much for integrative capacity! Yes, sooner or later every theory must come to such a nonexplanation. But the better theories take longer to get there. Paradoxically, theories that quickly beg the question seem more intuitively confirmable and realistic because they offer less hypothesis: They simply reiterate the phenomenal datum.

A drive theory points to something we can't all see. Klein seems much closer to the evidence when he says, "Motives arise from crises of incompatibility" (p. 182) or when he writes: "The 'imbalances' that make for motivational change are not the results of instinctual drives disciplined by the 'exigencies of reality'; they come about from a state of maladaptedness to new requirements" (p. 182). This seems so reasonable that we may not notice that it merely repeats what we want explained. It is not at all an alternative explanation. Drives disciplined by reality would *also* be a form of maladaptedness; it would be a *particular* form of maladaptedness. For Klein, nothing ventured, nothing lost. You can't lose if you say that change comes from maladaptedness: It can be proved by definition.

THE SELF: ORGANIZATION OR EXPERIENCE?

We have been introduced to the self as

. . . a single apparatus of control which exhibits a variety of dynamic tendencies, the focus of which is either an integration experienced in terms of a sense of continuity, coherence, and integrity, or its impairment, as cleavages or dissonance. I call this central apparatus the "self" [p. 8].

Note that here the self is an apparatus; the *experience* of the self is the "focus" of an apparatus.

We are used to the term "apparatus" in psychoanalytic theory. Klein wanted us to read him differently, but he didn't make it easy. His new apparatus, we are told, is distinctly not an "impersonal 'structure' with implicit mechanism characteristics." How is it different? Instead of "implicit mechanism characteristics," it has "a variety of dynamic tendencies," and instead of being an "impersonal" 'structure,' " it is a single apparatus of control (p. 8). I think Klein meant to imply that the self isn't like a conveyor belt, processing mental contents in a stereotyped way, but is more like a gyroscope doing whatever it must to balance the mind.

Thus Klein called the self "a grade of organization." And he told us that "the self is pictured as a receptive and responsive structure to which instrumental structures—ego—are responsive" (p. 182). This is a description of a superordinate schema, not an apparatus. And that is the most theoretically coherent meaning of the self in Klein's work. As such, it is not an explanatory term, which may be one of the reasons why Klein argued that we should demand less from explanation. The self is absent from psychoanalytic theory precisely because it is not explanatory: The unification of the mind is not a specialized operation. It is a covert ingredient in every specification. Any entity can be analyzed in terms of integration and differentiation (see chapters 15, 16). That is why Piaget can set up shop in any science.

What makes Klein's "self" a nontrivial concept is its ambiguity. It is not only a superordinate schema; it is also a subjective experience. Or perhaps it would be more accurate to say that the self, besides being an abstract, formal reference to schematic equilibrium, is also a set of subjective experiences which are *explained by* that abstract structure of inferred schemas. If we say that a failure of integration accounts for unintegrated components, we have said nothing at all. But if we say that a certain feeling of insecurity or shame, or tension, or painful life can be accounted for by this or that specific suspended decision, or inability to compromise, we may have said a great deal.

Even though the most *consistent* meaning of the self is the superordinate schema of schemas, the most *interesting* meaning of self is a feeling or awareness. Psychoanalytic theory has undertaken to explain subjective experience by abstract structures. Though Klein knew that explanation always involved abstraction (p. 3), he was nevertheless tempted to elide theory and make experience explain itself.

Consider Klein's statement that ". . . self-conception is what makes aims compatible or incompatible, and this self-conception is not inevitably a product of the tendency of drives toward discharge" (p. 184). Suppose we ask, whose aims are we talking about? One answer might be abstract, possible aims. Then the phrase would imply that we accept aims only if they harmonize with what we consider ourselves to be. But, of course, that isn't what the sentence means, because it would not explain conflict. So we must read the declaration this way: Our own aims, already possessed and defined, are felt to be compatible if we have one view of ourself and incompatible if we have another view of ourself. But once aims are considered to be our directions, rather than abstract options, they no longer stand apart from—

and under the rule of—the self-conception. *These* aims are aspects of the self, and a self-conception can't *do* anything to them—it cannot *make* them compatible or incompatible. In this sense, my aims amount to "me wanting." They *contain* the "me." It is deceptive to say that self-conception "renders" such aims compatible or incompatible when all it means is that self-conception is *at stake* in them. Self-conception is involved *in* the aims, and therefore in their compatibility or incompatibility. But this conclusion is a simple truism. It says: Our wishes are structured comfortably or uncomfortably. That's no news. It only seemed to be news because the self structure was first abstracted from a live experience and then equated again with a live experience. It is, I am afraid, the old Molìere explanation: opium produces sleep by virtue of its dormative powers.

This equivocation is so central to Klein's argument that it deserves a little elaboration. Suppose someone offered to prove that bare aims never conflict by pointing out that any two aims can co-exist if each resides in a different person. No one would contradict him. Suppose, then, he went on to argue that only a person's nature can make aims compatible or incompatible. He would still not find a challenger. Now, with this much agreement behind him, suppose the speaker felt free to propose that self-conception is what *makes* aims compatible or incompatible. His listeners would become uneasy. "This self-conception," they would exclaim suspiciously, "does it mean anything besides the unity of the person? If it does, you must tell us what more it means. If 'conception' simply means nature or structure, then you have gone no further than your first useless iteration: you are simply saying that internal conflict is not external conflict. But if 'conception' is a person's view of himself, then why not say that his conflicts determine his self-conception rather than the conception determining his conflicts?"

Klein's notion of "self-conception" gets its force from its logical implication of total mental structure, while its interest comes from the poetic connotation of a particular self-reflecting experience.

There is probably an ironic lesson here: the man who showed what a grab-bag the "ego" had become built his own theory around self-identity, a concept that wraps up every need and desire, every criterion for self-respect, and every safety requirement known to man. A term that thus catches into itself every conceivable end-point of action explains everything too effortlessly to be interesting. On the formal level alone, Klein's central term, self-identity, guarantees that his theory will be a mantric declaration that "integration (more or less) Exists." That so much can be written about self-identity is due to its double meaning as subjectively-experienced self, and as structure of mental integrity. The self-conception is in one sense a formal property: the *state* of compatibility of subordinate schemas. In another sense it is a living experience. There is also an in-between sense—a kind of health message theoretically inferred from a subjectively experienced tranquility (approximately equivalent to what slang refers to when someone is said to have "got it all together").

By mixing these senses, Klein managed to suggest that an experience of wholeness is both the act and the fruit of formal integration. Klein knew this brought him close to an eternally popular psychology of wholeness, and he knew its dangers. It can lead to an inspirational generalizing instead of a difficult unraveling (p. 55). In particular, such elevated concerns can replace the sexual disclosures which gave psychoanalysis access to unwelcome aspects of the self. Indeed, Klein seems to have perceived his mission as the creation of a self psychology that would preserve the psychoanalytic significance of sexual development. Without the special honor he paid to sexuality, Klein's over-all theoretical position would look strikingly like Sullivan's.[3]

IN A WORLD OF MEANING, SENSUALITY IS SPECIAL BUT NOT TOO SPECIAL

Klein assigned to sensuality two special attributes: Experiences associated with sensuality are hard to relinquish or forget (p. 87); and at the same time sexuality is peculiarly plastic. Plasticity seems to have had several meanings for Klein. It refers to the way a meaning floats loose from "modal activities." That would not by itself appear noteworthy. Meanings can always be detached from an activity—that's what meaning means. But if we compare sex with other "psychosomatic cravings" (p. 188), then this plasticity is outstanding (e.g., it contrasts notably with the behaviors inspired by hunger and thirst).

Sensuality, then, is a psychosomatic craving, capable of many different forms and imprinted early with a certain definition. Its influence breaks loose from specific, overt manifestations and becomes a dominant element in the meaning of any experience it is associated with.

Since sensuality fixates other aims, and since society insists that some of those aims be avoided, conflict is inevitable. Although Klein was determined to discuss conflict in terms of meanings, he was really dealing with conflict between demand structures that govern arousal.

If we keep in mind that schemas of meaning involve demand structure (p. 115) and are self-implementing (p. 92), Klein's account appears as a cross-sectional or state description of what others have described as a develop-

---

[3]Despite such a remarkable coincidence as his use of the term "dynamism" (p. 193), Klein did not refer to Sullivan, preferring to contrast himself with theory-poor thinkers such as Rogers, whose contributions, while similar in spirit, could be easily distinguished from his own by their disregard of "the dynamics of encounter, conflict, impasse and resolution" (p. 55).

ment of a sexual drive. The Freudian account depicts physiological appetites, modified by desires related to the environment. Klein felt that his was a radically different description because it allowed situational, self-regarding meanings to contribute to sexual motivation. But that does not really distinguish it from drive theory, which also requires structured channels (cognitive meaning), self-relevance (economic balance), and a pertinent situation (cathected objects) in order to explain motivation. Unlike Kohut, Klein agreed with the Freudian accounts of pleasure motivation. It was perhaps with some desperation that he sought to distinguish his own from Freudian theory: ". . . pleasure is not an end as it does not itself terminate action since we cannot identify it separately from the pleasurable activity" (p. 92). Did he suspect that he was passing grim and just sentence on his own theory? Can his basic terms—integration, identity, equilibrium—ever be identified separately from their instances?

In any case, the distinction between a conflict of meaning and a conflict of drive turned out to be harder to maintain than it was to initiate.

THE CRUSADE AGAINST DRIVE-DISCHARGE THEORY

To keep a fence between meaning and drive, Klein constantly referred to the refined forms of his schemas and the primitive (or general) forms of Freudian drive. A fairer comparison would either match the most generalized form of equilibrium theory with a general statement of drive theory, or else compare specific schemas with the particularized (structural) form of drive theory. Evenly matched, I don't think that they would look very different.

Of course, Klein was justified in rejecting Rapaport's (1960a) attempt to reduce meaning to inhibition, but otherwise one looks in vain for the error he tried to save us from. From his account one would think that Freudian metapsychologists explain all behavior in terms of a simple reflex arc. Klein did not take into account the layering of formulations on top of each other in the evolution and generalization of the drive-reduction concept. He was evidently not impressed with Ricoeur's (1970) argument that Freud's theory was a dialectical attempt to interconnect meaning with force. He argued that only in "clinical theory" do we see "appetite acting within a reticulum of meaning," (p. 91) but in fact that reticulum appears in all the reaches of psychoanalytic theory.

Indeed Klein himself recognized that metapsychology makes many references to meaning (p. 29). Despite that acknowledgement, he dealt with drive theory as though it ignored meaning. He felt entitled to deny that drive theory was a theory of human meaning partly because it did not discuss meanings from the point of view of the subject (p. 29) and partly because its explanations were poorly constructed (p. 100). As to introspection, the metapsychologist would reply that Klein's complex schemas are no closer to the way we ordinarily think about ourselves than drives are. (When we postulate an underlying something, it is really only a matter of style what word we use to name it. In fact, it may be more honest not to use a name from the "same class" as the phenomena [p. 57] to designate the entity that is supposed to underlie them.)

And as regards the second argument, that the way Freudian metapsychology refers to meaning is clumsy, surely that is beside the point. For better or worse, "binding" is how meaning is referred to in the energy theory. One could argue that the drive discharge theory is no good bcause it depends on a confused concept of binding. But the confusion is there because the drive-discharge theory insists on the relevance of human meaning, and for that reason saddles itself with the confused concept of "binding." One may criticize drive-discharge concepts of binding, but one cannot criticize the theory for *ignoring* meaning.

Why did Klein work so hard to attack a nonexistent drive-discharge theory from which reference to human meaning had been removed?

KLEIN'S PHILOSOPHICAL CRITIQUE

Klein would have answered that he fought drive-discharge theory in order to save psychoanalysis from a misconceived marriage with physiology. We should, he said, look for why's or motives, not how's or models. Yet his theory is replete with structures *doing* something (p. 91), with directed forces (p. 55), with "active but aborted wishes" (p. 52), with "blocked tendencies" (p. 184), with schemas that seek and provoke (p. 245), with physiological pleasures that induce, etc.

He claimed that models are unnecessary for clinical psychoanalysis: we need the concept of "repression" but we don't need a model of how it works. However, he did not explain where a word like "repression" would get its meaning adrift from any sustaining system. Indeed, it is only by grace of a model (from Piaget) that Klein could describe "schemas" so sparely and rely on them so heavily.

Klein suggested that psychoanalysis should proceed differently from other sciences. But since he granted to all science the same aim of finding coherences in data, his own reasoning implies that psychoanalysis needs special data, not special kinds of explanation. He suggested (p. 27) that clinical psychoanalysis is "more a process of seeing pattern or 'fit' than detecting causes in the patient's behavior" (p. 27), but he ignored the evidence that this is the way all science works (cf. Kuhn, 1970a).

If Klein was satisfied with a philosophical critique that is neither consistent nor profound, perhaps that is because it was not the inspiration for his work that he thought it was. If philosophical animus did not inspire Klein's attack on drive-discharge, what did? Could it have been the allure of an alternative system in which self and integration would be central terms? But I have tried to show that he dealt only roughly with the new self construct. It may be argued that a vision of it on the horizon was his lure and death stopped him there. Yet Klein's formulations of mental growth and action in terms of schemas are so general as to suggest that the construct itself did not deeply engage his ingenuity. If the principles of the new theory had been his muse, he would probably have been more fascinated by the details they could produce. For instance, schemas are not uniform atoms; if Klein had been very interested in them he would probably have elaborated a rank order of schemas. He knew that "meaning" is as abstract as "cause" (p. 3), but he made little use of the depths and varieties of this abstraction, and contented himself with general references to "meanings."

Had Klein been mainly preoccupied with, and immersed in, Piagetian concepts, I don't think he would have been so troubled by the rivalry between cognitive meanings and conative directions, between the self as a state of integration and as a perception, between physicalistic and formal description, between explanations of how and why. Piaget is comfortable with these polarities.

But if Klein's writing doesn't answer to philosophic needs, or to the lure of a new theory, then where does it come from?

REAL MISSION: HONOR MANY MOTIVES

Perhaps a cursory philosophical critique and a sketchy alternative psychology of the self sufficed as hand-maidens to another purpose. What, after all, were Klein's most powerful arguments? His attack on current psychoanalytic ego psychology is devastating. And he finally convinces us by repeated emphasis that man has many motives.

Klein demonstrated that the ego has become a ghetto for a crowd of miscellaneous aims, segregated to allow the rest of psychoanalytic theory a neater and grander causality. He became the advocate for the uncelebrated aims, herded into a corner of analytic theory. He looked for his enemy in the opposite corner. The polar opposite of multiple motivation would be an exaggerated uni-directional drive-discharge theory. Such a theory may not have existed in reality, but it *represented* the injustice he wanted to remedy, and so he conjured it up out of metapsychology and gave it battle.

Klein wanted to establish the multiplicity of motives. Motives are as plentiful as meanings. Let meanings, then, stand for motives. Call this a science of meanings, of why's, not how's. And make the self-feeling control the meanings, for that way no motive can pre-empt the causation of behavior: All wishes are equal before the great magistrate, equilibrium, which is the goal of integration. Piagetian schemas could be used to describe an endless variety of motivational structures. Sexuality will be a variegated assemblage of sensual experiences, deriving from many different sources, and serving many different aims. Sex is important, but it, too, is subordinate to the goal of integration. Like everything else, its meanings come from its implications for personal integrity.

Still, sexuality remains a problem because it is the way Freudian theory makes unity out of diversity. And, though Klein didn't want to let sex disappear in the suds of integration, neither would he permit the powerful undertow of a single tendency to drown particular meanings. He therefore allowed as an overriding aim only the absolutely minimum hegemony, the most abstract requirement of any organism: You might say that after Klein had cleared house, the only "drive" left was the organism's definition. The self is a theoretical cipher; it is an uncharacterized locus for aim in general. That the self tends toward integration says that we are dealing with an individual organism; it tells us nothing more and nothing less. That sparseness is a measure of Klein's fear that unifying theory obscures partial motives.

Anticipating that metapsychology would challenge him to account for the development of conflict out of unity and unity out of conflict, Klein answered in advance that, since he was concerned with meanings and reasons, he was not obliged to give a causal account.

Yet, as has been pointed out (Frank, 1979), Klein *did* offer causal explanations in the form of underlying systems. Both his discussion of repression and of reversal of voice refer to regular patterns of change. The plasticity of sexual pleasure says something about the *nature* of that kind of pleasure, something not statable simply in terms of experienced meaning but requiring the supposition of underlying continuities. Klein knew that he needed such constancies, but he thought he could get away with a weak predictive theory, which would be more experiential than a frankly causal one. Causeless laws: that is an old story—old and disreputable. It has no standing until the day empiricist philosophers solve the problem of induction.

THE MISLEADING CONFLUENCE OF REVISIONISMS

The irony is that Klein will go down in psychoanalytic history as a unitarian—a "self" psychologist—while in fact he was something more precious—a prophet of diversity in a land of system-builders. There is an enormous variety of patterns and motivations in the human organism that must be lumped together in a monumental theory of the mind (see, for example, Freud's [1915d] discussion of instinct groupings). Freud had to alternate between describing the mind as unitary and as divided (see chapter 15). Not everything can be said at once in such a theory: A certain minimum fineness of abstraction limits a theory of the mind.

I believe that Klein imperceptibly abandoned theory of the mind in order to do justice to the variety of its components. But theory abhors a vacuum. When one theory of the mind is relinquished, others instantly offer themselves as natural allies. It is my belief that these theories of the mind, each with its own animus, helped to divert Klein from a more modest and far more valuable exposition of the variety of interests and motives ingredient at the minute level of mental functioning.

Studies of child development suggest that the traditional psychoanalytic account of mental beginnings is only a rough guess, a clever backward projection of a theory that systematizes the developed mind (see Freedman, 1979). The mind of the infant is in some ways as multiform as his body. We would certainly get into trouble if we tried to write a "theory of the body." Moreover, the evidence of Mahler and Kohut suggests that at all stages of development we shall have to attend more specifically to needs that we are accustomed to submerging into larger categories. How to do justice to these scattered beginnings and unfamiliar mature needs without scuttling the whole project of theory of the mind – that was the central problem that Klein set for us. Spitz and Erikson have used the concepts of organizers for this purpose. Somewhat along the same lines, and following a lead of Klein himself, Gedo and Goldberg (1974) have tried to develop unity out of multiplicity, but only by artificially assigning primacy to certain needs at certain periods. Klein was one of the few who (besides exploring this latter possibility) also held out for a pluralistic mind.

What might Klein have done if he had not been distracted by unrelated cross-currents of dissatisfaction? Suppose no battle cries were heard of cause and reason, meaning and force, science and interpretation. Suppose nobody thought of the drive-discharge theory as a physiological gambit.

Then, I think, Klein would have taken one of two paths. Either he would have blended his multi-motive, developmental ideas with Freudian theory after the fashion of Loewald (1971), who holds that mind itself is an organism, and drives are derivatives. Or he would have disregarded over-all theory of the mind, and elaborated those areas that had been neglected, such as the assortment of vital pleasures and their early development. This would have required only the critique of the Ego.

Either way, he would not have had to make up a new theory of the mind. That would have freed him to use Piaget's principles for particular problems instead of stretching those principles around mental functioning as a whole – a stretch which (whatever organ system is encompassed), makes Piagetian principles either vacuous or circular.

24

Piaget's General Project

Peterfreund, Levenson, Schafer, Gendlin, George Klein, and the representational world school, all seek to eliminate the structural or partializing aspect of Freudian theory. But, although they agree on that, there is an axis along which they differ: how much interest they have in *transformations*.

In chapters 15 and 16, I argued that Freud, by describing the mind as both parts and process, was able to account for the transformation of a subject; he could say how a continuing personality can undergo change. When Hartmann (1927) insisted that psychoanalysis is not a phenomenology but an empirical science, he was reminding theorists that psychoanalysis had proposed to explain change—not just what a given mental state is like, but how and why it changes into another. Psychoanalysis differed from other theories of the mind in undertaking to describe mental transformations, both from birth to death, and from moment to moment. It is startling to see how marginal this main claim of psychoanalysis has become in the revisions we have examined.

Yet, despite the controversy about whether psychoanalysis is a natural science, it seems clear that nobody actually wanted *not* to have a theory of transformation. The revisionists seem to feel that transformations can be safely left to common sense ("once burnt, twice shy," etc.) while they straighten out alleged theoretical confusions, such as the invention of imaginary mental units and make-believe mechanisms. In fact, however, when psychoanalysis loses its partializing theory of the mind, it also loses its ability to describe transformations, that is, changes undergone by persistent substrates.

The revisions are all weak in this respect. But they differ somewhat in how much *effort* they make to recapture the old transformational power of psychoanalysis, in other words, how interested they are in remaining dynamic psychologies. The representational world school, when it is consistent, is near the static end of the spectrum. Toward the middle of the spectrum, Peterfreund's book on information processing describes utilitarian transformations within a motivationally static organism, and Levenson's book on perspectivism describes expressive transformations also in a motivationally static organism. At the other extreme, Schafer describes people as innovators, and so exclusively innovators that we can find within the theory no bounds (and therefore no regularity) to their innovation. Schafer acknowledges that there are limits to people's flexibility, but those limits fall outside the domain of his theory, along with any objective rules of transformation. Similarly, Gendlin portrays a mind that transforms itself, also without knowable constraints. In the more kinetic of these revisions, the principle of development is a dialectic or dialogic principle. (Schafer's principle of development is primarily a self-dialogue; Gendlin's is a dialogue between body feeling and symbolization.) Kohut points to needs that are more defined than Gendlin's body feeling, but he resembles Gendlin and Schafer in depicting growth as a dialogue. All three suggest that meaning comes from the collision between what is in a person and what response he gets. Schafer's person and Gendlin's person are changing beings. What their theories need in order to match the Freudian explanation of change is a principle of transformation, but because they are determined to be monists, they can only accept a principle of transformation if it avoids the old partializing "mechanisms." Enter the concept of equilibrium.

This concept seems custom made for the purpose. Equilibrium appears to explain transformation without invoking "parts." Both George Klein and Kohut tried to use the concept of equilibrium or homeostasis to recapture explainable transformation for psychoanalysis. George Klein especially recognized that if there was any way that one could avoid mental anatomy while still describing change, it would be the way Piaget did it. Piaget offered a persuasive, unified account of change that moved grandly across all disciplines. Not being tied to any one science, his account did not hypothesize any particular parts, and so it would be acceptable to holists.

In the last chapter, I argued that Klein did not succeed in his use of Piaget, but I left it open whether a more careful application of Piaget's principles would do the trick.

Even though Piaget did not himself offer a revision of psychoanalysis, it behooves us to see whether his method can be made to serve those revisions that appeal to dynamic equilibrium as the principle of transformation. While we are at it, we want to see what light Piaget can shed on the balance problems we have found in psychotherapy (as described in chapter 8).

II

Piaget is famous for his work on cognitive development, but his range of interest was hardly less universal than Aristotle's, and his system is understood best when set forth in its fullest generality. For although his empirical findings are bound to be – and have already been – modified, his approach remains an enduring paradigm. A good place to see Piaget's general approach is his book *Structuralism* (1970).

Piaget's subject is structure. He begins by telling us that structures are "systems of transformation," characterized by "wholeness" and "self-regulation." Reading that, one may rough out an image of some likely object of study – an organism, for instance. But then Piaget goes on to draw examples from mathematics, and now the reader has to conceive of a subject matter common to algebra and turtles. It is not an easy task.

The reason that Piaget's subject matter is so hard to pin down is that although the discussion is about technical developments in various sciences, the underlying concerns are major problems of philosophy. Among these problems Piaget deals indirectly with the following: (a) The problem of substance and essence: What constitutes a separate thing? (b) The problem of identity and change: What persists during change and how can it? (c) The problem of realism and nominalism: Are abstractions and generalities cooked up by the thinker, or do they have a reality in nature? (d) The problem of truth: What is the correspondence between mental representations and that which is represented? If his book were footnoted philosophically instead of scientifically, the names would appear of Parmenides and Heraclitus, Aristotle and Plato, William of Occam, Kant and Hegel, Leibnitz, Whitehead, Russell, Wittgenstein, George Herbert Mead, and really all the others.

Viewed this way Piaget's topic may seem fairly ethereal. But on the other hand, nothing has a more immediate, practical bearing on psychotherapy than a discussion of structure because psychotherapy boils down to structuring, being structured and studying structures. It is one of the many services of Piaget's book, then, to indirectly show where age-old philosophical problems are enmeshed in the psychotherapist's work. Rather than outlining Piaget's discussion of structures in the various sciences, I consider three of the underlying issues that Piaget implicity illuminates, which are relevant to psychotherapy.

The first concerns what might be called the *perfectability of descriptions*. It touches on the question of how final our theoretical systems can possibly be.

The many theories of the mind that compete for the psychotherapist's allegiance claim some degree of absoluteness. They do not claim completeness, because we all know that science has an expanding horizon. But however tentatively, theories suggest that the way *they* divide up the phenomena is the way we *all* do it; it is the way the mind is divided up or organized in reality. We are familiar with the battles between Melanie Klein and other psychoanalysts, between psychoanalysis and behaviorism, interaction theories and intrapersonal theories, cybernetic theories and process theories. People who are concerned with methodology have questioned whether psychotherapy models are real or simply useful. They ask where to draw the line between description and reification. The practicing psychotherapist may sometimes wonder whether his standard concepts are familiar myths or the way things really are. The theoretician looks for the "real" units of the mind: Are they quantities of energy, types of directional energy, psychic "institutions," thresholds, reflexes, habits, mental actions, internalized relationships, representations?

Piaget's answer is based on his belief that all things that have a real unity, which he calls structures, are basically rules of transformation among elements that are in a dynamic equilibrium. And a system of transformational rules, as G"odel has shown for the structures of logic, is never complete in itself but always requires a more comprehensive system to complete it. That more comprehensive system, on the other hand, depends on the existence of the first system as a content for it to systematize. Piaget concludes that not only may every structure be always still further structured, but indeed it must be, that is, each structure is integrated into a more comprehensive structure. Speaking loosely, it is as though every theory, besides explicit referring to many smaller descriptions of fact that it organizes, also covertly assumes a larger theory that lies outside its domain and provides its real skeleton. On the basis of Piaget's argument, it seems that if you think of a theoretical system without its implicit completion in a different and more comprehensive system, it has a degree of arbitrariness. It may seem to make sense out of lesser order descriptions, but it does not itself fully make sense until it, in turn, is organized into a structure of an entirely different kind.

Putting this into more familiar terms, and assuming that psychological classifications denote structures, we might say that there is no possibility of a classification that is the last word in describing mind. The ego and the id were not made in Heaven, nor were engrams or habits or families or dyads or societies or what have you. The way we slice up our data (if we do it well) reflects something about reality, but reality never tells us, "Enough, now you may lay down the knife." It seems to follow that our theoretical concepts are neither tentatively final descriptions nor myths. We should not be overawed by them but neither should we abandon them for unstructured states that claim to be less artificial, such as "feeling," isolated from thinking and talking.

This conclusion is related to ideas developed by Gill (1963), who suggested that in the case of mental structures, every form is a content to a higher order form, and Balint (1968), who challenged the absoluteness of the concepts embedded in the psychotherapist's language.

The second point that stands out as pertinent to psychotherapy concerns the gap between static descriptions and living development. In chapter 22, we described Gendlin's way of framing this problem. He claims that psychoanalytic theory outlines only mental "contents" and if you take it seriously there is no reason whatever to expect therapeutic (or any other) change. Contents are what they are and that's that. It is a rare psychotherapist who does not sometimes feel that his theory is best suited to console him for his patient's *lack* of movement. Even therapists who are not inclined to theorize become embroiled with this problem when a patient says, "But Doctor, how will knowing these things about myself help me to change them?" or, "Now that I know that, what do I *do* about it?" If a therapist is really allergic to theorizing, he will simply reassure himself that there is some enormous body of literature that must have answered this question many times over. But Gendlin is a theoretician–practitioner, and he reacted by developing a new process theory of therapy where all that exists is movement, and conceptual distinctions, such as ego/id and conscious/unconscious, fade into irrelevance. Interaction schools, like that of Jay Haley (1963), which portray psychic life as, so to speak, a reaction to the neighbors, have their own way of circumventing the paradox of change. (We can change neighbors without having to alter the anatomy of the mind.) Behaviorists also have an answer to this problem: reinforcements come and go; we are not stuck with ids that go on forever.

Piaget's solution to this knotty problem lies, I think, in his distinction between structures and their "functioning." Or rather, his contribution is to blur the distinction between structure and functioning. Having defined structures in terms of rules of transformation, he was able to say that a real structure is nothing other than a mutually interactive balancing. A structure is a set of preservative interdependencies, constructed while things are changing. For Piaget, being a structure means imposing organization, and that is the same as perpetually creating new structure. You can picture structuring embryologically or evolutionarily, but the most vivid way to picture it is the way that Piaget arrived at it, and that is in the development of human cognition. According to Piaget, the human infant is born with certain structures that, as we have noted, are neither abstract nor rigid. Like the restraint of a rubber band, these structures are patterns that regulate variations of action, as the action encounters external objects (e.g., the action of sucking as applied to a breast, to a rubber nipple, to a finger, etc.). When new objects are met, the structure (of action/perception) is modified, and becomes part of a larger structure of equilibrium both with the outside world, and with other of the infant's structures (e.g., sucking patterns are equilibrated with those involving sight).

Piaget said that we can split this process in half: We can focus at one moment on purely "structural" aspects (beginning with order, subordination schemes, etc.) which are the inborn reflex patterns, and after that we can focus on "functional" aspects (assimilation and accommodation), which are the ways those primitive organizations organize their substrate and are in turn reorganized by the world. But in fact this division into structure and function is an artificial abstraction, because in one way or another (one way in mathematics and another in biology) structures *are* things that assimilate and accommodate; that is partly what their being structures consists of. Structure is as structure does.

Put very broadly, a structure is something that organizes and is affected by its organizing. If you leave its functioning out of the picture, you have not got a complete picture of structure. You have artificially frozen a changing thing at an unreal, hypothetical, abstract, timeless present. If you do that in biology, you are forgetting the organism's progressive interaction with the environment, *which is what defines the structure*. Because structures exist just to assimilate and accommodate, it is easy to see how a thing—for instance, a pattern in the mind—can stay the same over a period of time and yet change in order to relate to more and new things: If you say the mind has a structured content, what you *mean* is that it will change in certain ways. Change is not some fortuitous thing inflicted on an otherwise unchanging specimen. So there is no need to push ponderous, static psychic institutions into motion. And there is also no need to abandon delineated concepts of the mind (which refer to structures) and cast ourselves loose in a sea of shapeless process. The paradigm is: (a) a structure is always changed by its structuring activity, and (b) no structure proceeds but from another structure. Gendlin (1964) comes closest to applying this outlook in therapy despite the fact that he is not sympathetic to the notion of structure. His work should be read in conjunction with Piaget's book to get an idea of Piaget's practical consequences.

Finally, there is an important problem that I think Piaget has raised but has failed to resolve. It is the problem of uniqueness. Piaget holds that everything can be structured. There is no limit to what can be described in terms of formal rules of transformation. There is no upper limit: we can always generalize further. But there is also no lowest order of elements that fit into a structure without themselves structuring something still more elementary. The smallest is still nothing but a general rule governing a type of transformation of something else. Thus a formal, mathematical account can ideally be rendered for all things, big and small. There is doubtless a very important sense in which this endless generality holds true, best exemplified in the ideal end-point of cognitive development, as Piaget has shown in his research. For instance, the child gradually acquires the notion of enduring objects, of his mother in various moods, of his mother's place in the world, of motherly traits, and so on. It may be that when the child grows up to be an experimental psychologist he will formalize the entire series, and put it into rules and equations. But what will he do with the structure that is his mother? What must be dealt with in that case is an individual, and if the man in the street used such words, he would surely say that one "limit of formalization" is reached in the notion of the individual (i.e., something that is unique in space and time).

Piaget was aware of this dimension, or at least aware that some people consider it a dimension. He disclaimed any interest in the "lived," always fencing it off with quotation marks. Concerned that his reputation as a psychologist might get him into trouble with more hard-headed thinkers, he protested that even psychologists—even (and that is the limit) psychoanalysts—are ultimately concerned not with "the lived," but with categorized structures that can be compared with each other. And in any case Piaget wrote *Structuralism* as an epistemologist.

Now it seems to me that an epistemologist has, if anything, rather less right than a psychoanalyst to deny that we are acquainted with unduplicatable, perishable individuals. For although as psychotherapists we deal with what can be communicated (and therefore duplicated) using concepts and comparisons, nevertheless when it comes to canvassing the full span of knowledge and experience, it must be admitted that we meet with, live with, and mourn individuals.

One of the difficulties of formalizing the rules governing the structure of an individual is that the rules would have to refer to unduplicatable moments of time. Individuals are what perish or can disappear. But formalizing rules, by their very nature, rise above local moments. Piaget is acquainted with an argument of this sort in the theory of Émile Meyerson (1930). Meyerson wrote that what scientists try to explain is change and the way they explain it is by finding that change is only apparent—that there is beneath it an underlying identity or persistence. Change is what provokes inquiry and baffles the mind; and a discovered, persisting identity is what answers questions and rests the mind. Change is mysterious; science tries to make it less mysterious by theoretically reducing it to a minimum. Science takes what is new and tries to find in it something old. One might suppose that Piaget would regard his work as an example—even, perhaps, a biological explanation—of Meyerson's point. After all, Piaget believed that an organism fits its new environment into those old structures as well as it can. An infant apprehends a lot of strange things by assimilating them into the familiar category of suckable. And Piaget never tired of emphasizing that the goal of apperceptive development is a map of the world in which every change is reversible, at least in imagination, with all novelty fading into a previously structured pattern. In Piaget's view the organism tries to avoid being thrown off balance by novelty and it ultimately develops a logical framework that makes it ready for anything. That, it seems to me, is also a perfectly Meyersonian exposition. But open Piaget's (1970) book and you will find the most curt dismissal of Meyerson imaginable. Piaget's argument against Meyerson is exceedingly odd. What he does is to take the concept of a mathematical group "which calls for a certain inseparable connection of identity and change" (pp. 13–14) and offer that as proof of "the compatibility of identity and change" (p. 21). Meyerson never said that identity and change were incompatible. On the contrary, he implied that they are always found together because his point was that science looks for the one in the other. What Piaget seems not to have recognized is that Meyerson was discussing things that *actually* change, concrete things in a real world that change as times goes on.[1] To enter a debate about the mysteries of time triumphantly armed with an example of changes "undergone" by a mathematical function shows, I think, an astonishing aversion to tangling with the concrete, individual aspects of the world. After recognizing the (really Meyersonian) struggle of the developing mind to overcome irreversible changes by means of reversible conceptualizing, Piaget seems to have become an advocate for one party in the struggle, and tried to protect the rationalizing mind from any irreducible irreversibility in the world that could frustrate it (although he had the grace to mention the concept of entropy as ungovernable).

His partisanship can be seen in his attitude toward the "savage" thought that Lévi-Strauss analyzes:

> And when he [Lévi-Strauss] speaks of metaphor as constituting a "first" or "primary" form of discursive thought, must we not take this to mean that there is something to follow after, or at least that there are "levels?" Granting that "thought untamed" (*la pensée sauvage*) is always present among us, does it not nevertheless constitute a level of thought inferior to the scientific? [Piaget, 1970, p. 115].

But Lévi-Strauss (1966) had already answered this question:

> The manner in which primitive peoples conceptualize their world is not merely coherent but the very one demanded in the case of an object whose elementary structure presents the picture of a discontinuous complexity [pp. 267–268].

A discontinuous world is a changing, concrete world of separate individuals, as contrasted with abstractions, space–time continua, and completely classifiable, identical members of logical sets. The first chapter of Lévi-Strauss's *The Savage Mind* is entitled "The Science of the Concrete." Lévi-Strauss's point was that, insofar as we deal with this aspect of the universe, we deal with it basically as the primitive does. That is something that Piaget, with his

---

[1]In his discussion of chemical equilibrium formulas, Meyerson discusses abstract "displacements," which correspond to Piaget's mathematical operations, as examples of the scientific escape from irreversible temporal change (pp. 222 ff).

evolutionary respect for the "higher" stages of cognitive development, would not allow. As a result, he was forced to deny the discontinuous elements in the universe.

Piaget (1970) admits this at the end of his book:

> It might seem that the foregoing account makes the *subject* disappear to leave only the "impersonal and general," but this is to forget that on the plane of knowledge (as, perhaps, on that of moral and aesthetic values) the subject's activity calls for a continual "de-centering" without which he cannot become free from his spontaneous intellectual egocentricity [p. 139].

It comes down to the question of whether this is true. Consider the esthetic plane: I think that the closest thing to art that a *continual* "de-centering" could lead to would be a textbook of trigonometry. As for the moral plane, ages of fruitless effort to establish a rational or deductive foundation of values do not make a good case for continual de-centering. And on the plane of knowledge, where we must admit that a continual effort at objectivity is indeed important, that effort is not sufficient to bring us in touch with the unique particulars that are also important to us in life. Piaget's account evaporates not just the subject but also the individual object, leaving only the "impersonal and general." He has not denied it. He said that this is the path we must follow. But how can we be content with a description of the "impersonal and general" when there is more to the world than that?

In the end, what difference does it make to the psychotherapist? No obvious difference, certainly, because in practice we think along any lines that are useful. Unlike theory, practical thought does not wait on epistemology. But a simplifier could put Piaget to bad use in therapy. If a therapist is heavily influenced by Piaget's description of ideal goals, and less attuned to the interests of the particulars that are blended in them, he will tend to look for something like a therapeutic alliance with an objective ego. He will see a clear difference between the realistic therapeutic relationship and transference. He will hope to dispel distortions. He will divide patients into those who can restructure the past and those who are stuck in it, those who can accommodate to the therapist's structures and those who assimilate him to theirs. The therapist may give up on assimilators.

Fortunately therapists inevitably get caught up in the feeling side of life as well as the cognitive. And for all Piaget's hints about a logic of feeling and the development of equilibrated affective schemata, affects occupy an uncertain and controversial place in Piaget's system. We will not know what influence Piaget can ultimately have on therapy until we know where affect fits in his theory. That is the subject of chapter 25, where we find a good use for Piaget in psychotherapy.

25

Piaget and Psychotherapy

THE PLACE OF AFFECT IN PIAGETIAN THEORY

Many people feel that Piaget elaborated the most fertile psychological theory since Freud. Although the relationship between the theories of Piaget and Freud is not certain, their overlap has fascinated a large group of theoreticians. Both the ambiguous relationship and the clear mutual relevance of the two systems were demonstrated by Peter Wolff (1960) in a brilliant monograph. Since Wolff's study, psychoanalytic theorists have made increasing use of Piaget's concepts, for instance Anthony (1976), Blanck and Blanck (1977), Nilsson (1977), Greenspan (1979), and Tenzer (1983). As noted in chapter 23, George Klein (1976) even attempted to recast psychoanalytic theory in Piagetian terms. Piaget (1973) in turn has recognized a similarity between his approach and the psychoanalytic.

If Piaget's bearing on psychoanalytic theory has excited much interest, the possibility that Piaget's ideas might shed light on psychotherapy is even more exciting because he has so much to say about a central question of therapy theory: How is interaction between person and environment transformed into psychic structure? Because Piaget devoted himself to that question, one expects his ideas to contribute to a unified theory of psychotherapy, transcending particular models of the mind, while justifying each of the therapist's activities. For instance, Lewis (1972) provides an example of how Piaget's concepts can be applied to psychotherapy in general, bypassing parochial theories of the mind.

Before we can use Piaget's system to describe psychotherapy, two tantalizing uncertainties must be resolved: (a) Piaget concentrated on how we learn about the physical universe, but as psychotherapists we need to know how people learn about other people. (b) The structures Piaget studied were cognitive, and it is not clear how affect and motivation can be brought into his account.

On the subject of how persons get to be known, Piaget was rather nonchalant. He suggested that the mother may be the first physical object to be seen as constantly enduring (Piaget, 1973). But he did not bother much about how one builds a representation of her personality or that of others. We would suppose that such a task demands more complex integrations than those needed to comprehend a nonhuman object. Piaget's (1962, 1967) study of the developing moral sense might have led him to that issue, but he was more interested in the transformations that lead to general moral rules than in the procedures by which the child decodes the parents' individual principles. (His studies do make a start on the problem of understanding another's personality.)

The problem of affect, however, is one that Piaget dealt with frequently. And his attention to it highlights a remarkable equivocation: He most frequently described affect as an energetic aspect of every schema, with cognition contributing the schema's structural aspect (Piaget, 1971a, p. 231; Piaget and Inhelder, 1969, p. 26). But at other times, he refers to *affective schemas*, as though they constituted a separate species of schema, with characteristics of their own, distinct from cognitive schemas (Piaget, 1962, p. 189). He wrote that affective schemas never became as reversible (i.e., as objective) as cognitive schemas (Piaget, 1962, p. 189). He even went so far as to say that affective interests may conflict with cognitive interest (Piaget and Inhelder, 1969, p. 129). His most systematic discussion of affect occurs in his theory of the development of moral judgment. There he proposed that impulses are gradually regulated under an evolving schema of the will, much as operational schemas are coordinated by logico–mathematical rules (Piaget, 1967).

Piaget's first suggestion—that affect represents the energic aspect of schemas, while structure represents their logico–mathematical rules—is too vague to be useful. What is *energy* in such a definition? We commonly experience great representational vividness, for example, unrelated to what is usually called affect. Perception seems to have an energy of its own. But if these "forceful" aspects of cognition are not what Piaget means by energy—if he is thinking instead of emotional interests *served by* cognitive schemas (Piaget and Inhelder, 1969)—then one would have to ask whether it is fair to say that affect is merely forceful and is not also structured. (It is the same problem as the paradoxical structure of the unstructured Freudian Id.)

Even if we can't see our way clear to describing affect as purely energic, Piaget may still be right to say that affect is present in all schemas. Thinking this way, we might be inclined to dismiss Piaget's second definition that gives affective schemas a category of their own. Can we even imagine an affective schema all by itself, devoid of cognitive elements?

For example, suppose affect were a built-in physiological response, releasing certain biological activities when triggered by the appropriate stimulus. In a Piagetian perspective, such an affect would be an analyzer of the world, and affective responses would still be a kind of understanding. Moreover, if we did not restrict our model to a purely thermostatic physiology (and even, in the last analysis, if we did), this response would have a range of adaptability to new circumstances, and that would amount to affective learning. In these respects our hypothetical affective schema would resemble an ordinary cognitive schema. But now let us try to drive a wedge between affect and cognitive schemas in the following way: Let us say that purely affective schemas lack the mutual regulation, internal anticipations, and universal appropriateness that characterize cognitive schemas, and therefore people do not feel these schemas to be a view of the outside world, whereas cognitive schemas are just that. (This would be something like the James-Lange theory of emotions.) But that would just leave us with a successor problem: We would have to describe the hybrid that is composed of an affective schema combined with a cognitive schema. Because, after all, thinking determines much of our feeling, and in any case, the affect that we deal with in psychotherapy, unlike a galvanic skin response, is projected into cognitive descriptions of the world (a good man, a frightening situation, a beautiful piece of music). Constructing a psychology from the marriage of affective and cognitive schemas might be similar to building a psychology out of internal releasing mechanisms, as, for instance, Bowlby (1969) has done.

As a practical man and a keen observer of children, Piaget knew that emotion biases cognition (e.g., Piaget, 1967). From the theoretical standpoint, however, he was most impressed by objective thought as a quantum leap *away* from bias. Intelligence, he felt, is no slight modification of instinct; it is a whole new approach to adaptation (although, to be sure, it inherits the vague legacy of instinct's mission). From Piaget's (1971a, p. 226) contrast of instinct with intelligence, we get some idea of what affective and cognitive schemas would look like if they were two species of mental life, existing side-by-side within the mind.

Yet we must ask whether the logico–mathematical system that Piaget regarded as the apotheosis of intelligence, really provides all the material that even bare intelligence requires. How well could intelligence get along without affect?

For Piaget, intelligence is roughly equivalent to objectivity. And he considered this objectivity to be the perfect way to preserve the subject from disruption by alien events. But there are two reasons to think that objectivity is inadequate to the task. The first is this: Piaget's logical intelligence has achieved its poise by abstracting from time, and therefore it is not equilibrated with real time. (I am speaking about the time we die in, not Einsteinian time.) Piaget (1969, p. 259) was well aware of this, but did not, I think, realize that it limits the usefulness of logico–mathematical intelligence as an adaptive or equilibrating organ. According to Piaget, "reversibility" is the main gambit by which the subject protects itself from the sting of novelty. But we live in an irreversible world, and cognizance of that aspect of things requires something beside logico–mathematical systems. That is probably where affect enters the picture. Very likely affect has something to do with the connection between our reversible physical concepts and our irreversible lives.

The second, related, limitation of logical schemas as a tool of adaptation is that they require, and indeed accompany, self-awareness. The airy mobile of abstract intelligence is planted firmly in the concrete block of personal subjectivity. One of Piaget's most important teachings is that the same physical and mental operations that analyze the world into enduring, orderly, external objects, are simultaneously interpreting the self as a separate being who looks at those objects from a particular perspective. Making allowance for one's perspective is the other side of the coin of perceiving independent objects. But making allowance for a perspective is tantamount to being aware of one's subjective feelings (however subliminally). *Local knowledge* (to borrow Geertz's term) gives us the latitude and longitude from which we measure the wider world. But the feeling of specialness that marks self-consciousness cannot come from logico-mathematics, for it is the essence of formal systems that no perspective is privileged. What else but affect can connect the objective world with the subjective standpoint that must be known in order to be discounted when viewing that world?

What these two objections amount to is that full intelligence must be able to cope with uniqueness as well as generality, and therefore cannot be exclusively composed of logico–mathematical schemas. The nonformalizable aspect of intelligence seems to be connected with affect. Therefore, we should be loathe to place affect into a separate domain from intelligence, even in the unlikely event that we were able to imagine an "affective schema" that was not at the same time a cognitive schema: intelligence simply has too much to lose by the divorce (Friedman, 1968a).[1]

This leaves us with our beginning question unanswered: What is the relationship between affect and cognition? Piaget frequently says that cognitive and affective schemas are always found together. I have just argued that

---

[1] I have not touched on the more complicated question of the relationship between the cognitive knower and his society, which Piaget freely admits to be a necessary support of cognition (1971a). If there were not affective binding to family and culture, an affect-free scientific structure would not emerge. That says something about the relationship of affect to cognition, but what it says is not exactly clear.

this is not because affect is a name for the energy of cognitive schemas. And I have argued that affect is not an antiquated coping system, like a mental vermiform appendix, that remains uselessly attached to an evolved, self-sufficient cognitive structure of equilibrium. What alternative relationship could tie affect so closely to cognition?

In order to answer that question, we must first figure out what Piaget means by structure. That was the subject of the preceding chapter. There I emphasized that one thing structures are not is autonomous, side-by-side building blocks of the universe. Structures are organizations. Structures include other structures and pieces of other structures. We can view the same thing as a structure or as part of a structure. Mind is a structure, and is also part of the equilibrium of the social structure, and so on. In fact, it appears that a structure might be one among several possible analyses of a given thing; alternatively, we can identify many different sets of data as "things" (cf. Piaget, 1970).

Then what was Piaget saying about his data when he described them as constituting a structure? *He was saying that he was able to see parts that function together to protect some essence or purpose from dissolution.* Piaget did not put it this way and the fact that structure embodies purpose is likely to be overlooked, both because Piaget buries particular purposes beneath general principles that conserve all purpose, and because Piaget's outlook is itself a way of describing an essence or purpose that cannot be otherwise described.

Piaget's organic structures are problem-solving systems, and the general problem that they solve is how to maintain their identity in changing circumstances. But we must add that for Piaget there is no way to specify the structure's identity except by describing the course it follows in adjusting to reality (unless, perhaps, by pointing to the limits of its adaptibility). *How then are we to know a structure when we see one? Only by observing a conservative purpose served by an arrangement of reactions.* And because we cannot see naked purposes or what it is that must be conserved, it comes down to this: that we identify a biological structure by its problem-solving *form.* Piaget spent his life describing what that form is.

The reason that Piaget could call so many things structures, and the reason that they overlap each other is that *any* reactive stability in an environment can be characterized as a structure. Even if we knew abstractly all about the general form of problem-solving systems, we still cannot pick out a particular structure unless we can see a particular problem that it solves. What we choose to take as its problem determines what structure we are examining. Because it is so general and protean, Piaget's approach might have remained, as it started, a philosophical system (Piaget, 1971b), if he had not seen an opportunity to apply it in an area where problems can be empirically separated and defined, and where (temporarily) stable solutions can be precisely formulated. That was, of course, the study of children's perceptive and cognitive development. There, fortunately for Piaget, we are able to isolate phasic solutions. And, moreover, we already know perfect solutions to which they approximate: Mature thinking acquaints us with the objective universe, the objective universe gives us independent knowledge of the child's problem, so we adults are able to pick out intermediate reactions to the universe that constitutes the child's attempted solutions.

We do not, however, enjoy the same advantage when we describe other structures. For one thing, if problems are solved in a continuously evolving rather than stepwise fashion, it will obviously be more difficult to isolate and diagram the actions that define the various problem-solving structures. (One wonders what results Piaget's method would have yielded if human development consisted only of increasingly venturesome sucking!) What is more important, if we do not know precisely what the problem is that the structure is designed to solve, the structure itself will be correspondingly vague. We will still, of course, be able to say that it follows the general principles of problem solving (i.e., responsive conservatism) but we will not be able to say what it solves or what it conserves, or how it is related to other structures. Another way of putting this is that if we lack a vision of the end stage, which would constitute an ideal solution to the structure's problem, we cannot see clearly its problem-solving nature, and therefore, we cannot delineate the boundaries of the structure we are considering. Piaget tried very hard to persuade us that logico–mathematical structures are the end stage and ideal solution to all problems, but we must conclude that this is a Platonic dream, and that these bare forms of equilibrium are merely the common denominator of many particular solutions to particular problems. As we have seen, they do not even completely describe general intelligence.

We are now in a position to say something about the relationship of affective to cognitive schemas. Cognitive schemas are ways of organismic functioning that answer to certain kinds of problems (problems that can be abstractly resolved). Schemas that involve affect are ways of functioning that answer to problems defined somewhat differently: These problems have cognitive aspects, but they are more specific problems than those solved by cognitive schemas, and they are probably less formulatable. And the individual person as a whole is a structure that is designed to resolve still more specific and less definable—perhaps even unique—problems.

In effect, some problems are rather general, and some are more specific. Even a very specific problem obviously taps as much general problem-solving ability as the organism possesses, ultimately, in man, mathematical conceptualizations. But specific problems require in addition other types of problem solving, on the continuum from cognitive to more totally organismic, physiological answers. We can pick types of schemas out of this continuum according to our ability to identify problems.

SOURCES OF PIAGET'S SUCCESS

So far this analysis has failed to produce any but the most commonplace and obvious theoretical tools for conceptualizing psychotherapy. How did Piaget manage to do so much better? Let us try to summarize what allowed Piaget to make so many empirical discoveries with his natural philosophy:

1. He recognized that all interchanges of the organism with the environment can be construed as problem-solving arrangements, the central problem being change and unfamiliarity.
2. He recognized that problem solving is cumulative; it draws on previous problem solving. This could be anticipated from the conservancy principle.
3. He recognized that cognition, like nutrition, is an interchange with the environment.
4. He took advantage of our abstract, final, common intellectual structures to pose specific problems to subjects in early stages of development. By comparing these attempted solutions with the final stages (mathematics and geometry) that he already knew, he was able to outline the structures of preliminary solutions and demonstrate their progression.
5. He was helped by the apparent, regular, phasic, discontinuous developmental stages, in this area (although their cause, and, to a lesser extent, their reality, is still debated.)
6. The discreteness of the logical problems he could pose to his subjects allowed him to dissect and compare their solutions. In other words, his separable questions allowed him to separate cognition into parts, and perceive how a whole is made of those parts.
7. Because the sort of cognition Piaget dealt with can be made explicit (it is formalizable), it was possible to show that the child forms structures before he is aware of them.

WHAT IS PIAGET'S LESSON FOR PSYCHOANALYTIC THEORY?

If this is what made Piaget's framework so productive, we may ask what brilliant new discoveries would emerge if the same procedure were applied to mental life as a whole, with its affective and interest aspects included. The answer, I am afraid, is anticlimactic. Looking over the previous summary, it seems to me that a theory of the mind such as Freud's is just such an account of overall, progressive, conservative, responsive, problem-solving systems, revealing the multiform purposes of the object when confronted by challenges.

That is not to say that Piaget's empirical findings make no difference to a theory of the mind. They clearly do, because he took one subset of problems and discovered a great deal more about them than was known when psychoanalysis was formulated. That increased knowledge, in turn, is bound to have an impact on other details of the theory, including the nature of childhood mentation, the significance of memory, dreams, and reconstructions, and the influence of maturation on the phenomenological environment.

Nevertheless, any comprehensive theory of the mind of the sort we are already familiar with, will qualify as the eagerly awaited extension of Piagetian principles to a larger field, because as we have seen, what can be carried over to the larger field is not any peculiarly Piagetian structures, but just his method of looking for stabilizing systems.

PIAGET'S LESSON FOR PSYCHOTHERAPY

It would seem that the most exciting question a therapist could ask of Piaget, namely, what kind of equilibrium is made of affective structures, is not in fact likely to elicit any very new kind of answer. It might be more profitable for the psychotherapist to ask what in the environment helps to equilibrate affective structures, because the psychotherapist is, in a way, an environment designer.

But when we do this we must be careful to use Piaget's system as a model for answering the question rather than as part of the answer, for we have seen that his analysis applies only to the most abstract problem solving. When Piaget discusses "decentering of cognition," and "reversible operations," he is referring to an asymptote of predictability and generalizability in the one aspect of our awareness that is related to the physical aspect of the world. Affective organizations are not on all fours with this kind of schema; they are not parallel even on a "lower" level. One should probably not speak about decentering or reversibility of affect in the same sense as we speak about decentering or reversibility in objective cognition. It would seem to be a category error even to deny objectivity and reversibility to affect, just as it would be to say that feelings have fewer angles than geometric figures. Instead we have to find the analogues of decentering and reversibility that apply to this more specific slice of human reactivity.[2]

---

[2]This is where I think George Klein (1976) erred. He tried to establish an equivalence of *techniques* by which cognitive and affective schemas are integrated. For instance, he thought that mentally representing oneself as active after a passive experience works to internalize affective experience in the same way that imaginatively replacing a displaced object helps to establish an objective schema. But *cognitive* reversibility strives to *erase* the difference between a displacement in one direction and in the other, while this can in no sense be the emotional aim of active reversal in fantasy. (That is true unless we picture the Indic religious experience as the end stage of equilibrated affective schemas. As a matter of fact, there is something in Buddhism that comes

Some of the principles for analogical application to psychotherapy might be the following:

1. Learning is a solution to a patient's problem, generally the problem of maintaining his purposes in the face of novelty and in the face of conflict induced by novelty.
2. The patient learns from his actions and from eliciting responses in others.
3. What he learns is simultaneously about himself and the other person; they are two sides of the same coin. That means that the patient simultaneously solves a problem of integrating the therapist into his purposes and integrating his several purposes most usefully to deal with the therapist.
4. Solutions have a relative stability, i.e., perception and self-feeling form a stable system: they are modifiable, but show some consistency (resistance).
5. These systematic solutions are reworkings of previous solutions; they would be impossible without their predecessors; they evolve along a necessary path.
6. The patient's new conscious awareness of something within himself already constitutes a revision (by generalization) of the previous solution to his problems.
7. For both the patient and the therapist, an awareness of the structure of the interaction comes before new awareness of the structures of the self and partner that determine the interaction.
8. The therapist only learns the patient's problems when he sees the solutions that the patient arrives at.

Now let us take these principles one by one and see if they shed any light on the therapy process:

Principle 1. In a Piagetian perspective, people are constantly solving problems. The only problems that are finally solved are the cognitive ones discussed by Piaget—he has selected them *because* there is a final solution to them. Presumably there are always problems that are more or less pressing, more or less unsolved, and the "more" is what we deal with in therapy.

Almost all therapies suppose that patients are trying to solve problems. Apparent exceptions are approaches that define problems from the therapist's viewpoint, those that say a person is only half-living or that "process"

---

close to carrying Piaget's attitude about cognitive decentration directly over into affectivity.) Piaget's cognitive reversal retraces, for instance, the path of a thrown rock, but who throws it is of no consequence to that schema. The personal perspective is recognized solely to establish its irrelevance. Since precisely the opposite is the case in identification with the aggressor, the similarity to Piaget's reversal is an illusion.

has stopped, and those that regard the patient as not his true self. But if the patient presents himself for treatment he must already be working on a difficult problem. Piaget's contribution is to summarize the problems as difficulties in maintaining one's purposes in the face of alien impingements (including impingements from within oneself). He thus reminds us that, no matter how benevolent and wise, one cannot substitute one's own purposes for the patient's.

This aspect of treatment is implicitly recognized in all those accounts of therapy that emphasize the overwhelming role played by the mobilization of hope.

Principles 2 and 3. Piaget says that learning ultimately comes about from operating on something. A therapist would be wrong to think that he makes patients' behavior instructive by pointing to it. The patient's actions are more aptly thought of as an experiment than as data. Without direction from the therapist, the patient continuously interprets the outcome of this experiment in terms of what he feels himself to be doing to the therapist; for him the therapist's interpretation is just one experimental result among others. This is one of the reasons for the psychoanalytic principle that intellectual under-standing alone is quite powerless to effect change.

A Piagetian view would emphasize that everything that the patient does, even if it is unknown to the therapist and invisible to the patient, is the manual by which the patient decodes everything the therapist does in response, whether it is the therapist's answering attitude, his general mood, viewpoint, or specific interpretation. That is true also for fantasy action of the patient and, alas, fantasy responses attributed to the therapist. It follows that it is exceedingly difficult for a therapist to know exactly what information he is imparting, or, as we see later, what it is that the patient is looking for as a solution. Respect for this principle can be seen in the psychoanalyst's restrained activity, his celebration of free associations, his protection of undisturbed marginal fantasies, and his nourishment of the transference.

It would also follow that it is quixotic to hope that the patient will first learn to see the therapist realistically and use that as a secure base for learning about himself. These two lessons (about himself and about the therapist) are learned at the same time by the same process.

Principle 4. We have noted that Piaget owed much of his empirical success to the stable stages of thought characteristic of certain age groups. It would have been harder for him to describe the principles that succeed each other if they progressed on an even continuum. The psychotherapist also would have a hard time if he could not fish out relatively stable systems of problem solving used by the patient. Therefore he has recourse to theoretical pictures of pathology and normality. A sophisticated and highly worked-out theory like psychoanalysis describes stages of problem solving at various ages, for example, psychosexual stages, whose contribution to mature solutions can be identified in adult patients. Theory also provides standard patterns of problem solving, for example "defense mechanisms" and their derivatives, and standard pathological dynamics. Holistic theories that shun static configurations must rely on a picture of a final, ideal stage of problem solving — an optimal solution (e.g., Gendlin, 1964). Ultimately such teleologic terms alone cannot adequately describe the therapy process (see chapter 22). But a theoretical picture of a final stage of development does help a therapist to conceptualize therapy if he also has vignettes of the steps that lead to it. For instance, the psychoanalyst is aided by supplementing his picture of oedipal conflict with (vague) pictures of how the oedipus complex is ultimately resolved, or more generally, how "object relations" are fully established and ambivalences are coordinated.

These pictures of relatively stable structures give the therapist the conceptual means to infer the patient's moment-to-moment problems in therapy.

Principle 5 . The principle that solutions are always reworkings of previous solutions is well known to the analytically oriented therapist. Psychoanalysis has always required an orderly progression in therapy. Premature interpretations are to be avoided, not just because they may be frightening, but also because they would be meaningless, or because they may be assimilated into unintended meanings. It is, however, an open question whether or not a therapist can really know what schemas the patient has or has not developed, and therefore what new use can and will be made of the therapist's activity. During the long passage of time spent in therapy, a patient may develop entirely unknown schemas that make the therapist's interventions useful in new ways without either party knowing exactly when or how (see chapters 11 and 34).

Principle 6 . Piaget's work serves to nail down the principle that consciousness is not simply a spotlight on otherwise unchanged structures. That is certainly not an innovation; Freud said that consciousness reorganizes its substrate. (Freud cited the changes made by verbal coding, and even went so far as to say that nonverbalizable unconscious contents lack relational concepts.) Many analysts have come to think of memory "revival" as always a reorganization of experience quite apart from defensive distortion. Furthermore, the psychoanalytic axiom that attitudes, feelings, and behavior change when unconscious schemas come into consciousness is reinforced by Piaget's demonstration that even in the logical sphere, consciousness reworks what it focuses on. If purposes are structured and structures change shape as one becomes aware of them, the action of therapy becomes less mysterious.

Principle 7 . That awareness of interaction precedes understanding of interactors is also a restatement of old wisdom. It is another reason that "intellectual understanding" rarely changes people. The tensions and gratifi-cations of therapy are the stuff out of which is sorted who the therapist is and who the patient is. From this point of view difficulties are Discovery at work, not Discovery on strike. Furthermore, whereas difficulties are constructive, success is instructive. That should make us less edgy about gratification in therapy and raise our concepts to a more professional level regarding "supportive therapy," "transference cure," "ego-relationship therapy," and so on.

Principle 8. A consequence of Piaget's approach is that we can know the patient's purposes only by the way he solves problems, and we know he is working on a problem only by the form of his activity. Can we detect problem-solving activities before we know specific problems?

Here is where we would expect the greatest help from Piaget, who was, after all, a specialist in problem-solving form. Perhaps his concepts will help us learn what sort of event is evidence that a novelty is being reduced to a familiarity. But that is not going to be easy because we have no independent way of determining what is new to the patient (cf. Levenson, 1972). Some primitive communication of anxiety often seems to help us. Dreams too have been used for this purpose, especially by Thomas French (French, 1958; French and Fromm, 1964). Transference is a traditional instrument for pinpointing assimilation and accommodation, but the epistemology of trans-ference interpretation is still nascent and increasingly interrelated with countertransference. I would maintain that any element of struggle in psychotherapy helps to detect problem-solving systems (see chapter 34). In a struggle, patient and therapist can orient themselves toward a common problem before arriving at a common definition which in fact may never be achieved (cf. Lichtenberg, 1983).

SUMMARY AND CONCLUSIONS

Let us now see where these thoughts have led us. First of all we have lost hope that Piaget's work holds the germ of a special theory of the mind for psychotherapists. Instead he gave us an approach that is not very different from the one used in constructing any comprehensive theory of the mind. He was wise enough to apply his concepts principally to the delimited problems of logic and mathematics, where we can independently specify adequate solutions. If we try to include more in our focus, especially affective arrange-ments, the result is not an expanded Piagetian psychology, but a dynamic theory of the mind such as psychoanalysis.

No doubt Piaget's approach usefully emphasizes certain features of theory-building that are specifically germane to psychotherapy. But even these are far from startling, and some of them come close to the commonplace principles of integration and differentiation. Nevertheless, I can see a number of possible contributions.

Piaget reminds us that structures are defined by purposes and purposes are exemplified by problem-solving activities. Piaget further reminds us that successful problem solving is progressively institutionalized and becomes a purpose in its own right. This helps to minimize the difference between affect and cognition in therapy, and therefore, between attachment to the therapist and understanding received in therapy. Problem solving is problem solving, and it is so regardless of the terms or level of the problem. Very personalized problems will necessarily be worked out in holistic, emotional, nondiscursive ways, and there is no puzzling gap to be bridged between experience and information as agents of therapy. Cognitive and affective solutions are simply abstractions from the overall preservation and modification of purposes. All reactions are a form of cognition and all cognition is a form of reaction.

The merit of a theory often stems from the puzzles it raises, in this case puzzles about what it is in psychotherapy that especially facilitates the universal activity of problem solving. Is the patient helped to solve his problems by the therapist's recognizing them? That is by no means a foregone conclusion because a Piagetian model is not an ordinary instructional model. But if it does help, then we must ask how the therapist knows what the patient's problems are. (Problems are not the same as complaints.) Are treatment problems the route to all the patient's problems? If so, why? Perhaps it is because the therapist also learns by solving problems and, just like his patient, he cannot operate on a vicarious experience in his head as creatively as he can learn from an actual one with his patient. Do both patient and therapist get to understand something between themselves by tampering with the relationship and watching the result?

Finally, this rather unstartling approach may yet help do one of the things we require from a general theory of therapy, namely, provide a spectrum for relating different types of treatment to each other. For instance, therapies might be assortable in terms of how much problem solving each fosters (see chapter 16).

PIAGET'S LESSONS FOR TRAINING

Perhaps the most intriguing relevance of Piaget's analysis to psychotherapy lies in the area of training. (Maybe methodological and theoretical problems always have more practical import for training than for treating.)

Piaget said that thinking is a kind of acting, or rather that various kinds of thinking are various kinds of action. Thinking is a balancing activity with cognitive consequences. (It is as though the old rough American pragmatism of learning by doing had been extended to "headwork.")

One kind of doing in psychotherapy is fitting events into a theoretical grid. As a matter of fact, in most therapies (those without protocols) this is as close to a job description as we can find; it is the activity of psychotherapy that sets it apart from other life activities. The practicing psychotherapist is constantly framing and reframing, categorizing and recategorizing.

But in Piagetian terms, another way to think about a patient is to interact with him.

Supervision routinely trains the first kind of thinking. It helps the trainee put what he sees into theory; in other words, it helps set up reversible schemas of a causal nature, so that he can mentally rebalance his understanding as the patient acts. (Supervision also trains empathy. The process of empathy may be elucidated, and its practice improved, by Piagetian considerations. Piagetian thought would tend to amalgamate empathy with other kinds of knowledge because some of the prelogical stages of cognition share many features with empathy.)

When a therapist urgently needs to re-establish his personal balance, he will do it any way he can. He may interact with the patient harmfully or irrelevantly. That is another reason why supervision concentrates on cognitive operations. If supervision can maximize the therapist's internal (mental) activity, his overt actions (comments, etc.) will probably be most flexible. Supervisors help the therapist to experiment with pictures of the patient to restrain him from harmful interventions. The danger in this approach is that the trainee will come to think of intellectual schematizing as a panacea for therapy problems and as such it will inevitably fail him. For interpersonal problems are more like examining a new substance than like working out a mathematical problem, and therefore reflection alone is unlikely to yield adequate schemas for coordination. Just as a patient cannot think about himself alone as fruitfully as with an interlocutor, so also a therapist cannot develop his views and picture of the patient if he just tries to work out schemas entirely in his own head. (Of course, while it continues, supervision provides the therapist a field for interactive exploration, but it must also foster a more permanent resource for the day when supervision has ceased.)

In addressing this problem it is useful to remind ourselves that Piaget's theory describes balance implicitly in terms of conservation (and development) of purposes. Psychotherapy training, as opposed to didactic teaching, can be viewed as the cultivation in the trainee of relatively stable professional purposes of a special kind that can be preserved in the greatest number of ways by extremely variable activities ranging freely over whatever problem areas the patient chooses or needs.

Something of the sort is doubtless intended when it is said that the job of the therapist is *to understand*. But by itself that term simply begs the questions that Piaget helps us to answer (see chapter 8). The imbalances that are felt in therapy are so gross and comprehend such varied affective schemas and operations that understanding in its ordinary sense is a will-o'-the-wisp. It will not always succeed in equilibrating therapist and patient, and when understanding does not make the therapist comfortable purely by virtue of its cognitive content, he will try to get comfort from it as an overt action: He will try to make himself comfortable by being an "understander," in which case what began as inquiry will become a kind of role playing, which partly avoids the problems at issue.

Piaget is no less exploitable for role-playing than any other theorist. When therapists read a developmental theory, they inevitably dream themselves into the drama. They identify with one of the characters; they select a role for themselves. Because most developmental theories discuss infants and mothers, therapists regularly translate the theory into practice by picturing themselves in a mother role.

What role are therapists led to identify with by reading Piaget? Piaget was most interested in children's relationship to the non-human world. Beside the subject child, the only character in the drama was . . . the experimenter. And so the therapist who wondered how he may resemble the separating mother studied by Margaret Mahler, will naturally ask himself how he may resemble the *experimenter* who figures in Piaget's inquiry. That role comes especially easily, because the analyst has historically been seen not just as a parent figure but as a naturalist.

However, it is a mistake for a therapist to identify with Piaget's observer. Piaget's observer is interested only in finding out how things are, not doing something about it. His subjects have no interest in him and nothing to gain from him. In fact, North Americans are often irritated by Piaget's indifference to pedagogy and melioration; he had no orthogenic interest. And so, since psychotherapists are paid to *do* something when they carry Piaget's ideas into the consulting room, their role as Piagetian observer is twisted more and more into the role of teacher. Indeed, a bizarre but logical extreme of this effort to make a therapist out of a naturalist is the unveiling of the psychotherapist as a science teacher (see Wiener, 1975). Once the therapist has succumbed to this illusion, he will regard the Piagetian stages as stations he is helping the patient to pass through. He will teach the patient about his actions, outside and inside the transference (in this case, life itself constitutes the experiment). Ego de-centering (loss of egocentricity) will be seen as a treatment tool: it will be equated to objective curiosity which the therapist favors. And the therapist will actively encourage, or at least applaud, "accommodation" to painful reality.

Because it connects therapy with the development of mind, this outlook is not without value, but it would be more convincing and profitable as an elaboration of Vygotsky (1962) than of Piaget. As an elaboration of Piaget's system, this application is marred by a fundamental error. In his experiments, Piaget himself was only a trivial part of the world that he described. The experimenter in Piaget's world was the child. In Piaget's picture there is just a child and a world. If a therapist looks for his analogue in that scene, he has nothing to choose from but the role of the world that the child is exploring. As a therapist, I am not an educator; I am the subject matter—I am at least part of what the patient is learning about, because Piaget said that a subject learns about his actions, and about himself, and about the objective world all at once and in the same way, with awareness moving from his actions to self and object. If that is the case, then it would be senseless for me to ask my patient to develop a special motivation for our project. He will either be in action with me or he won't. And if he is in action, he will necessarily have a motive of some sort or other, and it hardly matters what it is. His motivation boils down anyway to trying to preserve his balance, from which, if I play my cards right, all the other Piagetian stages will proceed. I am the patient's object of exploration, not his coach. The patient will try to adjust his actions to me, will succeed and fail in several ways, according to his several needs, re-adjust his actions accordingly, and thereby develop increasingly useful, sophisticated, adequate, integrated levels of awareness of what is out there (namely me) and what he is up to (who he is). But it will all come from acting on me. I presume his main action will be to influence my attitudes, and he will read his successes and failures out of that.

Admittedly, it is by no means clear how we should visualize interpersonal action in Piagetian terms, or what it is that the subject discovers by it, because the outcome is not the abstract, impersonal, reversible mathematics, or the physical grid that he achieves by acting on the physical world. But Piaget advertises his approach as a general biology, and it should be as applicable to psychotherapy as it is to evolution. In fact, it is useful to remember that if the Piagetian framework fits a patient, it must fit the therapist as well. The therapist, too, must operate by assimilation and accommodation to maintain an equilibrium in interaction with his patient.

That is the view elaborated in chapter 8. The therapist is not the experimenter but part of the experiment, and his reactivities are the reciprocal of the patient's learning activity. To speak the language of analogy, the therapist does not teach the patient how to throw a ball or how to walk: The therapist is the target the patient is aiming at. The therapist is the crawling limbs the patient is trying to coordinate. (In psychoanalytic terms, this point has been made by Winnicot, 1971; Tower, 1956; Myerson, 1981; and Lichtenberg, 1983.)

Can a therapist be taught to see himself as a medium in which the patient practices coordinating his own purposes? Such a training objective would not tell us what techniques must be learned because no formula could predict what schemas a patient will need to coordinate. As indicated in chapter 16, any theory of therapy based on a theory of the mind would help the therapist to be a universally usable medium. Every school will have its own descriptions and prescriptions. A Piagetian outlook would simply reclassify therapy difficulties as (partial) solutions to whatever the patient's problems are, leaving it to the various schools to decide how to describe them. From the standpoint of training, personal difficulties between patient and therapist would, paradoxically, be viewed as solutions to the therapist's professional identity problems. A Piagetian approach to training would encourage the trainee to solidify a professional purpose that is conserved rather than disturbed by interpersonal difficulty, so that the therapist will be balanced by leaning toward what the patient needs to work out. I discuss this in more detail in chapter 34.

26

Kohut's Mixed Theory

T o my knowledge, Heinz Kohut is the only revisionist who has ventured to construct a full theory of the mind. Because of that, and because it emerged slowly out of evolving theory and practice, Kohut's work is much harder to bring into focus than revisions based on a concise doctrine, or a simple model, or a special animus. Ornstein (in Kohut, 1978) offers a useful guide, but of course he views the system from within the system, where empathy is already given such a singular position that it can by itself account for the development of the theory. The outside critic will have to first cast the organically developing theory into a form that feels like a progressively developing argument before he can place it in the field of contesting theories.

What follows is an attempt to do that. It does not proceed from a statement of Kohut's theory, but from a kind of imaginary rewriting that tries to capture component tendencies. I cannot emphasize too strongly that it is not an exposition. Besides deliberately avoiding special terminology whenever possible, and ignoring the chronological sequence of explicit conceptual frameworks, my account artificially simplifies and separates strands of thought, some of them Kohut's and some which I hypothetically attribute to him. Much will seem distorted when removed from the balancing framework of the total corpus. One cannot learn Kohut's theory from this critique.

Because this is a theoretical review, no attempt will be made to judge what are, after all, the important issues, namely, whether Kohut's vision sorts pathology usefully, delineates clinical distress vividly, relates early to later experiences in new ways, and allows us to treat patients more effectively.

This essay was originally published in 1980, and Kohut continued to refine and extend his theory after that date. But since I am mainly concerned with the structure of his project I have not felt it necessary to make more than passing reference to his post-1978 work. (Elsewhere, [Friedman, 1986] I have discussed Kohut's final judgments on the theory of therapy, collected in the posthumous book, *How Does Analysis Cure?* [1984]). I will explore Kohut's theory of the mind in four sections: two sections outline divergent early trends, one describes the final outcome, and one evaluates the theory. I will then turn to Kohut's theory of therapy, discussing it first in the spirit of an earlier, and then of a later version, finally commenting on the overall therapeutic approach. The paper ends with a possible moral of the story.

THEORY OF THE MIND I

There are many open spaces in classical theory where one might have supposed Kohut's thoughts could be neatly fitted.[1] (To mention just one, Freud pointed to—but left for others to describe—the child's need to borrow strength from his father in order to master the oedipal dilemma.) Why, then, does Kohut end up working on a different theory?

I think the answer will be found in his starting point, and I think his starting point was his sense that patients' attitudes are only partly transference, if transference means holding on to a previous object in the guise of the analyst.

As Kohut saw it, patients reach out for the analyst in two nontransference ways. One is the mature fashion in which people satisfy already stabilized desires. The other is an immature way that asks not for satisfaction of a differentiated desire, but for a stabilizing response that will do for the petitioner what the mature person can do for himself.[2] We would be more likely to call it a need than a wish (1978, pp. 163, 225; 1971, pp. 45–46), because it seeks a basis on which to continue with all other aspirations, and its rebuff is associated with collapse or disaster, rather than with frustration.[3]

---

[1]Excellent brief summaries of Kohut's monographs may be found in Loewald (1973) and Schwartz (1978). Kohut and Wolf (1978) have also provided a concise summary.

[2]Kohut later came to believe that we never achieve complete self-nourishment, and that we always depend on some surrounding world that has personal value for us and in which our goals have meaning.

[3]Whether to consider such an important theoretical element a need or a wish is not simply a question of style. The difference between the two terms goes far to differentiate theories of efficient cause, such as the theories of psychoanalysis, from those oriented toward formal or final causes, as are equilibrium and object-relations theories. The same issue will come up in connection with homeostasis.

Kohut may have asked himself: Where else do we meet an undifferentiated, unconflicted need for someone to provide a sense of stable well-being? Experience, imagination, and psychoanalytic theory all answer that it is in the infant's relationship with his parents (reflected in the purified pleasure ego, primitive identifications with parental strength, etc.).

Most theorists assume that the means to meet this need are provided early in life, once and for all, for better or worse. What looks like a search for external stabilizing in later life is really the readjustment of systems formed in childhood, which remain the reservoir of well-being. We are accustomed to thinking that, however helpless he may feel, an adult's equilibrium depends on integrating and redefining established powers of his mind, as when a superego is modified in psychoanalysis.

But in certain adults Kohut believed he saw major patterned regulation forming for the first time on the scaffold of the psychoanalytic interaction. And whether, as he initially thought, this was a defensive regression, or, as he came to believe, it was a new push on a fixation, what impressed him was that it gave him a window on a central, infantile need for structured control of stimuli and affects.

Kohut does not seem to have been as interested in the way-stations between outside influence and internal regulation as those writers who struggle with introjects, identifications, presences, imitations, etc. Although he does not ignore the "mechanics" of structure formation (e.g., 1971, pp. 49–51), and although his later theory obliged him to make some distinctions between nuclear and other selves, his main approach to maturation is through the study of needs. The selfobject and its subdivisions are interpersonal terms, and their intrapsychic correlates are defects, not structures (cf. Loewald, 1973). Between the defect and the filled-in structure (ambition or ideal), gradations are mainly quantitative, having to do with stability and efficiency rather than type; that is, they are classified according to how well stimulation is supported and delimited. When Kohut compared the situation of an adult patient requiring stabilization from his analyst with that of a child seeking joy and comfort from his parent, he made the comparison not so much in terms of mental anatomy, but principally in terms of the problems the subject had to solve. Instead of speculating on learning procedures, his account dwells on the infant's tasks—tasks accomplished or failed (e.g., 1978, p. 869). I suspect he felt that similarities between adult feelings and childhood experience could best be traced through similarities in problem solving. His line of thought seems to have run like this: If mothering keeps the child in a state of well-being, what must the child do to re-establish that state when mothering is partially or temporarily withdrawn? Clearly, the child must replace the missing mothering aspect for himself. What did his mother do that he is biologically able to do for himself? His mother had modulated stimuli, drives, or feelings by organizing, balancing, encouraging, damping, directing, and defining them. Up to a point the child has the capacity to learn how to imitate these functions in her absence.[4] Kohut (1978) says:

> . . . the child incorporates the parent's drive-restraining attitudes in the form of innumerable benign memory traces . . . the child himself later acts in the same way toward the drive demands that arise in him (p. 370).

> Every shortcoming detected in the idealized parent leads to a corresponding internal preservation of the externally lost quality of the object (p. 433).

But if the gap between his need and the parenting response is too great for the infant to master, he will lose the good state and also miss a chance to take over a new way of regulating his tensions. (For example, tensions will not become ideationally well-defined.) He will continue to require specific responses from other people to recapture the good state. A patient who continues to require this at an age when reportable introspection is available offers us the opportunity to learn what an absence of structured regulation of tension feels like.

But are we warranted in attributing the need for environmental compliance to a lack of internal regulations? Does not everybody, no matter how mature, need some sort of compliance from the environment in order to feel good in some way? The answer is yes, but the requirements of good feelings are not all of the same type. As mentioned, Kohut found in various patients three types of claim on the world. There are claims which cannot be met by the environment because they are conflicted (e.g., transference). There are nonconflicted claims which continue to exist whether or not they succeed

---

[4]Kohut has allowed the impression to arise that he is engaged in removing psychoanalytic theory from biology. Some regard that as a virtue; others, as a betrayal of the whole psychoanalytic enterprise. I believe it is a false issue. Kohut does not hold that the child needs just anything and everything. An organism is naturally sensitive to only certain disequilibria. (The term "optimum stimulation" merely begs the issue.) Furthermore, the infant at any given time is capable of only certain self-regulations. Early in life, for example, he is biologically incapable of nursing himself. What he *can* do, by way of "internalization," must be as biologically built-in as what he cannot do is biologically excluded. Cleary implied in Kohut's theory are nascent schemata of autocontrol over internal and external stimuli, which can be exercised and extended by parental caring and further extended by small desertions. Those beginning schemata already contain patterns which define them as needs and which select from the parent's co-definition the appropriate elements, the elements which fit and delimit the original schemata (1971, p. 49). The parent's role in this complex interaction early in life is summarized as "soothing" and "stimulating." As the child's mind differentiates, the parent's regulation seems more obviously a way of giving the child a chance to fulfill specific personality needs. (This sort of progression is worked out in detail by Gedo and Goldberg [1973].) There is a sense in which infants and at least some adult psychoanalytic patients can be said both to imitate their partner and to create the image of the partner to imitate. In the infant the imitation of lost illusions is more apparent. But in all cases the essential function of the partner is to provide the material with which biologically and psychologically ordained propensities can build in the direction that they are programmed.

(personal styles of mature love [1978 pp. 310–311, 369]). And then there are claims similar to those of infancy, which are also unconflicted, but differ from mature styles of loving in this respect: if love is frustrated, it continues to search for fulfillment, but if this immature demand is not met, it ceases to function. We may say that it gives up. It seems to reflect more a need for a means than for a target. Although I do not believe Kohut made it an explicit argument, we find ourselves asking what kind of aspiration would cease to aspire if it did not succeed. The answer suggests itself: a need for organization and form would tend to be inexpressible without organization and form. You might say that mature needs follow an established conduit, but a need for a conduit would show itself as a failure of transmission.

I put this argument into Kohut's mouth because I feel that it is implicit in such phrases as the "central, empty, depressed, and deprived sector" of the psyche (1978, p. 878), "a weakness in the core of his personality" (p. 845), references to narcissistic configurations that are "insufficiently cathected and . . . thus liable to temporary fragmentation" (1971, p. 19), and views such as this: " . . . the experience of the fragmented body-mind-self and self-object cannot be psychologically elaborated" (p. 30).

We have now outlined a situation common to some adults and all infants, namely, a need for organization, modulation and stimulation. We would expect that need to be satisfied by everything that has been called psychic structure. In the course of his explorations, Kohut recognized a number of new psychic structures and elaborated old ones, such as the ego. But nowhere, I think, does he deny that every mental structure contributes to the sort of modulation he is interested in.

Because no conflict is involved in the need for structure, we can clinically observe the subjective feelings that identify the varying degrees of psychic structure along the ladder of growth. At one end, experience suggests that self-esteem, integrity, vitality, and confidence in one's affective stability are the kinds of adult good feelings that are at stake. At the other end of the ladder in infancy, we cannot know what is subjectively at stake, but we can remind ourselves that a need for structure means a need to regulate stimulation or excitement, and we may imagine that for the infant some sort of comfortable vigor is the feeling that results from age-appropriate success in establishing mental structure.

Let us call an unconflicted need for a stabilizing response from another person a narcissistic demand. We now have three clues that link a narcissistic demand with normal structural maturation. First, a narcissistically needy person's direct dependence on another's response is analogous to the dependence of the child's tranquility on his caretaker, and that suggests a lack of stimulus regulation. Secondly, the collapse of the person's striving when he is unsuccessful suggests that what he is seeking is structure. Finally, his undisguised presentation of this striving allows a psychoanalyst to track its ancestry through various states of pride and ambition all the way back to excitement regulation, and that derivation shows the whole chain to be related to a need for structure.

By so reading his patient's yearnings as direct manifestations of primary need for structure, Kohut was able to develop the phenomenology of basic regulations in some detail. I will oversimplify crudely in order to briefly fill out the account. The phenomenology includes a sense of idealization (at first of the parent-infant dyad, later of the parent, and finally of ideals). In its origin this factor is "related to drive control" (1978, p. 435). The phenomenology also includes a sense of confident self-aggrandizement. This factor is related to " . . . the drives [themselves] and their inexorable tension" (p. 435). In other words, from the primeval parent-child perfection, the maturing child differentiates two features: the controlling, defining, respected parental power and the parent's enthusiasm for the child's enthusiasm. The former grows into structures of pride, the latter into sources of ambition. Standards of performance come from the first; celebration of the self as performer from the second. A person needs something general to respect. And he must feel able to make himself special. Though interrelated, these needs have individual histories and manifest themselves in distinct ways throughout life.

It is now clear why Kohut was not content to elaborate the terms of existing psychoanalytic theory. Narcissism was not, for him, a subabstraction to be fitted into a large, abstract theory; it is no more abstract than gross, erotic lust. When the therapist is pressed for understanding and mutual adulation, he is at that very moment observing a demand for restraint and support of excitement; he is witnessing first-hand nothing less than hunger for psychic structure.

In infancy this hunger is satisfied by the parent's presence, supplemented by what the child has been able to adopt of the parent's attitude toward himself. In the course of adopting these attitudes the youngster perfects his secondary process, constructs his ego, and collects resources which will later be used to handle conflicting drives, such as those that contend in the oedipal conflict.[5] In all of these states his structure-hunger is satisfied by structures that accumulate as a by-product of *all* early interactions with the environment. In adult years unsatisfied hunger for structure (that is, hunger for channeling, defining, sustaining, and moderating of his impulses) appears as pressure on the analyst for a suitable response to *drives in general*. I propose this as the *tendency* of the first phase of Kohut's theory.[6] He did *not* actually make it his theory for the following reasons:

---

[5]Kohut later distinguished between the oedipal period and the presence of oedipal conflict.

[6]This tendency is illustrated in Kohut's (1978) statement that "Exhibitionism, in a broad sense, can be regarded as a principal narcissistic dimension of all drives . . . " (p. 438). And it is this tendency that Schwartz (1978, p. 442) picks up when he writes, "Ambitions and ideals, after all, are drives and objects seen solely from the point of view of the self." This latent tendency of the theory would make Kohut's argument for a separate narcissistic line of development a plea to

1. If the infantile good feeling is preserved by accumulating structural by-products of drive satisfaction, then self-feeling would be a simple marker of psychological growth. It would be the unconflicted *aspect* of the *whole set* of psychic structures.[7] It would follow that narcissistic deficiencies would never occur without concomitant disruption of object attachments. But Kohut believes that, on the contrary, a person may have narcissistic problems far in excess of object-libidinal difficulties.

2. Clinically, this sort of theory would not account for the conflict, repression, defenses, and resistances exhibited by narcissistic patients. In practice the analyst would find himself struggling to persuade the patient to integrate into his personality a need (for structure) that is supposed to be the patient's own wholehearted quest for integration itself. Such a proposition can scarcely be formulated, let alone argued.

THEORY OF THE MIND II

Looking back at Kohut's original perception with these difficulties in mind, we see that a distinction is called for. We have envisioned a patient making an appeal that is not a compromise between divergent wishes secretly aimed at the parents. We have pictured the appeal as whole-heartedly addressed to whoever will answer it. Now Kohut qualifies this by saying, in effect, that whole-heartedness does not mean unconflictedness or guilelessness.

How can this be? How can a wish be checked, or a disguise required if there is no intrapsychic conflict? Object libido needs restraint because some wishes for certain objects can court unacceptable risks. But it is hard to see how narcissistic libido can court danger of any sort if it is essentially structure-building and protective.

Basically, Kohut answers the riddle this way: What blocks narcissistic striving is the risk of losing a somewhat comfortable feeling in the act of seeking a more comfortable one. There is no specific danger from the outside world except the negative one of non-responsiveness (active or passive). Nor does the appeal hesitate because of a contrary wish. The patient does not say to his analyst, in effect, "I would like very much to appeal to you this way, but I cannot afford to, lest I lose this other, incompatible response I also desire from you."

---

attend to a specific phenomenological significance of familiar psychoanalytic configurations. And it would be consistent with his early use of "narcissistic libido" to refer to a "psychological meaning of the essential experience" (Kohut, 1971, p. 39n).

[7] The nature of Kohut's theory is partly determined by his sharp distinction between the conflict aspect of psychoanalytic theory and its maturational aspect (in which he was always more interested, judging from his early papers). Freud's theory hedged on this (see chapter 15; also Gill's [1963] important monograph testifying to this aspect of Freudian theory).

What the patient is afraid of—indeed correctly appraises—is that *he himself cannot handle the expression of his own stifled wish.* There are obviously *some* wishes that a person with a narcissistic personality disorder can express while awaiting the results. (In Kohut's terms, these are object wishes from either the transference or mature sectors in the analysand.) And then there are other wishes that he cannot risk. It is very much as though he has a separate set of drives which can be frustrated by their own immaturity, a frustration that is not due to a structural conflict. And indeed Kohut puts these aspirations on an equal footing with other drives by referring to the ego's task in *dealing with them* (1971, pp. 185–186).

In this vein, we might talk about a *drive* toward idealization and a *drive* toward grandiosity. A warning signal from the ego (a small sample of the catastrophic shame that would ensue) causes the drive to be repressed. In a state of repression it cannot be channeled and defined by reality, so it remains primitive and risky and increasingly fit for repression.[8] These special drives have their own impetus and their own fate apart from other drives. We can no longer say that narcissistic strivings are simply the structural needs served by exercising *any* drive. And, as they are special drives, we might suppose that their "object" is not as replaceable as the "object" of a general need for structure.

This brings us to the theory of the vertical split. Some patients retain a fantasied, inauthentic relationship with a parent, which provides a modicum of narcissistic fulfillment. To pay for this minimum contentment, some part of the aspiration must be repressed. That repression is the familiar kind that allows a partial and preferred expression to creep around it. Ordinarily, however (when there is no vertical split), narcissistic aspirations are repressed in a quite different fashion. They are inert, yet ready to respond to any suitable environment. (This is the horizontal split.)

Thus these strange drives sometimes behave like other drives, and sometimes they do not. Sometimes their stunted form is associated with a particular person and relationship, and at other times they are just stopped short in a dormant availability.

Moreover, at one point (1971, pp. 82–83) Kohut tells us of occasions when "the child's available libidinal resources already were bound too firmly on the pathological parent" to permit narcissistic use of more suitable objects. He thereby implies that narcissistic inclinations, unlike other drives, are not *ordinarily* fastened to particular people (except in the act of satisfaction), but that occasionally they may be fastened so tightly that they conflict with

---

[8]According to Kohut, a fantasy of grandiosity becomes wildly elaborated when sequestered in the unconscious. This poses serious problems for the theory since such a hot-house elaboration does not result from impact on the world or from interaction with other drives and interests. Is there a Jungian archetype that can supply ornate definition on its own?

drives toward other objects. Here, I think, the theory wavers: Are narcissistic aspirations merely the mind's consistent need for structure? Or are they particular drives that, like other drives, pick out objects and linger with them?

It is hard to describe the inhibitions of narcissism without making it seem like a drive. But it is like no other drive postulated. For if narcissism is no longer equivalent to structure, it still seems to be fundamental to structure in a way that other drives are not. These very peculiar drives can make structures on their own (e.g., the grandiose self), and when they are blended with other drives in the formation of structures such as the superego, they act as a binder (1971, pp. 186–187). We cannot rid ourselves of the impression that structuring is what narcissistic inclination *means*. It is as though all structures need the service of narcissistic "instincts," and some structures are built exclusively from such instincts.

I think that by the end of *The Analysis of the Self*, Kohut faced a crossroad. On the one hand he could describe structure-building. That is, he could extend the classical account of the birth of the ego, generalize the process to include the superego, coordinate specific feeling states with it, and advance the process forward from infancy into adult life. Alternatively, he could announce a newly-discovered drive, with a continually open (always anaclitically selected) object, which is ultimately channeled by the very structures it builds (and has as its object those same structures).

He never wanted to do either, but I think he wanted the advantages of both approaches. By the time of *The Analysis of the Self*, however, they were getting in each other's way. The painful struggles seen in treatment were jostling the theory of a straight-line, neutralizing matrix, and demanding that concepts of simple growth make room for concepts of specific goals. This tension forced a final reformulation of the theory.

THEORY OF THE MIND III

The Restoration of the Self (1977) shows us the path Kohut selected. Although he prudently refuses to give up the advantages of *any* theoretical framework, the dominant paradigm from this point on is aliveness and deadness. Development is not decided by the balance of conflicted yearnings but by the threat of extinction. The form of explanation is that a structure which permits survival (that is, permits cohesion and functioning) replaces one which does not. For example, a compensatory structure is one that matches the endowments of parent and child in such a way that a tolerable self can be made; in contrast, other perceived aspects of a parent which are rejected could not satisfy the needs of an integral self (pp. 82–83). Or, again, it is not the oral drive that determines the oral character; it is the fact that there is no other way to survive in some situations but through oral excitement (pp. 73–74).

The result of trying to describe in one formula something that looks a little like structuring and a little like drive activity is this: the self may have to make do without some assets if it risks more by seeking those assets, but it will try to acquire them when it seems less risky.

This self is a superordinate structure (1978, p. 756) that governs all other adjustments of the mind. The problem with such homeostatic explanations is that they are successful only when fully circular. If the self were the observer's notion of achievement, for example a "healthy" mind, the degree of its achievement would be informative, but it would not be a *cause* of any events in the subject's mind. On the other hand, if we regard the self as an actually existing superordinate schema, we must properly say that it is always fully realized in everything it does, and that is why we can explain everything by reference to it.

In these terms we *cannot* speak about a defective self. And we therefore cannot discover in it some promising dormant developments. If the psyche or self is impoverished, why, then, it is impoverished. There is less of it altogether, both to have and to want.[9] The homeostatic model simply tells us that whatever is conserved is what is conserving itself (see chapter 23). Such a circular conception of the self might be useful to a philosopher (it resembles a Hegelian idea), but Kohut is a clinician and must explain unfulfilled aspirations. He therefore tends instead to use the self as a name for whatever it is in a person's nature that determines what his ultimate satisfaction would be. Strictly speaking, of course, the potential for happiness – the shape of perfect happiness for a given individual – is always monolithic. But it is a more useful concept than a superordinate self because it leaves room for a discrepancy between someone's potential happiness and his actual happiness, and that can serve as an actual cause of events. For if you look at it closely, the discrepancy between potential and actual happiness is a definition of a frustrated need. But it is a need defined by its satisfaction, as hunger would be if it were defined as a state of non-satiation. With this sort of self used as a principle of explanation, the child is considered to be striving for whatever is ultimately in his best interest, and disturbance is caused by not having done with him what would have been most beneficial.

And what, on this view, can we say of the helpers? What defines the good parent, the skilled analyst? Basically, all we can say is that they offer whatever is necessary. Any handling, though it is sometimes called excitement control, sometimes empathic response, is ultimately defined by the satisfactoriness of its outcome. Although one must be grateful to Kohut for the evocative portraits of idealizing and grandiosity, these aspirations are so extensible that

---

[9]Loewald (1973) astutely points out that a self in need of a self-object is not yet fully a self.

they embrace almost everything. If a parent clings to an early merger, she frustrates a narcissistic striving (1977 p. 275). If she separates too early, that also frustrates a narcissistic striving. A seductive approach by a parent is "unempathic" (p. 188). A sensuously unstimulating approach is likewise unempathic (p. 274). Empathy and narcissistic need refer to the just-rightness of interactions.

A theory loses power when its variables are defined by their outcomes. But Kohut surprises us by demonstrating how much heuristic profit can be wrung from this circularity. By making effects (unsatisfactory outcome) define causes (unsatisfactory preparation), a circular explanation forces us to think as generally as we can, and thereby provokes larger questions than we might otherwise have asked. The proposition that exposure to traumatic incest is not what a person needed scarcely advances theory of the mind. But it may prompt the investigator to wonder, in general, what *was* needed in childhood, and he may then go on to ponder the job-description of parenting. Whatever logical status we assign his theory, Kohut is the last writer who can be charged with vacuousness or idle wordplay. His pages are rich with picturable human needs and agonies. His circular theory directs attention to that general import people have for each other which transcends their particular interactions. It enables him to tell us, for instance, a great many interesting things about the hard-to-describe meanings parents have for their children. In fact, it may be argued that in a causal system, "meaning" is always a circular term: the nature of its determinants is spelled out by the very meanings that result.

THEORY OF THE MIND: SUMMING UP

What is the relationship between Kohut's work and drive-conflict theory? Kohut says that they are complementary, like wave and particle physics. In a trivial sense all theories which look at the same thing in different ways are complementary. Such complementarity tells us nothing about the relationship of the theories. The concept of complementarity was not introduced by physics to explain, for instance, the relationship between a discussion of chairs and a microscopic account of wood. Technically, complementary theories are equally comprehensive, on the same level of abstraction, and mutually exclusive in some sense.

Is Kohut's theory incompatible with classical theory? Kohut can see an intrapsychic conflict between guilty man and tragic man (1978, p. 760). If that were possible, the two accounts would be components of a single system. (Light waves do not, to my knowledge, impinge on photons.) And although *representation* has a new significance for Kohut, he does not give it an independent definition. He asserts that he could dispense with it (1977,

p. 206), but since he has in fact retained it, one wonders how much his theory leans on the older one.

Is Kohut's theory as comprehensive as the theory it seeks to replace? In the final reckoning, Kohut offers a uniquely detailed account of ambitions and ideals and the tensions associated with them, but says little about such matters as mature sexual fantasies and the normal tensions associated with them. Kohut is much clearer about how someone is fulfilled by his career than about why he is satisfied by the way he makes love. Kohut feels that his best efforts have shown that what he has to say cannot easily be put into earlier psychoanalytic language (1978, p. 788). But as regards the issue of comprehensiveness, the question is one of relative facility: Is it easier to build particularistic Freudian concepts into large, personal directions than it is to make Kohut's self psychology specify the peculiar configurations of personal proclivities? If it is harder to build downward from Kohut's generality than upward from Freud's particularity, it still would not follow that Kohut's theory is superfluous. It is difficult to imagine anyone leaving Kohut's writings without carrying away a vital new truth about man. But it would be a supplementary, not a complementary truth. In other words, it would be an elaboration of an unstressed aspect of existing theory.[10]

If not complementary, is Kohut's theory perhaps a holistic Gestalt of what had previously been a history of atomic drives? We cannot make so sharp a distinction. Psychoanalysis has never suggested that an organism becomes human simply by weaving bodily pleasures together into an integrated pattern. The function of libido theory is to build blended human meanings out of these beginnings. The organization and transformation of meaning and affect is what psychoanalysis sets out to explain.

Kohut deals with the vitality and direction of aspiration in general. If his theory should turn out to be, in part, a generalization of psychoanalytic principles (comparable, perhaps, to French discussions of desire-as-such), that would not imply that previous theory ignored the whole person. (In rejecting such an invidious comparison, Schwartz [1978, p. 441] rightly contends that a competent psychoanalyst nowadays views his patient from multiple perspectives.) On the other hand, neither would it imply that Kohut's theory is simply a poetic point of view. Kohut's generalization is not just a perspective: it is a system, and that makes a big difference in the kind and number of coherences it can point out.

Finally, however, we cannot say that Kohut's theory is a systematic generalization of the psychoanalytic theory of the development of aspiration; it is actually a different *kind* of theory from Freud's. The difference between

---

[10]Lester Schwartz (1978) examines the applicability of complementarity to this theoretical debate, not only questioning whether the two theories actually converge on the same subject, but also whether Kohut really claims only parity for his.

the theories is that Kohut's permits him to say, for instance, that "the need of the budding self for the omnipotent selfobject's pleased acceptance of its merger needs . . . [is one of the] . . . primary configurations" (1978, p. 788). To designate a need for acceptance as an elementary configuration does not simply give it more honor. It constructs configurations on a new principle, just as if we made a basic principle out of a need for safety, or excitement, or tranquility, or beauty, or meaning, or fulfillment, or perspective. There are many ways of looking at satisfaction—of describing end-stages—of designating what shuts off action. There are many ways of describing the aim of life and describing failure.

No human phenomenon is so simple as to be adequately characterized in terms of drive and defense. A rigorous psychoanalytic description of a person would require a subtle, individualized portrait of psychic institutions, for which we do not even have a vocabulary. (Think of how lacking in nuance is the term "a harsh superego.") Therefore, we rely on personal acquaintance to supplement our categories, and if we lack that, we probably have very little specific knowledge. For psychohistory and psychobiography, Kohut's account offers at least as much understanding as drive-defense theory.

But theory of mind is a different matter. Theory needs particular perspectives to justify its choice of terms. When asked why it looks on things the way it does, psychoanalysis can answer that this is how one describes mentation as the product of a functioning entity. Committed to that goal, one selects dimensions which show how meanings are transformed by conflicting motives stemming from a single source (see chapter 15).[11]

Nonconflictual transformation is therefore not a psychoanalytically describable territory. Like objective reality, it is referred to in psychoanalytic theory. But, like objective reality, its neutral contents are not discriminated by psychoanalytic principles. A neutral zone may be described any way you like, according to your purpose. An attempt to build a theory of the mind on the ground of the "progressive neutralizing matrix" will not work. It leads necessarily to a circular account of causes in terms of satisfactoriness and appropriateness.

Kohut contends that empathy carves out its own categories. The most controversial premise of Kohut's method is his sharp separation, in the realm of psychology, of data-gathering from explanation (1971, pp. 300 ff.). Understanding and explaining are called "two opposing approaches" (p. 528). (His later work softened this opposition. See Kohut, 1984.)

---

[11]Kohut understood that psychoanalysis had been characterized "by a specific mode of theory formation" (1978, p. 337) in terms of "stable arrangements of groups of forces which are potentially in conflict with each other" (1978, p. 345). But he came to feel that this was too restrictive a definition.

We have no reason to believe that such a sharp distinction is valid. Indeed much evidence indicates that data are products of theory, however undeliberate. Infant observation suggests that the empathic reactions of caregivers may satisfactorily fall within a fairly wide range of infant accommodation. The most knowing parents' rightness is partly of their own making. There is no single way of grasping human experience, any more than there is one science of physical objects. Kohut has given us an extremely useful new grid for viewing human experience. But when it comes time for him to categorize his vision, he claims a higher truth for his abstractions because he underestimates their abstractness.[12]

Kohut's conviction that he has broken the epistemological barrier is naturally most provocative in matters of social and cultural advocacy. Can we be sure that he is not simply arguing for his preferences? To take one example, I think we can find support in Kohut's own work for the belief that what gives vitality to art, literature, and psychological theory is the plentitude of their constructs, not their ephemeral gestures of empathizing. That might lead us to fear that Kohut's dreams of a future generation preoccupied with the cultivation of empathy for its own sake is a vision of a culture that has nothing of value to celebrate.

Kohut's theory allows the practitioner to form extraordinarily useful new empathic configurations concerning the meaning and consequence of certain paramount affective constellations. In my opinion they are the most useful we have seen in recent times. This success suggests that psychoanalysis should enrich its stock of state descriptions (including forms of threat) which can be traced *en bloc* in their development and consequences. Kohut's work shows the advantage of outlining many independent lines of development, and pairing them with corresponding "structures" of organization. (For some of Kohut's earlier stress on the distinctness of the narcissistic line of development, see 1978, pp. 617, 767, 770, and 1977, p. 45.)

Since such descriptions are not theories of the mind, we should not expect them to invoke rigorous explanations of development. They must rest on various aspects of a fully worked out theory of the mind. Indeed it is just this combination of phenomenological specificity and theoretical ambiguity that

---

[12]Kohut thought that his new paradigm was a new way of seeing and not just a new conceptualization, so he thought he was offering more than a revision of theory (1977, p. 299). But every new Kuhnian paradigm represents a shift in perception. What we should ask is not whether Kohut's theory alters our perception, but how its perceptual revelations and bias compare with those of other theories. In answer, we might consider Gray's (1977) observation that "empathy" is often the phenomenological name for a tactful, selective attention to preoedipal configurations. This issue finds us involved in deciding what a patient's state "means." The nature of meaning remains highly elusive in all disciplines, and Kohut deserves our attention when he suggests that therapeutic leverage is what should control our decisions.

makes Kohut's theory more useful than other object-relations theories,[13] (not to mention humanistic, existential, nondirective, and experiential theories, which also find expansion in Kohut's work). His students are able to use drive images, structural by-product images, and homeostatic models, according to which of them at the moment keeps in view the story of the solidity and liveliness of the self.

THEORY OF THERAPY I

Kohut's theory has substantial therapeutic implications, and it is worthwhile to look closely at its probable effect.

We have seen the theory arise from the impression that, in order to sustain his basic aspirations, the narcissistic patient has a troubled but unconflicted need for an actual behavior by the real person of the analyst. For example, a claim for adoration may be psychic structure in statu nascendi, and if the analyst does not react to it at face value, he will inadvertently inform the patient that this primary need is unacceptable. Then what sort of response is called for? On the one hand these undeveloped needs for affirmation require an impossibly perfect match with the analyst. On the other hand failure to meet them is the very wound that caused the illness. How does the analyst avoid repeating the pathogenic trauma? Kohut frames his answer in deceptively familiar terms. The patient cannot retreat from the disappointing analyst, because the analyst uses interpretation to block regression (1971, p. 199). But since in this case the striving is unconflicted, its regression would not be the kind that seeks concealment and could not be blocked by mere recognition. In this context, therefore, we must suppose that blocking regression means stopping the patient from giving up (pp. 89–90). A way to stop someone from giving up is to make his project seem easier. How does Kohut's interpretation make a patient more hopeful? It conveys to the patient that his frustrated wishes are pointed toward growth and offers a tacit apology for frustrating them, which implies a promise of fulfillment. In this way the patient is induced to continue his project in the face of adversity, and that, according to the theory, is precisely how autonomous structures of self-esteem are built. The most conspicuous thrust of Kohut's therapy is this persistent tempting of the patient's shy narcissism.

---

[13]Space does not permit a listing of the many detailed parallels between Kohut's theory and British object-relations theory. The cardinal and defining similarity is the principle that the basic matrix of the personality is formed by a caretaker meeting an overall need for a satisfying experience, an experience originally defined by the ideal preseparation union with the mother and ultimately characterized by a sense of wholeness, vigor, strength, and identity. More particular strivings are characterized as theoretical artifacts or the result of pathological fragmentation.

Kohut is not the first theorist to suggest that there are some unconflicted aims which the analyst must simply encourage. But his view that certain treatments deal *chiefly* with nonconflicted growth needs makes him particularly suspect to those who are afraid that the analyst may not only begin, but end up in a fantasy role designed by the illness. I think this is of some concern to Kohut.[14] In different places he has emphasized, here the nurturing, and there the informational aspects of his technique (1977, pp. 135–136). He thinks it is useful to point out maladapted behavior (pp. 196–197). It is important to make connections and encourage memories. The aim of therapy is mastery based on insight (1978, pp. 507–508). But the fact remains that the most important assignment this theory gives to interpretation is to cement a growth-promoting therapeutic relationship. And Kohut is finally bold enough to say that "It is not the interpretation that cures the patient" (1977, p. 31). One stream of thought within his work is clearly experiential. But the intellectual, informational rationale is never given up during the construction of his theory. His students seem especially anxious to hold on to it (cf. Goldberg, 1978, pp. 146, 434–435). In the end, Kohut (1984) relinquished the intellectual rationale for treatment and allowed the experiential spirit to triumph. He finally believed that it is the experience of the empathic bond that effects the cure.

THEORY OF THERAPY II

But though, in Kohut's theory, insight seems to have to struggle to keep its pride of place, his theory of pathology increasingly gives interpretation another job than fostering a relationship. After initially apprehending the patient's narcissistic strivings as whole-hearted, unconflicted appeals, Kohut added that they are *not integrated* with the rest of his adult personality, and cannot be responded to as though they were. (See 1971, p. 20, where Kohut refers to "intrusions" of archaic grandiosity and self-objects into the realm of the ego.) It is, in fact, not possible for the analyst merely to gratify them, even if he wanted to; mediation is required (1971, p. 178). Split-off compromises must eventually be "explained" to the reality ego (pp. 178, 184). Failed needs are assimilated to successful accomplishments (pp. 178, 207, 226).

---

[14]Kohut's ambivalence can be seen in his description of certain maneuvers as "reluctant compliance." Although this is an honest enough name for a common practical dilemma, it does not make brave theory. Furthermore, the reader will wonder why it applies only to certain exceptional indulgences. How are they qualitatively different from what the theory requires at all times? If "reluctant compliance" applies to active participation, it must also apply to passive forebearance. Even the law binds a passive partner to an agreement he knowingly did not disclaim. Kohut did not see that he had to choose either a therapy riddled with reluctance or an entire therapy that was confidently, but only partially, compliant.

Whereas Kohut had warned the analyst not to allow an unexamined "therapeutic alliance" to assist him in narcissistic disorders, he now gives him license to rely on healthy aspects of the nuclear self (pp. 207–208). Although the earlier picture of the patient was somewhat that of an adult who needs to be a child again, it is now more evident that the patient possesses developed but unused adult capacities, and, just as in the transference neuroses, the analyst can expect him to solve old problems in a more mature fashion than he would have if he had been given the same chance in infancy (1977, p. 30). At last Kohut can comfortably use the word "transference" to describe a narcissistic relationship to the analyst. Since the patient has settled for less integration in exchange for more comfort, there is another variable open to therapeutic action besides the patient's unnecessary pessimism that can be lifted by a happy experience: there is also a reluctance to accept responsibility for incongruent wishes, which can be overcome by developing a more comprehensive schema. So Kohut's aim is the classical one of *integrating* wishes by inducing their exercise on an analyst who is both accepting and reflective. In its bare essence Kohut's final therapeutic rationale is not that the analyst soothes legitimate cravings. The rationale is that the analyst makes it possible for the patient to take up again the differentiation and integration of his needs. This is hardly a maverick idea. What distinguishes Kohut's approach is his insistence that the patient is differentiating and integrating his aspirations in the very act of exercising them on the analyst. It cannot be too strongly emphasized that Kohut's theory is a rare attempt to specify precisely how intensely motivated activity by the analysand itself acts to modify his motivation.

Does that mean that the analyst heals by gratifying? One can assume that the constructive remobilizing of aspirations is gratifying. But it is the momentum, not the gratification, that Kohut is after. His work may be read as an effort to identify in the analytic situation some of the refining and defining machinery that operates on meanings and goals throughout life.

If we closely examine Kohut's dictum that no unusual friendliness is called for in disturbances of the narcissistic transference, we see that the sign is posted not to warn us off a forbidden field of gratification, but to remind us that there is a *specificity* in the patient's need which would be obliterated by trying to calm him with irrelevant friendliness. (If the patient is so sick that there is no specificity in his need, then Kohut recognizes that the analyst – or rather the psychotherapist – may have to invent the form of friendliness by himself.) There is nothing wrong with gratification *per se*. Analysts have never wished to frustrate patients for the simple sake of austerity. Debate about gratification is a discussion of what does and does not stop the analytic process. Kohut argues that narcissistic need is a quest for personalized structure which is consonant with the analytic process. The analyst keeps the process going by gratifying the need. But that kind of need is optimally gratified if the analyst is imaginatively attentive. Anything from the analyst that is more personally friendly will be felt as a selfish imposition. (Kohut would say that it is overstimulating and sexualized.)

And yet commentators such a Martin Stein (1979) are by no means deceived when they remark on a special kind of gratification implicit in Kohut's therapy. The theme of this treatment is unqualified appreciation of the value and necessity of the patient's strivings. This fundamental exoneration leaves guilt looking for a locus. The result is that responsibility and blame tend to be shifted to the Other. Life failure is the fault of the parents.[15] Failures in the therapeutic relationship are the responsibility of the analyst, who cannot dismiss them as manifestations of inconsistent and misplaced demands.

Failure and discouragement are nodal points for any treatment predicated on growth. If failures are not the patient's responsibility, then treatment will fruitfully center on the therapist's failures.

Such a gentle, apologetic view of responsibility leads to an attitude of endorsement toward immaturity, which contrasts with the ambiguity by which analysts generally allow developmental arrest to be seen from either its growth-need or fear-gain side. Objectively, fixation can be viewed as a snug harbor from adult tensions or as the green shoot from a dying stalk. Kohut's therapist is biased to the latter view. It must be an impressive experience for a patient to have his pathology consistently given its progressive rather than its regressive significance—to be told that his immaturity is not a hammock but a launching pad, his incompleteness a purple heart from deprivation, not a badge of indolence, greed, and cowardice.

THEORY OF THERAPY: EVALUATION

Many features of Kohut's approach are strengthening exercises in grasping incontrovertible psychoanalytic principles: Not every two-person adult relationship is a diversion from a three-person relationship. An analyst should not become so used to frustrating the patient that he ceases to concern himself with each disappointment he inflicts. He should not be a therapeutic moralizer. He should try to find the reasonableness of the patient's attitude and, if possible, the inevitable claim or wish that it implements. He should

---

[15]A more subtle issue than responsibility is the mode in which mental contents are perceived. Gray (1973, 1982) points out that a focus on remembered life events registers these memories as documents of the life course, rather than as part of mental functioning. I understand Gray to be warning that the patient can become (willingly) trapped in an ethical drama, rather than (reluctantly) free to observe his own dramaturgy. Another consequence of this biographical reverence, according to Gray, is that the analyst takes on a supervisory role, a matter I refer to below.

remember that defensive behavior is also expressive. He should give patients a chance to exercise what they have been afraid to exercise. He should be aware that with his every act, no matter how routine, and his every statement, no matter how narrowly focused, he is commenting on the patient as a person. He should not force his patients into the intellectual frame that is easiest for the analyst. He should recognize that freedom from major countertransference does not make him harmless.

What possible dangers should be watched for as this approach is clinically evaluated? Is there a sacrifice of specificity? If the analyst is a generalized Other, to whom the patient appeals for wholistic sustenance, are particular imagos and needs lost from view?[16] Does the analyst dwell on a patient's resentment of exploitation (assuming that it is not the patient's true self that is in collusion), rather than summarizing the patient's divergent feelings—all of them authentic—concerning a particular bad bargain he made as a child? Is there a willingness to let everything be summed up as: "Mother didn't let me be me?" If some analysts do not see the forest of virtual abandonment for the trees of special dealings, a Kohutian must guard against elegaic generalities about the regulation of self-feeling, in relation to which all other interests in life are mere instrumentalities. (It is to Kohut's credit that he early recognized that fascination with primitive, global meanings can lead to neglect of more mature refinements [1978, p. 380].)

Are all-purpose concepts of excitation and control used as a standard, undifferentiated interpretation—for example, pilfering, explained by reference to inner disequilibrium (Goldberg, 1978, p. 393)? In its role as general stimulus moderator, does sexuality reveal to the analyst only a preceding discomfort? (If sex appears in some clinical reports as a kind of psychic mustard plaster, Kohut would probably attribute that to the type of case discussed.)

A worrisome consequence of a growth model of psychoanalytic treatment (as opposed to a conflict model) is the judgmental position in which it paradoxically places the analyst. An analyst who frequently gives a blessing is a critic. Such encouragement is far more controlling than the cynicism of the conflict theorist, for whom nothing is more deserving of a blessing than anything else, but then neither is anything less deserving. This problem should be kept in mind when an analyst reports that he said: "You try to do away with those feelings, or you feel you rightfully deserve to have them responded to. And in a way, or at one time, they should have been, you should have expected that" (Goldberg, 1978, p. 320).

His students' case histories occasionally suggest that Kohut's scrupulously self-critical technique can also be exploited by the therapist for easy self-

---

[16]This may be more of a problem for Kohut's students. One of them refers to a patient's relationship with his mother as transference (Goldberg, 1978, p. 344).

justification. One suspects that a patient's behavior late in treatment is empathically judged to be healthier than the same behavior early in treatment. It is not at all clear that the therapist's congratulation of himself for empathic correctness would have been awarded to the patient's mother for the same action (pp. 404, 414). In contrast to Kohut's theory, other theories, that do not speak of behavior as correct or incorrect or of needs as univalent do not offer this means or foster this urgency, to make of the scene what one would like it to be.

Since this approach carries with it an apology for empathic failure, patient and analyst may develop a shared faith that there is a perfect response to every demand. One wonders whether the notion of a perfect response (an object-relations axiom) might encourage an iatrogenic idealizing of the analyst. Kohut would be the first to agree that, however useful an idealizing transference might be, the slightest, indirect, vested interest in it by the analyst restricts the patient's choice of complementary roles. Any way that the therapist *tries* for a given role confines (restrictively defines) a patient. Will patients feel that they are being coached by Kohut's therapists in how they are to regard their analyst? Kohut might reply that one cannot attempt to understand without looking like an understander. But the issue is one of nuance. Does Kohut's high moral valuation of empathy transform an effort to understand into a dramatically fixed, care-taking posture? Does the analyst persuade the patient that he is a better parent than the biological parents? Are there times in treatment when it would be better if empathy looked like something else?

CONCLUSION

Whatever our theory of the mind, there is no reason to suppose that its *terms* are suitable for any particular patient. People experience themselves dramatically (*cf.* Schafer, 1970b). A theory of the mind is not a drama. Theory is there to help the therapist, not the patient. It may help the therapist to focus on important configurations. It may alert him to hierarchies of significance. But life experience is too rich to be captured in an abstract formula. Of all people, it is the psychotherapist who has elected to use the subtlest shades of definition to grasp life's immediacies. How dismal, then, that Kohut and his students are able to point to so many ordinary analyses which can only be characterized as extended sales talks for a theoretical schematism. Always present, perhaps, persuasion was never particularly welcome in psychoanalysis, except persuasion to be brave.

It stands to reason that a degree of stubbornness is needed to work on a subject so famous for its wiles as human desire. But that steadfastness should go to one's theoretical guidelines, not to one's perceptions and communications. There is nothing in classical theory that says exactly how an oedipal defeat will feel in an atmosphere of percepts, concepts, affects, moods, imagos, dramas, and strivings peculiar to a given patient. There must be as many varieties of oedipus complex as there are families. Theory does not need to wring a credo from a patient's lips.

I have argued that empathy is not some knowledge before knowledge. It does not provide a theory-free description. But in making so much of it, Kohut does remind us of the plasticity and receptiveness that is supposed to distinguish psychotherapists—their effort to accommodate their pre-existing mental and affective models as closely as possible to those of a new patient, and of a patient at a new moment.

Of course we must have our cognitive structures. My point is that we should have a great many of them. The fewer the intervening forms between a theoretical paradigm and a communication to the patient, the less likely we are to capture his reality and convey our own. Kohut's forms should be judged by their usefulness (as Kohut asks [see Kohut, 1978, pp. 435, 750, 891-892, 928].) After all, there is no precise way to map theory onto felt experience. If a patient accomplishes more by dwelling on what he wanted from his father than on his fear of him, he may, for all we know, be working free of a fear in that way. Kohut came to think of his theory as a radically new paradigm. But he deliberately left us the option of seeing many things his way without giving up our other ways of seeing them.

27

The Common Thread:

Holism

A theoretician today may regard personhood as an explanatory term rather than a tacit assumption. This kind of thinker gives more attention to main directions and less to partial aims. He dwells on formative processes rather than on persisting sectors of the mind. He speaks of wishes and meanings, not energies and discharge. The significance of a striving is more visible to him in its mature apotheosis than in its rude beginning. Consequently, he is more interested in how meanings change than in how they started. He doubts that psychoanalysis is a natural science. He borrows methods and even whole branches of knowledge directly from the Humanities at least as often as he applies analysis to the Humanities. In his descriptions, treatment looks more creative and less uncovering, less surgically authoritative and more a groping for perspective.

At least some of the spirit of this trend, if not each characteristic, is captured by Kohut, Schafer, Loewald, Gill, Lacan, Leavy, George Klein, and the representational world school (e.g., Stolorow). Of all current trends, this one seems especially humanistic, in the academic sense of that word, and we naturally wonder why humanism should have such a current influence. Is humanism, in fact, what inspires the trend? Or have these theories been piled into a humanistic corner by some other theoretical breeze?

These are hard questions, because the traits we notice seem to be old ones. They are foreshadowed in Freud's theory. And each has been emphasized by one or another venerable tradition. The history of psychoanalysis seems more a random migration than a march, both over time and around the world. Everything was there once before; and everything has been there continuously in some circle or other.

Why does a humanism come up again, now, in the mainstream of North American psychoanalysis? In what way is it new? What does it portend?

Tracing the path of theory is a task of staggering complexity, and I emphasize this here because I may seem to ignore it in what follows. I believe that conceptual clarity requires that, before looking at external influences, we squeeze all we can from the assumption that theory grows as a "next step" out of previous theory. Until we know to what extent that is true, we cannot know what other explanations we need.

In North America, until very recently, Heinz Hartmann represented the mainstream of psychoanalytic innovation. Hartmann's attention to certain problems pre-empted other approaches. His influence seems to have made the difference between earlier and later humanistic trends. While his work is almost universally esteemed, humanist theory often defines itself by taking what seems to be an alternative position, or rebelling against what is thought to be Hartmann's approach. Consequently, the humanistic aspect of current thought might be illuminated by placing it in relation to Hartmann's work. I suggest that Hartmann's goals were unsettling and that much of his achievement is often covertly used against him.

Hartmann is hard to discuss in the same way that Freud is hard to discuss. Although a system-builder, he was not a simplifier. He could not turn a blind eye to anything a reasonable man should be aware of, even though it might inconvenience his system. Nevertheless, we must try to find his central concern in order to trace his influence on subsequent theory.

Hartmann is generally credited with fastening psychoanalysis to biology in two ways: through instinct and through inborn apparatuses. We think of him as a natural scientist studying man's adaptation to the natural environment and showing how Freudian theory accounts for this by postulating mixtures of aggressive and sexual energies. And at the same time, we know that his wisdom cannot be reduced to a few clichés. Hardly an objection can be made to his popular image that he himself did not anticipate and make his own. Not being an ideologue, he seems to have found all the reasonable positions. But clearly he did have a central concern.

Consider Hartmann's (1958) argument in *Ego Psychology and the Problem of Adaptation* that includes the following passage:

> Actions, therefore, always imply intentions, acts of will, motives, etc. on the one hand, and (mental and physical) apparatuses on the other. Thus far investigators have paid little attention to the role of these apparatuses in the possibility, direction, success, and development of action [p. 100]).

What kind of theory pays little attention to the role of apparatuses in governing action? Hartmann tells us that it is a theory in which the "automatic character of the id" does not have to contend with any "structure and formedness" in the mind.

What would such a theory look like? A theory that neglected apparatuses would depict all mental products as defined by wishes. It would emphasize the unifying power of Freudian theory. In such an account, the constraints that mold wishes are the absolute fewest—wish is free to take whatever form it will.

That may have been a working model for some early practitioners, but it was never psychoanalytic theory. And by the time of Hartmann's book, ego psychology was well on its way. By that time, no one could ignore the old principle that wishes and fears produce a constant grid which adds meaning to momentary wishing.

Why was Hartmann not satisfied with that? Because he knew that defensive structures are not the only constraints imposed on wishes. There are also other mental characteristics which wishes have to reckon with. The mind has a nature to begin with.

This was not a new thought. Psychoanalysis is not spiritualism; it is the study of the mind as a thing—a biological thing, to be exact (chapter 14). Was it, then, Hartmann's mission simply to *extend* this biological comparison—to put the mind under the laws of adaptation and evolution that rule other organisms?

Contemporary biology was important to Hartmann. But adaptation is not the technical term it seems, when it is used as generally as Hartmann used it. He did not focus narrowly on avoidance of death or on reproductive success. His work is not filled with evolutionary speculation. He used the term in a more common-sense way. He reminds us how handicapped we would be without each of our human inclinations, even those we regard as vulnerabilities. He knew that human adaptation has mostly to do with the *human* environment. Adaptation thus comes down to being fully human. By emphasizing that "adaptedness" is relative not to the environment per se, but to an evolutionarily expectable environment, Hartmann implicitly made a point that is often inverted: adaptation is the preservation of an organism's character. If we think of the entity as mortal, the measure of adaptation is survival. If it is mind we refer to, adaptation means continuity of function. If the entity is a given organization of mind, adaptedness means being able to hold on to as much of it as possible. (Hartmann's way of saying this is that synthesis is equivalent to adaptedness.)

Hartmann is often cited when discussing man's need for external support, or his capacity to mold to the environment, or his ability to muddle through if given half a chance. Despite Rapaport's (1960b) exegesis, people often lose sight of the stubborn, proprietary aspect of adaptation.

In fact, adaptedness does not refer to the impact *of* the world. It refers to the imprint the mind puts *on* the world. The term, "average expectable environment," has only general roots in biology, anthropology, or evolution. In Hartmann's writings it is most elaborated in his definition of normalcy. Where is the average expectable environment to be found? Not on this or that continent, in this or that village. It is the shape of the soul. It is another name for the nature of Man. It specifies the set of meanings into which life's adventures will inevitably be placed. The average expectable environment is the broad, a priori gestalt of experience.

Well, then, if Hartmann did not judge mechanisms of defense to be sufficient structure, and if he did not intend to import anything very technical or specific from biology, what *was* his aim?

We recall that he said we should pay more attention to apparatuses. Apparatuses are constraints on intention. Here is Hartmann's message: there are more constraints on thinking and volition than analysts sometimes acknowledge. The mind is complex and is not uniformly amenable to one simple kind of understanding.

Defenses are not the only forms to which a mental action must shape itself. Even if we think of motives as including defenses, we still cannot ask a person, for example, why he chooses to see only in straight lines and not around corners. We cannot ask him why he reacts to events as though they occur in three dimensions, or why his superego responds to voices and not to ultraviolet rays. We cannot ask these questions, expecting to hear a wish or a concealment confess itself.

But that is not the whole story. The famous apparatuses of primary autonomy are only the most conspicuous unwilled constraints. Hartmann was just as interested in the brute facts that *develop* in the mature mind as he was in those that are set up at the beginning. The mind is designed to reason, but also, at times, not to reason. The plan that underlies the *variability* of our responses is as much a reflection of human nature as are the constants of vision. Our social and theological gods, our art and culture, are absolutely needed for our minds to work, whatever may be their origins in wishes.

Hartmann knew he was adding additional *influences* to the Freudian motives. But he also saw these nonintentional factors as a *way of looking at* the mind—a different *type* of meaning—the adaptational "point of view." He showed us that we can give more than one meaning, for example, to a social belief. It can have the meaning of its genesis, including drive and defense, and it can *also* have the meaning of an orienting point for assimilating experience. A social belief can have these two meanings (among others) for the person who holds it. And we who observe that person can give the belief both meanings if we choose.

By adding more constraints on intention, Hartmann complicated the story of mentation twice over. He added constraints as causal inputs and also constraints as different meanings. And he then crowned the ambiguity with the in-between term, "function." A function is a *meaning* of a psychic action besides the meaning provided by its history, and it is also a *performance* by the psyche and thus a causal influence on other actions, alongside the influence of instinct. "Function" reminds us that we now have on our hands not just the problem of connecting Freudian causes with other causes (for example, instinct with optical reactivities), we also have the problem of collating different types of explanatory *principles* into a unified theory. Rapaport (e.g., 1960) seems to have been aware that this might open a chasm within Freudian theory. As regards causality, he and Hartmann managed to couple "functions" to energy and stretched this hybrid across the chasm. As regards levels of meaning, however, Hartmann's "ego" remained vulnerable to George Klein's (1976) critique: nothing but its name covered the assorted explanations, meanings, and motives within it.

Hartmann was responding to a theoretical need of the times. It was the same need that inspired Waelder's (1930) essay, "The Principle of Multiple Function." Rubinton (1980) found that in four principal psychoanalytic journals from 1974 to 1979, Waelder's paper was the third most frequently cited pre-1940 source, after Anna Freud's *The Ego and the Mechanisms of Defense* and Hartmann's *Ego Psychology and the Problem of Adaptation*. It is not hard to see the nature of its relevance. Using terms characteristic of today's humanism, Waelder's paper is a reminder that there are many ways to make meaning out of a mental event, even within psychoanalytic theory. Waelder dealt with mental apparatuses as abstract designations for interests, or points of view, or meanings that can be read into or out of a mental event.

Hartmann showed how many constraints a mind is responsive to. Constraints are determiners or definers. To set out as many constraints as possible is to point out how many meanings something can have, or how many ways it can be analyzed. By using the phrase, "multiple appeal," Hartmann makes us think of meanings as though they were guided past magnetic influences on all sides. Waelder's phrase, "multiple function," expresses this more abstractly: a concrete mental event is analyzable into many abstract predicates. ("Function" is not as ambiguous in Waelder as it is in Hartmann.) Waelder is more philosophical, Hartmann more biological. Waelder talked of meanings; Hartmann seems to dissect anatomy. Essentially, they were calling attention to the same thing, and their similar popularity probably indicates how much this corrective was needed.

Waelder was a prophet. He saw that it was precisely Freud's ability to encompass the fullness of meaning within his theory that set him above the neo-Freudians who singled out one or another perfectly valid meaning as their only concern. But no matter how elastic it may be, a theory must have some point of view or it is no theory, and Waelder pointed out that, while psychoanalysis recognizes an infinity of meanings in human behavior, it also postulates what he called the "ontological primacy" of meanings derived from Freudian instincts.

So although in his paper Waelder did not try to connect all meanings to the Freudian ones by energic formulas, as Hartmann did, he was concerned in his own way to keep the terms of Freudian analysis paramount among the many perspectives on the mind it is possible to take.

From a very different perspective Balint (1937) also sought to introduce other determinants of meaning besides the automatic character of the id. The idea of libido unfolding its own meanings seemed to him plainly senseless and contrary to the evidence. For Balint, meaning was created in interaction with the world and especially with early care-givers. Like Hartmann, he felt that ego apparatuses put their stamp on meanings. But he also used Melanie Klein's view to add dimension. Why, we wonder, did he do that? Klein's "objects" were not Balint's. She described an epigenetic unfolding of fantasy, much as Abraham described an unfolding of libido types. If in both cases the meaning comes from inside, why should Balint find Klein rewarding and Abraham misguided?

I think that what the object-relations people take from Melanie Klein is not objects, but *situations* (see Segal [1967] on Kleinian fantasy). She used only very abstract wish forms (love and destruction)—much more abstract than libidinal vicissitudes. She described the rest of mental content as situations in which the child feels himself to be involved. It is her phenomenology that makes Klein valuable to the object-relationists, all the way down to Kohut. I think they celebrate her for changing theory of the mind from an explanation in terms of wishes into a demonstration of situations. Fairbairn carried explanation by situation to its extreme (see Guntrip, 1961, p. 279). With him, even the founding act of internalization is not considered to be programmed: it is invented by a person in order to handle a situation sensibly.

If we are dealing with a dramatic interaction among imagos, we can analyze it in many different ways, just as we can a real social event. All these theories have this in common: they expose the field of psychological explanation to a heterogeneous list of possible accounts.

Freudian theory does offer a common thread which links situational theories to tradition: it is the theme of internalization. Internalization makes the vague, uncharted world of situations familiar while it is being explored by the new humanists, just as it did for the older situationists. No wonder, then, that Schafer (1968) used *Aspects of Internalization* to try to finally ease the strains within the Hartmann tradition. Like Hartmann, Schafer said that representations are orienting points for motives. But unlike Hartmann, Schafer also implied that representations help to *define* motives. Representations seem to be both embodiments of aims and also the rocks and shoals through which aims navigate.

Here is how Schafer made visible the fundamental difficulty in Hartmann's theory: he accepted the principle that the mind cannot be reduced to one parochial type of meaning. But he also realized that other types of meaning cannot be given second-class status as "functions." He therefore tried to describe structuring in the uniform, all-embracing terms of motives and ideas. But it turned out that even this distinction is arbitrary; there is no fixed boundary between motives and ideas. In his effort to clarify the work of those who tried to hook up multiple meanings to specific Freudian meanings, Schafer revealed that there was no way to carve up a field like that for display. This conclusion was actually welcomed by the theorists of the representational world, for they imagine that we have a choice between being realistic and being theoretical.

But Schafer had a more profound response to his own work. He recognized that the anatomy of mind could not be illustrated in universal terms and that the subject which had all meanings within it was just The Person—alive and mentally moving. And he proceeded, with great consistency, to the step that logically follows from *Aspects of Internalization*, which was itself the step that logically followed from Hartmann. Schafer proposed to take human action as his subject matter and to turn his attention to the ways that meaning is abstracted from it.[1] It is, then, no accident that Schafer ended up with the most explicitly situational psychology in the psychoanalytic tradition.

Kohut (1977), on the other hand, compromised between a single-perspective psychology and a psychology of situations, first by supposing that what is internalized is not situations but their significance and, second, by describing that significance in terms so abstract that they encompass all possible meanings.

Lacan (1977a, 1977b) is the one humanist who *explicitly* regarded himself as Hartmann's opponent. Yet Lacan repeatedly implied that desire is subject to multiple constraints. Although he visualized those constraints in their linguistic incarnation—desire submitting itself to language—in point of fact, language sums up all of the social reality (and physical reality insofar as that is defined) through which desire must be objectified. It would be fair to say that language represents for Lacan all the interests and meanings that Hartmann felt were overlooked in a purely intentional psychoanalysis.

Finally, Loewald's (1980) ingenious organismic theory of the mind is another example of an apparent reaction to Hartmann that is in fact a continuation of his work. Hartmann (1927) can be read as arguing against

---

[1] Schafer (1970a), like the other authors mentioned, sees his relationship to Hartmann quite differently from the way it is described here. In his elegant appreciation of Hartmann's work, Schafer portrayed him as holding psychoanalysis to a consistent biological vantage point, thus making the options clearer and paving the way for Schafer to decide not to deal with psychoanalytic data from a natural science perspective. Schafer accepted "adaptation" as specifically, albeit vaguely, biological, the focus of an exclusive point of view that is different, for example, from a sociological approach. He therefore took Hartmann at his word when he claimed to bypass questions of self, intentionality, and meaning. Hartmann, however, realized that adaptation is largely to a man-made world, and it is hard to see what dimension of meaning can be excluded from such a vantage point.

Binswanger that the mind is not just meaning, but an organism, and so it cannot simply be *translated*, any more than an organism can be translated. Furthermore, Hartmann's notion of adaptation implies that the mind is like an organism: its variability in response to contingent circumstances, its effort to conserve its evolutionarily determined nature wherever it finds itself, the inter-relatedness of all of its parts, etc., are all aspects of an organism. The reference to apparatuses and fueling that characterizes Hartmann's terminology, makes Loewald's more explicit and consistent organism theory seem to be a radical departure from Hartmann's tradition, but it is really an extension of it.

Hartmann had tried to satisfy the demands of holism while protecting North America from holism's skeptical implications. No longer carefully titrated by his compromise, the full force of what I have called the new humanism is now felt by us. But Hartmann's work was not just a delaying action: it left a mark on holist theory. The holists who follow him respect Freudian schemata and insist that, no matter how open a situation may be to multiple interpretations, man has a shaped nature which constrains his volition, whether it be called language or the bipolar self.

I will now turn to speculations about consequences.

Freud's theory divided the mind into parts. By parts, I mean enduring, specific interests which endeavor to persist within a unity. Freudian structures are meanings relevant to conflict: they have little significance except in opposition to each other. By their conflict they can be referred to without knowing their details. The details can be supplied by the individual. Conflict serves as ostensive definition in Freudian theory.

When theory discards this way of picking out data and reaches for total meaning in the form of gross situations, the divided mind aspect of Freudian theory slips away, and its process aspect comes to the fore. The process aspect takes the form of a maturational continuum, a spectrum from undifferentiated to differentiated psychological form. Without the dialectical tension between the synthetic function on the one hand, and conflicting structural interests, on the other, there is nothing to prevent mind from becoming completely homogenized (chapter 15). The humanistic trend is humanistic because it is holistic.

The old conflict analyst had a clear treatment assignment: stand impartial among conflicting factions! The holistic therapist has got to find an equivalent stance that makes sense on his own terms. His stance has to foster growth of meanings—meanings that are not necessarily apparent, since they are not discriminated by internal self-contradiction. The therapist must adopt a practical style that will, in the first place, discriminate meanings and, in the second place, help to develop them.

I would say that putting a meaning on a situation amounts to taking up an *attitude*. Humanists, in effect, talk about how patient and analyst adopt attitudes toward themselves and therapy.

In actual practice, the old hunt for conflict continues, supported by the older theory which remains in the background. But in the foreground, the newer theories replace conflict-hunting with a study of attitudinal options – the dramatic forms that situations can be cast into, their internal logic and intertranslation. The new humanism has made us see that there is no human reality free from attitudes.

Attitudes are undeliberate interpretations. In our attitudes we do not see a situation as classifiable in a certain way: we see the situation *as* a certain sort of situation. The humanist tradition has sent us back to the elementary question of what decides the analyst's attitudes. So far, we have been given mostly prolegomena: we have been shown the kinds of meaning that *can* be extracted from a situation, the variety of metaphors and dramatic structures that are available. That is valuable, but it leads inevitably to the next question: How, *in fact*, does the analyst extract meaning? What are the determinants of his perception: A process theory forces this question on us more vigorously than does a conflict theory, which has built-in principles of definition. (Actually the problem of definition is always there for those who want to see it.) A process theory bravely stirs up tough questions about the perceptual psychology of the analyst. To answer these questions we will have to go far beyond what we are accustomed to call countertransference. We will probably have to consider how theory affects our watching people. We should see whether intellectual vulnerabilities and affective fascinations select our perceptions. We will want to know what gives the analyst a sense of conviction.

The humanist is wary of dogmatism. He knows that meaning is always creatively produced anew. To grasp such creative meaning, he finds it reasonable to cultivate his tastes, or his apperceptive appetites, instead of fashioning theoretical stencils to lay on his subject. Tastes might include, for instance, appreciation of esthetic modes, or the empathic appeal of a certain kind of situation. These may be ways a therapist interactively models meanings he does not quite know yet, a cardinal task for pluralistic meaning developers.

But we will not be satisfied with an account of how the therapist's attitudes are formed. We want to know why those attitudes are useful. Psychotherapists try to be imaginative, but they do not want to be simply imagining. We mean to capture reality in our perceptions.

The analytic community is scared by the nimbus of relativism and poetizing which clings to these theories. Not only does it threaten the practitioner's self-respect as a knower; it leaves him vulnerable to the old accusation that he operates by persuasion and the far more serious accusation that he is operated on *by* the patient.

Persuasion seemed most dangerous to psychoanalysts when science was thought to build up abstractions from neutral data. Deviating from that data meant that one had stopped elucidating and had started propagandizing.

Psychoanalysts therefore had to disown all the influence that a personal relationship inevitably brings. But these days, science is more commonly viewed as a particularly well worked out perspective in which the difference between hypotheses and data is not that great, and progress is achieved by a process similar to persuasion. Now it should be easier to come to terms with persuasion in psychoanalysis. The humanist study of metaphor and narrative shows this greater comfort with the role of persuasion.

Still, science is not rhetoric. The psychoanalyst has a theory that reassures him that his attitudes are neither manipulations nor gullibilities. It holds that underneath the patient's artful persuasiveness is a set of meanings which, although the patient cannot express it, is nevertheless already articulated in some way, and so, if the analyst's attitude corresponds to that hidden articulation, he will not have imposed anything, nor will he have been imposed upon (see chapter 34).

But it is precisely this pre-existing articulation that holism has challenged. What kind of articulation can the humanist call upon to ground *his* attitudes?

One of Schafer's (1970b, 1979) answers is typical. (It is not his only answer.) Along with some philosophers of history, he avoids skepticism by listing an exhaustive set of attitudes which ring all the changes. Formally, at least, if the analyst's attitudes are complete, they cannot be biased, arbitrary, or tendentious. This sort of validation supposes that the very nature of human aspiration traces a limited number of perceptible patterns. Aspiration is a trying for something in a not completely amenable world. Schafer's vision of reality implies a struggle with the environment—a struggle with only so many possible outcomes. The same may be said for Kohut's ambitions and ideals.

Intrapsychic conflict no longer carves up the phenomenal pie, but in another way, conflict still defines meanings. The humanist tradition takes Freud's medium-sized dramas and middle-level choices, and generalizes their agonistic structure. On the one hand, this agonistic framework is expanded into the largest dramatic emplotment of a human life. On the other hand, it is found in the smallest, commonest treatment transaction.

Indeed, we owe some of the renewed interest in therapeutic action to humanist study of the *general process* of meaning formation, steadily at work among the changing issues that occupy attention. For instance, a humanist will tell us that psychic reality changes when it is viewed differently. Lakoff and Johnson (1980) have recently argued that action is intrinsically metaphorical, and, therefore, change of metaphor (for example, the metaphor, "argument is war") will change the act (for example, argument might become a game). The broadest rationale for treatment is the provision of new opportunities, and because process theory is so broad, it calls on that rationale regularly.

Schafer (1979), for instance, aims to develop new possibilities for feeling autonomy; thus the patient is kept reexamining himself. But the patient does not want to see himself so variously; new perspectives happen because new *questions* arise. Schafer should tell us how those powerful questions are made to arise in treatment. Such questions are undoubtedly felt as problems, and that takes us, I think, beyond a literary perspective. We would especially expect an action psychology to deal with successes and failures as molders of meaning. Actions – even intrapsychic actions – are not performed in order to be observed.

Kohut's model more explicitly leans out of the humanistic framework. He proposes that the analyst's attitudes act as a lattice for the growth of a rough, preordained meaning – a meaning which makes an aspiration useful.

I make this point because it seems to me that the same humanism which is so stimulating to treatment theories can take a cloistered form which may make us completely forget about therapeutic action. Its civility tends to bleach out of theory what is most familiar in practice: wanting, fighting, discomfort, the push and pull of strong compulsion.

The best humanistic psychoanalysts realize that the models and metaphors and narrative stuctures that most need to be talked about are not the ones that come out of the patient's mouth or the ones that nestle in the analyst's head, but the ones that are enacted by these two people together.

Whether they make treatment look like simple clarification (as Schafer's does), or gentle acceptance (as in Kohut), or even a consistent evasion (as Lacan makes it seem), at some point all these theories imply that a meaning is not simply made *of* the patient, but that the patient is enveloped in an interaction with the analyst which *causes* him to develop new meanings. That implication needs to be elaborated.

In order to be useful to the theory of treatment, this school must study not only how meanings are encoded and deciphered, but why they change. If, for example, metaphor or model or narrative form determines meaning, we must require the humanist to tell us how, in the consulting room, a struggle over attitudes changes metaphor or model or narrative form. And I would guess that, for an answer, he would have to turn to empirical studies of conspicuous transformation of meaning, such as the history of scientific theory shift and the vast area of infant and child development.

One resource might be Piaget's theory, because it has such power to explain how purposeful effort inadvertently changes schemata. By slinging a ball at a target, a child learns some principles of physics, and therewith, something about his actions, something about his principles, and something about the target (Piaget, 1978). Perhaps a patient acquires an analogous comprehension when he tries to establish attitudes in his therapist and records achievements in terms of the therapist's reactions. Perhaps the therapist serves as an experimental reagent, whose evoked attitudes allow the patient to discover more and richer meanings and aims, a more integrated self, and more various affordances in his companions.

COMMENT

There are dangers in the process approach. If the old conflict theory were to disappear altogether, the therapeutic atmosphere might lose its peculiar blend of enticement and elusiveness, familiarity and estrangement, security and uncertainty.

If theory no longer studied a natural entity—a real, unknown substrate of action—the therapist would no longer be in touch with a central someone that the patient does not yet feel himself to be (cf. Loewald, 1960). To the therapist's ear would come only persuasive narratives and perhaps an over-whelming temptation to settle for a story.

Without conflict to assign him the humble role of impartial umpire, a humanist therapist might take on airs of nurturing mother, superior parent, or clever artificer.

These dangers are distant because Freud's theory will not quickly disappear.

As a supplement to Freudian theory, the new view offers us these considerable services: it reminds us that psychoanalysis is a matter of attitudes; it forces us to admit that, since meanings are made and not found, we have to face up to the nature of therapeutic influence; and finally, it encourages us to increase our stock of interactive appetites with which to pick out different meanings from the clinical field.

There are ultimately two great spurs to change: the sense of conflict and the sense of promise. They are as necessary for the freshness of the therapist's perception as for the patient's improvement. The humanists have found conflict too restrictive, and we may or may not agree with them on that score. But the therapist cannot lose if he cultivates many rather than few appetites and increases his susceptibility to configurations that will automatically engage him with some excitement. Theory is what gives him permission to become excited: the humanist trend expands his permission.

After all, and whatever language is used, in the final reckoning a patient carries away his own meanings, and a wide vocabulary of schemata makes it likelier that some of these will have been shared by his therapist.

SUMMARY

What looks at first to be mainly a humanistic trend in current psychoanalytic theory, on closer inspection turns out to be the later stage of a movement that started out in the 1930's with the intent of gathering into psychoanalytic theory all of the meanings that can be made out of a mental event.

In North America, Hartmann led that movement, but with such care not to let his holism dissolve the particular terms of Freudian theory that his holistic successors, who are less concerned about the theoretical framework, see themselves as moving in a different direction.

Since the newer holism is committed to a plurality of meanings, it has brought us closer to that aspect of treatment that *chooses* meanings—in other words, the analyst's *attitudes*. This is especially useful since, in practice, holism supplements rather than replaces the coherent orientation of Freudian theory.

If holism were to march out on its own, one might worry that psychotherapy would be changed into an esthetic critique, with insufficient attention to the dynamism of the wishes the patient trains on his therapist.

Holism would further its cause by studying the interplay of wish, effort, and meaning.

28

Summary:

The Need to Balance Perception

and Influence

Most of the revisionists I have discussed believed they were responding to philosophical errors in Freud's theory of the mind. I have argued that these philosophical objections to Freud's method are weak. But if that is so, we must wonder why the revisions have burgeoned. Of course, fashions change. But practice is arduous, and it is unlikely that teachings will converge to one focus unless they are drawn there by a demand of treatment. If there is a trend that is not compelled by theoretical necessity, it probably tells us more about the practice of psychotherapy. For we have regularly found that therapists show what their work is and what allows them to do it, by their restless revisions of theory and their repeated squabbles with colleagues. What is the practical outcome of these revisions?

We have seen that the new theories make more treatment-relevant pictures available to the clinician while reducing his authority to rule on them. The way these revisions do that is by their refusal to explicitly describe mental potential.

SYNOPSIS

In Part II, I argued that an important element of psychotherapy is a theory of the mind to which the therapist is dedicated. In Part III, I tried to show what a full theory of mind consists of, and how its completeness helps treatment. In Part IV, we saw how, nevertheless, a wave of holistic revisions rejected those requirements. And so, in this chapter, I speculate about why it is helpful for therapists to omit the very descriptions of mental potential that usually constitute a theory of the mind.

On the face of it, a disdain for hypothetical substrates seems to be part of an effort to get closer to the patient's experience, as though empathy were what the old theory of potentiality interfered with. I will argue that this is not true if we are referring to ordinary empathy. Ordinary empathy is never in danger. There is no special, private datum for it to pick up; the mind is through and through a mixture of public and private meanings. And ordinary empathy is not always therapeutic in its implications. It cannot be that the older theories of potentiality were rejected because they interfered· with ordinary empathy; it is not *that* empathy which the holists are seeking.

The holist revisionists are probably attempting to cultivate the special empathy that therapists employ. I argue that this empathy is not a peculiarly accurate perception of human meaning, nor is it access to purely private experience. Rather, it is a view of some part of a patient's experience as unavoidable because of its connection with the rest of his experience.

I propose that a therapeutic empathic focus is designed to make the therapist feel that he is viewing something in his patient that is already laid out in an inescapable form, while in fact what he sees is a movement that he has induced. Intense therapeutic empathy thus allows the therapist to remain naive of his manipulations fostering integration. I suggest that this is a necessary part of the therapist's psychology, accompanying whatever more complete theoretical apparatus he brings to bear.

The therapist needs to feel that he is seeing and not doing. That need is interfered with by a full theory of the mind, because a full theory, such as Freud's, outlines *other* ways that the patient could see himself and *other* ways that the therapist could see him. Because diagrams of potentiality induce in the therapist a kind of skepticism about any given appearance of the patient and any convenient image of what he is doing to the patient, such diagrams interfere with a sense of passive perception. Therefore, the newer, truncated theories omit reference to potentiality (and do not constitute full theories of the mind).

The therapist's empathic sense of *witnessing* change draws his attention to underlying continuities inside his patient and away from the rules that govern change. If therapist and patient assume that mental happenings are self-explanatory when properly tuned in on, they will be relatively less interested in how one mental happening is related to another. Immediate transformations, of course, will be attended to, but they will be experienced as part of an extended present awareness, as one large, introspective atom, so to speak. Some simple sequences may be acknowledged (such as disappointment leading to depression). But that is not where the focus of interest will lie.

Even Kohut, whose mixed system includes "experience-distant" hypotheses, insisted that those hypotheses had to be an expansion of experience, not a correlation of experience with something outside it, of the sort, for example, that infant observers chart.

HOLISM LEADS TO MORE PHENOMENOLOGICAL FORMS AND LESS ANALYST AUTHORITY

What is the practical outcome of these revisions? Here are two conspicuous results: (1) Theorists grant psychoanalytic significance to more meanings, to a wide variety of human situations, and in some cases, to an open-ended range of forms. (See chapters 19 and 27.) (2) Impressed with more types of meaning, the analyst's own familiar patterns lose their authority, and the patient's descriptions become more definitive.

These results are produced by a shift in theory. What type of theory moves in this direction? The predominant feature of these revisions is holism—the doctrine that the mind has no real divisions. Holism permits innumerable defined situations to be affiliated to theory. A holistic theory offers the least resistance to any proposed meaning because it has no status to give or to deny to any partial meaning. (In the original version of this summary [Friedman, 1985], I spelled out how each of the revisionists discussed in Part 4 developed a form of holism, granting significance to more situations and decreasing the analyst's defining authority. If my generalizations here strike the reader as arbitrary, I invite him to consult the details in that paper.)

HOLISM WORKS BY SHUNNING POTENTIALITY

A full theory of the mind, such as Freud's, identifies an entity with multiple potentialities that are described as parts (chapters 15 and 16). Structural theory describes the invisible but present source of what only happens later, or could have happened under other conditions. That is what potentiality means, and that is what theory of the mind describes. The new revisions all propose a greater number of visible situational forms for the therapist to work with—actual forms that can be spotted as they appear. In doing this, these theories neglect to characterize potentiality, that is, the unseen, enduring core of the person that has the power to make him different in different circumstances. The new theories try to connect the therapist with what is concretely experienced, and, to the extent that they succeed, they are powerless to describe what *can* happen, or what *has not* happened, or what one *wishes* would happen. (Incidentally, a refusal to describe potentiality is the essence of object relations theory, which therefore has every right to boast that it is what we are seeing in current trends.)

Needless to say, all theorists use a full theory of the mind when they treat people. They have to have a sense of people's dispositions and proclivities. And that means that all theorists have at least a tacit belief about the nature of potentiality. These beliefs about potentiality can be gleaned from the therapist's expectations, revealed in their clinical attitudes and interventions. Their implicit theories of the mind are often different from their written theoretical accounts. All the more remarkable and demanding of our respect is the effort of theorists to purge their thoughts of detailed reflections about specific potentiality, i.e., the persistent characteristics which determine a person's choices. These theorists are moving away from blunt statements of potentiality, such as "A conflict between these two wishes has been enshrined in such-and-such a defense, and thus prevents a discharge of aggression in response to such-and-such a provocation and such-and-such a fear." A statement like that names wishes, defenses, and aggression, none of which can be directly experienced. Depending on the outcome of the conflict, the same wishes and defenses and fears could be expressed in many *different* experiences. By means of such a description, a later, different experience can be related to a present core constitution. And what might have made possible a change that never took place can be described in terms of present dispositions. Statements of potentiality also include lawlike patterns showing the way that transformations take place. In contrast, the newer theories try to liberate perception from prejudicial expectations about potential change, and potentiality therefore has been swept under the theoretical rug (often with the excuse that it is a metaphysical matter). "Laws of thought" are then regarded as pompous imposters that do not really belong in the psychological domain.

Examples

Gendlin's (1964) theory is the best example of this enforced muteness on the subject of potentiality. In his account, there are no standing powers and mechanisms; only actual experience is described (see chapter 22). Levenson is also enigmatic on the score of potentiality. *The Fallacy of Understanding* (1972) presents a structuralist theory, and so it does not dismiss potentiality as an indescribable process of "development" of meaning, as process theorists do. But that refusal leaves potentiality even more problematic: in Levenson's account, actuality would seem to be all there is, and the reader is given little reason to hope that treatment can change anyone (see chapter 21). George Klein (1976) does not diagram potentiality. He does not show us an anatomy of the mind which could work this way or that. Potentiality is just alluded to. It is just whatever is at stake for the organism (that being the principle of equilibrium [see chapter 23]). On an explicit level, Schafer (1983b) simply avoids the issue. (He distinguishes between a mind with the potential to change and one without, but he has nothing further to say about the distinction [1973b, p. 283].) Theoretical commitments concerning potentiality are implicated in his practice, but they are not sayable in terms of his theory (see chapter 33).

Within Peterfreund's (1971) information-processing theory, the sum total of the component programs would seem to provide an explicit account of potentiality, but in fact what gives his model its "hard science" sheen is precisely his insistence on dealing only with actualities and leaving the real questions of potentiality undiscussed. The real locus of potentiality—what *can* happen, whether or not it *does* happen—is represented in his theory by the range of flexibility of the highest order program that determines the fate of the subprograms. He does not discuss that further (see chapter 18). The representational world school is almost a deliberate effort to reduce all that is real to what is actual (see chapter 19). Kohut (1971, 1977) alone, because his theory is an amalgam, does provide an account of potentiality, and it is probably for that reason that his new forms (conjoined as they are with specific *possible developments*) have turned out to be so extremely useful (see chapter 34).

WHAT IS THE ADVANTAGE IN BEING INEXPLICIT ABOUT POTENTIALITY?

My purpose here is not to criticize theories but to learn what treatment difficulties they answer to. If it is true that theorists have been trying to raise more configurations to analytic respectibility, and if they have been trying to diminish the analyst's defining authority, we would want to know what in the treatment task has demanded that movement. But we have an even harder question when we notice that these theories have neglected to describe potentiality. It is intuitively understandable that a therapist wants to recognize many relationships and forms of feeling. And it is intuitively obvious that a therapist is better off exercising modest self-restraint in labeling what happens in the consulting room. But it is not so obvious why a therapist would be better off without a theory of specific potentiality. Why stop referring to underlying reasons for what happens and to reasons for what could but does not happen? It is hard to see the advantage in avoiding the kind of theory that originally gave therapists their subtle perceptiveness. When psychoanalysis was born, states of mind seemed to be enriched by connecting them with other states of mind, actual or potential. The theory of the unconscious made trivial phenomena exciting by linking them to other states through newly discovered principles of transformation. A detailed theory of potentiality made *everything* about the mind more interesting and was unquestionably responsible for recruiting a new profession. While it may be hard to see what advantage there is in dropping such theory, there is probably some advantage or it would not be happening.

DO IMAGES OF POTENTIAL INTERFERE WITH EMPATHY?

On the face of it, this collection of revisions seems to be a rebellion against the analyst's overconfidence in his own definitions – definitions which reduce his perceptual forms to a monotonous few and estrange him from the patient's subjective reality. Is that the reason for getting rid of descriptions of potential? Is the analyst less sensitive to personal nuances if he carries around pictures of defined potentiality, which are "seen" by him but not immediately experienced by the patient (for example, a dynamic formulation or a metapsychological explanation)? But it is not evident that "knowing" how the mind works gets in the way of the analyst's perception. After all, these theoretical "prejudices" about the mind call attention to perceptions that might otherwise be ignored – and they are eagerly sought by all practitioners for that purpose. Even when preconceptions are used "reductively" in speculating about a patient, it is not clear how they interfere with the analyst's *perception*. One can worry that an analyst's *imagination* is limited by a theory that tells him how to sort his perceptions. But since he has got to have his perceptions before he can sort them, his awareness cannot be all that limited by his pictures of potential structure. (Nobody pretends to *see* egos, ids, etc.)

One simply cannot converse without apprehending his partner's situation and without getting close to his meaning. A *fortiori*, no analyst could be in danger of such estrangement. I conclude that schemas of potentiality did not force analysts to see their patients as mere two-dimensional, animated, theoretical phantasms, and we must look elsewhere for the reason that schemas of potentiality have fallen into disfavor.

EMPATHY THAT IS UNIVERSAL CANNOT BE THE GOAL OF THE NEW THEORIES

Even a grotesque, mythically rigid analyst, pledged to a narrow, Procrustean stereotype, would have had to be able to take in an infinite variety of human situations in order to reduce them to his doctrinaire formula. And *just to take them in* requires ample elastic empathy. Why would such an analyst ultimately find himself in need of radical means to enlarge his perceptive capacities? This is the complaint continually put to the self psychologists, and

I am not convinced that the self psychologists have made the most of the challenge.

Ordinary listening requires a much more empathic sense of the speaker's situation than is implied by the stark contrast of conceptual understanding and empathy. A hearer has to empathize with the speaker's intent, social role, psychological frame, immediate history, etc. The speaker has to do the same for his listener (Rommetveit, 1983). Even more interesting is the possibility that meaning is constructed *in the course of* this mutual adjustment (cf. Lichtenberg, 1983, p. 238, in psychoanalysis; Bakhtin [see Morson, 1983] in criticism; and Dore, 1981, in speech theory.)[1]

Kohut and his students have usefully incited a spirited debate about empathy. The question of how little deliberate theory we can get by with in grasping a person's state is an important one (Shapiro, 1981). Self psychologists have rightly demanded that we attend to the contrast between those moments when we seem to be viewing our patient from inside himself and the very different and more ordinary times when we see him as someone in *our* world of objects (Ornstein, 1984; Schwaber, 1981).

In general, however, Kohut's concept implies that empathy is something that *gives* more specific form *to* an experience that is reaching for definition,and is not a replica of a developed state. The question of empathy thus provides an opportunity to scrutinize the fluctuant quality of experience in general—an opportunity that is not always sufficiently appreciated. Theorists of empathy sometimes seem to regard experience as a finished datum: there, it would seem, sits private experience, and the only questions are how accurately and by what means it can be captured, and whether and how it is transmitted.

But reflection suggests that empathy is a *quality* of experienc*ing*, not a reproduction of an already experienced datum. Empathy cannot be defined in terms of its datum. It cannot be a perception of an inner world as opposed to an outer world. It cannot be an accurate image of subjectivity in contrast to a distortion by an objective prism. It cannot be any of these things, because the mind is reflexive: absolutely *all* ways of thinking about someone are also ways that he thinks about himself, and therefore all ways of thinking about someone match up to some part of his experience.

Questions about empathy are not primarily questions about communication or understanding, but about the anatomy of experience itself, whether isolated or communicated. The human mind is a (self-) perceiver, so the distinction of outsider and insider is often beside the point (which is one of

---

[1] This whole question of the relationship between language as a free-standing, propositional code and language as an expressive sign of individual, personal intention has given rise to a rich, ill-tempered literature in philosophy: think of Wittgenstein, Derrida, Gadamer, Ricoeur, Searles, Austin, and many others.

the reasons for a concept such as selfobject). Of course, the *act* of trying to share someone's world has enormous consequences. But there is no special perceptual vocabulary that such an act must use. What we ordinarily consider "distant" and "abstract" categories color a person's intimate experience as influentially as his pleasures and pains. (Consider the category of "heretic" in the old days, and of "narcissistic" in recent ones.) Philosophers have observed that a person's sense of himself is partly made up of how he is experienced by others. People imagine themselves as viewed from another's perspective (Mead, 1934). Along with everything else, the empathizer will therefore partly pick up an "outsider's" view of his subject, since that is already part of the insider's view of himself. Incorporating the outside view of oneself is an act of empathy with the outsiders, while on the other hand, we are often far less "empathic" with ourselves than are the outsiders who love us.

Many theorists have noted that empathy is a style of perception rather than a simple "tuning in." For instance, Shapiro (1981) describes empathy as a gestalt type of experience, and Lichtenberg (1981a) refers to empathy as picking out general aspects of experience rather than partial aspects. Loewald (1960) has the longest record of sifting this feature of empathy for its psychoanalytic significance. As we look for the incentive that inspired theorists to purge potentiality from their writings, it is important not to make the mistake of supposing that the potentiality described by a theory of the mind is, by virtue of its objective pretensions, a veil hiding the mind's subjective state from direct imagery. Such imagery was not what revisionists were seeking.

If we suspect that the theory of the mind, with its elaborate tracery of mental potential, is an impediment to empathy, it is not because theory of the mind makes it harder to see some special, private universe. Rather, theory must make it harder to think about that universe in some special, useful way, and that is the incentive for avoiding detailed reference to mental potentiality.

THE EMPATHY WORRY IS ABOUT HOW THE ANALYST EXPERIENCES THE PATIENT'S INTEGRATING

Every ordinary communication *is* (among other things) the creation of an empathic understanding of oneself in another. People *make* others feel toward them what they want felt. I need no special therapeutic expertise to respond the way someone is trying to make me respond. I suggest that what feels like special therapeutic empathy is not simply experiencing, through vicarious introspection, what the patient experiences through direct introspection: it is experiencing what the patient *might*—and, one hopes, *then does*—experience through introspection. I ask readers to test this assertion by close attention in their own practices.

Ordinarily, we would expect a state of mind to make itself known in its expressions. A conscious state of mind as it is experienced by the subject is close to a publicly available fact (unless dissembled). One of the reasons that empathy seems to be nonconceptual, and "from the inside," is that, in a peculiar sense, it is *not* a reproduction of the subject's actual state of mind, but is what *could* be discovered by him from his actual state of mind, given a different attitude (cf. Lichtenberg's [1981a] concept of an "observation platform"). It is not simply what the patient experiences, and so it is not transmitted in his words. And since it is not transmitted in words, it does not seem to be a public view. The reason that empathy touches on a private, insider fact is precisely that it is ultimately all that a patient *would* experience *if* he were "empathic" with himself: the more empathic with himself he is, the more he sees his total experience as a whole. And *that*, carried to its impossible extreme, would be something that only he could attain. Empathy is extremely private, but only asymptotically. As the name for an imaginary, polar extreme, empathy is a sense of all experience together, past and present. Any particular "empathizing" gets its name from some *degree* of connecting or integrating one aspect of a person's experience with another.

The various meanings of "empathy" have this in common: they refer to the gathering together of aspects of experience as interrelated. Empathy moves from an awareness of a part of a state of mind toward an awareness of the rest of the state with which it blends. In the process, what at first seemed isolated, and to that extent arbitrary, becomes an inseparable aspect of a whole experience, current and past, about which it would make no sense to say that one part could be different. We have all felt this interlocking effect of empathy. (A philosopher would say that empathizing is finding the internal relations that one aspect has with the rest of experience.) To empathize with an aspect of someone's experience is to sense it as inevitable because of its linkage with the rest of that person's experience. Sensing a patient's experience empathically is *sensing it in the mode of inevitability*. That is why empathy comes across as exculpatory, exonerating, and permissive.

Therapeutic empathy therefore confronts us with the difficult fact that experience is partly actual (in its fragmented phenomena) and partly potential (in its unlimited connectedness). It makes us want to say that we understand how a person feels, when it is perfectly clear from what happens next that he did not feel that way at all until we felt it for him, but yet that he feels different because we knew he felt that way already!

WHAT'S WRONG WITH UNEMPATHIC VIEWS IF THEY DO NOT SUFFER FROM INACCURACY?

What, then, shall we say about the outside/inside contrast, the concept/percept contrast, and the extraspection/introspection contrast which have been used to characterize empathy? What, after all, is the polar opposite of empathy? If empathy just designates the accurate grasping of human meaning, only tissue pathology would be unempathic. But we have just decided that this ordinary empathy is not the empathy that is at issue in the new theories. Nobody could have worried that psychoanalysts have been too conceptual and cold-blooded to understand what is said to them. But if there has been a worry about empathy that has contributed to the new theories, what danger was envisioned? What is the opposite pole of the kind of empathy that therapists are currently concerned about?

If, as I have argued, empathy is holistic perception of human meaning, then an unempathic attitude (if it is not simply being nasty or inattentive) would be one that perceives things mainly in terms of choice or decision. An unempathic person is simply one who takes the position that the subject's state of mind could easily be other than it is. And how easy it is to imagine it being immediately different is a measure of how unempathic is the viewer (who may well be the introspecting subject). Notice that, according to this definition, not every view of an act or attitude as flowing from a person's nature is an empathic one, since, like an angry jury condemning a psychopath, the viewer might see the whole person as choosing his life en bloc. In such a pseudoholistic image, the life experiences that make a person what he is are not reckoned into the whole, and the whole life is considered an option, rather than a product of mutually implicating, interlocking, determining, causative experiences and reactive feelings. But this is already a special case, and "unempathic" usually means not realizing that something about a person is inevitable by reason of his specific experiences.

My viewing someone's state as inseparable from his coherent self need not blind me to his feelings of internal conflict and incoherence. Conflict theory differs from holisitc theory, and Freudian attitudes differ from those of our revisionists, according to how they account for conflicted feelings. Freudian theory sees conflict partly as evidence of an uncompleted choice. Holism sees conflict as a defective mental state. Freudian theory allows one to imagine a cathectic shift that could reverse the outcome. (In others words, the theory outlines a specific potential for a different direction.) In contrast, a concerted empathic focus of attention stares at the inevitability of the stalemate (and may backhandedly resolve it in the process).

THERAPEUTIC EMPATHY AS A SENSE OF IMMINENT MOVEMENT

Empathy should be neither dismissed as a fad, nor worshipped as a wonder. In a general sense, it is a ubiquitous feature of human relationships. It is also a name for a concentrated focus of attention attuned to inevitability. When a psychotherapist is intensely empathic, though he has an endless vista of implications and ramifications, he is responding to a *narrow range of options* in the patient's experience and among the roles immediately available to him. Empathy should not be talked away, for instance, by calling it "merely" trial identification, because that makes something which is general and ordinary seem special and technical, as though we explain things by saying them psychoanalytically. Analysts should try to look at their world as much as they can in an ordinary light, adding theoretical concepts only when required. Progress will not come from encapsulating every phenomenon in a safe, old term as soon as it poses a riddle. Analysts should go out of their way to try to make a question show an aspect of theory that has been glossed over or left undeveloped. If psychoanalysis is to be a growing discipline, then, empathy will be used to explain trial identification rather than the reverse, *so that* empathy itself can continue to clamor for clarification.

Nobody would claim that Freudian theory is unempathic in the sense of failing to deal with how a person feels to himself. What the elaborate Freudian hypotheses do is to show paths to other feelings he might have about himself. Freudian theory describes latency and potentiality, not just inevitability and actuality. Potentiality is the roundhouse from which various end points can be reached by an individual. Tracks that are not used are experience-distant insofar as they are not used. But the mind is continually turning back on itself. What is experience-distant can trade places very quickly with what is experience-near. As we have seen, it is a peculiarity of experience that its actuality contains various levels of potentiality, such that someone can say, "That is exactly how I feel, and it wasn't apparent to me until you said it." Psychoanalysis originally claimed its domain by exploiting this odd feature of experience. It has not finished its work. (For example, theories of the preconscious do not abound.)

Arguing about empathy brings into sharp relief questions about the nature of experience that are exciting and disturbing to all psychotherapists. What interconnection and implication can feelings have an instant from now that they do not already have? Does this integration that is immediately available have a single or a foremost pattern? If, instead, an infinity of patterns can be found, do those meanings have an order of priority, as Freudian theory suggests when it refers to "closeness to consciousness"? (See also, the onion-skin analogy in Freud's [1895a, p. 289] model of concentric stratification and Gendlin's [1964] proposal of an implicit order of meaning formation in the experiencing process.) In what sense can we say that a form of wish is paramount when it is not what is closest to consciousness? Interest in empathy inspires us to ask how specified potentiality, in the form of theoretical constructs, can help the analyst to find actualities to empathize with. Do pictures of potentiality help only by providing forms of recognition? Or do they free the analyst from enslavement to the patient's current experience so as to allow other levels of meaning to crystallize?

Since there is a sense in which empathy is ubiquitous while the practical difficulty that inspired new theory must involve some variable, our inquiry requires us to consider relative empathic ability. How should this capacity be described in the terms I have used to describe empathy? What has empathic ability to do with regarding experience as inevitable, whole, and integrated? Of course, people vary in their *wish* to empathize. Anyone may *decide* to be "nonempathic," for good reason (for example, in quest of revenge). And people can "decide" to be empathic for self-serving reasons; empathic attitudes can serve masochistic, exhibitionism-modulating, trauma-controlling, and aggression-inhibiting purposes (Schafer, 1959). But we have evidence that, apart from their intent, people vary in their *aptitude* for empathizing with another person's experience. Daily life shows that non-empathic views are freqeuently default views: he who cannot form an empathic picture forms a non-empathic one as though he prefers it. We must be able to describe empathic ability by itself, disregarding its purposes and its genetic preconditions. Our question is not what facilitates empathy, but what it means to be able to empathize intensely.

It is a tricky question because, unlike other forms of apperception, empathy seems to have a component of action, and empathic capacity seems to refer not just to astuteness but to an inclination toward the subject. Empathy may operate at or below the level of consciousness, and the selection of level of response may be itself a form of empathy, as when we avoid hearing what someone does not want us to hear. (One investigator has found that, on this level, women are more empathic than men [Rosenthal, 1981].) It is a matter of vital concern to psychotherapy whether, seeing it as inevitable and indivisible, we can fully grasp somebody's thoroughly committed experience without reacting in such depth that it alters our behavior toward him. (Kohut often seemed to be uncertain on that point.) Or, to put it another way, if empathy pertains not just to the patient's perceptions, but to his consequent unconflicted, organically necessary strivings, is it *possible* to recognize his pull on us without at least slightly responding to it?

We have noted that *ordinary* empathy—the grasp of someone else's meaning—can be part of any attitude whatsoever, from concern to hostility to indifference. But now consider empathy as a sense of the inner necessity of a patient's feelings, and add to that that his feelings include his strivings which reach out to the therapist. Is there a sense in which the therapist's response *constitutes* the recognition of such an appeal? (That would mean that complete self-restraint in all reactions would impose a form of blindness.) This is a slippery walk. "Trial identification" is much more safely quiet and tentative. There are also other ways to describe the situation with terms that imply that the therapist retains his valuable neutrality. But using such terms may simply be a way of not asking whether the therapist's attitude has to actually *change* in the process of experiencing integrative empathy. The question is, when integrative empathy is experienced, does that by itself make it *impossible* for the therapist to act toward the patient in certain discordant ways? (In regard to this general question, see Tower, 1956.) In other words, we may ask how the therapist's empathy is different from that of the clever psychopath.

Partly to avoid the heresy of the corrective emotional experience, self psychologists have had to talk as though analysts (but not parents!) exercise empathy only *descriptively,* albeit nonconceptually (Gedo [1979] has seen this paradox.) In other words, in exercising empathy, analysts are supposed to be seeking a kind of description, but with a minimum of abstract explanation. That leaves the self psychologists open to the criticism that abstract concepts enter into all descriptions. But there are other sorts of recognition than descriptions. Most recognitions are not descriptions, but heedings. No formed concepts would seem to be needed for the way people heed each other all the time. Abstractions and concepts are also involved in heeding, but they do not function in the systematically structured way that concepts – and even whole theories – covertly set up "intuitive" psychoanalytic pictures or "experience-near" descriptions.

If empathy is both reflection and response, empathic ability may mean being sensitive to an appeal that while least active is also closest to actuality. In other words, empathic sensitivity might be more a function of knowing how a person is likely to change in the next split second than of knowing how he is at this split second. There has always been a place in psychoanalytic theory for this sort of anticipation, from the old image of ideas marching through the " 'defile' of consciousness" (Freud, 1893–1895, p. 291) up to the current doctrines on the correct order of interpretations. (As I will emphasize below, even if empathy is a sense of how things may move, it does not follow that it is felt by the therapist or the patient as such.)

This is an extraordinarily murky area, combining the phenomenology of experience as it moves over time with issues of standing motivation and defense. Most frequently, therapists find themselves empathizing privately and "statically." But even those quiet images imply expectations about how they might develop. And as a result of these "disinterested" empathic reveries, the analyst acts with expectations about how his actions will be received, and this suggests that his reveries are partly anticipations of movement.

And insofar as empathy is guided by a sense of what somebody is *trying* for, it is more a peering forward than a looking at.

In his important essay on this subject, Schafer (1959, p. 346) sharply distinguishes the will-less, contemplative act of empathy from its communicative therapeutic expression. But even while it is silent and devoid of apparent aim, empathy is, according to Schafer, "a form of experimental internal action" (p. 346). And Schafer goes on to say that in the analyst's own, apparently inactive empathizing "the boundaries of awareness are enlarged through discovery of new forms of experience as well as recovery and clarification of past experience . . . By new forms of experience I refer to new differentiations and syntheses, new distributions of intensities, and new criteria of relevance" (p. 346). If all these fluctuations are a part of empathy even in its quiet, contemplative, aesthetic aspect, is that not evidence that empathy is a sense of how experience can move? Surely empathy must have as many moods and rhythms as any other category of experience. But we may find that it always has an element of anticipation of development, even when that is not immediately apparent. A person's empathic capacity may have to do with a sense of how things will move when responded to in a particular fashion.

It is useful to superimpose Schafer's earlier views of generative empathy onto his more recent holistic account, for the latter is one of our revisionist theories. In the earlier paper, he wrote that "what is to be shared and comprehended [by generative empathy] is a hierarchic organization of desires, feelings, thoughts, defenses, controls, superego pressures, capacities, self-representations and representations of real and fantasied personal relationships" (1959, p. 345). Nowadays Schafer no longer appeals to hierarchic organization. What takes its place as the analyst's representation of the patient's structure? What is the way personal potential can be envisioned? Since his philosophy eschews potentiality, we must extrapolate an answer. It seems to me that Schafer now believes that the empathizing analyst shares (1) an expanded view of the world as the patient partially sees it, together with (2) a sense of other, accessible vantage points from which the world would look different (e.g., Schafer, 1973b). In other words, empathy is the vision of the patient's present experience against the sliding backdrop of just-around-the-corner shifts in perspective. The collection of these possible changes in viewpoint takes the place of Schafer's previous diagram of psychic organization. Now more than ever before, it seems to me, Schafer would be inclined to see generative empathy as a sense of what can *develop* out of the patient's momentary state.

If it still seems a little far fetched to regard empathy as a sense of how a state can change, a therapist should recall how different a given psychic constellation *feels* to him when he sees it as leading out into a different elaboration. How did Kohut help the analyst to understand narcissism? Certainly not by admonishing him to be more empathic. What he did was to show new developments available in its recognition (see chapter 34). Narcissism seems different to Kohut's students because of its new possibilities, though the students think they are just being more empathic about the old phenomena than they used to be. Although Kohut's is only an equivocal example of it, our revisionist theories have, in effect, been saying that therapists should be more openly expectant ahead of time about what can develop, and more convinced afterward that nothing else could have developed. They have done this straightforwardly by writing accounts that leave possibilities relatively blank.

Why would anyone feel a need to be more open minded about possibilities than Freudian theory permits? As far as ordinary empathy goes, a psychoanalyst who followed the rule to stay as close as possible to what is about to become conscious, could maintain many intimately shared forms with his patient and also many theoretical possibilities, since Freudian theory specifies potentiality in categories general enough to be filled by many individual meanings. Metapsychology certainly leaves room for local color. Freudian life dramas, such as the oedipus complex, are individualizable. Even supposing that Freudian theory was misused to allow analysts to be overly schematic, the theory certainly does not *demand* its misuse, and anyone who cares can call it back to its proper role.

After all, potentiality – the hidden dispositions to which events are a clue – acts as a lure for perception. The analyst notices what seems fruitful to notice, and an anatomy of dispositions makes many superficial bumps portentous. Theory inspires attention. Admittedly, by the same token, a given theory has to make light of some configurations, or else it has no shape at all. In other words, if one had little theory, one might fail to notice opportunities for lack of a template, while if one relied too much on theory, one might fail to notice opportunities because they do not seem relevant to cure; that is, they are not mentioned in one's theory as significant figures, pregnant with development. ("Resistance" is often used as the null class of potentiality for a given theory. The theory says, "Here I can find no promising latent developments.") That is one reason that new theories come into being. But why should one want to get rid of theory altogether and leave ideas about mental potential as unformulated as possible?

EMPATHY AS COVERT ACTION

The empathy debate has provided one clue to our persistent question: What seems real to the analyst may depend on both his impressionability *and* the momentary sense of what he can elicit. If empathy were just a matter of his impressionability, theory of potentiality, like all theory, would both help and hinder it. But if empathy involves a sense of momentarily inevitable movement, theoretical diagrams would mostly interfere.

I am suggesting that empathy is not a simple experience, but is a real or imagined action taken by the empathizer upon his subject. Does that seem too strong a statement? It is clearly *not* how empathizing feels to the therapist. Therapeutic empathy feels like following, not leading. It feels self-denying. That is because it makes everything secondary to visualizing the patient's experience as an integrated whole. It goes without saying that empathy shoulders aside the therapist's personal wishes (including those that are masked as therapeutic demands). But that is not all that is suspended. Among distractions which intense therapeutic empathy subordinates are those side-long glances at complex possibilities, both within the patient and between him and the therapist, that a theory of the mind fosters. Quite unlike the marshaling of a field of rearrangeable structures and forces, it is this feeling of being at the service of a single, beckoning phantom that gives empathy its special flavor of authenticity.

As with so many other aspects of the current discussion of empathy, Schafer (1959) anticipated this problem. He elaborated the defensive use of altruistic surrender in the exercise of empathy. He wrote, "We must, however, distinguish the altruistic component of generative empathy from altruistic surrender . . . As a dominant and inflexible basis for empathy, altruistic surrender soon proves unsatisfactory. It manifests itself in the rigid require-ment that the patient continue to remain in one psychological position in order to continue to be a source of vicarious unconscious gratification for the therapist" (1959, p. 355). (In general, Schafer's work deals convincingly with empathy as a central issue in treatment, about which the patient has more deeply conflicting attitudes than simply fear of disappointment.) But why would "the altruistic component of empathy" not have the same restricting effects as the analyst's personal altruistic surrender? It is a mistake to suppose that, once it is purged of personal pathology, a therapeutic approach no longer has expressive, interpersonal, prejudicing, and role-defining impact. Nowadays, when there are so many examples of the influence of school and tradition on empathic focus, Schafer might be less inclined to regard the therapist's characterological defenses as the only investment in empathy that can be rigid enough to press the patient into a confined psychological position.

THE ANALYST'S HOPE THAT UNDERLIES EMPATHY

An intent, empathic stance avoids the distraction of reacting in several ways at once to a patient; it avoids perceiving him as having various different potentialities at the moment (which would be a stance inspired by a conflict theory).

It should not be imagined, on that account, that an extremely empathic attitude is an easy one to adopt. Hanging onto a consistent empathic viewpoint can be stressful and demanding. It is certainly not a lazy impres-sionability, or an obedient acceptance of what the patient tries to convey.

In ordinary life, we grant just that much empathy to our partner as he asks or presumes in order, first of all, to give contextual meaning to his utterances, and secondly, to think of him the way he wants to be thought of. Any further imaginative intrusion into his situation depends on our personal *interest* in him or his situation; in other words, it depends on our wishes.

If, as therapists, we go further than the patient has asked and enlarge on his situation, we may well be countering a motive of his with one of our own. We are bent on satisfying a professional wish condoned by our theory, a wish to induce an integration of the patient's experience by our effort to experience it in an integrated way. This wish will have many intimate, personal meanings to both of us.

How does that wish compare with the kind of demand that is characteristic of the conflict investigator (e.g., Gray, 1982), who, in effect, asks the patient why he is managing himself the way he does in the analyst's presence?

In essence, the "empathizer" asks himself the same questions, though for reasons suggested below, he is not as likely to put the question to the patient. As mentioned earlier, he may actually be empathizing with a conflict in his patient. And, for his part, the conflict investigator is empathizing with the various aspects of the patient that he contemplates, since there is no other way to capture a human meaning than through empathy in its broad sense.

The difference is, as I have suggested, that the "empathizer" sees things under the sign of inevitability and unity. His attention is concentrated on singleness. He searches the patient's momentary state (including any feeling of conflict) for its (one) meaning. He looks for global, unused potentiality, rather than a pattern of multiple potentials. The global potential is a potential for articulation, maturation, and integration. The analyst's subjective feeling in pursuing this is similar to that of a photographer developing a film, rather than a fluoroscopist observing a barium swallow. The kind of theory which assists in this posture is a process theory rather than a structural theory. And the kind of attitude that it fosters is a justifying one because it stresses holistic inevitability. Schafer (1973a) has struggled to combine this empathic view with the assignment of responsibility and the distribution of multiple potentials, but fault lines in his theory show that these are incompatible demands (see chapter 20).

The fundamental polarity between an empathic vantage point and a conflict vantage point has to do with the degree of freedom that the therapist attributes to the patient at the moment. The empathizer sees limited plasticity both in the articulation of experience and in the relationship to the therapist. The conflict analyzer sees a great number of possibilities. He sees different ways that the patient's motives are shaping his covert experience right at the moment; he does not pick up just congruent echoing amplifications. He imagines different relationships the patient could right now have with him, given a shift in the field of forces, which would enable the patient to regard himself and his motives in different lights. He asks the patient why he is doing what he is doing, because he presumes that the patient could take an ironic view of his presentation, suspend his heart-felt experience in favor of another heart-felt experience, and play around with his role. (The patient has to stop *doing* to the therapist in order to look at his role, so he must have some other sort of doing available to him, some other role to occupy.)

What about the steadily empathic therapist? He is no more willing than the analyst of conflict to "let be." Both therapists want and expect—and have whetted their appetites for—something more. They differ in how much more the more is. Without this "wanting" by the therapist, patients would just convey what they choose and awaken what they want in the therapist.

Because the devotedly empathic therapist senses the next development to be the one avenue possible, the patient is not asked why he is behaving as he does. That would suppose him to have access to an alternate vantage point. Instead, the patient is simply treated as the more integrated person he could momentarily become, with the hope that he will be able to establish a similar integrative conversation with himself.

Naturally, these approaches are both parts of all therapy, representing the feelings of inevitability, on the one hand, and multiple possibility for the patient to reposition himself, on the other hand: human necessity and freedom. But insofar as they name a style, the conflict and empathy approaches *feel* like separate routes, because they are alternative postures for the therapist, each with its own type of strain. The therapist's attention is focused differently when it is concentrated in a narrow, empathic channel than when it flutters over many regions of possibility, exploring rules of transformation and substitution such as defense mechanisms. These ways of perceiving represent different actions on the patient, different types of hope and expectation, different therapeutic wishes and intrusions, different types of relationship.

THE EMPATHIC TRANSACTION

People who profit from empathic matching not only see themselves more clearly as a result but experience the matching as a way of being dealt with. They see it as a way they can be regarded by someone *other* than themselves. And they see it as a way that someone *wants* to be with them. The in-between status of selfobject in Kohut's theory pays homage to this mixture. Besides suggesting a pattern for self-observation, empathy is an assimilable way of being regarded from the outside, and that defines a *relationship* which has, as Kohut showed, a whole history of association to other empathizers.

For the therapist, empathizing feels as roleless and accepting as any fixed role can possibly feel. It is, in actual fact, the most flexible fixed role a person can adopt. It lets the therapist forget he is playing a role. By putting theoretical terms of potentiality out of his mind, the empathizer frees himself from the difficult obligation of monitoring his professional ambiguity. These reassurances go hand in hand: the reassurance that the perceived state of the patient is inevitable (and thus faithfully tracked) and the reassurance that the therapist has not chosen a particular, personal relationship with his patient.

CONCLUSION: WHAT NEED OF THE THERAPIST IS SERVED BY THE REVISIONS?

We have been trying to understand how it is practically useful to blur pictures of potential. It has not been easy to see how the therapist's perceptions or knowledge are enriched by avoiding theory, especially since theory does not really go away. Any particular empathic registration or description can be translated into as much theory and as much conceptual knowledge as you please. One can extract plenty of theoretical preconceptions about potentiality from what seems at first to be an intuitive perception. That may be why many analysts complain that self psychologists are taking proprietary credit for simple sensitivity.

If, however, we think of the *therapist's wishes and strivings*, the revisions become less mysterious. Is it legitimate to portray analysts as wishing, striving, intruding, expecting? Of course these must all be hedged about with qualifications and professional specifications. But no realistic picture of a therapist's activity can omit this dimension. There is no way for a therapist's attention to be directed—or suspended—if he is not wishing, striving, and expecting (see chapter 10).

Once we acknowledge the therapist's working psychology, we can understand how much difference it makes whether he operates with a view of delineated potentiality, as in Freudian theory, or a sense of holistic necessity.

If a therapist has a wish for a change that seems so inevitable that it looks not like a change but like an elucidation of what is already present, he will not want to see himself as entering a field of various potential responses. A theory of the mind will actually interfere—though not so much with his vision as with his liberty. He wants to see potential as already actual so that he can surreptitiously foster integration and imagine that what he accomplishes has been thrust on him.

In that kind of empathic act where a therapist tries hard to bring about a development so unavoidable that it appears to be simply what is already there, his frame of mind will be a holistic one: he senses himself groping for the patient's nuance rather than his own categories, and he regards his expectant intrusions on the patient as acts of perception.

This whole situation can be translated into theory of the mind (as Loewald [1960] has done so skillfully). But that does not make theory of the mind any more welcome to the therapist who is momentarily devoted to the act of empathy.

Of course, self psychologists know that empathic attitudes and their failures act as interpersonal influences. Indeed, Kohut felt that the experience of being empathized with is a fundamental lifegiver and structure builder. But those who routinize empathy show that they do not consider it to be a particular intrusion or intervention. If the therapist thought of empathic effort as an intrusion or action or intervention, he would also have to consider it an invitation to respond in a certain way and therefore a point of choice for the patient in his relationship with the therapist. Kohut *did* take that view when he dealt with defensive compensations, and, as we might have predicted, along with that view of empathy as an action on the patient, went a bit of old-fashioned theory and defined potentiality (and even some diagrams!) (Kohut, 1971, p. 185). But after layers of defense are peeled off, the empathist no longer views himself as acting within a field of possible responses; he thinks of his empathy not as an intrusion, but as a *match*: the shape of the *interaction* takes on the same aura of inevitability as the *perception* it responds to.

Why have theorists taken such pains to bolster this relatively unself-conscious wishing of the therapist, this wishing to be witness rather than agent?

First of all, it may be that these days patients need this approach more consistently than they used to. More patients may have less intrapsychic choice than they used to have, and therapists may not feel they can challenge the best relationship that can be arranged. Pathology has probably dictated theory. But it is hard to know to what extent, because there are other forces at work.

Second, there may be a cognitive dialectic involved in treatment. Therapists may need a heterogeneous mixture of choice and necessity in their sense of themselves, in order to organize their data. Perhaps they need the freedom from perceptual appearances that is provided by a theory of the mind, while at the same time they may need to feel coerced by reality, as though the way things seem is the only way they can be.

While having to empathize in the everyday way just in order to converse, the therapist does not always have to want to empathize in the exclusive, intent way that is currently advocated. In fact, therapists cannot always want to adhere to this mode. Other considerations are bound to intervene. The exclusive dedication that defines the empathic focus of attention sacrifices a lot of other useful states of mind, such as detachment, mobility, self-interest, playfulness, skeptical attitudes, and an ironic view (Havens, 1982; Schafer, 1970b). It seems likely that there is a natural cognitive rivalry between the need for immediately experienced integration and the need for mobility among potential integrations. The balance that needs to be maintained is not a balance between an intuitive process and a conceptual process, or between compassion and objectivity. It is a balance between the therapist's wish to force an immediate integration (not by impatience but by unself-conscious intention), on the one hand, and the therapist's wish to allow more uncertainty (not by tolerance, but by tentativeness), on the other hand.

Patients vary in their ability to make use of new freedom, and have different leeway at different times. Their capacity will influence how much the therapist looks to new possibilities and how much he nestles into what is already present. But probably no therapy is without some element of each effort (see Lichtenberg, 1981a).

Third, there may be a dialectic in which encouragement of the therapist's wishes alternates with their inhibition. Operating with a wish that feels like a perception may quite simply permit the therapist to give freer reign to at least that one kind of wish. In other words, a holistic, multimeaning, nonlabeling doctrine may legitimize a therapist's appetite. And reading back from that, we might conclude that some therapists may have felt estranged not just from their patients' subjectivity but from their own enthusiasm. I have suggested that theories emphasizing the therapist's defining authority also require him to be more restrained, while therapists are permitted more freedom by theories that depict patients as developing their own meanings out of autocthonous processes (chapter 5). We must all judge for ourselves whether different schools are noted for different sorts and degrees of enthusiasm. But if we decide that one reason for revising theory was to unwrap the therapist's strivings, we would be led to a more complicated picture of the stresses the therapist has to negotiate in his work.

SUMMARY

1. A group of psychoanalytic revisionists, including Gendlin, Levenson, George Klein, Schafer, Peterfreund, Kohut, and members of the representational world school, share a holistic approach that increases the variety of configurations relevant to psychoanalysis and lessens the analyst's authority to describe the field.

2. These theories are noteworthy for avoiding the description of specific potentiality, which is what theory of the mind consists of.

3. In an effort to see what practical need of the therapist is served by avoiding potentiality, I examine the nature of extreme empathic focus.

4. Ordinary empathy is just reception of human meaning. But extremely dedicated therapeutic empathy is visualization of a person in the mode of inevitability. In action, a dedicated empathizer wishes to induce an immediate integration that feels so inevitable that it seems to be a perception of a state rather than induced movement.

5. It seems likely that therapists need to perceive themselves partly as responding to inevitabilities as well as fostering changes. Theory of the mind

with its description of potentiality is anathema to the feeling of being entrained to inevitability.

6. Therefore, in order to help the working therapist, a full theory of the mind has to be supplemented from time to time with writings that are, in a strict sense, theoretically deficient. In that sense, these revisions operate as aesthetic or inspirational aids. That treatment requires such aids is a testimonial to how complicated the therapeutic interchange is.

V
What is a Psychotherapist?

29
Ambiguity as a Discipline

L et us look at psychotherapy with an innocent eye.

From an objective viewpoint what stands out about patient and therapist is that they are radically alone. They are unaccompanied by person, object, or common problem. There is no third thing to attend to. They have no common program. Nothing definite is on the horizon except the end of the hour.[1]

Now, we have a choice: We can dwell on the peculiarity of that picture for a while. Or we can make it evaporate with down-home descriptions, such as "the need for help," and "the work of understanding." If we tint the picture with our traditions before we look at it bare, both "help" and "understanding" will join "therapy" in the limbo of opaque, taken-for-granted concepts. So we look at it bare.

What is likely to happen when two people are settled together for 50 minutes alone and without an agenda? What do they do when nothing is provided?

WISHES AND WISHLESSNESS

One thing people always have with them is wishes. The patient's wishes drive therapy. Everyone knows that. But how about the therapist? Therapists take

---

[1] The therapist might as well tell the patient: "The only thing I can promise you is that I will throw you out in 50 minutes." Indeed, this solitary certainty is more often the tacit subject of conversation than is recognized. It is inexplicit because it seems to have been contractually agreed upon and disposed of.

pride in having no wishes except the desire to help patients sort out their own wishes. If therapists had wishes they would be seeking satisfaction, and few therapists believe they use patients for their own satisfaction.[2]

Psychoanalytic theory does not entirely support this position. The analyst's motivational structure is supposed to be a useful antenna (see, especially, Racker, 1968; Tower, 1956). Just as the patient's cooperation reflects earlier relationships, so also the analyst's work has deep meaning for the analyst (see Brenner, 1985).

Why haven't the therapist's wishes figured more prominently in the literature? The generic reason is that in describing professions such considerations are usually trivial. In fact, psychotherapy differs from other professions in that respect (chapter 31). But there are also two specific reasons for neglecting the impact of the therapist's wishes: (a) We don't usually imagine the therapist to be wishing on his way to work; his wishes are supposed to be activated by his patients. And (b) when made aware of his wishes, the therapist is supposed to savor them and spit them out like a wine taster, rather than letting them go to his head like a drunk (cf. Fleiss's [1942] metaphor of a tea taster).

What shall we say about these familiar images? They do capture something about therapy—something that has to do with the detachment caused by the therapist's objective theory; that was discussed in chapter 5. But as clear images, these are myths designed to make everybody feel better.

We therapists are not pianos waiting to be played on. No breathing person is without his own theme and aspirations. Nor are we containers. The germ of truth in the concept of projective identification unfortunately reinforces the myth that the therapist's feelings and reactions are caught by contagion from the patient. It is true that my reaction is often designed by my partner but the medium he works in is my own purposes.

As to the fate of our wishes, the second image is deceptive; it pretends that the unconscious can be entirely at the service of the ego. But we cannot bottle our unconscious. Access to the unconscious refers to maximum freedom in experiencing ourselves and our world. It does not mean command over what we will and will not allow our unconscious to do to us. (Some therapists seem to regard their unconscious as a handy dictionary of archaic terms; while the patient's unconscious remains a source of wanting and trying.)

In practice, therapists are not so shy about using their wishes to understand patients, but they may worry that this is exploitive. Yet we have to be realistic about the question of using people. As practitioners, we fit patients

---

[2]It is a curious fact that when therapists admit that they too have wishes, it is often very primitive wishes that they recognize, and self-treatment that they suppose is their unconscious objective (e.g., Whitaker & Malone, 1953). They seem to feel that the therapist can stave off ordinary desires but not psychotic ones.

into the preferred pattern of our life, and that means we use them. In contrast, a lawyer can argue that he leaves his client alone and gets his satisfaction from tangling with the legal system; the surgeon, that he uses bodies, not persons. These are not philosophical distinctions: patients have real and specific reactions to being used for a psychotherapy practice – reactions that they do not have to other professional uses. Being used for the practice of psychotherapy goes counter to the parenting or friendship or devotion that psychotherapy, unlike other professions, seems to promise.

The customary answer to this is that the therapist's use of the patient is not exploitive because his using is just the act of benefiting the patient. One need not disagree to see that this is neither deep nor clear. Is "benefiting" a good description of the therapist's momentary intention? If "benefiting" means answering to the patient's expressed need, then the desire to help has not been regarded as the right attitude for a psychoanalyst. Indeed, a formalist tradition, carried to its extreme by Thomas Szasz (1965) holds that the analyst's responsibility is just "to analyze." For most analysts, and all psychotherapists, the situation is more complicated. Freud's general command is to push a beneficial process forward in a practical way. To be sure, he implied that the therapist can use the patient as a source of knowledge, but only in a way that furthers the project. As it happens, a wish to understand helps to preserve the analyst's poise. Attending mainly to understanding, rather than to curing, the analyst is undistracted by temporary improvements and setbacks, and avoids being partisan toward material or invested in the patient's choices. With the fewest hostages to fortune, he is least manipulable.

Thus the profession recognized from the beginning that as regards the particulars of what comes up during treatment, the therapist does not try to be helpful in any ordinary sense of the word. And he is allowed to use the patient as a source of knowledge.

The word *understanding* has been dulled by familiarity, so let us refer to *knowing*. Knowing is more evidently personal and dangerously uncircumscribed. A wish to know might be many sorts of wish, and a therapist cannot be sure that some of them will not interfere with the patient. Even aside from the Biblical meaning, some efforts to know a patient might be considered exploitive.

But then any asymmetrical, personal relationship that is worth its salt is exploitive in the sense that if there is no way that you heedlessly want something from me, I obviously do not mean much to you. Like everybody else a patient wants to be (and is afraid of being) exploited because it is his only chance of an eager reception. (Lacan [1977a] has elaborated on this.) And for his own part, when a therapist does not feel exploited that is the time he wishes he had become a concert pianist or an ophthalmologist.

The patient's wish to engage the therapist is the material of treatment. He can engage the therapist only if he finds something the therapist wants from him. And so, to mobilize his strivings, he is given few clues about what the therapist wants (a good reason, incidentally, not to recite "ground rules"). At least in these terms the patient's wish to be exploited is well known. But the therapist declines the offer. (Or so he hopes.) For he knows that if he uses the patient to satisfy a desire, it will narrow the patient's freedom and his own attentiveness. It is easy to see why a therapist would prefer to have no wishes.

But if the therapist had no purposes, no wishes, no hopes or expectations—nothing to be satisfied or disappointed, nothing that could be excited—he would probably have no interest in his patient and certainly no searching interest. Nothing could be *elicited* in such a therapist and so he would have no personal reason to see, hear or do any one thing rather than another. And without a personal *reason* to react, no live, momentary particulars could be felt, let alone responded to (see chapter 10). He could usher the patient into and out of his office, and say things at predetermined intervals. He might even respond to key words he had learned in training. And that is where the relationship would end.

One form of wishing that therapists can comfortably recognize is that which shadows the patient's wishes. To empathize with the dramatic forms of a person's life—the shape and fate of his aspirations—we must write him into a drama of our own. We can see a person from within his own framework, but we cannot fully appreciate him without tentatively placing his framework in ours. In ordinary life this is hardly noticed because we recognize human behavior by automatically giving it moral significance, and that means that we place it in a framework of our own. (Schafer's action language expresses this fact.) We will not clearly perceive a striving unless we at least vaguely see a goal, and we will not identify something as a goal unless we apply to it an evaluation of our own. Of course we need not give it only one significance, and certainly as therapists we try to give it many. But however imaginatively done, "trial identification" involves identifying the patient with the therapist as well as vice-versa. This process is automatic and invisible in social intercourse. It only becomes conspicuous when we try to understand someone at a distance, as when we read a text or think about history. Philosophers such as Gadamer (1975) and Collingwood (1946) tell us that in these situations we tangibly locate our subject on the intersection of its "horizon" with ours. If we could not blend our own needs with an author's, we could not read books; if ancient struggles did not touch our present concerns, we could not write history. If we had to completely efface our own interests, we could only collect books and relics, just as our hypothetically selfless therapist would only be a receptionist.

But blending horizons is not simply an interpretive activity: It is a *using* activity. We read a book, study history, and engage a patient for our own purposes. In order to allow himself to be more than a receptionist, the therapist needs reassurance about his purposes. What calms his fears is his theory. Theory informs his background imagination with overt and covert expectations that are certified as legitimate: There are expectations of discovery, a promise of intellectual mastery, anticipations of intense emotional experience; there is an opportunity to exercise practical expertise. These intellectual, professional, and effectance motives are terribly important, although they are often regarded as trivial (cf. the quotation of Fenichel on p. 91). And they shade off into subtler but no less important motives, such as the wish to see an anticipated change or feel a hidden relationship, which are also stimulated and certified by theory. These anticipations of change may appear to the therapist directly as a theoretical formula, or they may take the form of theoretically conditioned alertness to a nuance in the patient's talk. Most therapists try not to be excited and we are rarely aware of these wishes that, moreover, can hardly be felt altogether at once. But although quiet, they are always present (see chapters 27 and 32).

In anticipating developments, the therapist is usually shaping them by his theory or his desire, although he feels that he is simply and eagerly open. In chapter 27, I suggested that recent theory is designed to foster this necessary illusion.

One reason that theory does not do justice to the struggle in therapy is that some of the therapist's wishes are embodied in theory not as wishes but as pictures of potentiality. (cf. Loewald, 1960). A theory, whether theory of the mind or theory of therapy, is a description of potentiality and its relation to actuality. The patient has an infinity of potential responses: A selection must be made, and it is made by the therapist's theory. Thus theory enshrines some of the therapist's hidden wishes. The therapist does not know that he is pitched up against his patient with these needs because they appear to him as theoretical knowledge. In other words, some of the therapist's wish-grid— what he wants, what gratifies him, what he scans for, what brings him to life, what makes him look forward, what allows him to see this or that instead of the other thing, what makes something salient at the perceptual level, all the aspirations that give human meaning to what the fellow creature across from him is doing—some of this is experienced by the therapist as just the way things are in the patient's mind. (It is easier to see the wishes incorporated in rival theories than in our own. For instance, if we are not gestalt therapists, we will read their theory as a description of the sort of behavior they like to deal with.)

Sometimes therapists do sense that having a theory means having desires, and because they would like to be completely accepting, they may from time to time convince themselves that they are not using their theory. They will say, "I am just listening," or "I am empathizing, not theorizing."

Disavowals of theory cannot be supported. Schafer (1980a) argues convincingly that listening in an "ordinary" way is untherapeutic. We cast what comes to us into patterns (see Spence, 1982). Kohut (1984) indicated that experience-distant theory always gives a particular slant to empathy by suggesting forms to "close on." Shapiro (1981) indicates that the biasing function of theory is not *de minimus*.

Theory does not have to take the form of pages in a book. Indeed, pages in a book can only suggest a theory, which always has indefinite extension. Every way of referring to potentiality and its relation to actuality is a piece of theory. If you are at all inclined to foresee change, or can imagine a change that might have happened but didn't, you are applying theory. When I try to cheer a friend, I am using an idea of how his mind works, and a picture of his potential cheerfulness or fun.

Any stance or attitude toward a person is a practical embodiment of theory. If the stance is peculiar, as in psychotherapy, it embodies a specialized or technical theory even if its user does not know how to put it into words.

When we talk about particular theories we refer to Freud's or Kohut's or Schafer's, and so on. But when we talk about theory in general we are, in effect, just referring to the therapist's implicit expectations about the patient's potential. No pretentious beard-stroking is implied. (Indeed, I believe that the most important task of training is to teach beginning therapists how to explicitly derive their implicit theory from what they find themselves doing. See also Harré's [1984] formula that the self is a theory.)

We may sum up with the conclusion that therapists have wishes; that at least some of their wishes are embedded in their theory; and that their theory is often tacitly embodied in their attitude toward their patient.

MANIPULATION AND GUILELESSNESS

Therapy bare is two people without plan or diversion, and it seems likely to be characterized by their wishes toward each other. If it did not sound so poisonous, or if we could rely on its industrial meaning, we should say that two people alone with nothing else to do will exploit each other.

A great deal has been written about the patient's wishes. I have suggested that the therapist, too, has wants, many of which are compressed into his theory, and that he therefore might be said to exploit his patient. Because he is pledged not to exploit, he does not want to see his wishes for what they are.

It is understandable that a therapist will pretend to be innocent of wishes, but it blinds him to the fundamentals of his work. People move toward their opportunities: They scan and define what other people offer in terms of their own wishes, and this is no less true of therapists than patients because it is part of the general way that people make human sense out of others.

But that is putting it too mildly because, as mentioned earlier, therapy schedules no objective project and so the therapy situation provides no external reflector to give meaning to one's gropings other than the reaction of the other person in the room. There is no car to emerge from an assembly line to tell the worker he has placed its doors properly. There is no tradition of courtesy or dignity to tell the patient that he has behaved as a person should in this situation. There is no news bulletin or original text or archaeological find that will show him that he has spoken a truth. From the patient's standpoint, all that will happen as a result of what he does or does not do is that the therapist will seem to feel one way or another about him, presumably because he is or is not approaching what the therapist expects (wants) from him. (Of course the patient has an impact on himself, but even that impact is partly a consequence of the therapist's apparent reaction: The patient picks up the echo of what he says and the resonator is his imagination of the therapist's perception.)

This strange situation has a bearing on the kind of meaning that the patient registers, and we can see it precisely because we are examining the naked situation of therapy before clothing it in fine words. Outside of therapy, social context allows one to respond (for instance) to just the propositional aspect of what someone says apart from his reason for saying it, and on the other hand we can get a separate sense of his motive for wanting us to believe it. But there are no social contexts (or few of them) to allow this sort of separation in therapy. A patient cannot really even know what is being pointed to in him if he ignores all the affective and wishful components of the therapist's communication. The situation is too undefined and fluid for that. (Chapter 11 wrestled with that problem.) The context is so undefined that a patient cannot even be sure what he himself is saying and why he is speaking, which is a source of much uneasiness.

People always have to scan others to find their own opportunities. But in therapy each party has to scan the other's wishes just to know what is said.

The aloneness of the therapy situation, therefore, can be expected not only to encourage the participants to seek satisfaction from each other, but also to understand themselves in terms of the other's response. Because the therapist has a theory to talk to as well as a patient he is not as vulnerable as the patient. And because the setting is arranged by the therapist, he seems to want that leverage. Like it or not, then, the situation is designed to make the patient insecure about his meanings. Both parties are at sea but the therapist has a raft and he has arranged for the patient to flounder.

We must go one step further. Not only are the therapist's technical efforts construable in an unpleasant light (as Haley [1963] has shown by projecting them onto a simple plane of power), but the technical aims are never his only motives. They are not even his only "proper" motives. He has supplementary, competing motives that are tacitly annointed by his theory.

Beside disguised wishes embedded in theory (wishes that are made to look like descriptions) we have seen that theory allows the therapist a number of auxilliary wishes that really feel like wishes. The theory organizes them and renders them "safe." But only up to a point. Consider the wish to understand, to prove oneself intellectual master of material, to anticipate and assimilate, to feel like a competent professional (see chapter 8). As time goes by, the therapist inevitably invests more and more in some understandings, and has more and more to lose if they are wrong. Desires for evidence flow together like mountain streams into a surging insistence on confirmation. (Cf. Kohut's [1979] first analysis of Mr. Z., and see also Spence, 1982.) One of the ways a therapist may exploit a patient is by using him as an amenable object of intellectual transparency. (That may not sound nice, but many a patient has profited from it, for an important function of theory is to give every patient a way of satisfying his therapist.) Most therapists know that one of the strongest forces in the consulting room, and the least controllable, is their own reluctance to give up a plausible understanding and agree to be lost all over again. It is one of the reasons Freud cautioned against formulating a case during treatment. Spence (1982) has shown that we cannot exercise this caution simply by waiting until a treatment is over before we decide meanings, because all hearings and understandings are progressively built up on hypotheses (some of them demonstrably false).

We cannot be too often reminded that the therapist's need for certainty exerts an influence on treatment. Many theorists have tried to loosen the therapist's attachment to his views. Philosophic critiques cast doubt on the possibility of certainty. Schafer (1970b) recommends an attitude of irony; Lichtenberg (1981b) and Havens (1982, 1986) show how useful not knowing can be; Kohut (1984) suggests that we postpone closure as long as possible. Schwaber (1983, 1986) instructs therapists to continuously reopen all closures. These observations are designed to relax cognitive demands on the therapist. Surely it helps for the therapist to have an open mind and feel free not to be always on top of things. But the nature of perception puts a limit on humility and tentativeness. The tendency toward closure often operates against the therapist's conscious wish. He may crave a new perspective and abhor the rut he is in, without being able to do anything about it. Even Kohut (1984), who has campaigned most vigorously against the adoration of knowledge, allows that receptivity requires the imposition of patterns. Therapists have been helped to avoid old forms of stubbornness less by Kohut's plea for open-mindedness than by his newly devised concepts for them to close on: new shapes of growth, of narcissism, and of transference. Restraint alone cannot hold back the drive for intellectual mastery; competing interests are necessary.

What, then, does check the need to understand? What counterforce operates on the therapist? We cannot hope to achieve flexibility through another way of grasping configurations. Once achieved, *any* kind of grasp, conceptual or intuitive, is an investment by the therapist and generates a wish for confirmation. (An empathic grasp may be even more prized by a therapist than a theoretical guess, since it reflects on his humanity.)

The only thing that can lessen a need to be right is another kind of need. To balance a wish for mastery, what is required is a different kind of wish, not a different mastery.

Such a wish might be for a meeting, for acquaintance, for liveliness, for fluctuation, and so on – almost any need that is not met by a case report. Our concern, after all, is not to clear the therapist's mind of opinions. Our objective is to find a rival satisfaction that will make opinions less important. Personal discovery, as when we meet an entertaining stranger, satisfies a different desire of the therapist than cognitive mastery. It is the variety of desire, not the absence of concepts, that makes concepts less gripping. (This amounts to looking at empathy as an appetite rather than as a cognition. The issue was discussed in chapter 27.)

The wish to know is also balanced by a wish to see something emerge. Development can satisfy a therapist even when he does not know how to categorize it. The desire to see change happen is deeply ingrained, especially in a therapist who is concentrating empathically. (See chapter 27 on potentiality.)

As Kohut (1979) found in retrospect, the therapist has only as much permission to meet someone new and see something move as his theory allows him. And his theory can give him that permission only by taking turns with ordinary perception. In other words, a diagram of the forms of potentiality must be able to yield to the particulars of ordinary perception. Turning it around, we might say that specialized knowledge of human potentiality must be able to give way to an appetite for personal discovery and a delight in surprise.

The situation is more complicated than it appears. We have noted in chapter 10 that one major purpose of theory is to permit, and another purpose is to forbid certain intuitive attitudes on the part of the therapist. The way theory liberates untheoretical responses has been beautifully described by the literary critic, William Empson (1947). Referring to how hard it has become for today's reader to understand poetry, Empson (1947) wrote:

> the habit of reading a wide variety of different sorts of poetry, which has, after all, only recently been contracted by any public as a whole, gives to the act of appreciation a puzzling complexity, tends to make people less sure of their own minds, and makes it necessary to be able to fall back on some intelligible process of interpretation . . .

> One's situation here is very like that of the visualizer who cannot imagine enjoying poetry without seeing the pictures on which he relies; any intellectual framework that seems relevant is very encouraging (as one sees from the

cocksureness of the scientists) whether it actually "explains" anything or not; if you feel that your reactions *could* be put into a rational scheme that you can roughly imagine, you become willing, for instance, to abandon yourself to the ecstasies of the Romantic Movement, with a much lower threshold of necessary excitement, with much less fear for your critical self-respect . . . The same machinery of reassurance, I suppose, is sought for in my use of phrases like "outside the focus of consciousness," without very definite support from psychological theory. *To give a reassurance of this kind, indeed, is the main function of criticism* [pp. 243–244, italics added].

This statement seems to me exactly applicable to a psychotherapist and his theory.

But theory cannot liberate the therapist's reactions unless it plays on his imagination. Psychotherapy is a perceptual activity, and it seems that such activities need innovation to maintain their liveliness. When forms of thought and perception become part of a canon they may lose immediacy and "finding power." Therapy needs innovative supplements to prevent ritualization. Those supplements may be revisions. Even if revisions are not justified, the old forms need renewal of some sort, critical appraisal, reframing, re-contextualization: the old forms need to come alive for the new therapist as they were alive to their inventors. The influential critic, Northrop Frye (1957) wrote of literary criticism, "One of the tasks of criticism is that of the recovery of function, not of course the restoration of the original function, which is out of the question, but the recreation of function in a new context" (p. 345). So we should not be surprised that newer theories have emphasized esthetic multidimensionality (e.g., Schafer, 1970b; Spence, 1982). They would naturally be inclined toward a holistic focus because that is akin to esthetic perception.

These considerations show us that the therapist's mixed perspective is better compared to blurred than double vision, and his ambiguity is more thoroughgoing than a mere double game. His discipline requires dedication to a distracting theory that in turn stirs responses that distract him from the theory. He turns to a theoretical framework that sends him back to his own, now enriched, devices. To be sure, we have seen in chapter 5 that ideology figures in psychotherapy. But the therapist is not by vocation an ideologist. His theory will not accept his full attention. Unlike an ideology, his theory does not bless either a static perspective or a defined role. The therapist shows his fidelity to his theory by seeing through its pretentions with the very skepticism it has furnished.

This is not as Delphic as it sounds. Although theory sometimes serves as an easy fix, when it is working properly it does not simply translate ordinary experience into expert terms, but incites to new ordinary experience.

In the next chapters I hope to do justice to the therapist's more stable, familiar roles. But first his defining characteristic—his commitment to ambiguity—deserves all the oxymorons we can give it.

THE TWO WORLDS OF THE PSYCHOTHERAPIST

If there were no theory behind it, the psychotherapy session would be a very strange meeting. It would be oppressive (because of its lack of mutuality), evasive (because it does not have a declarable objective), seductive (because it deliberately creates false hopes), impolite (because it assiduously avoids protecting the patient), pretentious (because the therapist acts as though he knows more than he does), mendacious (in seeming to promise what cannot be delivered, either as regards the relationship or the patient's ambitions), and so on.

The therapist should try to keep in touch with this ugly social reality—the relationship as it appears stripped of theory—because it influences the way his patient sees him, and accurate communication requires that the therapist know who his partner believes he is addressing.

Theories differ in how much they encourage a therapist to travel between the ordinary reality of the session and his theoretical hallucination of it. Theories that are concretely phenomenological or are composed of interpersonal formulas discourage checking back with social reality because they are already closer to ordinary reality. Theories that include high abstraction, such as Freudian theory, invite the therapist to move back and forth between social meaning and analytic meaning, because they describe the mind as an object and do not replace ordinary social reality with a favored phenomenology. The fact that therapists often ignore this advantage of metapsychology is not the fault of the theory. For instance, theory encourages them to recognize that they are not just training patients to extend their awareness but are also deliberately undermining their adult self-respect (see Tarachow, 1963). Even if therapists do not see this implication, theory has done what it can to allow for unpleasant social reality when it says that the therapist designs an environment conducive to regression. In contrast, more vivid theories, such as that of the holding environment, or the representational world, do not encourage the therapist to see how different his view of himself is from the way he actually appears. The less abstract the therapist's theory is, the more he will be trapped within it because it makes him feel that his professional persona belongs to the "real" world. (I am artificially treating the theoretical rationale and the social appearance as two, distinct worlds, whereas in fact they are extremes on a continuum composed of different mixtures of each.)

Because he reacts to a double vision—one an ordinary social awareness and the other inspired by theory—the therapist's response is highly ambiguous.

The ambiguity is his defining feature (see Hoffman, 1983). If the therapist behaved as he does while seeing the interaction entirely in its ordinary, social sense he would actually be the offensive charlatan he sometimes appears, silent in order to force the patient to reveal himself without reciprocation, anxious to establish hegemony for its own sake, and so on. (See Haley, 1963, for a full description of the therapist as bully.) He could not be described as trying out other potential relationships. On the other hand, if the therapist permanently forgot the social meaning of his behavior (a more common error), that is, if he saw himself exclusively against a backdrop of psychotherapy ritual, he would be a self-deceiving *apparatchik* who is so dedicated to professional forms and habits that he has forgotten how peculiar he is, and regards psychotherapy as a generalizable way of life. (Such an habituation may be crucial to certain therapies.) Perhaps some recent theoretical movements have arisen to correct this unworldliness. Therapists have to be reminded by Gill (1982) or Levenson (1972) about the ordinary meaning of their actions.

But although fleetingly wise to himself, the therapist's ambiguity is related to his basic naivety (cf. Bromberg [1984] on the analyst's innocence). He is not all those bad things previously listed (oppressive, evasive, seductive, impolite, pretentious, mendacious, etc.) because he is genuinely motivated by an unusual theory, which amounts to an unusual set of expectancies. He does strange things without meaning to, and partly without realizing it. He is not engaged in a power play—he is not thinking about power: He is hoping for, or expecting, or being excited by, the prospect of a development that his theory has sensitized him to. When his patient reacts to his incivility the therapist is then reminded of the other aspect of his behavior, for example, that he is maintaining control (as well as giving it up). If the therapist were so lost in his theory that he did not recognize that, he would not understand the patient's reaction. We are none of us so cut off from ordinary social reality that we can claim complete innocence when someone comments on the unfriendliness of our therapeutic position. (Even the wish to encourage someone is covertly patronizing.) But in the person of a good therapist the patient encounters someone whose mixture of motives is genuinely not what it seems, and it is the therapist's genuine quantum of innocence along with his guile that makes the interaction yield something fresh.

30

Disambiguating Postures:

General Considerations

Although psychoanalytic theory has always required the analyst to be an ambiguous figure, there is some uncertainty about how ambiguous he should be and in what way. Even the purpose of his ambiguity is unclear. When asked, I believe most therapists would say that their ambiguity allows the patient's fantasies to be discovered. But this reason is also given by therapists who do not encourage or work much with fantasies. Those therapists are probably making other uses of ambiguity. In the previous chapter, I suggested that the ultimate source of the therapist's ambiguity is his unsocial attitude and the peculiar attention that goes with it.

Ambiguity does not refer just to the concealment of the therapist's private life. It means that he is not an identifiable figure even in the consulting room. If the therapist has a reason to hide his political activity, the same reason should make him reluctant to style himself as his patient's teacher. A role is a role, whatever stage it is acted on. There is no difference in principle between a macropolitical position in the community and a micropolitical ideology in the office, even if all that is at stake is being a blank screen for fantasy.

And, as we have seen, there is more at stake than that. The therapist's ambiguity is an acknowledgment of the plain fact that therapy is different from an expectable social situation while yet being at every point construable in an ordinary fashion. Every interaction has an ordinary social meaning, but technical theory gives the therapist's reactions a different meaning as well. In therapy, even ordinary politenesses such as greetings are decided (permissively or prohibitively) by the therapist's theory and are therefore more ambiguous than they appear. If he chooses to be frank that is not the same as someone else being frank, because the therapist has (ideally) something else in mind by his frankness than does an ordinary frank person.

Arguments for greater therapy frankness must reckon with the significance of both mysteriousness and openness as *intentions*. The *attempt* to conceal something that one would ordinarily reveal, has consequences apart from, and far more important than, what is concealed. Conversely, if the therapist is frank about himself he is choosing to make the odd relationship seem more like an expectable relationship, and that conceals something about the therapist that concealment would reveal, namely, his peculiar role.

Advocates of frankness will say that inviting a one-sided intimacy reproduces a child-to-adult relationship or caricatures a patient–doctor relationship, which is far from ambiguous. They are right that the stance is perceived that way (as well as in other ways). But the therapist's ambiguity requires him to be no more eager to disavow a role than to cultivate it. If his rationale requires ambiguity, he must be indifferent to how it is perceived.

The fact that the therapy relationship is both similar to, and different from, an expectable social relationship produces constant uneasiness in both parties. That uneasiness can be sensed in the familiar terms of danger scattered through the therapist's thought and writing. *Seduction* and *manipulation* are examples. The therapist can neither clear himself on these counts nor accept the accusations. Anxious terms related to *patient distortion* are vain efforts to defend himself. The therapist must continually perform in a manner that always leaves him open to criticism.

That is one reason it is misleading to speak about "errors" in psychotherapy. Because contradictory duties are required of him, the therapist cannot help but err. He has only two choices: how much trouble to invite and from what direction. (In training, a therapist should not be shown where he missed the "correct" response. Instead he should learn which errors—or more exactly, what undesired consequences—he is likely to bring about by an action, and what trouble he prefers to what other trouble.)

It is intolerable to be always open to the charge of impropriety without being told what conduct would be proper. Accordingly, we have noted in chapter 8 that one of the therapist's balance problems is the problem of assuring himself that he is acting like a therapist. Therapists are especially sensitive to this challenge because acting like a therapist is almost impossible to describe except in platitudes.

Every time a therapist tries to correct an imbalance, he identifies with some stable image of a proper therapist. A therapist must have such a picture ready when he needs it. When in trouble, he will picture an unequivocal role no matter how forcefully his theory insists that he remain ambiguous. The therapist needs to feel he is playing his part correctly, and that need is pressing and inescapable. (A patient who makes it easy for him to feel like a therapist will reap unintended rewards.) A good therapist will probably have a favorite self-image in the front of his mind, others ready to glide into place when he has to back down from the dominant role, still others he can muster by force when he needs to dislodge a too comfortable relationship.

Ideally, training promotes skill in shuffling roles. In order to start functioning, a trainee needs to begin with an unequivocal role, but it must be one that he does not identify with and can easily relinquish. Considering that it is impossible to let go of an interactive role without a superordinate one to fall back on, this is altogether not an easy assignment for the educator! It is a problem that is discussed further in chapter 36.

Some studies suggest that time in service predicts a therapist's effectiveness better than the nature of his training. Might the aging therapist's increased comfort with his personal idiom relieve him of the need to hold onto a fixed professional identity? It is tempting (especially for older therapists) to assume that years of practice bring increased spontaneity, genuineness, and intuitiveness. But the advantage of those years may also come from a greater amorphousness, the older therapist identifying psychotherapy with whatever he does, while newer therapists justify themselves to the profession by adhering to structured roles. Not just spontaneity but role diffusion and randomness may accompany the aging therapist's complacency and irresponsibility as he moves into a benign senescence.

Thus, disciplined shiftiness may vary from therapist to therapist but whether to a greater or lesser extent, therapists continually seek relief from their ambiguity in the snug harbor of an unequivocal role. Of these roles, the most insistent are: Reader, Historian, and Operator—the last taking the form of educator, parent, physician, and so on.

Some people believe there is an alternative—the role of Observer, which is professionally reassuring while still being socially ambiguous. Although easy and familiar, this option is a mirage. What distinguishes a role is its aim. A reader makes sense out of verbalizable expressions; an historian seeks causes; an educator looks for his openings and judges his students' readiness. The role of Observer is simply all roles except Operator. It has been invoked mainly as a disclaimer of manipulation. It is not a role in itself.

Outside the scope of this book lie therapies that make the therapist's role quite clear. Many of these are popular and profitable. Some are modifications of the psychoanalytic program. They may offer a helpful experience and not call it therapy. New roles have been invented, such as EST "Trainer." These programs are more explicit and reassuring than ambiguous psychotherapy. They usually acknowledge the operative role more straightforwardly than does dynamic therapy.

What distinguishes the analytic tradition is that it never tried to make things clear by accepting manipulation outright. It tended to cast the therapist as reader and historian and, at the most active end of the spectrum—as a teacher. Even the role of teacher was challenged. In the 1920s, Ferenczi and Rank (1925) wrote:

A further result of such instruction was that, without noticing it, one pushed the patient into withdrawing himself from the analytic work by means of identifying himself with the analyst. *The fact that the desire to learn and to teach creates an unfavorable mental attitude for the analysis is well known* but should receive much more serious attention [p. 39, italics added].

(Today the role of teacher is often disguised for a new reason: Teaching implies a human nature, either as its subject or in its method, and the concepts of psychological causality and nature are out of favor in many quarters.)

Because I have emphasized ambiguity so strongly, I must make it clear that the therapist could not be ambiguous if he did not frequently seem to have a specific interest. Ambiguity implies the existence of many possibilities, and the possibilities have to be apparent. An ambiguous relationship is not the same as detachment. If the therapist had no relationship to his patient he would be unambiguously uninvolved.

At the other extreme are the multitude of possible relationships including the whole range of the therapist's and patient's transferences, most of which would be shunned by a psychotherapist, especially if the role was clear enough to be defined (as foster parent, lover, etc.)

In the middle, are those clearly disambiguating roles that a therapist can accept from time to time – the role of reader, historian, and operator – which simply represent ways of deliberately responding to human behavior: One can read behavior as a communication, analyze it as evidence (about the person's life course), or attempt to affect it.

None of these disambiguating roles amounts to psychotherapy but they are indispensable resting places for the therapist and each a planned rendezvous with the patient. The therapist's ambiguity is useful only because it flutters around these unambiguously defined interests – interests in making sense, tracing origins, exerting influence. They give the project some intelligibility. They create an atmosphere of relevance. Because of these recognizable roles there is an evident point to the therapy meeting. Each clear posture sets up its own field of forces in the consulting room. Each has unexpressed premises and inadvertent effects on the others. Separately they give the therapist a transient identity, and together they provide a tangible medium for his wandering attitudes, his elusive wishes, and his intransigent theory. Because his unambiguous moments are quite genuine the patient can feel that the therapist's underlying ambiguity is worth his being concerned about. The therapist "handles" his patient by shifting among these projects, or responding to all of them as a simultaneous chord. Dealt with on these diverse axes, the patient feels himself to be a three dimensional object – an object that gets its definition from his own newly discovered directions.

31

Disambiguating Postures:

The Reading Imperative

T herapists always seem to be deciphering. Their most frequent posture is that of reader. They are reading an allegory, or hearing a life story, or just following what is said.

Enthusiasts of hermeneutics (e.g., Ricoeur, 1981) tell us that all experience is reading, but when I say in this chapter that therapists are readers, I do not mean merely that they are reading the book of nature, but rather that they are tracing overt and covert accounts of happenings, as one does when reading a novel.

From time to time, the therapist's attention wanders from his reading. For instance, stories are not absorbing him fully when he wonders why the patient tells them. And sometimes the therapist attends less to the stories than to the opportunities they offer. For instance, compare the moment when a therapist is confirming his understanding (integrating his experience of the patient) with the moment when he is discerning what is most useful to the patient (so that the patient can integrate his own experience). We may see no difference in the way he acts. But when the therapist's interest is in confirmation he is more in the position of a reader, while at the other moment he is in the position of an operator, a teacher, a scientist of causes and effects, wondering what is closest to the patient's consciousness, or what the patient is hesitating to say. Several times in chapter 8 we glimpsed Winnicott reading his patient aloud while his patient conducted his own business. On one of those occasions (see p. 100, this volume) Winnicott confessed to "muddle." His confession referred to a muddled *reading* he had just made. But the act of confessing showed that he was thinking of its effect on his patient, and had adopted an *operative* posture that then superseded his effort to get the "text" right. Clearly, therapists maintain various attitudes at different times, but a reading attitude is probably the most frequent.

Empathy sometimes takes the from of reading, especially when it is a complex awareness. A therapist can be so moved by what he empathically "reads" that he is distracted from the effect his reading has on the patient. In a mood like that, the therapist most closely resembles the reader of a novel, and the patient's mind might be considered a "text," from which nuances of meaning are derived.

The drive to "read" patients is as strong as the drive to make sense out of letters on paper. Anyone can confirm this by attending a psychodynamic case conference, where total strangers who know almost nothing about a patient, comment with phrases such as, "This is a woman who . . . " Is this dogmatic style simply professional arrogance? I think not. These are the natural ways that we think about what we are reading, as when we say, "This is a story of a repentant murderer," "This is an allegory based on Greek mythology," "This is a sign intended to keep people off the grass."

The reading imperative was brought home to me forcefully when I asked a group of therapists to discuss the ordinary social meaning of excerpted therapy dialogues. My procedure enraged many skillful therapists. I could not understand why until I realized that, by restricting them to an analysis of isolated speech acts, I was interfering with their bursting effort to read the whole patient. It was as though I required them to study random pieces of typography from a book by their favorite author. They could not help searching for the story, and they hated me for willfully interfering.

From such examples one infers that the effort to read a patient is a continuous pedal-point, carrying a melody that may be independent of the therapist's conscious plans. When asked why they were angry, some of the frustrated therapists in my group were able to put the demand into words: "You need to know more in order to understand the immediate dialogue," or "Instead of trying to draw a meaning out of an isolated exchange, one should wait and watch, or ask the following questions . . . " But there were also therapists who could not put their anger into words, so tacit and elemental is the reading imperative. The force of the reading imperative was shown by what they felt compelled to do. They *had* to turn the page, so to speak.

The reading imperative looms large in training. A supervisor offers a reading of a patient. It sounds good to the trainee, who always imagined therapy to be like that. But when the trainee is alone with his patient, the experience does not feel at all like a reading. The supervisor therefore judges that the trainee is not paying attention to the text: he performs another demonstration reading. In the next uncomfortable meeting with his patient, the trainee still cannot see how the morass of tensions amounts to a reading, and now he is told that he has a reading block (countertransference).

If a supervisee does not want to discuss troubles, he can present an achievement, and achievements often take the form of piecing together a story. (That is sometimes zestfully described as uncovering "material," which also implies another story – a detective story – about the finding of the story.) There is scarcely a more welcome activity for supervisee and supervisor, or patient and therapist, than telling a story. Although it is not what they basically want to do, the opportunity to tell a story temporarily satisfies the patient, therapist, and supervisor. Telling a story is a good way to remain on the active end of things and avoid unpleasant uncertainties (see Schafer, 1980b). It also postpones the moment of truth regarding demands.

So pervasive is "reading" in psychotherapy, that the question may arise, "What else can the therapist possibly do?" In some respects the hermeneuticists are right that psychoanalysis is an attempt to give a therapeutic rationale to bare reading. Freud's account goes beyond reading (see Part III, this volume). But reading continues to be an ideal of psychoanalytic treatment. One finds it expressed in the puristic insistence on interpretation as the sole legitimate vehicle of analytic change. Because therapists' acts are considered suggestive, this tradition treats interpretation not as a speech act but as a communicable proposition, thereby placing it literally on a par with a written text. Eissler's (1953) classic paper illustrates this effort: In effect, he required psychoanalysis to try to approximate to a pure reading. Eissler's paper, which popularized the term, *parameter*, reminds us that there is indeed something else that therapy could be besides a reading, because it was to prevent psychoanalysis from degenerating into it that Eissler wrote his essay. The degenerate something else is personal influence.

But a patient is not a text. And how extraordinary it is that this needs to be said! Therapists have no impact on a work of art, but they have an impact on their patients. Therapists act out of expectations of potential responses from their patients – expectations engendered by vague, unscrutinized theories, or elaborate, published theories. Reading is a different activity. Reading a novel, we grasp the necessity of what happens; reading a poem, we feel the necessity of its expressions and even its typography. To be sure we understand a text by placing it in a field of possibilities (e.g., of genres and traditions). But we care not at all what other works the author had it in his power to write in place of the text we are reading. We are interested in the necessities that shape the single, artistic object. We ask, "Why is it necessary for Raskolnikov to surrender?" not, "What unrealized potential would have enabled Raskolnikov and Dounia to escape merrily to Switzerland?" The necessities are presumed; we hunt for inevitabilities if they are not immediately apparent. Appreciating art means understanding the way everything in the work fits together. (When some of the older psychoanalytic interpretations of fiction looked beyond artistic necessity and considered the author's unrealized potential, they went beyond – or stopped short of – an empathic grasp of the work as art.) And in this respect, art is just the most compact vehicle of meaning. The same principle applies to reading a letter, insofar as we want to know what it says and not whether its writer is of sound mind.

These simple truths do not in the least diminish the importance of recent discussions of clinical readings (e.g., Schafer, 1970; Leavy, 1980; Spence, 1982). Therapists need to be aware of how pervasive, complex, prejudiced, and perspective-bound this activity is, although it seems so simple and straightforward. But as we become more sophisticated about the subtleties of reading, we must keep in mind that a focus on reading draws the therapist's attention farther and farther away from the ambiguous amalgam of roles that he is enacting. For he is not just a reader. He works at *producing* texts. And he works at *inducing* readings. Therapy is dedicated to the *changes* that must happen in order that an integrated text may emerge, and in order that the patient will be attracted to alternative readings.

And for a mission to change patients, it is important that the therapist is not only a reader but appears as one both to himself and his patient. In point of fact, the theory in his head makes the therapist a different sort of audience from the one that a published writer controls. When the therapist "reads," he does so knowing that his "reading" will affect the intentions of the "writer." The therapist's theory tells him what the effect will be. And, aside from the particular effect he expects from his readings, the therapist *uses* his reading posture to (a) buy leisure and immunity from the patient's pressure, and (b) find a middle distance between objective theory and social reactivity.

Lurking behind his reading, the therapist's objective theory of the mind deconstructs desire and draws the therapist's attention away from desire to the component interests that are blended in it (cf. Ricoeur, 1970). Once filtered through the prism of theory, the patient's dissected wishes do not appeal to the therapist's live wishes, and cannot find answering attitudes. (Thus one hears that theory is dehumanizing, reifying, etc.) It is his obtunded reactivity that keeps the therapist from exploiting any one aspect of the patient: He cannot take at face value the patient's particular desires; they do not seem wholly real to him while he is regarding the patient objectively. The therapist who attends objectively feels less personal impact from the patient's transference. (The term, *transference*, is a token of the diminished impact.)

But a theory that deconstructs desire will not make sense out of what somebody is saying. When a therapist listens to the patient's account, imagines his childhood, or forms a vague image of events in treatment, he is creating narratives. Narratives get their sense from patterns of wish and event, forms of striving, succeeding and failing. Such patterns are found in dramatic forms or rhetorical tropes, well illustrated in literature and history. Narrative is a name for human activity presented as human activity. Narrative tropes may even be necessary for grasping non-human, individual sequences in time. In some respects, anyone who refuses to put action into a readable, narrative form, is staring right through action and not seeing it.

Seeing through action is part of the clinical attitude, but there would be little contact with the patient if the therapist had no narrative forms available to read. Therefore, theory comes not just with reductionist concepts but with bridges that link them to forms of the play and fate of desire, which is what a "reader" watches.

The art historian, E. H. Gombrich (1960) has shown that, in order to represent reality, graphic artists need (and culture provides) ready-made images to serve as first approximations. Therapists, too, need such forms in order to recognize "texts" in their patients. One of the reasons that recent, holistic writings dwell on the self, on narrative, and on representations, is the need for an alphabet of self-defined, perceivable, dramatic configurations that can be picked out of the therapy scene and studied.

But although empathic reading brings the therapist closer to the patient than a reductionistic theory of the mind, it, too, keeps the therapist at a distance from the patient. The reading mode is, after all, rather self-involved. We do not contemplate our family and friends that way. (I am told that some therapists recommend the "psychoanalyzing" of novels precisely because that practice cultivates distance-taking and encourages analytic neutrality with patients.) A reading selects only a few possibilities of interaction. Just as a case history inspires little love or hate (although it may instill respect and compassion), a reading-acquaintance limits the way a therapist can use his patient. And the patient who receives a "reading" reception will be frustrated in his wish to be needed. He has been fictionalized.

But that does not mean that the reading-therapist is without wishes or that the textualized patient is powerless. If there were no wishes or temptations there would be no happenings (chapter 10). In the reading posture, the therapist's wishes are circumscribed, not interdicted. He is confined to cognitive and esthetic enjoyments, but these are not negligible. A reader is drawn by one of the most powerful of human compulsions—the urge to dramatize. The wish to get the whole story is not a tame one. I will make no friends by saying so, but an observer must record that therapists are helplessly grateful to patients who make themselves readable, and resentful of patients who do not.

32

Disambiguating Postures:

The Therapist's Historicism

_____

The therapist's reading will always turn into a history. Perhaps we do not need history to understand the words, "I feel bad." But we probably cannot hear that without supposing an antecedent reason for the pain, and then it is no longer just a reading. And certainly when the patient says, "I got a 'C' on my exam and I hurt," we are clearly in the realm of history (on a microscopic scale) with all the inference and causality and continuing objects that history presupposes. Of course there is a difference between believing that a particular academic defeat actually turned into pain and hearing someone talk about academic defeat as a cause of his pain, just as there is a difference between a history and an historical novel. But it is not possible to understand a sequential allegation without thinking historically, at least imaginarily. Nobody disputes that.

The term _narrative_, is now a popular way of referring to history that can be either real or imaginary. Narrative is a description of a sequence as though it were intelligible. And because it comprehends both fiction and history and is non-committal about belief, it is a key term for those who wish to depict all of therapy as a reading. This homogenization of fact and fiction is a much more radical challenge to the therapist's historicism than the older doubt about the extent to which factual historical detail is attainable and useful in therapy.

The radical challengers use the neutral word, narrative, to level histories down to stories. They get away with it because causality today has few champions to hold the line between history and fiction. Whereas the old-fashioned, here-and-now therapist asked only that explanations be confined to recent influences and current advantage, a purely "reading" therapist regards even current motives as a mere story. The narrative critics not only hold that the past in which the patient believes is just a story, but that the therapist's understanding of how the patient got such an idea is also just a story. The patient's memories, the therapist's opinion of them, and the patient's use of both memory and opinion are just readings and more readings.

In the last chapter I argued that, although the literary critic may restrict his thinking, a psychotherapist cannot be satisfied with simply "reading" his patient. One non-reading role a therapist must play is that of historian. In order to make that point, I take issue with four current attempts to shake history out of psychotherapy. The antihistorical claims I argue against are: that (a) one can describe the mind in non-causal ways; (b) one can adopt a useful language in which truly historical propositions do not appear; (c) history proper is alien to the therapist's concern; and (d) history in general is a fatally defective enterprise if it pretends to be anything more than storytelling.

Concluding that a psychotherapist always does some historical thinking, I then consider what place historical thinking occupies in psychoanalytic theory, and what effect it has on the therapeutic proceedings.

CAUSES CANNOT BE KEPT OUT OF MIND

We are embedded in time, and therefore every apprehension is a historical reconstruction. Listening to someone speak, we fill in missing or indistinct links in his message, and guess his intent over and over again.

In doing this, we make causal inferences, just as we would if we were studying the Bodhi Tree of Sri Lanka. Out of this comes a paradox that bedevils discussions of reconstruction: In some ways the mind's cumulative nature marks it off as a peculiarly historical study, but in other ways the mind's historicity levels it down to the common lot of things in general.

On one hand, "reconstruction" is simply the understanding of any individual thing. On the other hand, as Leavy (1980) beautifully demonstrates, the human specialties of talking and listening are so intrinsically self-reconstructive that in them distinctions of past and present blur into transcendence, making history a living presence in the human soul alone. Because meanings of the past are developed in the present act of dialogue, we seem to have a more immediate acquaintance with a person's past than with that of an impersonal object.

This double aspect of human life, as part of nature and unique in it, corresponds to the twin threads of causality and signification that are intertwined in reconstruction, the one thread representing man's natural history and the other his reflectiveness. Some people think that these two threads lead to two different kinds of knowledge: knowledge of man as an object, and knowledge of man as a person. We do not feel the same need to invoke formal laws of cause and effect to understand our friend as we do to understand his fever. But this distinction between knowledge of man as an object and knowledge of man as a person becomes less persuasive when we recognize that the quintescence of personal knowledge—mental (self-) reflection—is simply the act by which a person makes an *object* of himself, and even of himself-making-an-object-of-himself. Leavy (1980) writes "Mind speaks for itself: everything else is spoken about" (p. 31). But that is not the whole story, for when mind speaks for itself it also speaks about itself, and in exactly the same way as everything else is spoken about.[1] Signification cannot be separated from causality.

It cannot be sufficiently emphasized that memory is not merely an exploration of subjectivity: Memory is one of the ways that a person gets outside of himself and looks at himself as situated in the world. (A Piagetian would not forget this.) That is true, a fortiori, for reconstructive thinking about oneself.

Theorists who think they can separate the thread of significance from the thread of causal efficacy dislike inferred reconstruction because it treats a person as though he were a thing. But in order to appreciate what an alleged memory means to a patient we have to give it some possible reality. And that requires every therapist to attribute at least a vague lifeline to his patient. Accordingly, the concept of causality is hidden even in existential theories of treatment.

Whenever we look past *what* someone says and judge that he would not be talking that *way* unless he had certain experiences, we are employing causal inference.

NO LANGUAGE WITHOUT ALL LANGUAGE

We always have a choice of rhetoric. (Schafer's brilliant article on "The Psychoanalytic Vision of Reality," 1970b, is an important exposition of that principle.[2]) But only within natural languages. If we were to grant one style the status of a language, as Schafer (1983b) does, we would lose the ability to investigate the reasons for its adoption. Speech grows; it is structured by a language over which we have no control (cf. Gadamer, 1975; Lacan, 1977a). Every bit of our experience uses every bit of our natural language to construct

---

[1]For the most extreme elaboration of this point, see Harré (1984), who carries the argument to the untenable conclusion that the mind is just an hypothesis.

[2]But isn't it a step backward to think of the freedom achieved by treatment as an improved telling, rather than a loosening of constraints? It seems perverse to describe a change in attitude as a change in behavior. If we change a disposition to speak, it is the disposition and not the speech that should interest us, especially if its benefits go beyond easier communication.

external and internal narratives. What in effect Schafer has been suggesting (as I argue in chapters 20 and 33) is that psychoanalytic treatment is a subtle rhetoric, and his contribution should be labeled not as a special psychoanalytic language, but as an effectively suggestive psychoanalytic influencing technique. As a rhetoric, its usefulness can only be explained by a psychoanalytic theory composed of all language including causal and structural terms.

HOW RESTRICTED IS THE PSYCHOANALYTIC UNIVERSE?

Narrative order is indeed variable, and the storyline in which an analyst imagines his patient is partly selected by theoretical or personal preference. Nevertheless, narrative form is not just chosen; it is also constrained by a great number of forces, interests, and concerns, and indeed there is always all at once a multitude of narratives going on within any one conceptualization, and each narrative restricts the choice of the others. Much of what seems to be a matter of dramatic choice in the way we present ourselves is forced on us by a subliminal infrastructure of compelled narratives beyond our conscious control. The passage of days and years, the larger size of parents than their young, what tends to please and hurt people, the limits of human power, and so on are not items that we select or reject according to plan. Gadamer (1975) points out that the observer is obliged to receive knowledge the way it flows to him in the stream of time; his station plays an involuntarily formative role in his interpretation.

To emphasize the voluntary, craft aspect of narrative is analogous to stressing the poetic aspect of momentary experience. There is truth in both views, but a partial truth. All experiences use these modes of configuring, but conversely, the material for these configurations is every other kind of awareness. By calling thinking *narrating*, Schafer's existentialism artificially separates human freedom from life's material and causal flavor. (For a poignant reminder of our dual nature, see Burke, 1978.)

It does not do justice to the intrinsically conglomerate nature of thought to say that psychoanalysis deals only with meaning and is therefore not a natural science, or that the only sense we can consistently make within psychoanalytic theory is the sense that is made by a patient of his own experience. After all, even Schafer (1980a) specifically states that analysands not only tell about themselves but show about themselves. They make sense not just in their language, but through their use of language as well as by means of nonlinguistic behaviors. A patient may eventually make declarations that match the therapist's inference. And, hoping for that, the therapist may find it useful to treat his surmises as though he were being told something. But in fact, he may have made his guess the same way he guessed last Sunday why his dog ran barking to the door, and not the way one decodes a narrated message.

Schafer (1985b) has begun to elaborate the role of "actual" events in the practice of psychoanalysis. He acknowledges that analysts do not think just about psychic reality but also about the analysand's "actual" environment and the influences he was subjected to. These are not just meanings to the patient, but "actual" facts and events. But Schafer saves his anti-natural-science relativism by shackling "actuality" in eternal quotation marks. Those marks are intended to warn us that "actuality" is not an independent fact but a description conforming to agreed convention and to common sense.

Schafer seems to be saying that we cannot help supposing "facts" while we are busy organizing narratives and communicating with each other. That is what Kant found. Because thinking always involves certain categories, Kant concluded that these categories are part of the nature of understanding. No language can escape reference to things and causes.

PERSONAL STYLE AND REALITY: THE FREUDIAN CONNECTION

So far, I have argued that understanding a person's mind requires an understanding of many other things, and that there is no limit to the kinds of terms we use to describe it; that the authority for ideas about persons is as broad as our fund of knowledge, and, by the same token, everything we know about the world contributes to our reconstructions of personal history.

Freud believed that what we have learned from many people illuminates what we are shown by each of them, and, further, that we can find a sense common to many types of observation that is not told by the patient in words. (That is the procedure of natural science.) In particular, Freud assumed that we all know something about personal situations beside the individual twist given them by the patient's unique associations, and Freud depended on this contrast between reality and individual experience to make sense of the individual's behavior. To this extent, Freud's procedure was more that of the historian than of the literary critic or the pure phenomenologist. Freud did not confine himself to the internal criticism of a patient's speech considered as a text. His interest in brute reality makes him as uncomfortable to literary students of meaning, as his interest in meaning makes him uncomfortable to object relations theorists. Freud was interested in both fact and thought, and the notion of reconstruction lies right at the heart of his way of welding the world of personal meaning to the world of impersonal fact.

Consider the case of the Wolf Man (Freud, 1918). There Freud argued at length for the historical truth of his reconstruction only to confess at the end that his argument was unconvincing: these memories may not be memories after all. *Non liquet* is the well-known conclusion.

The reader wonders why Freud argued so vehemently to such an indecisive conclusion. What had his persistence accomplished? Probably this: Although he had to concede the possibility of a false attribution, he had satisfied himself that the reconstructed event was not an invention. An inherited schema would serve his purpose as well as a memory.

If verisimilitude of memory was not what most concerned Freud, what did? Was it psychic reality, in the sense of a subjective past? Probably not that alone. The fact that something was imagined a long time ago rather than a short while ago is interesting only to the extent that it altered the perception of – and interacted with – the real environment as time went by. Without that consequence, the mere antedating of mental states would be a trivial game. Freud was not solely interested in showing that new fantasies borrow pieces of older fantasies. What he sought to establish in 1918 was that the meaning a child makes of his experience is influenced by an unwilled imprint on him, and *for that reason*, the construction of contemporary hopes and fears can be graphed.

Any curl of the mind may be useful, but not every shape was designed for its use. Above all, Freud wanted to establish a nonmotivated substrate of mentation. What he could see emerging from the patient's material was not just purposes but inflicted fact. If that nonpurposeful fact was not historical events, perhaps it was the event of heredity.

For Freud, the primordial reconstructions of the Wolf Man's infancy had an importance beyond their representational accuracy. They pointed to just-given, unwilled matters-of-fact, which connected wish and purpose to a realm without. Freud was investigating the mind as a transforming (interpreting) agent. Mental states come from transformation, and there is always something to transform. Fantasy transforms previous states of mind. But there is always something for the mind to work on, even at the beginning, at which time, if material is not given by the environment, then it is phylogenetically given. Of course, what is "given" is always described in terms of potential affective and purposive meaning. Otherwise it would be a stimulus in the realm of physics, and there would be no way to connect it with mind. But the "given-ness" of the material links it to a world of other types of causation. Freud (1909a) explicitly described the synthesis of nonsignificant materials into significant events.

To say that Freud studied man's transformational capacity is simply to repeat what has often been said by others, that he combined a doctrine of causes with a doctrine of symbols. It is the causal aspect involved in reconstruction that a hermeneutic psychoanalysis is bound to reject.

Freud's discussion of the Wolf Man illustrates this combination of causal and symbolic theorizing. If Freud had been interested only in causality, he could have agreed with his adversary that wishes serve a current purpose, and he would have needed to show only that current purpose was produced by earlier events. If he had been interested only in the process of symbolizing, he could have accepted his adversary's view that the materials used by fantasy are current events. But Freud wanted to trace the antecedents of the elements *represented* in the fantasy to the earlier states that *caused* it. Transformed experience is both a consequence of something prior and a new representation of it. It is a new meaning as well as a summation of previous influences. As a summation of effects, it holds innumerable further meanings.

Schimek (1975) has presented a plausible argument that Freud gave up the seduction theory in order to achieve a more universal theory of the mind. Viewed in this way, Freud's project was to find the primary matters of fact out of which mental life is built.

Mental life is produced by nonmental forces arising from the body and from other entities, and it also refers back to them. The concept of psychic reality was not a trick to avoid dealing with the relationship of objective and subjective worlds. Psychic reality is a response to another reality, either contemporary reality, past reality, or phylogenetic reality (the last, a built-in feature of the person as a physical entity.)

That is why reconstruction always refers to a reality that imposes itself on someone and is not willed by him. Reconstruction is a part of the effort to understand the mind as both symbolizing and a matter of cause and effect.

Freud attempted to embrace both the historical and biological descriptions of the mind within the core of his theory, and so his theory runs the gamut from supra-individual forces to personal family dramas—from mechanisms of action to nested and evolved meanings. Understandably, many theoreticians would like to deal with these aspects separately, or to banish one or another of the heterogeneous models of explanation. But efforts to purify the theory of the mind do not look promising. In Part IV, I have tried to show why that might be expected.

Reconstruction takes psychoanalysis out of the purely hermeneutic realm; it introduces a great many other entities than the mind.[3] We have no choice but to think in roughly the same way as Freudian reconstructions are made; they represent the necessarily causal ways in which we think about people.

PROBLEMS OF HISTORY

Historical knowledge is problematic. How do we decide what life means or meant to someone else, if not by filtering it through our own meaning? Historians and philosophers of history have had a head start of several centuries in trying to solve this problem of accommodating biased perspec-

---

[3]For this reason, knowledge of infant development cannot be totally excluded from psychogenetic conceptions, however complicated the relationship may be.

tives to objective truth. (For a summary of attempts to find a universal vantage point, see Mandelbaum, 1971; Gadamer, 1975.)

Psychoanalysts have been shielded from this trouble by the finitude of the lives they study. Psychoanalysis places itself among the biological rather than the social sciences partly because the short history of an individual has a more constant pattern and limited outcome than the long history of the human race. No one knows how Man will end, but everyone knows how each man will. We do not consider it unreasonable to talk about what it is that childhood prepares us for. But if someone asks what is the purpose of the species, we know he is a theologian or a poet.

Out of place in sociology, history, and the evolution of language, the concept of maturity helps to make psychoanalysis a biological study. Because maturity brings limited possibilities, it provides a natural schema for selecting and describing earlier meanings.

It might seem, then, that psychoanalysis can evade the problems of history because the drama of development is given by nature, rather than being imposed by artful narrative. That is true, however, only to the extent that maturity is measured in nonvolitional terms. For example, we do not need a specifically historical model of human development to account for the perpetuation of the gene or senescence. But if by maturity we mean an integration of purposes, then it will not be described without a history of desire, a history that isolates and combines wishes, and shows their interaction. (Besides Kohut, Loewald [1978b] and Schafer [1970b, 1980b] contribute to this discussion.) The "point of the story" has to be ferreted out of the sequence, just as the historian must find a "logic" in history. So, after all, the psychoanalyst is faced with the same problem as the historian in giving coherence to a sequence of aims.

That means that the theory of the mind has itself a dramatic structure, insofar as it deals with the individual's path to mature aspirations. For that reason various psychotherapies can be distinguished by the morality play implied in their theories of the mind. One can almost always find in them forces cast as evil or reactionary, and these characterizations may be a major determinant of differential psychotherapeutic effects. On the subject of the implicity dramatic configuration of people's lives and treatment, Schafer (1980b) has been the most eloquent.

Understanding things dramatically is an aspect of empathy, and the kinship of history and psychoanalysis is exemplified by the shared problem of empathy. Philosophers of history such as Herder, Dilthey, and Collingwood have noted that history requires a primary capacity for representing the meanings of more or less remote people, for, if primary deciphering had to come from contemporary historical theory, then historical explanation would be circular. Similarly, in his plea for renewed psychoanalytic curiosity, Kohut (1977) emphasized the reliable capacity of the human being to make sense out of another human being's meanings, untutored by sophisticated theory. He did not say that we can approach a subject with a blank mind, but he held that interpersonal recognition is not completely dependent on disposable conceptual constructs.

Some theoreticians have reacted as though Kohut has urged the cause of extrasensory perception. But it should be pointed out that, as far as we know, (no one yet having shown how to construct an inductive logic) even simple perception of objects depends on some machinery of recognition that builds objects out of properties: yet we hear no complaint that this faculty implies an extra sense. As Cassirer (1929) pointed out, if we did not possess the capacity to read something else into our sensations—to see them as signs of what lies beyond them—nothing could teach it to us. This same reasoning tells us that if we did not have (or find unfolded within us) an initial capacity to arrange perceived stimuli into forms of human meaning and intention, no data would ever take such shape. (I do not speak of the development of this capacity in the infant; however, it is beginning to appear that it is accomplished very early.[4]) The issue is not whether we possess a special capacity for empathy, but rather which manifestations of it involve learning. (A good example of this kind of debate is the Chomsky–Piaget conference on the capacity for—versus the learning of—language [Piattelli-Palmerini, 1980].)

We do not need to subscribe to a formal theory to be aware of the world, and by the same token there is a sense in which we can listen to patients "atheoretically." But this means also that no single hearing of a patient can claim final authority, just as no theory in physics tells us that only one way of experiencing an object is correct. It would seem that empathic accuracy is not confined to one reading. And this is as much a problem for the psychotherapist as it is for the historian. It is no accident that philosophy of history and psychoanalytic critiques are both concerned with how narratives make sense and whether "making sense" is the same as making up a sense.

Comparisons of the psychoanalytic enterprise with the historian's have been made for some time. (See Novey [1968] for an earlier discussion, and Leavy [1980] for a more recent one. Schafer's "The Psychoanalytic Vision of Reality" [1970b] is exemplary.) Kenneth Burke (1954) writes: "Human conduct, being in the realm of action and end (as contrasted with the physicist's

---

[4]In considering this problem, it might be useful to reflect on Hesse's (1980) idea that within our theories there are no completely fixed "observation sentences," but just more or less tenacious ones—the more tenacious ones playing the role of observations. If this is true, "theory" might change "empathy." Schafer (e.g., 1980b) evidently shares this view. On the other side of the argument, Lakoff and Johnson (1980) "ground" basic metaphor in brute physical facts of experience, implying a fixed order of explanation in our understanding. Trevarthen (1980) argues from observation of children that some understanding of intention is biologically determined, but this leaves open the possibility that even these basics are conceptually rearranged with expanding experience.

realm of motion and position) is most directly discussable in dramatistic terms" (p. 274). White (1973b) suggests that narratives connect events involving human aims by arranging them according to grammatical tropes and dramatic forms. Speaking philosophically, one might say that while comprehension of the objective world requires one to think in terms of entities, comprehension of human desire requires, in addition, models of narrative art. (Langer [1953] describes memory as a kind of protofiction, which transforms a ragged chain of mental events into experience.)

History, and that large part of psychoanalysis that is history, employs rhetorical figures to train the observer to spot organization that can then be studied.[5]

The problems of history afflict every backward-looking feature of treatment: memories, screen memories, anamneses, recollections of yesterday's analytic hour, and so on. We can challenge every one of these with questions of validation, perspective bias, changing versions of a supposedly fixed reality, the difficulty of catching meanings as they existed before they were mixed with the newer concerns that inspire the search, and the like. The same challenges even apply to therapeutic communication: To what extent do therapist and patient visualize the same thing when they talk about the past, and how do they communicate if they do not?

But it is reconstruction in its classical sense that is most burdened with

---

[5]At the same time, however, we must be careful to note that neither science nor history is entirely composed of a single mode of thought. Harré (1970) makes that quite evident in the case of science. Kuhn does far more justice to the variety of cognitive activities in science than is sometimes appreciated (see, for example, Kuhn, 1976). In the case of history, attention should be paid to Mandelbaum's (1980) criticism of Hayden White. In effect, Mandelbaum points to the various categories of objects and projects that the practicing historian actually deals with before even getting to the choice of narrative style or interpretive principle. White is the chief advocate in the field of historiography of the doctrine that an arbitrary, preliminary narrative configuration puts together the primary field of study. But even White admits that narrative begins only after we form the idea of some entity (in the case of history, the State) for the narrative to be about. Even this supreme tropologist tells us that there is more to history than tropes. Almost all philosophers of science (including Kuhn) accept science's claim to be ruled by reality, although they may disagree about where and how the authority is exercised. And historians, for all their philosophical speculation, do not regard the past as an absolute invention. Schafer makes passing reference to familiar cognitive criteria of coherence, consistency, comprehensiveness, and nondisconfirmation. The casualness with which he sprinkles these binding formal criteria over the heavily stressed optional perspectives tilts his work toward an unnecessary relativism. If the philosophy of science chose to dwell on what was common to Bohr and Democritus, and left the formal criteria of theoretical sufficiency to a footnote, even physics could be made to look like one of the fine arts. (I believe that Schafer has been led into this disrespect for the interrelation and implications of cognitive criteria by the shallowness of the English school of language analysis [see chapter 16].) We should not say, therefore, that either science or history is defined simply by specialized views of the world, but rather that we can be introduced to the world only in specific ways, and that when we deal with human strivings, those ways of being introduced have dramatic form.

these problems. A classical reconstruction is the analyst's spoken inference about the patient's distant past, based on, and purporting to causally unify, a number of important aspects of the patient's current life.

A reconstruction is supposed to draw support from many aspects of the patient's behavior and experience. But its clues can never be as redundant as those to present perception. Inasmuch as it counts more on inference, a reconstruction must invoke theory more explicitly than other awareness.

Schafer (1980a) has eloquently described how theory uses narrative structures to prepare data for study. Each analytic school prefigures its field with these sagas: It does not discover them in the course of a treatment. Alternatively, one can say that the discovery of a characteristic life history includes more theorizing than is involved in simply listening to someone. Despite the trained belief of the schooled analyst that reconstructions are forced on him by experience, unprejudiced listening would in fact yield little of psychoanalytic interest. Indeed naïve listening is Schafer's (1980a) marvelous definition of countertransference. The knotty intermixture of theory and observations in analytic data is not fully appreciated by those who propose to separate a "clinical theory" from the rest of psychoanalysis. As the historian, Munz (1977) points out, meaningful data are meaningful because they are part of a causal sequence.

Classical reconstruction puts the analyst's causal theory most on the line. Causality is an aspect of every historical narrative. The historian Hayden White (1973a), who comes closest to Schafer in holding that dramatic forms shape our view of history, also provides a whole menu of explanations—causes—that must be added to narrative form to make up a historical account and he has recently (1980) added entities as prerequisite for narrative.

But although analysts have a causal theory with hypothetical entities to support their reconstructions (chapter 16), they have today, as a group, less confidence in their histories than professional historians have in theirs. We must say that, on this score, Freud (1918) was overly sanguine about the reliability of his method. Most of us would not agree that some analytic evidence is suggestion-proof, or that the total evidential gestalt will override any observer bias. Studies of the "Clever Hans phenomenon" (Sebeok & Rosenthal, 1981) show the hazards of such confidence. And we have been disillusioned by the proliferation of contradictory "discoveries" by various analytic schools. Too many apodictically presented etiologies look far-fetched today. Too many others have been put on the defensive by experience outside of psychoanalysis, especially with infants. Such writers as Schafer make us uncomfortably but inescapably aware that all communication is suggestion (cf. also Burke, 1950).

It is in vain that analysts claim as a research sanctuary a unique order of existence (psychic reality) where appearance is the same as reality. The plausibility of any inference whatever always rests on a wide range of ordinary experience, with its ordinary vulnerability to illusion.[6] We would have little confidence in any extrapolation from analytic data if we had no extramural memory of our own childhood and knew no young of any species.

Even when we try to ignore objective conditions, we only tune in on an early psychic reality if our idea of it is plausible, that is, roughly compatible with the situation as we otherwise imagine it. Certainly Freud used evidence from any quarter. Whatever history will finally say was the primary reason Freud gave up the seduction theory, it will have to record that he regarded implausibility as one legitimate argument (cf. Freud, 1897).

SKEPTICISM ABOUT RECAPTURING THE PAST

If fantasy can create images of the past, and if the unconscious does not distinguish between truth and imagination, or past and present, then it would seem that the mental record offers no privileged confirmation of conjectures about its history.

Skepticism is also fed by the difficulty of broadly describing so complicated an affair as a human life. Dwarfing piecemeal interpretations, reconstructions were meant to be grand summaries. It has become apparent that such summaries can be made only with the help of a lot of a priori organization and patterning, without which an infinity of alternative ways of construing the data is possible. (The concept of overdetermination is used to gather in a few of these other ways of construing.)

Meanwhile, analysts have become more inclined to think of trauma as chronic strain rather than discrete events. And there has been a swing in either prevalence or diagnosis toward character pathology, which is not a pathology that is neatly accounted for in narrative form or explained with hypotheses that are easily matched to memories.

For all these reasons, and influenced by a prevalent literary model of interpretation, reconstructions these days are likely to be thought of as organizing the present rather than mirroring the past. Novey (1968) already inclined to that view. Loewald (1978b) has worked it out in detail. Schafer (1979) endorses it. One finds it in Leavy (1980). Schimek (1975) presents an intriguing conceptualization of this approach. The focus today is on current process, with pictures of the past giving form to latent meaning in the present.

---

[6]Theoreticians frequently use the concept of psychic reality to evade the question of whether a reported or reconstructed event actually occurred, while accepting that the earlier psychic reality of the *impression* was itself a positive historical event. This assumption goes far beyond empathic grasp and supposes a secure, objective knowledge of long causal chains of mental states.

THE RATIONALE FOR RECONSTRUCTION

I do not think it is sufficiently appreciated that with all these changes in psychoanalytic theory, and despite radical revisions in the picture of treatment, what seems most durable in psychoanalysis and related therapies is its historiographic procedure. Schafer, the least causal of theorists, is one of the most temporally inclined. Even analysts who hold that some kinds of infantile trauma never become mentally represented still feel that it is useful to bring those facts to the patient's attention as historical events. One might wonder what point there is in telling a defective person a historical (event-laden) story about his deficiencies. Freud (1909a) after all, held that psyches are built by a sort of primitive historical reconstruction early in childhood. If one believed that, then one would naturally regard it as helpful to subject those founding histories to revision. But Gedo (1979, 1981) holds that what distorts personality is not always ideation; yet he is inclined anyway to remedy it in the same way as Freud, although he supplements Freud's procedure with other kinds of interventions. Likewise, Gill (1982), who makes treatment seem to hinge on visualization of bias, is nevertheless careful not to belittle reconstruction, sometimes implying that people hold on to transference until they understand its genesis, although at other times he implies that perceiving and dissolving transference may occur in the same act.

Examples abound: Winnicott (1974) suggested that because the fear of insanity is learned from a state actually experienced in infancy, the patient must be told that what he is afraid of has already happened to him. Winnicott thereby advanced two hypotheses at once: one about the origin of a fear, and the other about the effects on a patient of telling him a story about the origin of his fear. They are very different hypotheses, but Winnicott treated them as one question. In concerning himself primarily with the question of origin, and assuming that its revelation is therapeutic, Winnicott illustrates the historicity built into the psychoanalytic tradition.

For Greenacre (1980), the curative force of history is so evident that she regards treatment not based on it as a magical hope. But we should remember that everybody's treatment seems a magical hope to non-believers. Skeptics can point to patients who have turned reconstruction into a magic rite of self-invention. And we all know poorly trained therapists who chant reconstructions to tame discontent and bewilderment.

Leavy (1980) suggests that it is the interpretation of transference that gives analysis its historical thrust. That is true, however, only because the Freudian conception of transference is historical (as Kohut's, for example, in many respects is not). Schafer (1979) shows how exploration of the past is used to capture the vitality of the present (analytic) experience, but we can grant this without yet understanding why, according to Schafer's theory, it should be so. Schafer implies that the analysand's problem is the narrative in which he imagines himself, and narrative practice helps him to live more authentically. But if narration were needed only as a kind of perceptual training it would not have to reach far into the past. Narration must be grandly historical only if the past is causally important and not just narratable (so that what needs attention is not just *thoughts* like, "I am what I have been made," or even "I am what I have always told myself I am," but also what the formative influences actually were.)

Loewald (1978b) ventures a bona fide theory of the mind, so he is able to say more explicitly how a patient's present intermixture of defined and undefined, complex and simple intentions can be elucidated by understanding earlier and later phases of its development.

Although authors draw the dividing line in various ways, it seems that no therapy will be regarded as psychoanalytic if it slights the value of constructing life histories even though it might claim to resolve the transference in some other fashion.

There are dynamic treatments that are not primarily historical, for instance, those of Sullivan, Horney, Levenson (1978), Gendlin (1964), the gestalt therapists, transactionalists, systems therapists, and so on. Why, in contrast, is history so important to Freudian analysts?

Originally, the historical approach made sense because the patient was thought to be suffering from the unconsciousness of a noxious experience. When it was recognized that neuroses are not built on bare memory but on purposeful fantasy, it became harder to say how historical discovery could release a patient from bondage.

Insofar as psychoanalysis is a study of conflict, it would logically try to disentangle elements from their compromised amalgams, so that they can be woven into new syntheses. A reconstructive project would make available the sources of discomfort and sources of new competence. Against this, it might be argued that dissecting the present no more recaptures the past than pulverizing a tree yields its early forms. It is this sort of reasoning that leads to a therapy in which speculating about the past is just one way of exploring current meaning. (See in this connection, Greenacre's [1981] misgivings about those "constructions" that are simply thematic analyses of a patient's life, and Greenacre's [1975] reference to Moore and Fine's [1968] "constructions," which specify early feelings but not formative events.)

But I think that as long as psychoanalysis employs an overwhelmingly historical procedure, it is implicitly committed to the view that, taken together, the myriad cognitive and emotional consequences of historical events can be integrated only in one or another picture of a single past reality. And that would be true even though the earlier perceived world was already colored by meanings from previous psychic configurations.

That does not imply that memories are accurate perceptions. Although they are evidence of the past, memories do not distinguish past fact from present elaboration. Only causal analysis (as in judging coherence) can make the historical distinction. Thus, it is not true that whatever a person remembers or reconstructs ipso facto constitutes his past, nor that he acquires a new past by revising his memories. Although psychoanalysis turns out not to be archaeology, it may properly be compared (as many have done) to art history. Art history shows a present influenced by its past, a present that refers to its past, and a present that refers through its past to an outside reality perceived in the past. Of course, the past appears differently in different contexts, but that is true of every object of perception. It is only in a manner of speaking that we can say that each artist has a different past. Not just anything that an artist takes to be the art of the past is necessarily art of the past. He can be mistaken.

THE PROBLEM OF RELATIVISM

If relativism means that we can say anything we like with equal justice, it excludes the very notion of reality. But if it only means that there are many ways to formulate reality, then it is a trivial corollary of the concept of reality. Reality is something on which there can be many perspectives (by many people and at different times).

In a sense, a perspective depends on the questions that are addressed to reality (cf. Collingwood, 1946; Popper, 1958; Toulmin, 1972; Gadamer, 1975). Reality is what is common to the different answers, each elicited by a different question addressed to the same subject. Reality is not relative; the relativity of answers to their questions is what makes reality absolute.

In order to understand what reality has been perceived by someone (or oneself at a different time), one has to know what questions that person addressed to it, as well as the answers he elicited.

Freud (1909a) set this out very clearly. He supposed an interested organizing activity, which he called "curiosity," that makes experienced fragments into a meaningful whole. Curiosity, in turn, is guided by intimate interest in intimate partners and therefore turns those fragments into dramatic, personal (object-relational) narratives with human significance. Freud used his understanding of the subject's early sexual interests to decipher the reality that they organized.

For treatment purposes, we can ask what personal problems questioned reality. Then we would say that, in order to infer from memory or its equivalent what the reality was that a patient confronted early in life, we must know what problems he met it with. We, as observers, will necessarily search that same reality with our own questions, but at first all we have to go on are answers to the *patient's* problems. So, given the patient's "answers," we must find the problem with which the patient formerly confronted reality.

That is where difficulties of the hermeneutic circle come in. For it would seem that the only way we can know what the subject's problems were is by looking at the answers he believes he got. We learn his old interests from the resultant memories. But how can we understand the reality reflected in those memories unless we already know what interests at the time refracted it? We can not know his question except in terms of the answers, but we can not know what reality was illuminated in those answers unless we know what questions surveyed it.

Schimek (1975) shows that Freud sought primal forms of experience that could cut through this circle. Schafer (1980a) argues that psychoanalysis postulates standard human questions and interests that analyze reality. (It does not follow, as he seems to imply, that this assumption is a convention; it is actually a risky prediction that these were indeed the child's questions.) Gedo (1979) and Gedo and Goldberg, (1973) have provided an array of new guesses about how the child questions his early reality. (But these may be challenged as arbitrary. One might ask: "How do you know that this need is uppermost at that age?")[7]

If we could revive the original problems (questions) that the patient addressed to reality, we would know what grid he used, and we could then translate the present answers into the past reality. Can we revive the old questions? The assumption is made that this is what happens in the transference. Transference is supposed to give us the needed categories for decoding the present record of the past. In other words, we reawaken the patient's archaic cognitive–affective grid, capture the past perspective he himself once had, and use that perspective to identify the reality that he was up against. By saying that, of course, we have only removed the problem to another plane. For we now must wonder how to decode the transference. If we had an objective description of the analytic relationship, we could ascribe distortions to the patient's strivings. But we have no such objective description (see Friedman, 1973a). Indeed, it is likely to work the other way: we are likely to use the patient's history to define his bias in the treatment relationship. It is notorious how reliant we are on genetic hypotheses to make sense out of the interpersonal field. Schafer (1979) describes psychoanalysis, quite fairly, as moving between past and present in this mutually enlightening fashion. The hermeneutic circle is thus involved again.[8]

But the circle needs to be broken, and Schafer suggests that psychoanalysis

---

[7]It is safer to enumerate early interests than to rank them, especially after earliest infancy. But theory of the mind and theory of treatment seem to require a postulated hierarchy. George Klein (1976) tried to combine the empirical strength of assorted "vital pleasures," with the theoretical power of hierarchical organization, unsuccessfully, in my opinion (see chapter 23).

[8]The philosopher, Karl Popper (1958) correctly sees problems as the speculum of reality, but I am not sure that his description of the "logic of situations" sufficiently acknowledges how difficult it is to identify a problem belonging to a different time or a different person.

does that by *assuming* typical life events. We impose these on the transference in order to perceive it, and we do the same with personal history. If so much is what we impose, then what can we know? I think the answer to this question can only come from a study of the way problems between therapist and patient are experienced. Most of that work remains to be done.

RECONSTRUCTION IN TREATMENT

No action has just one meaning. A formal rationale is but one aspect of an intervention, the aspect that fits the therapist's idealized picture of how treatment works. In order to move from an ideal, self-congratulatory outline of treatment to a naturalistic picture of it, we must catch as many meanings and effects of technique as possible. We have to separate what a therapist does from what he means to do because what he means to do is just one part of the event.

We will not accomplish this if we believe that inadvertent fallout of good technique is just transference or resistance. Transference and resistance bathe everything in treatment. And a science of conflict should easily grant original ambivalence to all expressions and reactions. Therefore, there cannot be a simple, veridical "take" on a therapist's procedure (see Levenson, 1972).[9]

Resistance is just therapeutic action viewed from the other side (cf. Friedman, 1969; Schafer, 1973a). Thus when Kris (1956) lists the ways that reconstruction can be used in the service of resistance, the experienced

---

[9]Gill (1982) recommends constant attention to the nuances of the analyst's activities, even the possible meanings of attending to possible meanings. He writes chiefly of practice. In theory, Gill tries to hold a middle ground between the relativistic position that interpersonal reality is not univocally definable (p. 96), and the non-relativistic position that we can make at least a conceptual distinction between present-cognitive and historical-affective apprehensions of the analytic scene, which roughly correspond to realistic and biased views (although he also realizes [p. 85] that there is no clear distinction between attitudes determined by the past and present). Gill's disinclination to push relativism to its fanatical extreme also prompts him to distinguish between the analyst's technical behavior and his personal behavior (pp. 104, 105). Such a distinction must surely be available to any profession. And it is necessary for teaching. But it would be unfortunate if therapists thought that they could identify separate actions as technical and personal in the actual process of treatment. In practice, although an analyst's attitude may be more or less influenced by technical intent, it remains *his* attitude. No abstract process speaks through him. Nor does an analyst add personal style to an impersonal behavior, as a waitress adds a pickle to the hamburger she brings. In analysis there is no plate of food; there is only an analyst. Thus, in practice a reconstruction is a whole activity by a whole person, embodying all of the meanings and motives that go into an act. In practice, a reconstruction is not any more a technical than it is a personal behavior: it is a behavior with a technical rationale and personal significance to both patient and analyst.

practitioner will see in them universal overtones of all reconstruction (more or less conspicuous and requiring more or less attention).

How does reconstructing affect the parties of the therapeutic relationship? In sorting out effects I make an oversimplified distinction between cognitive and relationship aspects.

COGNITIVE IMPLICATIONS

Focus

As a description of the therapist's vantage point, *free-floating attention* is a relative term. It is not absentmindedness, reverie, transcendental meditation, or untetherdness. Purpose is not completely forgotten. Cognitive grids are required to isolate relevant features of the continuous and thickly interlayered field of study. The great psychoanalytic configurations that serve this purpose are well known. Most of them have to do with personal history. Schafer (1980a) describes them as the means by which significance is picked out. When the classical historical configurations are supplemented, it is usually by other historical configurations. (For instance, Gedo [1981] finds images of symbiosis and soothing useful as familiar configurations with which to make sense of phenomena.)

Every hearing makes shapes out of the wishes and fears confided, but therapists have wanted more stable landmarks than these fluctuating contemporary pictures. A general reconstructive bias is a way of focusing on a hidden "essence" for the therapist's mind to work on. In its narrower sense, reconstruction arises from supreme ambition to unify one's focus. A reconstructive program looks for a structure common to many expressions. In the therapy project, reconstructing sets up both a discipline (to look behind appearances) and an evasion (of its ambiguity). This *type* of focus affects treatment even when no particular reconstruction is offered. A feeling of mastery may be gained by the reconstructive intent, quite apart from the achievement.

Does a focus require belief? It seems to me that if reconstructions are a way of seeing phenomena as expressions of an underlying reality, then they must be felt to approach reality. A therapist who uses naïve reconstruction to focus his gaze will think differently from one who merely plays with possible forms. Whatever their similarities, an historian is not a poet. He has a different mental set, personal psychology, and influence. The difference is important to treatment.

Does that mean that it would be impossible for a psychotherapist to give up doing history, and take to fabricating personal myths? Many writers (Ekstein and Rangell, 1961; Novey, 1968; Leavy, 1980) acknowledge that false history can be useful. A therapist might suggest new possibilities of past experience without any conviction that they are true. He might try playful combination and recombination of "memories."

Flat-out myth-making has the virtue of being more flexible than real belief about the past. The great service rendered by Lacan, Schafer, Leavy, and other dialecticians is to loosen the analyst's frantic grip on his prized picture of his patient. Linguistic solipsism, literary skepticism, hermeneutic circularity, all encourage a healthy profusion of frameworks and a deeper dimensionality to cope with the constant, bullying need for closure.

Even when they are just toyed with, reconstructions are powerful sense makers. The form of a reconstruction seems to have a usefulness of its own. One reason is that reconstructions conveniently package multimodal structures and causal schemas in a way that can be quickly and easily assimilated. In addition, reconstructions implicitly sketch a "mug shot" of the "enemy" that treatment is supposed to fight. It is thus not surprising that new, helpful ways of visualizing patients often come in reconstructive forms (e.g., Winnicott's (1965) true self and false self). And many practitioners use them as experimental visualizations ("This patient behaves just as though . . . "). Conviction does not seem to be necessary for that sort of usefulness.

But a frankly playful structuring would change the nature of the therapist's curiosity. No longer a naïve historian, the playful therapist's curiosity would shift to the current scene; and there, I suspect, it would be just as realistic and naïve as a historian's curiosity. We can play with some variables, but there will always be others that we must take dead seriously for the game to go on.

Problem Type

One useful way of studying a feature of therapy, is to ask what sort of problem it characteristically presents to the participants, how nearly they share that problem, and how their solutions collaborate or clash.

Perhaps the most important type of problem created by reconstruction-oriented treatment is the demand that all transactions between patient and therapist must be finally put into propositions. In contrast, a psychotherapy oriented to the present can be as much or as little discursive as one pleases; it does not have to be discursive at all. The only psychotherapy that can be said to use the exchange of propositional information as an indispensable instrument, rather than a replaceable tool, is a reconstructive therapy. It is its reconstructive orientation that makes psychoanalysis, for instance, inescapably discursive. And it is this paramount discursive form imposed on all the other problems of patient and analyst that gives analytic therapies their gross identity.

Discursiveness, in turn, gives the therapist's cognition flexibility, which would be impaired by other activities. In describing a life course, the therapist is freer to believe what he wants (despite Freud's protest to the contrary) than he would be in hypnotizing, play-acting, personally reacting, or directly empathizing. For, no matter how active or capricious the therapist may be in these other activities, the demands of the situation hem him in; he is restricted by the patient's response. In contrast, the therapist who receives data as part of a distant, debatable story, instead of being entrained by impressions immediately received, can calmly reflect on the possibility that the patient's presentation is deceptive. And his freedom makes a problem for the patient, whose natural intent is to compel attitudes in his analyst.

In short, a reconstructive attitude makes the therapist an elusive audience. But his is a special, precise kind of elusiveness, for although he cannot be forced to imagine as the patient dictates, he readily shares the dramas he does imagine with his patient. Freudian theory encourages detailed disclosure of the analyst's imaginings. One of the strengths of the Freudian life history is that it can be nuanced without dissolving into vague generalities. Generalities are avoided by the famous particularity of analytic reconstructions. (It might be useful to compare life-history formats of different schools, such as that of Kohut or Gedo, with regard to how much reorganizing flexibility they allow in proportion to how much specificity.)

This particularity can only be had in a discursive treatment (i.e., a treatment conducted as an exchange of propositional information). In the process of historicizing behavior, a reconstructive therapist gives that behavior elaborate ideational content, expressible in detailed propositions. By contrast, assigning a present meaning to behavior does not offer as much opportunity for ideational elaboration. One can see this limitation in Wilhelm Reich's (1949) wonderful characterology, where the life-historical aspect of character is only roughly sketched. (But see Gill's, 1982, warning that history can also be used to escape current nuances.)

In general, reconstructive conversation rings the changes on current experience by multiplying the number of ways that a patient is compelled to visualize himself as an object as well as a subject. The opportunities and frustrations attendant on this activity constitute a characteristic problem for the parties in psychotherapy.

RELATIONSHIP IMPLICATIONS

Authority

As Schafer (1979) points out, the therapist knows the present better than the past. The patient, of course, is closer to his past than is the therapist. But as to what is forgotten—and that is the subject of reconstructions—the situation may be reversed. A therapist may act as an expert guide to the patient's past, with the patient a novice explorer. (The analyst "knows" from theory that there was an oedipal conflict, although he must guess where it manifests itself.)

Even when offered tentatively, a reconstruction is one of the clearest demonstrations of authority at the therapist's disposal. That is by no means to be pictured as bullying. Patients usually want their therapists to be authoritative. Reconstructions may be conceived of as opportunities for patients to see their therapists as authorities.

The role of reconstructive authority is not to be confused with dogmatism or historical realism. Those are other issues. Here I refer to the role and relationship that is set up by a reconstructive attitude.

Although the image of authority that reconstruction gives the therapist probably acts chiefly as a gratification,[10] nevertheless it is well known that a conspicuous battle between patient and analyst often occurs around some critical feature of reconstruction (see Kohut, 1979 for an illustration).

Reconstructions may be helpful to the patient. They are always convenient for the therapist.

The patient will react to the therapist's investment in cognitive authority according to his own needs. Nowadays this particular interactive meaning of reconstruction is likely to be diluted by constant revision, tentativeness, and collaboration in venturing reconstructions, in the fashion described by Schafer and Leavy.

Closeness and Distance

The reconstructive attitudes make a difference in the closeness of the analyst to the patient, and it does so in a number of ways. In one obvious sense, the therapist virtually inserts himself into the patient's childhood, and accompanies him as a sympathetic adult. To have one's growing life tracked and recorded with interest is an important part of being parented, as becomes apparent when tragedy prevents it from happening. This experience is undoubtedly related to the construction of a sense of self and to the process of mental organization described by Loewald (1960). In this way, then, reconstruction is bound to make for intimacy.

In addition, the reconstructing therapist is partisan, because causal structures offer an implicit exoneration.[11] That tone is lacking, for example, in a presentistic approach such as Horney's. One of the ways that Schafer makes

---

[10]I see no way that a line can be drawn between "idealization" and simply seeing the analyst as expert, because the patient has no way of objectively judging his analyst's expertise (perhaps nobody does!). Freud and the earlier theorists were more comfortable with this fact than most contemporary theorists are.

[11]In a criminal trial, psychogenetic reconstruction is more likely to be the approach of the defense psychiatrist than of the prosecutor's witness.

propaganda for personal responsibility is by regarding history itself as a voluntary narrative rather than a mirror of causality. Even if that propaganda were not supplemented by the deliberate rhetorical bias of his action language, it would increase the burden of the patient's responsibility, despite Schafer's appreciation of life's hardships and his understanding of situational inevitability. In contrast, the analyst who offers adult company in a journey through retrospective childhood, and acknowledges the passivity of the present in relation to the past, and the past in relation to the outside world, acts as the patient's apologist even though he may be unearthing earlier responsibilities the patient had managed to "forget." (Schafer does not eschew these positions, but they are not prominent in his later theory.)

Reconstructive efforts allow the therapist to be close without feeling compromised: He can express reactions to a patient, as though to a different person in a different place, that would be seductive in current interchange. The distant focus can make it look as though the therapist had escaped personal entrapment when he is actually reacting to his partner (in this connection, see Gray, 1982).

But the distant focus can also *protect* the therapist from affective entrapment. Reconstruction spares the therapist from being structured ("press-ganged" as Fairbairn [1958] put it) by the patient's behavior; it allows the therapist to take a greater distance from the patient. The concept of transference is an example of how reconstruction removes the therapist from the imprint of the patient (cf. Szasz, 1963).

Disclosure of the Therapist's Attitudes

The therapist's attitude is revealed more openly by reconstruction than by anything else in his standard repertoire. Of all his activities, it is in reconstructing that the therapist tells most clearly how he thinks treatment works.

Moreover, compared to an interpretation, a reconstruction is rich in sweep and cast of characters; it makes a more dramatic statement, and is thus more personal in its point of view. Being dramatic, it is also moralistic.[12] Schafer (for instance, 1970b) has shown that the style of a narrative is an expression of an attitude. One of the most important challenges in current theory is Schafer's demonstration of the expressive value of narrative description. The

---

[12]This has sometimes been overlooked because of the personally exonerating quality of reconstruction. Because the patient himself is not judged, the general evaluative nature of reconstruction is sometimes hidden (except to those who identify with groups, for example advocates of the women's movement). The moralizing of reconstruction seen in object relations theory and self psychology, although frequently attributed to those analysts' neglect of the patient's active role in constructing his own experience, is really the moralizing seen in all reconstruction, but magnified by the broader brush strokes used by those schools.

psychoanalyst is never farther from being a blank screen than when reconstructing the patient's past.

Finally, not only does the therapist reveal his theory of treatment most explicitly in making reconstructions, he also reveals a very specific type of curiosity, and in showing his curiosity the therapist reveals what it is that makes him feel he has accomplished something. His ambitiousness is specified.

Collaboration on a Project

The hunt for the past is an easily grasped, definable project. It has none of the ambiguity of the rest of psychotherapy. It is one activity that can be as clear to the patient as to the therapist.

People hunger for a clearly visible project, and they want to know what is being done to them. Reconstruction satisfies both needs. Observe in some nonanalytic psychotherapies how uncomfortable patients are with a relationship that, not being social, is also not visibly task-oriented or marked by tangible milestones. Reconstruction is bound to ease this situational pain, entirely apart from any value it has in producing change. Generally speaking, even the therapist is hard put to say how treatment works. Hence, the specifically historical project is reassuring to both parties, and that reassurance will be one of its most substantial effects, whatever theoretical mandate it carries. That is why it is so important as a disambiguating posture.

A visible project is important not just for the cognitive mastery it allows. It also provides a measure of how well things are going. There is an imaginable end-point. That end-point may not be the end-point of treatment, but it is a visible target: to discover the truth about the past. The feeling that "we are getting there" is important in making sense out of any activity. Reconstruction is a relatively easy way to elicit that feeling.

Recovering the past can deflect disappointment: ("We have not yet learned what we need to know. There are important areas that are still obscure. We can name them.") Deferring disappointment, reconstructions also interfere with premature closure by saying that there is more meaning to be had.

But undoubtedly the most significant fact about reconstruction as a project is that it is not only a clear project but it is a project that offers the clearest opportunity to clearly collaborate (as a partner in building a knowledge of childhood history). As Kris has shown, this can be used as a resistance, but according to our stated principle, resistance simply reveals one of the constant invisible meanings of a therapy.

Of course, a patient can see himself collaborating with the therapist in other efforts. But such collaboration is less explicit; indeed it is a matter of debate (for instance, under the heading of working alliance). In contrast, the ambition of the therapist to discover the past is not disguised, even if he observes Freud's caution that it is not a psychoanalytic aim in itself. An invitation to collaborate with a skilled, respected researcher in a project of great importance to both parties cannot fail to put an imprint on the patient's experience of treatment and the consequent treatment situation. It also, of course, gives the patient an opportunity to overtly oppose the therapist, but opposition is more interesting when it is more hidden.

We cannot minimize the psychological value to a working therapist of a potential criterion of completeness and adequacy—and therefore competence—and that is what reconstruction offers. Reconstructive achievement is not the only criterion of therapeutic progress nor indeed the currently prevalent one, but its potential value in that regard will always give it a special allure.

There is, moreover, another important meaning that reconstruction is bound to have. Reconstruction is an easily specifiable by-product of treatment. To those who believe in it, it constitutes "discovery" in a more ordinary sense of that word than other aspects of treatment. Other wisdom accumulated in the course of a treatment is also considered research. But nothing can approach the unambiguousness with which a reconstructor views a reconstruction as a finding. Consequences of that fact bearing on the therapist's stance, and on how a patient can hope to fit or manipulate the therapist's needs are legion, and need hardly to be mentioned. (Schafer's relativism is an antidote to distortions arising from the therapist's pride of discovery.)

The therapist is in the peculiar position of having to fight off roles such as that of healer or parent, which the relationship presses on him. Probably the most attractive substitute for the role of healer is that of historian. And thus the project of reconstruction will necessarily appeal because it provides an acceptable kind of disinterested curiosity—a counterirritant to an attitude that must be avoided. At the same time, reconstruction allows the patient to throw up a bridge between the sort of passionate interest he wants from the therapist and the very different kind of passion the therapist is willing to offer.

Finally, it must be said that reconstruction enjoys the status of the oldest activity in the tradition of psychoanalytic treatment. Besides its usefulness as a cognitive focus, as an area of authority, as an instrument of closeness and distance, as a tangible project that mediates between the aims of patient and therapist, reconstructing feels like psychoanalyzing, historically and culturally, and that, in turn, must have an impact on the therapist's presentation of himself to his patient.

33

Disambiguating Postures: The

Therapist as Operator

As we saw in chapter 31, many therapists try to isolate one clear role, such as reader-of-a-text, to do away with ambiguity for good. We should add that the therapist's craving for a straightforward role is reinforced by his wish for a single sort of under-standing as a goal. Because he frequently describes patients novelistically rather than biologically, he may narrow his target to hermeneutic under-standing, and excuse himself from the complexity of natural science.

One tradition alone has a right to do this: Writers who regard the individual person as a theoretical construct (e.g., Foucault, 1971; Harré, 1984) may consistently pair knowledge of persons with a single type of understanding, because they believe that the individual person is a recent cultural invention. If a person is a hermeneutic construct to begin with, he can be exclusively assigned to hermeneutics for examination.

But psychotherapists do not have that luxury. In their work they *address* individual persons, and we saw in chapter 32 that this involves not just "reading" their "stories" but also viewing them historically.

And that is not all; reading and history do not exhaust the ways a therapist thinks. Whenever a therapist contemplates not just his patient but the therapeutic interaction, he has in mind two people who will inevitably understand each other in as many ways as they can. The same thing is true of this book: Our subject is certain practices and objectives that have generally been called psychotherapy, especially in North America (and especially in the middle of this century). No specialized dimension of meaning has been reserved for our investigation. The observer of a practice has to accept any sort of knowledge that his investigative net catches. Ours is not a speculative subject and we are not free to set up axiomatic conventions for it.

Taking therapy as it is and watching what is done, we understand in all kinds of ways that the therapist understands his patient in all kinds of ways, and we see that each type of understanding employed by a therapist has its special impact on his patient. And now it must be noted that understanding the effects of each type of understanding is itself another form of therapeutic understanding.

We have identified reader and historian as roles that the therapist can identify with in his work. It is now time to note that a therapist does not just act out roles but also considers their utility. You can contemplate lives and treatment and trace causes and still not be a therapist. You are not a therapist unless you propose to do something to a patient.

We have noted that the role of operator is least loved, and for good reason. It does not take long for a therapist to learn that he is most likely to get what he wants if he does not appear to want anything. A therapist will not squirm when he is mistaken for a reader or an historian, and his work will not be visibly hindered by those appearances. But once seen as a manipulator, he has the devil of a time accomplishing his purpose, even if the purpose is just "getting" the patient to experience something differently. Much of this book has been concerned with how the therapist feels about "getting" the patient to do something. In this chapter, I recapitulate the reasons that the role of operator must be continually disowned. Later I illustrate, through a comparison of Merton Gill and Roy Schafer, the kind of operating a therapist performs willy-nilly, and what hinges on this role in the therapeutic interaction.

I
WHY ARE THERAPISTS SHY ABOUT BEING OPERATORS?

We have previously noted several drawbacks of the operative role: The patient can use the therapist's effort to create a familiar interaction instead of risking a new experience (chapter 4). Manipulating the patient makes it difficult to free the patient's voice from the therapist's suggestion (chapter 10). The operator's action is ultimately defined by the patient and it is therefore less planned than it seems (chapter 11). Actively operating interferes with passively perceiving; operations must be inadvertent in order to allow something to appear to the therapist as an independent datum (chapter 28). I shall summarize these problems in reverse order.

Operating is at the Expense of Perceiving

In chapter 28, I suggested that when therapists operate, they do it from two bases: They operate from a schematic idea of what can come to be, which constitutes their theory of the mind. And they operate from a sense of imminent movement, which feels like communion with the patient's current state, and which is incompatible with pressing the patient for compliance.

I do not wish to set up a typology with two categories, like the contrast between knowledge and intuition, or understanding and empathy. I am referring to feelings about awareness, not modes of awareness. Cognitively, schematizing and sensing are not sharply separated from one another. Indeed, I have argued that theory infiltrates not just the therapist's schematic anticipations but also his sense of immediate reality. When theory acts as a schematic anticipation, it leads to a presumption; and when it influences the sense of available liveliness, theory leads to a "perception." Both reactions reflect the therapist's belief about the patient's potentiality. We are not concerned here with how a therapist proves his theory or his discoveries. We are considering how he can do his job. What is essential to the therapist's work is that he experience two different feelings—one type that apparently certifies a datum, and another that apparently correlates data (to oversimplify along the lines established by Kohut [1984]). A feeling of being guided by an abstract schema predominates in the therapist's sense that behind what the patient says is something quite different that the patient cannot see (e.g., a repressed or strongly defended wish). Again, abstract schemas predominate when, involved in a struggle, the therapist feels that a force inside the patient is opposing the work (for example, resistance). By contrast, one can see a predominance of a sense of movement when a therapist feels he can see around the corners of the patient's momentary awareness to something that the patient will also see if he looks there (cf. Lichtenberg's [1981b] "observation platform"), or when the therapist senses that the patient really wants something he has not solicited but might ask for if encouraged (cf. Gill's "allusions to the transference" referred to in this chapter).

These days, as seen in chapter 28, the distinction has becomes invidious, with a sense of movement being praised and theoretical schemas denigrated. Therapists have pushed conceptual expectations farther and farther from awareness, trying to make themselves innocent observers. I have suggested that it is not accidental that these therapists are unable to say why therapy is therapeutic. Theory of the mind has been shrunken and discarded precisely in order to free the therapist's momentary interaction from self-consciousness about his influence. Therapists who welcome revisions may feel that theory of the mind has overprepared them, curtailed their spontaneity, blunted their perceptiveness, formalized, starched, and dehumanized their dealings with patients. Holism can be thought of as a crusade to allow therapists to feel more responsive and less operant.

We have seen that this campaign has two objectives: One is cognitive and above-board: The therapist wants to know what credence to give to what he thinks. He wants to ground himself in reality, even if reality says his ideas are fictions. He wants to know that he is not fooling himself (see chapter 27). All serious thinkers have that need. The other urge is necessarily unacknowledged and less deliberate: The therapist wants to be able to discount the influence of his own desires at some point, so that he can feel instructed (see chapter 28).

Operations are Defined by the Patient

In terms of theory, the therapist cannot simply see himself as an operator because the nature of his operation depends on what story the patient tells himself about it (see chapter 11).

Although the naive reader or historian finds it impossible to say why his understanding alters the patient, the naive operator suffers from the opposite handicap: Although willing to talk about altering his patient, he cannot elucidate what he did to accomplish this. Of course he tells himself his own story about his actions, but he does not explore the patient's story of therapy, and that is, after all, the effective story. Like the behaviorist, a naive operator cannot trace the detail of his impact. For that he would need hermeneutic help. Lacking an individualizable phenomenology, he prepares programs of procedures. The brief therapy modalities are packages of unknown significance, so familiarly labeled that we need no longer care what the patient makes of them and the only question we are inclined to ask is which package to use and when to use it.

Of course, programmatic therapists who roll up their sleeves and go right to work without worrying about how they look to the patient are not the only ones who accept an operating role. Psychoanalysts regard the psychoanalytic situation (the couch, minimum analyst input, induced regression, etc.) as an efficient cause, if not of therapy, at least of therapeutically useful states. And there are accepted principles of effective psychoanalytic technique. But analysts have always recognized that they cannot simply see themselves as unequivocally operating even with these few devices and principles. They are required to leave the meaning of their operations open, and therefore cannot say in advance of the patient's report that they are doing this or that defined thing to him.

It is the usual therapy ambiguity. One of the most useful phrases in the working therapist's vocabulary is: "It's all grist for the mill," which, carried to its extreme, implies that in the long run the analyst's operations are inconsequential, their meaning being assigned by the patient. On the other hand, there are writers, such as Tarachow (1963), who believe that the analyst does so much operating (largely by inaction) that the patient needs a measure of masochism to put up with it.

One of the most fascinating attempts to cope with this equivocation about whether the analyst is an operator is Isakower's (1957, 1963a, b) suggestion that an analyst should not allow himself to think what he cannot usefully tell his patient. Isakower did not mean that the analyst should censor himself. He was suggesting that the analyst does not so much learn to think how to be useful to the patient as he learns to think in a way that is itself useful to the patient. In other words, he believed that the analyst should develop a habit of "reading" that has a beneficial effect (because of its accuracy and relevance) without the analyst having to intend an effect. He called that cultivated habit "the analyzing instrument." Like some recent descriptions of therapy as a reverberating amplification of the patient's meanings (Levenson, 1983; Michels, 1983a), Isakower portrayed the analyst's thinking as companionate rather than operative. But Isakower did not ban operative thinking; he indicated that there are times when it is proper for the analyst to consider how his companionate thinking operates on the patient (his main point being that supervision is not one of those times).

Not everyone is convinced that it is possible to dissolve the role of operator in the role of reader that way, as shown by the fact that Isakower had to argue against a prevalent style of supervision in which effects *on* patients are discussed as well as impressions *of* patients. Most analysts are willing to think about analytic technique even during treatment.

Operating is not Freeing

Therapists do not want to give patients a fulcrum for transforming therapy interaction into an old, stereotyped pattern, and they know that their pushing can be used this way. Furthermore, therapists want therapy to free the patient's voice and not transplant the voice of the therapist. For both reasons, therapists would like to think that they are describing rather than inciting. Yet the therapist is clearly responsible for making something happen or at least giving it a chance to happen. A therapist may picture himself as a reader, but he cannot get by with merely reading to himself. At some point he has to own up to "manipulating." The role of agent is sometimes modestly restricted to just "reading aloud" (e.g., see Winnicott as cited in chapter 8). But even that risks putting words in the patient's mouth and, worse still, suggesting that the therapist has a stake in the truth of his beliefs and their therapeutic value. Therapists are always looking for a middle ground between trying for something and just seeing what happens.

In psychoanalysis, the operative role appears when the analyst thinks in terms of resistance. Broadly speaking, the analyst tries to "clear away resistances." But that statement is unacceptable because it is too blatantly manipulative. Therefore, if we ask an analyst what he tries to "get" his patient to do, he will probably say that he tries to "get" his patient to see his resistances in such a way that they no longer function as resistance. Here the goal of "seeing" (interpretively and historically) softens the image of operating. (The phrase, "analyzing resistances" combines nuances of both reading and operating in one image of a reading-that-alters.) But even though the image of operating is softened, any doctrine that directs the therapist's efforts to one sector of the field of process is bound to make the therapist's role seem operative. And the approach will seem even more operative if it regularly directs him into a center of tension. Thus if we compare Merton Gill's *The Analysis of the Transference* (1982) with the general body of Roy Schafer's recent work (as found, for example, in *The Analytic Attitude* [1983b]), Gill's focused attention makes him seem more operative than Schafer, whereas Schafer's concern with style rather than subject matter makes him seem to be a "reader." (I believe that it is Gill's conspicuously operative approach that makes him look like a "wild analyst" to Schafer [1985a].)

Taken together, these two authors provide an unusual opportunity to see where operating fits into therapy for, although their approaches seem divergent, they turn out to have instructive similarities: Gill's apparently operative approach and Schafer's apparently reading mode are both deliberately couched in "reading" terms, and yet both implicitly rely on the therapist's specific operations.

Furthermore, the operations themselves turn out to be rather similar (i.e., reacting to something in the patient as though it had actually been presented to the therapist, although it is not fully on stage.) The differences are just as instructive. On the literal level, the contrast of Gill and Schafer shows us what happens if the therapist manifests different proportions of reading and operating. And, more fundamentally, the work of Gill and Schafer illustrate two different estimates of the cost/benefit ratio of therapeutic ambiguity as against the usefulness of the role of operator. The comparison also raises the dizzying question of whether there are specific occasions when the therapist will be more ambiguous if he operates than if he does not, a question that hinges on how and where meaning is latent in the patient's mind.

II
CONTRASTING THE OPERATIONS OF GILL AND SCHAFER

Gill and Schafer have much in common. They are both responsible for major metapsychological clarification, Gill in *Topography and Systems in Psychoanalytic Theory* (1963), and Schafer in *Aspects of Internalization* (1968). Both have now decided to approach psychoanalysis as an intrinsically noncausal study of human meaning, rather than a natural science.

Both of these theorists talk to the clinician with the authority of supremely gifted analysts, offering compelling advice about technique. And the message of each is, to begin with, so humanly plausible, so daily confirmable, and so historically respected (the transference as reference point; the analysand as author of his own experience), that one is startled to notice how different they make treatment seem. Gill recommends a rather single-minded pursuit of reference to the analyst, evaluated broadly for degree of bias, while Schafer recommends a broad panorama of accounts, momentary and historical, introspective and interactive, demonstrative and discursive, evaluated narrowly in terms of personal responsibility.

I suspect that most clinicians find themselves thinking in each of these opposite ways at different times. At times, they think that what makes analysis work is generally what Schafer says and, at other times, that what makes analysis work is always what Gill says. I might summarize these differences by saying, vaguely, that treatment sometimes seems to get on by pictures and sometimes by pressures.

Both Gill and Schafer make our examination more difficult than it need have been by their relative indifference to the theory of psychoanalytic action. It seems that when the natural science model is abandoned, so also is systematic interest in the analyst's impact on the patient (though, in fairness, few theorists of any stripe grapple with the nature of curative action).

It is a relative neglect. Both writers have much to say about what produces therapeutic change. But it appears as incidental clinical wisdom or as marginal reference to accepted theory, with little elaboration. Both are more interested in describing the analyst's activity than in saying why it should be useful (although Gill allows himself access to the Freudian terminology and thus connects with its various rationales). Both Gill and Schafer require us to infer their theory of influence from their general exposition, aided by a few parenthetical comments.

GILL

Gill's practical suggestion may be abbreviated this way: An analyst should discuss the patient's troubled reaction to him. He should find a reference to himself in whatever the patient says, even to the point of asking for it if he cannot see a clue (Gill, 1982, pp. 111, 124). This principle leads to a constant hunt for—and translation of—covert allusions to the transference.[1] Moreover, while looking for the patient's reaction, the analyst should seek a plausible explanation of the patient's view in what the analyst has actually

---

[1] ". . . if the transference idea is not already conscious, the analyst makes it so by interpreting allusions to the transference in the explicit nontransference associations" (p. 115). "In summary, I advocate another shift in emphasis, in addition to giving priority to the analysis of resistance to the awareness of transference. Even after some aspect of the transference has been brought to awareness, instead of priority going to the resolution of such transference by relating it to contemporary or genetic extratransference material, it should go to further work within the analytic situation" (p. 120).

done to him.[2] He should then work out with the patient what bias the patient has contributed to that perception.[3]

The aim is to collaboratively discover the patient's transference distortions within a setting that makes them less necessary.[4] Accounts of other matters are interesting principally in the way they are used to express feelings about the analyst, or the light they shed on the patient's view of the analyst.

Gill leaves to accepted technique the matter of what the analyst does when the patient talks directly about the analyst. He does recognize that even at those times, the patient may be covertly expressing still other transference feelings (pp. 16, 74; Gill and Hoffman, 1982, p. 179). As to personal history, Gill finds it helpful in dissecting the patient's bias (Gill, 1982, pp. 95, 123). But he warns that genetic interpretations are frequently used to discount the patient's real experience of the analyst and the analyst's actual responsibility for it.[5]

Gill's Primary Rationale: Resistance

Gill says that he is led to his recommendations by a consideration of the nature of resistance. If we put Gill's use of Freud's definition of resistance (p. 46) together with his other comments, the argument runs like this:

Resistance is the patient's way of dealing with his analyst so as to protect his investment in primitive gratification. A patient can do this in two ways. He can avoid "specific and regressive involvement with the analyst." Or, once involved, he can refuse to see that involvement as regressive and optional.

If the patient has an intense, fixed view of the analyst, the analyst should

---

[2]"Just as the patient attempts to find a realistic basis for his experience of the relationship, so must the analyst find as plausible a realistic basis as he can for his interpretations of this experience. In doing so, he underscores the importance of what is actually going on" (p. 111).

[3]"The overcoming of resistance to the resolution of the transference means that the patient must come to see that certain attitudes are indeed transference, or at least to recognize the role played in his attitudes by what he brings to the situation" (p. 117).

[4]The transference is resolved during its analysis by two factors: "First, the clarification of the contribution of the analytic situation to the transference leads to the recognition that the way the patient has experienced the analytic situation is idiosyncratic. The patient must then perforce recognize his own contribution to this experience, that is, the contribution from the past. Second, barring impeding countertransference, the examination of the transference inevitably involves an interpersonal experience with the analyst which is more beneficent than the transference experience" (pp. 178–179).

[5]"It is not that contemporary extra-transference and genetic transference interpretations have no value, but the danger is always that they will be employed as a flight from the immediacy of the transference within the analytic situation. They are the interpretations most likely to lend themselves to defensive intellectualization by both participants, and their repercussions on the transference may well be left unexamined. This is not to deny that contemporary and genetic material may have to be *clarified* and even interpreted to gain clues to understanding the transference. It is work with extra-transference material as such, without any reference to the transference, that I find questionable" (pp. 122–123).

help him recognize his bias, and the transference will resolve itself. Although the analyst is not an authority on reality, he and his patient can reach an agreement on what might have been seen differently. When the patient becomes aware of his prejudice within the range of possible perspectives, the prejudice no longer traps him, and the transference dissolves.

If, however, the patient does not explicitly talk about the analyst, the analyst must look for his subject matter in the patient's covert allusions. At such a time, the patient is resisting awareness of the transference or resisting experience of the transference (the distinction is not elaborated). This kind of resistance is overcome by showing the patient the covertly transferential nature of what he does say. The analyst helps the patient to see the resisted attitudes by acknowledging their plausibility.

Thus Gill's first rationale for his procedure is that the transference should always be interpreted because that is where the resistance is. But then the pressing question is: Where is the *transference* manifested? And we must answer that it is everywhere. Anything the patient does has some relationship to the transference, because it happens in the presence of the analyst.

Transference and resistance are reflected in every effort of the patient to adapt his old wishes to his new, psychoanalytic existence. But when we look at the matter that way, we might be inclined to take up Gray's (1973) position rather than Gill's and state that the analyst is interested in *everything* that is presented to him, in regard to how it is arranged for his attention, not just in allusions to the analyst's behavior. To put it another way, we would not necessarily expect allusions to the analyst to be veiled expressions of one focal reaction; we would expect allusions to the analyst to appear as a continuous shaping of the patient's productions according to the myriad valences of the transference at the moment of speech. (These allusions could be discussed both intrapsychically and interpersonally. In practice, for example, Gill is as interested in a patient's need to comply as he is in his semijustified grievances [Gill and Hoffman, 1982, p. 102].)

We may grant Gill's point that the patient's behavior is partly caused by the analyst's attitudes. An analyst should want to know how he deserves the patient's reaction. And he would satisfy himself on that score most *easily* if the patient were reacting to some discrete act or attitude of his. But although it would make his task easiest if the patient's reaction were always that specific, the mind was not created for the benefit of analysts, and we cannot assume that its reaction will always be of that sort.

I conclude that one would not be forced to adopt Gill's technique simply by being convinced that resistance is entirely expressed in the transference and must always be dealt with there. Equating transference with resistance does not tell us how best to call attention to either transference or resistance in treatment. That is a separate question, involving issues of *influence* and not simply definition of concepts. I believe that Gill is actually concerned with influencing the formation of meaning, and it is his concern with that issue, rather than a simple need for theoretical clarity, that inclines him toward interpersonal terms. For purely theoretical purposes, intrapsychic and inter-personal definitions would do equally well. Resistance can also be described intrapsychically. Situations between people also have intrapsychic meaning. As I read him, what properly inspires Gill's sympathy for interpersonal formulations is his recognition that *the forces that determine the outcome of the treatment relationship* are inevitably interpersonal. The analyst must do something to insure that the patient can see things with a freedom he is not used to. Therefore, Gill is not content to make allusions explicit: he wants to seize the attitudes they represent and undermine their hold on the patient's world view. In the context of this operation on the patient, "resistance" has to be an interpersonal term. In passing, we might note that Gill's theory is even more interpersonal than those theories according to which the analyst amplifies the patient's meanings by "resonating" with them (e.g., Levenson, 1972). Such theories are probably describing the same transaction that Gill has in mind, but their language hides the specific, directional pressure that Gill acknowledges (and which we are more accustomed to in the analytic literature).

Gill's Secondary Rationale: Interpretation

Gill knows that a shift of meaning has already occurred when an unrecog-nized perception is acknowledged (p. 178). Acknowledging it probably allows modification by other thoughts. But what is more important, I think, is that a forbidden perception is embedded in one context while an allowed percep-tion is embedded in a different context. Gill is vague about this shift in contexts, because it involves the effect of the therapeutic relationship on the patient's meaning (p. 119), and he is extremely ambivalent about that. A " 'corrective emotional experience' [is] *not sought for* as such, but [is] an *essential byproduct* [!] of the work" (Gill, 1982, p. 179, italics added; see also, p. 93).

The equivocation so honestly set forth here is found throughout Gill's writings on treatment. Being anti-authoritarian, he wants to work by enlight-enment alone. But his interpersonal paradigm shows him that meanings arise through interaction. He thus finds himself caught between the tradition that regards meanings as already prepared within the patient's mind, needing only to be discovered by analysis (as, for instance, in Ferenczi and Rank [1925]) and the tradition that describes meanings as newly created in psychoanalysis (e.g., Lichtenberg, 1983). Positioned in the middle ground, Gill says, in effect, that an experience of regression is actualized by calling attention to its incipient overtures.

But it can happen that a person is able to live out a certain role and relationship *because* he keeps it secret from himself. So the old question remains with us whether interpreting the transference "widens and deepens" it or, on the contrary, diminishes it. It is difficult to answer this question because there is no one transference. Interpreting may enlarge one transference and discourage another.

Even on superficial questioning, patients confess that talking freely about the analyst is not only too intimate a surrender (for example), but also a spoiler of the desired, tacitly felt relationship. Every contradictory thing that has ever been said on this subject seems to be true. Transferences that are not mentioned, let alone analyzed, are the strongest transferences. Interpretation, or even simple discussion of a transference, tends to dispel, not enrich it. But *also*, transferences that are not picked up and discussed may remain gray, bland, dull, rudimentary, and scarcely felt.

Gill (1982, p. 124) recognizes that an undiscussed transference attitude may be much more intense, real, and intractable than one that has been discussed. He also believes (p. 22) that allusive themes that are not picked up continue through the hour (and presumably beyond). He holds that transferences account for the outcome of treatment to the extent that they are not discussed; if they are discussed, the outcome has more to do with newly achieved flexibility and less with transference (pp. 119–120). These beliefs imply that interpretation *dispels* transference. But overall, Gill holds that calling attention to them maximally develops transference.

It seems to me, however, that as Gill encourages some transferences, he disposes of many more by his behavior as an analyst. (Very generally, as a good analyst, Gill tends to behave like someone who neither wants nor appreciates any one attitude from his patient more than any other, and that by itself demolishes a lot of transferences!) I think it best to say not that Gill catches the transference in *flagrante*, but that he shatters an inhibiting transference by encouraging the one alluded to.

In any case, Gill feels that although the analyst helps a transference perception to become flexible by making it explicit, he will make it still more flexible if he contrasts it with reality. The analyst does not authoritatively define reality; but together with the patient he sets out an array of possible meanings, against which the patient's bias may be seen by contrast.

Since Gill does not want to rely indefinitely on positive transference, it is important for him to believe in an independent incentive that inspires flexibility. That incentive is provided by a neutral reality (a range of neutral possibilities) which the patient's cognitive sensibility cannot deny when it is presented to him in discussion with the analyst. Gill strongly believes that the essence of the psychoanalytic method is that it accomplishes its goals by verbal clarification of the patient's experience of the analyst.

To facilitate the comparison of experience with reality, Gill relies on a distinction between cognitive and affective apprehensions. The distinction between cognitive and affective responses is another example of Gill's mid-position between those who feel that formed but concealed meanings are revealed in psychoanalysis and those who feel that psychoanalysis develops meanings into something new. Since he uses separate categories of cognitive and affective meaning, Gill should be able to say that treatment helps patients appreciate how they have cognitively twisted the truth to suit their needs. On the other hand, his policy of canvassing all the ways that the truth can be perceived, each presumably with its own affective bias, seems to be directed toward altering or expanding the patient's wish-forms, and from this standpoint, the distinction between cognitive and (psychogenetically determined) affective reactions would seem superfluous and misleading. The Gill of *Topography and Systems* would not have had this problem.

Other Rationales for Gill's Procedure

If resistance can be nebulous in form and origin, and if calling attention to transferences cannot be counted on either to encourage or to invalidate them, we would need another rationale for Gill's technique. It should not be hard to find one. What the analyst *does* when he carries out Gill's procedure is, after all, something complex and forceful, regardless of his definition of resistance.

To appreciate this, one should again compare Gill's approach with Gray's (1973). Gray typically draws the patient's attention to an interaction of two conflicting tendencies, both of them evident to the patient. Therefore, Gray does not have to "sell" his patient on a hidden content. Gill, however, has to make his patient aware of one hidden feeling. He must have some power to make the patient acknowledge what he did not previously acknowledge. Gill implies that the analyst's willingness to accept the patient's feelings without rancor has a corrective effect. True, he warns against deliberately adopting a sympathetic attitude as a "corrective emotional experience" (in the sense of a posturing manipulation). However, Gill's account does seem to imply that the analyst's readiness to see the patient's perceptions as reasonable is at least partly what allows the patient to acknowledge them. And that implies that the patient formerly regarded them as unreasonable or intolerable to the analyst (see Gill, 1982, pp. 59-60). The very act of self-revelation may create ill will toward the analyst who is seducer and audience, and it might also be freed up by the analyst's acceptance of the ill will. (Once again it must be noted that Gill himself does not *want* his accepting attitude to be the decisive factor; he wants the decisive factor to be his clarifying of the patient's experience. I am elaborating what I believe is the rationale implied by his procedure.)

The covert allusions which Gill finds it useful to draw out are unpleasant. His clinical examples confirm that. What Gill takes as the focus of analytic work is not just anything referrable to the analyst, but the *trouble* a patient has with his analyst that he is not able to admit to himself. Gill is interested in troubled feelings. An unavowed transference feeling might lurk in a pleasant reminiscence. But Gill does not encourage the analyst to say something like this: "You talk about enjoying the movie yesterday with your husband; perhaps you enjoyed our session last Thursday." Only if the analyst perceived her comment as an invidious comparison with the misery of the analytic session, or an expression of the patient's hope for what she has not gotten from the analyst, or a discomfort about acknowledging her enjoyment of the analyst, or some such *troubled* feeling, would yesterday's happy experience appear to the analyst as an allusion fit for analytic work. It is not the allusion per se but trouble that gives the analyst his opportunity.

But trouble is not merely a useful fulcrum for forcing the patient's perceptions. It is also important as a signpost for the analyst. As Spence (1982) points out, anything can be seen as related to anything else. If we were to follow the rule to look for what is being expressed covertly, it would hardly tell us what to make out of process, unless we had some reference point. Transference is a good reference point. But it is too broad a concept to discriminate details. and I believe that one of the attractions of Gill's procedure is that it offers specific, disturbing actions of the analyst as a reference point for parsing process.

Of course, Gill could say that whatever is unexpressed is troubled insofar as it cannot be expressed. (This would entail the thesis that feelings and thoughts are always explicitly stated unless there is a countervailing force.) But then we could take anything as a present but stifled meaning. Absence would prove presence; nothing would be excluded. On the other hand, manifest trouble narrows the field a little, provided, of course, that one has a way of identifying it.

By orienting toward trouble, dissatisfaction, or complaint, Gill finds a specific way of decoding the patient's communication. That is one rationale that may be offered for his method.

Another rationale might be that Gill has found a way of isolating a patient's problem as something that the analyst can also feel as a problem. One cannot depend on what a patient *says* is a problem. And we cannot assume that what feels problematic to the analyst is a problem to the patient. The way Gill identifies a *shared* problem is by sensing that he has disturbed the patient in a way that the patient has difficulty correcting. (Its inexplicitness shows that the patient has trouble correcting it.) In addition, by this means, Gill trains the patient to become sensitive to a certain kind of problem. (By contrast, Schafer is more variously problem oriented.)

Third, Gill gives the patient instructions: he shows him that the analyst is important to him. I believe he indicates that this is what the patient should be attending to, although he denies that he does that (Gill, 1982, pp. 66, 111).

Gill has a way of finding a specific, personal, immediate problem with the analyst that the patient is working on and throws his weight behind certain efforts to solve it.

Let us look closely at this procedure from a phenomenological point of view. If it is an analyst's reaction that makes it possible for the patient to take action (to "come out with" what he is alluding to), that suggests that what held him back in the first place was mistrust of the analyst. By his approach, Gill has shown that he is not like the patient thought him to be. That difference gives the patient leeway for the new possibility of explicitly acknowledging what he has covertly implied (pp. 119, 178). (This was also Strachey's strategy.)[6]

To put this another way, if Gill persuades a patient to recognize a reaction that he formerly concealed, he must have found something which was almost ready to be revealed. He has seen it manifested in a way, though not a way that the patient could look at and explore. Gill has found a problem that is *near* a new solution. (Gill implies that it is a substantial problem, involved in a conflict, since he holds that mere "muddles" are not the kind of things addressed by analysis [p. 137]. Although Gill's position seems to me the most cogent, others may want to consider that work on allusions sometimes amounts to a didactic clarification of the patient's subliminal perception.)

Let us sum up the influence that the analyst brings to bear when he follows Gill's advice. (1) As recommended by Ferenczi and Rank (1925), he induces engagement. (2) As Strachey (1934) recommended, he forces himself on the patient in a way that is different from the role he has been assigned by the patient. (3) He sees where the patient is about to—but has not quite—let himself do something different and draws him out (following the familiar rule to operate with what is closest to consciousness).

SCHAFER

Schafer makes three claims: He seeks to reform psychoanalytic theory. He claims that his is the best description of how analysts think. And he believes that troubled people who adopt his approach will become less troubled.

The last of these claims is the most relevant to therapeutic action and the least systematically set forth.

In essence, Schafer says that troubled people observe themselves faultily. In their self-deception, they mistake what they are doing, and (though this is less clear) they also do things incorrectly.

---

[6]Note, by the way, that Gill hints that the analyst should not just elicit the patient's alluded-to needs, but also sometimes heed them by modifying his behavior! (Gill, 1982, p. 179; Gill and Hoffman, 1982, pp. 91–115).

Moreover, once we distinguish, as we should, action plain and action observed, we realize that there are four possibilities in this regard: faulty action that is accurately observed, faulty observation of action that is just right, faulty observation of faulty action, and accurate observation of action that is just right (1973a, p. 273).

"Faulty action" may seem self-explanatory, but that is only because we automatically think of it in realistic, or even physical, terms. Thus, as Freudian metapsychologists, we can easily picture an id-mover forcing an ego-executor to perform an action partly designed by a superego, which in the end fails to satisfy the urgent wishes, or relieve the feelings of guilt, or bring about a tolerable relationship with the world. The purposes which initiated the action not being met, we would judge the action to be faulty. But that is not what Schafer means by "faulty."

> [As Freudian metapsychologists], for each instance of an action, we provide a designer, a mover and an executor; implicitly we view the action as a manifestation of that "agency." . . . I propose that it is clearer . . . to speak of one person's doing a large number of actions, each of which may be looked at from many points of view, i.e., may be defined variously as an action. Each action may be defined variously by the agent as well as by independent observers (1973a, p. 271).

In Schafer's relativistic universe, "faulty action" is paradoxical. We are exhorted to discard our naïve belief in a ghostly mind of motives which mental actions can serve well or badly. The actions themselves are the mind. But if mental actions build psychic reality, how is it possible to err? What more can be said but that we do what we do, and that is that?[7]

Schafer says more about what the fault is in faulty observation: in general, it is acting unheedfully, inattentively, unobservantly, or inaccurately (1973a, p. 273). More particularly, people may observe themselves faultily by assigning responsibility to pieces of their mind rather than to themselves as persons, as when they say to themselves:

> I inhabit a world of autonomously acting mental entities. These entities include thoughts, feelings, desires, attitudes, impulses, prohibitions, and judgments. They act on me or on one another, and these actions take place in me or around me in space. The actions of these entities [are] more evident at some times than others. They cause my suffering and my gratifications. At best they are only sometimes or partly subject to my influence or control.

---

[7]". . . there cannot be more than one reaction to one situation and . . . there cannot be more than a relatively narrow range of similar reactions to a group of relatively similar situations. Clearly different actions must imply clearly different situations" (1973a, p. 269).

Examples:

I couldn't seem to shake off the sad feeling about my childhood.

The thought of revenge suggests itself.

My anticipation of today didn't let me go to sleep . . . [1980a, p. 74].

Somewhat more equivocally, Schafer suggests that blaming the outside world is also a kind of faulty observation. Schafer does not deny the impact of the world. To some extent he seems to regard the assumption of responsibility as a narrowly psychoanalytic rule of thumb:

> Thus, the analyst *as analyst* sees the analysand as continuously selecting, organizing, and directing his neurotic existence . . .

> Passive experience—the representation of oneself as passive in relation to events—is, of course, of the utmost significance in psychological development and psychopathology. I am emphasizing that it is intrinsic to psychoanalytic understanding to regard passive experience as a mode of representation that can never tell the whole story of any psychological event or situation . . . More and more, the analysand indicates a readiness to accept the responsibility of his life as action. This acceptance has nothing to do with ideas of omniscience and omnipotence, however, in that it does not imply a belief on the part of the analysand that he has caused his whole life or can cause it from now on. Nor does it preclude his having "passive" experience (passive self-representations). But more often than before he says, "I will" and "I won't," rather than "I must" and "I can't." More often than before he says, "That's the way I see it," "I decided," "I chose," "I know" and "I prefer" [1973b, pp. 187-188.]

To summarize, then, faulty self-observation disguises responsibility by exaggerating external influence and by pretending that reactions to it, instead of being decisions of the person himself, arise from reified aspects of him that he visualizes as independent agents and forces. The language used to dodge responsibility is a language of disclaimers.

Schafer's Featured Rationale

Why should using disclaiming language cause trouble? Schafer acknowledges that it frequently does not cause trouble. People use disclaiming language all the time in ordinary speech. However, some people, for some reason, disclaim agency and responsibility "excessively or desperately," and these are the people we call neurotic and treat with analysis (1980a, pp. 75-76). Characteristically, Schafer does not concern himself with why one person disclaims variably, while another does so excessively and desperately. Nor (so far) does his mission require him to *describe* excess and desperation: disclaiming is simply something people do more or less of, and if they do a lot of it, that is both a manifestation and the substance of a psychological difficulty. Schafer does suggest that people who do a lot of disclaiming are those who view their wishes and aims as thoroughly and devastatingly incompatible (1980a, p. 65), but he makes it clear that conflict is simply what disclaimers proclaim; it is not the *cause* of disclaimers. As a matter of fact, the notion of actual, conflicting aims is itself a typical disclaimer — a misleading division of an individual into reified aspects of himself. In truth, Schafer tells us, such an individual is simply acting "in a conflicted manner."

Schafer's approach is to deal with human beings solely as narrators. Consequently, a person's use of disclaimers is an ultimate fact and neither requires nor allows an explanation (which would in any case just be another narration). Although an analyst can talk with his analysand about the way disclaimers were developed, that account is just a rephrasing of the disclaimers in an alternate language.

Needless to say, this is not a position that can be held to consistently by a provider of services. At the very least, references to unhappiness and satisfactoriness have to be worked into the account. And since Schafer is an extraordinarily insightful therapist, he has a great deal to say about help, but much of it is in the nature of *obiter dicta*. I believe he has deliberately adopted an informal style of discourse to avoid a systematic statement of such substantive matters as pain, because he foresees that a systematic statement would edge toward something he would consider mechanism.

Conflicts have no reality in action language apart from their description. They do not need to be compromised in order to be resolved; action language simply makes conflicts superfluous. Helped by analysis, misperceived "conflicts" may be replaced by plain conflicted acting, but the latter is not necessarily harmful. An analyst who faithfully adhered to this position would treat neuroses the way Oxford language analysts treat Philosophy — by exposing problems as cognitive "muddles." As a clinician, fortunately, Schafer is second to none in his respect for the reality and intricacy of human unhappiness. By a literary tour de force, he transmutes his voluntaristic theory into an infinitely more compassionate vehicle than the *actually* exonerating rival theories of causal forces and constraints. (In this, his stylistic skill is assisted by the equation of action and situation: in a sense, a person is compelled by his situation, but he does not have to be in that situation!)

In any case, since disclaiming does not cause conflict or prevent its resolution, our common rationale for prescribing honest self-confrontation will not work here, and it becomes the reader's task to collate those of Schafer's remarks that amplify the word "faulty" in "faulty perception."

Implicit Rationales in Schafer's Work

Schafer (1980a, p. 70) says that the passive mode is "by far the more burdensome or threatening in that it throws into question one's ability to regulate and understand one's own conduct." This doctrine faces more difficulties than its casual formulation suggests. First of all, as Schafer observes, the passive mode is frequently used in everyday thought and speech, which is strange if it is burdensome and threatening. And it seems odd that people who are especially burdened and troubled would cling to a burdensome and threatening mode. (In general, of course, any noncausal theory of analytic action will make it easier to say why hermeneutics helps than why it is needed—just as the causal aspect of Freudian theory makes it easier to say why a patient remains disturbed than how it is possible to help him.)

Indeed, Schafer, the clinician, knows that ordinary language may make people happier than responsible language. (For example, he recognizes that a disclaiming mode may make a person feel less alone [1980a, p. 75] or more emancipated [1973a].) In addition, Schafer implies that disclaimed action may somehow allow a person to live with motives and aims that are "felt to be drastically conflicting," although, as we have seen, what this means is unclear, since we have been led to believe that feeling oneself to be possessed of a conflict is *equivalent* to disclaiming.

In any case, since language varies with respect to disclaiming, some trade-off of burdens and benefits must be involved in the choice. What are the specific benefits for which Schafer recommends responsible language? We are told that action language opens up more options to the patient and gives him the power to unify the scene of his experience (1980a, pp. 70, 74, 75; see also, 1973a, p. 283).

We might add that an analyst who is good at finding coherent meaning will seem to be giving personal approval: Schafer (1979) refers to the analyst's "appreciative attitude." The fact that appreciation helps an analysand face responsibility suggests that he has been evading responsibility because he disapproved of himself and because he believed that people such as the analyst would also disapprove of some of him. Since Schafer's appreciation of what seemed unacceptable reveals a fittingness and coherence, we might say that integration is what both appreciation and nondisclaiming language foster. That the goal of treatment is to increase integration and flexibility is also implicit in Schafer's theory of situations (e.g., 1973a, p. 274) and explicit in his stated goals (1973a, p. 283; 1973b, pp. 187–188). Since a person's action is equivalent to the situation he senses himself to be in, remaining ignorant of one's action is tantamount to remaining ignorant of the details of one's situation.

Events, Schafer says, exist only within an interpretation; they have a meaning only in the context of a person's interests. We may assume, then, that when a person sees how he constructs experience, he will also see his interests more clearly; he will see how experience could appear otherwise; and as a result, he will see how his desires could be variously accommodated and combined. What is at stake is how many possible worlds we can live in and how many interests we can acknowledge.[8] But that is more a goal than a rationale. How is the *procedure* supposed to work? Here are some ways.

Providing Useful Perspectives. . The analyst's creativity provides a model of how the analysand could synthesize his awareness if he should wish to do so. I single this out as Schafer's featured rationale. It is the only one he is comfortable with, because its emphasis on the analyst's *creativity* does not seem to require Schafer to commit himself to a natural science statement about the world or the mind. He need only say that some *descriptions* of analysands are *helpful.* (Of course, that *is* an empirical proposition, but not one that calls attention to its hypotheticalness or to its positivistic implications.) Schafer's philosophy does not allow him to advertise the other rationales widely because he wants to avoid a theory of human interaction; other rationales cannot be limited to the realm of hermeneutics.

In suggesting that he can show the analysand a *better way* to think, Schafer echoes the Freud who tried to persuade his patient that there are advantages to giving up the pleasure principle. But Freud used interpersonal means to persuade the patient to give it a try. What does Schafer use? Sometimes he seems just to count on the obvious usefulness of his way of thinking, as educating analysts have always done. We are familiar with educating analysts who treat deficiencies of reality testing; Schafer treats deficiencies of available narrative forms. But that is only one of Schafer's approaches. There are many more.

Interfering With Simplification. The analysand gives directions to the analyst about how he wishes to be seen. (He simplifies himself.) Schafer does not take directions from his analysand: he describes that as avoiding countertransference (1980b, p. 43). How does he avoid taking directions? By refusing to settle for a single view and by refusing to accept ordinary speech. The action language is a distractor. Schafer superimposes a different style of

---

[8]Schafer (1973a) finds that some people are more limited in this regard than others. He implies that if a person does not have enough complexity to draw upon, he can never detach himself from the particular experience he has constructed. Apparently *this* person's passivity is not a refusal to acknowledge agency, but is a sign that there really is no other story to tell. And if that is the case, then we have here a paradox of a *truthful* disclaiming, reifying, and projective language. It is another example of how Schafer's fidelity to clinical experience constantly strains the skeptical philosophical corset in which he encloses it. How could a voluntaristic theory such as his ever conceivably account for a *built-in* limitation of perspective?

narrative on the patient's. A new reality is layered over the patient's reality. And the new reality contains many alternate realities. (Schafer does not dwell on what that does to a relationship.)

Interchange Between Showing and Telling . Schafer (e.g., 1980b) emphasizes the interconvertibility of what the patient shows and what he tells. Evidence can be considered an account, and the way the patient chooses to speak can be evaluated as evidence about him. Of course, there is no point in drawing these two together if they are not, in fact, different. But though converting a showing into a telling begs the philosophical question of the difference between a manifestation and a communication, it is a useful *technique* for the analyst. By using it, an analyst can quickly reflect varied images to the patient in the form of a narrative, acting *as though* the patient had made the statement he has in fact avoided. (Schafer [1980a, p. 80; 1983a, p. 153] includes Gill's maneuver as one form of this practice.) When he converts a showing into a telling, the therapist slips out of the audience role and claims his own narrative freedom. Narration is a way that ideas can be shuffled. And Schafer is fully aware of this.

This, too, is a way of preventing the analysand from controlling the analyst. An analysand might please Schafer by self-agency talk. But there is *no* way he can prevent the analyst from noticing a disclaimer on a metalevel.

Schafer responds *as though* the patient actually intended to reveal what he conceals. That is standard psychoanalytic procedure. Schafer's peculiarity is that he makes the procedure sound merely formal ("I will tell a different story now, according to the Freudian rules"). However, as we have seen, Schafer admits that there are people who do not have a variety of covert intentions that can be appealed to, and hence are unable to profit from this translation, even though he can tell them just as many different stories as he tells analyzable people. This proves that the analyst must touch actual *intentions* and not just provide possible story lines. Thus Schafer, no less than Gill, picks up something that is covertly intended and phrases it explicitly. This also highlights the appeal function of language and sensitizes the patient to that aspect of his communication.

Viewing the Analysand's Activity as the Solution to a Problem . Narration is not arbitrary composition: it is designed to answer certain questions. The analyst wonders what is being solved by the patient's action (1980a, p. 80). That is equivalent to seeing what situation the patient feels he is in (according to Schafer's equation of action and situation). A disowned action is a secret problem. Schafer extends that further than Gill; he is willing to observe bias in a story, as well as allusion to trouble with the analyst, and he perceives *many* allusions to the analyst besides unhappiness. Thus Schafer's is essentially a theory of the discovery of problems, attunement to problems, and the definition of problems in the context of talking with an analyst. But he does not have the specific problem-finder that Gill has. (He uses disclaiming grammar as an alerting signal, but he does not rely on it.)

Self-Effacement. Schafer reminds us that, ideally, the analyst demands nothing of the analysand. The analysand can do no wrong because he can do no right (1980b, p. 44). Schafer's emphasis on redescription unsettles any arrangement the patient thinks he has made with the analyst. When the analyst regards what the patient inadvertently reveals as a narrative, he makes it impossible for the analysand to hold onto a role or to control the relationship, and therefore the analysand cannot "satisfy" the analyst. To put it more crassly than Schafer does, the analyst's job is to note how the analysand is always "up to something." In order to do this, the analyst must have no requirement of his own which can be used as hostage. By having no desire of his own that can be met, Schafer is really chasing the analysand's desire (his appeal) down the corridors of narration that temporarily confine it. (I think that is how Lacan would have viewed it, and, by the way, Lacan could have made a good case that this deconstruction and multiplication of narratives shows that a narrative is just what is *not* important in this treatment.)

GENERAL COMPARISON

The initial warrant for the comparison of Schafer and Gill was that, more than most theorists, each seemed to focus with preponderant intensity on one of two contrasting aspects of psychoanalysis, the development of long-line pictures of the patient, on the one hand, and the determined agitation of the therapeutic relationship in pursuit of transference experience, on the other. (By contrast, for instance, a theorist who made the concept of *interpretation* central to his exposition would subsume these two aspects in his primary term, or distribute them here and there among side issues, and *his* theory would be more usefully compared with theories of nonverbal influence.)

As we might have expected, this macroscopic difference faded when we looked at the details of the two theories of therapeutic action. There we found them far more alike than different. The difference between these representations of analysis is not, after all, that one shows us the analyst making pictures of patients while the other shows us the analyst pushing patients toward interaction. We are left, then, to wonder what substantial (though more limited) problem Schafer and Gill deal with differently that gives rise to the misleading initial contrast. If we can identify the real difference, we may find a more workable way to study the contrast of psychoanalysis as a picturing and as a forcing procedure.

Despite their many similarities, the different styles of Gill and Schafer do foster different poetics of treatment. The atmosphere that Gill describes is one of accepted discord resolved into mutual investigation; the atmosphere Schafer describes is a mutual investigation enriched by intermittent discord.

The main practical difference that follows from Gill's greater specificity (and prejudice) is that he takes on a more fixed role with his patient. That is partly because his focus is more obvious and his therapeutic wishes more identifiable. His implied instructions to the patient are more specific. The patient can "satisfy" Gill, so to speak. (There is here a tradeoff of comprehensive subtlety for powerful, local practicality.) Patients can see Gill's visible wish to distinguish what is distortion from what is not. (Gill is acutely aware of the hazards his technique runs in the area of predictability and routinization; see, for example, 1982, p. 125.)

FUNDAMENTAL ISSUES IN THE DIFFERENCES

The most important difference between Schafer's emphasis and Gill's can be seen in Gill's attention to disguised complaints about the analyst as a sign of imminent mobilization of wishes.[9] He implies that other expressions of underlying wishes will not be as useful as covert complaints. He believes there is something special about these allusions among all the ways a patient's behavior reflects his feelings about the analyst. In other words, he seems to suggest that there is such a thing as a main meaning of the patient's communication.

Of the three issues on which Gill is most divided—objective reality versus relativism; interpersonal experiencing versus understanding; transference allusions as a main meaning versus allusions as useful openings—the last is left most to the reader to work out. Gill (1982, p. 64) says in one and the same paragraph, (1) that transference meaning is just one meaning, chosen by the *analyst* for its usefulness, and (2) that a topic is chosen by the patient for its allusiveness to the transference. When Gill (p. 22) suggests that an allusion continues to organize the entire session, he seems to be saying that it is the real, main meaning. (We may ask whether it carries over into the next hour, and, if so, how the accumulated, concatenated meanings can be sorted out.)

Whether there is such a thing as a main meaning is one of the most troubling and interesting questions in the psychotherapeutic enterprise. (It is a slightly different question from the problem of defining a given aspect of meaning, as discussed, for example, in Gill and Hoffman [1982, p. 179].) I believe that if one were to carry to the limit the idea that allusions to the

---

[9]"Imminent mobilization of wishes" is my term, not Gill's. It refers to the patient's temptation to override a resistance to the experience of the transference.

analyst are the main meaning of a patient's communication, it would ultimately lead to this: the sign that something within a patient is nearest to development is that it pushes the analyst off balance. That "something" is then no longer just a message, but is a virtual act (in the interpersonal sense of act, not in Schafer's sense). It is not a compromise formation in the ordinary sense; it does not correct or solve the problem. It *invites* the analyst into a *possible* situation. The analyst's felt imbalance is the sign that the patient is offering to share a problem with him. If the analyst responds one way, he will inspire hopeful elaboration; if he responds another way, he will shut off that elaboration, regardless of how many other clues to the same issue he picks up. Therefore, a single allusion will not necessarily go on knocking at the door indefinitely, and if we regard the allusion as the main meaning of a given utterance, then the main meaning is more nearly expressed by some of what the patient says than by the rest of it.

There are nodal points where the patient tests a solution to his problem with the analyst more tangibly than at other times. He sketches a structure within which he is prepared to move. The analyst may infer other "true" structures, and he may bring those other structures to conceptual fulfillment, but the patient's meaning may not be able to develop and enlarge itself within them. These other responses may not mean the same thing to the patient as the ones his allusions invited, even if all of the patient's references were semantically equivalent. It is only in taking up a position vis-`a-vis the allusion to himself that the analyst is heard to speak to the problem that the patient is having with him. Thus, it is not just *what* the analyst says that matters. It is also the very *doing* something *at that point* that says something to the patient (because that is the moment when the patient is half intending to do something to the analyst). This, of course, was Strachey's message.

Gill seems to offer a theory of the mind in which meanings are summed up by a bid to the object world and take on new meaning depending on the answer to that bid. (See also, process theorists, such as Gendlin [1964].)

The objection to this, which I would associate with Schafer, is that everything a patient does is a nodal point for some meaning or other. And probably the truth lies in between these arguments. Perhaps one should say that the patient's illocutionary meaning (the gestural or manipulative force of what he says) is carried more in some aspects and moments of his communication than in others.

But let us return to Gill. If the patient's meanings are of a sort that will move according to how the analyst receives them, then we should be able to describe what happens in terms of the patient's perceptions as well as his wishes. The question of whether meaning shows itself in special, privileged manifestations, or whether it is uniformly manifested in everything the patient does, then becomes the question of whether some of the patient's actions more than others put the analyst's *role* especially in question. (Strachey was involved in this debate also.)

Of course, the analyst is always being cast in some role or other. The question is whether this casting is more experimental, fluctuant, or unstable at some points than at others. Gill tries to find a place where the patient says: "I *almost* see you this way, which bothers me, and I *almost* see you in such a way that I could do something about it." If the analyst does not notice that juncture, what would have happened may, in fact, not happen, despite other conversation about those visions.

Suppose that is so. Suppose there are special crossroads within the patient's production. The next question would be whether at *all* times, *somewhere* there is such a special crossroads. Neither Gill nor Schafer believes that there is always a nodal point. Gill implies that although direct references to the analyst may conceal indirect ones, nevertheless, when the patient talks about his feelings for the analyst, no one part of his communication as opposed to another is in principle a privileged vanguard approaching new meaning in the same way as allusions to the analyst were a vanguard while he was not talking about the analyst (though it is hard to understand why allusiveness should disappear simply on account of the topic of discussion, and in practice Gill seems to continue to pick up allusions). And Schafer, although in practice he undoubtedly responds at points of maximum urgency, does not describe privileged moments or invitations to share a problem. (Schafer's theory would not seem to comprehend layers of greater and less intensity or importance within a patient's mental state.) Yet, for that very reason, Schafer (like Gray) is more able to remain alert to "allusions" even when the explicit topic *is* "the transference."

A similar contrast applies at many levels. Though not directly named by Gill, the arousal of old hopes figures dramatically in his model and not particularly in Schafer's. Schafer, however, is more adept at describing choices made by patients at lower levels of urgency and aspiration, where we might not be inclined to use such a big term as "hope." In general, I am sure, Schafer does what Gill suggests, and Gill does what Schafer suggests. But Gill's mandatory procedure is optional for Schafer.

One finds Schafer, but not Gill, discussing new metaphorical coinage and the creation of new meaning by describing old. (Gill acknowledges that the transference is a new, creative emergent, but he is more interested in what is old about it.) On the other hand, Gill, by his particular injunctions, shows us the interactive process as something with its own metaphorical power to create meaning. (I elaborate this possibility in chapter 34.)

Ultimately, Schafer reaches the same conclusion as Gill: events are describable only in narrative, and narrative is dictated by interests and questions. Thus, the narrative that the patient makes out of the analyst's intervention depends on what the patient is interested in at the time the analyst acts. (Michels [1983a] has shown how this answers many puzzling questions of theory of technique.) It follows that the story the analyst tells is not all that the patient will incorporate into his own story; the patient's internal narrative especially notes when, and in response to what, the analyst tells his story about the patient's story. New meaning and metaphor thus arise for the patient by the way the analyst's actions and attitudes *fit* into the live play of the patient's impact on him.

But Schafer's terms are borrowed mostly from literary criticism, and so it is easier for him to talk about how a person makes sense out of his experience than how a person affects someone else's sense-making. He finds it useful to dwell on the patient's responsibility in configuring his childhood (as against the passive imprint childhood events made on him). He has more to say about each of the two narrators in an analysis than about their impact on each other. He has chosen an esthetic, solipsistic, autonomous slant for its practical usefulness. As Schafer describes it, action is creation. But in that case, action is akin to Piaget's assimilation, and Schafer is left with few means to describe what we *usually* call action, that is, something that has *impact* on somebody else, action *on* the analyst and the analyst's action *on* the patient — therapeutic action in general. Schafer dwells mostly on how one transforms one's own experience.

Gill, on the other hand, writes less ambitiously about how meaning is formed, but he describes what kind of event makes somebody else's enfolded meaning blossom. Gill shows how what *happens* between analyst and analysand — and not just how it is narrated — puts a new aspect on a meaning.

Although Gill does not realize it, he is functioning as a natural scientist when he suggests that, to get a certain result, the analyst has to react in a special way at specified, actual space-time points, while Schafer seems to feel that various actions can be taken at various points, depending upon the analyst's chosen description of the patient, since what is at stake is simply a "reading" of the patient.

Schafer (1959) earlier described generative empathy with great refinement and nuance, but even at that time he was more interested in the analyst's psychology than in the nature of his effect or influence. He was more interested in what generative empathy looks like in detail than in how and what it generates. (One of the few interactive effects he mentioned there is "giving permission" [p. 367].)

In his later writings Schafer has further elaborated the analyst's epistemology and has added a great deal about the patient's. We hardly notice that what is missing is the relationship between the two. The connection is probably undescribable in a strictly relativistic account.

Schafer is very clear on the various ways that a patient can perceive the analyst's help — for example, as a feeding. The analyst may see it, on the other hand, as strengthening the ego. How can the analysand make good use of what the analyst does, even though he construes it so differently? We are not told. Nor is it said how the one can come to a different experience of the other's activity, and how they can participate in the same activity, although Schafer does count on this progressive agreement.

Schafer (1959; 1983a, pp. 126–128) has hinted that the patient takes what he needs from the many possible meanings in the analyst's interpretation. He has not continued that line of inquiry. He would certainly agree that the patient selects meanings not only from interpretations, but from the entire analytic situation (see chapter 34).

WHAT ARE ALLUSIONS TO THE TRANSFERENCE?

The psychoanalyst views his patient's behavior as a series of attempted solutions to problems, avoiding dangers and courting satisfactions. In order to highlight the problematic aspect of experience, the psychoanalyst tries to make a situation tolerable that exposes his patient to the most severe emotional dangers and the most risky lures. The analysand finds himself left to his own devices more radically than in any other human relationship, while at the same time seeming to be unreasonably accepted and protected. (Nunberg [1928] portrayed that situation most clearly.)

How do Gill's allusions to the analyst fit into this project? First of all, experience reveals a *spectrum* of allusions. At one end of the spectrum are explicit, conscious, withheld thoughts, while at the other end are implications that neither party will ever be aware of—occult ways in which the patient's behavior is affected by the analyst's presence, his actions, his character, his significance, and his meaning to the patient.

At the explicit end of this spectrum are those occasions when the patient actively challenges his own solution to a problem. At those times, the patient has in mind a specific complaint, or perhaps a plea: something addressed to the analyst to make him do one thing or avoid another; some effort to readjust the analyst's place in the world of the patient's desires. Having addressed the analyst this way in his mind, the patient nevertheless proceeds pretty much as he has already been doing. After imagining a different way of dealing with the problem, he continues to deal with it as before. In effect, he has challenged his own solution, but decided not to accept the challenge. Yet his imagined action is felt by the alert analyst.

Moving toward the other end of the spectrum, one encounters a range of less explicit, less consciously rehearsed references to the analyst. In these instances, the patient is dissatisfied with the way he has been dealing with his problem concerning the analyst, but he is less willing to challenge it even imaginatively. Despite his misgivings, however, the patient has toyed with a different approach to the problem. The inclination to deal with the analyst in a different way shows itself in aborted actions directed toward the analyst. These actions can be described as initiatives for a different relationship; they can also be described as requests that the analyst be a different "object." But they are more and more covert the farther we move on the spectrum toward unknowable "body English."

This is, of course, just one way of stating the well-known function of conflict in treatment. What needs to be emphasized, however, is that the different possibilities of handling conflict about the analyst are not just different imaginings about him, but are different approaches to him, different attitudes toward him, speaking to him in a different voice, abandoning agreed-upon assumptions, claiming different entitlements, reconstruing the entire psychoanalytic set-up, etc. For a patient to entertain alternative possibilities may mean that he is considering taking seriously something he had been treating as provisional or seeing something as real that he had pretended to regard as formal, or finding a personal meaning in what he had previously tried to believe was a professional convention.

These are not simply times when the patient is withholding part of a response. They are times when he would be talking in a different style, i.e., bidding for a different relationship. It would *feel* much different to talk *that way*, and the patient is not entirely ready to experience that different feeling. He knows he would invite a different response from the analyst, or perhaps require it, and in any case, it is not certain just *what* it would lead to. The different approach would gather up synoptically a great number of vaguer wishes and fears and would force issues that cannot be known ahead of time.

We need more detailed phenomenology and theoretical description of the various states of mind that underlie very inexplicit allusions to the transference. The two theoretical concepts that have done duty in those areas, the concept of the preconscious and the idea of the transference neurosis, now need to be spread out and dissected. We often describe a patient's course of treatment as an initial holding-out from—and then falling into—a transference neurosis. Gill's terms are most adequate to that kind of situation. But there are other situations that require a more complex description. Not every resistance to awareness of a deep transference simply draws upon characterological or floating transference. It seems that Freud was right after all: there can be profound transferences that paralyze a patient by their very nature. For example (although is it not Freud's), strong feelings of need and an expectation of abandonment can make a patient reluctant to take initiatives that would intensify his plight.

If we were to say that all allusions lie in the preconscious, we would bypass what we most want to know about, which is the conspicuous difference between the preconscious idea that needs only to be attended to in order to be voiced and that other kind which is unconscious in the sense of being actively denied, but is not part of the system unconscious inasmuch as it might become plainly voiced in a slightly different context a few moments hence.

What distinguishes allusions that need only to be mentioned in order to be confirmed from allusions whose message is indignantly denied? I believe that it is not always a questions of readiness to experience a transference neurosis, nor is it always fear of the specifics of the transference, nor is it necessarily the armor of character transference or a penumbra of floating transferences that stand in the way of individualized regressive transferences. All of these are clearly present in some situations but not in others. I suggest that the most universal variable which decides how much the analyst can exploit allusions to the transference is the degree to which a patient is willing to accept uncertainty. Of course, it might be said that this is simply a function of how frightening the potential transference fantasy is, but that is an empirical question and should not be decided by theory. Very indirect allusions to the transference, especially those whose translation is strongly resisted, may represent an unforeseeable attitude toward the analyst, an attitude that would have been born had the statement or provocation not been aborted. The uncertainty may be as frightening as the particular transference theme that has been stimulated (Myerson, 1981). As we have seen, both Gill and Schafer recognize that patients vary in the basic flexibility of their outlooks. Logic requires that Gill and Schafer, and the many analysts like them who believe that transference is a new synthesis, not just a repetition, must grant that the patient faces a vast uncertainty in allowing transference to blossom. Obviously, as the transference is clarified, particular dangers replace the initial uncertainty of the venture, but that does not mean that it was the developed fears in their particularity that most immediately inspired initial resistances. In these terms, then, one might say that Gill seizes the moment when the patient has an incentive to risk overturning the whole analytic arrangement. Following Gill's advice, the analyst acts as though he had already been dealt with in that different way, and so the uncertainty is reduced and the risk already taken.

It has often been remarked that psychoanalytic treatment requires a subtle interplay of responsibility (intensity of feeling) and irresponsibility (playfulness and tentativeness). A degree of tentativeness is what allows experiments with real action. But if, *per impossibile*, an analysis were conducted entirely as make-believe, the analysand would never have actually taken a risk or experimented with images and relationships. That is reason enough to follow Gill in insisting that the patient address the analyst directly, spelling out the details of his perception and pinning down their consequences by personal allegations. After an allusion has been turned into a direct statement, the patient stands in a different relation to the analyst.

When presented with relatively explicit allusions, the analyst has a great opportunity to effect change and a corresponding liability if he discourages it. The patient shows more of his wish, and the wish is more open to participation from the analyst. If the analyst misses those points, he says directly that he will not participate in that kind of change, does not want it, or is threatened by it. The most powerful argument for Gill's procedure is the negative one: a simple silence in the face of an obvious allusion is one of the most intrusively personal statements an analyst can make.

But what about the analyst's response to messages at the other end of the spectrum — those subtle explorations of different solutions in the form of a hint of behavior or a highly analogical allusion? Certainly, any debate that Gill will stir up has to do with this end of the spectrum. What is the effect of the analyst's picking up the kind of bid that is not willingly, imminently, or pressingly offered?

Picking up that kind of allusion has a number of special consequences: It is more instructional. In defining a *very* covert allusion, the analyst has a lot of freedom. As Gray (1973) points out, problems appear on many levels of generality. Thus the analyst's statement of an unformulated reaction will be much more arbitrary and authoritarian than when he echoes an already formulated thought. The patient is pushed more conspicuously toward what and how the analyst wants him to think, and what kind of hypothesis the analyst is interested in. Gill even offers patients samples of what he is after, i.e., *ways* of calling into question the analyst's own action. And finally, interpreting very hidden allusions tends to destabilize the patient's control of messages, his conscious intent, and his definition of what is happening (until daily routine domesticates the analyst's technique). We should not judge these consequences according to whether or not we like the picture. What needs to be asked is what we sacrifice in pursuing allusions at the extremely inexplicit end of the scale, since for everything we do we pay a price.

WHERE ARE ALLUSIONS FOUND AND HOW ARE THEY ILLUMINATED?

Interaction is a unilaterally continuous, as well as a turntaking process. A patient continuously reacts to the way he himself is behaving. Even if it were supposed that there is a single stimulus to his productions, he would, by those very productions, set up further stimuli for himself.

This fact is most forcefully presented by Gray (1973). Whatever the analyst has done that initially stimulated the patient's allusion, Gray can see still other allusions to the analyst develop during its production and elaboration. Indeed, the *reason* for the patient's allusiveness may sometimes be more apparent in the shifts and transformations that occur while he is expressing his allusion (for example, a shift from an account of aggressiveness to one of caring) than in the link between what the analyst did and how the patient responded. Because Gray's focus is on the patient's reaction to his own reaction, he has less need than either Gill or Schafer for a neutral reality to arbitrate the patient's accuracy.

In practice, the contrast is a little like the difference between understanding a boater's reluctance to put his canoe in rapids and watching him paddle clear of underwater rocks. Gill might be compared to a coach who says, "I will help put your canoe in the rapids, and we shall see what concerns you in those waters!" (Gill *pulls* tentative reactions into full perception or accusation.) Gray watches the patient in action and charts the rocks he is instinctively avoiding. (Gray *points* to the already visible efforts of the patient to solve problems he has set up for himself.) Gill wants the patient first to feel a passive reaction to the analyst and not to start by reflecting on his mode of dealing with the analyst. He wants the patient to register the experience first as an emotionally charged perception and only later as a motivated, or even motivating, perception. (Understandably, then, Gill wants to know that he has a way of eventually "correcting" the perception.)

We should not exaggerate the practical differences between these approaches. Both will alert the patient to the analyst-figure he has been subliminally imaging, and thus both will enlighten the patient about his own behavior and the construction of his experience.

However, if what the patient is responding to are extremely subtle stimuli in the image of the analyst, the analyst will not find them by hunting for localized perceptions. Even though it may be the analyst's best policy to assume that if he looks hard enough he will find what he did to provoke the patient's reaction, he may anyway run the risk of interrupting the display of the broad picture by fastening onto the moment. Furthermore, if the analyst took it as a rule of thumb to look for the immediate source of the patient's reaction in a currently identifiable feature of the analyst's attitude, that would tend to focus on the perceptual rather than on the imaginative sphere. It might distract him from the legendary kind of literal transference where the patient talks to figures of his past; he might obscure the patient's reaction to him in the role of mere interlocutor. Admittedly, Gill is right that this picture of transference has been unconscionably overworked, but can we say that it is *never* a good description? (Actually, Gill leaves that question open [e.g., 1983, p. 234], allowing that his approach may turn out to be the correction of a common technical error rather than a comprehensive description of analytic procedure.)

As Gray might say, the transference of defense may not take the form of a specific image. For the analyst to say, "You are talking to me as though . . ." does not necessarily entail, "You have observed me to be. . . ." In order to see how the patient is "talking as though," one must scan the broad text, since self-presentation occurs in all shapes and sizes and ultimately, as Schafer would say, in the shape of an entire treatment.

In this respect, only Gray consistently and exclusively watches the appeal function of the patient's activity — the relation of speech to wants, fears, etc. In contrast, both Gill and Schafer are concerned with error. I know that sounds strange, since both Gill and Schafer are modest about objective truth. Yet Gill places great importance on separating bias from consensually validated perception, and Schafer establishes an acceptable set of narratives (and has recently [1983b] added criteria of reliability and objectivity).

THE ANALYST AS PROVOCATEUR

But it is not all truth-finding and story-telling for Gill and Schafer. Each also has a powerful way of creating an experience of change. Gill "calls" his patient on the half offer of a different style of behavior toward himself. His personal, particularistic, incident-focused efforts are clearly more important for their experiential component than for the subsequent sorting out of reality. His interventions induce different *actions*. And Schafer's emphasis on responsibility exerts a steady pressure that must make patients *feel* their hidden dealings with the analyst which were formerly obscured by disclaiming figures of speech.

It should not surprise us that plausible programs, though oriented toward the discovery of truth, should turn out to be, in part, stimulating manipulations. The truth of desire cannot be established during a routine mode of scrutiny, because the very routine would eclipse signs of appetitive control. The data base, so to speak, would dry up. An analyst might snuff out the pilot light by too programmatically taking up only allusions to himself, or by ignoring those allusions when they are pregnant. In each case, the patient's general atittude to the analyst would not be allowed to fluctuate, although he might oblige the analyst with playful excursions regarded as "part of the game." A fixed pattern of allusion detection would become a training in assertiveness. A fixed pattern of ignoring allusions would be a simple training in introspection. The mainstream of psychoanalytic tradition has always endorsed a combination of random attention and orderliness. (Gill [1982, p. 179; Gill and Hoffman, 1982, p. 137] is aware of the dangers of a fixed program, but it is not clear how he avoids them.)

There are, then, two dangers in a fixed program of detecting allusions: (1) subtle strivings might be ignored, and (2) unpredictability, with the attendant possibility of new solutions, might be minimized.

Is it possible to respond to the appeal function of language both continuously and unpredictably? I believe there is evidence that this can be done in nondiscursive ways, but it would not accomplish a psychoanalysis, probably because, though it would keep uncertainty alive, subtle discrimination requires wandering, truth-seeking narrative. Although varied talk about many things can itself become routinized and secure, still, if handled correctly, it allows the analyst to spot subtle reflections of his influence without setting up a standard, routine interchange. Only with a variable base of curiosity can the analyst avoid a fixed relationship which will confirm the patient's transference meaning. (Gill writes about the need for spontaneity, but he does not integrate that with the rest of his discussion.)

As always, the big problem for theory is the relationship between discursive and nondiscursive elements in treatment. What, for instance, happens to the transference when treatment does not *seem* to be concerned with transference? Presumably, transference is then being elaborated anyway. But how can we know it is not also being modified at the same time? And what happens when the transference *is* being discussed? Presumably, something of the same sort is going on. In other words, despite efforts to neaten the schema, one never stands outside transference looking at it, and one never stands inside transference without changing it. (Schafer captures this truth in his description of multiple histories.) Surely, working on the transference does not mean talking about the analyst. The difference between exploiting the transference and analyzing it cannot simply be a matter of whether there is a lot of talk about it or just a little. The desired effect has to do with (1) experiencing the transference, and (2) experiencing some varied perspectives on it. All the authors discussed in this paper agree on that. If they do not say it that way, it is because they fear being tarred with the brush of the dreaded corrective emotional experience. It is time to shake off the concern of heresy that clouds this issue. Some kind of manipulation is involved in any deliberate procedure, and we can make our distinctions while accepting that fact. Psychoanalysis brings new perspectives to the patient with the help of many verbal propositions. It is hard to imagine how else so much detail could be delineated. But change hinges on the resultant intensity and new variability of core attitudes.

Gill is doubtful that analysis can elicit intensity and variability without an explicit focus on transference. (He argues this against Loewald [Gill, 1982, pp. 78, 79].) There is indeed reason to worry that an analyst who relied on an implicit relationship to both nourish *and* readjust the transference would lower his guard and collude with the transference. But Gill offers no argument to support his belief that an analytic response is collusive if it is not a discussion and no argument to show that the only response that lessens the rigidity of a patient's transference is transference talk. Gill is readier to admit that some of the net effect of treatment comes form unanalyzed positive transference than he is to admit that some of the resolution of the transference might occur nondiscursively. That leaves him with an acknowledged but unclassifiable debt to the aspect of the analytic experience that goes beyond cognitive discovery.

CONCLUSION

These considerations suggest that flexibility of outlook is the goal of treatment; that it is achieved in a complex fashion; and that it can be fostered during the recounting of many different things.

Psychoanalytic theory would benefit from cross-matching the focus on transference with the story-telling tradition, in order to describe how transference talk tends to produce new images, and how acts of visualization (narratives, etc.) loosen transference frames.

Gray (1973) points out that the analyst is involved in the patient's own representation of his life and history during the time he is in analysis. There must be a complex interplay of adjustment and readjustment simply in talking to the analyst about analyst-soaked life events. (Strachey understood this.) In other words, an allusion to the analyst is already present in the anticipated audience reaction to—and interest in—even untold stories. Allusions to the analyst are not confined to the aspect of speech that encodes a reference to some particular action or attitude of the analyst. Seen from this standpoint, Gill's allusions are simply the most therapeutically powerful allusions, when they are available.

According to both Gill and Schafer, the ultimate achievement of analysis is flexibility, and that may be said to be the common denominator of all statements of analytic aims. It is also a commonplace, embodied in many technical prescriptions, that the patient's ultimate flexibility has something to do with the analyst's flexibility. Looking further into theory as well as practice, it is evident that the analyst's flexibility has something to do with what he is interested in, that is, in the nature of his reactivity.

Bearing this in mind, we should view Gill and Schafer as offering not two grossly different pictures of treatment, but slightly different instructions for training the analyst's interest, and the effects of following these instructions should be empirically studied.

SUMMARY

1. Schafer seems to be mainly concerned with how life histories are designed. Gill seems primarily interested in eliciting hidden allusions to current inter-

action with the analyst. But actually the common goal of both authors is to provide the patient with more ways of experiencing than he is accustomed to.

2. Gill believes that the appeal function of the patient's languages shows up in references to the analyst's specific behaviors. Schafer believes that the appeal function is often less focused. The two authors therefore train the analyst's curiosity along slightly different lines.

3. Although they do not emphasize it, both Gill and Schafer assume that the analyst's attitude changes the meaning of the patient's potential alternatives enough to make those options newly available. And, though they do not emphasize this either, both authors believe that something like awareness of a neutral reality further induces the patient to revise his old certainties.

4. The analyst's actual influence is most forthrightly exemplified in Gill's persistent unpacking of transference allusions.

5. The patient's allusions to the analyst can be thought of as more or less faint efforts to change the way he handles problems that he encounters with the analyst. If the analyst ignores these allusions to himself, he will actively discourage new ways of dealing with conflict. (For an adult, transference is a new way of dealing with conflict.)

6. Because Gill's effort is specific and visible, the analyst who follows his instruction may compromise his neutrality, and may give patients a way of implementing old patterns by "cooperating" and by not "cooperating," whereas it is harder for a patient to "cooperate" and not "cooperate" with an analyst who is influenced by Schafer. (This difficulty has not escaped Gill's notice.)

7. More work needs to be done on the phenomenological gradation between "deep" preconscious and "tip-of-the-tongue" preconscious. A fixed program of seeking allusions to the transference may obscure subtler references to the analyst that arise not from nameable perceptions, but from generalized expectations that manifest themselves in the patient's overall self-presentation. To see how the patient tailors his overall appearance for vital purposes, it may be necessary to encourage the longer narratives that Schafer examines.

34

How It Fits Together:

Performable Model and

Metaphor

W hatever a therapist is doing, whether reading meaning, understanding origins, or fostering change, the patient sees an image of himself reflected in that activity. (That point was elaborated in chapter 11.) What the therapist reflects is not necessarily what he has read, figured out, or deliberately promised. His awareness tints the mirror, but his experience is not the patient's, and we can never understand therapy unless we know what the link is between the two experiences.

In the last chapter, we examined two therapy programs (those of Gill and Schafer) that seemed to differ in degree of manipulation. We found that in fact they both work the same way, that is, by actively anticipating a new reality of the patient. Their disagreement was really about which of the therapist's wishes best demonstrate his anticipations, and how much he should disguise his anticipations in order to preserve his ambiguity. If therapy works by anticipation, the next question is the one raised in chapter 11: How does the therapist's anticipation stimulate the patient's invention? I suggest that, within an ambiguous relationship, reading, understanding and manipulating create a living model or a performed metaphor (or a new map or a novel theory) of the patient as he would be if he were already what he will become through treatment. I suggest that in doing this, therapists follow a procedure that is used whenever we try to configure the unknown. We do the same thing, for instance, when we venture a new scientific theory, coin a new metaphor, or try out a model of an obscure subject. In the privacy of their thoughts, therapists are following this procedure when they look for sense in the interaction. And their outward response guarantees that the patient will go through the same procedure.

Using a cognitive, theoretical model, therapists react to the patient's approaches in such a way that a living model of a more flexible patient is enacted in the consulting room. Words are used in this process, but the metaphor or model that is built is a prolonged, infinitely detailed experience, as untranscribable as life.

Psychotherapy is a physical event, so the changes it induces cannot be equated with developments in scientific theory or the invention of literary metaphor or other adventures of ideas. Yet I suggest that all innovative processes, whether ideo-motor or purely conceptual, share a common form. If we look first at the general means by which we find something new in an old universe, and then add what is unique to therapeutic discovery, we may see how the elements of therapy come together to produce therapeutic effects.

In the first part of this chapter I reflect on theory change, metaphorical expansion of meaning, and the maps and models that represent them. I hunt for the special quality of psychotherapy models, metaphors, and so on, that allows the therapist to explore a patient, bearing in mind that his exploration has to change what is explored.

PHILOSOPHY OF SCIENCE

Current philosophy is not necessarily more authoritative than older philosophy. But philosophy of science is now being discussed in a way that is especially germane to psychotherapy.

Consider the well-known symposium, *Criticism and the Growth of Knowledge* (1970), edited by Lakatos and Musgrave. This is a debate that calls into question the older, positivist distinction between observation and theory. Here, Karl Popper (1970) has the most confidence in neutral observation, insisting that the progress of science requires it to submit to a non-theoretical challenge. But even he does not see the challenge as an array of truths that might be assembled into a better theory. Although Popper's work is part of the empiricist tradition, he does not regard a theory as a report dictated by indifferent facts: He thinks that a theory is an imaginative guess that at best can boast that it has survived challenges. With Popper at one end of the spectrum, and Thomas Kuhn (1970b) at the other, the argument has moved away from the older debate about whether theory is compounded out of theory-free descriptions to the last ditch question of whether there is even such a thing as a theory-free test to which a theory can be submitted. Popper thinks there is.

Kuhn replies to Popper that if we look at the actual history of science, we find that theories are not automatically discarded when they run into difficulty. Up to a point, scientists tolerate inadequacies while exploring a theory's strengths. Science would not go far if a theory was discredited by its first failure. It may later turn out that an early failure was due to a trivial appendage or a faulty formulation. Kuhn, Popper, and others such as Imré Lakatos (1970), have pursued these considerations into a much needed analysis of what exactly a theory is.

One stimulus to the rethinking of theory was Kuhn's (1970a) provocative explanation of scientific conservatism and revolution: The puzzles that a theory solves are themselves delineated by the theory. A scientific theory is, in effect, a way of both formulating and solving puzzles. The theory is learned by practice on exemplars; it is an on the job training in seeing the world a certain way. The fine detail of science depends on the diligence of this application, and that in turn requires a standard of competence set by a scientific community. Historical and social forces affect these arguments, but as science advances its practitioners become insulated and indifferent to the laymen's understanding. In effect, the specialty community is riveted to the challenge of elaborating its own way of analyzing reality. There comes a day, according to Kuhn, when the theory's anomalies (puzzles that it frames but cannot solve) accumulate, and those deviant scientists who have been focusing their attention on the anomalies win over the community to a new way of approaching reality.

This description of scientific revolution has been debated for a quarter of a century. There is certainly no agreement on the subject, and Kuhn himself has not settled on a dogma. But he has continued to affirm these principles, which are of interest to psychotherapists: Nature does not come divided into categories; only a theory can introduce a thinkable reality to a scientist; the theory does that by offering authoritative examples of how to question nature, which train scientists to ask and answer questions in a certain way; and a major change in theory involves something like a switch in gestalt because the most elementary terms of the old theory already suppose a view that is incompatible with the new one.

Fundamental to Kuhn's position is the fact that, although you can point to an individual such as John or Mary, you cannot point to a natural class such as ducks or swans. Neither the concepts nor the examples of *duck* or *swan* come with instructions telling which instance goes with which label. We learn divisions of nature by example—examples that may come to exemplify something different as we obtain new information. Someone points to one animal and then another, calling both ducks, and eventually we learn to distinguish ducks from swans, although we may wish to change our groupings if we find some unforeseen type of beast. In the same way, scientists use a model as a demonstration without knowing exactly how much of the model applies; these models are practical aids to attention, not abstract definitions. (See also Hesse, 1980a, on the interchangeable roles of fact and hypothesis in a scientific theory.)

Something like a model, therefore, can never be dispensed with by science. It can never be melted down to a literal, unequivocal, binding abstract formula. And it follows that a model cannot be exactly translated into another formula (see Kuhn, 1979, p. 415). An outdated scientific theory can be referred to by a new theory, but cannot be exactly translated into it. The replacement of an old scientific model by a new one will appear as a switch in metaphor—metaphor not being used here to mean simple substitution of a comparable term or the selection of some aspect of the original meaning, like a simile, but rather a new way of seeing. The metaphor is a new model, redistributing individuals among natural families.

RHETORIC

In this respect, change of theory shares a problem with rhetoric. Rhetoric currently fascinates scholars in many disciplines who see the classic figures of speech as cognitive options and not just oratorical ornaments.

Kenneth Burke (e.g., 1950) was early in this revival. He showed how thoroughly our common-sense world is experienced in shapes of rhetoric and therefore appetite. Burke does for the social world what Kuhn does for the world of science: Both authors imply that we know and learn by draping experience over suggestive models. These models are the kind that function as metaphors rather than as blueprints. For instance, physics uses the solar system as a model for the atom. The model is metaphorical because its resemblance to an atom is not fully specifiable. Analogously, the student of rhetoric cites the image of a river god as a way society can sum itself up without explicitly declaring its principles. (See also Pepper, 1942; Geertz, 1983.)

Burke wrote that all evocative predication (he called it identification, that is, identification of one thing with another) is rhetoric; it has a tendentious gist. More recently the argument has been advanced that history makes special use of bias as a cognitive tool. Tendentious organization seems to underly every meaningful story. Hayden White (1980) describes historians as relentless moralizers (see chapter 32).

This line of argument suggests that science reforms itself by attending to new exemplars that function as suggestive models. A suggestive model might be a type of problem together with its solution (Kuhn), or it might be a visualized structure (Arnheim, 1969). Similarly the meaning of ordinary experience may shift when it is reported in a new figure of speech. When that happens, the change agent is metaphor because figures of speech have the metaphorical effect of presenting something in a particular light without argument.

METAPHOR AND MODEL

In order to characterize psychotherapy, I find it useful to consider the peculiar power that is shared by metaphor, model, and map, which enables them to represent unknown properties of the world.

As we have seen, Kuhn believes that scientific models are useful because their metaphorical indeterminacy allows for exploration. Max Black (1979) holds that metaphors concretely model indeterminacy and thus help to visualize possibilities. Other theories (e.g., Henle, 1958) also stress the importance of metaphor for modeling new knowledge. It has even been suggested, as an escape from the incommensurability of scientific theories alleged by Kuhn, that metaphor allows one to peek around the corners of a man-made theory and visualize the natural joints of the universe (Boyd, 1979).

This kind of speculation is in marked contrast to the idea that metaphor is poetic synonymy—a mere substitution of an uncommon word for a more ordinary one. Those who regard metaphor as word-substitution usually appeal to the fascinating work of Roman Jakobson (1956, 1959, 1960). Jakobson points out that neurological defects reveal that the brain has separately destructible faculties (a) to summon words and concepts that are similar and (b) to summon words and concepts that go together. Jakobson referred to these types of relatedness as *metaphor* and *metonymy*.

Some writers (for example, Lacan, 1957) believe that therapeutic change is greatly illuminated by Jakobson's discovery that language operates on the axes of substitution and contiguity. Using Jakobson's extremely formal terms while implicitly trading on the more creative nuance of *metaphor*, others have gone so far as to suggest that treatment consists of converting a predominance of one of these functions into a predominance of the other (see Levenson, 1978, p. 13; Watzlawick, 1978).

But it seems to me that the *usefulness* of a certain pattern at a certain moment must be explained by a different analysis, such as the one Ricoeur (1977a, 1978) has undertaken.

After a painstaking survey, Ricoeur concludes that metaphor is not one word standing in for another, but is the message of a whole sentence. It is a propositional twist that accompanies discovery. According to him, metaphor makes use of a general faculty of imaginative schematism and it is that power that permits the expansion of knowledge.

Ricoeur's theory implies a Piagetian function for metaphor: the structured language may be thought of as a preexisting schema; metaphorical anomaly ("live" metaphor) represents the challenge of novelty. As the metaphor becomes a standard colloquialism, the language, which accomodated to the live metaphor, now assimilates the dead one.

Seen in this light, metaphor serves language the way a new disciplinary matrix, in Kuhn's sense, serves science. A live metaphor and a new matrix are open-ended models that orient the mind toward a new way of abstracting. They both inspire one to slice up the universe differently, promising that the slicing will happen in a systematic and realistic, although unfamiliar way, and they do that without forecasting the characterization (or marking the slices) ahead of time. Both the scientific practice and the metaphoric identification support a new exploration without actually specifying it. They are both models, in that we are introduced to them ostensively rather than discursively. (See Harré, 1970, on the need for nondiscursive supplements in science.) And they are both metaphors in that they are not equivalent to anything in the preexisting framework.

The use of metaphor and open-ended model as indispensable ways of picturing the world, is now a frequent subject of discussion. Goodman (1976) proposes that a metaphor makes a familiar method of analysis work toward "the sorting and organizing of an alien realm" (p. 72). Lakoff and Johnson (1980) suggest that the unexplored but tangible structure of a metaphor helps to understand more amorphous aspects of reality, such as the realm of feelings. Their book argues that metaphors are grounded in body orientation, and are thus ultimately shaped by reality. We have noted Ricoeur's (1977a) belief that metaphor is not carried by a single word, but is a product of at least a full sentence. Lakoff and Johnson go further: They draw attention to the web of hierarchical and overlapping metaphorical *systems* that structure experience. (Perhaps it is this extensive systematic quality that distinguishes businesslike, epistemological metaphors from the sporadic colorful poetic metaphors that catch our attention.)

Harré (1970) argues that science aims to discover underlying substantial realities, and that (some) models serve as provisional nominees for the substantial things we are investigating. These unknown things can therefore be further investigated in the workings of the model. "Live" metaphor (i.e., metaphor that is creative rather than conventional) can be found in Harré's work in two guises: One is the kind of model that has only partially known applicability. The other is a seemingly nominal classification that has begun to look as though it might actually separate natural kinds.[1]

Arlow's (1979) richly informed discussion of metaphor in psychoanalytic communication concludes with a comment on metaphor in psychoanalytic theory:

> metaphors constitute the only way by which what was hitherto unknown may be organized and conceptualized in a novel way. Any new term for a set of

---

[1] I am indebted to Dr. Arnold Goldberg for calling my attention to the work of Rom Harré, who sums up the exploratory use of models most satisfactorily to my taste. The example of Harré shows that one can acknowledge perspective bias without giving up ontological reality and, indeed, Harré, Immanuel Kant and I would argue that bias actually presupposes an objective reality (see chapter 16).

relationships not previously discerned will ultimately have to be expressed in some form of metaphor, because of the very nature of human thought and language. (p. 383)

MAPS

Another way of talking about rough reference is in terms of maps. By itself, a simple map can only tell what categories to look for and how to connect them with each other. It cannot identify the real things these categories designate that are embedded in the flux of life. We can wave a road map at the scenery forever and it will not shout "The party is over *there!*" It is up to the reader of the map to find the road that corresponds to the printed lines. For that reason, a child can play with a map without learning anything about the neighborhood. And similarly, people can use conceptual "maps" without learning much about the world. For example, they can imitate professional chatter in order to affiliate with a group. Fortunately, theoretical maps are usually not used to parrot speech but to learn a communal language, and that means acquiring skills in classifying, and learning to sharpen one's perceptions.

But suppose a tentative map is introduced that is the first of its kind. Imagine, for example, the first map of scenic locations. Such a map immediately serves as a suggestive model for discovering divisions in nature. Unlike the use of a road map, finding correspondences between such a new map and reality amounts to making empirical discoveries. The process is a lower level version of Kuhn's "normal science." It employs an open model, and prescribes exercises for feeling out its applicability.

After a map has been established as a formal diagram of a delimited aspect of reality (and that is what we usually mean by a map), it has become something different. Like an exploratory map, this mastered map might also be called a *model*. But it is no longer an open model; it is the kind of model whose applicability is exactly known, just as it is exactly known how a miniature automobile does and does not correspond to a passenger car, and how a blueprint corresponds to a building. An established map is a product, not a part, of the scientific process of discovery.[2] The relationship between a

---

[2]For a more technical discussion of what I have here oversimplified, see Harré (1970). Harré argues that we propose a model as corresponding vaguely to an underlying reality, and we try to modify it to depict reality exactly. Goodman (1976) makes a more precise distinction than I between diagram, model, and metaphor. But my point can be followed into Goodman's discussion if we suppose that the newly introduced map has taken on its form from a different domain where it is already established (for example, an aboriginal map of a territory drawn along the lines of a totemic diagram)

new type of map (or a model of indeterminate applicability) and a standard map (or completely specified model) is comparable to the relationship between a new, "live" metaphor on the one hand, and a simile or "dead" metaphor on the other.

In live metaphor, open-ended models, and imaginative maps, one thing is understood through the understanding of another thing, even while the logic of the comparison is still unknown. That is quite different from an understanding achieved by abstract concepts that formally and explicitly declare their lesson to begin with. Indeed, the authors we have looked at imply that abstract concepts are never rich enough to explain anything but formal systems.

PERFORMABLE METAPHOR

Faithful to my view of metaphor, I have been discussing metaphor (and models and maps) metaphorically. We usually think of maps as pictures. Models are things that can be pointed to. Metaphor is a linguistic term. Yet we also know of a map (a *mandala*) that is used to find transcendence. We are familiar with a sort of model that can only be enacted, for example, a stage play (see Gadamer, 1975). And if metaphor extends propositional meaning to new areas, then surely its function is frequently served by action. Indeed, action is by far the most common way that people develop new categories. The historian Oreste Ranum (1980) proposes an interesting example. If he is right, the system of slights and courtesies that Richelieu evolved around Louis XIII gradually altered the nature of French royalty. That is an especially colorful instance of what happens all the time in everyday life.

In ordinary interaction we do not usually interpret other people's motives conceptually; we conspire with them in action to build a virtual model of who they are. (A sociologist or anthropologist may then identify the model and interpret it conceptually.) We treat other people's treatment of us as illustrating one thing or another. Indeed, psychotherapy is socially peculiar in encouraging a patient to go beyond implicit attribution and say outright what he is and what he thinks the therapist is. And to develop this awareness the patient may first have to note how he feels he has been dealt with and, more usefully still, how he is dealing with his therapist. That we ordinarily interpret other people's meanings by reciprocal attitudes rather than by theories does not mean that attitudinal interpretations or actions have philosophical priority over conceptual ones, or that conceptualizations are artificial reifications. They are both ways of registering abstractions drawn from concrete experience. My point is just that attitudes are among the many ways of abstracting. (Goffman [1974] provides countless illustrations of this.)

MAKING INTERACTIVE MODELS BY RESPONDING TO EFFORTS
METAPHORICALLY

In his thinking, the psychotherapist uses theoretical models not unlike those used in other inquiries. But he applies them to a peculiar subject matter, and he brings about another model that is quite peculiar. Therapists study a subject that they and their patients are constantly *producing*, namely, the therapeutic relationship (see Schafer, 1959, 1970b, 1979, 1980b). This situation is not without parallel in literature and history. Versions of history have "made history," and literary meaning is a joint product of reader and text (Gadamer, 1975; Barthes, 1979).

But there is a vast difference between academic study and the therapist's thought. Neither the poet nor the historical past inscribes a message directly onto the beholder's sensorium. A patient, in contrast, works partly in the medium of his therapist's feelings and attitudes. That is the patient's intention. (Lacan, [1977a] deserves great credit for seeing the importance of this fact.) Rather than studying, for example, an artistic *work* influenced by completed purposes, the therapist surveys an outpouring of *effort*, because he is himself (partly) the canvas and pigments the patient uses. It is about that field—the spirit of the patient's effort—that the therapist develops his firmest convictions, and a model that discriminates aims within that field is the one that helps him the most.[3]

What is special to the therapist's discovery is his tendency to make structures out of efforts to elicit structures within him.

There is no kind of awareness a therapist does not use: He is a reader grasping dramas; he is an historian analyzing the Now into past purposes and constraints; he is a psychologist employing a causal theory of the mind's workings. All of these can be purely academic enterprises.

But the working therapist must bring his form-making to bear on the patient's eliciting efforts. He does not just make sense out of what the patient conveys. He does not simply offer his mind as a stage for communication in order to observe what is enacted there. The therapist scrutinizes the stage directions that order him around; he does not simply obey them. His specialty is not to feel what the patient wants him to feel but to feel the patient

---

[3]Schafer's (1973b) ingenious action language gains plausibility from the fact that the paramount datum in psychoanalysis is the patient's effort, rather than the kind of perfected structure other disciplines study. It does not seem to me, however, that any one "language" or level of abstraction, is adequate to the simplest experience. How much less adequate, I should think, would be a language unable to cope with a characterizable subject, yet forced to describe a synoptic, multilayered psychoanalytic event! Just to apprehend even appetitive pressure on the analyst, one must structure it into discrete wishes, aims and purposes by models of substance. In chapter 20 I tried to show why the action language, which I regard as the least important part of Schafer's important project, cannot succeed.

wanting him to feel. His eye is placed short of the point at which the beam converges to an image, for he is interested in what the rays can produce beside that image. What he sees is not the real image that the patient projects but a virtual image on an intervening lens.

Hans Loewald (1960) is the master of what might be called the Theory of the Virtual Image. He described how growth comes about when a yet-to-be-built, virtual object within the patient is responded to by a therapist. He proposed that the patient internalizes the interaction between his relatively raw (unconscious and preconscious) expression and the therapist's integrated view of it and then appropriates the integrating gradient for his own use in processing his own experience. I suggest that to experience one's expression in terms of another's integrated meaning is to participate in a performed model or metaphor.

Loewald recognized that, if the goal is "structural change," treatment cannot simply translate one set of particular experiences into another; it must change the way experience is processed. (The technical implications of changing process rather than contents has been elaborated by Gray [1973].) This is accomplished by a meeting of the patient's intention and the analyst's response. That interaction carries a message of continuing usefulness. A message based on a type of interaction can be internalized as a process because, like a metaphor, its application is not finally determined. The patient experiences a way of feeling himself, rather than simply a description of himself. The therapist makes interaction into a model or metaphor by reacting as though the personal interaction signifies a hidden structure of wishes, a potential structure of perceptions—in short, the inner structure of the patient's mind. The patient will make many specific readings of this metaphor over an indefinite period of time. Because the interaction is the metaphor, all of the therapist's exploratory means—all of his interpretive, historical and causal forms—must ultimately find a foothold in how he feels that he is being handled by the patient.

THE ROLE OF THEORY IN PERFORMABLE MODELS

To some extent, it is enough that the therapist subscribes to a theory of the mind to ensure that a model of the mind will be enacted with his patient. That point was elaborated in chapter 16. A belief in any theory sensitizes the therapist to intentions, and distracts him from the effects intended. Even the simple act of retranslating what the patient is doing ("he is defending against an impulse"; "he is expressing an impulse"; "he is seeking affirmation," etc.) modifies the thought-pictures inflicted on the therapist. More powerful theoretical visions, such as transference, splitting, disillusionment, and so on, bias the therapist's whole receptivity and deflect his reactions in major ways.

But not all theoretical beliefs are equally effective deflectors. An unrealistic model will not compete sufficiently with the therapist's ordinary social reactions. And it will not be as promising to the patient. A model is realistic if you can turn it around and look at it from many sides. If it looks to the eye as it feels to the hand it captures the imagination more powerfully. A performable model will be most usable if the therapist's reactions that define it are multiform and converge on a useful potential. Each act of the therapist will reinforce the others and will signify more opportunity. That is the point where it makes a practical difference how complete a theory is. For example, an incomplete theory that fragmentarily refers to the oedipus complex or to separation anxiety, but does not answer questions about the relationship of these to other configurations, or say how they bear on habits and growth, will not in the long run produce as coherent a virtual image as the full Freudian theory. By themselves, such isolated fragments as transference, defense, representation (in the sense of a form carried over from the past) will not nudge the therapist's reactions toward a coherent, ongoing pattern. With only these scattered biases and without a complete theory of the mind, not as many impingements on the therapist will be reacted to as though they were related to an underlying form. (It would be a mistake to suppose that a fragmentary theory makes for a more flexible therapeutic relationship. Incomplete modeling leaves the therapist with a patchwork of fixed pictures. The bias it gives him is a specific palette of character types and limited dramatic forms. In contrast, a complete theory biases the therapist's reaction in the direction of an undefined pluripotential mental entity capable of transformations.)[4]

Far too often, theoretical completeness is regarded as just a matter of intellectual refinement. Ironically, the practical power of theoretical completeness can be overlooked precisely because it is so pervasive. The completeness of a theory often makes itself felt simply in the coherence that is implied in the therapist's reactions. For instance, we may react to hostility as a defensive manifestation of a desire without consciously accepting a theory of drive or psychic structure. In that case the logic of our reaction (which, even without our permission, pays homage to those intricacies) will orient us

---

[4]Observing infants in the first months of life, Stern (1985) calls attention to the cross-modal, choreographic coherences that constitute the primary data for earliest learning. And he cites evidence that a mother, influenced by her own prejudices, "interprets" her infant's behavior by triangulating his inner vital structure with complementary behavior of her own that does not imitate the child but translates the dynamics of his state into a different dimension. From the infant's side, this teaches about an "it" within him. From the mother's side, such a participatory interpretation of her infant's efforts is like understanding a work of art. While it is always dangerous to transpose the mother–infant relationship onto descriptions of therapist and patient, these findings suggest that there are many, subtle ways that theoretical coherence can affect treatment, extending far beyond simple verbal consistency.

quite nicely toward a mental entity, and it is always the logic of our action, whether we have thought it out or not, that will define the metaphor we enact with our patient.

The more complete a theory is, the greater is its power to collate the various impressions the patient makes on us, especially over time. The integrating vortex induced by a theory comes from its elaboration of both process and structural models of the mind. A powerful theory makes the therapist feel that he is responding in terms of a specific future form, even while he is reacting to an inchoate momentary appearance: A powerful theory allows its believer to tacitly feel the developmental consequences of an immediate, raw appeal.

Many therapists have been helped by British object relations theory when it says to them, "This person before you has a false self and feels weak. You must persuade him to show his true neediness or else he will not build something better." Although this theory fails to say what precisely will happen when the patient reveals himself as needy and unguarded (growth being an undissectable given in this account), even such a simple map will discriminate aims by defining them in terms of the therapist's theory.

It is something more, however, when we are told by Kohut, in effect, "From a life-long motive, this person is doing something to you (in a representational act—a kind of play that we are always engaged in with other people) which if you respond to it in a specific way, will build foreseeable and evident structures."

Both instructions say, "See the patient's behavior as an illustration of this or that theoretical notion." What Kohut's message does that the other does not is to design an attitude that collates the patient's varying impacts on the analyst as though the analyst were face to face with a hidden germ of internal strength. The impacts become for him not just symptoms of something potentially valuable, but varying glimpses of that value itself.

THE ROLE OF WISHES IN PERFORMABLE MODELS

Every therapy enacts a meeting with a hidden self (see chapter 16). That enactment is explored differently by patient and therapist and has different meanings for them. The patient explores the interaction according to his personal and tacit inclinations. But whatever the patient's interests may be, it is the therapist's job to make sure that what ultimately gets explored is a model of the patient's hidden self. The therapist insures this by his pattern of response.

The psychotherapy relationship is an open-ended model because it is a concrete structure of interactive events that shows how new meaning can be assigned to strivings, thoughts, and feelings, even though it is not known to begin with exactly how it will shed that light (see Schafer, 1977). (By contrast, an ordinary relationship is more like a simile or a closed model, because its fixed roles and customary relationships pick out fixed features of the parties' constitutions and give them implicit meaning ahead of time.) Likewise, one can view the therapy situation as a performable metaphor, in that the therapist treats the patient's actions as though they were manifestations of something central and essential. The patient experiences himself differently through the new relationship, and that is a metaphorical understanding.

For instance, Kohut's theoretical model instructs the analyst to feel a ("narcissistic") pressure as an effort toward independent security, although it used to be felt as a dead-end claim. The analyst is instructed to feel the pressure as though it were a step toward consolidating the self. In his mind's eye, the analyst practices being handled by the patient to achieve that goal. During treatment, the analyst's specific sense of how he can be manipulated in this way is a template that registers those aspects of the patient's pressure that Kohut wants him to perceive. The analyst's cultivated readiness to be used for that particular kind of "play" (a deadly serious kind of play) translates the theoretical or discursive model into an action model that allows him to discover a new aim in his particular patient.

Historical causes, personal dramas, and theory of the mind are extremely important in preparing the therapist to observe new configurations. And so is the drama of treatment that links them. But we must not forget that if these structures help the therapist to find new configurations it must be because they truly match similar models and metaphors that the patient experiences with a therapist who is working that way. The therapist's truth is dependent on the consequent truth found by the patient. (This is the point Ricoeur [1977b] makes in his article on the truth claim in psychoanalysis; see also Habermas, 1968). What guides the practicing therapist is some perception of an answering construction on the part of his patient. Unfortunately, it is not at all clear what we should mean by "answering," or what that perception feels like. Yet without such constant signals of confirmation, we could not long track a seamless clinical happening faithfully and coherently.

What prompts the patient's announcement of an "answering" meaning? Perhaps he sees an opportunity in his therapist's receptivity (see French, 1958, p. 40), and betrays some special "élan," from which the therapist senses how much play his attitudes afford the patient's strivings. (On this point, see Gendlin, 1964a.) If the therapist can never know for sure exactly what an interpretation means to a patient, he can probably tell that it means a great deal or very little.

Reasoning along these lines, we would expect therapists to be grateful for a theory that gives them an appetite for states of unstable meaning and uncertainty of aim. After all, an appetite is the sort of orientation that selects continuously, minutely, and without deliberation, because its reward is not distant and theoretical. A theory that trains an appetite for situations that are ripe for change provides its own ostensive definitions. With such appetites, the therapist will find concrete examples of theoretical concepts like a guided missile finding its target.

What in general is this appetite an appetite for? It is for a pressure from the patient, a pressure that gives promise of a buried liveliness or expressiveness as postulated by the analyst's model of mental growth, and is consequently experienced by him with gratification. Classical appetites include the taste for conflict, especially when directed toward the analyst. (There are many other examples in clinical theory.)

New theory often modifies treatment by cultivating a new appetite. Kohut's theory is an example. Intellectually, Kohut's theory is organized around a theme of the analyst's open receptivity. But at the practical level, one finds that the Kohutian's modeling power is achieved not by freedom from prejudicial forms, but by a bias toward forms such as reactions to disillusionment. Obviously Kohut did not discover the reaction to disillusionment. What he did was to describe growth in a way that encouraged his followers to develop a special appetite for that sort of thing. The model or metaphor these therapists enact with their patients is different from what it would have been if disillusionment was something they only knew about but had no particular appetite for. (For that reason arguments stalemate when they turn on whether some newly featured aspect of human nature has or has not been previously known to therapists.)

We can see appetites functioning this way more clearly in a new theory because we do not take them so much for granted. Consider the Kohutian therapist. Unlike many of his colleagues who take a dim view of "unrealistic" longings, the Kohutian does not seem to recognize disappointment as the final state of a vain effort. He reacts almost as though the awful feeling is a reassuring image of how the patient can profitably use him. Small wonder that he develops a taste for disappointment reactions. Covert disappointments stand out readily from the scene because they are fundamentally wanted by the therapist; they carry natural highlights. At the same time, the patient often indicates that the therapist's reaction to his disappointment has allowed him to make something new and complex out of his defeated state. The theory has given the practitioner both a natural analyzer of phenomena (in the form of a professional desire), and a built-in receiver for signals of metaphorical relevance, especially pressures from the patient and ways the patient handles him. Reacting on the basis of these sensitivities, the therapist completes a model of the patient that can be used in different ways by the therapist according to his theory, and by the patient according to his aspirations. The metaphor, which is what they are exploring, is not something said by the therapist, nor a set of propositions in his head (although these contribute to it). Nor is it a charade designed to teach the patient a lesson (for that would model a pupil rather than a hidden self). The metaphor lies in the structure of the action between therapist and patient.

Like a blind person reading with fingertips, a patient scans the therapeutic model with his wishes. And he picks out the model's shape from the therapist's reaction to his wishes. What is the patient looking for, as he learns this new model of himself? He is looking for the therapist's wishes. We all want to be desired, loved, preferred. We want someone to find his or her satisfaction in us. Wishes seek wishes. More exactly, our wishes specify which of our actions and attitudes, which of our "selves," we would like someone else to find satisfying. (As previously mentioned, Lacan was one of the few to see the great import of this fact for therapy, and his convoluted style is, to a small extent, excused by the "hall of mirrors" phenomenon he was describing.) The patient tries to find out how his wishes fit with the therapist's. Insofar as the patient trains his wishes on the therapist, it is the therapist's wishes that are most important to him.

Unlike Richelieu's one-sided creation of a special king-ness (see p. 513, this volume), psychotherapy enacts a model that is determined by what each partner's wishes evokes in the other.[5]

Details of the interaction model depend on what the therapist is "after" at any moment, and how that relates to what the patient is after. We have noted many times that one use of theory is to help the therapist find what he is after in *everything* the patient is after. The therapist's wish to understand does that, but a wish to understand is too amorphous to focus a specific response at a specific point. Theory helps when it develops enthusiasm for particular efforts of the patient.

DO THERAPISTS EXPRESS WISHES EVEN IN INSIGHT THERAPY?

Picturing an interplay of wishes between therapist and patient will provoke two objections. The first is that such a picture, if it has any use at all, portrays only turgid and volatile treatments, and not therapies where experience is packaged in cognitive forms.

But what we are discussing is not really an issue of cognition versus affect, or insight versus relationship. A wish, an appetite, or a proclivity is illustrated as well by the therapist's alertness to a promising turn of events as it is by his worry or excitement. In a relatively cerebral exchange we will find signals of the therapist's determining wishes in the local "feel," that the therapist's familiar theory takes on with this one patient. Or we might see the shadow of a wish in the way the therapist automatically tailors his customary profes-

---

[5]Of course, it is an oversimplification to call even Richelieu's invention one-sided. Human beings can only be influenced by responding to their aspirations. If people did not want to respect and be respected, Richelieu's ceremonies would have played to no audience.

sional response to a particular patient. These nuances show the patient's personal tug on the therapist, and we have seen that such a personal pull can only fasten on wishes (chapter 10). Most wishes are expressed subtly and tacitly (chapter 11). For much of the time during which a performable model is being built, there may be no actual interchange at all, because the patient experiences an imaginary interplay with his therapist even when he is alone.

IS PERFORMABLE METAPHOR SUGGESTION?

The second objection to including therapist wishes in the formula of therapy is that psychotherapists are supposed to keep their gestural input to a minimum. Psychoanalysis, which is our paradigm therapy, is famous for the pains it takes to minimize the analyst's personal gestures.

And yet analysts recognize that the minimum is not nil. Many features of the analyst's role qualify his neutrality. From the time of Wilhelm Reich (1949, p. 49) and Waelder (1936), theorists have acknowledged that each comment of the analyst betrays a selective perspective. (See also Myerson, 1977.) Nothing human can be exhaustively or univocally described, and the analyst's choice of description is a function of who he is. Loewald (1960) describes a special forward-looking, structuring attitude of the analyst. Schafer (1970b) characterizes the analyst's coloring attitudes in detail (making it clear that they should be multiple and flexible). And, after all, analysts undergo training analysis not just to rid themselves of interfering illness, but also to gain access to a full repertoire of attitudes, a fact that can only be denied if we regard the unconscious as a mere lexicon.

Nevertheless, not everyone feels that the therapist's limited perspective always slants his response. Moreover, when such therapist "sets" are accepted as part of therapy, it is often on condition that they be regarded as uniform, non-specific, personally unexpressive elements, unavoidably built into the treatment situation.

What worries therapists most is an *individualized* signifying attitude (i.e., a personal attitude of a therapist personally aroused by a particular patient). It is precisely this aspect of Kohut's theory, for example, that has raised some theoretical eyebrows. An individualized, metaphorical interaction with a patient might constitute suggestion, and suggestion is condemned for interfering with the patient's autonomous reshuffling of his own meanings.

In particular, the "bad" example of Franz Alexander (1956), with his "corrective emotional experience," is held up as a warning to theorists who talk about nonconceptual, discursive, noninterpretational elements in therapy. Ironically, that aspect of treatment, although noted by him, was not Alexander's prime concern. He worked with an enlightenment model. He believed that good analysts know they are being "set up" by patients to confirm a false picture of reality, and intuitively lean over backward to avoid entrapment (Alexander, 1956, pp. 78–102). Sometimes they choose bare neutrality as their artificial attitude, but the patient may subvert this, or manage to see it as a repetition of a childhood environment. And Alexander would ask us to admit that, despite all precautions, the analyst might be a poor example of general reality because of his own peculiarities. Therefore, Alexander argued, although exceptional analysts might work intuitively, it would be far better for analysts to know what they are trying to do, and do it more deliberately. They should consciously judge what attitudes need to be avoided, and then deliberately avoid them. The purpose of the emphasized attitude was not to give the patient what he craved, but the reverse: It was to thrust on him against his will an experience that would destroy his illusions. It was not a matter of making patients feel good. Still less was it a way of making up to the patient for previous deprivations. For Alexander it was a lesson about reality that counted. Alexander was a "realist." The patient was misperceiving reality, and Alexander was resolved to demonstrate reality to him: "At the same time recognizing and experiencing this discrepancy between the transference situation and the actual patient-therapist relationship is what I call the 'corrective emotional experience' " (1956, p. 41). The corrective emotional experience is not a paradigm of a nonrational, influencing therapy. It is the unfortunate isolation of a rationalistic component in psychoanalytic treatment.

Admittedly, Alexander was an avowed influencer as well as a promoter of reality. But that was paradoxically because he did not want to exercise transferred parental influence. Unlike most analysts he did not see regression as a path to change. He regarded regression as defensive, and distrusted it. That led him to campaign purposefully against the wish for dependence. His frankly controlling strategy was dictated by concern for the patient's reality testing.

If Alexander is a bad example of something, that something is not manipulativeness but naiveté. He thought that a pathogenic issue might be simple enough and wrong enough to be symbolized by the analyst in a single contrary attitude.

To see how the therapist's wishes can be used for more creative modeling, it is useful to compare Kohut's "corrective emotional experience" with Alexander's.

Alexander used himself as a model of reality, and he therefore regulated his reactions to illustrate the "real" Alexander. His posing was required because he wished to interfere with the patient's prejudice about external reality. (He endorsed conventional analytic neutrality if it succeeded in shaking the patient's preconceptions.) Nothing could contrast more sharply with Kohut's theory. Kohut was not interested in correcting the patient's errors. He did not wish to instruct him in the reality of the world. He did not try to stop the patient from doing one thing or force him to another. He wanted to nurture primitive strivings because he respected their power to construct reliable strengths. Therefore, we may say that his response was designed to create neither a vision of Heinz Kohut, nor any other picture of external "reality," but an open-ended model of a relationship that allowed new meaning to be given to old motives. The analyst colludes with the patient in modeling this, much as one would participate with a child who is playing an adult role. (I regret the patronizing connotations of this analogy, and use it simply because it is easier to picture play with children than among adults. Play may be regarded as a performable model; see Vygotsky, 1933.)

It is important to note that Kohut's mission was not to make the patient see his analyst as an empathic person, but to make the patient feel how his wishes combined with the analyst's attitudes to attain a new significance. (In all fairness, it should be said that Alexander hoped his reality training would accomplish this objective; that line of thought is more evident in the work of French [1958].)

If this view is correct, it may explain why therapists are limited in their treatment style. Most of them know that some patients do better with other therapists. Therapists can usually imagine the style they cannot provide. If they can imagine it, why can't they follow it? Therapists will say that they do not like the needed style, or that their personality is not suited to it, or that the needed style is not real treatment (although they may think that real treatment stands no chance with this patient). But isn't there another reason? Therapy depends on cultivated appetites, and these are not simply a matter of choice. The therapist does not deliberately select a behavior from moment to moment. It would be truer to say that his action "happens" because it makes sense to him. And it makes sense to him because it fits into the type of exploratory interactive model that his appetites tend to build. Because a therapist orients himself around a tacit virtual model, it is probably impossible for him to copy a style on a play-by-play basis. Intellectually, he might recognize each move as appropriate or even inspired, but it will not *feel* reasonable to him if it is not part of a more general focusing plan.

Looking at matters this way may help us see the family resemblance in diverse psychotherapies. In our view, a therapist is someone whose theory and appetites give him a central sense of another's untapped potentiality with the result that his explicit understandings do not seem to arise out of a fixed relationship. As long as there is some reality in the therapist's vision of the patient's potential, and as long as the therapist maintains the ambiguity that this vision sustains, we would expect the patient to find the meanings he needs. The interactive metaphor from which the therapist reads those meanings might have had other, equally useful shapes corresponding to the variety of therapies (and therapists), but the patient's reading might be the same for all.

VI
Implications

35

Conclusion:

No Resting Place

W e started this book by noting the discomfort involved in therapy, focusing especially on the therapist's discomfort.

First we looked for reflections of discomfort in theory. On the surface, theory made therapy look rather comfortable, partly by denying that the therapist has wishes that can be toyed with. Under scrutiny, however, theory shows the imprint of the therapist's wishes.

Then we looked at the stress from the standpoint of the therapist's experience. We saw him maneuvering to keep his balance in several spheres. We noticed how hard it is for him to keep balanced with no social means of expressing his wishes. He must act artificially, but he does not even have many artifices: His profession has few conventions and only vague justifications.[1] And he dare not build a stable platform by establishing his artificiality as stock-in-trade (by explaining his purpose to the patient or assuming the patient's consent) for that would transform his behavior into a rigid, personal wish, and he seeks to avoid that. He will have wishes, but they cannot be defended and they cannot be confessed.

Because his task simultaneously encourages wishes and makes them un-thinkable, the therapist comes to feel his urges as professional knowledge about the patient rather than as a desire to change him.

---

[1] Some therapists seize on the few conventions that they have as constituting a definition of psychotherapy (see Friedman, 1976a), and that serves to justify the conventions. But this self-justification deprives the enterprise of meaning. ("Why do you psychoanalyze this man?" "Because he is there.")

But I have suggested that ultimately it is undisguised, though minute, wishes that determine what looks real to the therapist and what stimulates him to act. At the finest points of process, almost by definition, professional wishes have to become personalized. It is wishes – any kind of wishes – that scan for individual potentialities in an individual partner. Conversely, because a partner's potential in itself is undefined, its specification depends on what is asked of it, in this case by the therapist who says, in effect, "I am drawn to *this* in you." Blatant, open wishes select specific potentialities too decisively to suit a treatment that intends to explore freedom. A therapist who openly asks for this or that, biases the patient's choices. Fortunately, a therapist's blatant wishes are counterbalanced by the perspective he gets from his theory of the mind that puts him in the position of a natural scientist. Theory finds *things* to look at within the patient. Things can be seen to have the potential for many different developments, aside from their appeal to the therapist's wishes. Everyone assumes that people have dispositions, so everyone uses a theory of the mind. But the greater elaboration of theory in psychotherapy dilutes the therapist's personal attitudes, causing him to regard his patient as a natural object and not just as a character in the therapist's own life drama. (For example, *transference* is a natural science theory that discounts the therapist's reactions.)[2]

Psychoanalytic theory of the mind keeps the therapist's wishes general and mobile. Talking to someone who is dedicated to that sort of theory, the patient confronts new possibilities. He may find this freedom partly in the way the therapist describes him. But basically, the way the patient discovers a new and not always pleasant freedom is by having his actions on the therapist treated as expressions of a complex and variously operating mind (see chapters 16 and 34).

We noticed that a theory of the mind does not say how it should be applied at any particular moment. For one thing, unique individuals and moments are not indexable in a general theory. But there is a more significant reason for the gap between the therapist's theory of the mind and his experience of

---

[2]Apparently for this very reason, François Roustang (1982) has taken transference to be the central term of analytic theory. He writes, "Theory is then no more than a form of protection through which the analyst avoids the transference" (p. 59). Many of my principle points have been discussed by Roustang in a Lacanian fashion, among them: (1) The therapist's need to theorize in order not to be assimilated to the patient's universe, along with his need to stop theorizing when responding to the patient's particularity. (2) The therapist's need to recreate his theory out of newly felt problems. (3) The partly ideological use of theory in practice. (4) The danger that the therapist will freeze the patient's transference if he settles into the role of theoretician. Roustang also writes about analytic theory as the embodiment of the therapist's desire, though here it is difficult to tell whether his ideas coincide with mine. If, when he writes that theory embodies the therapist's fantasies, he means that theory is the therapist's vision of potentialities, then our views converge considerably. (I am indebted to Paul Stepansky for pointing out how closely Roustang's thoughts parallel mine.)

the moment: His most important datum is the *impact* he feels, and impact means that the therapist's own wishes and attitudes are affected. The therapist would like to have the most general, objective attitudes, but if he did not have particular attitudes he would not feel an impact, and he would have no receptors for the patient's meaning. He must keep particular dramatic attitudes alive within himself even though they pull him away from abstract, objective theory of the mind. A therapist who could not be put on the spot would probably never know what is happening.

Probably one reason that therapists periodically get angry at theory of the mind is that it tends to immunize them from the patient too effectively. Freudian theory is obliged to squeeze together part and whole, structure and process. It combines fortuitous events and personal life-dramas with perennial forces and inexorable developmental processes. It must include object-like views, even though it is not restricted to them. Annoyed by all the objectivizing veils between themselves and the patient, some modern theorists want to get rid of the object, mind. Their philosophical argument is weak but that is all the more reason to respect their efforts as a sign that explicit theory of the mind is sometimes inconvenient for a practitioner.

A therapist without a technical theory of the mind would deal with a patient as he pleases. No theorist wishes to encourage that. The new theoretical minimalists are no more cavalier than the old metapsychologists about therapeutic discipline. They do not want to unleash uninhibited social attitudes toward patients. And to prevent that from happening, they all necessarily assume a theory of the mind and of therapy. But they keep it secret from themselves. They do not allow themselves to recognize how they address an inner reality and they do not recognize the natural science predictions that guide them in their responses.

These new theorists bring into bold relief a special need of therapists. We see them trying to feel one thing and to avoid feeling another: They do not want to feel that they are eliciting a potentiality from a person (actualizing a latent property of an object). They would rather feel that they are reading a communication from a person (receiving the message of a text). Accordingly, they want to feel that what the patient is doing to them is not a doing but a showing.[3] And they want to feel that what they are doing to the patient does not exploit causal rules of transformation, but just offers earnest witness. Theory of the mind is hidden so that the therapist can sense some of his encouraging anticipations as passive perception rather than actions.

We concluded from this that a therapist needs to act as a desirer and partner without feeling that he is imposing his desires or succumbing to temptations. Therapists fail to declare all their theoretical baggage not

---

[3] Schafer (1980b) converts a showing into a telling, and a telling into a showing, but it seems to me that his implicit intention is to make it all come out as a telling.

because they are dishonest, but to leave themselves free to register human meanings as passive perceptions. I can think about a rock as an object, and I can study its impact as an object. But although I can think about a person as an object, I cannot perceive his human impact on me that way. I first recognize his action by responding from within a drama that we share, and it is from that drama that I derive all further meaning, including theoretical classification. If I then turn around and hold myself responsible for dramatizing the event, I will never get to be an audience: I will never perceive this person's effect on me. (The reason case histories are so extremely unrevealing is that we don't feel the patient's punch.) If I see myself only as having elicited a reaction from a biological organism, which would have been a different reaction if I had experimented differently, I will not perceive a human meaning. To be sure, a person *is* a biological organism, and our theories regard him as such. But at some point in our dealings with him, we have to feel that he has *decided* to show us more of his internal state and that we are receiving the impact of his intention, and not just that we are producing more and more predictable reactions by our maneuvers. We must feel that we are not just getting what we are trying for, not just manipulating a mechanism.

We can make this clearer by comparing the therapist's modes of awareness with two uses of language: reading and conversation. Like the therapist's perception and his theoretical understanding, both conversation and reading require a theory of the mind. In conversing we use our knowledge of human nature as a basis for manipulating our partner when we need to make his meaning and our meaning clear. In contrast, texts require us to make do with what is already given, and our knowledge of the way people behave does not show itself in personal approaches to the author. We can feel passively receptive to texts and only literary critics are aware of how active our understanding is. Psychotherapists have to feel themselves in both positions at once. They alternately exhibit and hide their interpretive theory. And they write theory that alternately exhibits and hides the importance of theory.

Therapists always picture treatment as a reading. If this model encourages relativism, it is because reading is specifically a way of not seeing the mind as an objective entity. In other words, a reading posture is designed to avoid sketching an abstract schema of potentiality, so that the therapist can feel directly and unequivocally touched by the patient.

But, although the therapist needs to partly hide theory from himself in order to see the patient dramatically and "textually," therapists also need to believe that they are dealing with a natural being whose propensities may be classified and researched. Nor is that an "inhuman" attitude. It is common sense (see Schafer, 1980a). But therapists carry the ordinary natural science understanding of mind to an extreme. Ordinarily we are more concerned with how a person is than what he might become. Therapists want to keep the patient's potentiality more boldly before their eyes than ordinary life requires. They do not do that by constantly thinking about theory. They do it by adopting a special, expectant attitude that shows dedication to a theory. Even when the theory is forgotten, the expectant attitude continues to testify to the dedication. (In chapter 5 we noted the positioning effect of theory: The positioning effect can outlast detailed memory of the theory.)

Dedication is what makes the difference. In ordinary life, common-sense theory of the mind carries people just to their own points of interest in their partner. But dedication to a theory of the mind, at its very least, inspires in the therapist a searching hope to always see something more than what he sees, and that expectation makes his current feelings about the patient tentative and unspecific. Obviously, something strong enough to temper affective reactions deserves to be called dedication. Dedication to—rather than the mere use of—theory is also shown in the therapist's stubborn confidence that development will occur if interference is cleared away. These are both extreme consequences of viewing a person as an object (that is, having a description of his potential activity and supposing his mind to have continuing parts with various functions.)

In summary, the therapist has to have wishes, and he has to have a view that precludes wishes. He has to feel that he is observing history while he is in fact making it. He has to feel that he is watching something happen, although he is actually trying to bring it about. He has to feel that he is reading when he is really conversing. He has to feel that things are determinate when they are up for grabs. He has to feel innocent but responsible. He has to feel that he is objective when he is biased, distant when close, impassive when needy.

Nor is this mandatory confusion a pastiche of attitudes, assembled for assorted purposes. It is one mission, designed to pull together maximum (potential) freedom with momentary (actual) liveliness in the patient. The confusion of attitudes within the therapist diffuses his abstract, theoretical vision into the personal drama he enacts with his patient. It allows the therapist's personal attitudes to play on the patient without forcing the patient into a reciprocal role, as attitudes usually do to a partner. If the therapist were just someone with wishes, his wishes would set just one kind of scene. (Even the wish to be helpful would do that.) But because they are wishes of someone dedicated to a theory of the mind, they search out a variety of possibilities. Yet the therapist's net contribution to the treatment scene is not theoretical information but attitudes modified by theory. Even when the therapist and patient talk in "psychological" terms, what makes a difference to the patient is the personal attitude that is conditioned by the larger view. The therapist's attitudes are the patient's data. Whether it is the therapist's knowing the patient or the patient knowing the therapist, human action is grasped first by moral evaluation. But because moral evaluation forecloses other attitudes, theory of the patient's mind as a natural object invites him to be other than the dramatic character he currently portrays.

It is the therapist's responsibility to accept the paradoxes and embarassments of this discordant job. He cannot pass the responsibility along to some justifying formula, as I am guilty of doing in these pages. It is just as injurious for the therapist to think of himself as posing in an ambiguous role in order to expand the patient's meaning, as it is for him to think of himself as an innocent bystander. If the therapeutic alliance masks the manipulative aspect of the therapist, the role of a smart dodger masks his real caught-up-ness and impressionability. If the therapist wholeheartedly tried to avoid being manipulated, he would miss the details that can only be perceived when his native appetites are inadvertently stirred and his unplanned enthusiasm evoked. Lacking the credulity that Havens (1982) writes about, such a surgical therapist would not be able to appreciate the patient's life. (Cf. Schafer [1979] on the analyst's appreciative attitude.)

Psychotherapy, then, is a continuous effort to accommodate incompatibles. Perhaps it is some consolation that they are the great incompatibles: time and permanence; uniqueness and generality; law and chance; percept and concept; fact and value. Isn't that the expectable burden of a practice that deals planfully with freely creative individuals? No wonder that we find parallels in history and art, whose subjects also are both in time and above time.

There is no way to stretch someone without stressing him. Hope and illusion go hand in hand. We have seen that the stresses of psychotherapy result from, and result in, various contradictory attitudes. Each attitude is an illusion from the point of view of another attitude. Whenever possibilities are being explored, illusions are in the offing. Uncertainty about what is illusion is the heaving sea on which therapy floats. It is the source of fluctuating malaise and strain. But I must emphasize that it is not just the patient who rides the waves; it is the therapist as well (and the supervisor, and the funder, and everyone who has anything to do with therapy). That is important. If the awful prospect of collapsed illusion haunts therapy, nevertheless illusions cannot all evaporate together, nor is either party immune to the hazard, and there is some comfort in that. The therapist has to see through himself if he is to operate well. He must be able to view himself wryly. (Cf. Schafer [1970b] on ironic vision.) But he cannot afford to be cynical about himself, any more than he can be cynical about his patient. He has to know that he is always deceiving himself, but he has to feel that he is mostly genuine.

Once again we see how important theory is. Theory helps the therapist to maintain his illusions while seeing through them. I have tried to document that throughout this book. And I must emphasize that theory performs this acrobatic feat both intellectually and by molding the therapist's posture.

Insofar as theory harmonizes the discordant tasks, it makes therapy look more settled than it is.

But there is a limit to how much serenity theory can insure, and that is not because we are frail, but because theory is composed of views that cannot be logically fused into a momentary attitude, as witness Freud's part-theories and process theories, and his surpassing sense of drama. Freud's theory is a dialogue of multiple considerations. Revisionists skim off one or another homogeneous perspective from among his many modes. They do away with instincts. They adopt a clinical theory. They use Freudian life histories. They select defense mechanisms. They may preserve only the procedure (although that is a paradox because two people alone in a room can hardly be considered a method even if "instructions" are given.)

Hovering over all particular theoretical debates is the question of the place of theory in general. Theory is needed. It is all that distinguishes the therapist from the rest of humanity. Theory is always used, even when it is not evident. Yet even theoreticians are ambivalent about theory. Some worry that if a therapist is a theorist he cannot be a reader. If he is interfering with his "text," he is not absorbing it. If he is thinking like a natural scientist, he cannot be recognizing the Sophoclean drama. Some fear that if a therapist applies a theory of things to the realm of persons, he will be making up a pseudobiology out of his personal myths.

If nobody loves theory, it is probably because too much is expected of it. What a science of individuality can do is to make practical difficulties tolerable. It cannot make them go away, for then we would have only a science of generalities. If one wants to see exactly where theory enters psychotherapy *in flagrante*, one should skip over occasions when a therapist savors a theoretical image, and look at the times when he is desperately trying to maintain a necessary illusion without faking it.

For example, theory lets the therapist pose as a knower, but theory also whispers to him that he is not by any means the kind of knower that he comes across as, and that he is creating an illusion that makes the patient feel more profoundly understood than is humanly possible. It is not just a matter of transference. The therapist's avoidance of any one perspective leaves the patient only the option of addressing him as an unlimited knower. Lacan (1977a) recognized the power and inevitability of that illusion. But that is not fraudulent because the therapist does honestly think of himself as a knower, that is, as a natural scientist. The same combination of illusion and authenticity applies to the sense of the therapist's straightforwardness and collaboration with the patient. In each case, the therapist is genuinely committed to an illusory role, and it is his theory that manufactures and "deconstructs" the role. As an illustration, I recommend the treatment reported by Winnicott (1972) and referred to extensively in chapter 8. Unless they have exactly Winnicott's orientation, readers will be startled by his basic certainty, which is evident behind the particular confusions and muddles that he frankly confesses. The certainty of his framework must have its own effect, and yet Winnicott, who cannot be imagined to have ever pretended to magisterial authority, tried to use interpretation to *dispel* illusions about his wisdom (1972, p. 587).

In chapter 1, I noted that theory makes treatment seem deceptively stressless. In the light of subsequent chapters we must modify that. Theory seems tranquil only if we look at one part of one school at one moment in history. Even then, treatment looks civil only if we caricature the theory. In a large panorama, dialectic tension and downright warfare appear within theory itself. But it is one of the uses of theory to lend itself to simple caricatures that countenance a given role for the therapist's momentary rest. And it is these useful caricatures that falsely beautify treatment.

Theory that gives a semblance of harmony to clashing demands is one of the few comforts a therapist can honestly come by. (It is like Bakhtin's [1981] and Ricoeur's [1984] notions of narrative.) There is no other comfort. There is no escape from falseness. A therapist cannot unequivocally position himself in an equivocal role: that is a self-contradiction. He can be more or less flexible, ironic, philosophical. But at a given moment, he cannot be without an attitude. He can understand a pose when he is caught out or when he catches himself out. But he cannot prevent it from happening. Of course anyone can just accept a fixed role. That is probably the best definition of "supportive therapy." At that point the therapist might more accurately consider himself a counselor, an advisor, or friend. He is no longer pursuing the goal of psychotherapy, although the patient may experience a therapy fortuitously related to the therapist's efforts.

The therapist's main predicament is not that he is asked to be more mobile than is possible. Nor is it the problem of the photographer who must engage a moving object from a stationary position. These are problems, indeed, but the basic problem is greater and more awful.

The problem is that, considering how the therapist sees himself compared with what he is actually doing, therapy is not entirely honest. I return to the litany: The therapist has to be manipulative, but not intend to manipulate. He has to try for something and not care about it. He has to engage in mutual seduction and yet forswear it. He has to exploit a patient and be selfless. The therapist is always in a false position. And he is not even squarely in a false position. The therapist has nothing to confess, if he is doing his job. He was not hired to be good; he was hired to do therapy. An apologetic attitude would be a useless burden to the patient. But a smug attitude would be imperceptive. If the therapist is not fooling himself, he is not doing his job. And if he continues to fool himself always in the same way, he is not doing his job. There is just nothing a therapist can legitimately do about this problem except work on it through theory and practice, recognizing what he owes to which of his beliefs and where those beliefs fail him.

People help others in many ways. Therapists can make themselves comfortable and still help patients. Patients may be given less than maximum freedom and still be helped. Some patients may be helped more by a comfortable therapist who stays closer to an ordinary social relationship than by one who is wierder. Some patients seem to require mainly one or another role to bring out what they need brought out, and they seem to profit from a certain amount of settled, mutual deception. We could run the gamut on this: some patients may need more or less seduction, exploitation, control, and so on. I say that casually here only because I did not take it as my subject. It is not a trivial matter. Psychotherapy should account for these differences just as any natural science accounts for differences in its field. But my point is that, whatever is helpful in these more defined relationships, what keeps them from replicating ordinary life is whatever element of anomaly they retain, even if that remaining anomaly is just a background hint or nostalgic memory of a therapeutic ideal, or an occasional odd shift in the therapist's attitude at a crucial moment when the momentum of the interaction would normally have led to a destructive outcome.

* * *

Is there anything to be said for psychotherapy as a human enterprise apart from its individual outcomes? What would we write about it in an anthropological epitaph? Just as one can scientifically appreciate the improvement of imaging techniques in radiology apart from their practical usefulness in medicine, we may ask what psychotherapy has to say for itself, *sub specie aeternitas.*

I suppose we could say that it was an example of human discipline—both the intellectual discipline of figuring out the mind, and the personal discipline of pushing the limits of individuality against the confines of social forms.

Man is not satisfied with any limit. He paints his face. He flies to the moon. He looks behind his own thoughts. And in the end, he is not content to have his meanings assigned to him by a social field, even though society is his own collective construction. Perhaps therapy is an effort to break free of the one thing that most constitutes the human condition—our definition by others (cf. Lacan, 1977a, b). Meaning is always social, but the social framework varies in rigidity, producing meanings that are more or less conventional.

It is true that psychoanalysts sometimes describe their method as a socializing maneuver. They note that they draw patients away from fantasies about their original families into the larger world of public meanings. Viewing public reality as a monolith, some critics have charged that treatment standardizes life. But in fact, when compared to a family fantasy, public reality offers fewer constraints on what a patient can make of his strivings.[4] Giving up the pleasure principle means using one's motives more variously.

That would explain two striking features of psychotherapy: Therapy is uncomfortable. And therapy is relatively useless in traditional societies. (It is utterly destructive—and therefore futile—to try to detach someone from his lifeline.)

Psychotherapy is only superficially related to those perennial healing procedures designed to reunite alienated persons with their community (Frank, 1961). Of course psychotherapy arose from a society that had a reason to foster it and was bound to be congruent with its times; that is a mere historical tautology. But beyond that it must be granted that Frank's socialization theory of symbolic healing does have a practical bearing on psychotherapy. Because therapy is uncongenial, both parties tend to move it into a fixed, reassuring, socially defined relationship such as the one Frank describes. Should therapists and patients finally succeed in that, there would be no more psychotherapy, though talking treatments and healing ceremonies flourish till the end of time.

---

[4]Nothing misses the mark more than the old libel that the profession of psychotherapy is bent on adjusting people to their environment. Individual therapists, of course, must answer for their own behavior. But this criticism is often leveled by people who want to "free" random strivings to fit into a tiny, virtuous community.

36

Training

A solved problem is as useful to a man's mind as a broken sword on a battlefield.
  — Sufi Proverb

PRINCIPLES OF TRAINING

We can practice psychotherapy forever without asking what it is, and we are sometimes better off not knowing. Training is a different matter; unreflectiveness does not help it at all. In the next few years, the profession's survival may depend on the educator's choice of principles. What are his options?

Bureaucratic Principles

In the future, practitioners will be paid for some treatments and not others. Educators have an advantage: they will always be freer because they are not paid for a particular procedure. But that makes public policy even more dangerous for them. Educators do not have to ask themselves whether their interest matches the paymaster's. They can find ways to accomodate to outside demands, and no opportunity is more treacherous for a profession that lacks established principles or techniques than a chance to accomodate to extra-professional convenience.

Those who look forward to the world of tomorrow will point to the useful discipline that a funding challenge brings. And they will argue that anyone concerned with mental health must respect reality, especially fiscal reality.

There are also other benefits: Fading prosperity has brought a new interest in comparative psychotherapy; outcome studies are underway; patients are profiting from their therapists' new flexibility; trainees are being exposed to more treatment styles and being prepared for more contingencies than they used to be.

But dangers accompany these opportunities. Bureaucrats want to monitor psychotherapy the way they monitor other treatments, and they have every reason to want to. But it is not honest for *therapists* to accept that as their challenge because they do not know, to begin with (and we are still at the beginning), whether it is good for them to plan treatment the way a surgeon does. The previous chapters have suggested that, in fact, it is not a good way for therapists to think; our survey implies that psychotherapy runs counter to the needs of quality control.

The therapist must give the bureaucrat what he asks for. The only question is what he should teach about enforced bureaucratic activities. One might think the answer simple and uncontroversial: He should teach that a bureaucratic activity is a bureaucratic activity. But people do not like to see themselves compromising. It feels shabby to be now more, now less sincere. An educator risks his self-respect by relaying orders from outside. He may feel more honorable when he assimilates the must to the ought. Isn't it better, he may ask, to transmute the bureaucratic requirement into a learning experience? Maybe we will think more clearly if we think like surgeons. Maybe it will keep us on our toes. Maybe it will sharpen our use of terms. And, after all, even before money problems made it mandatory, many schools already honestly advocated a hard-headed evaluation of treatment results. (Case conferences have been conducted in that spirit for years.)

In fact, it may transpire that this was the best choice—that by sheer coincidence, bureaucratic pressures forced psychotherapy to do just what it should have done.

But then again it may turn out to have been the wrong choice. My point is that the profession does not know yet; it dare not let itself find out by weighing the financial rewards. Architects can cater to society's demands while independent principles of engineering ensure that buildings do not collapse. Psychotherapy has no independent tool to safeguard treatment while styles of thinking go in search of money. Thinking is the only tool a psychotherapist has. Genuine therapy may involve some peculiar dishonesties, but they are the special dishonesties inherent in doing therapy. Other motives must be clearly labeled. If an educator tells a trainee to select target problems in the first 6 months of a patient's treatment because he thinks that works best, well and good. But if a teacher suggests making a list of objectives because the controller wants to see it, he should say so. Otherwise he will add an irrelevant form of make-believe to an activity already overburdened with illusion, and imperceptibly mold the provider's idea of therapy to fit the inspector's. Inspectors have a different competence.

Bureaucratic reality concerns what we must write in a record. It has nothing to do with what we think about what we write. Considerations of bookkeeping and social policy are properly involved in choosing patient and illness priorities, allocations of public monies, even modalities of treatment. But they have absolutely no jurisdiction over the principles of psychotherapy. What could be more obvious? Yet, because the profession does not agree on those principles, it is ill equipped to respond to nonprofessional demands in a principled manner. Psychotherapy is endangered by its unformed state, which leaves it open to inadvertent decisions based on irrelevant considerations. It has to be more on guard than any comparable practice. (Psychoanalysis enjoys a much greater consensus, but it is doubtful that even analysis would have survived without its private institutes.)

Psychotherapy Principles

If the paymaster cannot tell us what is essential in psychotherapy, neither can the pharmacopeia of therapies. We cannot excuse ourselves from selecting principles by simply teaching all modalities. Even if it were possible for one staff to teach them all with equal vigor, trainees would stagger away believing that there are no principles but just different ways of talking. (Probably few trainees would stagger into a program with such a blurred identity.)

How about using psychoanalytic principles? Nobody who has read Parts III and IV of this volume will be surprised that I see no alternative to including psychoanalytic theory of the mind in a curriculum for therapists. Psychoanalysis is the most developed psychotherapy, both in practice and theory, and has been most extensively tested educationally. Unfortunately, one of the least developed aspects of psychoanalysis is the theory of therapeutic action. Its most general principles—those that are shared by other therapies—are the ones that are least understood. And it is with those that the teacher of general psychotherapy is most concerned, because he must prepare the student for various treatment arrangements.

If training guidelines should not be dictated by public policy, cannot be evaded by flipping through modalities, and will mostly not be found in psychoanalysis, what can orient the teacher of general psychotherapy?

The question answers itself: Therapy remains a puzzling business, so it is appropriately taught as a research project inquiring into its own nature. The trouble with this maxim is that therapy is difficult and upsetting, and trainees cannot be expected to begin it armed only with puzzles.

The usual compromise between the beginner's need for security and his need for education is to teach trainees to *do* their *work* (mostly by modeling), and to *think* about their *patients*. I believe that trainees should learn to think about their work and not just about their patients. And the main thing about their work that they should think about is the problem they have with it. If a beginner learns a way of thinking about problems, he will be able to extend his intellectual competence to all the modalities on the market.

It has to be admitted that thinking about practice problems often interferes with handling them: It exposes too many bewilderments and leaves them unsettled. A trainee will find equilibrium one way or another, and if a gyroscope is not provided, he will devise his own. How to arrange for the beginner to balance himself without developing unchallengeable habits may be the principle problem for psychotherapy training.

At any level, trainees demand a model for action. And teachers offer one, counting on later experience or analytic institutes to make it reasonable and flexible. But in fact people do not give up hard won security. Training time may be the last thinking time. Even technical terms may become unavailable for later conceptual understanding, once they are established as the armature of the earliest treatment stance. (*Resistance* is a good example.)

Can teachers do better than supply a dogma for action, hoping that later training or cynicism will eventually soften its edges?

Investigative Principles

The bane of training is the unspoken myth that the therapeutic situation is normal.

What most obviously makes therapists regard therapy as normal is that they live with it. But we have seen other, more profound sources of the ideology of therapeutic normalcy. Let us review a few of them.

First, and least important, is the fact that it is easier to think about therapy as natural, than to move back and forth between its (theoretical) normalcy and its (social) strangeness (see chapter 29).

A more powerful incentive is the therapist's wish to feel a partnership with his patient (see chapter 1).

A third motive is the therapist's need to feel he is watching rather than arranging something, so that he will have a passive perception to work on (see chapter 28). In chapter 35 we saw the therapist maneuver to escape an uncomfortable duplicity that results: trying to be an innocent witness while covertly inciting what he watches. The therapist must disguise his wishes, and while he is learning his craft these wishes can only show up as expectations of proper (normal) patient behavior. Such expectations of proper patient behavior are part of the earliest imprinting on a new therapist and they are thoroughly gratuitous, unsupported certainly by psychoanalytic theory, and accurately sensed by patients as a double bind that requires them to be both absolutely free, and also dedicated to satisfying their therapist.

To be sure, everything human is natural. No relationship is invented *de novo*. Therapy has been compared to child rearing; being analyzed has been compared to falling asleep and dreaming. But whatever the value of these comparisons, no sensible person would say that therapy is raising a child, or that being in analysis is talking in one's sleep, and psychoanalysis has never suggested such simple equations. Yet many therapists vaguely feel that analytic theory presents therapy as a biological stage in the patient's life cycle, guided to its natural maturity by a "good enough" analyst, who is part of every human being's "average expectable environment." In this view, it is not so much the analyst as the contrived analytic situation that is portrayed as a blank screen. In a negative hallucination, the therapist discounts the way he shapes treatment by his physical movements, his selection of office furnishings, his holidays, his instructions and appointments, and his unsociable choice of what he will and will not do. He cannot see what all the world knows: that he has invented and insists on the most artificial relationship known to man.

The clear and foremost purpose of this mind-set is to allow the therapist to think of himself as not personally trying for anything: He is simply being a normal psychotherapist. All the trying belongs to the patient (except that when the patient tries to do what the therapist wants, that is not thought of as trying but merely being a "normal" patient.)

Now, a student in a general psychotherapy program is unlikely to see the sort of patient who will behave as he "should." His are not "normal" patients, by psychological standards, and therapy does not "happen" in its "natural fashion." Of all the tough problems a beginner faces, this is one he should not have to struggle with, because it is perfect nonsense.[1]

Once we acknowledge that therapy is therapy precisely because it is not a normal interaction, we can meet the trainee where he really is.

The abnormality of psychotherapy is an ineradicable problem for both partners. No help comes from society's equilibrating rules. Both patient and therapist must struggle to keep their balance. As he begins this strange

---

[1] Jules Coleman (see Acknowledgments), found a way to give trainees a natural behavior as therapists, without inventing a fictitious "normal" therapist–patient relationship. As he arranged it, things did not have to go "normally" for his trainees to enjoy and therefore cultivate a therapeutic interaction. Beginners were not required to play-act the role of a therapist, or conduct themselves in the "normally" outlandish fashion that requires the patient to play a "normal" supporting role. Consequently the awkwardness that afflicts both parties in therapy was both accepted and good-naturedly overcome.

Coleman's method, carefully thought out and parsimoniously taught, leaned heavily on his unique personal gifts, and cannot be reproduced. (Proof of that is that few of his trainees agree on what he taught, or what chief skill he inculcated. I have no reason to assume that Coleman would accept my understanding of his purpose.) Still, his writings, and teachings where known, should be consulted for an unequalled vision of the tasks of training.

vocation, a therapist must learn to see what just threatened his balance a moment ago and how he then regained it.

Observing how one's balance was upset is not the same as identifying countertransference; it is a more neutral judgment than that. It does not assume that the problem is purely personal. It does not suppose that one has been more vulnerable or undisciplined than he should be. It does not even begin by supposing that one has learned something the hard way about the patient. It means detecting an interpersonal problem. Spotting interpersonal problems that force adjustments during a session may be a more fundamental skill than the ability to identify transference and countertransference. One can define individual dynamics more accurately if one has not prejudged how much or little the therapy situation itself contributes to the stress. After recognizing what is being coped with, then a trainee may come to see how he has reacted more desperately than he needed to because of his personal concerns. And he can see which of therapy's many frustrations and opportunities the patient has capitalized on, guided by his transference.

When I suggest that the therapist should not begin by identifying transference and countertransference per se, I am not implying that he should begin by sizing up the situation objectively (as a transactional theory might require). Interpersonal problems cannot usually be detected in a neutral way. What feels like neutrality is often insensitivity or preoccupation. The therapist does not identify therapy difficulties by taking distance, but by allowing himself the emotional leeway to respond to many of the patient's affects with many affects of his own. Such a broad vocabulary of feeling can spell out how he makes a problem for the patient, and how the patient deliberately puts pressure on him (sometimes by avoiding trouble).

To help them identify problems, therapists should be trained to sympathize alternately with themselves and with their patient (good patient/bad therapist; bad patient/good therapist). Once the problem is located, the therapist's wishes will be visible, and that will make the patient's predicament clearer. And the supervisor can use the trainee's wishes that are now in full view to draw out the trainee's implicit theory of therapy, which he did not know he owned and never pursued to completion. By retrospectively tracing how he recovered his balance, the trainee becomes conscious of his implicit expectations, and his expectations are his theory. As I have argued in chapter 12, theory is always being used knowingly or unknowingly by all therapists, new or old. Most often their theory appears only when they are asked to pull apart what they have just done. ("What did you hope to accomplish by that, and why would you expect to accomplish it that way?") The therapist's practice betrays the influence of more beliefs than he thought he had. When we draw these beliefs into the light, and inquire into their justification, it is amazing to see how theory comes to life, visibly sprouting from the reality of the work.

Obviously this kind of supervision requires time. The conventional 45–50 minute interval is totally unsuited to the task. A short format forces the supervisor into a "reading" mode: If 2 hours of treatment events consume 30 minutes of supervision, the logical thing for a supervisor to do with the remaining 15 minutes is to give the "text" a quick read. And that, as we have seen (chapter 10), is a sadly misleading caricature of how therapists think.

Elaboration of aims, consequences and alternatives, rationales and speculations, requires at least $1\frac{1}{2}$ –2 hours. That is the kind of time enjoyed by a continuous case conference or problem seminar, but individual supervision is where the approach belongs, because that is where the finest pressures and concerns can be hunted down with the least distraction.

SPECIFICS OF SUPERVISION

Emphasize Problems

After the trainee has been involved in the perplexing business of therapy for 1 or 2 hours, the logical question to ask him is whether he had trouble, and if so, how he thinks he could have avoided it. Whether or not he is able to identify trouble, the trainee is asked: "What were you hoping for from your patient? What were you expecting from him? Why would you expect him to behave that way in this situation? Of what use would it be for him to do what you expected? What more can you do to facilitate it?"

This represents a slight shift of focus from the patient. It is a focus on trouble, or, if no discomfort is identified, it is a focus on what the therapist brings with him to the hour, for that implicitly constitutes trouble.

The next question in supervision might be: "What did you do as a result of the patient's meeting or not meeting your expectations? And what does that show about how you think people work?" (If the trainee has presented a problem, then the order of inquiry is reversed: First, "What did you do in reaction?" and after that, "What does that show about what you wanted? And what do your wants show about how you think the mind works?")

It may be objected that this sort of supervision ignores the whole point of therapy. Shouldn't trainees try to understand their patient's psyche in depth? Of course they should. But they will never achieve a useful understanding of the patient if they do not know what activity he is engaged in. If a trainee knows what is happening, he can proceed toward the center of the mind that is acting. Unfortunately trainees are often so primed to understand their patients that they feel frustratingly detoured when made to scrutinize an hour's process, like a spectator so fascinated by the idea of a movie that he cannot be persuaded to turn away from the projector and watch the screen.

Of course supervision deals with patients. But the inquiry about the patient, some of it highly impressionistic, takes place in and around questions about the therapist's expectations, tactics, and theory. The trainee is asked, "How did the patient make you feel? What does that show about the patient's main concerns? What does the patient want that is different from what you want?" That inquiry goes on against a backdrop of the humanly probable responses to interpersonal situations: The supervisor might comment, "Maybe it's only natural that the patient reacted this way, but he could have reacted that way: What does it show about him that he didn't?" (This picks up Gill's [1982] treatment technique in its teaching mode: Why, out of all possible construals of a situation, does the patient pick just this one?)

Whenever possible, therapy problems should be traced first to the inherent difficulties of therapy. Countertransference problems appear most genuine and workable when they emerge as a personal reaction to a difficult or impossible task. In that context, they do not need to be coaxed out by a supervisor. (This, incidentally, is also a training corollary of Gill's treatment paradigm: If someone sees the logic in his reaction, he is also likely to see its idiosyncrasy, whereas if he does not see the logic in it, he probably does not really know what his reaction was, although he may confess his "overreaction" obediently.)

Make Technical Terms Grow Out of Problems

We must not let technical terms befog reality. We have a tendency to camouflage unnatural situations and make them seem natural by giving them familiar labels. ("Of *course* I see patients only on a fixed regular schedule, . . . that is Reality.") It is fair to say that for most therapists the chief value of technical terms is to normalize their unnatural work. That is bad for training. In training, these terms should be demonstrated as born from trouble, and trouble is not hard to find: It is the soup in which the trainee and patient are stewing. If sophisticated nuances are not included when a term is first introduced, they are not likely to join it afterward. If for simplicity's sake *regression* is introduced as though it were an autonomous process like respiration, a therapist may never in his whole life realize that he is personally *trying* to put the patient in a childlike position, and he will not realize that the patient's reaction is not just an attitude to regression, but an attitude to someone who wants to infantilize him.[2]

---

[2] Because I have earlier taxed the reader's endurance with the paradoxes that qualify these statements, I need here make only brief reference to the other side of the story: (a) The nature of the patient's reaction depends on the nature of the patient and not just the situation. (b) The patient has his own regressive wishes: It goes without saying that nobody can be tempted to do something he has no wish to do. (c) The therapist's infantilizing is just one facet of the ambiguous therapeutic relationship; the therapist's genuine non-manipulativeness is also a facet (see chapters 28 and 33). (d) Regression is not *just* being like a child (chapter 4).

Resistance will probably be the first technical concept to arise. If a trainee learns that resistances naturally spring up in patients like mushrooms in a forest, he will probably think that way forever. In contrast, if he sees to begin with that he uses the term when his wishes conflict with the patient's, he will then not be so helpless (or harmful), because that is the kind of frustration he has met with everywhere in his life. He will be able to use his ingenuity to develop the meaning and handling of resistance for the remainder of his career. The educator should see to it that technical terms remain doorways to problems of treatment, which is what they originally were, and not let them masquerade as answers. If this is not done at the beginning of a professional career, it will probably never happen.

Practice Ordinary Meanings

One of the most remarkable features of psychotherapy training is the way it desensitizes trainees to nuances of meaning that life has already taught them. Meanings that would be picked up instantly at a cocktail party are over-looked for hours in therapy. They are overlooked not because deep meanings seem more important, but because it is a strain to superimpose a (bizarre) therapy interaction on an (expectable) social one. The therapist would rather act as though both parties have decided to conduct an odd (therapeutic) conversation, and so a protective blindness develops to ordinary social messages. Now, it goes without saying that teachers must make the trainee comfortable with his strange new role by acknowledging its pressure, and offering the companionship of a helpful theory. But while they are easing him into a life of oddity, the trainee must be reminded of the ordinary gestural meaning of conversation. Half the task of training is to encourage a trainee to understand strangely. The other half is to help him to perceive normally. Training often accomplishes the first challenge only to fail at the second.

Despite every effort to prevent it, parochial patterns of treatment begin to seem normal when practiced daily. It is essential to drill trainees in variant meanings of utterances and interchanges, in order to keep them in touch with the (normal) social reality from which they are withdrawing, as they become comfortable with (abnormal) therapeutic penetration. (Cooper [1985] describes an analogous problem: the beginning analyst's abandonment of his ordinary psychotherapeutic skills.)

By drill in variant meanings, I mean something like this: "What might that sentence mean? What does it mean with that inflection and what does it mean without it?"

"What kind of a response is that? What would you think if somebody answered you that way at the Christmas party?"

"If somebody said that to you at home, how would you feel?"

"What does that suggest that the patient wants you to feel about him?"

"What would you say two other people were doing to each other if they had an interchange like that?"

"If you heard that from an actor, how would you assume the playwright wanted you to understand the character?"

This sort of drill does not favor interpersonal conceptualizations as against intrapsychic ones. That debate has no place here. No theory of the mind denies that language is social. And so, apart from any other consideration, understanding must begin with ordinary social meanings. No matter how personal the meaning one is after, it is available only through manifest content of some sort. However deep our sounding, it always starts from the surface.[3] Process reports usually show a great many surface beginnings that are missed by the therapist. A therapist who is pretending that therapy is normal has an incentive not to hear a really normal meaning. He may anesthetize himself to normal meanings so that he can imagine that the transaction is entirely on the level to which he has become professionally acculturated. Training usually initiates this self-blinding.

Supervision Should be Mostly a Private Relationship

Inasmuch as the therapist shares an abnormal relationship with his patient, and moreover, one that has no final description, his difficulty is the best indicator of what is happening and, therefore, the best point of departure for teaching. And if training takes difficulty as its point of departure, it encourages trainees to find problems. Now, every psychotherapist knows that if we want our partner to look for problems, we must create what Schafer (1983b) calls an atmosphere of safety. In supervision that means, at the very least, that the trainee can count on confidentiality.

In other words, if therapy is an abnormal relationship, then a training program should exude tolerance. The presenting therapist should feel himself talking to a supervisor who takes it for granted that dilemma is the only normal feature of therapy. Of all people, psychotherapists should be the first to realize that a judgmental attitude does not just testify to high standards, but reflects a certain view of reality. Preoccupation with evaluation of trainees says something about how treatment is perceived. If a training program tries to be therapeutic by understanding its own trainees pathographically, it will encourage them to take a normative approach to the treatment situation. A standardizing view says louder than words that there

---

[3] There are therapists who think they can simply bypass the manifest content of speech. I believe they misunderstand what they are doing. What looks like primary "depth-hearing" is simply selective attention to one or another aspect of manifest communication—for instance, imagery, or innuendo, or phatic and prosodic features, or as the Lacanians prefer, lexical elements. Can anyone imagine analyzing a dream without accurately registering its manifest report? (Come to think of it, Spence [1982] finds that it frequently happens inadvertently.)

is such a thing as a normal, natural, expectable, right course of treatment, with a proper relationship of mutual cooperation between patient and therapist, and that there is something disturbingly wrong with one or both parties if treatment departs from that mode. After all, if there can be errors, there must be a correct behavior. If indeed there is such a thing as a normal therapy, then a watchful, monitoring training program will teach it well. But if, as I have argued, therapy is not like that, such a program will be misleading.

We have all heard horrible stories of training institutions (usually abusing a captive clientele of social workers) that admonish or even discipline trainees for what (almost beyond belief) is called "resistance" to the institution. Such blatant Orwellian corruption of the term cannot fail to filter back into the therapy situation. I am not concerned here with the inexorable creep of power motives into all things human. My point is that, no matter how sophisticated its didactic teaching, an institution's behavior can covertly suggest that the therapeutic relationship is a normal part of life. It goes without saying that educators are obliged to use their skills to help disturbed trainees when that is necessary and possible. And no reputable program actually deals with its trainees as though it were treating them. Nevertheless, it is not always sufficiently appreciated that when a training program fusses about personal and professional evaluations, it tends to make trainees feel that work difficulties are a shame, that problems are unwelcome, and that performance should be measured against a normal, expectable process. This is not a plea to be kind to trainees. Indeed, many psychiatric residents complain if they are not regularly evaluated. Their demand for evaluation is a request for the kind of reassurance that, being characteristically unavailable in their chosen field, is precisely what they should be learning to do without.

There are, then, two reasons for institutions to avoid unnecessary student evaluations: (a) People highlight problems when they feel safe. (b) Normative monitoring is a misleading hint about the nature of treatment. Evaluations are useful in many ways. The question is: What do they sacrifice? What they sacrifice, I think, is the main message that training should transmit.

Modalities Should Always be Compared in Detail

One of the many reasons for showing trainees different styles and theories is to dispel the illusion of naturalness that clings to the dominant model. From the height of a comparative view, trainees can observe their own assump-tions. But we will fritter away that opportunity if we lay out the various schools of psychotherapy like so many instruments on a tray. The most trivial and evanescent lesson of comparative psychotherapy is: "You can think this way, or that way, or another way." To get the real value of the comparison, all the models must be drawn into one, continuous critical discussion. ("How does this school represent what the other calls 'resistance'?")

*Teach Creative Receptiveness by Proper Theory
and Technically Relevant Humanities*

What chiefly protects therapists from the delusion that there exists a normal psychotherapy is their ability to imagine themselves involved in all kinds of human dramas as they listen to the patient and feel the interaction with him. This important capacity does not, I think, depend on training. Therapists can be counted on to pick up from the profession's "popular culture" any exciting, new ways to view therapeutic interaction. Greed for forms is so great that only the most faithful ideologue will settle for the kit he was given in training.

The question is whether sensitivity to dramatic forms can be increased by deliberately incorporating the Humanities into the psychotherapy curriculum. I suspect that immersion in art and literature during training does not regularly broaden the therapist's perceptions or make him as flexible as educators have understandably hoped. I seriously doubt whether there is a correlation between a therapist's breadth of culture and the variety of his therapeutic templates.

It is the therapist's theory and not his general culture that permits or forbids patient-receptor appetites and templates. Theory does that partly explicitly, by setting up canonical images of life (e.g., Oedipus complex, primal scene). Partly it does it by prescribing a stance that then indirectly allows certain appetites and images to flourish (e.g., a taste for conflict). And theory releases the therapist's creative freedom by acknowledging the ironies of treatment, for it is the ironies of the task that inspire the therapist's most plentiful and unexpected images. Without borrowing from outside the field, the educator can encourage flexibility simply by painting an honest picture of therapy.

That is not to say that the Humanities have no place in a psychotherapy curriculum. Although therapy may stand to gain little from the use of literary works as *Bildung*, or as helpless, make-believe patients on which to inflict one's theory, criticism in the Humanities may be made to comment directly on the work of treating real people. Nothing could be more relevant to the therapist's perpetual growth than E. H. Gombrich's (1961) study of the way artists use historically developed forms to apprehend visual reality, or Rudolf Arnheim's (1969) study of pictorial form as a general medium of discovery. Even though it is now in disfavor, I would think that Heinrich Wölfflin's (1929) hypothesis about epochal changes in artistic vision has much to teach practitioners immersed in shifting theoretical world views. Philosophers concerned with the different ways that the world can be represented, for example Nelson Goodman (1976, 1978), offer provocative reading for people whose profession requires them to abstract variously and innovatively from vague material. Philosophers of history speak directly to current problems in theory and practice (see chapter 32).

Reading poetry and doing psychotherapy have something in common. Therefore, poetic criticism is germane to psychotherapy education. For instance, I. A. Richards' *Practical Criticism* (1929) might be used to show how difficult it is to understand literal meanings in an abnormal (in his case poetic) context. At the other extreme, William Empson's (1947) undogmatic study of the power and ubiquity of poetic ambiguity should be as helpful to therapists as it has been to literary critics, in loosening first impressions and tracing obvious evocative power to the braiding of less obvious meanings.

But sensitivity to ambiguities in poetry is no guarantee of a flexible response to patients. A flexible response to patients is a function not just of the therapist's associative net, but of what it is he associates to. A therapist may give no play at all to the social surface of speech while ringing all the changes on what he takes to be its underlying Ur-text. He may associate to etymologies and not to rhetoric. To make sure that the trainee does justice to the surface communication, it is helpful for a supervisor to say frequently, "Yes, that sounds plausible. It struck me differently. Can you think of any still different meaning it might have? I will try to think of another one myself."

PERSONAL OBJECTIVES

So far I have drawn conclusions about training from the nature of therapy. I have argued that if therapy is the problematic, unsettling, and ambiguous sort of thing I have made it out to be – if therapy is not a normal activity; if the therapist is often off balance; if he always has a theory at work – then training should take the form I have suggested.

Now, at the risk of redundancy, I look at training from a different standpoint. Here I begin with the equipment that a therapist needs, and ask how a training program can help build it.

The preceding chapters suggest that the therapist's equipment generally consists of (a) a formal theory (including patterns of human development), (b) figurative schemas for capturing social situations, and (c) appetites for aspects of personal encounter. If that is true, then training should maximize these assets.

Let us begin with the piece of equipment that has been least acknowledged: appetite.

Appetites

As memories of training dim, therapists drift toward their native style. Native style includes all of the therapist's equipment, cognitive and affective. But nothing in native style is so influential as interpersonal appetites.

The educator reads conflicting morals out of this story. On the one hand, he realizes that training must be a powerful experience if it is to leave even the slightest imprint on lifelong practice patterns. Because the trainee's native style has almost everything to say about what he will finally do, and training almost nothing, the slightest concession to native style may forfeit what small influence training has. On the other hand, the student's native equipment is part of what makes therapy work. In fact, special talents are so important that many patients can be treated only by therapists with certain personalities.

In some ways, then, training is designed to overcome a natural bent, whereas in other ways it must be reinforcing.

A problem-centered approach that prods the therapist to constantly work out his own theory teaches a discipline (the designing of rationales) that will remain relevant to whatever he wants to do in the future.

That is fine for theory. But as for appetites, a problem-centered approach is merely permissive. How are appetites actually encouraged or instilled?

Appetites are the ultimate finders of direction and deciders of action, even when the therapist is generally guided by theory. The satisfaction a therapist's appetite finds is the ultimate warrant that he has made contact with reality, and so a trainee's appetites will automatically cultivate themselves as they are satisfied. Successful appetites flourish. A therapist adds an appetite to his repertoire when he is effective at the very time that he is satisfied. Nothing else will cultivate an appetite. An appetite may be of a special therapeutic sort, such as genuine curiosity, or a wish to see everything make sense, or a delight in discovery, or the love of puzzles and mysteries, or a pleasure in matching images, or a taste for irony, or a zest for uncovering buried liveliness. Or a therapist may have an appetite for an ordinary social role, one that is not specifically psychotherapeutic and certainly never taught, such as a preference for an avuncular role, or pleasure in being someone who educates or socializes others, or being charming, or fascinating, or inspiring. Whatever the appetite, it is encouraged when the patient responds in a way that is both satisfying to the therapist and clearly better for the treatment than what was happening before it was brought into play.

We have seen that theory, and therefore training, first govern this process by blessing or restricting appetites, so that they can or cannot be tried out. The patient's positive response then confirms them in the repertoire (or, if negative, lets them wilt). If a useful appetite is permitted or encouraged, then it will educate itself. Anyone who has supervised beginners knows that often his most memorable teaching is that a therapist may enjoy himself. A supervisor can have no more dramatic experience than watching what happens to a treatment when the therapist suddenly finds a way to enjoy it.

This enlightenment is more likely to happen if the supervisor encourages a not-too-cautious experimentation. Moderate risk-taking helps to decompress the beginner's crushingly exaggerated sense of the patient's fragility.

In addition to encouraging individual proclivities, some common appetites should be fostered in every therapist. Our thesis suggests that we should coach trainees to sniff out slight, momentary, out of character shifts in a patient's style, or some small, expandable disturbance. We should be reluctant to let a supervisee settle for an unexciting therapy. And one way to maximize excitement is to cultivate in him a taste for trouble. Although everyone seeks balance, a therapist should learn to have fun with trouble, so that he will automatically gravitate to change points. Therefore, educators must make sure not to offer just schemas that make peace with predicaments. We do not want to diminish a worry by taking the larger view. ("It isn't you she's angry with: It's her father.") Nor should we transform the crunch of trouble into contemplative mush. It may be less exalted to ask, "What can you do about it?" than, "What does it represent?" but such tactical questions keep the reality of the problem in view as a problem.

Supervisors are in a position to make it seem that expertise means being in command. They should avoid that. The supervisor has as good an opportunity, and a better reason, to show his trainees that expertise lies mainly in spotting predicaments (for trainee and patient) and in seeing those problems in many alternate ways.

If a beginning therapist comes to feel that he is most expert when he is most vividly in trouble, he will develop a taste for personal liveliness strong enough to compete with all the familiar pleasures of theory and schema. And if the therapist is able to enjoy a patient when the patient gives him *unclassified* trouble, he has learned quite a lot of therapy.

Schemas

Now let us turn to the therapist's second type of resource: his schemas. By *schemas*, I mean the recognizable situations, the mini-dramas, that make human sense out of what the therapist sees. The Oedipus complex is a schema. So are the paradigms of infantile situations re-enacted in therapy; so also are images of splitting, resisting, faking, compensating, fusing, projecting, part-object-making, the narrating of life stories, the disavowal of responsibility, and so on. In fact, I use the term *schema* here to refer to all the therapist's mentation insofar as it is marshalled for ad hoc recognition rather than to serve a tight system of theory and treatment.

Today, schemas are more widely shared among therapy sects than they used to be. Ecumenism prevails, even in the analytic community, and certainly in psychiatric residencies. And because therapists unashamedly snap up schemas (more readily, for example, than appetites), the educator does not have to worry so much about schema poverty in his trainee.

But he does have to worry about schema flexibility. A training program should advertise schemas as wonderful readings that we are happy to find and happy to abandon, not talismans that we touch to make sure we are all together and all professional. No educator can be proud of students who measure their proficiency by the ease with which they cast information into these schematic terms.

Schemas should be taught as creatures of the moment. According to Gombrich's (1961) principle and chapter 10 (this volume), nothing can be perceived without models, and schemas are such models. They should be superimposed on each other and discarded at will. If we hold on to them steadfastly, they become more important than the patient, who exists, so to speak, only to illustrate them. Schemas should be cultivated as perceptual aids, not as understandings of persons. Therapeutic consistency is adherence to principles, not to pictures. The educator's eye is on flexibility.

Here again we see how advantageous it is for training to organize itself around problems. Just as a taste for problems is the most general appetite to be cultivated, so the most useful function of schemas is to feel out problems with the patient. Unfortunately, schemas are often used to paint a picture of a patient for another therapist as when making a referral. That is bad. What is good is using schemas to define the difficulties patient and therapist have in treatment. Another therapist does not learn much from a description of the patient's dynamics and life problems. Nobody should leave training thinking that this communicates an essence. On the other hand, almost any description of trouble with a patient tells another therapist a very great deal. And every graduate of a training program should know that.

Theory

We have discussed training in appetites. And we have discussed training in schemas. Now we must think about the place of theory in training.

My arbitrary definition of schemas as fragments made it easy for me to argue that they must be kept flexible. But when conventional depictions are part of an elaborate theory, the contrary is true—they must connect with each other coherently or be expelled. A jumble of vivid images is good preparation for perception, but a wretched excuse for a theory. One of the toughest tasks of training is to prevent students from taking perceptual schemas too seriously and aspects of theory too casually. The terms of theory must be shown to be more than a convenient way of looking at things. They must be shown to be mandated by conceptual and practical necessity.

Our investigation has led us to believe that the theory of therapy and its theory of the mind cannot be properly taught in isolation from practice. It is not even sufficient to teach it concurrently with practice. The terms of theory of therapy arise out of practice problems, and theory has to be related to those problems. That is why I have recommended tracking down theoretical presuppositions during supervision, exploring logical and systematic entailments.

But time is short and theory is long. Some brief approaches must be found to do justice to theoretical responsibility. We must settle for pointing out paths that need to be followed in answering theoretical questions, even if there is no time to actually follow them. In supervision and case conferences, sample scrutiny will have to stand in for a full Socratic dialogue.

Another way of hinting at systematic responsibility without teaching a whole theory, is by comparing one theory with another. In this way, one can demonstrate similar compulsory chains of justification in different systems. And the terminology of each theory is reinvested with problem-solving meaning when we show that different theories run up against common problems. (Incidentally, if this is not done in a program that teaches several theories, another message will be given, namely, that theories have no roots, and are simply rhetorical devices.)

To summarize, if schemas are presented as useful pictures, then their fragmentary nature does not entitle them to rule perception beyond the moment, and flexibility is what the educator will foster. But if an interwoven theory is to be taught – and it is the argument of this book that such a theory is essential to psychotherapy – then its systematic construction cannot be bypassed, nor the reason it came into being set aside, lest students get the idea that a theory is just one untranslatable set of rigid, arbitrary pronouncements (for example, a psychoanalytic "world view," consisting of oedipus complex plus psychic energy plus erogenous zones, etc.). What the educator has to do is to illuminate the interconnected way the theory works, and the routes through which its meaning comes, by continually cross-translating theory with other theories and with the trainee's practice problems (not just his practice).

APPENDIX

I wish I could provide examples of the sort of supervisory discussion I have in mind. But supervision does not usually produce a record.

As a substitute, I append reports on a continuous case conference for trainees of assorted levels. In this conference we took no responsibility for treatment (leaving that to individual supervisors) and used the occasion to raise any questions and challenges we wished. After each meeting I tried to summarize in writing the questions that had arisen and the answers that were offered, and a few additional ones. One of the therapy sessions was discussed by two different groups.

I am afraid that a report of a conference is tedious without a glimpse of the treatment. But I wish only to illustrate the teaching inquiry and for this purpose the details of the cases are irrelevant.

The reader should bear in mind that these were spontaneous, unstructured discussions. They were, it is true, influenced by my own interests and hunches, and my educational prejudices affected the way I arranged and classified what came up. But I tried to include all the major points that arose. And the terms in which the report is written are those that the trainees offered (although the questions are usually mine). For that reason, the similarities and differences between the two groups' responses to the same first session are interesting.

Report on Our First Meeting (First Group)

The group mainly reacted to *conflict* between patient's and therapist's wishes.

1. The patient *resists questioning*. She does not satisfy the therapist's wish for answers.
2. She *makes him take more initiative* than he wants to. (He wants her to elaborate. She makes him keep asking.)
3. She wants *his* view; he wants her to reflect on her own view.
4. One of us felt that she did not seem very committed to treatment, and was likely to disappear or grumble during each session.

What General Problems Did This Raise?

1. The patient shows *resistance*. (I postponed this. Later we will have to ask what *resistance* means as a technical term, and how it guides the therapist's actions. What does resistance resist? How is it overcome?)

2. There is a *power struggle* between patient and therapist. She was described as demanding, controlling, and "doing" instead of thinking. The therapist, on the other hand, refuses to let her plan the conversation.

The therapist seems to want to *train* the patient. This briefly raised the question: Are patients supposed to do a certain something? And if so, what is it, and how do you get them to do it?

3. By her style she *insulates* herself from the therapist, while he, on the other hand, wants her to be more *open*. Yet when she does directly engage him, he wants her to be *less* free that way.

Is this a *paradox*?

Some of the group felt she should get more interested in herself. But aren't her questions very sincerely concerned with herself? ("Am I crazy?") Doesn't the therapist really want her to be *less* concerned with herself? (To say, for example, "This is me, for better or worse; I don't *care* what I look like to you." i.e., a "disinterested" self-presentation.)

If a patient fearfully tells you to deal with him distantly (e.g., by a question-and-answer format), how can you make him feel closer? If you do it his way, that's distant. If you don't, that may be *more* distant, equivalent to not dealing with him at all.

4. Some of the group felt that the patient was making trouble for the therapy. (I believe there was also some feeling that you're not supposed to say that. But what therapist doesn't *think* it? It was clearly the group's first impression.)

We also heard a counter argument that what the patient is doing is exactly what is needed, because that's what the treatment is addressed to.

Is this *another paradox?*

We can *say* it is all grist for the mill, but in practice, we have to *do* something. (Nothing is also a something.) Won't our reactions say Yes or No to a patient?

Finally We Got to the (?) Underlying Problem

We said: *The patient is seeking reassurance.* That's *why* she asked so many questions, cooperated so stiffly, kept her distance, tried to control everything etc.

What should the therapist *do* about anxiety?

The group suggested:

1. Decrease her anxiety by telling her that others feel the same. But won't that make her personal reasons seem irrelevant? Won't it suggest that we are only interested in "abnormal" feelings?" Won't it imply that the therapist is a judge of normality, and he may have some other, more unfavorable judgments, now or later?

2. Train her to tolerate anxiety: Tell her that therapy will accomplish more if she lives with that anxiety and turns her attention to her own thoughts and imaginings.

Is it possible for someone to make that change voluntarily?

3. Lower anxiety *and* encourage her to live with anxiety, by "reassuring" her this time, and suggesting that she change her focus in the future.

But won't this be heard as a criticism that she wants forbidden things, and has transgressed? Won't it sound like a confession that the therapist was forced by pity or weakness to do something wrong?

4. The therapist could accept the question, celebrate it and elaborate it, as follows:

Is she implicitly asking whether he thinks she's crazy? Or oversensitive? Is she asking whether treatment is working right? Is there a question about whether she is allowed to ask questions at all? Does she wonder whether she has any say about how the treatment goes? Is she exploring whether the therapist is the only one who has to be satisfied, saying, in effect, "Don't you have to satisfy me, too?"

Maybe making these implicit questions explicit would decrease her anxiety by admitting the logic of her concerns, or maybe it wouldn't. It certainly wouldn't *answer* her questions. She would see that the therapist is evading. This response may turn out to be the same as all the previous ones, but in a more slippery and slimy form.

Summary of Technical Problems We Raised

1. Training patients: How? Why? What?
2. How to do what we want to do without fighting for control.
3. How to accept impingements on ourselves for purposes of study, without prejudicing them by the inescapable need to react. (We may know more later in the therapy, but we have to act now.)
4. Should we relieve patients' anxiety? If so, how can we do it without joining them in routines we would rather they questioned? If we don't relieve anxiety, why should the patient change his behavior?

How Should We Decide Answers to These Questions? What Does Theory Say?

Your theory?
The therapist's theory?
Others theories you have heard about?

Report on Our First Meeting (Second Group)

Should one *teach* the patient how to be a patient? (We didn't discuss what the therapist wants him to learn.)

A Paradox

If you try to *get* the patient to *do* something (e.g., to behave like a good patient), then you have to interact with the style that he brings with his illness. We have seen our patient arrange for her therapist to be active and intrusive, even though he does not want to be.

What possible solutions are there to this paradox?

Should one focus on the *transference* early? (We did not discuss what that means.)

How? By asking: "What do you think about me?" How else?

Permissiveness

1. How do you distinguish permissiveness from *unsupportiveness*, or *mysteriousness*? How is it different from saying, "Go out on a limb?"

2. Should you be permissive of the topic ("talk about anything you wish"), or should you be permissive of the wish behind it? How would you show tolerance of a wish? (We didn't really explore these questions.)

3. What if there is more than one meaning to the patient's production? Permitting one of them may forbid the others.

E.g., Suppose she wants to talk about anything (including sex) but doesn't want to volunteer anything. Then if the therapist lets her talk about just whatever she wants, he is simultaneously forbidding her to demand his initiative. Shall we say that the second wish should *not* be permitted?

4. How can you be permissive while you are "educating" somebody to be a patient? In other words, do you go *with* the patient? Or do you try to get the patient to go *your* way?

Anxiety

When you spot anxiety do you:

1. Try to reduce it? Why? How?
2. Try to maintain it, so that it can be explored?
3. Try to increase it, so that it will show itself more clearly?

If you choose 2 or 3, how do you know that the anxiety you are dealing with is the original one, and not a new anxiety arising from dealing with a cruel therapist?

In particular, we have seen at least these initial anxieties in our patient:

1. How crazy am I? How odd—screwed up—shameful—weak, am I? What horrible things am I unwittingly revealing?
2. What do you think of me? How do you feel about me? I can't quite tell, and I wish you'd give me a clue.
3. Do I have any rights here? Can I do the same to you as you do to me, e.g., ask *you* questions? Do you have to cater to *me* in *any* way? Will you feel that *I* have to be satisfied (by getting an answer), or is it just I who have to satisfy you?

How common do you think these anxieties are in psychotherapy? Do they occur only or especially at the beginning of treatment? What happens to them as treatment progresses? What role do they play in the effectiveness of treatment? What do different theories say about this? What is the effect of increasing or decreasing anxiety involved in *these specific questions?*

Report on Fourth Meeting

Segment Examined

She said she was nervous about coming to the session . . . because she could not put her feelings and her troubles into words . . .

(We speculated that she had stage fright, was worried about doing well, misunderstood the task required of her.)

The therapist selected the last formulation. He instructed her not to worry about reasons for her behavior.

What is the Therapist's Theory of Therapy?

1. Patient should *free-associate*. That means trying not to exercise conscious control over what comes to mind.
Problems:

(a) it involves work, but it must be free. (The freest talking is natural talking, which is not free-association.)

(b) the patient should talk as though no one else is present, but that is impossible.

(c) people vary in the reverie-nature of their cognition.

(d) free-association requires an interest in one's own thoughts, but that is already a goal. It is not literally "free" but is serious and purposeful.

(e) free-association requires the reporting of the restrictions and hesitations that are noticed. That requires directed attention.

(f) free-association is an impossibility, and the point is to observe which specific ways it turns out to be impossible. (Nobody said anything about playfulness.)

2. Free-association reveals an *unconscious reality*, a second reality, a different way of looking at oneself and relationships. (A pattern can be detected.)
Problems:

Why is a therapist necessary? Why not just free-associate alone? The answer is:

3. Free-association meets *resistances*, which the therapist must deal with. What does that mean? *Distortions* are introduced. What does that mean?

There is an inner, essential purpose or meaning, which is disguised. The therapist deciphers the coded form and presents the truth to the patient. *Why* are there distortions? The patient experienced things as painful in childhood, and by habit continues to protect himself against them until the therapist reminds him, and he then experiences them as not so painful, because now he is grown up.

4. When the distortions in the patient's experiencing are shown to be unnecessary, the patient can conduct his life and experience his relationships in a more fruitful? unconflicted? way.
Problems:

Why is self-knowledge useful? We postponed answering this.

Does the patient discover the reality of himself just from the therapist's demonstration of resistances? OR does the relationship between patient and analyst play a part?

How Does This Theory Apply to This Patient?

1. She won't free-associate. So how can therapy begin?

2. She is instructed in the need to free-associate. But she still does not do it.

3. Is it a resistance not to free-associate? Is that so very different from a resistance manifested *within* "free"-associations?

4. Is the therapist in the positions of saying:

"If you weren't so obsessive-compulsive, I could treat you for your obsessive-compulsive neurosis."

"If you weren't so mistrustful, I could cure you of your distrust."

"If you accepted everything about yourself, and felt confident that I would too, I could cure you of your insecurity."

Is the therapist requiring her not to have her troubles in order to treat her?

We are finding that the *problem of training a patient to be a patient,* is the same thing as the *problem of overcoming resistances.* (Or, better, vice versa.)

Until we can say why a person is better off knowing himself, we may find it hard to say what his incentive is to free-associate. (We have already implied that there is an incentive *not* to free-associate.)

Critique of This Theory

1. A patient may continue "distorting" not just from sheer habit, but because of persisting wishes. How do you change wishes?

2. It may not be a question of distortions after all. This patient may really "find" herself in just the accused role she fears/desires. (In a later session, the

patient actually gets the therapist to concede that this is what occurred.) How does the therapist manage not to be part of the situation that patients put him in? (Somebody noted that when the patient says that her fear is that she will be asked questions she can't answer, the therapist repeats his question.)

What Acts on the Therapist Besides His Theory?

The same thing that always affects a therapist: *He has to work with what he gets!* It's no good wishing for something else. (Although some of us suggested that we might try waiting for something else.)

What Does This Patient Offer?

Sorry. She is not primarily interested in just *reporting*. (Who is?) She is *seeking* (reassurance, as to normalcy, interest, leverage, etc.). She *complains* (in a somewhat indirect fashion, about being used for teaching purposes; about the therapist saving his thoughts for his supervisor; about not being asked reasonable questions; about being misunderstood to mean more than she says.) She *accuses* (about the same things). She *defies* (his evident wish for her to rattle on). She *teases* (by "worrying" about confidentiality and then "solving" the problem, and much more later on in treatment).

Whatever happens in this treatment is going to happen about complaining, seeking, accusing, complying, defying and teasing.

Question of the Week (Please consider carefully)

If she *had* "free-associated," would she *not* have been doing some things like complaining, seeking, accusing, complying (especially complying), defying, and teasing? If she were doing both together—free associating and interacting—which would be visible? Should one heed only the report and not the action?

37

The Future

Psychotherapy is one form of ideational help among many. (See Frank [1961] for a view that minimizes the differences.) It depends on a special interplay of theory and practice, and it is vulnerable to anything that interferes with that interplay. It suffers when theory is dislocated from practice, as in an aggressively pragmatic atmosphere, or when therapists do not bother to reflect on their experience, or when theory reflects mainly on itself.

Psychotherapy is threatened by the intrusion of public policy, because that fosters tendentious thinking while the profession depends on honest self-scrutiny. If psychotherapists start to think of themselves the way they present themselves to third parties, they will become extinct. Recent commercially packaged group experiences may show the sort of symbolic help the future holds: bags of tricks and mottos; influences of some sort that do something or other. The profession will not be saved by comparative outcome studies of processes in which nobody knows what interaction occurred, why it occurred when it did, or what momentary meaning it had. We have no National Endowment for Hermeneutics to support the study of the independent variable (i.e., what gets across to the patient).

Psychotherapy is also threatened by overconcern about the scientific status of psychoanalysis as the paradigm theory. Nobody knows what science is. Psychoanalysis will not be helped by forcing it into or out of some otherwise defined discipline. Let it walk in its own shoes, whatever they are. To my mind, the most important virtue of science is that it is one sphere where people really try not to think just as they please. That is hard enough for human beings, and if psychoanalysts and psychotherapists can bring themselves to do that, they will have done a great deal, even if they do not progress in knowledge and power as rapidly as the "hard" sciences do. The main thing is not to surrender the interest in objective reality. (This is not to belittle scrutiny of the nature of psychoanalytic knowledge; it is just a plea not to cage psychoanalysis.)

Obviously the fate of the psychotherapy profession is more uncertain than it seemed 30 years ago. Yet in some ways it is better off. Thirty years ago no profession was as ragged or questionable as general psychotherapy. Psychoanalysis was more fortunate: It had a theory and a procedure. It had a curriculum, standards of performance, and a *lingua franca*. It was adorned with learned journals and subtle spokesmen. Psychotherapy had none of these. A handful of illustrious figures spoke seriously for psychotherapy. But its periodicals were filled with recipes, practical hints, and shared experience. Detailed and subtle reflection about what, after all, is a matter of detail and subtlety, was confined to the analytic literature. Psychotherapy was taught in a make-do fashion with whatever scraps of theory and procedure it could snatch from psychoanalysis, therapists being too grateful for the scraps to worry about their place in a non-analytic setting, or to fuss about the mutual compatibility of random items carried over from a systematic psychoanalysis. The general rule was that a therapist should try to think and act like a psychoanalyst whenever possible, never mind the specific momentary rationale.

Many general psychotherapists, even while reflexly assuming a psychoanalytic posture, or experimenting on the basis of assimilated analytic concepts, derided psychoanalytic theory as a useless indulgence. The general psychotherapist looked on analytic writings as "nit-picking." And for their part, theorists, who were mostly psychoanalysts, customarily thought it ridiculous to waste painstaking theory on the cluttered, amorphous, inconstant phenomena of psychotherapy.

Almost nothing has changed. But the "almost" is important. Today fewer people want a full psychoanalysis, whether because their troubles are different, or their means fewer, or their interest less. And there has been a shift in psychoanalytic theorizing, partly the result of its wider application, but probably also due to the intratheory tensions I have discussed. This has changed the relationship between psychotherapy and psychoanalysis.

This change in intellectual climate and practice pattern, together with increased crowding of curriculum by promising neurosciences has left educators undecided about their new mandate. Should they think of analytic theory as exotica, and leave it for analytic institutes to teach to subspecialists? Or should they regard analytic theory as a basic science, even more essential to generalists than to analysts because the generalist must devise his own situations? Whatever they decide, it will not be as random a decision as it used to be.

The analytic literature is now concerned with treatment processes and meaning change in general. Thirty years ago theorists did not feel the need to enlarge their vocabulary, as is necessary to deal seriously with "parametric" problems. Nowadays psychoanalysts concern themselves with issues that are properly psychotherapeutic because they are fundamental to all talking therapies. The tradition and habits of reflection cultivated by psychoanalysis are now available to psychotherapy.

Why do I make so much of this one gain for therapy? Access to a careful literature is important not only because a profession needs something more than a how-to literature. Literature is important to psychotherapy because theory is a living, practical *piece* of psychotherapy. A theoretical literature does not just confer professional dignity; it conserves and arranges the fundamental machinery of treatment.

Personal influence is almost infinitely variable. Therapists affect patients in many ways. People have always influenced other people's lives, and they will go on doing it, deliberately and undeliberately, in formal and informal settings, often with profound benefit. Personal helpfulness is not in danger of disappearing, and no special measures need be instituted to conserve it.

Psychotherapy, on the other hand, will thrive where theory and practice do their intricate dance, and it will die when they stop.

But never before has general psychotherapy had the opportunity to intertwine practical problems with careful reflection. If, in the worst case, the end is near for it, these final years will be its best.

References

Aaronson, D., & Rieber, R. W., ed. (1975), *Developmental Psycholinguistics and Comunication Disorders*. New York: New York Acad. Sci.

Alexander, F. (1956), *Psychoanalysis and Psychotherapy*. New York: Norton.

Allport, F. H. (1955), *Theories of Perception and the Concept of Structure*. New York: Wiley.

Amacher, P. (1965). *Freud's Neurological Education and Its Influence on Psychoanalytic Theory*. New York: International Universities Press.

Andersson, O. (1962), *Studies in the Prehistory of Psychoanalyis*. Stockholm: Svenska Bokförlaget.

Anthony, E. J. (1976). Freud, Piaget, and human knowledge: Some comparisons and contrasts. *The Annual of Psychoanalysis*, 4. New York: International Universities Press.

Apfelbaum, B. (1966), On ego psychology: A critique of the structural approach to psychoanalytic theory. *Internat. J. Psycho-Anal.*, 47:451–475.

Arlow, J. A. (1975), The structural hypothesis—theoretical considerations. *Psychoanal. Quart.*, 44:509–525.

_____ (1979), Metaphor and the psychoanalytic situation. *Psychoanal. Quart.*, 48:363–385.

_____ & Brenner, C. (1964), *Psychoanalytic Concepts and the Structural Theory*. New York: International Universities Press.

Arnheim, R. (1969), *Visual Thinking*. Berkeley: University of California Press.

Austin, J. L. (1962), *How to Do Things with Words*. 2nd ed. Cambridge, MA: Harvard University Press.

Bakhtin, M. M. (1981), *The Dialogic Imagination*, ed. Michael Holquist, trans. C. Emerson & M. Holquist. Austin: University of Texas Press.

Balint, A. (1943), Identification. *Internat. J. Psycho-Anal.*, 35:97–107.

Balint, M. (1937), Early developmental states of the ego. Primary object-love. In *Primary Love and Psycho-Analytic Technique*. London: Hogarth Press, 1952, pp. 90–108.

_____ (1968), *The Basic Fault*. London: Tavistock.

Barthes, R. (1979), From work to text. In: *Textual Strategies*, ed. J. V. Harari. Ithaca, NY: Cornell University Press, pp. 73–81.

Basch, M. (1973), Psychoanalysis and theory formation. In: *The Annual of Psychoanalysis*, I. New York: Quadrangle/New York Times Book Co., pp. 39–52.

Beres, D., & Joseph, E. D. (1970), The concept of mental representation in psychoanalysis. *Internat. J. Psycho-Anal.*, 51:1–9.

564

Bergler, E. (1937), Symposium on the theory of the therapeutic results of psycho-analysis. *Internat. J. Psycho-Anal.*, 18:146–160.

Bernard, P. (1975), The limits of absolutism: Joseph II and the Allgemeines Krankenhaus. *Eighteenth Century Studies*, 9:193–215.

Bernfeld, S. (1944), Freud's earliest theories and the school of Helmholtz. *Psychoanal. Quart.*, 13:341–362.

———— (1949), Freud's scientific beginnings. *Amer. Imago*, 6:163–196.

———— (1951), Sigmund Freud, M.D. 1882–1885. *Internat. J. Psycho-Anal.*, 32:204–217.

Bernheim, H. (1884), *Hypnosis and Suggestion in Psychotherapy*, trans. C. Herter. New Hyde Park, NY: University Books, 1964.

Bibring, E. (1937), Symposium on the theory of the therapeutic results of psycho-analysis. *Internat. J. Psycho-Anal.*, 18:170–190.

Black, M. (1979), More about metaphor. In: *Metaphor and Thought*, ed. A. Ortony. Cambridge, MA: Cambridge University Press, pp. 19–43.

Blanck, A., & Blanck, G. (1977), The transference object and the real object. *Internat. J. Psycho-Anal*, 58:38–44.

Boring, E. (1950), *A History of Experimental Psychology*, 2nd ed. New York: Appleton-Century-Crofts.

Bowlby, J. (1969), *Attachment and Loss, Vol. 1*. New York: Basic Books.

Boyd, R. (1979), Metaphor and theory change: What is "metaphor" a "metaphor" for? In: *Metaphor and Thought*, ed. A. Ortony. Cambridge, MA: Cambridge University Press, pp. 356–408.

Braid, J. (1846), The power of the mind over the body. In: *Readings in the History of Psychology*, ed. W. Dennis. New York: Appleton-Century-Crofts, 1948, pp. 178–193.

Brenner, C. (1985), Countertransference as compromise formation. *Psychoanal. Quart*, 54:155–163.

Brett's History of Psychology (1953), ed. R. S. Peters. London: Allen & Unwin.

Breuer, J., & Freud, S. (1893–1895), Studies on hysteria. In: *The Complete Psychological Works of Sigmund Freud: Standard Edition*, 2. London: Hogarth Press, 1955.

Bromberg, P. M. (1984), On the occurrence of the Isakower phenomenon in a schizoid disorder. *Contemp. Psychoanal.*, 20:600–624.

Burke, K. (1950), *A Rhetoric of Motives*. Berkeley: University of California Press.

———— (1954), *Permanence and Change*, 2nd ed. Indianapolis, IN: Bobbs-Merrill.

———— (1978), (Nonsymbolic) motion/(symbolic) action. *Crit. Inq.*, 4:809–838.

Cassirer, E. (1957), *The Philosophy of Symbolic Forms*, Vol. 3. New Haven: Yale University Press.

Chomsky, N. (1972), *Language and Mind*. New York: Harcourt, Brace, Jovanovich.

———— (1980), *Rules and Representations*. New York: Columbia University Press.

Coleman, J. V. (1947), The teaching of basic psychotherapy. *Amer. J. Orthopsychiat.*, 17:622–627.

———— (1948), Patient-physician relationship in psychotherapy. *Amer. J. Psychiat.*, 104:638–641.

———— (1949a), Distinguishing between psychotherapy and casework. *J. Soc. Casew.*, 30:244–251.

———— (1949b), The initial phase of psychotherapy. *Bull. Menn. Clin.*, 13:189–197.

———— (1953), The contribution of the psychiatrist to the social worker and to the client. *Ment. Hyg.*, 37:249–258.

———— (1962), Banter as psychotherapeutic intervention. *Amer. J. Psychoanal.*, 22:69–74.

———— (1968), Aims and conduct of psychotherapy. *Arch. Gen. Psychiat.*, 18:1–6.

———— (1971), Adaptive integration of psychiatric symptoms in ego regulation. *Arch. Gen Psychiat.*, 24:17–21.

Collingwood, R. G. (1946), *The Idea of History*. London: Oxford University Press.

Cooper, A. (1985), Difficulties in beginning the candidate's first analytic case. *Contemp. Psychoanal.*, 21:143–150.

Cranefield, P. (1966), The philosophical and cultural interests of the biophysics movement. *J.*

Hist. Med. & Allied Sci., 21:1–7.

Davison, T., Bristol, C., & Pray, M. (1986), Turning aggression on the self: a study of psychoanalytic process. *Psychoanal. Quart.*, 55:273–295.

de Santillana, G. (1941), Aspects of scientific rationalism in the nineteenth century. In: *The Development of Rationalism and Empiricism*, ed. G. de Santillana & E. Zilsel. Chicago: University of Chicago Press, pp. 1–51.

Dewald, P. A. (1972), *The Psychoanalytic Process*. New York: Basic Books.

Dore, J. (1981), Conversation as accountability practice: Ethnopragmatic analyses of language meaning and function. *Cog. & Brain Theor.*, 4:201–216.

Durkheim, E. (1895), *The Rules of Sociological Method*. 8th ed., tr. S. A. Solvay & J. H. Mueller. Chicago: University of Chicago Press, 1938.

Eissler, K. R. (1953), The effect of the structure of the ego on psychoanalytic technique. *J. Amer. Psychoanal. Assn.*, 1:104–143.

Eisley, L. (1958), *Darwin's Century*. Garden City, NY: Doubleday.

Ekstein, R., & Rangell, L. (1961), Reconstructions and theory formation. *J. Amer. Psychoanal. Assn.*, 9:684–697.

Ellenberger, H. (1970), *The Discovery of the Unconscious*. New York: Basic Books.

Empson, W. (1947), *Seven Types of Ambiguity*. London: Chatto & Windus.

Fairbairn, W. R. D. (1955), Observations in defence of the object-relations theory of the personality. *Brit. J. Med. Psych.*, 28:144–156.

———— (1958), On the nature and aims of psycho-analytic treatment. *Internat. J. Psycho-Anal.*, 39:374–385.

———— (1963), Synopsis of an object-relations theory of the personality. *Internat. J. Psycho-Anal.*, 44:224–225.

Feffer, M. (1982), *The Structure of Freudian Thought*. New York: International Universities Press.

Fenichel, O. (1937), Symposium on the therapeutic results of psycho-analysis. *Internat. J. Psycho-Anal.*, 18:133–138.

———— (1941), *Problems of Psychoanalytic Technique*, trans. D. Brunswick. New York: Psycho-analytic Quarterly.

Ferenczi, S., & Rank, O. (1925), *The Development of Psycho-analysis*, tr. C. Newton. New York: Nerv. & Ment. Dis. Pub.

Flavell, J. H., & Wellman, H. M. (1977), Metamemory. In: *Perspectives on the Development of Memory and Cognition*, ed. R. V. Kail, Jr. & J. W. Hagen. New York: Wiley, pp. 3–33.

Fliess, R. (1942), The metapsychology of the analyst. *Psychoanal. Quart.*, 11:211–227.

———— (1953), Countertransference and counteridentification. *J. Amer. Psychoanal. Assn.*, 1:268–284.

Fothergill, P. G. (1953), *Historical Aspects of Organic Evolution*. New York: Philosophical Library.

Foucault, M. (1971), *The Order of Things*. New York: Pantheon.

Fraiberg, S. (1969), Libidinal object constancy and mental representation. *The Psychoanalytic Study of the Child*, 24:9–17. New York: International Universities Press.

Frank, A. (1979), Two theories or one? Or None? *J. Amer. Psychoanal. Assn.*, 27:169–207.

Frank, J. D. (1961), *Persuasion and Healing*. Baltimore: Johns Hopkins Press.

Franklin, B. (1785), Report of Dr. Benjamin Franklin and the other commissioners charged by the King of France, with the examination of the animal magnetism, as now practiced at Paris. In: *Foundations of Hypnosis*, ed. M. Tinterow. Springfield, IL: Charles C. Thomas, 1970, pp. 82–128.

Freedman, D. (1979), The sensory deprivations: An approach to the study of the emergence of affects and the capacity for object relations. *Bull. Menn. Cl.*, 43:29–68.

French, T. (1958), *The Integration of Behavior, Vol. 3*. Chicago: University of Chicago Press.

———— & Fromm, E. (1964), *Dream Interpretation*. New York: Basic Books.

Freud, A. (1936), *The Ego and the Mechanisms of Defense*. London: Hogarth Press, 1948.

_____ (1965), *Normality and Pathology in Childhood*. New York: International Universities Press.

_____ (1969), Difficulties in the path of psychoanalysis: Confrontation of past with present viewpoints. In: *The Writings of Anna Freud*, Vol. 7. New York: International Universities Press, pp. 257–268.

Freud, S. (1888a), Hysteria. *Standard Edition*, 1:41–57. London: Hogarth Press, 1966.

_____ (1888b), Preface to the translation of Bernheim's *Suggestion*. *Standard Edition*, 1:75–85. London: Hogarth Press, 1966.

_____ (1891), *On Aphasia*, trans. E. Stengel. New York: International Universities Press, 1953.

_____ (1892), Letter to Josef Breuer. *Standard Edition*, 1:147–148. London: Hogarth Press, 1966.

_____ (1892–3), A case of successful treatment by hypnotism. *Standard Edition*, 1:117–128. London: Hogarth Press, 1966.

_____ (1892), Preface and extracts from Freud's footnotes to his translation of Charcot's "Tuesday Lectures." *Standard Edition*, 1:131–143. London: Hogarth Press, 1966.

_____ (1894a), The neuro-psychoses of defence. *Standard Edition*, 3:45–61. London: Hogarth Press, 1962.

_____ (1894b), Extracts from the Fliess papers. Draft E. How anxiety originates. *Standard Edition*, 1:189–195. London: Hogarth Press, 1966.

_____ (1895a), Studies on hysteria. *Standard Edition*, 2. London: Hogarth Press, 1955.

_____ (1895b), On the grounds for detaching a particular syndrome from neurasthenia under the description "Anxiety Neurosis." *Standard Edition*, 3:90–115. London: Hogarth Press, 1962.

_____ (1895c), Project for a scientific psychology. *Standard Edition*, 1:295–343. London: Hogarth Press, 1966.

_____ (1897), Letter #69. *Standard Edition*, 1:259–260. London: Hogarth Press, 1966.

_____ (1898), Sexuality in the aetiology of the neuroses. *Standard Edition*, 3:263–285. London: Hogarth Press, 1962.

_____ (1899), Screen memories. *Standard Edition*, 3:303–322. London: Hogarth Press.

_____ (1900), The interpretation of dreams. *Standard Edition*, 4 & 5. London: Hogarth Press, 1953.

_____ (1904), On psychotherapy. *Standard Edition*, 7:257–268. London: Hogarth Press, 1953.

_____ (1909a), Notes upon a case of obsessional neurosis. *Standard Edition*, 10:155–318. London: Hogarth Press, 1955.

_____ (1909b), Analysis of a phobia in a five-year-old boy. *Standard Edition*, 10:5–149. London: Hogarth Press, 1955.

_____ (1910a), The future prospects of psycho-analytic therapy. *Standard Edition*, 11:139–151. London: Hogarth Press, 1957.

_____ (1910b), 'Wild' psycho-analysis. *Standard Edition*, 11:221–227. London: Hogarth Press, 1957.

_____ (1910c), The psycho-analytic view of psychogenic disturbance of vision. *Standard Edition*, 11:211–218. London: Hogarth Press, 1957.

_____ (1911), Formulations on the two principles of mental functioning. *Standard Edition*, 12:218–226. London: Hogarth Press, 1958.

_____ (1912a), The dynamics of transference. *Standard Edition*, 12:97–108. London: Hogarth Press, 1958.

_____ (1912b), Recommendations to physicians practicing psycho-analysis. *Standard Edition*, 12:111–120. London: Hogarth Press, 1958.

_____ (1913), On beginning the treatment. *Standard Edition*, 12:121–144. London: Hogarth Press, 1958.

_____ (1914a), Remembering, repeating and working-through. *Standard Edition*, 12:147–156. London: Hogarth Press, 1958.

_____ (1914b), On narcissism. *Standard Edition*, 14:73–102. London: Hogarth Press, 1957.

_____ (1914c), On the history of the psycho-analytic movement. *Standard Edition*, 14:3–66. London: Hogarth Press, 1957.

_____ (1915a), Observations on transference-love. *Standard Edition*, 12:159–171. London: Hogarth Press, 1958.

_____ (1915b), Repression. *Standard Edition*, 14:146–158. London: Hogarth Press, 1957.

_____ (1915c), The unconscious. *Standard Edition*, 14:166–204. London: Hogarth Press, 1957.

_____ (1915d), Instincts and their vicissitudes. *Standard Edition*, 14:117–140. London: Hogarth Press, 1957.

_____ (1916–1917), Introductory lectures on psycho-analysis. *Standard Edition*, 16. London: Hogarth Press.

_____ (1917a), A difficulty in the path of psycho-analysis. *Standard Edition*, 17:137–144. London: Hogarth Press.

_____ (1917b), Mourning and melancholia. *Standard Edition*, 14:243–258. London: Hogarth Press.

_____ (1918), From the history of an infantile neurosis. *Standard Edition*, 17:7–122. London: Hogarth Press, 1955.

_____ (1919), Lines of advance in psychoanalytic therapy. *Standard Edition*, 17:159–168. London: Hogarth Press, 1955.

_____ (1920a), Beyond the pleasure principle. *Standard Edition*, 18:7–64. London: Hogarth Press, 1955.

_____ (1920b), *A General Introduction to Psychoanalysis*. Garden City, NY: Garden City, 1943.

_____ (1923a), The ego and the id. *Standard Edition*, 19:12–59. London: Hogarth Press, 1961.

_____ (1924), A short account of psycho-analysis. *Standard Edition*, 19:191–209. London: Hogarth Press, 1959.

_____ (1925a), An autobiographical study. *Standard Edition*, 20:3–74. London: Hogarth Press, 1959.

_____ (1925b), The resistances to psycho-analysis. *Standard Edition*, 19:211–224. London: Hogarth Press, 1959.

_____ (1926), Inhibitions, symptoms and anxiety. *Standard Edition*, 20:77–178. London: Hogarth Press, 1959.

_____ (1937), Analysis terminable and interminable. *Standard Edition*, 23:216–253. London: Hogarth Press, 1964.

_____ (1938), An outline of psycho-analysis. *Standard Edition*, 23:144–207. London: Hogarth Press, 1964.

_____ (1940), An outline of psycho-analysis. *Standard Edition*, 23:144–207. London: Hogarth Press, 1964.

_____ (1950), Extracts from the Fliess papers. *Standard Edition*, 1:173–280. London: Hogarth Press, 1966.

Freund, J. (1968), *The Sociology of Max Weber*. New York: Pantheon.

Friedman, L. (1965a), The significance of determinism and free will. *Internat. J. Psycho-Anal.*, 46:515–520.

_____ (1965b), Fact and value: new resources for esthetics. *Psychoanal. Rev.*, 52:117–129.

_____ (1968a), Drives and knowledge: A speculation. *J. Amer. Psychoanal. Assn.*, 16:81–94.

_____ (1968b), Japan and the psychopathology of history. *Psychoanal. Quart.*, 37:539–564.

_____ (1972), Difficulties of a computer model of the mind. *Internat. J. Psycho-Anal.*, 53:547–554.

_____ (1973), How real is the realistic ego in psychotherapy? *Arch. Gen. Psychiat.*, 28:377–383.

_____ (1974), The nerves of the mind. Review of Collected Papers of Adrian Stokes, *Contemp. Psychoanal.*, 10:511–521.

_____ (1975a), The struggle in psychotherapy: Its influence on some theories, *Psychoanal. Rev.*, 62:453–462.

_____ (1975b), Elements of the therapeutic situation: The psychology of a beginning encounter. In: *American Handbook of Psychiatry*, Vol. 5, 2nd ed., ed. D. X. Freedman & J. E. Dyrud. New York: Basic Books, pp. 95–113.

―――― (1975c), Discussion of "Is psychoanalysis a social science?" by Paul Parin. *The Annual of Psychoanalysis*, 3:385–391. New York: International Universities Press.

―――― (1975d), Letter to the editor. *Internat. J. Psycho-anal.*, 56:123–127.

―――― (1976), Defining psychotherapy. *Contemp. Psychoanal.*, 12:258–269.

―――― (1977), A view of the background of Freudian theory. *Psychoanal. Quart.*, 46:425–465.

―――― (1979), Marie Coleman Nelson's paradigmatic therapy: A variant reading. *Mod. Psychoanal.*, 4:19–37.

―――― (1982), Sublimation. In: *Introducing Psychoanalytic Theory*, ed. S. Gilman. New York: Brunner/Mazel, pp. 68–76.

―――― (1984), Lover's quarrel or incompatibility? Discussion of Jarl Dyrud's paper, "Sartre and psychoanalysis." *Contemp. Psychoanal.*, 20:253–256.

―――― (1985), Potentiality shrouded: How the newer theories work. *Psychoanal. Quart.*, 54:379–414.

―――― (1986), Kohut's testament. *Psychoanal. Quart.*, 6:321–347.

Frye, N. (1957), *Anatomy of Criticism*. Princeton, NJ: Princeton University Press.

Gadamer, H.-G. (1975), *Truth and Method*. New York: Seabury Press.

Galaty, D. (1974), The philosophical basis of mid-nineteenth century German reductionism. *J. Hist. Med. & Allied Sci.*, 29:295–316.

Gardner, M. R. (1984), Discussion of Vann Spruiell's paper, "The analyst at work." *Internat. J. Psycho-Anal.*, 65:39–43.

Garma, A. (1962), Symposium on the curative factors in psycho-analysis. *Internat. J. Psycho-Anal.*, 43:221–224.

Gedo, J. (1979), *Beyond Interpretation*. New York: International Universities Press.

―――― (1981), *Advances in Clinical Psychoanalysis*. New York: International Universities Press.

―――― (1986), *Conceptual Issues in Psychoanalysis*. Hillsdale, NJ: The Analytic Press.

―――― & Goldberg, A. (1973), *Models of the Mind*. Chicago: University of Chicago Press.

―――― & Wolf, E. (1976), From the history of introspective psychology: The humanist strain. In: *Freud: The Fusion of Science and Humanism: The Intellectual History of Psychoanalysis*, ed. J. Gedo & G. Pollock. Psychological Issues, Monogr. 34/35. New York: International Universities Press, pp. 11–45.

Geertz, C. (1983), *Local Knowledge*. New York: Basic Books.

Gendlin, E. (1962), *Experiencing and the Creation of Meaning*. Glencoe, IL: Free Press.

―――― (1964), A theory of personality change. In: *Personality Change*, ed. P. Worchel & D. Byrne. New York: Wiley, pp. 102–148.

―――― (1967), Values and the process of experiencing. In: *The Goals of Psychotherapy*, ed. A. Mahrer. New York: Appleton-Century-Crofts, pp. 180–205.

―――― (1968), The experiential response. In: *Use of Interpretation in Treatment—Technique and Art*, ed. E. F. Hammer. New York: Grune & Stratton, pp. 208–227.

Gill, M. M. (1963), *Topography and Systems in Psychoanalytic Theory*. Psychological Issues, Monogr. 10. New York: International Universities Press.

―――― (1976), Metapsychology is not psychology. In: *Psychology versus Metapsychology*, ed. M. M. Gill & P. S. Holzman. Psychological Issues, Monogr. 36. New York: International Universities Press, pp. 71–105.

―――― (1982), *Analysis of Transference*, Vol. 1. Psychological Issues, Monogr. 53. New York: International Universities Press.

―――― (1983), The interpersonal paradigm and the degree of the therapist's involvement. *Contemp. Psychoanal.*, 19:200–237.

―――― & Hoffman, I. Z. (1982), *Analysis of Transference*, Vol. 2. Psychological Issues, Monogr. 54. New York: International Universities Press.

Gitelson, M. (1962), The first phase of psycho-analysis. Symposium on the curative factors in psycho-analysis. *Internat. J. Psycho-Anal.*, 43:194–205.

———— (1964), On the identity crisis of American psychoanalysis. *J. Amer. Psychoanal. Assn.*, 12:451–476.

Glover, E. (1937), Symposium on the theory of the therapeutic results of psycho-analysis. *Internat. J. Psycho-Anal.*, 18:125–132.

———— (1955), *The Technique of Psychoanalysis*. New York: International Universities Press.

Goffman, E. (1969), *Strategic Interaction*. Philadelphia: University of Pennsylvania Press.

———— (1974), *Frame Analysis*. Boston: Northeastern University Press, 1986.

Goldberg, A., ed. (1978), *The Psychology of the Self*. New York: International Universities Press.

Goldsmith, M. (1934), *Franz Anton Mesmer.* London: Arthur Barker.

Gombrich, E. H. (1960), *Art and Illusion*. New York: Bollingen Foundation.

Goodman, N. (1976), *Languages of Art*. Indianapolis, IN: Hackett.

———— (1978), *Ways of Worldmaking*. Indianapolis, IN: Hackett.

Gray, P. (1973), Psychoanalytic technique and the ego's capacity for viewing intrapsychic activity. *J. Amer. Psychoanal. Assn.*, 21:474–494.

———— (1982), "Developmental lag" in the evolution of technique for psychoanalysis of neurotic conflict. *J. Amer. Psychoanal. Assn.*, 30:621–655.

Greenacre, P. (1975), On reconstruction. *J. Amer. Psychoanal. Assn.*, 23:693–712.

———— (1980), A historical sketch of the use and disuse of reconstruction. *The Psychoanalytic Study of the Child*, 35:35–40. New Haven: Yale Universities Press.

———— (1981), Reconstruction: Its nature and therapeutic value. *J. Amer. Psychoanal. Assn.*, 29:27–46.

Greenson, R. R. (1967), *The Technique and Practice of Psychoanalysis*, Vol. I. New York: International Universities Press.

Greenspan, S. I. (1979), *Intelligence and Adaptation*. New York: International Universities Press.

Grossman, W., & Simon, B. (1969), Anthropomorphism: Motive meaning, and causality in psychoanalytic theory. *The Psychoanalytic Study of the Child*, 24. New York: International Universities Press.

Guntrip, H. J. S. (1961), *Personality Structure and Human Interaction*. New York: International Universities Press.

———— (1969), *Schizoid Phenomena, Object Relations, and the Self*. New York: International Universities Press.

Habermas, J. (1968), *Knowledge and Human Interests*. Boston: Beacon Press, 1971.

Haley, J. (1963), *Strategies of Psychotherapy*. New York: Grune & Stratton.

Harré, R. (1970), *The Principles of Scientific Thinking*. Chicago: University of Chicago Press.

———— (1984), *Personal Being*. Cambridge, MA: Harvard University Press.

Hartmann, H. (1927), Understanding and explanation. In: *Essays on Ego Psychology*. New York: International Universities Press, 1964, pp. 369–403.

———— (1956), The development of the ego concept in Freud's work. In: *Essays on Ego Psychology*. New York: International Universities Press, 1964, pp. 268–296.

———— (1958), *Ego Psychology and the Problem of Adaptation*. New York: International Universities Press.

Havens, L. (1982), The risks of knowing and not knowing. *J. Soc. Biol. Struct.*, 5:213–222.

———— (1984), Explorations in the uses of language in psychotherapy: Counterintrojective statements (performatives). *Contemp. Psychoanal.*, 20:385–399.

———— (1986), *Making Contact*. Cambridge, MA: Harvard University Press.

Heilbreder, E. (1973), Freud and psychology. In: *Historical Conceptions of Psychology*, ed. M. Henly, J. Jaynes, & J. Sullivan. New York: Springer, pp. 249–256.

Heimann, P. (1962), Symposium on the curative factors in psycho-analysis. *Internat. J. Psycho-Anal.*, 43:228–231.

Henle, P. (1958), Metaphor. In: *Language, Thought and Culture*. Ann Arbor: University of

Michigan Press, 1965, pp. 173–195.

Herbart, J. F. (1891), Textbook in Psychology. In: *History of Psychology: A Source Book in Systematic Psychology*, ed. W. S. Sahakian. Itasca, IL: Peacock, 1968, pp. 86–91.

Hesse, M. (1980), *Revolutions and Reconstructions in the Philosophy of Science*. Bloomington: Indiana University Press.

Hoffman, I. Z. (1983), The patient as interpreter of the analysts's experience. *Contemp. Psychoanal.*, 19:389–422.

Holt, E. B. (1915), *The Freudian Wish and Its Place in Ethics*. New York: Holt, Rinehart, & Winston.

Holt, R. (1962), A critical examination of Freud's concept of bound vs. free cathexis. *J. Amer. Psychoanal. Assn.*, 10:475–525.

_____ (1976), Drive or wish? A reconsideration of the psychoanalytic theory of motivation. In: *Psychology versus Metapsychology*, ed. M. M. Gill & P. S. Holzman. Psychological Issues, Monogr. 36. New York: International Universities Press, pp. 158–197.

Hymes, D. (1964), *Language in Culture and Society: A Reader in Linguistics and Anthropology*. New York: Harper & Row.

Isakower, O. (1957), Problems of supervision. Curriculum Committee Meeting of the New York Psychoanalytic Institute, November 20, 1957.

_____ (1963a), Minutes of the faculty meeting, The New York Psychoanalytic Institute, October 14, 1963.

_____ (1963b), The analyzing instrument. Minutes of the Faculty Meeting, The New York Psychoanalytic Institute, November 20, 1963.

Jakobson, R. (1956), The metaphoric and metonymic poles. In: *Critical Theory Since Plato*, ed. H. Adams. New York: Harcourt Brace Jovanovich, 1971.

_____ (1959), Sign and system of language: A reassessment of Saussure's doctrine. *Poetics Today*, 2:33–38, 1980.

_____ (1960), Closing statement: Linguistics and poetics. In: *Style in Language*, ed. T. A. Sebeok. Cambridge, MA: MIT Press, pp. 350–377.

Janet, P. (1925), *Psychological Healing*, trans. E. & C. Paul. New York: Macmillan, pp. 153–154.

Joergensen, J. (1951), *The Development of Logical Empiricism*. Chicago: University of Chicago Press.

Jones, E. (1915), Professor Janet on psycho-analysis. A rejoinder. In: *Papers on Psycho-Analysis*, 2nd ed. New York: William Wood, 1918, pp. 373–382.

_____ (1953), *The Life and Work of Sigmund Freud*, Vol. 1. New York: Basic Books.

Kantor, J. R. (1969), *The Scientific Evolution of Psychology*, Vol. I. Chicago: Principia Press.

Kaplan, L. J. (1972), Object constancy in the light of Piaget's vertical décalage. *Bull. Menn. Clin.*, 36:322–334.

Kernberg, O. (1966), Structural derivatives of object relationships. *Internat. J. Psycho-Anal.*, 47:236–253.

_____ (1974), Contrasting viewpoints regarding the nature and psychoanalytic treatment of narcissistic personalities: A preliminary communication. *J. Amer. Psychoanal. Assn.*, 22:255–267.

_____ (1975), *Borderline Conditions and Pathological Narcissism*. New York: Aronson.

_____ (1976), *Object-Relations Theory and Clinical Psychoanalysis*. New York: Aronson.

King, L. (1975), Medicine, history and values. *Clio Medica*, 10:285–294.

King, P. (1962), Symposium on the curative factors in psycho-analysis. *Internat. J. Psycho-Anal.*, 43:225–227.

Klauber, J. (1968), On the dual use of historical and scientific method in psychoanalysis. *Internat. J. Psycho-Anal.*, 49:80–88.

_____ (1972), On the relationship of transference and interpretation in psychoanalytic therapy. *Internat. J. Psycho-Anal.*, 53:385–391.

Klein, G. (1969), Freud's two theories of sexuality. In: *Psychology versus Metapsychology*, ed., M. M. Gill & P. S. Holzman. Psychological Issues, Monogr. 36. New York: Basic Books, 1976, pp. 14–70.

————— (1976), *Psychoanalytic Theory: An Exploration of Essentials*. New York: International Universities Press.

Klein, M. (1952), The origins of transference. In: *Envy and Gratitude and Other Works, 1946–1963*. New York: Delacorte Press/Seymour Lawrence, pp. 48–60.

Kohut, H. (1971), *The Analysis of the Self*. New York: International Universities Press.

————— (1975), Letter, April 10, 1975. In: *The Search for the Self*, ed. P. Ornstein. New York: International Universities Press, 1978, pp. 899–900.

————— (1977), *The Restoration of the Self*. New York: International Universities Press.

————— (1978), *The Search for the Self. Selected Writings of Heinz Kohut: 1950–1978*. Two vols., ed. P. Ornstein. New York: International Universities Press.

————— (1979), The two analyses of Mr. Z. *Internat. J. Psycho-Anal.*, 60:3–27.

————— (1984), *How Does Analysis Cure?*, ed. A. Goldberg & P. Stepansky. Chicago: University of Chicago Press.

————— & Wolf, E. (1978), The disorders of the self and their treatment: An outline. *Internat. J. Psycho-Anal.*, 59:413–426.

Krieger, L. (1975), Elements of early historicism: Experience, theory and history in Ranke. *Hist. & Theor.* No. 4, Beiheft 14: Essays in Historicism, pp. 1–14.

Kris, E. (1956), The recovery of childhood memories in psychoanalysis. *The Psychoanalytic Study of the Child*, 11:54–88. New York: International Universities Press.

Kuhn, T. (1970a), *The Structure of Scientific Revolutions*. 2nd ed. Chicago: University of Chicago Press.

————— (1970b), Logic of discovery or psychology of research? In: *Criticism and the Growth of Knowledge*, ed. I. Lakatos & A. Musgrave. Cambridge: Cambridge University Press, 1–23.

————— (1970c), Reflections on my critics. In: *Criticism and the Growth of Knowledge*, ed. I. Lakatos & A. Musgrave. Cambridge: Cambridge University Press, pp. 231–278.

————— (1976), Mathematics vs. experimental traditions in the development of physical science. *J. Interdisc. Hist.*, 7–31.

————— (1979), Metaphor in science. In: *Metaphor and Thought*, ed. A. Ortony. Cambridge: Cambridge University Press, pp. 409–419.

Kuiper, P. (1962), Symposium on the curative factors in psycho-analysis. *Internat. J. Psycho-Anal.*, 43:218–220.

Lacan, J. (1977a), *Ecrits: A Selection*, trans. A. Sheridan. New York: Norton.

————— (1977b), *The Four Fundamental Concepts of Psycho-Analysis*. London: Hogarth Press.

Lakatos, I. (1970), Falsification and the methodology of scientific research programmes. In: *Criticism and the Growth of Knowledge*, ed. I. Lakatos & A. Musgrave. Cambridge: Cambridge University Press, pp. 91–196.

————— & Musgrave, A., ed. (1970), *Criticism and the Growth of Knowledge*. Cambridge: Cambridge University Press.

Lakoff, G., & Johnson, M. (1980), *Metaphors We Live By*. Chicago: University of Chicago Press.

Langer, S. K., (1953), *Feeling and Form*. New York: Scribner's.

————— (1967), *Mind: An Essay on Human Feeling*, Vol. 1. Baltimore, MD: Johns Hopkins University Press.

————— (1972), *Mind: An Essay on Human Feeling*, Vol. 2. Baltimore, MD: Johns Hopkins University Press.

Langs, R. (1975), Therapeutic misalliances. *Internat. J. Psychoanal. Psychother.*, 4:77–105.

————— & Stone, L. (1980), *The Therapeutic Experience and Its Setting*. New York: Aronson.

Leavy, S. A. (1980), *The Psychoanalytic Dialogue*. New Haven: Yale University Press.

Levenson, E. A. (1972), *The Fallacy of Understanding*. New York: Basic Books.

_____ (1978), Two essays in psychoanalytic psychology. *Contemp. Psychoanal.*, 14:1–30.

_____ (1983), *The Ambiguity of Change*. New York: Basic Books.

Lévi-Strauss, C. (1966), *The Savage Mind*. Chicago: University of Chicago Press.

_____ (1970), A confrontation. *New Left Rev.*, 62:57–74.

Lewis, W. C. (1972), *Why People Change*. New York: Holt, Rinehart, & Winston.

Lichtenberg, J. (1981a), Implications for psychoanalytic theory of research on the neonate. *Internat. J. Psycho-Anal.*, 8:35–52.

_____ (1981b), The empathic mode of perception and alternative vantage points for psychoanalytic work. *Psychoanal. Inq.*, 1:329–355.

_____ (1983), *Psychoanalysis and Infant Research*. Hillsdale, NJ: The Analytic Press.

Loewald, H. (1960), On the therapeutic action of psychoanalysis. *Internat. J. Psycho-Anal.*, 41:16–33.

_____ (1971), On motivation and instinct theory. *The Psychoanalytic Study of the Child*, 26:91–128. New York: Quadrangle.

_____ (1973), Review of "The Analysis of the Self," by H. Kohut. *Psychoanal. Quart.*, 42:413–425.

_____ (1978a), *Psychoanalysis and the History of the Individual*. New Haven: Yale University Press.

_____ (1978b), Instinct theory, object relations and psychic-structure formation. *J. Amer. Psychoanal. Assn.*, 26:493–506.

Loewenstein, R. M. (1963), Some considerations on free association. *J. Amer. Psychoanal. Assn.*, 11:451–473.

Luria, A. R. (1981), *Language and Cognition*. New York: Wiley.

Mahler, M., Pine, F., & Bergman, A. (1975), *The Psychological Birth of the Human Infant*. New York: Basic Books.

Mandelbaum, M. (1971), *History, Man and Reason*. Baltimore: Johns Hopkins University Press.

_____ (1980), The presuppositions of metahistory. *Hist. & Theor.*, 19(4):39–54.

Mannheim, K. (1936), *Ideology and Utopia*. London: Routledge & Kegan Paul.

Margolis, J. (1975), Puccetti on brains, minds, and persons. *Philos. of Sci.*, 42:275–280.

Maslow, A. H. (1968), *Toward a Psychology of Being*, 2nd ed. New York: Van Nostrand Reinhold.

_____ (1970), *Motivation and Personality*, 2nd ed. New York: Harper & Row.

Mauss, H. (1962), *A Short History of Sociology*. London: Routledge & Kegan Paul.

May, R. (1958), Contributions of existential psychotherapy. In: *Existence*, ed. R. May, E. Angel, & H. F. Ellenberger. New York: Basic Books, pp. 37–91.

McGinn, R. (1985), A principle of text coherence in Indonesian languages. *J. Asian Stud.*, 44:743–753.

Mead, G. H. (1934), *Mind, Self, and Society*. Chicago: University of Chicago Press.

Meissner, W. W. (1973), Identification and learning. *J. Amer. Psychoanal. Assn.*, 21:788–816.

Mesmer, F. A. (1779), *Mesmerism by Doctor Mesmer*, trans. V. R. Myers. London: Macdonald, 1948.

Meyerson, E. (1930), *Identity and Reality*, trans. K. Loewenberg. London: Allen & Unwin.

Meynert, T. (1885), *Psychiatry*. New York: Hafner.

Michels, R. (1983a), Contemporary psychoanalytic views of interpretation. In: *Psychiatry Update*. Vol. 2, ed. L. Grinspoon. Washington, DC: American Psychiatric Press, pp. 61–70.

_____ (1983b), The scientific and clinical functions of psychoanalytic theory. In: *The Future of Psychoanalysis*, ed. A. Goldberg. New York: International Universities Press, pp. 125–135.

Mitchell, G. D. (1968), *A Hundred Years of Sociology*. London: Duckworth.

Modell, A. (1968), *Object Love and Reality*. New York: International Universities Press.

Moore, B., & Fine, B., eds. (1968), *A Glossary of Psychoanalytic Terms and Concepts*, 2nd ed. New York: American Psychoanalytic Association.

Morson, G. S. (1983), Who speaks for Bakhtin? A dialogic introduction. *Crit. Inq.*, 10:225–243.

Mourelatos, A. P. D. (1970), *The Route of Parmenides*. New Haven: Yale University Press.

―――― (1973), Heraclitus, Parmenides, and the naive metaphysics of things. *Phroneses*, Suppl., 1:16-48.

Munz, P. (1977), *The Shapes of Time*. Middletown, CT: Wesleyan University Press.

Myerson, P. (1977), Therapeutic dilemmas relevant to the lifting of repression. *Internat. J. Psycho-Anal.*, 58:453-462.

―――― (1979), Issues of technique where patients relate with difficulty. *Internat. Rev. Psycho-Anal.*, 6:363-375.

―――― (1981a), The nature of the transactions that occur in other than classical analysis. *Internat. Rev. Psycho-Anal.*, 8:173-189.

―――― (1981b), The nature of the transactions that enhance the progressive phases of a psychoanalysis. *Internat. J. Psycho-Anal.*, 62:91-103.

Nacht, S. (1962), Symposium on the curative factors in psycho-analysis. *Internat. J. Psycho-Anal.*, 43:206-211.

Nilsson, A. (1977), Adaptive and defensive aspects of the individual: A system approach to adaptation in relationship to a psychoanalytic anxiety model. *Internat. Rev. Psycho-Anal.*, 4:111-123.

Nisbet, R. A. (1966), *The Sociological Tradition*. New York: Basic Books.

Nordenskjöld, E. (1928), *The History of Biology*. New York: Tudor, 1942.

Novey, S. (1968), *The Second Look*. Baltimore, MD: Johns Hopkins University Press.

Noy, P. (1969), A revision of the psychoanalytic theory of the primary process. *Internat. J. Psycho-Anal.*, 50:155-178.

Nunberg, H. (1926), The will to recovery. In: *Practice and Theory of Psychoanalysis*, Vol. I. New York: International Universities Press, 1948, pp. 75-88.

―――― (1928), Problems of therapy. In: *Practice and Theory of Psychoanalysis*, Vol. 1. New York: International Universities Press, 1948, pp. 105-119.

―――― (1932), *Principles of Psychoanalysis*. New York: International Universities Press, 1955.

―――― (1937), Symposium on the theory of the therapeutic results of psycho-analysis. *Internat. J. Psycho-Anal.*, 18:161-169.

Ornstein, P. (1984), The empathetic vantage point: Its clinical and theoretical consequences. Grand Rounds, New York Hospital-Cornell Medical Center, Department of Psychiatry, March 28.

Pepper, S. C. (1942), *World Hypotheses*. Berkeley: University of California Press.

Perls, F. S. (1966), Four lectures. In: *Gestalt Therapy Now*, ed. J. Fagan & I. L. Shepard. Palo Alto, CA: Sci. & Beh. Books, 1970, pp. 14-38.

Peterfreund, E. (with J. Schwartz) (1971), *Information, Systems, and Psychoanalysis: An Evolutionary Biological Approach to Psychoanalytic Theory*. Psychological Issues, Monogr. 25-26. New York: International Universities Press.

―――― (1973), On information processing models for mental phenomena. *Internat. J. Psycho-Anal.*, 54:351-357.

―――― (1975), Letter to the editor. *Internat. J. Psycho-Anal.*, 56:128-129.

Piaget, J. (1951), *Plays, Dreams and Imitation in Childhood*, trans. C. Cattegno & F. M. Hodgson. New York: Norton, 1962.

―――― (1967), *Six Psychological Studies*, ed. D. Elkind (Trans. A. Tenzer & D. Elkind). New York: Random House.

―――― (1969), *The Child's Conception of Time*, trans. A. J. Pomerans. New York: Basic Books.

―――― (1970), *Structuralism*, trans. C. Maschler. New York: Basic Books.

―――― (1971a), *Biology and Knowledge*. Chicago: University of Chicago Press.

―――― (1971b), *Insights and Illusions of Philosophy*, trans. W. Mays. Yonkers, NY: World.

―――― (1973), The affective unconscious and the cognitive unconscious. *J. Amer. Psychoanal. Assn.*, 21:249-261.

_____ (1978), *Success and Understanding*. Cambridge, MA: Harvard University Press.

_____ & Inhelder, B. (1969), *The Psychology of the Child*, trans. H. Weaver. New York: Basic Books.

Piattelli-Palmerini, M., ed. (1980), *Language and Learning: The Debate between Jean Piaget and Noam Chomsky*. Cambridge, MA: Harvard University Press.

Pollock, G. H. (1976), Joseph Breuer. In: *Freud: The Fusion of Science and Humanism; The Intellectual History of Psychoanalysis*, ed. J. Gedo & G. Pollock. Psychological Issues, Monogr. 34–35. New York: International Universities Press, pp. 133–163.

Popper, K. (1958), Back to the presocratics. In: *Conjectures and Refutations*, 2nd ed. New York: Basic Books.

_____ (1970), Normal science and its dangers. In: *Criticism and the Growth of Knowledge*, ed. I. Lakatos & A. Musgrave. Cambridge: Cambridge University Press, pp. 51–58.

_____ (1974), Intellectual autobiography. In: *The Philosophy of Karl Popper*, Vol. I, ed. P. A. Schilpp. La Salle, IL: Open Court, pp. 3–181.

Pribram, K. H. (1971), *Languages of the Brain*. Englewood Cliffs, NJ: Prentice Hall.

_____ (1976), Signs and symbols and language. Presented to the Symposium on Brain and Behavior, William Alanson White Institute, New York City, January 24.

Puccetti, R. (1975), A reply to Professor Margolis. *Philos. Sci.*, 42:281–285.

Quen, J. (1976), Mesmerism, medicine and professional prejudice. *NY State J. Med.*, 76:2218–2222.

Quine, W. V. (1981), *Theories and Things*. Cambridge, MA: Harvard University Press.

Quinton, A. (1972), Freud and philosophy. In: *Freud, The Man, His World, His Influence*. Boston: Little, Brown, pp. 72–83.

Racker, H. (1968), *Transference and Countertransference*. New York: International Universities Press.

Rangell, L. (1982), Review of "The Psychoanalytic Dialogue" by S. A. Leavy. *Psychoanal. Quart.*, 51:127–132.

Rank, O. (1936), *Will Therapy and Truth and Reality*. New York: Knopf, 1945.

Ranum, O. (1980), Courtesy, absolutism, and the rise of the French state, 1630–1660. *J. Mod. Hist.*, 52:426–451.

Rapaport, D. (1942), *Emotions and Memory*. Menninger Clinic Monograph Series #2. Baltimore: Williams & Wilkins.

_____ (1944), The scientific methodology of psychoanalysis. In: *The Collected Papers of David Rapaport*, ed. M. M. Gill. New York: Basic Books, 1967, pp. 165–220.

_____ (1951), The conceptual model of psychoanalysis. In: *The Collected Papers of David Rapaport*, ed. M. M. Gill. New York: Basic Books, 1967, pp. 405–431.

_____ (1960a), *The Structure of Psychoanalytic Theory. A Systematizing Attempt*. Psychological Issues, Monogr. 6. New York: International Universities Press.

_____ (1960b), On the psychoanalytic theory of motivation. In: *The Collected Papers of David Rapaport*, ed. M. M. Gill. New York: Basic Books, 1967, pp. 853–915.

_____ (1967), A theoretical analysis of the superego concept. In: *The Collected Papers of David Rapaport*, ed. M. M. Gill. New York: Basic Books, 1967, pp. 685–707.

Reich, W. (1949), *Character Analysis*, 3rd ed., trans. T. P. Wolfe. New York: Noonday Press.

Ribot, T. (1886), *German Psychology of Today*, trans. J. M. Baldwin. New York: Scribner's.

Richards, I. A. (1929), *Practical Criticism*. New York: Harcourt, Brace.

Ricoeur, P. (1970), *Freud and Philosophy*, trans. D. Savage. New Haven: Yale University Press.

_____ (1977a), *The Rule of Metaphor*. Toronto: University of Toronto Press.

_____ (1977b), The question of proof in Freud's psychoanalytic writings. *J. Amer. Psychoanal. Assn.*, 25:835–871.

_____ (1978), The metaphorical process as cognition, imagination, and feeling. *Crit. Inq.*, 5:143–159.

_____ (1981), *Hermeneutics and the Human Sciences*. Cambridge: Cambridge University Press.

Ritvo, L. B. (1970), Reporter, Panel on "The Ideological Wellsprings of Psychoanalysis." *J. Amer. Psycho-Analytic Assn.*, 18:195–208.

_____ (1974), The impact of Darwin on Freud. *Psychoanal. Quart.*, 43:177–192.

Rommetveit, R. (1983), On the dawning of different aspects of life in a pluralistic social world. *Poetics Today*, 4:595–609.

Roustang, F. (1982), *Dire Mastery*. Baltimore: Johns Hopkins University Press.

Rosenthal, R. (1981), Pavlov's mice, Pfungst's horse, and Pygmalion's PONS: Some models for the study of interpersonal expectancy effects. In: *The Clever Hans Phenomenon*, ed. T. A. Sebeok & R. Rosenthal. New York: N. Y. A. Sci., pp. 182–198.

Rubinstein, B. (1976), On the possibility of a strictly clinical psychoanalytic theory: An essay in the philosophy of psychoanalysis. In: *Psychology versus Metapsychology*, ed. M. M. Gill & P. Holzman. Psychological Issues, Monogr. 36, pp. 229–264.

Rubinton, P. (1984), Classics in psychoanalysis: I., Publications through 1939. *Behavioral and Social Sciences Librarian*, 3(4):69–75.

Ryle, G. R. (1949), *The Concept of Mind*. New York: Barnes & Noble.

Sandler, J. (1983), Reflections on some relations between psychoanalytic concepts and psychoanalytic practice. *Internat. J. Psycho-Anal.*, 64:35–45.

_____ & Rosenblatt, B. (1962), The concept of the representational world. *The Psychoanalytic Study of the Child*, 17:128–245. New York: International Universities Press.

Schafer, R. (1959), Generative empathy in the treatment situation. *Psychoanal. Quart.*, 28:342–373.

_____ (1968), *Aspects of Internalization*. New York: International Universities Press.

_____ (1970a), An overview of Heinz Hartmann's contributions to psychoanalysis. *Internat. J. Psycho-Anal.*, 51:425–446.

_____ (1970b), The psychoanalytic vision of reality. *Internat. J. Psycho-Anal.*, 51:279–297.

_____ (1973a), The idea of resistance. *Internat. J. Psycho-Anal.*, 54:259–285.

_____ (1973b), Action: Its place in psychoanalytic interpretation and theory. *The Annual of Psychoanalysis*, 1:159–196. New York: International Universities Press.

_____ (1973c), Concepts of self and identity and the experience of separation-individuation in adolescence. *Psychoanal. Quart.*, 49:215–233.

_____ (1977), The interpretation of transference and the conditions for loving. *J. Amer. Psychoanal. Assn.*, 25:335–362.

_____ (1979), The appreciative analytic attitude and the construction of multiple histories. *Psychoanal. Contemp. Thought*, 2:3–24.

_____ (1980a), Narration in the psychoanalytic dialogue. *Crit. Inq.*, 7:29–53.

_____ (1980b), Action and narration in psychoanalysis. *New Lit. Hist.*, 12:61–85.

_____ (1981), Notes on the noninterpretive elements in the psychoanalytic situation and process. *J. Amer. Psychoanal. Assn.*, 29:89–118.

_____ (1983a), The place of psychical reality in the analytic dialogue. Grand Rounds, New York Hospital-Cornell Medical Center, Department of Psychiatry, April 20.

_____ (1983b), *The Analytic Attitude*. New York: Basic Books.

_____ (1985a), Wild analysis. *J. Amer. Psychoanal. Assn.*, 33:275–299.

_____ (1985b), The interpretation of psychic reality, developmental influences, and unconscious communication. *J. Amer. Psychoanal. Assn.*, 33:537–554.

Schimek, J. G. (1975), The interpretations of the past: Childhood trauma, psychical reality and historical truth. *J. Amer. Psychoanal. Assn.*, 23:845–865.

Schopenhauer, A. (1847), *On the Fourfold Root of the Principle of Sufficient Reason, and On the Will in Nature*, 2nd ed. London: George Bell, 1897.

Schur, M. (1966), *The Id and the Regulatory Principles of Mental Functioning*. New York: International Universities Press.

Schwaber, E. (1981), Empathy: A mode of analytic listening. *Psychoanal. Inq.*, 1:357–392.

_____ (1983), Psychoanalytic listening and psychic reality. *Internat. Rev. Psycho-Anal.*, 10:379–392.

_____ (1986), Reconstruction and perceptual experience: further thoughts on psychoanalytic listening. *J. Amer. Psychoanal. Assn.*, 34:911–932.

Schwartz, L. (1978), Review of "The Restoration of the Self" by H. Kohut. *Psychoanal. Quart.*, 47:436–443.

Sebeok, T. A., & Rosenthal, R., ed. (1981), *The Clever Hans Phenomenon*. New York: N. Y. Acad. Sci.

Segal, H. (1962), Symposium on the curative factors in psycho-analysis. *Internat. J. Psycho-Anal.*, 43:212–217.

_____ (1967), Melanie Klein's technique. In: *Psychoanalytic Techniques: A Handbook for the Practicing Psychoanalyst*, ed. B. B. Wolman. New York: Basic Books, pp. 168–190.

Shands, H. C. (1963), Conservation of the self. *Arch. Gen. Psychiat.*, 9:311–323.

_____ (1976), Structuralism and genetic epistemology in psychiatry. In: *Piagetian Research*, Vol. 5, ed. S. Modgil & C. Modgil. Windsor, Eng.: NFER.

Shapiro, T. (1979), *Clinical Psycholinguistics*. New York: Plenum.

_____ (1981), Empathy: a critical reevaluation. *Psychoanal. Inq.*, 1:423–448.

Spence, D. P. (1982), *Narrative Truth and Historical Truth*. New York: Norton.

Spitz, R. A. (1956), Transference: The analytical setting and its prototype. *Internat. J. Psycho-Anal.*, 37:380–385.

Stein, M. H. (1979), Review of "The Restoration of the Self" by H. Kohut. *J. Amer. Psychoanal. Assn.*, pp. 665–680.

Sterba, R. F. (1934), The fate of the ego in analytic therapy. *Internat. J. Psycho-Anal.*, 15:117–126.

Stern, D. (1977), *The First Relationship*. Cambridge, MA: Harvard University Press.

_____ (1985), *The Interpersonal World of the Infant*. New York: Basic Books.

Stewart, W. A. (1967), *Psychoanalysis: The First Ten Years. 1888–1898*. New York: Macmillan.

Stolorow, R. D., (1978), The concept of psychic structure: Its metapsychological and clinical psychoanalytic meanings. *Internat. Rev. Psycho-Anal.*, 3:313–320.

_____ , Atwood, G. E., & Ross, J. M. (1978), The representational world in psychoanalytic therapy. *Internat. Rev. Psycho-Anal.*, 5:247–256.

Stone, L. (1961), *The Psychoanalytic Situation*. New York: International Universities Press.

_____ (1967), The psychoanalytic situation and transference; Postscript to an earlier communication. *J. Amer. Psychoanal. Assn.*, 15:3–58.

Strachey, J. (1934), The nature of the therapeutic action of psycho-analysis. *Internat. J. Psycho-Anal.*, 15:127–159.

_____ (1937), Symposium on the theory of the therapeutic results of psycho-analysis. *Internat. J. Psycho-Anal.*, 18:139–145.

Sulloway, F. (1979), *Freud: Biologist of the Mind*. New York: Basic Books.

Symposium (1937), On the theory of the therapeutic results of psycho-analysis. *Internat. J. Psycho-Anal.*, 18:125–189.

Symposium (1962), On the curative factors in psycho-analysis. *Internat. J. Psycho-Anal.*, 43:194–234.

Szasz, T. (1963), The concept of transference. *Internat. J. Psycho-Anal.*, 44:432–443.

_____ (1965), *The Ethics of Psychoanalysis*. New York: Dell.

Tarachow, S. (1963), *An Introduction to Psychotherapy*. New York: International Universities Press.

Tausend, H. (1959), Report of scientific meeting of the Los Angeles Psychoanalytic Society, March 30, 1959. *Bull. Phila. Assn. Psychoanal.*, 9:111–112.

Tawney, R. H. (1926), *Religion and the Rise of Capitalism*. New York: Harcourt Brace.

Tenzer, A. (1983), Piaget and psychoanalysis: some reflections on insight. *Contemp. Psychoanal.*, 19:319–339.

Titchener, E. (1929), *Systematic Psychology*. Ithaca, NY: Cornell University Press, 1972.

Todorov, T. (1984), *Mikhail Bakhtin: The Dialogical Principle*, trans. W. Godzich. Minneapolis: University of Minnesota Press.

Tomkins, S. (1980), Affects as the primary motivational system. In: *Feelings and Emotions*, ed. M. Arnold. New York: Academic Press, pp. 101–110.

Toulmin, S. (1972), *Human Understanding*. Princeton: Princeton University Press.

Tower, L. E. (1956), Countertransference. *J. Amer. Psychoanal. Assoc.*, 4:224–255.

Trevarthen, C. (1980), The foundations of intersubjectivity: Development of interpersonal and cooperative understanding in infants. In: *The Social Foundations of Language and Thought*, ed. D. R. Olson. New York: Norton, pp. 316–342.

Trosman, H. (1976), The cryptamnesic fragment in the discovery of free association. In: *Freud: The Fusion of Science and Humanism: The Intellectual History of Psychoanalysis*, ed. J. Gedo & G. Pollock. New York: International Universities Press, pp. 229–253.

Vygotsky, L. S. (1933), The role of play in development. In: *Mind in Society*, ed. M. Cole et al. Cambridge, MA: Harvard University Press, 1978, pp. 92–104

——— (1962), *Thought and Language*, ed. & trans. E. Hanfmann & G. Vaka. Cambridge, MA: MIT Press.

Waelder, R. (1930), The principle of multiple functioning: Observations on over-determination. *Psychoanal. Quart.*, 5:45–62, 1936.

Walmsley, D. M. (1967), *Anton Mesmer*. London: Robert Hale.

Wangh, M. (1974), Concluding remarks on technique and prognosis in the treatment of narcissism. *J. Amer. Psychoanal. Assn.*, 22:307–309.

Watzlawick, P. (1978), *The Language of Change*. New York: Basic Books.

Weiner, M. L. (1975), *The Cognitive Unconscious: A Piagetian Approach to Psychotherapy*. Davis, CA: Psychological Press.

Whitaker, C. A., & Malone, T. P. (1953), *The Roots of Psychotherapy*. New York: McGraw-Hill.

White, H. (1973a), *Metahistory*. Baltimore: Johns Hopkins University Press.

——— (1973b), Foucault decoded: Notes from underground. *History and Theory*, 12:23–54.

——— (1980), The value of narrativity in the representation of reality. *Crit. Inq.*, 7:5–27.

Winnicott, D. W. (1960), Ego distortion in terms of true and false self. In: *The Maturational Process and the Facilitating Environment*. New York: International Universities Press, 1965, pp. 140–152.

——— (1962), The aims of psycho-analytic treatment. In: *The Maturational Process and the Facilitating Environment*. New York: International Universities Press, 1965, pp. 166–170.

——— (1963), Dependence in infant care, in child care, and in the psycho-analytic setting. *Internat. J. Psycho-Anal.*, 44:339–344.

——— (1971), *Playing and Reality*. Harmondsworth, Eng.: Penguin.

——— (1972), Fragment of an analysis. Annotated by A. Flarsheim. In: *Tactics and Techniques in Psychoanalytic Therapies*, ed. P. L. Giovacchini. New York: Science House, pp. 455–693.

——— (1974). Fear of breakdown. *Internat. Rev. Psycho-Anal.*, 1:103–107.

Wittels, F. (1931), *Freud and His Time*. New York: Liveright.

Wittgenstein, L. (1922), *Tractatus Logico-Philosophicus*. London: Kegan Paul.

Wolff, P. H. (1960), *The Developmental Psychologies of Jean Piaget and Psychoanalysis*. Psychological Issues, Monogr. 5. New York: International Universities Press.

Wölfflin, H.(1929), *Principles of Art History*, trans. M. D. Hottinger. New York: Dover.

Wolstein, B. (1976), A presupposition of how I work. *Contemp. Psychoanal.*, 12:186–202.

Wundt, W. (1873), Principles of physiological psychology. In: *Readings in the History of Psychology*, ed. W. Dennis. Appleton-Century-Crofts, 1948, pp. 248–250.

——— (1897a), Lectures on human and animal psychology. In: *Psychology: A Source Book in Systematic Psychology*, ed. W. S. Sahakian. Itasca, IL: Peacock, 1968, pp. 128–129.

——— (1897b), Tridimensional theory of feeling. In: *History of Psychology*, ed. W. S. Sahakian, Itasca, IL: Peacock, 1968, pp. 126–127.

Wyss, D. (1966), *Psychoanalytic Schools from the Beginning to the Present.* New York: Aronson, 1973.

Zetzel, E. R. (1958), Therapeutic alliance in the analysis of hysteria. In: *The Capacity for Emotional Growth,* ed. E. R. Zetzel. New York: International Universities Press, 1970, 182–196.

_____ (1966), The analytic situation. In: *Psychoanalysis in the Americas,* ed. R. E. Litman. New York: International Universities Press.

Zilsel, E. (1941), Problems of empiricism. In: *The Development of Rationalism and Empiricism,* ed. G. de Santillana & E. Zilsel. Chicago: University of Chicago Press, pp. 53–94.

Author Index

Subject Index

as entity, 184–85, 186
in insight therapy, 510–21
for mastery, 434–35
role in performable models, 517–20
of therapist, 427–32
  potentialities in patient and, 528
to see change, 435
Wish-entity, expression of, 184–185, 186

Wolf Man, case of, 452–53
Working through, 239
Würzburg school, 166, 167

Z

Zeno's paradoxes, 234, 316